The Foxfire 45th Anniversary Book
Singin', Praisin', Raisin'

The Foxfire 45th Anniversary Book
Singin', Praisin', Raisin'

**Edited by Joyce Green, Casi Best,
and Foxfire Students**

Anchor Books
A Division of Random House, Inc.
New York

The Foxfire Fund, Inc.
PO Box 541
Mountain City, GA 30562-0541
706-746-5828
www.foxfire.org

Library of Congress Cataloging-in-Publication Data
The Foxfire 45th anniversary book : singin', praisin', raisin' / edited by
Joyce Green, Casi Best, and Foxfire Students.
p. cm.
ISBN 978-0-307-74259-9 (pbk.)
1. Appalachian Region—Social life and customs. 2. Folklore—Appalachian Region.
3. Appalachian Region—Biography. I. Green, Joyce, 1940–
II. Best, Casi, 1991– III. Foxfire magazine.
F106.F695 2011
974—dc22
2011007737

www.anchorbooks.com

Printed in the United States of America
10 9 8 7 6 5 4 3 2 1

Only Gone from Our Sight

Words and Music by Reagan Riddle, Recorded by The Primitive Quartet

God calls loved ones home, yet our pain He can feel,
He always knows best, He can comfort and heal.
Remember, my friend, weeping lasts for the night,
We'll see them again; they're only gone from our sight.

Only gone from our sight to the beauties of Heaven,
Only gone from our sight to a city so bright,
Where the flowers of God are blooming forever,
Keep looking beyond; they're only gone from our sight.

This book is dedicated to the memories of
Robert Murray, Foxfire curator extraordinaire,
and Marie Carter, gift shop comanager,
who are only gone from our sight.

Dedication
To Those We Miss

Acknowledgments

Over a period of six months, a group of dedicated individuals have worked earnestly to see *The Foxfire 45th Anniversary Book* come to fruition, and so many people have contributed ideas, time, knowledge, and information toward the finished project. We would like to sincerely thank present and past students of Rabun County High School for much of the content you will read through the sections of this book. Due to his love of gospel music, we would also like to dedicate the music section to Mr. Mark Earnest, Rabun County High School principal, and thank him for his commitment to and support of the Foxfire program. We would especially like to thank students Brittany Houck, Alyssa LaManna, Katie Lunsford, Kayla Mullen, and Kelly Smith for their many hours of interviews and transcription. We would not have been able to meet our deadline without their help.

We want to recognize Rabun Gap–Nacoochee School, Billy Joe Stiles, and William Thurmond for their information, input, and help with the history and information used in the Farm Family stories. We also thank Mrs. Dorothy Carnes for the picture she provided of the Woodard family, and the Clerk of Court staff of Habersham County and the Northeast Georgia Regional Library for their assistance with research on some of the crime stories.

Former Foxfire book editors Margie Bennett, Kaye Collins, and Lacy Hunter Nix brought their expertise back to the mountain and provided knowledge and help that made this whole thing possible. They proved to be such valuable assets, and their contributions were enormous. Kaye Collins sacrificed her summer vacation from teaching and spent countless hours in the archives of Foxfire, training students, researching, writing, interviewing, and providing guidance to those of us who were new at this task. Lacy Hunter Nix stepped in to fill a void in the middle of the project, and her knowledge and dedication proved to be a godsend. Margie Bennett, longtime Foxfire teacher and ally, even worked from a hospital bed in Tennessee and was so willing to tackle any task, whether it was interviewing, transcribing, writing, or just securing permission slips from contacts to have their stories published. Sheri Thurmond worked extensively on the Farm Family section and conducted several interviews. Teresa Gentry was instrumental in getting this book project off the ground and also interviewed and edited several articles. Museum curator Barry Stiles and former student Ben McClain also provided expert knowledge and helped to organize and write many of the how-to articles.

Special thanks go to Rev. Delbert McCall and Reagan Riddle, who allowed us to use the lyrics of their songs, and to all the musicians who allowed us to record their musical compilations for a CD. Lee Carpenter worked tireless hours to format tons of material and get it ready for publication. His creative ability and sense of design provided the needed touch in the book's completion.

Finally, our deepest appreciation goes to the contacts whose stories are featured within these pages. This book would not have been possible if they had not been willing to share their lives with our readers. And then there's Ann Moore, Foxfire's president and chief executive officer. Ann is a remarkable woman who remained calm during the most stressful times even though she carried the heaviest burden of us all. She sacrificed meals and sleep and worked through her vacation to provide the direction and guidance we desperately needed. She proofed all the copy numerous times and was definitely the glue that held us all together. I truly admire her dedication and commitment to Foxfire and our contacts and students.

—Joyce Green and Casi Best, editors

In addition to the acknowledgments from our editors, I, too, want to thank everyone, especially the writing staff, who played such a huge part in the compilation of this book. My appreciation to Lee Carpenter, as well, who spent many nights after his regular job, pulling the book together as a whole for us; the excellent design is also his work. Lee is a patient man! He always allowed us to make last-minute changes and rewrites, and though it may have been a bit stressful, he took it all in stride! I also want to acknowledge and say a special thank-you to the two editors for all that they have contributed to bring this book to fruition. As you can see, so much of the work that is included was accomplished by them. Casi is a former Foxfire student who made a huge contribution to Foxfire during her high school years, and she continues to do so. While a student, she contributed over three hundred volunteer hours to us, in addition to her classroom work. She is an intelligent, wonderful young Christian woman whom I think the world of. She is now at Piedmont College becoming a nurse, and she will be a great one! Joyce Green: What in the world can I say? She is so incredibly creative, as you can see from her introduction to the book, her section introductions, and the songs she wrote that we've included here. What you don't know is that she is a wonderful person, a great teacher, a brickmason and carpenter, an interior decorator, a beautiful singer and talented musician, and a caring Christian wife, daughter, and mother. Joyce is so talented in so many ways! Without her dedication to this book and the untold (and unpaid) hours she spent writing at night, on weekends, and during the final stages of this draft, we would not have been able to put this manuscript to bed on time. With sincerest appreciation to Joyce, Casi, Lee, and our book crew members for this latest, terrific addition to the Foxfire collection.

—*Ann Moore, president and executive director*

Contents

Banjo Ringing Loud and Clear, Mountain Music in the Air

When Ann Moore, Foxfire's president, approached me about being coeditor of *The Foxfire 45th Anniversary Book*, I knew immediately that I wanted our readers to be engulfed in the Appalachian mountain music that is near and dear to my heart. The mellow sounds of the guitar, the whining of the fiddle, the high pitch of the banjo, and the lapping notes of the big standing doghouse bass are the pure sounds of traditional music that draw in the audience like a moth to a flame. Once you have been captured by its rich and pure melodies, you will never be free.

Music has been a part of my life for as long as I can remember. From the time I was three years old, I traveled with my daddy, an old-fashioned Baptist preacher, to churches all over northern Georgia, South Carolina, and North Carolina to attend their monthly singings. The pews were always full, with people spilling out to the porch and yard and even huddled outside the church's open windows. Many drove long distances to savor the sounds of the pure Appalachian music. There was no air-conditioning, only the paper fans provided by the local funeral homes and an occasional breeze drifting through the tall windows.

Sometimes our travels took us to tent revivals, where folding chairs were placed in straight rows on the fresh wood shavings covering the ground. The smell of recently cut grass, which had been trimmed with a sling blade around the perimeter of the newly erected tent, mingled with the smell of the new shavings from the local sawmill. If it rained, sometimes water would begin to drip on your head from holes worn in the tent from many years of use. The roughly hand-painted sign, which read REVIVAL, was visible from its strategically placed anchor near the roadside. The music was mostly bluegrass gospel with the groups playing strictly acoustic instruments. Usually this included a guitar, banjo, mandolin, and possibly a fiddle. The sound was mellow and the harmony tight.

Occasionally, these singings featured southern gospel groups accompanied by a piano. I longed to play the piano, but my parents could not afford to buy one, much less pay for lessons, so I would sit at the kitchen table, carefully press the wrinkles from my dress with the palms of my hands, and pump away at the make-believe pedal on the floor. It was about this time in my life when my uncle Eddie bought me a guitar. It would be the second one from him. The first had been a small plastic version when I was three years old. That toy guitar had brought me many hours of enjoyment as I sat on a swing made by my dad from an old board with the words JESUS SAVES painted on the seat. This one was a real wooden guitar. I was so proud of that old used guitar. I still own it after fifty-some years. He, along with my mom and dad, taught me a few chords, and I learned to play rhythm well enough to get by. I love the guitar, but to this day I still dream about playing the piano.

As the years have passed, etching their ever-lingering reminders in my face, my love for bluegrass has continued to become more ingrained in my being. I grew up listening to the music of the Carter Family, Bill and Charlie Monroe, the Blue Sky Boys, the Stanley Brothers, Jimmie Rodgers, and the Delmore Brothers, just to name a few. Wayne Raney of WCKY, in Cincinnati, Ohio, and the Grand Ole Opry could be heard above the static on the old cracked red radio we owned. Mr. Raney, the DJ, would announce and play music for a while, play his harmonica, sing a few songs himself, and then sell baby dominicker and red leghorn chickens to his listening audience. He also sold and shipped hundreds of harmonicas across the country through the years. The slow, fast, happy, and sad ballads told stories that bounced off the cardboard-ceiled walls of our little country home. The aroma of Mama's homemade cake, baking in the old woodstove, would fill each room while the sound of Daddy's chopping ax was daily splitting wood for the heater that kept us warm during the cold winter months. There was no running water in the house; an aluminum dipper floated on top of the spring water that had been carried to the house in a two-gallon aluminum bucket. Beside the bucket was a matching aluminum wash pan placed beneath the hand towel hanging from a nail driven in the wall. We all drank from the same dipper, washed our hands in the same water, and dried on the same towel.

The station from Greenville, South Carolina, was the only one we could pick up on our old black-and-white television. I often strained to watch *The Roy Rogers Show*, *The Lone Ranger*, *Sky King*, and *Sergeant Preston of the Yukon* through the snow and interference that were ever present on the screen. Although these programs were entertaining, my favorites were always the music shows. I tried to never miss *The Porter Wagoner Show*, *Flatt and Scruggs*, and *The Wilburn Brothers Show*. These were not only music to my ears, but I could actually see the entertainers. I loved the sound and admired the fancy "show" clothes that they all wore. The wagon wheels adorned with rhinestones and jewels distinguished Porter Wagoner's clothes from all the others. The ladies' full-skirted ballroom gowns were often clenched with both hands and raised to knee length as they broke out into a buck-dancing routine.

So many talented groups rise out of the hills of Appalachia. Deciding who would be included in this edition was a very tough decision. The groups you will learn about throughout these pages, whom you can also listen to on a companion CD available directly from Foxfire, are just a sampling of the talent that enriches our area. You will experience the music of well-known, well-traveled, award-winning groups like The Primitive Quartet, The Gary Waldrep Band, Curtis Blackwell and The Dixie Bluegrass Boys, and David Holt; multitalented miracles like Johnathan Bond and Young Harmony; talented songwriters and performers like Dale Tilley and Morris and Greg Stancil; and true diamonds in the rough like LV and Mary Mathis, who had never recorded any of their music until now. Whether it be from the stage of the Grand Ole Opry, the Stompin' Ground in Maggie Valley, or Old Mater Farm in Sylva, North Carolina, the voices of the Crowe Brothers and Mountain Faith will awaken your senses to the true sibling harmony experienced only in family music. George Reynolds and The Foxfire Boys are the true soul of the Foxfire music program. From the classrooms of Rabun County High School to the World's Fair in Knoxville, Tennessee, to the Olympics in Norway, The Foxfire Boys cut their teeth on bluegrass music under the direction of their mentor and teacher, George Reynolds. Each of these groups submitted one song to be featured on the CD (see www.foxfire.org). Information on how you can obtain more of their music is listed at the end of each article.

While music was a dominating factor in the social gatherings of my childhood, I also vividly recall the stories shared by family and friends while sitting on the front-porch swing listening to the rain beat against the rusty old tin roof or stretched out on a patchwork quilt around the woodstove as the poplar logs popped and cracked on a cold wintry night. The stories of crime, murders, ghosts, legends, and "haints" would often bring chills to your spine and sometimes keep you awake for hours just listening to the strange noises of the night. We have shared a few of these in the "Knoxville Girl" section of this book.

The older generation often refers to yesteryear as the good ol' days, but the days were not always good. People often suffered heartache and pain, but the love of God, country, and family is so evident in all the stories printed within these covers. From the farm families to the family farms to just stories about life, these people shared a love for one another and a moral obligation to society that we have lost somewhere along the way. It has been an honor and a privilege to be a part of *The Foxfire 45th Anniversary Book: Singin', Praisin', Raisin'.* I will always treasure the memories and be thankful for times spent with contacts; my coeditor, Casi Best, who was and is the "best"; and the Foxfire book staff during the summer of 2010. It has been good to reflect on my childhood and share the countless memories of the childhoods of another generation. God richly blessed me with a loving, hardworking family who instilled in me the desire to love and care for my fellow man.

—*Joyce Green*

Born in 1991, I am a mere nineteen years old. If you mention iPods, Wi-Fi, netbooks, text messaging, iTunes, or anything of today's modern technological world, I'll know exactly what you're talking about, or at least recognize the name; however, mention a water dipper, a mess of greasy white half runners, a sling blade, or a two-horse team used for plowing, and I'm lost. Many people blame this lack of knowledge on today's society, but I blame it on the children of today's society. My generation should be more intrigued about our heritage and should have the desire to not let who we are fade away.

Several years ago I began to notice that when my grandparents and great-grandparents would tell stories, I couldn't follow along without having to ask, "What is that?" I was fascinated and wanted to learn about what my family members had to do "back in the day" just to scrape by. *The Foxfire Magazine* class paved the way for me to learn more than I ever imagined about my heritage. As a freshman in high school beginning the class, I started conducting interviews, meeting the knowledge-filled elders of our small community, hearing their remarkable life stories and advice, and simply falling in love with the Foxfire purpose of preserving the Appalachian heritage.

The remainder of my high school career I was blessed to have made so many new friends through Foxfire and been named *The Foxfire Magazine* editor for three years. I was beyond blessed to have the opportunity throughout school to work at The Foxfire Museum and Heritage Center with Robert Murray, doing anything and everything imaginable. Now that I've graduated from high school and am in nursing school at Piedmont College in Demorest, Georgia, Foxfire still holds a special place in my heart and always will. Not only are they assisting me to continue my education through the Julia Fleet/ Foxfire Scholarship Program, but also Ann Moore, Foxfire's president, approached me about being a part of this forty-fifth anniversary book crew. When she said that I would be working side by side with the people I grew up with here on the Foxfire property, I did not have to consider the opportunity a minute longer. This project has been a once-in-a-lifetime experience that I will forever cherish. My relationship with the Foxfire contacts and staff grows stronger each year. I will always be grateful that God allowed my path to cross with such an incredible organization.

Throughout this process Joyce Green and I have traveled all around the South meeting inspiring families and talented groups and hearing true-life stories that are unbelievable. I recall several occasions on this journey when God's presence, whether during a singing or an interview, was so real it felt as though I could reach out and touch Him. Within the following pages you will experience stories that will leave you with cold chills traveling up and down your spine. Whether they are caused by God's remarkable ability to raise people from the dead, His warning power to let people know they are crossing the line, the endless stories of generations having to labor for their shelter, the gruesome Appalachian murders, or even the ghosts that still appear, I assure you that by the end of this book you will have no question of God's existence and will be filled with appreciation for the world that we live in today, as well as gratitude toward your ancestors, and occasionally think to yourself, "You've got to be kidding!"

The majority of citizens today have food to eat, a place to lay their head at night, means of transportation, and clothes on their back. A very wise woman once told me, "We all have the same things. It may look a little different, sound a little different, taste a little different, and not be exactly what we hoped for, but ultimately we all have the same things." Throughout this process I've realized just how blessed I am and that my generation truly has no idea what hard work consists of, what a hard life actually entails, and, sadly, no idea what our ancestors endured.

If you remember anything from this book, I hope it is this: Every person has a story, and they're simply waiting for someone to say "hello."

Happy forty-fifth anniversary, Foxfire!

—*Casi Best*

The Foxfire 45th Anniversary Book
Singin', Praisin', Raisin'

"People will forget our past if it isn't recorded."

Foxfire's History

Ya know that old trees just grow stronger,
And old rivers grow wilder ev'ry day. Old people just grow lonesome
Waiting for someone to say, "Hello in there, hello."
—John Prine, "Hello in There"

Foxfire began at Rabun Gap–Nacoochee School in 1966. While Foxfire can be proud that it has helped preserve a way of life that was quickly disappearing, as a former Foxfire student, the thing I am most proud of is the lasting ties created between the old and the young. Over the years Foxfire students have not only interviewed hundreds of people—recording their stories and their knowledge—they have also said, "Hello in there." Lasting friendships, sharing both joy and pain, were formed between these hardworking, Bible-believing, family-oriented old-timers and the skeptical, self-centered teenagers who interviewed them. Having been one of those self-centered teenagers, I realize what a difference getting to know, love, and respect the elders of my community has made in my life. I visited with Lawton Brooks many times over the years. I shared his joy when a grandchild did something well. I shared his sorrow when his wife of many years, Florence, passed away. My sister and I cried at his funeral. Lawton Brooks had a lasting impact on my life, just as Aunt Arie, and many others, influenced me and all the other students. Lawton had a rich, full life, with numerous friends and a caring family, but he also was willing to make room for me in his heart. Lawton taught me that hard work won't kill you, that God always provides what you need, that hard times build character, that family is more important than anything, and that age has no effect on lifelong friendships! I also learned that everyone has a story to tell, something to share. They just need someone to listen and care.

Foxfire's impact on a former principal, a former student, a Foxfire contact, and a former staff member are shared in the following narratives, with a closing letter at the end of this anniversary edition from President Ann Moore, bringing Foxfire's past into the present. Their stories epitomize the idea that this was about much more than writing stories, being published, and getting a grade. It was, and is, a way to connect with other people, both young and old, who may or may not be different from you—people who are just waiting for someone to say, "Hello in there, hello."

So if you're walking down the street sometime,
And spot some hollow, ancient eyes,
Please don't just pass 'em by and stare,
As if you didn't care. Say, "Hello in there, hello."
—*Kaye Carver Collins*

Morris Brown was principal at Rabun Gap–Nacoochee for thirty years. He was an early champion of the Foxfire program and remained a loyal supporter until he passed away. His early support of the program was instrumental in Foxfire's success.

Morris Brown: I was enthused about Foxfire from the start and, after all these years, I am still enthused about it. Of course, I had no idea that Foxfire would grow to what it has. I thought it would be a local project that would last for two or three years, at the most get a little statewide publicity, but to dare dream of what did happen, of course I never dreamed that. I didn't figure there was enough material to last over two or three years, because I just couldn't see enough material in a little community like this to keep it going for a long period of time. I just figured it would be something local.

I can't really take any credit for the enterprise itself, although I did try to create an atmosphere in school for individual teachers to use their talents for the benefit of the students or the school itself. I supported them. We tried to make facilities and everything—but money—available to them. The only thing that I guess I did was to help provide the environment that could give birth to a project such as this. It would have been very, very difficult to get a project like this started in the public schools. It was a little new, and we had a little more leeway. The county school superintendent and the school president, Dr. Karl Anderson, were very supportive of us. I think the school and Foxfire came together at the right time to do this. Also the time that it was, people were going back to the "Mother Earth" thing. There was a big interest in it, which helped. We were sort of dumbfounded, to be frank with you, by Foxfire's success [laughs]. It came along just at the right time; the people were thinking about the "going back to nature" sort of thing and becoming a little bit more aware of our ancestors' contributions to the life of today. When it became a best seller of Doubleday, I think we were as surprised as everyone when it just really skyrocketed as far as the income from the selling of the book itself. To expand as it has is just unimaginable!

My daughter, Jan, was one of the editors for the three years that she worked with Foxfire. I was quite familiar with the class. Foxfire operated for a year out of my daughter's bedroom! Jan was in English class when the name was given. The students tried to decide on a name. They talked it over and finally came up with the Foxfire name. Foxfire is a little plant

PLATE 1 **"Foxfire seemed to bring out the best in people."**
Mr. Brown and his daughter, Jan

that grows back in the mountains and glows when the moonlight hits it in the right spot. It's hard to see. So they thought, "Well, we are just a small school—maybe we could call the magazine *Foxfire* and see if we could bring a little light to our county."

At its inception, Foxfire students would bring in the local citizens about whom they were writing. Many times we had programs built around their appearance at school. They had certain talents they would share with the students or at an assembly program. Whether it was musical, whether it was storytelling, or they had a certain skill to share, we made available to them, and to our students, assembly programs.

I've seen many students who were just so-so students, lackadaisical about their work, didn't seem to care whether they made a seventy. As a result of being in the Foxfire classes, they seemed to wake up, find skills or desires or goals they had not been aware of. If it had not benefited the school, it would have eventually died out. This is something that the whole school, student body, teachers, administrators, and the community itself could be proud to be a part of. It was a benefit to all the students. Even those not directly involved got some benefits by seeing it in operation. They were exposed to a culture many of them had never seen.

Foxfire seemed to bring out the best in people. They became more self-assured. It helped them to zero in on what their skills were and what they wanted to do. This was a by-product of the actual work that went on in a Foxfire class. I am sure it gave them a good feeling to see something down on paper that they had put together and to see their name in print. You know how it makes you feel to see your picture in the paper or see an article you've written? That sort of thing—it increases your self-worth.

From year to year the Foxfire program just kept growing and growing. It seems to me that its objectives when it first started and now are the same. It's just expanded some. It has grown and expanded. I think that the goals that were set out—to make education interesting, to learn by doing rather than just reading—they're just as much in evidence now as they were then. I can't see that the basic philosophy between then and now has changed much.

I am sure educators everywhere, colleges, high schools, and what have you, have looked at this and perhaps studied it. I am sure that their teaching and learning interests have been enhanced because of the Foxfire projects. As I say, see what can be done, see what high school students can do when they are interested in something, and they are motivated. It's not only the people here in Rabun County who benefited, but I am sure teachers and teenagers all over the United States have had their own lives, teaching methods, and learning processes enhanced because of the Foxfire project.

It's something new every time you pick up a magazine. You read about some individual who's done this or experienced that; it's not like reading yesterday's paper. It's new, fresh, and told in an interesting way that makes people not put it down until you finish reading it. I've seen in the response section of *Foxfire* magazine, on occasions where people have written in and said, "Once I started, I couldn't put it down till I finished it!" It's because of the uniqueness of it and the fact that it brings back memories of their childhood to those who read it. It just makes a memorable experience.

All in all, it's been one of the brightest ideas that has originated in this county. It certainly has been successful at Rabun County High School, and I know it's meant a lot to them. It's an experience to have something and see it grow and succeed. It gives me, our teachers, and the community a good feeling to know that we are part of a national thing. The publicity has become widespread over the years. Not many counties as small as ours have experienced something like this. [**Editor's note:** We sincerely miss our wonderful friend Mr. Brown, who passed away in 2009.]

Rosanne Chastain Short helped write Foxfire's Book of Wood Stove Cookery, *later expanded into* The Foxfire Book of Appalachian Cookery. *When she heard this summer about the illness of one of her coauthors, Kim*

Hamilton [McKay], she dropped a note to Ann Moore, Foxfire's president, with the following story attached. Rosanne's story exemplifies the feelings of most of the students who went through the Foxfire classes, so we thought it was perfect for this forty-fifth anniversary edition.

Rosanne Chastain Short: Every so often I find myself in a north Georgia gift shop, completely lost in flashbacks of thick mountain foliage, bumpy dirt roads, and sweet grandmothers standing in front of wood-burning stoves, countertops full of glass canning jars, and kitchen tables laden with fresh produce. Grinning like a kid in a candy store, I thumb through a copy of *The Foxfire Book of Appalachian Cookery*, fighting the urge to grab the closest tourist and say, "Look, this is me; really, I did this—want me to autograph a copy?"

I am continually amazed that thirty-one years later a summer job project continues to hold space on store shelves. Foxfire summer students Kim Hamilton [McKay], Dana Holcomb [Adams], and I spent two summers planning, visiting, researching, and interviewing what felt like hundreds of Appalachian cooks, including our grandparents. We traveled to the elegant Swan House and lunched with the ladies of the Atlanta Historical Society to view wonderful antebellum books of handwritten "receipts" [recipes]. We had our first taste of kiwi, something never seen in our small rural grocery stores in the late 1970s.

With almost a half century of wisdom, I now shudder, remembering the three teenaged Rabun County High School girls scrunched into my two-seater MG Midget, never giving the first thought to a seat belt, a vision that stands in stark contrast to the fight with my granddaughter's five-point-harness car seat I curse each time she visits. Without a care in the world, we set off each morning that there was no staff meeting held in the old log chapel, where students and staff alike sat on the wooden plank floor, mist-covered mountains visible from the open door, the scent of coffee in hand-thrown [pottery] mugs. Little did we know that it was our first taste of a truly democratic process that would ruin our tolerance for future starter jobs with petty managers threatened by our opinion. It was a summer of freedom—talk of cute boys, strict parents, college, and endless possibilities for our futures, a celebration to end an era, the last vestige of life before the pressures of tuition bills, mortgages, endless housekeeping chores, and running the carpool.

We zipped along Highway 441 with the convertible's top down, radio blaring, wind in our hair, packed lunches, my camera, a ratty tape recorder, and backup batteries stowed in the tiny trunk. Every day was a new adventure. With no GPS or navigation application on a cell phone (actually, none of us had heard of a mobile phone), we bounced down the mountain roads, finding our way with vague directions scribbled on a recycled piece of typing paper—from a real typewriter. As the photographer in the group, I would occasionally pull over to shoot roll after roll of black-and-white film if something related to gardening or food caught our eye. Holding photo credits for the majority of photographs in the original *Foxfire's Book of Wood Stove Cookery*, I was always behind the camera.

My grandmother, Lettie Ruth Chastain, was the impetus of my interest in the Foxfire classes. The summer after our move to extreme north Georgia, we talked while picking blackberries in her field, a sharp eye out for snakes. She told me how much she was enjoying reliving the old times through her Foxfire books. Never a strong English student, I knew the classes offered at my high school were for what would later be known as "language arts" credit, and the seeds of an idea were planted that hot summer day. I made my granny a promise over those five-gallon buckets of juicy berries to interview her for the Foxfire books.

Those summers were filled with fodder for the future *Foxfire's Book of Wood Stove Cookery* as I spent hours in her kitchen watching her pull a large, faded-green Tupperware container full of flour from underneath the kitchen counter. She would snap off the lid, make a well in the center, and scoop a couple of fingers into the Crisco can. Never breaking eye contact, she would patiently explain the process—"You just mix you some grease and milk in your flour, then roll 'em out on your pan"—her agile, lined hands making finger indentions in the dough. I once asked for her recipe. "Recipe, for bread?" was all she said, with a chuckle. Snacks were leftover homemade biscuits with a thick slice of garden tomato; our afternoons were spent stirring a large black iron pot filled with Brunswick stew, cooking over an open fire in the backyard. We cooled down from garden work in front of the television, snapping green beans or shelling peas until our fingers were raw. Those days were deadly dull for a fifteen-year-old girl with a *Tiger Beat* magazine hidden under her pillow, never dreaming they would later serve as precious memories.

One of the last things my grandmother told me was how very sorry she was that she could not make my son one of her hand-sewn baby quilts. On my next visit I brought my own baby quilt, tattered and worn, to let her know the work she had put into it a quarter century before would be once again enjoyed. Today that forty-nine-year-old quilt hangs in my granddaughter's bedroom. It did snuggle my son and, in turn, his child, soon to wrap its love and warmth around a new grandbaby. Three generations have experienced the love stitched into each small piece of blue and pink fabric.

In contrast there is a crocheted bedspread that hangs over the bay window in my study made by the even hands and temperament of my maternal grandmother. Both of these strong, caring women's handiwork represents, like the antique clock in our living room from my husband's lineage, an intricate part of the history that is our lives. Although I have photographs of both grandmothers and my husband's ancestors, a vast chasm lies between how much of these personalities I can share with our grandchildren. The difference lies in a high school English project. The tape-recorded interviews, which became articles published in *The Foxfire Magazine* and later books, are an eternal piece of her life and personality that I can share with my descendants. We can reach out and touch her work, a quilt made with pieces of my father's baby clothes, feed sacks, and leftover cloth, as they hear her words read from that tattered magazine and know the significance that the art of quilting held in her life. The recorded tape, spoken in her rural north Georgia accent and tucked away in the Foxfire archives, can allow them to catch the smile in her voice. I am forever grateful for preserving this precious piece of my granny and saddened that I did not have the foresight to interview my maternal grandmother or my grandfathers. In the naïveté of my youth, I thought they would all live forever.

PLATE 2 **"Every day was a new adventure. With no GPS or navigation application on a cell phone (actually, none of us had heard of a mobile phone), we bounced down the mountain roads, finding our way with vague directions scribbled on a recycled piece of typing paper—from a real typewriter."**

In juxtaposition to those days of no computers in the classroom, I use this story in a college communications class that I teach online to adult, evening, and weekend students at Brenau University. With much grumbling about time constraints and busy family duties, they head out with handheld video cameras, PDA devices that record and take photos to fulfill the assignment of collecting a story from a family elder. The results make my heart sing. With enthusiasm these busy adults rarely have the energy to express, they post messages in our virtual classroom, telling how much the exercise meant to them and thanking me for the assignment. More often than not, they conclude their findings with plans to continue to collect family stories.

As an administrator in higher education and a freelance magazine writer with delusions of grandeur for my young-adult fiction, I look back to that summer day in my grandmother's garden and fondly remember the knowing smile she gave my grand plans. It has come full circle. The voice that the Foxfire staff, sitting on the rough, plank floor of the old log chapel all those years ago, helped me find has led not only to a career but to a lifelong passion to share that experience with my own students as they capture the stories of their own heart.

Lawton Brooks, a longtime friend of Foxfire, was interviewed by students more than twenty-five times from 1970 until 1998.

Lawton Brooks: I used to go 'round with Suzy Angier, a former Foxfire staff person, and hunt people to interview. That Foxfire was the best thing that ever happened to Rabun County! That done the kids more good than anything; it gave them so many different things that they could do. I think it's wonderful. People will forget our past if it isn't recorded, but I will never forget! I think Foxfire has been a benefit to me. I've seen lots of things and done lots of things that I wouldn't of done if it hadn't been for Foxfire. When Foxfire first started, I never thought to myself it would make it. I thought to myself, "Will that ever be worth anything to anybody?" It has, though! It built up fast, too, and it's still a-goin'!

PLATE 3 **"I used to go 'round with Suzy Angier and hunt people to interview."**

I've got Foxfire books everywhere! I wouldn't take the world's fancy for them. I get them out ever' once 'n a while and go through them. It's one of the best things that has ever come along. *Foxfire 3* has more about my old life than any of 'em. It has the whole story. I get a lot of letters, and I've had three or four people who've come by from Texas to get me to sign their Foxfire books. They come from everywhere! They come all the time, dad blast it! All the time! I've made a lot of friends with Foxfire on account of I got to meet so many different people. I had two come from California! I've signed more books out of Florida than any place. Every place in Florida, I reckon, has 'em. You can go anywhere and pick up a Foxfire book, in any town you go to. I'd never thought they'd went like that, but boys, they went! Didn't they? People are still huntin' them. They ain't no one gettin' mine! I'm keepin' mine!

Margie Bennett joined the Foxfire staff in 1972. Over the years she has worn so many hats at Foxfire! She started primarily as the typist, but because of her various talents, she rose to be, among several other things, a coteacher in the Foxfire classroom. Margie's love for the kids and for the elders of our community endeared her to all who met her, and even though she left in 1988 to pursue other opportunities, Margie has always been just one phone call away anytime Foxfire has needed her.

Margie Bennett: Sixteen years, 1972 to 1988, could anyone have told me I would have the most fun of my life doing things I was never trained for and being with teenagers almost twenty-four/seven *and* getting paid for it? I began by typing *Foxfire 2* the summer our family, my husband, Bob, and our teenage son, Bruce, moved to Rabun Gap–Nacoochee School for Bob to work with the boarding students through the campus work program and outdoor environmental program and Bruce to attend tenth, eleventh, and twelfth grades and graduate from there.

I learned a lot that summer, and I was having a ball. One thing I still remember quite clearly was on my second or third day working for Foxfire, several of these older students asked if I'd like to go meet Aunt Arie Carpenter, a widowed lady who lived alone in nearby Otto, North Carolina. Of course, I jumped at this opportunity, so we piled into the Foxfire Blazer—a very warm July day—and one of the students drove us there. I was introduced and we visited with Aunt Arie a short while, and then something was mentioned about her garden. The kids got the hoe and rakes, and we all went out to her garden to weed. Several hours later, very hot and sweaty, we bade Aunt Arie good-bye and headed back to school. The kids dropped me off at my house and drove back to the office. I collapsed in a swing on the front porch and felt terrible. I suppose that was heat prostration, but I survived their initiation and felt I had earned my place and passed the test to stay with Foxfire. I

PLATE 4 "Several hours later, very hot and sweaty, we bade Aunt Arie good-bye and headed back to school." Aunt Arie with visiting students, working in her garden

didn't think about it till later that they were probably planning to make me or break me!

After that, I often drove up to Aunt Arie's by myself and had a cup of coffee. We just wanted to be sure she was all right and didn't need anything. There have been lots of others that we tried to keep in touch with; there were no telephones, you see. We might have a tape recorder with us, so if Aunt Arie had something to tell us about that we wanted to record, we'd do that. She welcomed the attention. We asked her so many things about her husband and their life together, and she was so philosophical about her life. That's how we came to publish a whole book just about her life and how she made and did things. [**Editor's note**: *Aunt Arie: A Foxfire Portrait* is available at www.foxfire.org.]

When I came to work for Foxfire, Suzy Angier was the only other adult working to help the teacher, taking the students on interviews and getting magazines ready for the publisher. Foxfire's original goal was to help ninth- and tenth-grade students get interested in school, to find something different to do at school, so they'd stay in high school to graduate.

By the time I got there, royalties from the first Foxfire book were coming in. That summer of 1972 was about the time that IDEAS [Institutional Development and Economic Affairs Service], an educational program located in Washington, D.C., got in touch with us to host a program to start similar cultural journalism magazines in schools around the nation.

The goal at that time was to reach out to a lot of high schools with specific cultures, which we did, so magazines like *Bittersweet* in Lebanon, Missouri; *Salt* in Kennebunkport, Maine, along the coast there; *Dovetail* in St. Ignatius, Montana; *Tsa'Aszi* in Ramah, New Mexico, and many more were created. Foxfire students who were home from college for the summer hosted representatives from these areas, teaching them how to interview contacts in our community, photography skills, magazine layouts, etc. In fact, a book came from these experiences, *You and Aunt Arie*, which was published by the *Salt* magazine students. Those same Foxfire students went to the areas where these young people lived, staying in their homes for several weeks to get their magazine staffs started with their own productions. Remember, the focus, as well as learning to interview, was to keep these students interested in school and writing.

There was a section of land, an old apple orchard, on the side of Black Rock Mountain available, and The Foxfire Fund was able to purchase it in 1973. At first, there were no buildings there, but we began to buy old log cabins and rebuild them with the help of a group of adults who were builders and, in addition, some Foxfire students during the summer months.

I typed the final copies of the *Foxfire* magazine and book articles there in a cabin furnished as an office. This was in the days of IBM Selectric, Ko-Rec-Type, electric typewriters—long before personal computers came

PLATE 5 "While writing articles, they were actually learning proper English and grammar *and* getting out of the school day once in a while to interview." Foxfire student Brenda Carpenter, Mrs. Addie Norton, and Margie Bennett

our way. Today, in 2010, Foxfire students are able to transcribe their own articles on computer and actually lay them out for the printer with a computer program.

The magazine was one idea—to write about their families, their Appalachian backgrounds. While writing articles, they were actually learning proper English and grammar *and* getting out of the school day once in a while to interview, to work in a darkroom printing pictures they'd made with Pentax cameras, all the elements of production of something printed to sell to their families and neighbors. It worked, and most of them *did* graduate, and some went on to college. Several of those students returned from college to actually work at Foxfire in *real* jobs.

Pat Rogers was probably the first to join our staff—about 1973; then a few years later, Mike Cook and Paul Gillespie were back from their years in college to teach video skills and photography, and George Reynolds, already a teacher from Virginia, to teach Appalachian folklore and music. Foxfire now had an income from educational grants, donations, and sale of the magazines.

In 1976, a consolidated high school for all the seventh through twelfth graders in Rabun County was being planned and built in the south part of the county. The Foxfire staff and students at RGNS met and voted to move to the new school. The principal for the new school met with us and worked out an agreement, providing Foxfire with classrooms and an arrangement where students in the *Foxfire* magazine class could get regular English credit; George was approved to teach music classes to students interested in banjo, guitar, dulcimer, fiddle, and other stringed instruments. Their specialties were primarily country and traditional mountain music. Enrolled were mostly students who did not want marching band or orchestra. In September 1977, the new school was opened as RCHS [Rabun County High School]. It was fun to have a large new classroom—with a darkroom and lots of space for tables and desks—and to be able to hire the new teachers from royalties of Foxfire book sales to teach photography, video, and Appalachian music. For English credit, Appalachian folklore and the regular magazine classes were taught with *The Foxfire Magazine* as the product. I took students on interviews, helped them write transcriptions of those interviews with pencil, paper, and a cassette tape recorder, helped them print their photographs, and guided them through the layouts of their articles for the Foxfire magazines. At times, I taught the magazine classes, and I even went back to college and got my master's degree in education. Since we had now moved our classrooms from RGNS to the new high school, we needed office space somewhere in addition to the new classroom. We had a part of the classroom there where the students processed subscription orders and answered letters from our readers, but it was not sufficient to handle all the business we now had, and our bookkeeper, Ann Moore, needed space for the expanded business we were dealing with. We refurbished several of our log cabins for office buildings and later some for residences. I worked there part of some days and helped in the classroom at the high school the remainder of the time.

About 1978, Bob came to work for Foxfire, establishing an outdoor education and environmental program for students at Rabun County High. It was shortly after this that we were involved in building a two-story log dormitory building, and our family—Bob, Bruce, and I—moved there and became the host family for overnight visitors to Foxfire. Also, there were several times when we became temporary parents for students who needed a home while their families were going through problems. There were six bedrooms and a bath upstairs, and we had a bedroom, bath, kitchen, large living and dining room on the first floor. We were a regular bed-and-breakfast of sorts. So we were truly with Foxfire twenty-four/seven!

In 1978, we were approached by Hume Cronyn—yes, the movie star—and Susan Cooper, an author, to consider a play about the people of southern Appalachia. Not long before this and still upsetting to many people in our area, the movie *Deliverance* was filmed here, depicting some of the local characters in such a derogatory way that most of us were dubious of anything Hollywood. Others thought about the TV show *The Beverly Hillbillies* and *knew* they were sometimes thought of as Li'l Abners. We were all very dubious about being a part of anything like either of these scenarios.

However, Hume won us over. The play *Foxfire* was written with our input, and produced and first opened to the public in 1982. All the Foxfire staff was invited to fly to Minnesota and meet and visit with the members of the cast. In fact, we took with us a film that had been made of Aunt Arie—her daily life and conversations—so Jessica Tandy, Hume's wife, could see Aunt Arie's mannerisms and emulate them as much as possible without looking "hokey" or artificial. The play was a success and Hallmark made it into a movie with Hume, Jessica, and John Denver as the principal actors. I still see it being played occasionally on the Hallmark channel, and in this area, particularly Georgia and North Carolina, it is often a summer stage play. [**Editor's note:** The Hallmark Hall of Fame movie *Foxfire* is available at Hallmark Gold Crown stores.]

In 1986, spurred on by the interest we were getting from teachers and administrators around the nation, we began a teacher outreach program. School groups and individual educators were asking to visit our classrooms and have our staff and students talk to them about getting their students interested in experiential education. And they were inviting our students and staff to come to their schools and talk to their teachers, administrators, and students. The descriptor "experiential education" and John Dewey's methods began to crop up. We started a newsletter and corresponded with them. Sherrod Reynolds became the coordinator for this program. That interest is still going strong with teachers from around the nation and even Australia and New Zealand, England, Scotland, Canada, and elsewhere. Students now come to Piedmont College in Demorest, Georgia, to enroll in Foxfire teacher-training classes being taught by Dr. Hilton Smith (another Foxfire staff member at one time) and his colleagues.

Each year we would invite all our contacts on a spring Saturday and have a picnic and music and visit with them. We just wanted to have a good time with these people who had given their stories to us. We would bring them all together, and we'd be amazed! See, a lot of these folks were older and didn't travel much, so students and staff would go pick them up at their homes or their grown children would come and bring them. They got to talk to one another, and we would have interviews galore right there with two older people who used to know and visit with one another. That was fun—watching the fellowship they had as they reminisced about the old days. The students were there, and it was like an old-time family reunion. We did all kinds of things at the Foxfire gatherings. We ate and talked and enjoyed one another's company. The contacts looked around at the different cabins, and we showed them the traditional artifacts we had collected through their donations. We hosted those people, and they were the center of our attention.

We lived on the Foxfire mountain for several years, and then an opportunity came for us to move back to RGNS to establish a middle school, at first for seventh and eighth graders, and then later sixth-grade day students. The Foxfire staff encouraged me to go for it. That was in 1988; however, I've never been far from Foxfire. It was an exciting, challenging, and fun time in my life.

A Beautiful Life

William M. Golden, 1918

Life's evening sun is sinking low,
A few more days and I must go,
To meet the deeds that I have done,
Where there will be no setting sun.

Each day I'll do a golden deed,
By helping those who are in need;
My life on earth is but a span,
And so I'll do the best I can.

I'll help someone in time of need,
And journey on with rapid speed;
I'll help the sick and poor and weak,
And words of kindness to them speak.

While going down life's weary road,
I'll try to lift some trav'ler's load;
I'll try to turn the night to day,
Make flowers bloom along the way.

In the Good Ol' Days

Personal Stories of Appalachia

A Beautiful Life

In the Good Ol' Days

My memories of yesterday take me back to a simpler time when kindness toward, caring for, and a sense of obligation to your fellow man was much more evident than it is today. During times of hardship, sickness, and death, neighbors were neighbors, and they came bringing food, providing support, and lending a hand with whatever chores needed to be done. When a family member died, the community came and filled the table with fresh-baked and home-cooked food prepared on an old cast-iron woodstove. Those meals were served with fresh butter and buttermilk made in an old-fashioned churn and cooled by the tumbling waters from a nearby spring. I've heard it said in the South, "If you give us a bowl of tater salit and a banana pudding, we can have a funeral."

In this section you will experience an example of how these family morals and traditions have survived the test of time. The story of how a group of high school students banded together and worked to fulfill the wish of a dying man, Sammy Green, will help to renew your faith in mankind. It is obvious, as you read this story, that many of the values of former generations are still being passed down today throughout these mountains we love.

Madge Merrell and Jack P. Nix will take you back to the times of one-room schools, first automobiles, and just plain hard living. Times were tough, but love, faith, and family ties were abundant. You will also laugh through the humorous recollections of Lillie Billingsley and David "Lightnin'" Callenback and experience the sad and happy moments in the lives of Carlee Heaton, Coyle Justice, Vaughn Billingsley, Allen English, and Tommy Irvin.

"A Beautiful Life" is sung by choirs and congregations across this country every Sunday morning. It speaks volumes about the morals and sense of responsibility of a past generation. While listening to these lyrics you can almost see an old dad cutting a load of wood for a neighbor in need or a loving mother providing care for a sick friend. As you read the following stories, remember that "life on earth is but a span," so try to do the best you can.

—*Joyce Green*

"Praise the Lord, Sammy's quit smoking!"

~An interview with Sammy Green~

In December 2006, I went on what I believed was going to be a normal Foxfire interview. Much to my surprise, not only did I meet a unique and very sweet man, I just fell in love with Sammy Green. At the time, he was living with Sherri Gragg, a wonderful woman of no relation to Sammy who stepped up and took responsibility when it became apparent that he needed somebody to help out around the house now that he was getting older. Sammy lived with Sherri for about eight years and would tell you straight up, "I have went to bed hungry many nights, but not since I been living with Sherri, and I always have clean clothes to wear, too."

—Casi Best

My name is Sammy Oscar Green, and I was born in 1933—May 12, 1933, so I'm seventy-three years old. I was born in Cherokee County, in Murphy, North Carolina. That's my hometown. I never did get married, so I don't have any kids, and I left home when I was sixteen.

My parents were Sammy Winslow Green and Birdie Cearly. Daddy carried meal [cornmeal] and ground corn. After he got done carrying the meal, he ground corn the rest of the day on the water mill. Mama carried water for Mrs. Stewart; she'd get two dollars a day for it, so that wudn't much money. Mrs. Stewart didn't do nothin'; she didn't have to. She was a millionaire. She had so much money in a nail keg that she put two smoothing irons on it to hold it down, and she didn't put it in the bank. Son, they was millionaires; they didn't have to do nothin'. That's the reason she hired Mama to carry her drinking water.

All of my brothers and sisters are dead and gone; they ain't none of them living but me. I had three brothers and two sisters. The second boy died at ten years old. He had the rheumatic fever, and back then we didn't have any doctors, so there was nothing we could do.

I never did get to get an education; I just got to go to school for two years. The school was so old back then that it was just about ready to fall down. It caught a'far' [afire] and blowed up. Then they built a big, nice, new schoolhouse. We'd walk four miles there and back to school.

Us kids would go to church for fun [laughs]. We'd haul corn till four o'clock that evening and go home and take a bath in a warsh [wash] tub. Some people don't even know what a warsh tub is. Me and my youngest sister would beat my brothers and sisters home and wash in the water first. It'd make 'em so mad they couldn't hardly stand it. Our parents would whoop

[whip] 'em if they started to bother us, though. When we'd get ready, we'd have to walk six miles to the church and then six back. Now people've got cars and won't even go to church [laughs]. Most all of my childhood memories are of church. My brothers and sisters, and me, all grew up together in our hometown. We never did anything to get in trouble; we was good kids.

One time this man gave me a good squirrel dog. My brother Clint said, "That dog ain't no 'count; that's why he just give 'im to ya." Me and Clint went huntin', and me and the dog went one way, and Clint went the other. I come home with twenty-seven squirrels. I asked Daddy how many squirrels Clint got.

Daddy said, "He didn't even get a mess. How many did you get?" I said, "I got twenty-seven—got seven hits over yonder at one tree. The dog run to it seven times." Clint went over there to the hole where I'd put them squirrels and pulled twenty-seven out. He said, "Mama, feed that dog plenty of cornbread 'cause he's a good un [laughs]." He told me that he'd take the dog the next time, but I said, "Oh, no! I'm taking the dog." I went again and got twenty-two squirrels. Mama said, "Shew, look at them squirrels a-comin'." I had to skin all of 'em; Clint couldn't skin 'em. Daddy was like me; he loved to eat squirrel. He could just run that hind leg through his mouth and that was it; all the meat would be gone [laughs]. Boys, we liked 'em thangs.

PLATE 6 "There wudn't many people that went to be baptized the Sunday that I did because it was just thirty-five degrees."

Me and my brother would go huntin' and get back there in the woods and eat a can of Viennas [sausage] for dinner, supper, and then a can for breakfast. We'd keep stuff cold by keeping it in the spring. We'd hunt squirrels and rabbits all the time for food. Sometimes, we'd hunt deer, too. I killed two ol' bucks in my lifetime. I never do get to hunt for 'em no more. I never have eat much deer meat no way.

When we were growing up, Mama and Daddy stayed at home and just us kids would go to church. We went to Ranger Methodist Church. That's where I got saved. I was around sixteen or eighteen when I got saved. There wudn't many people that went to be baptized the Sunday that I did because it was just thirty-five degrees. That preacher said he'd like to have somebody to help him, but I guess nobody wanted to help with it being thirty-five degrees [laughs]. He was baptizing people by hisself, and I guess it'd be a hard job.

I used to smoke, but I laid 'em thangs down one day, and I ain't smoked any since. I told my preacher, "I ain't smoked a cigarette in a whole week." He said, "PRAISE THE LORD, SAMMY'S QUIT SMOKING!" [Laughs.] I guess that has been about forty years ago. I can smell the smoke from someone else's smoke, and I just have to go, "Shew!" [laughs] because it smells so bad. Now I go to church over at Ole Country Church in South Carolina, and we got a good preacher, too; I love it.

I've worked a little here and yunder, all in Georgia though. When I first left home I went and worked at a steel mill down in Marietta, Georgia. It was so hot that I had to quit working after three years. You just couldn't stand it. I can just remember the sweat rolling off of ya. Me and three other boys carried the steel out. While I was there in Marietta, people were getting robbed. My first cousin got robbed. He worked in a church house, in a' ol' English church, and he couldn't find his money. They'd even took his pocketknife— his eight-dollar pocketknife. Well, I had my money all in hundred-dollar bills. I had put three thousand dollars in a Prince Albert 'baccer [tobacco] can and put 'bout an inch of 'baccer over it, so if they got in my pocket, then they wouldn't find but close to ninety dollars in it. I didn't want 'em to steal that money after I'd worked like a dog for three years fer it. They woke me up one night. I didn't see nobody, and I was glad, too [laughs]! They got the money from my pocket, but that ninety dollars is all they got. They never did find no money in that can. Nobody would've ever thought 'bout looking in a 'baccer can for money. I was smarter than they was. They wudn't getting my money after I'd worked like a dog. That was the money that I used to come home on; I caught the bus back home. Marietta's a long ways from North Carolina; it's down there near Atlantar [Atlanta], Georgia.

After that I come back home. I just went back to cutting pulpwood and logs again. I had done that all my life, so that's all I knew how to do. I'd snake logs; that's where a man would get up and pull the logs out to the big ol' tractor area for the other workers. I also worked for a guy digging bushes. He said, "Sammy, if I make good, then you'll make good." The first day I worked for eight hours. He said, "You want me to pay you now so you'll have some money to pay for your room?" We was staying in some little town nearby.

I thought, "Well, it won't be much, but I'll do well to buy my dinner." He gave me one hundred dollars, and I came near of faintin' [laughs]. I said, "You mean I made one hundred dollars today?" He said, "Yeah. I told you, if I made good, then you'd make good, too." He done what he said, too. When I worked with him, I bought me a tractor and paid three thousand dollars for it. The road patrol caught me and charged me forty-five dollars because I didn't have no tag or lights. I told 'em that I didn't think I needed all that. The next day the sheriff told me that I could drive my tractor up and down the road just the way it was. He told me the man that stopped me wudn't no road patrol, and he wudn't supposed to charge me. He told me he just made hisself forty-five dollars. I said, "Well, he shore did. That was the last forty-five dollars I had, and he took it."

One time a friend of mine, Garr Haney, tried to get me to shoot a game of pool. I said, "Garr, I ain't never shot a game of that stuff in my life." He told me to throw fifty cents in that pot, and he'd shoot it for me. He hit that ball, and the fifteen got to the hole and he said, "Stay there, baby; stay there, baby." He asked me if I won it, what was I gonna do with it? I told him I was gonna give it to Mama to buy us something to eat with. He said, "That's the best thing you can do." He won me seventy-three dollars, and I bought groceries with it.

My brother-in-law was a stealer. That boy tried stealing my gas. He stole it one time, and I decided I'd wait and catch him. I got me a tank and waited, and I seen him pop that tank, and I popped him. I shot him there in the hind part [laughs]; boys, he squalled [cried]. He never did come back to get his cans, so I sold 'em for ten dollars. They wuz brand sparkling new, too. I got part of my gas back! That boy was too sorry to work and then went up and down the roads stealing people's gas. I never stole a drop of gas in my life. I learnt better than to do that.

Before my mama died, I took care of her for about six weeks in the hospital. Then she had a stroke and passed away. After that, I took care of Daddy for about three years. I had to pay for their funeral bills by myself; I had nobody to help me. I think I spent about three thousand dollars for their funerals. I walked sixteen miles to buy their tombstones, and the boy let me have a set for two hundred dollars since I walked that fir [far]. I thanked the man a lot. That two hundred dollars was hard to pay, but that three thousand dollars for the funeral bills was the hardest for me to pay fir.

One time when I come home from Marietta, my sister wanted to borrie [borrow] five dollars to buy a pair of slippers. I told her she couldn't buy a pair of slippers for five dollars, but she might buy 'em for ten, so I give her ten. I went on out to the poolroom and set there and watched my brother shoot two games of pool. He lost twenty dollars on 'em games. You just as well to pour a pan of hot whiskey in my face. I hated to see twenty dollars throwed away. I went back out to the bus station, and he come out there and me and my sister was there. She said she wanted to borrie ten dollars, and I asked what she wanted with another ten dollars. She said she wanted to get her a dress; she said there was a flowerdy dress up there in the store, and she wanted it to go to church in the next day. I told her she couldn't get a dress and everything that goes with it for ten dollars. I told her she might get it for twenty. She told me that I didn't pull her down; I raised her up all the time. I said, "You know what I just seen Clint do a while ago? He shot two games of pool and lost twenty dollars—go get your dress." She got the dress and was in it for church the next day. When Shirley come home with her new dress, Clint was there. Clint said, "Sammy, they got a big ham up there in the store that they wanted to sell for ten dollars. Why don't you take one of them ten-dollar bills up there and buy it?" Shirley said, "Yeah, I'll go up there with ya." So me and her went up there.

PLATE 7 **"I told him I was gonna give it to Mama to buy us something to eat with." Sammy's aunt, Ada, and his mother, Birdie Cearly Green**

I told 'em at the store that Clint had told me that they had a ham for ten dollars, and they said, "Yeah, git ya one of 'em, and while you're at it git ya one of 'em fat hens out there, and it'll be good for supper." I said, "Shirley [Shirley was holding the hen], you better hold that chicken way out away from you; that chicken'll mess you up sure 'nuf [enough]." Kenneth Stiles [store owner] offered me a good deal on some meat, and I told him that if he could tell me how I could get home with my mule and keep 'em from running away from smelling all that meat, then I would buy it. He told me to hold the mule real good, and he sent his wife in the store to get some old newspapers. He rolled that meat 'bout six inches deep and laid the meat down in the wagon and laid rocks around it to hold it down. He told me, "That mule won't ever know that that meat's on the wagon, Sammy."

We got back home and Daddy said, "Sammy, what'd you give for all this meat here?" I said, "I give Kenneth Stiles twenty dollars for it." He said, "He give it to ye, didn't he?" I said, "Well, he said he'd let me have it for twenty dollars, and I was glad to get it for that." Back then you could buy dinners a lot cheaper. I'd get five drumsticks, breasts, mash taters [mashed potatoes], pinto beans, coffee, and cornbread, all for seventy-five cents back then.

A Special Note About Sammy Green

At the conclusion of Sammy's interview, when the tape recorders had been turned off, he began to share his concern about not having any insurance or any way to pay for his funeral expenses. He was the last living member of his family, and while Sherri had been generous enough to take Sammy in and care for him for the past seven or eight years, he did not want to leave a financial burden on her.

After the interview in December 2006, Sammy's health took a turn for the worse. In March 2007, Sammy was admitted into the hospital and the medical staff decided they had done all they could and needed to call in hospice. We [students] decided to raise the money to bury Sammy. We took this on as a Foxfire class project and were able to involve other classes at our school in our effort to help Sammy.

I met with Sammy again to let him know that we were preparing a bluegrass music barbecue benefit for him to raise money for his funeral expenses. At that meeting, I asked him if there was anything special that he might want to have at his service. Much to my surprise, his only reply was that he had always wanted to be buried in a simple pine box. I remember thinking, "A pine box? How in the world are we going to accomplish that?" I knew if anyone could help us, it would be a local funeral home director, Lloyd Hunter. Mr. Hunter was so sincere through the whole process and provided us with the dimensions for a pine box. He also said he would be honored to perform Sammy's funeral, when the time come. So, with the dimensions of a pine box in hand, I went to the industrial

PLATE 8 Six ninth-grade industrial arts students built the pine box for Sammy Green's burial and served as pallbearers when he passed away: Jake Welch, Harrison Sumlin, Jordan Coalley, Ethan Hunter, Austin Gragg, Colby Nichols

arts class at Rabun County High School. After hearing my request, the boys were shocked, but after hearing the entire story, they, too, were more than willing to help fulfill Sammy's wish. Throughout the process the boys learned that we had become Sammy's family. They took a stand that I never would have expected: They said they would be privileged to be the pallbearers at Sammy's funeral.

When all the benefit preparations started, it was just a few small-town high school kids who saw a need and wanted to meet it. Little did we ever know that it would become a nationwide event. Sammy's story was broadcast on channel 32 TV news out of Toccoa, Georgia, and the Neil Boortz national radio show, as well as in The Atlanta Journal-Constitution, The Clayton Tribune, and numerous other outlets. We received a phone call out of Elberton, Georgia, from a couple who own a small granite business. They had seen Sammy's story on the news and wanted to help. They expressed how it would be their privilege to donate a headstone for Sammy. And the agriculture students at the high school assisted us the day of the benefit by cooking all the barbecue. From all the publicity and the people who came out the day of the benefit to eat and hear the bluegrass bands who volunteered their time, we were able to raise enough money to pay for Sammy's funeral; we even had some money left over for the hospital bills.

Sammy expressed to all, time and time again, how grateful he was for everything we did, and for everyone who participated in the benefit. He said we all gave him a sense of peace and a will to live, just by knowing that people still cared for him. Sammy had no idea, when he agreed to a Foxfire interview, *that he would gain a whole host of people who cared for him and would become known as his family.*

Sadly, Sammy left us and went to be with his Heavenly Father on August 18, 2009. Friends of Sammy, including the New York Times *reporters and photographers, attended Sammy's viewing at Hunter's Funeral Home in Clayton, Georgia, to see our promise to Sammy fulfilled. Only about two dozen people attended Sammy's funeral, several of whom barely knew him but had been touched by his story. Sammy wore overalls and a blue button-up shirt, just as he had requested. The pallbearers were the six boys who had built Sammy's pine box in the high school industrial arts class. As they marched to the graveside, with Sammy's favorite gospel tunes being played softly on the guitar in the distance, we were all filled with honor that we could help such a man fulfill his dying wish.*

Acts 20:35 says, "It is more blessed to give than to receive." I realized this through Sammy Green. Sammy touched more lives than he ever knew, and he will forever live on in our hearts.

—Casi Best

PLATE 9 **"When Sammy agreed to an interview with me, neither he nor I imagined this story would sweep the nation and touch the hearts of millions." Sammy with Casi in Dillard, Georgia**

"Don't you ever stop by my house again asking for whiskey."

~An interview with Madge Merrell~

My first article as a new student in Foxfire was published in the edition of The Foxfire Magazine *featuring former teachers. When Mrs. Green, one of my Foxfire teachers, suggested Mrs. Merrell, I knew she would be perfect. Mrs. Green and I arranged to meet Mrs. Merrell for the interview at the nursing home in Highlands, North Carolina, where she resides. When we opened the door to Mrs. Merrell's room, we were greeted with a big smile. Throughout the interview I was more and more amazed by the amount of information she shared. I thought, "Wow, this woman is almost ninety-nine years old, and she is still as sharp as a tack." In her fifty years of teaching, she watched countless children grow and mature. In addition to teaching, Mrs. Merrell also had many priceless experiences, such as living in a tent on the side of the road, seeing the first car to ever come to North Carolina, and learning to drive at the age of sixty-two. Life wasn't always easy for her, but she made the best of her situation.*

—Samantha Fountain

My name is Madge Dillard Merrell. I was born June 25, 1907, down there at Chattooga, right under the shadow of Chimney Top Mountain in North Carolina. I had the happiest childhood in the world. My daddy's name was Tom Dillard, and my mother's name was Susan Fugate Dillard. My father died October 31, 1947. He was the county commissioner, a school board member, and all kinds of stuff. He was deeply involved in politics. My mother died May 31, 1949—eighteen months after he did.

PLATE 10 "We called him Dink."
Mrs. Merrell and her older son, Dink

I was born where Chattooga Club is now. My mother said I was the least [smallest] baby she ever saw. I didn't weigh but about three pounds—I got lost in my clothes. I survived, and I was the happiest child. As long as I was around where my mother was,

I was happy. I had a happy childhood. My parents were Christians, and they never let anything stop them from going to church. Regardless of anything, we went to church. We would go to church in an ox wagon. I now belong to the Methodist church. I have belonged to the Methodist church for eighty-five years. I am their oldest member ever. I also hold the longest voting record in Jackson County.

We had plenty of food when I was growing up because we lived on a farm. We had plenty of food and lots of love. We all loved each other. We had very little money, but we didn't need any money; we had everything. We were very happy. I had four brothers and two sisters. All my brothers and sisters and I were born in Cashiers, North Carolina. I was the fourth child. My last brothers and sisters were far apart. One was seven years younger, and one was thirteen years younger. All of them are gone now; all of my brothers and sisters are gone.

We were always warm in the winter and cool enough in the summer. My mother would always come out on the back porch and say, "Come to the house, children. Supper is ready." My mother had a gristmill; you know, that you ground cornmeal in. You took the toll [a portion of the corn] out of cornmeal you ground for people. You took a gallon of toll out of a bushel of cornmeal to grind it. I used to go with my mother down to the river to grind meal. I would walk down there and listen to the water. My daddy was in timber all of his life. He cut timber and logged with horses and cattle. That is what he did, and my brothers did, too. One brother worked on the highway. He worked with men to build roads.

I saw the first car that ever came to the mountains, driven by Henry Ford, so they told me later. It scared me to death that day. Of course, it made the awfulest noise. I climbed the bank, and I tried to get away from that monster. It was scary. I didn't know what to think [laughs].

Since we didn't have a doctor, when my family got sick, my mother went out and got yellow root, and she boiled it. I used to have tonsillitis, and I had blisters that big [motions with her hands the size of her blisters]. She would make us warm medicine with Jerusalem oil. Oh, do you know what that is? Don't ever find out. That is the awfulest stuff. She used that when we got sick. When we got a cold, she would put flannel on our chests. She would make it hot and put all kinds of concoctions on it. It was not hot enough to blister us, but pretty hot. We had different things for whatever was wrong with us. I remember the cough medicine she made. She put alum in it and a little bit of whiskey and a little bit of honey, and it seemed like a couple of other things, but those three I remember. It would help a cough. My mother was our doctor.

For entertainment when I was growing up, we had parties and square dances, and we had all kinds of, you know, no-harm activities. Nobody was drinking. We would get together at night and have us a party. We would play different kinds of games. We went to square dances. One night I went to a square dance, and there were forty-two couples on the floor. The big thing with us though was going to church and singing at church. We had singings, and maybe we would have a preacher up there at the schoolhouse during the week. He might be there with us to sing and read. That was the big thing with us back then. We had a good time. We never knew who would come home with us after church on Sunday. My mama always said she cooked for the man in the woods—meaning anybody might show up to eat.

I went to school in Cashiers until I was in the seventh grade. My dad wanted me to finish high school. We didn't have any high schools in Cashiers or Glenville, so I went over to Western Carolina to the high school, which was affiliated with the college at that time, and I finished high school there. I stayed over there as a boarding student. We had eleven grades when I was in high school. I didn't finish high school until I was nineteen because I missed a year of school. We could stay in the dormitories at Western. That was a happy time, too. When I finished high school, I went back to college there for about a year and a half. Most of the teachers who taught school back then did not go to college. I had more education than most of the teachers. You didn't even have to have schooling to teach during the war because they didn't have any teachers.

I started teaching when I was twenty-one. The first year I taught was up in Canada in Jackson County, North Carolina. They called it Little Canada. Little Canada is really in the boondocks, about one and a half hours from Cashiers. I had seventh grade. It was very primitive up there where I stayed. There wasn't even a john [restroom] up there where I taught, or where I stayed either. We had a spring where the children got water to drink. They used a dipper. I bought them one of those collapsible cups, and they wouldn't drink out of it because they had grown so used to that dipper. They loved to use that dipper. I thought the collapsible cup would tickle them, and they wouldn't have to use that dipper. It didn't tickle them at all. The first year I taught, I got one hundred dollars a month, I think. Out of this amount, I paid about twenty dollars for board and lodging. One year I got paid fifty-two dollars a month during the Depression.

I went from Little Canada to Cashiers to teach. From Cashiers I went to Bull Pen [Pleasant Grove]. The school at Bull Pen was a schoolhouse, and the community also used it for a church. It had two rooms in the front of it—one of them they called the cloakroom, and one was where you put lunches. We walked every day to school. It was a mile exactly from where we lived to the school. I took my lunch with me to school. The kids brought theirs, too, something like the fried cabbage from the night before. They had two rooms up on the stage where they dressed if we had a program. We didn't have any electricity. It got pretty dark sometimes. We had wood. We used wood to heat the building. We had a boy who built fires for a while for me. The stove was one of the long ones. It had a door where the ashes were. We had to take the ashes out.

I married Merrett Merrell on June 9, 1930. I had already been hired to teach at Cashiers when I married. After I married, I got pregnant. At the end of my school year, my oldest child was born June 9, 1931. His name was M. H. Merrell Jr. We called him Dink. Four years after I had my first child, I had my second child, Curtis Ward Merrell. He was born June 28, 1935. My oldest son, Dink, died a few years ago; he died January 10, 2000. Curtis, my youngest son, died August 20, 1960—he was twenty-five years old. When my oldest son went to school, he could wear a pair of overalls a week. He would pull them off when he got home and put him something on to play in. I had two children and a husband that was sick a lot.

After my children died, I just didn't want to live anymore. I give up all reasons for living, but Dink left me grandchildren. I just couldn't leave them. Both of my children were born in June. Of course I had to have a babysitter. When Curtis, the last one, was born, I had taught school in Bull Pen for three years. We had a cabin that we lived in the first year, and it had lizards and everything else in it. I always felt like a snake was going across my foot. It scared me to death. The second year we lived in a house, which belonged to Cecil White, right across from where you turn up to the schoolhouse. It had cracks in it this big [motions with hands to show the size of the cracks]. We lived there that winter, and the next winter we didn't have no place, so we bought us a tent, and the family built a wooden floor and stretched the tent over it. They really did do a good job on that tent. And then they built me a little kitchen about twice as wide as that door [pointing to the door]. I had bought a new woodstove, but I didn't take it with me down there. The furniture store found a little step stove—just a tiny stove to cook on. They loaned that to me, and I cooked on it, and it cooked real good. We had a woodstove that was tin, but that was the warmest winter I ever spent. We had a lot of birchwood to burn. We had chickens and had plenty of eggs. I think we butchered a hog that winter. We had good food to eat down there. Mr. Rochester would come and eat with us. He sure did enjoy his meal. He would burp real big and say, "That sure was good." We raised most of the food for our family. I grew carrots, beans, corn, lettuce, radishes, and all kinds of stuff in my garden. My husband got out and got apples and had them ready for me to can when I got home. Women would can, make jelly, and all kinds of things like that.

The tent we lived in was so close that we almost lived in the road. One afternoon, it was almost dark, and some men came by, and they said, "I want to buy some whiskey." I said, "I want you to understand that I am a lady and that I am a schoolteacher. I am teaching school down here, and my family is with me. Don't you ever stop at my house again asking for whiskey!" But I can understand why they did it. Why would a tent be out there in the middle of nowhere? What fool would live on the side of the road in a tent? I couldn't be too hard on them. I never knew what became of that tent, but we had a good time.

When I taught at Bull Pen, I was the whole thing—the teacher, the principal, and all. I remember one day, they had a school committee meeting. Each community had a school committee. My uncle was on the school committee, and, of course, my daddy used to be. They come and spent a while with me to watch me teach. They were the ones that recommended the teacher. The county paid me.

One year I was going to get my children their Christmas presents—well, what I could. I let one of the teachers take my voucher to the bank, and she lost it. They found it under the carpet. They had swept it under the carpet, but they did write me a check. One Christmas, the first Christmas we were at Bull Pen, I went to Sylva, North Carolina, and bought the children their Christmas. I bought them new shoes and some clothes and a little wagon—a little red wagon. We made chains—red and green chains—to put on our Christmas tree at school. That is all we had, but it looked real pretty.

We lived at Bull Pen for three years, I guess. I don't know what happened down there at the Bull Pen School. The parents got to where they didn't want to send their children to me to teach. Some of them moved to Cashiers so they wouldn't have to send their children to me. I continued to teach school at Bull Pen with just two or three children. The funny thing about it was that when I was appointed to teach back at Cashiers, I had to teach their children again. That just killed them, I know.

I went back to Cashiers after I left Bull Pen. We bought property at Cashiers in 1932. We bought twenty-two acres for four hundred seventy-five dollars. It had a house on it, but it was a sawmill house. They had seed in one of the rooms and hay and everything. We hired a man to rebuild it. I was still teaching school, and they said that they would have it ready for me. My husband and the babysitter moved us to the house by horse and wagon. You just couldn't believe how happy I was. It was a mile from my house to the schoolhouse.

One day I had my children lined up. I didn't even have to tell them to line up in front of the steps. This little boy—he was about ten or twelve, I guess—was lined up. His name was George Hunter. The principal came

PLATE 11 **"My husband and the babysitter moved us to the house by horse and wagon." Mrs. Merrell's home in Cashiers, North Carolina**

along and had a magazine in his hand. It was just about as heavy as that one [pointing to a magazine]. Then he hit him over the head with that magazine. I said, "Let me tell you something. As long as I teach at this school, don't you ever do that again! You go over there and discipline your own students." He would go and drink coffee in the lunchroom, and I would have to quit teaching to go over there and discipline his kids and make them be quiet so I could teach. "Now, I mean it," I said.

He said, "Mrs. Merrell, I want to see you after school." I told him that I didn't have a thing to say to him after school. I just walked on like a big fat dog. He tried his best to get me to quit teaching there, but I had my contract. I told him there wasn't anything he could do to get me to quit teaching. I didn't want to teach with him either. He knew I didn't. In later years, the church bought the Cashiers school and made a church out of it. It is still in Cashiers. Now it is a bakeshop.

I remember when I was teaching that some of my students would have sore feet. I had a balm of Gilead [*Populus candicans*]. Do you know what a balm of Gilead tree is? It is mentioned in the Bible. I would take that and pine rosin [resin] and make a good salve out of it, and I would tear up any old rag that I had or that anybody had given to me, and I would take it to school. I had an old porcelain wash pan, and I would put water in the pan and put it on our stove and heat it and get it good and warm. I would have the children put their feet in that wash pan, and I would wash them up. Then I would put some of that salve on their feet and tie a clean cloth around it. Their feet would heal up.

When my students misbehaved, I had a hickory [to whip them with], but I usually had good children. I didn't have to use that hickory much. My children would march up to the door and form their own lines. I think they knew from the beginning that I was the one that would tell them what to do and what not to do. That helped a lot. I showed them a lot of love, too. I played with them. I was good to them—just as good to them as they let me be. I am a good teacher. The reason I say that is because I love the schoolchildren. I want them to do their best. If they are teachable, I will teach them how to read and spell. I had the sweetest students; I didn't have hardly any discipline troubles.

The big children would help the little ones. That's the reason I got as much in as I did because they would help them while I had another class. I taught everything for grades one through seven. I taught geography and history. It took me all day long. At one school I had forty-five students. The boys were as big as I was, and the girls were, too, but they were not as old. I had a good time with them. I would get out with them at recess time, and they would play. The girls would play in one place, and the boys would play in another, but they had the queerest ideas down there. We got one of the first radios, and they thought if they talked about us at their houses that we could hear them. I will never forget; they said, "You better watch what you say. She can hear you." They thought we could hear them through the radio. They would come to our house at night to listen to music. We listened to the Grand Ole Opry. That was when it was so popular. We heard Loretta Lynn, and Hank Williams was on there, and Roy Acuff.

I retired in the early eighties. I just got to where I couldn't teach on my certificate [due to state laws governing certificates]. I was in my eighties when I stopped teaching completely. I kept driving until I was eighty-four. I took a lot of correspondence classes. One afternoon I was doing correspondence work, and I felt somebody at my back. Have you ever felt like someone is behind you, at your back? I felt somebody looking at me, and I turned around, and there was a rifle barrel pointed at me coming in the door. It scared me to death. That man thought it was funny. I said, "That wasn't a bit funny. You could have caused me to have a heart attack."

I substituted for about fifteen years at the old Glenville School after I retired. I also taught adult school at night sometimes. They hired me to teach night school at people's houses. I made twelve dollars a week. I went to the houses and taught. I let them tell me what they wanted to learn. When I would go to their houses, you know, some of them could write, but they couldn't write very well. I would help them with that.

One of my former students who I still love is Delbert McCall. Delbert has done well. He is a preacher and still comes to visit me. Delbert's mother,

PLATE 12 "One of my former students who I still love
is Delbert McCall." Mrs. Merrell with her great-niece,
Renee White, and a former student, Delbert McCall

Danie, had a hard life. She was married to John Crowe, and he died, leaving her with three children—Mildred, Bessie, and Lee Roy—to raise. She then married Clarence McCall, Delbert's father, and had three other children: Joe, Wanda, and Delbert. Clarence McCall had cancer. Danie had such a hard time. She done all she could. After Clarence died she bought some property from us, and some men moved an old house from Bull Pen onto the property. The house was in the woods next to me. Danie's children would come through my field on the way to and from home. We had a big ol' hound dog that my son, Dink, and Delbert's brother, Lee Roy, played with. They had picked her pups up and looked at 'em and threw rocks at her and aggravated her—she hated them. She hated for anybody to bother her. She would bite; I knew she would. I told them never to come through my field to my house because that dog might be loose one day. Luckily, they never got bit. I had two black walnut trees in my yard, and one day when Delbert came by I had hung out my white sheets to dry. When I washed them, I would put a little lye in sometimes, and I would boil them to get them white. That day, I looked up, and Delbert had a walnut in each hand ready to throw at my sheets. If he had hit my sheets with them black walnuts, I never would have gotten the stains out. He was ready to, but I put a stop to that. He never has forgot it. When he was little, Delbert liked milk and bread. I would have him a glass full of milk and some bread when he got home from school. Delbert sings and plays the guitar. I don't remember him singing when he was a child.

He has brought me his tapes, but I think the first song he sung to me was when I was up yonder in the hospital [the hospital is connected to the nursing home where Mrs. Merrell resides], and his aunt was in the hospital. He come up next to my bed, and he took my hands, and he sung "Amazing Grace." He sure can sing. I would like for him to sing for me when I die.

I used to read a lot. I read everything that came out. I was an avid reader. That's what hurts me so bad, sitting here not reading. [Mrs. Merrell cannot see well enough to read now.] I read everything—all the local things. My daddy told me, "Honey, read. Just read." I would read the current books that came out. I would go to the library and read. Like I said, "If you can read, you can move mountains." Out of all the books I read, the book *Little Big* really stands out in my memory; that was a story about the Appalachian Mountains. Also, the Hannah Fowler books that were written by Janice Holt Giles were real good. I had them at home. I had *Hannah Fowler* and some more. The Hannah Fowler books were about a girl who went to Texas to teach school, and she was a lot like me.

When my husband died, Dink, my son, said he would be willing to let me stay in Cashiers if I would get my driver's license. I was sixty-two. He come and bought me a little Ford Falcon. I went and tried to get my driver's license that summer. I want to tell you, everybody in the country tried to help me. The teachers tried to help me, and the driver's education teacher helped me—even the sheriff tried to help; everybody wanted me to get my driver's license. You know, I got my driver's license when I was sixty-two. I tried out all summer. A woman, Daisy Watson, would ride with me to Highlands, North Carolina, to try out. I wouldn't have ridden with me knowing that I couldn't drive any better than I could. I finally got them in August. I drove for years, but I wasn't that good of a driver. I knew a woman who wanted to go get her license, and nobody would ride with her but me. You know, you have to drive so much with someone who has a license before you can get them. Nobody would ride with her, so I told her, "I will ride with you." I went with her, and she finally got them. She was like me; she wasn't the best driver.

This girl that comes and helps me sometimes asked, "How did you get your nice complexion?" I told her that I didn't put any soap on my face. I said, "Well, I credit it a lot to God for taking care of me all the years and for being with me through the valleys and the high mountains. Also, growing up I didn't smoke, and I didn't drink. I ate the right kinds of foods. I had good genes. I had to have had good genes." That is what I attribute to my longevity.

You asked about my favorite president. I think President Roosevelt was sent by God. I thought he was the finest man. When President Roosevelt was president, he made jobs for people. It was back during the Depression. I will tell you, Jimmy Carter was the most Christian. Billy Graham said he was the only Bible-toting president we ever had, but Jimmy Carter was too good for all that mess. He couldn't work with them. They were too sinful. I liked Bill Clinton. He just got caught up in it all. The economy sure was balanced when he was president. I hope we do not have a woman president. I don't want them to put that off on a woman.

Looking back on my life I think . . . my husband died January 7, 1969. Even when my first child died, I still had my husband and my other child. When Merrett died, I still had my son. When my last son died, I don't see how I lived through it. I guess it is because of my grandchildren. All of my grandchildren live in Macon, Georgia. I have three grandchildren and seven great-grandchildren.

I am still as active as I can be here in the nursing home. Two mornings a week, I have devotion. We have singing and usually memorial services. At night, we have trivia. Some of them are as smart as me, but I still try. I am pretty good at Bible trivia. I have been exposed to the Bible my whole life. In my earliest recollection, it was one of the things that was right there.

Editor's note: *Mrs. Merrell passed away from a brief illness just after the completion of her article, so she never saw it in print. She is greatly missed by her family and friends, and we will always treasure the memories and stories she shared with us. She was a very special lady.*

"So that's pretty well my eighty-nine years."
~Jack P. Nix tells us about his career~

On a hilltop overlooking the remnants of his parents' farm, Jack P. Nix lives with Ruby, his wife of more than sixty-five years. This home is the one they built in retirement after Mr. Nix served more than a decade as the state school superintendent for Georgia during the 1960s and 1970s. The middle son of a farmer, and a student who disliked school, Mr. Nix nonetheless went on to a long and accomplished career in education.

As we spoke on a warm July morning, Mr. Nix shared his memories with me in a straightforward, unaffected manner, describing everything from his own schooling to an appearance before a Washington congressional committee matter-of-factly. On a few occasions, however, his emotions did betray him. The broad smile on his face when he talked of his industrial agriculture students left me with no doubts of his sincerity when he shared how much he enjoyed them. After all these years, the frustration of dealing with a governor who was adamantly opposed to integration was also still very clear. And when he spoke of his wife, Ruby, and his very accomplished children and grandchildren, the smile that shone from his eyes said much about a man who loves his wife and family.

When I called Mr. Nix to request an interview, he expressed surprise that I would want to know about his tenure as state school superintendent, given how many years had passed since his retirement. However, with Mr. Nix, as with so many of our Foxfire contacts, I am, once again, reminded of the old adage that the more things change, the more they stay the same. Mr. Nix described a legislature and teacher community occasionally at odds as to who was best to make decisions concerning public education. He talked of the importance of giving students the opportunity to produce something of value in the process of their education. His own life story tells of how a dedicated educator, while simply doing his or her job, can change for the better the entire trajectory of a young person's life. Those lessons are as valuable today as they ever were. And, though I would claim Mr. Nix if I could, we are not related.

—Lacy Hunter Nix

I'm Jack Phillip Nix, born October 6, 1921, about one o'clock in the morning, my mama said. I started school in 1926. It was a one-room school with about forty students and one teacher. I went to that school for about two weeks, and they consolidated it with the Cleveland, Georgia, schools. We had a teacher for each grade then. In the first grade we had a "Baby Ray." It was a book, a Baby Ray book, and we studied that book for a whole year, but you didn't get out of the first grade that year. You stayed with Baby Ray one year and the first grade one year. Then you went on to second, third, fourth, fifth. So it really was kind of a kindergarten, too.

At that time we were having to pay to get to go to school. My dad had timber cut off our farm for firewood to be used at the school. If you didn't have that, it would cost you two dollars and a half a month to go to school. There were schools in the United States back in the 1700s, but they were private schools or organizations, one or the other—no state money for it and no public money going into it. It was all private. I believe it was about 1919 or 1920 that we got a poor-school fund started. The legislature appropriated twenty thousand the first year. Can you imagine twenty thousand for the whole state?! Then they finally got it up to a hundred thousand, but those were still awfully poor schools. In 1870, they worked out the constitution that would make it legal for the legislature to appropriate school funds for public education.

When I started school, you didn't even have to have a high school diploma to teach school. I believe it was about 1940 that the state board passed a policy that if you got any state money, then you had to have a college degree. That's when we started really putting colleges of education in most of the four-year institutions.

All my elementary and secondary education was in White County, Georgia. I went to Cleveland and graduated in 1938 from high school. I stayed out of school two years and a half before I went to college. I didn't like school. I had a teacher that never taught me, but he became interested in me, and talked me into going to the University of Georgia. This teacher was Bud Moss. He came here as a vocational agriculture teacher. He borrowed some money from Dad to buy a carload of cans. He built a canning plant. He needed cans, so he borrowed some money. The county board of education didn't have money to let him have. He would buy these cans, and when he canned stuff, people paid him for canning. About every week or two, he'd come out here to the farm and make a payment. He kind of liked me and invited me to go to Lake Rabun to the 4-H place there one summer with his students. I was the only outsider in the outfit, and while we were there, he talked to us about everything there is to talk about, like going to school. So he talked me into going.

One day he had me get in his car and took me to the University of Georgia and enrolled me in school and found me a place to stay. I got room and board for sixteen dollars a month, and my tuition was twenty-seven dollars and a half a quarter. I graduated from high school in 1938, and I started college in January of 1941. I graduated from the university in August of 1943. I spent two and a half years and received my degree. Later, I received my master's and my six-year on the GI bill as a veteran.

During the two and a half years I was out of high school, I worked here on the farm. We had a mowing machine and a hay rake. In the fall of the year, I would go around the community cutting community members' hay for them and raking it. They'd pay me for the length of time I worked. It didn't cost anything for the horsepower because we always had the horses. I saved up about two hundred and twenty-five dollars, and that paid my first year of college. The day before Bud came to pick me up to take me to Athens to get enrolled, I told my dad, "Well, tomorrow I'll be leaving." He reached back in his pocket and pulled out his checkbook. He said, "Here's you a checkbook. Don't break me up, but live like the other boys." He couldn't have said anything that made me anymore stingy [laughs]! I have a little book upstairs in the attic in a footlocker where I wrote down everything I spent—cost me eighteen hundred and some few dollars to get my degree.

My mother used to sell a lot of milk and butter. People would come out and buy her vegetables. She had a little glass in the cabinet in our home where she kept the money. When I'd come home from school, she'd slip me a five-dollar bill or something like that, so I'd have some "walking around" money. They were proud of me. I was the first one in our family to ever graduate from college. My sister, just older than I am, went to college for one summer. She taught school for one year on a high school diploma, but then she got out of it. From me down, we all graduated from college. There were nine of us, and I was the middle one, four boys and five girls.

I met my wife, Ruby, on a bus. I was hitchhiking home from the university. I could hitchhike from Athens to Gainesville pretty easy, but there wasn't much traffic on the road then from Gainesville to Cleveland. I'd have to catch a bus in Gainesville. I had met her sister once before when I was getting on that bus, and I saw her back there. I went back and sat down with her, and we started talking. She said, "Oh, I want you to meet my sister." I looked over the back at her, and she was curled up in the double seat. I said, "Where do you go to school?" She said, "I'll have you know I teach school." Those were the first words we said to one another [laughs]. She was teaching school in McIntosh County, way down on the coast of Georgia. A fellow from Union County was principal down there, and he talked her into going to work with him. We went together about three years. Then when I was out in Texas, training troops, I called her one day and said, "If you'll come out here, we'll get married." She caught a train and came out, and we were married August the eighth, 1945, at nine forty-nine at night.

I went to Habersham County, Georgia, and taught vocational agriculture one year after college. Then I went into the military, World War II. I took my basic training in Florida at Camp Blanding. They sent me to Fort Benning, Georgia, to go to Officer Candidate School; finished that, and, in May 1945,

I guess it was, they sent me to Texas. I trained troops about three or four months, and then they sent me to Okinawa, Japan. I stayed there exactly one year. I was education officer for the island—wound up running a radio station for the whole island, the Armed Forces Radio station. I had fifteen enlisted men, and we would go up on top of a mountain. We had a shortwave outfit, and we'd turn it on at night, after we'd go off the air, and talk to people in Africa and Asia and different places, just playing around with it. After a year I had enough time in to come home.

I came home and went back to teaching school in Banks County—taught school for ten years. We showed steers at the Atlanta Fat Cattle Show. To get a project, the students had to have something that was tangible. They learn faster when they have something like that. I had it worked out with the Northeastern Banking Company there in Commerce, Georgia, that if I brought a boy down there that needed some money to buy a calf, they'd loan it to him on my name, only I didn't have to sign anything. This boy and his dad would sign, and when we sold the calf, we'd go back and pay it off. So if he had money left over, he'd put it in his pocket. That was an enticement for them to do a good job. The Future Farmers of America [FFA] chapter and I got together, and I said, "Look, if one of these calves dies, we have a problem about paying it off. From now on, what about just adding five dollars to the expense of buying a steer, and I'll put that five dollars in an insurance fund." We had one calf to die, and we paid it off out of that insurance fund. I don't know whatever happened to the insurance fund. They still had it when I became superintendent.

One year we had, I believe it was, fifty-four steers down there at the Atlanta Fat Cattle Show. Some of those boys had never even ridden on an elevator or eaten out rather than eating a regular meal at home. They'd eat a hamburger. It was educational all the way around. One year we won the FFA class, and that boy got two thousand dollars for his steer. The restaurant people would come in and buy the steers. They'd beef them [slaughter them for beef] and say, "The grand champion of the Fat Cattle Show," and people would buy steaks better that way.

My students put in an indoor toilet at the high school in the basement of the library building. The superintendent wanted me to lay out a drain field. I did that, and when we got through, I told the board of education, "I saved you a whole lot of money by laying that thing out, digging those trenches, putting gravel and those pipes in, and covering them back up. Now, why don't you buy us a tractor?" So the county board bought us a tractor for the kids. We used that tractor to go out and plow their acre of ground for cotton or corn or whatever they wanted. It was interesting! I never had a job I didn't enjoy.

Then I ran for county superintendent. No one else would have it, and I was elected. Earlier, we had a fellow by the name of Clarence Tucker who was superintendent and had been for several years. He was a native of the county. One year, a young fellow who was a Baptist preacher, Ted Sisk, from Stephens County moved over to Banks County because he dated a girl from Banks County. He ran against Mr. Tucker and won. He and I surveyed the entire high school layout where we built the new high school. I became real close to Ted, and he became close to me. When his term was about over, I went by his office and said, "Ted, are you going to run again?" He said, "Why are you asking?" I said, "Well, if you don't run, I'm going to run, but I won't run against you." He said, "Well, I'm not going to run, but don't you tell anybody." I didn't tell anyone until qualifying day, and I went in and gave my check. That was all it cost—the entry fee—because no one tried to run against me.

I missed the kids more than anything else after I became superintendent. Before that, I'd take them camping every summer. We had a little canteen at the school there, and we'd open it at recess and lunch and sell Cokes and candy. We made enough money to buy a truck. We had a small truck, and then we bought a ton and a half. When we did that, I could haul the whole chapter at one time—twenty, almost thirty boys. They'd bring in groceries from home, and we'd go camp out for a week. I'd get pup tents off of the war surplus, and I had enough for every camper. We'd do our own cooking. I'd take those boys to a movie one night—just load them up on that big old truck and take off. That's what we also used to haul steers to Atlanta for the cattle shows. I enjoyed the high school boys about as much as anything.

I stayed there as county superintendent for three and a half years, then the state board of education had me come to Atlanta. I issued teachers' certificates for ten months. Then I was director of vocational education for the state and built area technical schools like Lanier Tech and most of the buildings over in Clarkesville at North Georgia Tech.

Then, in the fall of 1965, the governor called me and said, "Dr. Purcell is going to retire, and if you would like to have the job, we want you to be state superintendent. He's got one year left. During that year you'll have to run for the office." That summer I had to run for the office statewide, but no one would have it, and I was elected. In January 1966, I became state superintendent. I went in as Dr. Purcell went out. I only had an opponent one time in sixteen political years. I beat him in his own county.

The state of Georgia didn't have a school building program till the fifties. I'd get appropriations to allot funds to local systems based on the state board policies. I got special education and the arts funded, too, and I also introduced a bill to provide school-bus drivers with state insurance and retirement, and it passed. Georgia was the first state to pass funding for the school lunch program with state money. My school lunch lady, Josephine Martin, came to me and said, "There's not enough federal money. We can't have a decent meal with that. We need some more money." I said, "Well, Congress is not appropriating enough." She said, "We can get state money, maybe?" We introduced a bill, and we got state money—so much per meal served.

About the time I left was the time Jimmy Carter got his finger into education and tried to get my job appointed by the governor rather than elected by the people. I took the position that the people had children in school and the position was too important to let one man make the decision—the people ought to elect the superintendent.

I went to Washington one time to see Senator Sam Irvin of North Carolina. He and his committee wanted me there to talk about federal involvement in the state education program. What had happened was that we were getting so many reports on the amount of money we were receiving from the federal government. It was terrible. We had about seven, eight percent of federal funds coming into education, but we had stacks and stacks of forms we had to fill out—teacher, principal, local superintendent, then myself—I had to consolidate all that and send it to Washington. I got all those forms with blanks and made a copy of them, put a red ribbon around them, and caught an early-bird plane to Washington to Senator Sam's committee. When I sat down in a chair, he said to the whole audience, "What's that you have there, Superintendent?" I said, "This is the red tape that the U.S. Office of Education sends out and gathers." He said, "Well, what do they do with it?" I said, "Well, I asked one time, and the man who answered my question took me into a room and showed me where they stacked them on shelves in that little room. They stayed there and gathered dust." It bothered him. That really got to the U.S. commissioner of education. You see, when the Congress passes a bill and the president signs it, it then goes back to that agency for the agency to hire the lawyers and everything to try and determine what the bill said. By the time the lawyers and the staff got through adding rules and regulations, we had an undue amount of regulation. For instance, civil rights were coming with integration. We had to keep records there for a while that if there was any discipline problem involved with a minority student, we had to keep that person's name and the date that they had complained, what it was about, and send the reports to Washington. There were only seventeen states that had to do that, just southern states. The way Congress passed the bill, it only included the seventeen states. I mentioned to Senator Sam's committee that day that "we'll solve the integration problem in Georgia before you do in Boston and Chicago and New York and Los Angeles." It wasn't long until there were demonstrations in Boston after Georgia schools had successfully integrated.

I guess the biggest challenge I faced was trying to work around with Lester Maddox when we had integration. He didn't want the schools to integrate. He said, "You don't mix hawks and crows," and shook his head. I guess working with him was probably one of the most difficult things I had to do. I'll have to say this for Lester: He was the easiest governor to work with, at the same time, because if he told you something, you could bet on him doing it. He kept his word. If he said, "I'll do so and so," he'd do it. If he said, "No," he'd fight you tooth and toenail.

I suspect a vocational tech program and kindergarten for little kids were the best things I have ever done. I may not ever be noted for it, but

PLATE 13 **Mr. Nix served more than a decade as the Georgia state school superintendent.**

building all these vocational technical schools—there have been thousands of students who have gotten a job because they were able to go through a mechanics course or bricklaying, typing, or shorthand or biology. That's one thing I am really proud of.

The other thing is having kindergartens. See, we had kindergartens in Atlanta and Columbus. That's all. They paid for it with local money. It was illegal for me to pay for it with state money when I was state superintendent. I was in Israel, Tel Aviv, for the federal government. I was on a trip with seven other state superintendents for the government, and we didn't have anything one morning, and I started walking around on the street. I ran into a little school and found out it was an elementary school; they had a kindergarten. I went in and sat down in that classroom all morning, watching what the teacher and the students were doing. When I came back to the States, we had a state board meeting, and I told the state board about it. I said, "It's amazing what those little kids can learn, how fast they pick up stuff at that time. We need to have kindergartens all over the state for everybody." What I argued with the legislature, when I was trying to get kindergarten through, was that the way it is now, the children all come to first grade and, without kindergarten, it's hard to keep them all in the seats for the first month. It takes about a month to get them all to sit down at the same time. I said, "This is a readiness program. We're getting them ready to learn. It's not necessarily teaching the three Rs, but they will probably get some of that, and they will learn their colors and things like that."

The state board finally passed it, and I put it in my budget for the next appropriations and the governor kicked it out—Jimmy Carter kicked it out the first time. Then, the next time, Jimmy was still governor, and Maddox was lieutenant governor. Maddox helped me keep it in the budget. We got it in the budget at one-fourth the amount needed per year for four years. When I retired, I got the last fourth. That was for all children. I couldn't have done it if they had given me all the money to start with because I didn't have enough teachers or classrooms. I had to get that ready.

I retired in August of 1977 when I was fifty-five years old. I had been on the road and, as you can see [shows me his notes], I would write as I would ride around. My writing shows it, too. I retired and moved up to Gainesville, Georgia, because there were a lot of medical facilities there, and I knew I was getting older. I built a house and lived in it for three years, then I bought half of my daddy's farm here in Cleveland and built this house; I've been here since 1982. I started with a herd of cattle till Ruby had a pacemaker put in, then I sold all the cows. I just devoted my time to looking after her because she has had two open-heart surgeries and can't do a whole lot of cooking or anything like that. So that's pretty well my eighty-nine years!

"But he was a stinker, that boy of mine."

~An interview with Lillie Billingsley~

I never would have guessed one person could be so interesting until I met Lillie Billingsley. She welcomed my teacher, Mrs. Holly Cabe, and me into her home in Scaly Mountain, North Carolina, with open arms. Mrs. Billingsley was so kind to us that day—something that I will never forget. She relived her childhood and shared ninety-one years of memories with us, including some of the ways young people had fun "back in the day."

—Viola Nichols

I was born the nineteenth of August in the year 1914. When I was born, I was born over there in Blue Valley. I don't know how long we lived there. I guess I've lived here in Scaly, North Carolina, about sixty-five years, right here in this house. We was doing good back then. All of us young people were 'tending the churches; we didn't have much places to go in them days like y'all do now, so we went to church right down here. [She points down the road.] We'd just have a ball down there because we didn't understand their kind of religion. They did some funny things down there; their religion down there was always different from ours. They used to get up and dance, and some of them would just fall out in the floor. The women, they'd usually bring wraps and lay them down in the back of the church, and when they'd take them fall-out spells, this old lady, she'd get the coats and the wraps off the wall and lay them over the women.

I didn't know nothing about it, and I still don't know nothing about it. Course, I don't mean nothing by it, and I love everybody. We just went to cut up and have us a big time; everyone did it. We didn't go for nothing bad; we just went to see and be seen, if you will, and to have a good time, and we did. We really had a good time down there.

PLATE 14 **"Jim and me, we didn't have a car; we walked everywhere we went." Lillie Billingsley in 2006**

Now, some of the boys was pretty rude. They'd get out around the sides of the church, and lots of them drank back in those days, too, and they'd look through the windows and make ugly faces at the church members inside. Some of them would throw things through the windows. Some of the church members would get up there and get to shoutin' like they do down at the church, and them boys would throw things through the windows at them. A lot of the boys would sit on the back row and drink. They would get their little half-pint bottle out of their pockets and take 'em a drink. Then they would put it back in their pocket. We was just there for a ball—just a good time.

My son, Jimmy, pulled a big joke down there one time. He was the biggest thang you ever seen; he was the cutest thang. He was full of life and fun, and he wanted to enjoy himself, and he did so. He would put on a dress and the whole thang, and he'd get a brassiere [she motions to her chest] and make him some boobies, and then he'd go to church. At church there was a man that liked the women awful good, and he'd run after any one of them that would even look at him, and those that didn't look at him, he'd chase them, too! And Jimmy, he'd go to church down there. But he was a stinker, that boy of mine—he was a stinker indeed! And, boy, was he good-looking, that boy of mine. But I thought all my children was good-looking, so it don't make no difference. Anyway, Jimmy dressed up like a girl, and he decided to play a trick on this man that liked the women real good. So Jimmy would wave, real shy-like, at the man that liked the women, and the man would just perk up and look at Jimmy and smile. Jimmy just kept it going. He would peek around the corners at the man and just wave. He had the man chasing him all over Scaly. The man would foller [follow] Jimmy up the road and down the road.

Dolly [Mrs. Billingsley's sister] married Dub. Jim [Mrs. Billingsley's husband] and Dub were brothers, so sisters married brothers. It's about all the same thing; she married Dub just like I did Jim. I was married, I guess, three months before Dolly was. Jim and I were married at the courthouse in Franklin, North Carolina. Jim and me, we didn't have a car; we walked everywhere we went, but we didn't have to walk up to Franklin. We rode with the justice of the peace. After the wedding, he brought us back here to Georgia, and then we walked right up that old rough mountain to the Mud Creek Country. On the way, there was a place they called the Devil's Den with big rocks. We come by that and stopped and looked at it, then walked on up to the neighbor's house to just stop and rest a while. John Carpenter's house is where we stopped, and he and his family wanted us to spend the night, so we did. We spent the night that night, and then we walked all day the next day, and we come on up to where my mother and father lived.

PLATE 15 **"I liked Jim the best; he was a sweetheart."**
Jim and Lillie Billingsley in 1957

We stayed with them for all that summer, and I remember they helped us get started. My daddy said, "I got a good farm and plenty of land and all the plows and everything you need; you can tend all the land you want to tend. You'll get everything free, and that'll get what you need to get a house and stuff and get you started." That was from the ground up, you know. He did; he gave us that land, and we grew potatoes that year, and we had a big turnout of cabbage. We had a little old Ford truck that we used to haul the cabbage on down to Georgia.

We bought us two beds—two little iron beds—and a kitchen buffet. We made our own mattresses. It was fun to do because everybody back in those days was in poverty. One feller didn't feel no better than the other because nobody had any food to eat, and that's how it really was. We got on our feet. Mama gave me pots and pans from her house and some things out of her pantry to help us get started on. I didn't know much about cooking, but we got by.

Then we started raising our family, and we had a big family. There was Juan [pronounced Joo-ann], Gene, Ruth, Jimmy, Jo-Ed, Bobby, Homer, Gail, and Alice. Then we had two twin boys at the last part of it, and I lost both of them. Well, I had Jimmy, Juan, Bobby, and Gail while we lived here at this house. We had one little hospital, that was all. We had doctors that come to your house. They come to everyone who was expecting a baby. The doctor give you something just before you had your baby to keep your kidneys straight. One little bottle of medicine was all he give you. You eat for the health of your baby, so that it would make it. But now, whenever you go to have a baby, he don't give you nothing for your kidneys.

Then we moved from that place on down here to the Billingsley place, where Jim's father and mother's family lived. So one day, Jim, he come out in the country here to the store. We had killed a young-like hog, and then we put it in the smokehouse. The smokehouse was right outside the kitchen, so you just stepped right into the smokehouse. I was ironing one day, and I only had two children then. I had Ruth and Juan; they were my babies. Well, I was busy ironing and I smelled smoke, and I thought, "Oh! The smokehouse is on fire!" So I run out the door there, and the flames were flaming up, and my babies was in that house asleep. I saw there was nothing I could do, so I remember that I sat the iron down, and I went up the hill so that the Vinsons could help me. They was eatin' dinner and they had company, and they just throwed down everything. Arthur and George Vinson and Priloh came to help me, and Violie asked me, "Lillie, where's the children?" And I said, "They was in the bed asleep." "Lord!" she says, "let's get those children!" So we run down the hill and we got my babies out of the house, and they were all right.

I had some nice furniture in the living room and some even nicer stuff upstairs. Me and Priloh went and got what we thought was best, and we got my kitchen buffet out; I liked it pretty well. We lost everything we had at that time and moved from there on up here. We didn't have no house to move to, just more or less a shed. We stayed with Dub and Dolly that summer while we built our house. We worked on it, Jim and me did—we worked on our house till it was good enough to live in. We came up here and worked at night on the house. We just put our babies to bed and went and worked on the house. We lit our lantern. We didn't have power through here then. I mean, Dub and Dolly stayed with our babies at night, and we came over here to work on our house.

My parents were very strict on me. I didn't get to go nowhere. I only got to stay out until ten o'clock, and I never had dates with very many boys. The first date I ever had was with Fred Dryman, a feller that lived down below us. He walked me home from the Church of God. Then I met Jim. I liked Jim better. I'll never forget what L.C. [someone Lillie used to date] said one time. He said, "I used to go with Lillie and I loved her very much, but that d—— Jim took her away from me." I liked Jim the best; he was a sweetheart. Us young people, we didn't have no cars, and we'd get out and run around 'bout like you do now. After church, you know, we went to the Baptist church when we weren't up here at this church down here [Church of God]. Jim and me would go up there to Salt Rock Gap and sit on them big picnic tables until it was time to go back to church that night. Ever' Sunday, that's what we did because, you know, there wasn't no cars. Poverty days was something else.

The young people in our community used to get together and dance— for fun, you know. I was too young to fool with any of that, so I'd just watch. All I remember was that the man used to say, "Get your partner and round 'em up." And around Christmas, they'd have candy pullin's. [**Editor's note**: See the explanation for candy drawings in *Foxfire 2*, pages 372–74, and *Foxfire 3*, page 322.] I was just a kid; I wasn't even datin' anybody because I wasn't big enough. I'd go along with my sister or brothers. So we'd go to the dances, and they'd have candy pullin's. All the young boys that had girlfriends, they'd buy a box of candy to take. Some of them would get peppermint; some got sassafras and all different kinds of candy. They would put the candy in two dishpans and put a towel over each dishpan. And then the couples would go side by side and put one hand under the towel. If they got a piece of candy that was the same, they got to keep it and put it in their pockets. If the candy was different, you would have to put it back. They worked at that all night long, and they had a good time and enjoyed that. I'll tell you, when we was kids, times was rough, but we always got through it. And we had fun doing it.

Editor's note: *We lost Mrs. Lillie Billingsley in September 2010. We feel blessed to have had the opportunity for her to share her friendship, recollections, and stories with us. She will definitely live on in our hearts and memories.*

"He had his head stuck up, and Mama shot him."

~ Memories from David "Lightnin'" Callenback ~

David Callenback is a true individual whose stories are classic Appalachian folklore and tall tales. I have known Lightnin' (my family and I have always called him Lightnin') for over ten years. My family has enjoyed late nights listening to stories of his childhood: getting a "whoopin'," deer hunting, fishing, and pulling childhood pranks.

David grew up on the outskirts of Clayton, Georgia, in a small community called Chechero [pronounced Chur-cha-row]. He describes the rough times he and his family survived and what they had to do to make ends meet. David's father, Ralph Callenback, worked at a local sawmill while his mother cooked and cleaned their small house, worked in the garden, and tended to other children and any animals they had at the time. North Georgia was in an economic recession during most of David's earlier life. He speaks of the lack of jobs throughout the community and the desperate attempts of its residents to make money. Ralph Callenback, in an effort to support his family, ran moonshine for years before he was caught by revenuers. He, however, was sentenced to only a fine because he was the sole support for his huge family.

Despite a childhood of hardships, David Callenback has a congenial and humorous personality. He always greets everyone with a smile and sends them away laughing because he has a gift for storytelling, a gift evident in the following pages.

—Russell Bauman

The name's David Allen Callenback. I was born in Rabun County on February 5, 1958. Well, there wuz eleven of us. We all grew up on Chechero, and most of 'em moved out when they got big enough. I stayed on Chechero until Daddy got so old till he couldn't go, and he moved in with my brother Clifton. My other sisters and brothers, they moved to south Georgia, and I moved over here to Clayton. It got so cold down there a lot of times we had to go out and saw up wood, but there weren't no chainsaw, and we had to bust it. I wrung a lot of chicken necks and catched 'em and eat 'em. I killed hogs. It got so cold that your hands would just freeze, and you couldn't hardly scrape 'em. You cut 'em up and hang 'em up in the smokehouse and sawed 'em down.

My daddy worked at a sawmill for about twenty-eight years, and he didn't make a whole lot of money. I think he told me he made a dollar an hour, and when all the rest of us got big enough, we had to work. A lot of us that weren't big enough to work went to school and come in and worked in

PLATE 16 **"I could keep up with him . . . he could lay about four or five hundred [cement blocks] a day. He named me 'Lightnin'."**
David Callenback and his wife, Glenda

the garden all evenin' and busted wood. Startin' Sunday, we went fishin' and deer huntin'.

He bought that place from my grandpa for ten dollars. Most of us were raised up in that one house there. I caught the school bus at seven thirty every morning, had to wait out there and it rainin' and cold, and everything else. When I got back to the house, I'd coon hunt—stay out all night; then I got to chasin' the women. My daddy barred me. He put me up for about two months. He took my gun, and I couldn't hunt. My dad was making moonshine early down there on the creek in the morning, and we went down there and loaded it [the car] down, and he was supposed to meet us. So we loaded the car and come on, and come along two o'clock, the sheriff come up to the house and said, "Your daddy's in jail," said he caught him down there and blowed his still up. He had all his liquor hid up under the leaves; it cost him a hundred seventy-five dollars for making moonshine, so we quit making it. I quit helpin' tote sugar to it and everything 'cause I didn't want to go to the chain gang neither.

Then I got a job on the Youth Corps. I believe I was nineteen. No, I was sixteen on the Youth Corps workin' for Casey Jones, and I was helping him pick out tires. He give us forty dollars a pop. I'd take twenty, and I'd give Daddy twenty.

I wanted a shotgun, but Daddy said, "No, you can't have a shotgun unless you pay for it 'cause I'm not buying you one." So I saved my money; Daddy signed for a shotgun, and I went squirrel hunting. The first squirrel I shot, it flew all to pieces and the gun kicked me off the hill. I come home with my mouth busted, cryin', draggin' my gun. Daddy said, "Well, you're gonna have to be tougher than that if you want a gun. If you want that twelve gauge, you gotta grow up, or I'll just buy you a small BB gun." I was sixteen then, so I quit fooling with it, and I got tough enough to shoot it.

Daddy said, "Well, I need to get up the hill to the chicken house," 'cause he had his whiskey hid up there under his hay, but it was so slick, he couldn't get up there. He finally got up there, and he was gone and gone. After a while, Mama heard him a-singin'. Mama said, "I thought he was feeding the chickens." I said, "I thought he was." She said, "Go up there and see." So I went up the back way, up through the woods to the chicken house. He 'as setting up there drunk, a-singin', and the chickens just a-cacklin'. Mama said, "How's your daddy?" I said, "He can't make it!" She said, "What's wrong with him?" I said, "He's drunk!" Daddy said, "I can make it. Just hang on." There was a big car hood layin' there. Daddy started gettin' on the car hood and said, "Boy, give me a push." So Daddy got on the car hood, and I give him a push, and he went down the trail. There was a big bank, and he went down the bank. He went right down through the yard right off the bluff there. He's layin' down there, and he's skint, but he's still a-singin'. My other brothers, Cliff and Frank and Junior, drug him back up there and put him in the house. Mama said, "What happened to you, Ralph?" Daddy said, "Well, I got up there and had an upset stomach, and I sucked some eggs," and said, "It made me happy." Mama said, "You got any more of them eggs?" Daddy said, "No, I ain't got no more of them eggs." Ma told me, said, "Go up there and look under one of them boards." I went up there, and he had him a hole dug and had him some boards over it and there it was—half a gallon—and it was half empty. Ma said, "Bring it down here." Eugene was sick with the cold, and we couldn't take him to the doctor. She made him some medicine with it and stirred it up, and he drunk it. He got over being sick.

Let's see, I went to work for Kenneth Dailey. I was about twenty-two then. I went to work for Kenneth Dailey layin' block, and he was one of the best block masons I guess there ever was. He had a knack for it. I could keep up with him. I toted mud and block, and he could lay about four or five hundred a day. He named me Lightnin'. That's where that name come from, and it's just been like that. We built a lot of houses. I worked for him about four years, and I moved to south Georgia. I worked in a cotton mill, and I didn't like it 'cause down there it was ninety degrees every day, and the skeeters [mosquitoes] was bitin'. So I come back to the mountains up here to stay with Daddy and them.

Me and my brothers and sisters, there was eleven of us. All the boys slept in one room, the girls, another. The boys would get out and have pillow fights and pinch each other. "Oh God! No, please, they're bitin'! Oh Lord!" They'd go to hollerin' and jerkin', and here comes Daddy with a big hickory. I mean, there was so many of us, it 'as just like a herd of cattle, you know. We'd all be out in the yard playin'. One'd be in the creek; one'd be in the garden; one'd be in the rosebush; one'd be up on top of the house; one'd be up tarin' [tearing] the wood out; one would come out with chocolate all over his face so you couldn't see his eyeballs. Mama runnin'; Daddy runnin'. Poor old Daddy had to drink to make it. I mean, his nerves were shot. Poor old fella, he would start hollerin'. He'd start with the oldest: "Bill, Pauline, Junior, Frank, David," and he'd go on down the line, "Whar y' at!" We'd go, "Here, here." Dad said, "Thar's one of 'em gone, missin' one—Johnny!" Johnny said, "Here I am." He said, "Whar you at?!" He'd be up under the floor diggin' in the dirt. He'd come out with dirt all over him. Daddy'd get him a hickory. "David, what are you a-doin'?" I said, "I ain't doin' nothin'!" I'd be up thar just a-pullin' corn. It wasn't even ripe. Daddy said, "What are you doin' with the corn?" I said, "We're gonna cook it!" And, boy, he'd fly up thar with the hickory, and he'd strike me. He said, "The corn ain't ripe!" I said, "But it's long and green." He said, "Yeah, but it ain't ripe."

We made a garden in the bottom, and it did good, but the creek down below, it belonged to that T. B. Lee man, and he told us we could make a swimmin' hole. We dammed the creek up with big rocks, and we forgot about the garden up thar. We got it so high that the water backed up over Daddy's garden over there. He come in that day, and all his pretty taters and everything were under about two or three inches of water. Daddy said, "Boys!" Here we was down there doing belly busters, jumpin' off the rocks just like a stair step in a line, just like ducks just a-laughin' and a-kickin'. Pauline said, "Watch me go in the air!" She'd go in the air and hit the water, and here comes Frank, fall on y' and nearly kill y'. Dad said, "U-hoo!" There he was with a hickory, and I said, "Oh Lord!" Daddy said, "Who flooded my garden?!" I said, "I didn't have nothin' to do with it." Every one of us said, "No, Daddy, no. Somebody did it this morning, but none of us had nothin' to do with it." Daddy said, "Oh sure, look at the mud on them hands, boys. Look. And the moss all pulled out of the bank. Look. And the big rock y'all rolled. Tar [tear] that thing down!" We had to tar it down, and he said, "Now! Go up yonder and ridge all them taters back up." Daddy said, "When they get ripe, you gonna have to dig it." And, Lord God, it was a big garden!

Come fall of the year, it was ripe, and I wanted to go fishin'. Daddy come up from sawmillin' and said, "Y'all better have them taters ridged." I made up my mind. I said, "I ain't ridgin' no taters." I said, "I ain't doin' it." I said, "I'm goin' fishin'." Mama said, "You better ridge those taters, or your daddy'll beat you to death." I said, "All right; I'll ridge 'em." Went down there and took a hoe and covered the whole tater up with dirt, and there was about four big rows, long as from here to that house over yonder. Frank said, "I bet that ridged 'em good enough!" We went down there. Boy, we was jerkin' out trout! Frank said, "I got eight." I said, "I got nine." Frank said, "I got ten." Boys, here come Daddy with a pole, said, "Yeah, and one or two is gonna get a big strikin'!" Said, "Who done them taters?" I said, "I didn't do it. It was Linda and Pauline." He said, "Frank and David, up here, up here, stand up here." And, boy, you a-talkin' about getting' a whoopin'! I was a-jumpin' and a-bouncin' and a-hollerin.' Frank dropped my fish in the creek and left me. He went up there and was a-yellin', "Mama, Mama!" Dad said, "Come here, boy"; he struck Frank. Had to get down there and uncover every one of them taters. By God, next time Daddy said to ridge the taters, we ridged 'em. We didn't cover 'em up. We sat way back and looked. Frank said, "That looks pretty even. Dad will like that." I said, "I hope he does. We'll go fishin' now."

If you did good all week, he'd get paid on Friday, and he'd take you up to the store. There was a store about two miles, and you walked up 'ar [there]. You could get a co-cola then for a nickel and get a big Sugar Daddy for about six cents, and I mean you could chew two hours on a big Sugar Daddy. Oh, it was worth it, boys. A co-cola was rare back then. Turn that baby up and drink that baby and chew on that big Sugar Daddy. You come around that road just right behind Daddy with the overalls on. We wore overalls and the brogan shoes, and, you know, we always got our hair cut in a flattop, nearly off. All our ears stuck way out 'cause we didn't have no hair. Here we was right behind Daddy with a big Sugar Daddy. Linda said, "Mine's about gone. Wanna trade?" I said, "I ain't a-tradin' you! You eat your Sugar Daddy. I'm just a-easy suckin' on mine. Move outta my way! I work with this Sugar Daddy!" Linda said, "I'm gonna tell Mama that you were mean to your sister." I said, "I don't care what you tell Mama." She got down there and said, "Mama, David wouldn't trade Sugar Daddys." Mama said, "What happened, Linda?" Linda said, "I ate all mine and David wouldn't give me a lick." She said, "David would just barely lick his with his little bitty, short tongue."

Linda told Jesse Faye to take the meanest dawg I ever had in my whole life and let him down in the well in the bucket. Said, "We'll fix that thing," said, "we'll get rid of that thing, and Daddy'll never know it." Linda reached over to catch the dawg (a big walker) and got him by the collar, and, when she went to put him in the bucket, that thing took ahold of Linda's finger, and

Linda had a big mouth. You could hear her half a mile: "Whaaaaaoooooooo, Lord have mercy!" Daddy came runnin' out of that house. "What are you doin' to that dawg?" And that dawg said, "Yalp, yalp!" waggin' that tail, and Jesse Faye always told the truth. She never lied. She said, "Linda was gonna put the dawg in the bucket and drown it." "Well, Linda, come in here." We had iodine back then, baby, and, boys, he poured that thing full of that iodine, hit Linda like fire, and she was a-screamin', jumpin' around the house. He told me, said, "Didn't you step on a nail the other day?" I said, "It's fine, Daddy. Thar ain't a thing wrong with my foot." He said, "Come here, David, and hold that thing up thar." I said, "No, it's fine, Daddy!" He said, "That thing looks black. Come here, Mama, with a needle and open it." I said, "No, it's fine, Daddy." Mama took that needle and opened that thing up, and he poured it full, and I took a hot foot jumpin' around the house, screamin' and hollerin'.

Daddy said, "Do you want to go turkey huntin' in the morning?" I said, "Yeah, I'll go with ya." Daddy said, "Well, you're seventeen. You never killed a deer or turkey. Let me call him [turkey] up, but you git down below me. He's gonna come to you first, but let him get real close and shoot him. Don't be a-movin', or he'll be gone." So we got out thar bright and early that morning about four o'clock, and I about froze to death. I was mad. I said, "Thar ain't no turkeys this early in the morning." I was sittin' over thar, and the sun came up. I a-heard *gobble, gobble, gobble.* I said, "Daddy, right down thar . . ." Boy, I made Daddy mad. He said, "Shut your mouth. Sit down." I set down, and Daddy called him and called him, and I just set thar. I just had that gun layin' thar. I didn't know to have it ready. I just had my gun up thar lookin' through the woods. Here he come with his head up and his tail all spread out. I said, "Goll, thar he is!" I grabbed my gun, and he was as fer as from here to my mailbox, way too fer to shoot. I fired down on him and cut bushes ever'ware [everywhere], and the turkey went *brrrrrrrhththththththththt.* Daddy said, "Dang almighty, boy, can't teach you nothin.' You shootin' a hundred yards." I said, "But, Daddy, he had a beard that long!" Daddy said, "It ain't gonna do you no good 'cause you ain't gonna get it!"

So next time he took me, we got up thar, and Daddy says, "Now let him get close like I told you, but have your gun ready." So I sat up thar. Daddy called and called, and I seen him. I seen him comin', and just when I heard him stop, he had his head stuck up. I was too fer. I let him come on up. I was gonna shoot him when another one walked out right above it, and I didn't know that it was a hen. I killed it dead. Daddy came down thar and said, "That's a hen." Boy, he got a hickory and striped me all over. He said, "You ain't supposed to kill hen turkeys." I said, "Daddy, you said a turkey." I said,

"Is that not a turkey?" Daddy said, "Can't you see? A hen ain't got no beard, but a gobbler's got a big ole long beard. Why didn't you shoot the one right by him that had the beard? Both of 'em was close enough." I said, "Well, I'll just kill one myself. I ain't foolin' with you no more." Dad said, "Well, just pitch a fit. I don't care." He said, "I ain't takin' you no more." Mama told me, "Don't worry about your daddy. He got a bad temper."

Mama took me out thar way up on the hill. Mama told me, "I'll show you something." She built a cage out of w're [wire], and she took a hoe and dug a little ditch. She said, "Take this corn and put a little in thar." I put the corn in thar. She said, "Go back and just wait." She said, "They'll eat the corn, and we'll bait them two or three times." I'd go back every mornin' and the corn'd be gone. About that fourth time I baited it, I went up thar, and thar he was in the pen, the big gobbler. He went in that pen, but he didn't have enough sense to come out. He'd go 'round and 'round with his head stuck up just lookin', but he wouldn't go back out the same way he come in. I said, "Mama, Mama, come out here." Mama come up thar. Mama said, "That's the way to get a turkey." I said, "Now, how you gonna get him out?" Mama said, "Right here." She had a little bitty, short twenty-two rifle. Mama said, "Just like this." And she put her hand over one eye like that and t'k [took] the rifle and went SNAP! He went flop, flop, flop, flop. I said, "You killed him!" She said, "I was showin' you how to." I reckon I pulled him out, and Mama said, "We'll fool your Daddy."

T'k him down thar, and Daddy was in his favorite rockin' chair with his pipe in his mouth. He said, "Ol' David and all them a-turkey huntin' ain't killed nothin'." Mama said, "Well, he's a lot better hunter than you are, Ralph!" Said, "Look here!" Mama held him [the turkey] up and said, "He don't need no shotgun—killed him with a twenty-two rifle." Daddy said, "Lord have mercy, how'd you do that?" And you know, Mama ought to have told me not to tell. I said, "Hit him in a pen. He had his head stuck up, and Mama shot him." She smacked me right in the mouth. She said, "You tell everything you know." Daddy said, "Baited him?" I said, "No, Mama did." Daddy said, "Baitin's illegal. That ain't playin' fair."

Daddy was raised over on Germany Road. His original people come from across the waters. His great-granddaddy was a full-blooded German. His mother and Grandma Caroline was a three-quarter Cherokee Indian. I believe thar was seven of them. Thar was four boys and three girls, and they was all raised, every one of them, on Germany Road.

I made it to the twelfth grade by the hair of my chinny-chin-chin. Gamblin' and smokin' and pitchin' quarters against the wall, I got a whoopin' six times for that, and he [principal] couldn't break me, so he put me in the lunchroom dumping dishes. Every time some smart aleck come up, he

throwed the tray and mashed my fingers against that rubber thing that held
the trays. I'd get mad and throw a cup back at him. So he [the principal] took
me out of thar because I was always getting into it, and he put me back thar
washin' them big ol' pots. Lord, I sure did hate that. I had to scrub and scrub.
He said, "If I catch you at this again, I'll put you back in there. You can either
play football or soccer or something to stay out of trouble." So I decided that
I'd go into football. Well, I played football there, and I couldn't do no good,
so I went into basketball 'cause I was taller. I got good at basketball 'cause
I could run out there and make a hook shot. But, you know, we went to
Franklin, North Carolina, and they 'as this big ol' long-legged fella. He come
runnin' down through thar and stole the ball right out from under me, and
he run up thar and made a big hook shot and made it. I said, "I'll be durn!"
He's out there celebrating and, a' course, we got beat. Me and him got into it,
and they throwed me off the basketball team. Coach Rumsey said, "You ain't
supposed to get mad when they steal the ball and beat you." I said, "Well,
if he hadn't stole the ball, I's gonna make the shot, and we would've won."
He said, "It don't matter, though. You too slow." I said, "I can't keep up with
a race car." He told me, "This is what I'm gonna do." He said, "I'm gonna
git you a job, and every day, fourth and fifth period, you can mop the gym
floor." And, boys, I liked that. I went in there and mopped the floor. There
wasn't nobody in there, and I'd shoot the basketball and kick soccer.

There's a lot of good people down on Chechero. Most of 'em always
stuck together. Down there, they was just neighbors, and they'd help each
other because times was hard. If you wanted like a bushel of corn, and they
had it, well, they'd give it to you. If you wanted a ride to town or something,
they'd always take you to town and wouldn't charge you nothin' to go to the
store and back or somethin'. They'd let you squirrel hunt on their land and
deer hunt on their land. They didn't care just so long as you didn't throw
down a match on their land and burn down their land or nothin'. Every
now and then they'd allow loggin', you know, and they'd sell timber, you
know, stuff like that. Most of them old people are about gone now. They
wasn't much government land on Chechero. Most of it's all private owned,
you know. They hand it on down through the generations, you know. When
the old ones die off, they give it to the boys and the girls, and they hang on
to it.

I seen Mama and Daddy walk from Chechero up Smith Mountain with
a big ol' snow on the ground, and I bet you a dollar it was five or six degrees.
They'd walk all the way to town to work. I seen 'em do that several times. I
seen it pourin' down rain, and they got a taxi: Moon Smith, back in them
days. It seemed like he charged seventy-five cents to a dollar to bring you
home, and most times they didn't have seventy-five cents or a dollar, so they

just walked home. If some of the people who lived there on the road seen 'em goin' home, they would've brought 'em home.

When you makin' just a dollar an hour, you couldn't afford to do nothin.' Of course, you know, they take out taxes on you just like they do now, and if you got eleven kids, you know. People had to sell coon dogs and hogs and chickens and, Lord, I mean everything. I seen Daddy raise five and six hogs, some of 'em four or five hundred pounds apiece—killed 'em and sell the meat. People come by and buy a big ham or somethin', or he'd take it to a shootin' match, and they'd shoot on it, you know. Somethin' like a quarter on it or fifty cents on it, and he could make money that way 'n' stuff. He fooled with cane one time, made sorghum syrup, but he didn't make too much money at it. It cost too much to fool with it. He got into honeybees, and the honeybees 'ud always sting the children, and Mama made Daddy get rid of all the honeybees.

I helped Daddy tote sugar to the still, and usually you had to tote it way up a big bank about three or four miles. Daddy always waded a branch. That way, you didn't leave no trail. The revenuers usually would ride down the road and see a trail like that, and they'd know that it was a still. Daddy would wade the branch up to the still, and we'd tote sugar to it and wade back down the branch, and there wasn't no trail. He run it usually at night or in the mornin' when it was pourin' down rain—'cause of the dampness, you know. You couldn't smell it. That's the other thing; you could smell it if it was a clear night. He always tried to keep it where you couldn't smell it. It seemed like Daddy sold it for ninety cents a gallon. It was pure corn. I mean, you could drink a pint, and you couldn't stand up in a twenty-acre field. I mean, it had the power to it! I tried it.

I tried some when I was young. I's probably 'bout fifteen, I guess. I tried some at the still, see. It was comin' out of this spout, what you call a "worm" comin' down. He's runnin' a jug under there, and I stuck me a pint bottle that I'd found and washed out up under there. I run it full, and I sticked it up under my coat. Daddy didn't pay no attention. When I got up to the house, me and my brother said, "Let's try some of Daddy's squeezin's." I said, "All right, we'll try it." So we opened it, and I took a drink of it. I mean, it went down smooth. I said, "It ain't got no power to it. It tastes like water." He said, "Give me a drink," and he turned up a big drink. He took two drinks, Frank took two, and Cliff took two. We got up, and I fell out the back door. Frank fell on top of me, and here come Cliff. We 'as all piled in thar. Daddy come out there and said, "Lord have mercy, them boys have been in my squeezin's." I said, "No, Daddy, I run it out of the still in a pint bottle and brought it home." Daddy said, "Lord, son, you, whoa, you shouldn't've done that." I said, "We'll be fine." We got out there just a-laughin' and sangin'.

Boys, the next mornin', I woke up and my head felt like a fifty-five-gallon drum. I thought I was gonna die. I said, "Oh, my Lord!" I was just a-rollin' and pukin' out there. I said, "My God, that corn's rotten; that's the rottenest corn I ever drunk." Daddy said if I'd took it and let it age a long time, it'd be all right. That's the only one that I ever drunk that Daddy made.

Somebody come and bought it from him. I don't know who it was, but some of those'd come and buy it by the case from him. So many people got to comin' to the house that the sheriff seen all them cars, and he come down there. Daddy had to quit sellin'. So he'd just make it and leave it in the woods, just put it in the case, and the man that'd come to buy it'd just pick it up there. They loaded and hauled it out until he got caught. He had to quit. See, they'd a-sent him to the chain gang, but he told the judge, "Look, judge, I got eleven children. They all barefooted, and half-nekked, and about starved to death, and if you send me to the chain gang, my wife can't keep 'em up. If you sent me to the chain gang, the state is gonna have to take care of my children." So he turned Daddy loose where he didn't have to feed eleven children. That's smart thinkin' in them days. See, if Daddy had played it smart, they wouldn't've caught him then, but I think Daddy had tried some, and he was about full and he was up there. He always blowed the harp. He had his harmonica with him, and he was up there playin'. A man come to pick it up, and he got to blowin' the car horn. Daddy kept a-right on playin', and the law pulled up behind the man and said, "What are you doin' blowin' the horn?" The man took off and left, and they took off after him. The other law behind 'em stopped, and here Daddy was a-blowin' a harp. They heard Daddy blowin' the harp, and he was still up there at the still. He had about fifteen or twenty cases stacked up on top. He said, "Hey, Ralph! What are you gonna do with them?" He said, "I'm gonna sell them." "No, they gotta go with us." So he took it all, and they chopped the still. Well, I believe he told me they chopped the still up with an ax and took all the liquor. They gave him, it seemed like, a hundred-and-seventy-five-dollar fine, and they told him he couldn't be around anybody that drank no more or ran stills.

I imagine the law poured it out or sent it to Atlanta because some of it might not have been safe to drink. I don't know. I know what Daddy made was safe because he made it out of corn. He said all you do is take corn and put it in a tow [burlap] sack and put it in a creek, and it'll sprout. It sprouts through that sack. Then you take it to the mill. He had an old-timey mill that he'd take it to, and he'd grind it up. Daddy'd make corn mash out of it, and he'd put it on the still and cook it and run it through that still through that worm to that big jug he had down there. He made it out of corn, yeast, and sugar and somethin' else. I can't remember what it was. There 'as somethin' else that he did to give it the kick, but I don't know what that was. I believe,

PLATE 17 **David showing off a prize bluegill he caught on Lake Burton in Rabun County, Georgia**

it seems like a bale of sugar was fifty pounds. Fifty pounds a bale, I believe it was. It was Dixie Crystals, and if you bought too much in one store, then they'd catch you there because you were buyin' all that sugar. He said he was doin' a lot of cannin', but, see, they didn't believe that. That's when they first got on to him makin' liquor.

Me and my brothers were goin' fishin' for trout, but we couldn't find no fish bait. It was so dry, and there 'as a big hornets' nest hangin' on the limb. I said, "Right there's the bait, boys." Cliff said, "Reckon how many're in there?" Frank said, "Well, a man told me in town the other day that the way to get a hornets' nest is to cut you a stick and stop the hole up, take you a knife and cut the limb off, and stick the nest down in the water. It'll drown 'em." I said, "Well, that makes sense." And we all agreed, you know. Frank said, "Well, I'm the one that's got a knife, so let me try." He was always the bravest one. He cut him a stick. He whittled it down and said, "That about right?" I said, "That's about the size of the hole that'll fit." Well, he went up there. He got it in, but they was comin' in out in the air. Boys, when he stopped that hole up, I mean you talk about pourin' it to Frank! They just started comin' in out of everywhere, and one popped me right the side of the head. I took off, and them things followed us plumb to the creek. I had to jump in the creek, and I like to never got 'em off me. I run home cryin' to Ma, all swelled up like a bullfrog. Mama said, "Is the stick in the hole?" I said, "Lord, yeah." She said, "They won't leave that nest. They'll sting you if you get ten foot of it." Daddy said, "Wait a minute. I'll get the nest for you tonight." So he took a long cane pole and tied him up a big ol' *Clayton Tribune* on it and lit it and stuck it to it. He said, "Here's your bait." He went up there and got the bait. We went up there the next day, and we caught eight or ten big, brown trout. I guess that's one of the biggest browns I ever caught. It was about eighteen inches long. I caught him down yonder on Big Creek.

Daddy got snake bit and like to died, and the house burnin' up that time were some of the worst times I remember. If your house burnt back in them days, all your neighbors usually would just come and rebuild it and wouldn't charge you nothin'. Then if their house burnt, you just returned the favor if you could get the lumber. Lightnin' hit my house through the meter. Back in them days they just had these switch boxes stuck to the wall, and they had these fuses, you know. It was just cobbled up, but it worked.

Times have changed, 'cause, you know, there wasn't a whole lot in Clayton. It wasn't big like it is now. I mean, you come to town and things were a lot cheaper than they are now. When I was a boy, you could buy a twelve-gauge shotgun brand new for twenty-seven dollars and a half. Now they run anywhere from ninety-eight to one hundred and seventeen. Haircut is eight dollars, and back then you'd get a haircut for seventy-five cents. When you buy a pair of boots, you buy the best boots made for twenty dollars. Now they're hundred 'n' fifty, hundred 'n' sixty dollars. Things changed completely around from what they was thirty years ago. They were usually all just local poor people tryin' to make a livin' is what it was. There wasn't no such thing much as sellin' wood because nobody would buy wood. They cut it off their own land. A few people had gas. A few people back in them days had a lot of money, and they could afford gas, but most of 'em burnt wood, either that or coal. Now people go to town every day. When I was a boy, people went to town just only on the weekends. Friday evening and Saturday was their day to go to town, and they did all their grocery shoppin' and buyin' clothes, haircuts and shoes, huntin' supplies, and sewin' supplies at one time, and never did come back until they was out again. You see, a lot of people back then owned a lot of land. If a man had a lot of money back then and bought a lot of land and had it now, he'd be well off. Nobody had the money to buy it; it was cheap. I remember you could buy it for two hundred fifty dollars an acre, but where in the world would you get the two hundred and fifty? That was the trouble 'cause they weren't no jobs, you know—sawmillin' and makin' whiskey or farmin'. They wasn't much money in farmin', for sure. What in the world is a man supposed to do?

I just wish a lot of them things I bought way back when I was young, I had kept because it'd be worth somethin' now. Them ol' barlow knives now is worth a lot of money. I bought a lot of 'em for fifty cents when I was a boy. Now, if you've got a regular Barlow, the original, and it's old, it's worth money. You can still buy 'em new, but they ain't like the old ones, you see. The old ones was made better, and they had better metal in 'em. I was like any other boy; I just throwed 'em down.

When old-timers was raised up, a dollar was a dollar. They didn't go out and just spend it like you do now. I've seen Daddy make a hundred dollars, seem like to me, last six months 'cause he never would let go of much of it at one time. You could take twenty dollars to the grocery store, and two people couldn't tote it [what you bought]. Now you can take twenty dollars, and I can tote it 'cause it's only one bag full, and it ain't full, you know. I mean, groceries was cheap, you know. You could buy a big ol' slab of meat for it seemed like thirty-five, forty cents, and people was just barely gettin' by on that. Granny would can stuff and then sell it. She'd take blackberries and beans and stuff, and people in the community would come by and buy them.

Daddy never did drive, and I often wondered how he raised eleven children and went through all that and still lived to be eighty-two years old. He's a tough un. He ain't got no teeth now, but that's the way it is, you know.

If it come, you know, like Christmastime, usually you got an apple and an orange and maybe a fire truck. We never did really have a big tree or an artificial tree. It didn't matter to Daddy what it looked like, just a pine tree. He'd just stick it in a bucket of sand and put anything he could find on it, like balls and socks—you know, to sort of decorate it up. That dang ol' heater would get hot and get to smokin', and it'd put your eyeballs out in there, and I told my brothers, "We'll see if ol' Santa comes tonight. That heater pipe's red-hot. Let's see how he get down that." He said, "You got a point. We'll peep." Well, we was a-peepin'. It was Santa Claus all right, but we didn't think it was Daddy in a Santa Claus suit. Junior leaned over and whispered, "It's Santa. It ain't Daddy; it's Santa. He got that big ol' long beard and that red suit on, black boots." I said, "Well, how in the world did he get down the heater pipe then when it's red-hot?" Junior said, "I don't know, but he's in here." Linda said, "Yeah, that's Santa!" Boy, Daddy heard that and here he come, and I jumped in the bed snorin'. I wasn't movin' a muscle. He said, "Linda, what are you doin'?" Linda said, "In the bed," said, "is that you?" Daddy had the door shut. Said, "Yeah, that's me. You stay in that bed."

I woke up the next mornin' and had me a big ol' stick of peppermint

PLATE 18 **"I often wondered how he raised eleven children and went through all that. . . . He's a tough un." David's dad, Ralph Callenback**

candy, and I had me a big ol' orange. I opened my present, and I had me a wagon. Best Christmas, I guess—ol'-timey Christmas—where all the boys got a wagon and the girls all got dresses and stuff. No, we all had a wagon but Eugene. Eugene had a BB gun. He wanted a BB gun, and he got a BB gun. We was all ridin' around, and I thought it was just a miracle to get a wagon, a red wagon. We went down that hill, and comin' around that curve there, I could do good guiding the wagon around the curve. Frank said, "I'll tell ya what we'll do. Let's get up here on this hill and make us a racetrack. Here's the checkered flag." He went in there and got a pair of Mama's new panties and put them on a stick. "That's the checkered flag." I said, "Frank, I don't know about this." He said, "Yeah, it'll work." He said, "Now here's the line. We all start. Linda and Pauline, Jesse Faye, you push, but push us at the same time." Boys, I'm a-tellin' y', we was a-comin' down through there! I passed Frank! I cut the corner in front of Eugene, and Eugene and Frank run over my wagon. Boy, it just knocked a big dent in the red paint, and I was sick, cryin'. Lord God, I was up there: "Whoa, Lord, my wagon!" There was a dent in my wheel, and me up there tryin' to fix it. Frank was down there and had the pole up: "I win! Champion!" Boys, here comes Mama. "Where'd you get them panties?" she said. "Don't jump on me. Frank got 'em." She said, "They's mine, they're new, and you drived a hole in 'em." Frank said, "Oooh, Lord!" Boy, she got in there, and she wouldn't whup you hard. What she'd do is take a hickory and give you three or four licks—*wham, wham, wham, wham.* "You sorry?" Frank said, "No." *Wham, wham, wham.* "You sorry?" "Yeah."

But I mean, if Daddy flew in on y', I mean, he'd pick you off the ground. So we got out there, and I told Daddy, "I wrecked my wagon. Eugene run over it." Daddy said, "What 'us you doin'?" "Racin'." "Well, I'll tell you what. We'll take a hammer, and we'll beat it out." He took a hammer and beat the side of it out. I got my front end fixed back, and I went up there to my uncle Jess's. He said, "I got some red paint, boy; I'll fix you right up." Uncle Jess was cross-eyed. He was born that way, and he had one big ol' tooth in the front was all he had. He just was grinnin', and he painted it. Jess said, "Now I tell you what let's do; you get in your wagon, and I'll pull you behind my horse." He had a little ol' buggy. I got my wagon, and I tied it to his buggy and just drivin' along purty. We was fine just drivin' down the road with th' wagon hooked to it [buggy], and he pulled me and that little ol' buggy around through there. There was this snake come off the bank and coiled up. It was a copperhead layin' on the side of the road, it bein' summertime, and that dang horse seed [saw] that snake, and he went straight up in the air and let out a big kasnort [snort]—went down through there and come loose—throwed the dang buggy, Jess in it. Threw Jess plumb down. There was big blackberry patches on the side o' the road, and he went rollin'. I took off behind him and I went rollin'. I got tore all to pieces that time. I had a big ol' knot on the side of my head, just a-bellerin'. Daddy said, "Wh'd you do now?" I said, "Uncle Jess was pullin' me behind the buggy." I said, "The horse stepped on a snake and took off."

Daddy said, "I tell you what, Jess." He said, "You gonna have to do somethin' with that horse. He's wild. You can't do nothin' with that thing." He said, "I don't believe he would have done nothin' if he hadn't seen that snake." Dad said, "No, he's wild. He was jumpin' like that." Jess said, "Did you ever ride him? Did you put a saddle on him?" Dad said, "No, I've got a saddle out there in the barn." Jess said, "Maybe that's the problem. Maybe he's never been rode. Maybe he needs to be broke, and he'll be all right." They was sittin' at the table passin' the jug around. Jess took a big drink and give a big toast, and Daddy took a big drink and give a toast. Ma said, "Look at the two old fools sittin' there." And, you know, after a while their eyes got to rollin' and said, "Yep! We're gonna ride him now!" Ma said, "Get in the house, kids. Get in the house 'cause they gonna get killed." They said, "We got him!" They got him with a bridle and a saddle on him and tied him up under there. Jess said, "Now you hold him!" So Daddy had ahold of the reins, and Jess got up on him and said, "He's holdin', no problem." He give him the reins, and what does he do now, he set there. Now, Daddy had a big ol' bullwhip, a big leather bullwhip there. Daddy reached over and got that bullwhip, and went *kapowow*! That thing took off, and he was a-buckin', Jess a-hangin' on. Jess got him an ear. That thing 'ar gon' through the woods and throwed Jess up through the barbed-wire fence, down on it. Daddy run down there, and it kicked Daddy right in the belly and just rolled Daddy down on the ground, Daddy just layin' there. Dad said, "Ruby, Ruby!" Ma said, "I ain't a-foolin' with you drunks!" Ralph said, "Lord, we gotta go to the doctor!" Went down there, and that barbed wire just cut him all to pieces. My neighbor over there had an old forty-one truck, it seems like it—I believe it was—and we went over there and put him in the flatbed. Took him over to Doc Dover. Daddy come up here, and he was gonna git patched up. Went in there, and, Lord have mercy, you know back then, they just sewed you up with catgut or anything. I mean they just sewed them up, and Jess come out there and said, "Lord God, where's Ralph?" I said, "Daddy in thar gettin' patched up." Daddy come out there, and they sewed his ear up and his nose. Daddy said, "I tell you right now. I been thinkin'. I believe we did somethin' wrong with that horse." Ma said, "Well, ye', fools." Dad said, "Well, there got to be a way." Ma said, "Y'all ain't got a bit o' sense." She said, "You gotta coach it." Walked out there, he [horse] stood there, and I took corn and stuck it up to his nose and I'd pet him and say, "Whoa, Brownie. Whoa, boy." I got on him and rode him, and you had to be gentle with him; then you just pet him and be gentle with him and put sugar in your hand and give him corn, but if you took your foot and tapped him in the side, he'll take off, boy! He'd stick that tail up, a-lobdy, lopdy, lop. He'd jump a fence higher than this trailer. That thing, I wouldn't ride him much, you know.

One time when me and Daddy was fishin', I looked, and here come a big storm. I looked, and we was about three miles from town. I said, "Oh, mercy." Lightnin' just a-poppin', and they 'as a big rock cliff down there. Lightnin' was bad here'n scared me! He said, "We gettin' under this rock cliff down there." We eased right under that rock cliff. Daddy always had a big army coat on, and he always took cornbread and onions with him in his coat. He had all kind of goodies under there, you know. We was sittin' up under there eatin' onions and cornbread. Daddy got to movin'. He was wearin' them big ol' baggy overalls, and he got to pinchin' somethin'. Said, "Wait a minute." And, boys, there was yellow jackets pourin' out from under there. I looked, and it was a-hailin' so hard you couldn't see. It was either the hailstorm or the yellow jackets, and Daddy said, "Which one should I do?" All of a sudden, one got up under there, and, boys, it popped Daddy right up under the neck. He moved, and he went out in that rain in that creek, and I got up on the bank. I was a-beatin' them off my britches, and I mean, my britches was yellar [yellow] with 'em. He said, "Where's that big paper you had?" He said, "I got a match, and if it ain't too wet, I'll burn 'em out of there." The nest was on top of the ground, and we burned the nest. He walked up there and burned it. We was on the lower end, with others comin' out in the air. They'd turn around and fly off. Mama got worried and called the sheriff to come look for us. We got up on the road, and here come the sheriff. Sheriff asked, "Are y'all all right?" Dad said, "Yeah, it was a bad storm."

Well, the real good times was seein' Mama cook on the woodstove and Daddy killin' a deer and bringin' it in, the family reunions, takin' us squirrel huntin', fishin', all the time, goin' to the store and buyin' candy, and the first guitar I got and I learnt how to play, and people comin' by on Sund'ys and sittin' under the old tree and havin' picnics. We'd talk about coon huntin' and how many coons we caught and just everybody bein' a neighbor, you know. Those were the good times, you know, just bein' with your brother and sister, your family, you know. We've had a good life, and that's just the way it is.

"I don't feel like I'm Republican; I know I am."

~An interview with Carlee Heaton~

Carlee Heaton has always been a man on a mission, first being inducted into the Georgia Racing Hall of Fame and now for the Lord. After a big ol' hug from him, as we walked through the door, I began to notice that his induction was well earned. Every wall of his living room, even overflowing into the bedrooms of his home, was filled with trophies from all over the United States and photos of Mr. Heaton with all-time-great race-car drivers. However, as Mr. Heaton reminisced upon the good ol' days, with some occasional added details provided by his wife, Joan, I quickly knew that he was a man who would teach me not only about racing but also about how to handle what life throws your way. Mr. Heaton describes his hard childhood, which was filled with labor; his unique experiences in the Army, including spending major holidays with General Eisenhower, later President Eisenhower; and most of all giving up the hobby he loved so much to serve the Lord.

—Casi Best

My name is Carlee LeRoy Heaton from Salem, South Carolina, and I was born in 1928, the fourth day of November, so I'm eighty-one years old. Got almost six years in the Army; got two honorable discharges. I retired from BFGoodrich chemical company after seventeen and a half years on swang [swing] shift in Louisville, Kentucky. Then I came down here and went to work for Duke Power, and I worked eighteen and a half years for them and then retired from them. I had perfect attendance ten, twelve, or fifteen years out of the eighteen. Never was late a minute. Me and my boys both worked for them, Dwight and Eddy. Eddy got killed in '97 right over here between Walhallar [Walhalla], South Carolina, and Westminster, South Carolina, and things ain't been the same since; they sure ain't. He was killed when he was forty-two. I never did introduce you to my boss there [pointing to his wife]; we met in 1991, and we didn't get married till 2008. Anyways, it's been a long time [laughs].

I went to the school in Salem, but it burnt up in 1942 or '43, somewhere along in there. They took us over to Salem to a Baptist church. They went in there, put curtains up for the fourth grade and fifth grade, and they had four or five classes in the church. We done that till they got the school built back.

Growing up was real hard around here because it was the Hoover days, and there wasn't no jobs. All my uncles run sawmills, and I worked at a sawmill after I was eleven years old. My daddy made me quit school and start

PLATE 19 **"I never did introduce you to my boss." Carlee and his wife, Joan**

workin' in the sawmill helpin' him haul the lumber and stuff. I worked all of these mountains up in here pullin' logs with a one-horse team of horses. Both of my uncles, my mama's brothers, were well off, and one of 'em was a police officer here in Oconee County for forty-two years. I worked with him at the sawmill till I went in the Army, but I'd go help Daddy in the sawmill to keep it from being so hard on him. He'd go to town on Saturdays with the paycheck, come back, and get a quart or gallon of kerosene to go in the lanterns, a piece of fatback meat, and a sack of flar [flour], and we'd make that do us. Sometimes we'd get a pack of pinto beans, and, once or twice a week, we'd eat pinto beans. The rest of the time, we'd eat gravy and sometimes gravy and biscuits. Me and my mama and sisters would go down on the creek and get blackberries, strawberries, and grapes and make jelly. She'd cook 'em biscuits, and we'd have jelly biscuits. Mama made our clothes for us. My sister's bloomers [underwear], petticoats [slips] and stuff were made out of flar sacks. We went to the corn mill and had our flar and meal ground. My daddy and uncle would raise wheat and stuff, and we'd get wheat from them and have it to make flar out of. They's a flar mill in Salem and a corn mill, too.

We didn't have electricity. We had an outside bathroom and used kerosene lanterns. We grew a garden, too. We'd go pick cotton, peas, corn, and work in other people's fields, hoe their farms, and pull the weeds and the dried leaves off the stalks of corn. Take some strang [string], tie it all up, and when it dried put it in the barn for the horses and cattle to eat. We plowed with a mule. My daddy had one ol' mule.

We had an icebox and there was an ice truck come from here in Walhallar. He had a wagon with a mule pullin' it, and he'd chop us off a twenty-five-pound block of ice. We'd keep it in our icebox and keep our milk and butter there. We'd take that box to the creek and pond up the creek. Me and my sisters would get our water from a spring. We would build a fire and fill that tub full of water, so Mama could boil our pants and stuff. We worked at the sawmill, and all that rosin and stuff was hard to get out of ye clothes. You had to boil them and take a paddling stick and beat 'em. We'd pick probably one hundred and fifty to two hundred pounds of cotton at Christmastime and would come out here and sit at the gin. We'd pick blackberries and cotton and everything else to get enough money to get us a little sack of oranges at Christmas and a little bag a' candy and an apple or two. And, we thought we was in Heaven when we got all that. We really did. We'd pick cotton after everybody else had done quit pickin' it, and they'd give us the cotton left in the field just to get it out. We'd pick it every evening after we come outta school and brang it out here and sell it in Walhallar at Christmastime to get us something. Back then if you had a pair of overhaul [overall] pants and a white shirt, you was in Heaven. But, even though it was hard, it really was better back then.

I was nineteen when I went into the Army. My basic training was in Fort Jackson for thirteen weeks. Roosevelt was in office when I went in the Army. He died in 1948, see, and I went in in '48. I was goin' to Seattle, Washington, whenever they had his funeral. I was Army training when I got to Spokane, Washington; the Columbia River was 'bout three or four miles wide, and the deep hole was 'bout four foot deep. We couldn't even get off the train; we had to ride on up there. We's just a-hopin' that the railroad tracks wouldn't give away. Truman was president after Roosevelt. Truman stayed in there until 1951, and he went and fared [fired] MacArthur. He messed up the whole world when he done that because MacArthur would have whupped them Koreans. He had 'em 'bout halfway whupped when Truman fared him. Truman fared him because he knew MacArthur

PLATE 20 **"That's why I drove for Eisenhower."** Mr. Heaton's Army photo

was gonna win that war. I think Reagan was the best president we ever had. He was the best and the smartest one that we ever had. He'd tell it like it was, and the rest of 'em is just liars. Ronald Reagan and Nixon—if they hadn't impeached Nixon, then things would have been differ'nt. I don't feel like I'm Republican; I know I am [laughs].

I only had two sisters, no brothers, and they are both dead now. One of my sisters' husband went into the Army and retired there. I didn't stay but five years and seven months in the Army 'cause really I couldn't stand goin' overseas in that boat. Liked to have killed me, boys. We went over on a ship, and I got so seasick that I liked to have died on that thing. I offered to pay my way back here whenever I came back from Germany, and they wouldn't let me. They made me ride the ship for eleven days. When I got off that ship in New York, I said, "Mister, if they get me back on one, they'll have to kill me 'cause I'm not goin' back on one." They said, "No, you gotta go with us and stay with the troops."

I said, "Well, when you get me back to South Carolina and I get my discharge, you can kiss this Army boy good-bye 'cause I ain't comin' back." That's why I didn't go back and retire in there. I'd go AWOL right now before I'd ride one of them ships again. I sure would 'cause it just kills me. I can hear that thing screakin' now, and it felt like it was just gonna break half into with me twelve or fifteen miles out from shore. I knew I couldn't swim it [laughs]. Up in Alaska it's rough up there in that ocean, and over in Germany, too. They ain't no way nobody can get another ship out there in case something happens either.

I tried to get in the Navy, but I couldn't 'cause I was color-blind. I did everything 'cause I wanted to be a sailor and after I went down there to Anderson, South Carolina, to try to get in, they sent me a letter sayin' I could get in the Army, but couldn't get in the Navy. So I went ahead and joined the Army in 1948 and went down to Fort Jackson for thirteen weeks and come home for eleven days on vacation. Before I went to Japan, they sent me a letter sayin' if I'd come to Greenville, South Carolina, they'd take me in the Navy, and I'm sure glad that I didn't get to go. I stayed in George Patton's Third Army Division for sixteen months in Fort Knox, Kentucky. I marched a many a day up and down the streets there for big generals like General Martin Clark. We'd get twenty-four breaks goin' up through there in the hot summertime. You see them guys falling out just like flies. Eighty-five or ninety degrees, and you got twenty-five to thirty men lined up marchin' through yunder [yonder] for two, three, or four miles and you just give out. You have to stay in step, or someone will reach in and pull you out. The ol' Army used to be tough, but I sure did love it.

We was fixing to go overseas, and I got in a fight with a guy from

Arkansas and broke my fist, and they put me in the hospital for 'bout three weeks. Instead of sending me to Japan, they sent me to Alaska for nineteen months, then I come back here and stayed in Fort Knox for 'bout fifteen months. Then I went to Germany and stayed over there for twenty-three months. I drove all over Germany, England, and France. When I went to Germany in 1951, they sent us to [one of] Hitler's youth schools. He used to take all your kids up to that mountain place. He had big barracks built down in the mountains and then big ol' shars [showers] in there and horses for 'em to ride, ever since they was little kids. After we won the war, they sent us back there, so that's why I went all over Germany driving big wheels around. I had a good recommendation for driving, and that's why I drove for Eisenhower. He was a five-star general then, and I drove for him when I was in the service in Germany, on two different occasions. In 1951, Thanksgiving and Christmas, I stayed in the field with him all day—just drove for him all day. That ended up being President Eisenhower. He left me over there and come back over here to run for president, then he extended my time over there for eleven more months. I left there in February or March of '53. I come back here, got married, went to Louisville, Kentucky, and got them boys that I was in the service with to get me a job. One of them was working at the Pepsi-Cola place, and he had a buddy that worked at BFGoodrich. That guy told me that if I'd come up there and do good work that they'd give me a job. I'd have to work for ninety days before I could get in the union, but I had good recommendations. Eisenhower wrote me a recommendation, and they hired me at BFGoodrich. I was the only man that had ever worked there that didn't have a high school education. So I worked the ninety days, and they set me up to first-class pay. Top money back then was when I made $16.10 an hour, in 1989.

My wife went with me to Kentucky. That's where Dwight was born at. We stayed up there till my daddy died. Before my daddy died I lived down here on Lake Tamykee. I went and bought my mama and daddy a home here on Lake Tamykee. After my daddy died my mama wanted to stay down there by herself. I brought my two boys down to live with her, so she wouldn't be by herself. First thing ya know my wife wanted to come back down here to Walhalla, South Carolina, because her people was here, so I sold my house up on Lake Tamykee and come back down here, and bought this place. I bought my mama a trailer and put it right here next to me; then, after she died, Joan's mama lived up there in Franklin, North Carolina, and the man she was goin' with [dating] died, so she wanted to come down here. So we let her move in this trailer here. She lived there till she died 'bout two or three years ago. Life's been rough, but you gotta keep on goin'.

I quit smokin' in 1981. Me and Dwight and another boy from Salem went huntin', and I'd usually carry a pack 'n' a half of cigarettes and went in the woods and climbed a tree 'bout twenty-five-foot high and the wind was just a-blowin'. I reached to get me a cigarette and didn't have but one. I thought, "Lord have mercy, I done messed 'round and come up here with no cigarettes." Then I got to thinkin', "I'm just gonna quit." I went down there and told Dwight, I said, "Dwight, I'm gonna eat this sandwich, smoke this last cigarette, and that's it. I ain't smokin' no more." And that's what I done. I got me some of 'em butterscotch candies, and I kept puttin' 'em in my pocket; even when I worked at Duke Power, and the guys would take a smoke break, I'd put me in a piece of that candy and keep that in my mouth.

Joan: They bet each other a steak dinner if they didn't all quit. If they stayed quit, then they didn't have to buy, but the ones that started back had to buy the others a steak dinner. He's the only one that stayed quit.

Carlee: I used to work with J. R. Lamb, a founding member of The Singing Christians, at Duke Power. He was on my crew. My boss, Charles, told me, said, "Carlee, you take J.R. You and him build that wall back yonder."

J.R. said, "Okay, I'll work with ye." And we got back there to that wall, me on one side and him on the other side, and I's over there beatin' on a log and cussin' a little bit. J.R. would say, "Carlee?" I'd say, "What?" He'd say, "Boy, I'm right over here across this wall from you and you cussin' like that ain't helpin' us build this wall any faster. You quit that cussin' and you and me will build this wall, but that cussin' ain't gonna help us none at all." So I quit cussin' [laughs].

He'd tell me some days that he was old and 'bout outta horsepower, and I'd say, "J.R., you just tell me what to do, stand back outta my way, and I'll do your work for ya." He'd say, "Boy, I sure do thank ye." We worked in them nuclear power plants for a long time, boys. I like them nuclear power plants, if they'll just keep the maintenance up on 'em. Let me tell ye somethin'. Lot of people don't realize it, but some of 'em pipes over there that the steam goes through and goin' 'round 'em curves like a stovepipe, first thing ye know four to six years from now that pipe's gonna get thin. When that steam goes out, you oughta see some of 'em things blow up. It'll blow four to five hundred foot in the air. Just blows everythin' and the buildin's all gone. Keep maintenance up on 'em, and they'd be fine. If they mess 'round and go to sleep and forget 'bout somethin', then somebody's gonna get killed, but they ain't no way them plants over there that we built is gonna blow up. You oughta see the concrete and stuff that we put in them things one hundred and fifty or two hundred foot down yonder in the ground and solid concrete; there's just no way. I worked building the plant and worked in it after it was in operation, too.

I have been racin' ever since 1950. Racin' over there in Germany was on the highway and not on a track. Eddy drove my race car ever since he was 'bout thirteen or fourteen years old. We have raced everywhere. Raced in North Carolina, in Georgia, all over South Carolina, and just all around. They called him "Fast Eddy." After he left, got killed, Lee got to be 'bout eleven or twelve years old, and he started driving my car. Lee's Eddy's son, my grandson, and he drives for me now. He lives up in Long Creek, South Carolina. I drove my cars, too, back in my younger days. I liked to have got killed in 1962 in Orangeburg, Kentucky. Took me about three or four months till I could walk again. When I got to where I was walkin' again, I quit racin' 'em round tracks and started drag racin'. I had a fast car then. I won all of these trophies [points to the shelves]. We ain't got 'em all in the house no more, but that trailer down there is full of trophies that I won all over Kentucky, Indiana, Tennessee, and Ohio. I'm in the Georgia hall of fame for racin'. I race Chevrolets. I run that car right up yonder [points to a picture], and we won many a races with that thang. Buck Simmons, he's the winningest race-car driver they's ever been in Georgia. On my mama's one hundredth birthday, Buck had just won his one thousandth race, and he come and took a picture with my mama. My mama was one hundred, two months, and two days old when she passed away. She rode in that truck every race we ever went to, though.

PLATE 21 **Carlee's race car**

Joan: He drives fast, not only on the racetrack, but he drives fast on the highway. We was goin' down Highway 11; we was headed to the racetrack, and he was goin' eighty-five miles an hour in a fifty-five-mile zone and the highway patrol stopped him. My son was about ten years old, and he was sittin' in the back of the truck. The law was not to have a child in the back of the truck, but he was sittin' in a little chair back there. Well, he gets his license and shows it to the trooper, and they go back to the back and talk. He's talkin' about huntin' and racin' and all the cop does is write him a warning ticket and says, "Mr. Heaton, you save the speed for the racetrack."

Carlee: He knew I was broke [laughs]. If you make any money racin', then you always stick it back in somethin'.

Joan: Um-hum. Like them ten-thousand-dollar motors you gotta have.

Carlee: Things have changed since I was growing up. People are a lot different. People will lie to ya now. Back whenever I was a kid, you couldn't find nobody that'd tell you a lie hardly. If they told ya something, they meant it, but nowadays you gotta sorta have one of 'em separators to separate the bull from the cow. I would change a lot of things if I could go back and live my life over. I'd start goin' to church and listen to what my mama said whenever I was a kid 'cause we used to walk four or five miles every night to Brush Arbor, and my daddy would be somewhere drunk. Me and my mama and my two sisters would go to church every time we got a chance. Things have changed a lot for me the past few years 'cause used to be you couldn't get me to go to church. My wife kept baggin' [begging] me to go and baggin' me to go. She was tellin' me how much the Lord liked me and how good He'd been to me, so finally I decided to listen to her a little bit and I started goin'. I met Delbert McCall, pastor of Ole Country Church; he had preached my mama's funeral and my boy's funeral and I liked him, so I started quittin' racin' and goin' to church. It was real hard to do, but I done it. I been that kinda guy that whatever I want to do I can do. I may not can do it as good as you can, but I won't give up. I just don't give up. I'd tell young people today to get in church every chance you get and praise God 'cause He sure loves us all, or He wouldn't have done what He done. I just wish I'd done it a long time ago instead of wastin' all that time, but the good Lord liked me, or He'd took me out of here a long time ago.

"Most of the toys I had was homemade."

~ Coyl Justice shares childhood memories ~

Coyl Justice and Mildred, his wife of many years, live in a modest home in the Betty's Creek community of Dillard, Georgia. Sharing space with their home is the nursery they began many years ago, along with a lush vegetable garden. On a warm July morning, I visited with them to discuss Mr. Justice's secrets for planting native azaleas from seed [see the article on page 461 in the how-to section of this book], as well as his life as a son of the mountain communities that we here at Foxfire call home.

Walking their property during our interview, I saw the results of many years of hard work. Greenhouses were filled with many varieties of plants, and many more bushes and trees filled the grounds. In their vegetable garden—a work of art in and of itself—Mrs. Justice shared sweet red raspberries straight off the bush, and Mr. Justice showed me his method of keeping deer out of his garden, a small green shed housing a radio that broadcast mostly sermons from one of the local Christian radio stations. Explaining that the only other station the radio could intercept was a rock 'n' roll station, Mr. Justice told me how he had initially believed his idea to be a failure because the music did little to deter the deer; however, when he discovered the Christian station, too, he also happened upon the curious realization that deer evidently don't care for preaching!

Before our morning was complete, Mr. and Mrs. Justice had generously selected two plants they thought would make good additions to my own yard, for which they wouldn't hear any suggestion of payment. When our interview was over, they invited me in as a guest to share a midmorning snack with them, and sitting in their kitchen, we spoke of our faith and families. I saw the kindness with which they treated each other and the affection with which they spoke of their children, grandchildren, and great-grandchildren.

Mr. Justice and his wife were witness to the tremendous changes that took place in the mountains over the course of the twentieth century. They have known both hardship and the comfort of having enough. They have accepted great joy and endured terrible tragedy. Yet they do not merely survive but thrive, devout in their faith and with joy.

—Lacy Hunter Nix

It would take a long time to tell you my childhood memories, but they are some good memories. I was born on Betty's Creek in Smithbridge Township, in North Carolina. I have four sisters and three brothers, including me. There is seven of us in all. We had a good time. I had two boys that I played with almost all the time—they were O'Neal and R. L. Burrell. After

PLATE 22 **"I met Mildred going to square dances." Coyl and Mildred Justice standing in front of one of their greenhouses**

I got grown, they moved out of the community. That was probably one of my favorite childhood memories, gettin' to play with them. We stayed in the creek, in the woods, climbed trees, and all that—we did it all the time. Day after day, when we was not havin' to go to school, we did that.

My earliest memories were when the school was up in what they call the Last Chance Schoolhouse. That is up at the foot of the mountain, down on Mama Daisy Justice's. I used to go over there a lot. I was too young to go to school, but I used to go over there, and they would let me recite poems. I do not know how I remembered that, but that's one of my earliest memories. Slippin' off from home and goin' to where Dad had some mean steers—that was very dangerous—and I would slip off and get in the pasture with those steers. Sister Helen would come and get me. I do not know why I did not get hurt, but I never did. That was when I was real small.

Some of the fondest memories was gettin' to go to school at the Last Chance Schoolhouse, and then sittin' around in the house listening to Dad and all the older guys tell big stories about huntin', and all that stuff, and about World War I. That's just about it, besides going to Franklin, North Carolina, with Dad and Mom. I didn't get to go much, but I remember I was overjoyed with stuff like that. That is some of the times that I got to go with them, but most of the time when we were at home, we had to work. I was too young lots of times to work, but we had to hoe corn. That is not a very good memory, watchin' Bob and all the rest of my family that was older than me at work. Dad would get Bob in the field to hoe corn, and he would slip off. He had a wooden-wheel wagon, and me and him would be on that wagon. Dad would have to get a hickory and head him back to the cornfield. When he got his back turned, Bob would be back on that wagon. That was kind of fun.

Back when I was real little, Dad worked in the woods all the time. I remember him talkin' about having to work a year to pay his taxes. We raised what little food we had. To buy coffee, chickens, and cows, sometimes we would have two or three hogs, and we would kill one and sell it to buy coffee and flour and all that stuff. Then the Work Projects Administration [*sic*] come along in the early thirties, so that's how he supplied food and clothes for us. We didn't have a lot, but we had shoes at least in the wintertime. When it got close to Christmas is when we got shoes.

School was pretty good till the first few years. I was scared to death— scared of the teacher and everything else, but that was when I started in the first grade. School was pretty good. They had a school at Mulberry just above where Newman's Chapel is now. That's the first time that we went to school. I was in the first grade. Dad had took some kind of contract with the county to bus the children from Betty's Creek to Mulberry to school. They was only two teachers, and I think it was first, second, third, and fourth grade in one room and fifth, sixth, and seventh in the other room. There was only two teachers, and they had a job! They just had their hands full because everybody wouldn't mind the teacher very well. Dad had a little pickup, and he made what we call a camper shell now on the truck, but it was homemade and people laughed about it. They called it the chicken coop because that is about what it looked like. That is how we rode to school—in the back of it. It wasn't too warm, but we were out of the wind and rain. That is how we got to Mulberry School.

I suppose it's a lot different from our children growin' up and when I went to school. Now they cannot discipline with a hickory or ruler. When I went to school, if you done something and did not mind the teacher, then you got your hand bent back with a ruler and got the palm of your hand blistered with it. Then they also used hickories; now you can't do that because of the way things are. There was not a lot of after-school activities. Bob drove the school bus, and he was always waitin'. We just had to get on the bus. Sometimes they had a basketball game, but it was outside. The Otto School and the Mulberry School would play. They would have a basketball game ever' once in a while, but not much.

Most of the toys I had was homemade, like the wooden-wheel wagon.

Sometimes if you could get a grown-up to make one, then it would really fly—down a hill of course. We made the wheels out of either black gum or pine, and, you know, you had to make the wheels as round as possible. Some of them jumped up and down. When I got a little bit older, Dad bought a wagon—just a red wagon. We wore that wagon out till nothin' was left. That is 'bout the first toy that I remember. Course we got some small cars and toys like that, but not much. That is what we had to play with.

Some of the chores were carry in wood, and we had to go get the cows. Sometimes the cows were hard to find, 'specially in the summertime. We would turn them out in the mountains, and sometimes they would forget to come home, and we would have to hunt cows. We fed the hogs, hoed corn, and in the fall we took the feed to the cows.

Christmas was always a good time of the year—a good feelin' time. We did not get much for Christmas; we got an orange, an apple, and a couple pieces of candy. Then, when the wagon come along, that was somethin', but that is about all we got. Somebody in the community would dress up like Santa Claus, and that was a lot of fun. I never did know the difference till I must have been twelve years old, 'fore I didn't know there wasn't a Santa Claus. I mighta knowed it, but I did not want to believe it.

Dating was not like it is now. You had to be so old, 'specially the girls. The boys was all too bashful to ask a girl out. If they did—and if they accepted—then you had to go in and get 'em. You did not have a car, and you did not go on the outside and holler for them to come out. You had to go in and meet the parents, and, you know, now it is not that way. You either go to the house and honk the horn, and they come out, or they meet in town. We had to go to the house and get 'em. I used to date a girl over in North Carolina 'cross Warrior. She had to slip out because her daddy was real strict. I was scared to death of him. That was before I went in the service, but I don't know how I got over there. One of my sisters lived over there, and that's how I met her.

I didn't have much of a social life. We did just about everything that you could think of for fun when I was growing up. We did not get into mischief. We had lots of fun with things that kids would not even think about now. Some things we done was normal things back in that time. There wasn't anywhere to go, and nobody had a vehicle. We had square dances from house to house. It was lots of fun going to candy drawin's and all sorts of parties. [**Editor's note**: See explanation of candy drawings in *Foxfire 2*, pages 372–74, and *Foxfire 3*, page 322.] We had lots of different kinds of parties. It was a lot of fun just goin' from house to house. If you went from house to house like we done now, you'd probably get run off. Then people did not care because that is all we had to do. Even where we had the square dances and things, the people welcomed the youngsters. A lot of 'em was old that went to square dances. We had three or four places that we did have square dances. One was Hap-n-So on Patterson Creek. We had a lot of square dances there. I used to pick a mandolin and a guitar. Brother Bob did, too. We was the ones who made the music most of the time for the square dances. We went to parties all the time. We had parties, and we had candy drawin's. I don't know who done it, but they bought all sorts of different colors of candy; that is how we usually met the girls. We could go with the girls, and you chose a partner. You had to go around the house, and then it did not matter about the heat 'cause we used wood, and the houses was all cold anyway. You drew candy; they broke it up real small, and as long as you could get a piece that matched, you could keep drawin', but if you got a different color than your partner then you had to go back around and try again. We had corn shuckin's and all that stuff. That is 'bout all they was of a social life. As times got better, Billy Long had a truck that he hauled acid wood in [**Editor's note**: See explanation of acid wood in *Foxfire 9*, page 367], and we all got to go to town on Saturday afternoon in that truck. We all got to go to town, and he never got in a hurry. He always waited on us. He wouldn't run off and leave us 'cause it was a long way from Betty's Creek to Clayton. He would bring us all back home. Sometimes it would be before dark.

When I went out on my own is when I got drafted in the service—kindly got broke away from home that way, but when I came back home, I met Mildred. I think we dated for about two years, and then we got married. We, Brother Oakley and me, tore down a loggin' camp. We built a house out of that loggin' camp. It was just old rough lumber, and it had a kitchen, dining room, and one bedroom. There was also a living room. We did not have enough strips to strip up the cracks, so you could see whatever was going on outside. You did not have to look out the window. You had a couple of windows in the house. That is how we got started off, and that is how I got broke away from home.

I had three children—Gary, Mickey, and Julia. Gary passed away. Mickey is here. He works on old cars all the time, and he's real good at it. Julia is married. She's got three children, and she lives in Tallulah Falls right now.

Right now I am retired. I worked at the Aerospace Industrial Development Corporation, now known as A.I.D., a division of RBC Bearings, for thirty-five years. When I was there, we made parts for Lockheed aircraft, the Navy, and for the Air Force.

Me and Mildred got a nursery, of course, and we work in the nursery. We have lived here for fifty-some years. I started soon after we moved here, you know, tryin' to learn. I don't know how I done it, but I did—with her help. I started rootin' azaleas and rhododendrons and things like that. It went from there and—somewheres along the line—some things I couldn't root, not readily, 'cause I didn't know how. So I got started on the seed. Things that I can't root, I growed from seeds. Native azaleas, for me, is hard to root. Some of 'em will; some of 'em won't. But if you raise 'em from seed, it's easy. I learned by trial and error. I've got lots of books, and I belong to the Rhododendron Society. We get the magazine every two months, and they publish a lot of different things that people do, and I learned a lot from that because anything that I could find that people done things easily, or easier than I could do it, then I'd try it. That's how I got started. I had lots of failures—Mildred could vouch for that—and I still do. Even this time I threw away fifteen flats of seedlings that I had done something wrong with; I don't know what, but I had to dump all of 'em. Every once in a while, you will get a disease. You'll get things like mites and spider mites and things, and I have a terrible time with spider mites. But I'm finally gettin' rid of the spider mites. I used to root roses, and the spider mites made me quit just about because I couldn't find anything that would kill them. You know they have little webs, and they will get inside the leaf; you can't find spray that will penetrate, but hopefully now I have found somethin' that will penetrate.

We had, most of the time, three ladies helpin'; Mildred's sister was one. When we'd be plantin' these, they never did get the act of sowin' seeds. I couldn't trust 'em. I'd always sow 'em myself and cover them up. I guess that was me. They probably could have done it better than me, but I didn't trust 'em. You know it's a onetime deal once you sow 'em, and if that's all the seed you have, then you just lost a year. They'd try to sow some sometimes. They'd always cover 'em too deep—or at least I thought so, but they was really good at takin' 'em out of the seedbed. [**Editor's note**: At this point in the interview, Coyl's wife, Mildred, laughs and speaks up to tell me her opinion on the subject: "He sows them too thick. He sows them so close together that you can't get them out." Coyl laughs, too, and acquiesces: "That's what she tells me, that I sow them too thick. An' I do."] You had to take 'em out with a toothpick 'cause they was so little and put them in individual cups. And that's what they done. They was better at that than me. You know women is always better at somethin' like that. I don't know how many a day we would take up. You know the seed plant is very small, and you can fit thousands in one flat. It looked pretty good. You can do mountain laurel and rhododendron, but the mountain laurel—it takes two years to root the mountain laurel, but you know in two or three weeks, they'll come up in seed. So it makes a lot of difference.

We grow plants of all kinds. That is what I love the most. We grow lots of plants, not as many as we used to, but we still grow a lot of plants. I'm still

PLATE 23 **Coyl Justice demonstrating the tumbler he uses to make compost for his daughter-in-law**

tryin' to retire and get out of the business, but I think people don't want me to. I feed the birds, and we have, I don't know how many birds. We have a man from Atlanta that comes up here in the summertime. He takes pictures of the birds. I think he puts them on television; well, I saw them one time on television. He came last summer and stayed a week. He didn't stay with us. He came every day for a week and took pictures of the birds. We got a lot of birds.

I do not know of a life-changing event that would be worth talkin' about. Everythin' was pretty normal, I guess. The thing that changed me the most was when our son Gary passed away. That probably changed both of our lives forever. It just was not the same—never will be. Of course we have both of the other children, grandchildren, and great-grandchildren, but it is not the same since he passed away.

From the time that I was growing up till now, life has changed a lot. When I went to World War II, Betty's Creek didn't have any power. There mighta been a couple of cars up here, but we didn't have any power. Betty's Creek didn't get any power till I came back out of the service. That was 1946 to 1947, somewhere in there. After World War II, things began to change; we got power up here, and they built a new road. It used to be about six miles up Betty's Creek. Now, from my house to Dillard, it is about four point two miles. There has been lots of changes, and the different plants [factories] have all moved in. When I was growin' up until I went to the service, they wasn't jobs; only workin' in the woods, cuttin' timber, things like that. That changed rapidly after World War II. We done a lot of walking and a lot of hard work, and since the plants have come in, and we got jobs, it has made it a lot easier. So life's been pretty good.

I got a lot of advice, but it would take too long to tell you! The best advice I could give children would be—and this would go to the parents, too—go to church, stay out of drugs, stay out of drinkin', and lots of other things. Children that are raised to go to church—and parents treat them like they're supposed to—they're not going to do drugs. They're not going to drink, but they might try. Most all children is going to experiment, but if taught to go to church, then they won't do that.

I like Christianity, not religion. Everybody's got religion, but to me it's a serious thing. I have been a Christian ever since I was probably fourteen or fifteen years old. That does not mean I lived a Christian life all the time because I went out in the world. When you're saved, and you know you are a Christian, you always come back. When you're young, you know, you sow your wild oats, but when you get saved you might get out in the world. You always come back. I have enjoyed my Christian life. It has not been easy, but I enjoyed it.

I don't think I would change a thing. I am happy like my life is, and I don't think I would change a thing. If I had a million dollars, I wouldn't change a thing.

"The first airplane . . . we thought it was the Lord a-comin'."

~An interview with Vaughn Billingsley~

On an autumn afternoon, Kasie Hicks, another Foxfire student, and I took a trip to Vaughn Billingsley's home. When we arrived, I knocked on the door, and the friendly, warm smile of his wife greeted us. As Mr. Billingsley sat in his favorite La-Z-Boy and shared with us the fascinating story of his life, the fireplace warmed our backs and felt so homey. The interview lasted for a little over an hour, and then we turned off the tape and just chatted.

Today Vaughn Billingsley, father and grandfather, is the owner of a successful nursery. In fact, he recently patented a hybrid, an oak-leaf hydrangea, which he lovingly named "Vaughn's Lillie" after Lillie, his wife of many years, with whom he fell in love after he, as he likes to tell, winked at her.

With his childhood stories, Mr. Billingsley took me "back in the older days," and he showed me what it was like growing up years ago, when life was slower but much harder.

—Lacy Forester

My name is Vaughn Billingsley, and I'm old. I think I'm older than I really am. I'll be sixty-four on my birthday, July the ninth, 2003. I had one sister and two brothers: Barbara and Jack and Darrell. I was the oldest. I was born in the house. There wasn't no doctor. The doctor finally come and saw how Mama was. [Having me] about killed her. I was a big ol' baby. I think that she passed out. I can't 'member, though.

Well, my relationship with my parents was pretty good. Mother said I was stubborn as a mule, and I had to get whoopin's a lot. My daddy bought and sold cattle. He grew cabbage and was a truck farmer; he did other jobs, too. I believe that after school, we had to work as gardeners an' everything. We didn't have no time to play. We all just worked, kids and grown people. We hoed the field and picked cabbage ever since we was little kids. We got out there, and we had to do all the plowin', too. We did the plowin' with a team of mules.

I went to school up at Scaly Mountain, North Carolina. We had a two-room schoolhouse, and there was four grades in it. We had primer, then we had first, and then we had the "high first." We spent four years getting into the second grade. We didn't have no buses much. They couldn't haul us all, so we went to the fourth grade there in Scaly. I don't remember none of them teachers ever tryin' to help me to learn how to read any. We caught these buses to Highlands when we was in the fifth grade.

Well, there wasn't no favorite memories from my childhood. 'Bout all I can remember is bein' cold and hungry, raised up in the Depression, and didn't anybody have no money. It was rough. We was raised on beans and taters. One evenin', me and this boy went out, and we was hungry, so we decided to pick persimmons at James Miller's. We climbed up in that tree so that we could get the 'simmons off of it and eat some of 'em. Well, it was gettin' cold that evenin', and the sun was goin' down. It must have been six below zero, and we was up there, and the cold wind went to blowin'. We got so cold, we liked to not have got down out of that tree. It's a wonder we hadn't froze to death. We finally got out of the tree, and we got up close to a chestnut log. There was logs layin' all over the pasture. They was dead, so everyone let the cows pick around 'em. Well, we both laid down on the ground, and it was froze. I have never been so cold. It's a wonder we made it through that, but I told him what to do. I said, "Let's get up and start runnin', and we'll just run all the way home, just hard as we can run. The harder we run, we can get warmed up." We didn't get no 'simmons at the end. We runned just as hard as we could run, and by the time we got home, we was good and warm.

There was no way of ridin' [in a vehicle]; if y' got in a hurry, was goin' anywhere hurryin', then y' had to run. We went either by walkin' or by ridin' a mule. Some people had a wagon and wheels. You would walk to town and back, or ride in whatever you could hitch. Not many people had a rig. My mother one time was goin' to town, and she got out and started walkin', and some guy come along and picked her up. She never would tell who it was. But she got out, and she asked him, "How much do I owe you?" He said, "Oh, about a nickel and maybe get a box of soda." Some people would have to catch a ride with the mailman when he would come through. They'd catch him then. In my life, that's how it was.

I remember the first car I ever seed. It scared me to death. Me and my cousin Gene was out. We lived in an old log house down on the edge of the road. We was the only house back in there. We heard somethin'; we turned around and looked, and there was an old Model T comin' down the field there, down on the old road, and it was goin' *durp, durp, durp*, comin' down through there. It scared us to death. We jumped up and run in the house and crawled under the bed. I can remember getting just as far as I could up against the wall, and we were just a-screamin', scared to death.

The first airplane we ever seen, we thought it was the Lord a-comin'. We seen the little white thing up in the air. Well, I was the one who seen it. I was out in the yard, and I seen that. I went to hollerin' for everybody to come and look. They all come out and looked and looked. Mama come out on the porch; she looked up and said, "Well, the Bible said that in the last days that He would send signs and wonders from the heavens before He comes." I thought that was the truth.

Well, I don't know if there ever was a doctor when we got sick. We just rode a mule to get to the doctor. If you could catch somebody or know somebody and get them to take you to the doctor, you'd be in good shape. There wasn't a lot of people around then—might be a mile or two apart. I guess we lived three or four miles from where we saw the vehicle, and that was the closest place out. We lived just as far back as we could get without comin' out somewheres else.

Well, we'd just get out, and we'd run around and go to the swimmin' hole when I was growin' up. They was a swimmin' hole up there in the creek. We'd stay all day in the creek; then we'd go, y' know. They didn't care, I don't reckon—Mama and Daddy didn't. They'd let us go until it got dark, and we'd stay gone all day. If we didn't go to the swimmin' hole, then we'd go huntin' or somethin'—squirrel huntin' or rabbit huntin'— whatever you could get and make a little extra money off of. Muskrat was all the way up to three dollars. I mean, a big muskrat was just about as much as a hog.

When we was kids and would get to go huntin', that was a treat. I remember the first time that I ever went squirrel huntin'. I found some shells in the backseat of the car that we had borrowed to go coon huntin'. I found me some shotgun shells, and I asked Daddy, I said, "Can I take your gun over there and go squirrel huntin'?" He sat me down and talked to me a little and taught me what to do and how to act. He told me that if I seen a squirrel not to shoot until I saw it move and knew for sure that it was a squirrel. "Don't waste a shell," he said. So I went up across the edge of the field and into the woods. I had to walk about a mile or two up there before I could go huntin'. I walked up quite a bit, and there was a squirrel sittin' on a limb, just sittin' up there, lookin' at me with his tail bowed up over his back. It was a perfect picture. Well, I remember standin' there, waitin' for it to move. I waited and waited, and it never did move. It just sat there and looked at me. I said to myself, "Well, I know that's a squirrel, so I just better shoot it." So I did, and out it fell, so then I went on around until I finally killed one more. Then I went home 'cause I was pretty happy over killin' those two squirrels. That was my first time.

It was pretty nice to get candy bars and things like that back then. My aunt and uncle owned a store. Burt, our uncle, give us a candy bar. I think it was a PayDay or somethin', somethin' with nuts. We had never had nothin' like that, and we couldn't believe that he had give it to us. We thought there was somethin' wrong with it. We went on and looked and unwrapped 'em, and we got halfway away from the store to a little place, and we finished unwrappin' them, and, boy, we thought they were molded or old or somethin'. Really, he just wanted us to have them, I think, because we had never had none or nothin'. I finally tasted around enough a little bit to see if they was soured or anything, and then we went for it. It was the best thing I'd ever had.

I joined the Army when I was eighteen. You had to be eighteen to join the Army, I guess. I went through basic training and all, and I graduated the Army in '55, '56, or '57. I can't remember the exact year. I had to come back, but I met a girl when I was in the Army up in Illinois, and I went back up there to see her. We never got married or anything, but I liked her. I worked in Illinois for a while—ten years, in fact—and me and my wife got married up there. Them Yankees didn't get me; one of them liked to got me, and I really liked her, too. She was from Wisconsin, and her name was Rita. She was Catholic, and I was a Baptist, and that's kinda the way that went. They said, "You gotta become a Catholic or either raise the kids Catholic, and that's the only thing that will prevent you from marryin' her." I said, "Well, you know, I don't know; I don't believe I could ever baptize my kids Catholic." And she said, "Well, they'll come and baptize 'em while you're not there." I said, "They would do that, me not bein' there, my own kids' baptism?" That's kinda where it come apart.

I left there and came back down to Washington, D.C. The people I was workin' with came down from Washington to start a new business, a new job—a big job—a water plant. I helped move all that down there; then I came home for a while. I decided to call and maybe go back. I called the boss, asked him, "Would you have a job?" He said, "I've always got a job for you." I said, "Well, what about the scale? The Washington scale ain't near as much as Illinois." "Oh," he said, "We're gonna do better than that. I'll give you your own job."

Well, you know, I reckon I kinda had everybody fooled. See, I couldn't hardly read; I just had bad eyesight. I saw double all my younger life, and I couldn't ever learn to read nothin' at school. It never worked, couldn't. Saw, you know, everything was up and down instead of lines. After I got my glasses and everything, I kinda learned how to read on my own. I read slow. I mean, you know where the thing that comes across the TV? If you're watchin' some of those Mexican movies, then they write out what they said? I can't get all of that—'bout half of it, maybe two-thirds of it. Sometimes I can get all of it, but not usually. Anyway, that's what happened with my education. I wanted a high school education, and I remember wanting that, you know, and I said, "Well, I'd like to have that, a high school education." No Billingsley had ever finished high school up to that point, but I had to quit. I went four days in the eighth grade; it was just too humiliating.

I just couldn't stand the pressure, you know. They'd ask you to stand up and read, and the teacher wouldn't wait for you to figure out which letter was which, you know. I just couldn't take it. I told my dad, I said, "I ain't goin' back," and he never said nothin'. I didn't. Then I hurt my eye coon huntin' one night, and I went out there and told the doctor, I said, "I hurt my eye—jabbed a stick in it. I think I about knocked it out. I can't hardly see nothin', and it hurts pretty bad." He done an eye exam on me, and he said, "It's gettin' no better; it's getting a little worse?" He said, "No, you didn't do this a' coon huntin'." I said, "Yeah, I jabbed a stick in it—limb hit me in the eye. Somebody turned one loose on me." He said, "Well, they's a little bit of a scar there, but," he said, "that ain't what's botherin' you. You've had this since you was born." He went into the detail of how to show me, you know. I said, "Well, I don't reckon there's nothin' wrong." I always just argued, even when I was a Christian. You know, the Lord tells you. I would argue with that pretty good, you know. Anyway, he showed me. He said, "Now I'll show you." Then he flipped his thing and said, "How many lines do ya see?" And I said, "Well, I see two." He said, "How d' they look?" And I said, "They look like a V, a big, long, slim V, touchin' at the bottom." "Now," he said, "how many you see?" And I said, "One." He flipped it back, and every time he flipped it, he said, "That's what's the matter." Said, "You're seein' double." So he give me the glasses to correct that, and I began to kinda learn how to read.

PLATE 24 **"I saw double all my younger life, and I couldn't ever learn to read nothin' at school." Vaughn Billingsley as he tells the story of his double vision**

I come back from up north and growed cabbage at the farm. We had a bunch of work—just a mule and a hoe or whatever y' had. By the end, I had two hundred and two dollars. Anyway, before I left, I still had some money. I took off and started to caddie, and I had to get up at four o'clock in the mornin'. I'd be the first one there, and I'd get out early. We made three dollars a day, all day, to be a caddie. I couldn't save enough money doin' that—didn't make enough on that job—so I packed my clothes and took off. I caught the bus and got off at Cornelia, Georgia, and caught the train. I went back to Chicago. I had very little money. I had to ration out everything, so I couldn't spend it or nothin'. I just had to stay wherever I could. I got a little ol' job for a dollar and ten cents an hour. I had to ride a bicycle six miles a day, and in the wintertimes, it was awful cold. It got all the way to thirty-two below one mornin'. I just couldn't ride that bicycle to go to work, so I called in. They said, "What's the matter?" They called me "Bill" up there. They said, "What's the matter, Bill? Is your bicycle froze up?" I said, "Yeah, just a little bit. I don't know what's the matter with this bicycle." You had to pedal it hard downhill to make it go. Anyway, I worked there a while, and then I got another job.

I was workin' in a bowlin' alley. After about a year, I guess, or close to it, I met this girl named Sara Lee. She came out there one time. Her daddy was on a bowlin' league, so she just come down there with her daddy. So me and her got to talkin' for a little while, and all of her girlfriends came up to me when she went to the bathroom or somethin', and they asked if I knew who she was. They would say, "She is Sara Lee." I didn't care. I had seen and eaten them cakes before. I seen them in the store. I didn't pay no attention to it. I just figured it was the only bakery around there. Anyhow, at the bowlin' alley, I made one hundred and twenty-five dollars in two weeks to take home. That was pretty good pay at that time. I got enough to buy me an old car. I was doin' all right. I knowed some old buddies around there and this girl, and they would give me a ride every once in a while to work and back. All I had to do was call 'em and ask for one. I met them at the bowlin' alley. They'd play at the bowlin' alley down there, and then they'd take me home some.

I never owned my own place. I had one feller let me sleep in his garage. He had a car lot. He had a car and owned this buildin', and he would let me sleep in there. Man, it was warm in there; run out of fuel one time because all the radiators froze and busted, and I didn't have no place to go.

After I got saved and born again, filled with the Holy Ghost—now, I didn't speak in tongues, but I was filled with the Holy Ghost, and it happened to me just exactly—see, big ol' dummy me didn't know nothin'— but it happened just exactly like the Bible said. Teachin' and meetin' and teachin'—I was able to read. I read the Bible, and that thing came alive. I read it day and night and studied it. I'd sit and tears'd just pour, reading the Bible. It's so real. And a lot of people, if you don't have that spirit, it's a barbaric-type thing, a comic-book-type thing, you know, 'cause it's all impossible except you've got to leap through faith. From then on, you know, things got off of that, and I quit goin' to church. You quit goin' just a few times, and Satan will getcha. He can offer everything, like he's the god of this world, and it's all in his hands. He can getcha ticked off at all the church members or your neighbors, and take a polished shoe and unshine them. He's super sharp. I just quit, and I ain't been back yet, but I know, and that did happen to me—that ain't no fluke. That did happen to me; it changed all my insides, my heart and everything.

Satan is something, boy. He'll getcha. I used to pray that the Lord would take me away if anything I started to do was gonna belittle Him in any way, in His ways. I prayed that He'd take me on out. I said, "I'm ready to go; just take me." It ain't thataway; it didn't happen thataway. You have to be tested as though by far [fire], to see what works out, to have a good testimony. I was so happy; somebody come under conviction with, you know, the spirit just come. I would just melt down and go to telling 'em what the Lord done for me, how happy He made me, and they just couldn't take it. Some would just get right, right there; some are preachers and stuff now. That's the awfulest thing to have to think back how you got out of church and quit after so much happiness and everything.

Well, anyway, back to the workin' deal. I came back from Illinois, and he [his supervisor] said he was gonna give me that job, you know, to do my own thing, that was like building a factory where they built factories and power plants and stuff like that. Well, I knew—that scared me, obviously. I said, "Well, they probably have rolled blueprints as big as a thirty-gallon barrel. I won't be able to; I can't even read very good, just enough to kindly know." I couldn't hardly read a Christmas card or nothin' after I got to where I could see, and it just scared me off. I didn't go.

I had an old Mercury car; it was rusted to pieces. I bought a new '60 Chevrolet car, a two-door coop. I thought it was gettin' kinda wore [worn out]. See, Bucket Head [referring to himself] traded it for another '60 Mercury that rode real easy. I thought, "Well, mine [the new car] worked, but that's the way it was built." See [it was] a big, old heavy thing, and they'd fixed it and painted it and everything, and I traded mine—even paid a little boot, five or six hundred dollars. I told some of them that I made such a car trade that I could be out in the woods and think about that car trade an' my face would turn red! I used to have a red face, you know; my face'd be red, and they'd ask me, "What's your face so red for?" I'd probably thought about that car deal! I made such a bad trade that every time I think about it, I can be out huntin' by myself and think about it, and my face'll turn red, you know, just fumin'. It was a bad trade; I got beat so bad. I never ever traded another one after that; I just put 'em somewhere, give 'em to somebody, or sell 'em for whatever you can get for 'em. I didn't go back, so that old rusty Mercury, I fixed it up and sold it to a feller down there in Otto, North Carolina, for five hundred dollars. There went my whole new car for five hundred bucks— that's all I got out of it—that I bought; I paid thirty-two hundred for it at that time. I paid steady payments, and I got it paid off. It was a fast car; Lord have mercy, it was so fast, had that big motor in it. When I came back down here, and I took that old car and sold it, I went down sixty-four [Highway 64] out of Franklin and bought a '53 Chevrolet pickup. It had a new rebuilt motor in it. It's hard to imagine; it was in good shape, didn't have a dent or nothin' in it. Of course, this was in 1960; it was [nearing] ten years old. I gave three hundred fifty dollars for it, for a pickup that looked like new, wasn't bent or nothin'—had a new rebuilt motor.

Well, it [Billingsley's Nursery] just come gradual on. It started off we didn't have nothin'. Me and my brother started to haulin' a few bushes, some of the Chastains was a-talkin', and they had dug some around, and they'd dug one of those wild azaleas. I had done that all my life, dug for this fellow out of Atlanta to come up here, buy 'em for ten cents apiece off of the farmers and government or whoever had 'em and sell 'em like that. I knowed how to dig 'em. I could really pop 'em out; it wasn't nothin' for me. They said they'd sold one of them for fifteen dollars. I said, "Lord, help! I can dig one of them and sell 'em for a dollar apiece and make plenty of money!" So me and him [Vaughn's brother] got to talkin', and I said, "Let's take that pickup and dig us a load of mountain laurel and honeysuckle and just wild stuff and maybe get us a few boxwoods off of somebody for a dollar apiece." He said, "All right," so we did. We made eighty dollars apiece. We got us up a little load and went, and in one day, we made eighty dollars apiece. So we come back and got another load. Some woman said she'd like to have boxwoods, so we went back and bought a bunch of boxwoods. We got back down there, and she said, "Well, I'll have to go see the property owner, see if it's all right to put 'em in, see if he wants to buy 'em." Boy, there we sat, mouth open then! We just left. We finally sold 'em, but we didn't make but forty dollars apiece with all the gas and everything comin' out of that. I told 'im, I said, "This ain't gonna work. I thought we'd be into something, but it don't look like it's gonna work," so we just pulled off. Finally, one day I told my brother, I said, "Well, I think I'll get up a load and take in by myself; might make enough for one guy." It was my truck and everything. I did; I made pretty good money for a day's work—made a week's pay in a day. It took one day to load it and one day to sell it, and I just kept going back. It wasn't no time till nearly everything I took was promised. I'd just go around and deliver it, make three or four hundred dollars a day. It just went on like that. Then I got to doin' landscape and studying that. When I started, I found that I was kind of an artist like drawing pictures or anything like that. My daughter teaches art down there at the school. She's talented; that's a genetic thing like music.

Well, I just kept fooling with that, and I got to doing landscape, and a feller up there in North Carolina, they put in that golf course up there, Wildcat Cliffs Country Club. That was the second golf course in Highlands.

It was big; it was nice. They wanted to try to get somebody to do the landscapin', so they went down to Franklin and asked a local landscaper about takin' the job and doin' all the landscapin'. "Lord," he said, "I'm nearly eighty years old; I can't do nothin' like that." They said, "Well, would you recommend someone?" His son did it, too, sold bushes, and his son-in-law did. God, I guess he sold more bushes than anyone, the son-in-law, but, you know, they'd just dig it anyway—bare root it. I'd go down there and buy some bushes from the landscaper—turned out me and him dug 'em the same way, real nice balls. Of course, I was sellin' to a landscape architect; I had to do it that way. They asked him, "Well, could you recommend somebody?" And he said, "If I gotta recommend somebody that I know will do the right thing, it'd be Vaughn Billingsley." He said, "He'd dig it and put it in; it'd be done right. He does it; that'd be the only one I know." Well, they just called me straight; that's what really got me kicked off—had that whole golf course. I'd just work on both sides of the streets at the same time, pockets so full of money—couldn't hardly have time to go to the bank or nothin', just bulging with money 'cause you didn't have to argue price or nothin'. I tried to do unto them as I'd want them to do to me; then the reputation came. A lot would come, say, "You fix it. You've been recommended, and give me the bill when you get done." Money was not an object nor price, so that got

PLATE 25 **Vaughn's nursery business in Rabun Gap, Georgia**

me off to the races. I used to have to dig out of the woods, and everybody had bushes, had 'em planted in rocky ground that they couldn't use, awful hard to dig. Sometimes you'd find a patch that you could really dig more and get about all of them. It was always when I'd come home from Highlands that I'd see that big bottom down there that they used to grow beans and cabbage. [**Editor's note**: The site to which he refers is the current location of Billingsley's Nursery in Rabun Gap, Georgia.]

One day I came home, came in, and my daughter said that land [I wanted] was for sale. The landowner was a schoolteacher, and I went to school with her. My daughter was substituting for the landowner, and during their working together, she told her, she said, "I want to sell that." She had gotten into it with a farmer who leased it that had it in cabbage all the time. The farmer had farmed it so long he felt like it was his, and she wanted to go up on the price of the lease, and he said he wouldn't pay it or something. He just wasn't gonna do it, so she said, "Just stay off of it then," but he didn't stay off—just kept goin' on it—and she sued him then. He didn't go to court; she won the case. My daughter said, "She's gonna sell that." She had about thirty acres there. I called her, and she said, "Yeah, I wanna sell it." I said, "How much you gonna ask for it?"

She said, "Well, the bottom land is a floodplain, which you can't grow nothing on. It is forty-five hundred dollars an acre." Well, I had done bought some down there and paid twelve hundred an acre for it. I told her, "I ain't got no problem with that. Let's just go ahead and draw that up." She said, "Well, it won't work like that. There's eight acres more up there against the road. It's thirty thousand dollars an acre; you have to buy that, too." That's eight acres—two hundred forty thousand bucks—and that money then was money.

I said, "Well, all right. I'm gonna take it—not even gonna ask you to come down on it, but one thing I'm gonna ask you is not to mention nothing about the deal to nobody. If I want it told, I wanna be the one to tell it." She said, "Oh, that's fine. I won't mention it." I went through all that tryin' to buy other pieces of land. The news got out that I was fixin' to buy that. Everybody would see you around town and go straight and offer more and say, "Hold on. I think I know someone who can get you a lot more," and stuff like that.

I guess we can just say that back in the older days it was a lot harder than it is today. Most kids don't have to work. They only work if they want to, and we didn't have any of them nice cars or airplanes. Yeah, you kids sure have it easy. One thing I can tell y', though: Get a job and a good education, or y' ain't gonna be nothin' in life.

"You either moonshined or you sold corn to moonshiners."

~ Memories from Allen English ~

Allen and Betty English are members of a generation who have seen great change come to the mountains. Born in an era when most women birthed their babies at home with the help of a midwife, when wood served to both heat homes and cook food, when most people grew their own food, and before industry came to the area, Allen English spoke of a time when the rhythms of daily life were quite different from what we know today. In those days, he told me, families were close, sharing time together as a natural part of daily life rather than another item on a to-do list. Neighbors depended on one another in times of need, knowing that the time would come when those who had assisted would need assistance and those who had needed help would provide it.

I met Allen and Betty several years ago, not as Foxfire contacts but as friends of my father's. My dad shared with Allen an interest in hunting and fishing and an enjoyment of well-crafted guns. In fact, it was a relative of Allen's who acted as a father figure to my own father many years ago and taught him a love of the outdoors that he has passed on to his own children. When I went to interview them on a July morning, I found them just as I remembered them from my younger years: Allen, cheerful and friendly, and Betty, sweet and hospitable.

As he spoke of people who were happy simply because they were comfortable—by which he meant they had enough to eat, enough wood to heat their homes and their cookstoves, clean and sturdy clothes to wear, and bodies able enough to do the hard work required to put food on the table and keep the homes warm—I could not help but think of the financial crisis our great nation has experienced recently and wonder if we, as a people, will relearn the value and joy of gratitude for having enough. As we talked of his life and interests, I heard in Allen's conversation the rare quality of a man who honestly appreciates life's simple but great pleasures: fishing trips that bring home fresh and delicious fish to eat, hard work that produces a yard full of colorful flowers, time with family that leaves a legacy of happy memories, and an honest life well lived.

—Lacy Hunter Nix

Well, we grew up here in the country. I was borned in Tiger, Georgia. My parents lived in a log house, and I was born in that house in 1941. They didn't have a maternity hospital, and Ms. Lizzie Keason was the midwife. She's been dead for several years, but I can remember her. Before she passed away, I grew up old enough to remember her. She was the midwife. I have one brother and four sisters, and I was next to the youngest. I have one sister younger than me. My parents were Oscar and Clara English.

We worked; we grew most everything we ate. At a young age, we very seldom went to town. We had to make our own entertainment, and we would make our own toys—wooden-wheel wagons. We'd roll 'em off the hills and stuff like that when we was kids. And we had the creek down here, and in the summer, why, we had us a swimmin' hole. We had some neighbors, and they was some kids that would come around. Well, we did everything—stuff like horseshoes. Of course, we played in the creek, played cowboys and Indians when we was young, stuff like that—things today that kids don't play or even know about.

There's one thing that I tell a pretty good bit. Bob Joe Scroggs, he lived over in a house right straight across from us over there, and we'd get a big tire, like a big transfer truck tire, and this was a pasture up there that was steep. We'd carry that tire up there, and he'd get balled up in it, and he'd come down the hill, and they was two fences an' the woods down there, and he'd come plumb down that hill and through them barbed-wire fences. It didn't hurt 'im, but he didn't try it again [laughs]! Stuff like that was real excitin', but you'd think, why would anybody in the world get in a tire and come down that hill like that and a-knowin' that that barbed-wire fence was out there!

We was on up pretty much in age, toward teenage, when we went to town to the movies and things. On Saturdays, we would go to the Saturday matinee up at the theater there in town. Really, we just had to sorta entertain ourselves, but we worked a lot even at a young age. We worked in the garden and fields and things like 'at, and it wasn't somethin' we dreaded, 'cause it just come natural that we did such as 'at.

The families back then was real close together. On Saturday night, a lot of times, we'd just get together, and you'd talk, and there's one thing we'd always do in the wintertime. We'd grow popcorn, and we'd pop a big dishpan full of popcorn and stuff like that.

School was somethin'; it was fine, but we were not really, in ways, excited, 'cause in ways we was sorta carefree kids. It took us a while in the fall to get used to going back to school and sittin' there all day instead of out roamin' the country. We'd have to do our homework, and that was number one when you come home. You did that first, and then you did your evening work. And, then, if there was extra time, you might get to play some, but that homework was first—doin' your work and then your evening chores. And when I got older, I even milked the cow, and we had to feed the hogs. All that stuff had to be taken care of and get wood. If it was winter, you had to get wood in for the night. We burnt wood, and that was our source of heat and cookin' also. Mother, she cooked on a woodstove, and, o' course, we had a wood heater. That was the source of heat. That was one of the number one things; you had to have that done. I come along right amongst the girls, and my brother, he was much older, and he'd already gone out, so all that kinda work, I mostly did that. And the girls, they'd help in the house a pretty good bit, but my main job was to get wood in and stuff like that. Another job that I had was to always help Mother cook breakfast. That was one job that I did. And I still know a lot about that today [laughs]. That's a good meal.

They was very few people here when I was a child, and it was a farmin' community. All these houses here now, they wasn't here. There was an old gentleman that lived right here, right below the house. He had a small house, and we lived here, then one other one over there. And that was all the houses right in here, and now everywhere you look, they's a house. Like I said, it was thinly populated, and we did farming. It was sorta more carefree, I guess. Everybody in the community was tight-knit people. If you needed help with something, you just called on your neighbor, and then you returned the help. As far as money, they was never any money changed hands—just help—and that made it seem like a tight-knit community. Back then they wasn't so independent. People were more open to one another, but you see people today right around you, they don't even speak. Used to, everybody was very close.

We went to church. That was a big part of family life. We went out here to Liberty Baptist Church. We looked forward, when we was kids, to stuff like Bible school, reunions, and Christmas plays. We looked forward to that; it was special and different.

Besides farming my dad did some heavy construction for several years, and in later years, he went to work with Game and Fish. My mother primarily stayed home until they opened the shirt factory [Clayburne Manufacturing in Clayton, Georgia], and she worked a few years up there, but she didn't work many years. She was mostly a professional cook. Before that, they was some things that probably wouldn't be approved of today; I know they wouldn't be approved of today. Just like a lot of others, we come from a moonshining family. I mean, it was a way of life; it wasn't something that we liked to do, but it was something we had to do. The plants [factories] only hired so many people, and they was a lot of people in the county, and they was just so many jobs. We did do that till we got older, and when we could find jobs, we'd quit. And, back then, you didn't consider it as wrong; a lot of people did it. It was just a way of life for a lot of people. That's a reason a lot of the farmers, they farmed and stuff like that, but you couldn't sell corn to make a livin'. You either moonshined, using it to make the liquor, or you sold it to moonshiners. 'Course, you couldn't make a livin' in this country a-farmin'. It just wasn't that big.

It was very hard, but we always seemed to be happy; it didn't matter if we had a whole lot, but we always had plenty of food, we had clothes and a good place to live. That's something we never did hurt for. They's some people that did, but we didn't. By no means was we rich, but I'd say we were comfortable, and when you are comfortable and things like that, you are happy. That's what probably made the family and the people around here happy. They didn't have a lot, but that's what made folks close-knit; they was comfortable. They had enough. T'day it seems like some people, they can't get enough; no matter what they got, they can't get enough.

My teen years were pretty good. A' course, like some other kids, I did play some ball and stuff like that and went through that. Seemed like I was very glad to see that high school get over. As soon as that was over, I went into the service; I went into the Navy and then into [Army] Special Forces, and then, when I got back, why, I met—I knew Betty before I went in, but when I came back, why, I looked her back up, and then I married her. She was from Rabun Gap, Georgia, and I was from down in these parts. We didn't date before I entered the service, but I worked just briefly at a service [gas] station in town, and that's how I got to know her. In fact, I'd slip and buy her cigarettes [laughs]. And I had to pay for 'em! She might not approve of all that t'day, but I think it's been fun [laughs]! Forty-nine years—last June

PLATE 26 **"When I came back, why, I looked her back up, and then I married her." Allen and Betty English**

the second was forty-nine years since we were married. It seems like when we got together that we sorta just knew we was meant for each other. And we've had a good life. We've got a son and daughter, and they are good people. I've got five grandchildren. [**Editor's note**: At this point in the interview, Allen points to the pictures of his grandchildren and great-grandchildren and beams as he explains, "That's the great-grandkids. That's the sweeties. We're fixin' to have one more great-grandkid in October. Two, and we're fixin' to have the third. It's gonna be another girl."] Our great-grandchildren live out in Peachtree City, and we don't see 'em as much as we want to. We'd like to see 'em all the time, but we can't. Well, there's one thing about it: We can spoil them and send them back home to their parents! We've got one grandson, and he's special. He was twenty yesterday; he was just twenty years old yesterday.

When I first got back from the service, I couldn't find work and, for a brief time, I made moonshine again until finally I got on at Rabun Mills [Burlington Industries]. Then I went back to the shirt factory just a little while again, and then Atlanta Braves for about five years. When I worked with the Atlanta Braves, the Braves bought the old Camp Dixie for Boys in Wiley, just south of Tiger, and they built baseball fields and everything, and I overseen all of that. That was 1969, and they went through '75. They built the fields and ever'thing, but it was primarily a tax write-off for 'em. They brought a lot of underprivileged kids here, but, of course, they had a lot of rich kids down there, too. They did sell it. Most of the land in the camp was bought by the Braves' employees, and there's still a lot of them down there.

Then I went with Southern Company, Georgia Power, and that's where I retired from. In the meantime, I did a lot of other things. I built custom guns; I worked on a lot of other people's guns. That's where, I guess, my real love was—doing work like that—but it just seemed like I had to stay with Georgia Power for security reasons—insurance and everything like that. How I got into gun building was, I used to watch my dad. He had a mechanical ability, and he worked on everybody's guns in the community and around, from town and everywhere. He worked in his shop and in part of the house over there, and he never charged them anything. It was just something he liked to do. He'd work on 'em and fix 'em for them people, and I watched him. That's how I really got into it. And I built "custom" guns. How I really got into building custom guns is, I would see 'em in them books an' ever'thing, and I wanted one of 'em, but they were so expensive. And I said, "Well, if they could build 'em, I could, too," and I built one of 'em. And then from that, I built some guns, and I put over eight thousand dollars' worth of gold in one of 'em. Very expensive guns—us country boys, we couldn't afford that [laughs]! People like Richard Childress bought my

PLATE 27 **"Shoot, I can afford to hunt with a pretty gun!"**
Allen English holding his personal gun

guns. He owned Childress Racing; people that are multimillionaires and people with the Braves' organization bought my guns. I sell a lot of guns to New York; some of the buyers are Cornell [University] people. People had to have money because you couldn't build those guns cheap. T'day, most of them that I build, I hunt with; they are just showpieces. Of course, I'll hunt with one of 'em. I tell people, I say, "Shoot, I can afford to hunt with a pretty gun [laughs]!" Most people wouldn't put that kinda money in 'em. They was a few people here in the county that surprised me that did do that—have me to build them guns.

One of the biggest changes here in the mountains is the people that moved in here—that's, I say, the biggest change. The people that moved in here, they really wanted this kinda life. Well, when they got here, they didn't really like it, and now they want to change ever'thang. The original people don't mind the new people so bad, if they'd just leave their ways where they come from. Well, it's just like the churches, the government, and just ever'thing. Just like our church; it's a country church and always will be, and you've got people from Miami and Atlanta, you name it. And every one of those has dif'rent idies [ideas] from where they come from, what they want, and they want to change everything, and what you end up with is a bunch of people that can't agree on anything.

Of course, the way of life here changed; you don't get up and go tend the crops anymore. You get up and go to a job, but, really, that is one of the biggest changes that has been in this country—the migration of people that have come here, and then they want to change everything, you see. The way I look at it is, if I went into a different area, I would at least go there, see what goes on, and see if I liked it. Well, if I didn't like it, why, I wouldn't go. It's changed the way people relate to each other very much—very much.

They have different idies, dif'rent things; a lot of them don't get along, and it causes people to not associate with one another.

I'd like to see Rabun County back up twenty years, but you can't do that. It would be more of a slower, laid-back time. Like t'day, you have to make x number of dollars to survive here. Back several years ago, the money, a' course you always had to have money, but it wasn't the big, main important thing. Today you've really got to have some money, or you just don't survive, but, like I said, I'd like to see Rabun County more of a laid-back place, but we won't see that again, unfortunately.

One thing that I think the young folks should do is that they should communicate more together and be more sociable and stuff like that and not be so independent. They should do that. Of course, get an education, go to church, and stuff like that—stay away from drugs and alcohol and bad stuff like that. I'd like to see the young people go to church. I think they would be much better off. That would be my number one thing.

One thing that I like—Betty didn't ever foller [follow] it too much, but I love to hunt and fish. And I did a lot of hunting and fishing when I had time. I killed a lot of deer and caught a lot of fish, and I really enjoyed that. I still enjoy it and go when I can; 'course, age is catching up with me. I still enjoy it, and I've got a pond down here, and I play with it. I've got some big fish in it, and I catch 'em and smoke those fish. I love smoked fish. We love fish, and we love deer meat, turkey, and stuff like that. I do a lot of things, I say, for Betty. See all the flowers in that thing [points to several large flower beds outside]? That's a hobby for Betty and I, but we're gonna have to cut back on some of the things that we do like that. We won't cut it all out, but we're gonna have to slow down on some of it; it's getting to be a pretty big job.

I think the secret to a long and happy marriage is primarily give-and-take. It's very hard. It's hard to give, and it's hard to take sometimes—get togetherness, doing things together. Betty and I, we discuss a lot of things. It don't matter whether it's a small thing or a big thing; before it happens, we generally discuss it. If we agree on it, then we can go with it, but the number one thing for a long, happy marriage is togetherness. Me and Betty have to be "one"; we can't be separate. She can't go her way, and I go mine. We gotta go together. [**Editor's note**: Betty, who has been sitting with us throughout the interview, smiles and nods in agreement.]

I've really, really had a good life, and I've really enjoyed it. Of course, people like Betty have helped me; she's my right-hand person. And, of course, the kids were good. Really, I don't think that they would be a whole lot that I would change about my life because I've really enjoyed being, you know, the type person I am and my friends and everything like that. I don't think that there would be a lot that I would change.

"Castro, he invited me to come see him."

～Tommy Irvin on forty years as ag commissioner～

Tommy Irvin is the longest-serving agriculture commissioner in the United States, retiring in 2010 after over forty years of service in that role. The son of sharecroppers, he had to quit school at the age of sixteen to support his family after the sudden death of his father in a sawmill accident. From those humble beginnings of paying crops in exchange for rent and decorating Christmas trees with eggshells, Commissioner Irvin has traveled the globe, meeting world leaders and promoting Georgia's agricultural commodities.

My sister, Sheri Thurmond, and I first visited with Commissioner Tommy Irvin at his home in Habersham County—an unassuming brick ranch house with a giant magnolia tree out front. He was an imposing presence—filling the doorway with his six feet, five inches of height as he greeted us. As we talked to him about his life, it quickly became apparent that although he had no "basic formal education," he is well spoken and, more importantly, remains deeply concerned with doing a good job for the people of Georgia during his tenure of political service, which first began in 1956.

Later, I met with Commissioner Irvin at his office in the Department of Agriculture in downtown Atlanta. The walls surrounding his office were covered with dark wood paneling and bookshelves—all filled with mementos and pictures from his years in office—everything from pictures of family members, world leaders, and Irvin's trips around Georgia, to framed newspaper and magazine articles, a little red wagon, and awards and plaques.

I truly believe that many people are born with gifts. Commissioner Irvin's gifts are public service and public speaking. He read from a prepared speech only once. As he said, "I couldn't read a speech. I tried, and I was a failure, so I don't like to feel failure a second time." Instead, he prepared a few talking points for each of his two hundred–plus speaking engagements per year and gave impromptu speeches based on these notes. He went on to say, "I've had people, even today, that would compliment me for never turning down an invitation. I was hands-on about what we got going on in this department."

During both interviews, Commissioner Irvin emphasized the importance of education. Although he did not have the opportunity to complete his education, he ultimately came to where he is because he cared about education and wanted his children to have the best. He obviously made an impression upon the people of Georgia, as they elected him to serve as commissioner of agriculture ten times.

Arty Schronce, director of public affairs for the Department of Agriculture, was instrumental in completing the second interview with Commissioner Irvin, and I thank him for his assistance.

—Teresa Thurmond Gentry

I was born in Lula, Georgia, in '29. I'll be eighty-one years old next week, the fourteenth day of July [2010]. I had two brothers and two sisters. I was the oldest in the family. You probably may be aware of the fact that I'm really a product of a father and mother that were sharecroppers. Being a sharecropper, a portion of what you paid on the farm for the rent was paid in crops, since you didn't have any cash.

My grandfather on Daddy's side died of rheumatic fever when he was just a kid. Grandmother was a Dixon—Florine Dixon. My grandmother on the Irvin side was a beautiful lady. You can tell that from her picture. The Dixons—most of them were identified by some of the historical people [members of the historical society] in Habersham County.

My grandmother Hogan was of the old-fashioned way to do things. She would never cook anything on Sundays. She would cook it on Saturdays, put it aside, and serve it on Sunday. That's coming back in style, I noticed in some media recently. History, idn't [isn't] it? Well, I can remember it. I 'us [was] little when I was at Grandma and Grandpa Hogan's home; they had a big, long table, and you'd have a bench seat and move up to the table. We were called in to dinner by the big bell in the kitchen. We would line up, sit on that bench at the big long table; it was probably as long as from here to that wall (about eleven feet). The Hogans were White County folks.

We always had biscuits and cornbread for a meal. We fared better than you think we would. We would trade eggs or chickens off the farm, or an extra ham, for coffee and sugar and things that you couldn't produce on your farm. The economy in those days was entirely different than what it is today. We were poor, but we didn't know it. Everybody else was as poor as we were. You didn't have any money back in those days. It was the bartering system—we didn't have any money back in those days, so we traded for what we needed.

Tell you what we used for Christmas trees, since we were so poor: we used to stretch cotton out and put that on that tree. You might take shelled eggs and anything else you could do to dress up a tree.

We made a lot of our toys. When I was a young lad, we made our own wagons. We'd get a hickory tree and cut it, block it off, punch a hole through it, put you a little rod through it, and build on it and have something that you could play with, but not much steering. You'd also use it to go to the corn mill. Back when I was a young lad, we had a corn mill that was run by waterpower and a little dam over it. We used to catch the water running down the race to turn the wheel on the gin in the mill. It's also where we'd go swimming at. I have a little red wagon now that my staff gave me years ago. I remember I told 'em I always wanted a red wagon.

I remember my daddy would take his cotton to an Irvin distantly related to us who run a store in Cornelia, later where Belk's had their store. And we would take what we received for the cotton and get our overalls, shoes, wearing apparel, and coats—things Mama couldn't make or didn't have the material to make. And you may be aware that my daddy got killed in a sawmill accident, and I didn't get to finish school. I was sixteen. My daddy and I were big buddies. He taught me a lot, even though he was uneducated to the point he could hardly sign his own name. He took me under his wing, as you called it in the old days. Taught me everything about how to survive in the world at that time.

My brother is still living. When he was a little lad, he crawled up on a chair and fell backwards in a bed of hot coals in the fireplace. The only heat we had was the fireplace. I remember I pulled him out of that fire. I went screaming to Mama. I remember she come runnin'. She laid her hand—put it in some rendered lard we kept after we had killed our hogs—she put that on the burn, wrapped it up in a towel, and asked our neighbor to take him to the doctor. The closest we had was in Cleveland. I remember the doctor told my mother, says, "If y'all hadn't a' handled it the way you handled it, he wouldn't a' survived." He's gotta big patch there now where he didn't have any hair on the back of his head.

I tell folks I guess I learned how to drive on an old Model T. I knocked the steps down. Back in those days, the [porch was] sort of high off the ground, and you had to have three or four steps going up. I knocked the steps down, and my daddy gave me a good thrashin' for it.

Well, most of the things we had back then . . . you grew everything you ate, so you'd have all kinds of potatoes—what we know as sweet potatoes and what we call Irish potatoes now, and corn to make cornbread. You usually had a little patch of wheat to make flour out of if you had a place close enough around to thrash it for you. You raised your own hogs; you had your own cows. We even had cows after I moved here and built this house after I was married. This house, I built it in '53.

We had mules. My daddy would plow in those red hills up there in White County. When he'd get hot and thirsty, he'd tie up the mules to something stationary. Daddy always liked mules, not horses. Everybody wanted to know why. Daddy would say, "They're more reliable." He would go down to a branch head and lay down and siphon water up. Sometimes he'd take a wheat straw and use that for a straw. Wheat has a straw . . . had a hollow. You can see what they have when they have a straw now. It's fabricated, but it didn't have the uniqueness of the original wheat straw.

Well, back in those days, we had one cotton gin right across from where Chattahoochee Baptist Church is in White County. My father and mother are both buried there. Mr. E. T. Irvin had the cotton gin. I remember that when you got ready to harvest your cotton, people would bring it in on their wagons. And you'd have those wagons lined up one right behind the other. Most people had people in the family that picked cotton. My mother and I—she could always do more than I could—we'd pick a bale every two days. It takes about eleven hundred pounds of cotton with seed to make one ginned bale, which will weigh around four hundred fifty to five hundred pounds. At cotton gin time, Daddy would close the sawmill down and be a worker in running the gin, and he was good at it. My daddy was a hard worker. A real talent that person was—he was my buddy. My mother used to work at the sawmill, too.

I can remember in World War II . . . I was just a kid and was too young to serve—all of the other young men were going off and were old enough to go into the service. That 'uz the big war.

After we moved from White County to Habersham, we eventually moved into a farmhouse that my father had purchased. He was smart enough to know he didn't want to always be a sharecropper. He wanted to own his land, grow his own crops, and create his own revenue. This place where we gave a fourth of your cotton and a third of your corn as rent—that's what you called a sharecropper. Daddy was a tenant farmer in the Rogers's house. It had no inside facilities. The house was already occupied by the Rogers family, and what our family did when we moved in, they give up one room, and we all had to sleep in that room. We'd eat out on the porch. It was so hot for us. Best I remember we moved in about this time of year, around September. And that's when I moved down to the corncrib. We cleaned it out—no corn in it. I took me—you didn't have mattresses—you kind of had a heavy-duty quilt, padded cotton in it. That's what I slept on. Oh, by the way, there was a side part of that crib where you could drive a wagon into it. The people who owned it were up on all the things you do to do things right. I think they had a mesh war' [wire] inside, so the rats couldn't get in there.

We moved into this house with an old fireplace called the Shelton Place. That was the first place my daddy was able to borrow the money to buy, and he didn't borrow the money from a bank. He borrowed the money from individuals. Well, the only heat we had was a big fireplace, and this particular house was a dual fireplace—had a fireplace on each side. One room was where you slept. The other room is where you cooked and eat, and you had those fireplaces farred [fired] up. That house had four rooms and a hallway, which was unusual back in those days. You'd have a hallway from one side to the other without having to go outside. At that Shelton Place is where Daddy let me have my own cotton patch. Even though he got killed in that work accident before harvesttime, the cotton money that I made out of my cotton patch allowed me to not be a tenant farmer—to buy a patch of land and own a patch of land. Best I remember, I think that money I got out of that cotton, I was able to get in the sawmill business. I got up early and stayed up late. I did everything myself. I was fairly well successful.

As I said earlier, my daddy got killed in a sawmill accident, and I really grieved deeply when I lost him. I know that I was in the truck with Fred Bowen. He worked with Daddy at the sawmill. We got him in the truck. We went down to Stephens County Hospital in Toccoa, Georgia, and they pronounced him dead when we got there.

The Rogers family was associated with us before we even moved into the house up at Dick's Hill where I slept in the corncrib. If you did something for one, you did it for the whole family, and we had to keep an eye out for each other. After my father's death, one of the members of the Rogers family, Delmus, married my mother. She was widowed, he had never been married, and she had a second family with him.

I guess back in those days, if you turned five, you could go to school. We would have what you would call a summer recess. You had a time to plant the crops and a time to harvest the crops. You didn't have lunchrooms back in the school in those days. You had to paper bag it. Your mother would make you—in the summer months—make you sandwiches that were picked out of your garden. You may have heard this before, but I tell folks that it's amazing that my political career later on caught on and that I was a sponsor of the constitutional amendment that allowed the use of public funds to pay for the school lunch program.

I know that I have told a lot of people how I got started in the business world, but I started out in the lumber business. As I said earlier, I got in the lumber business from what I made out of my cotton patch. Daddy allowed me to have three acres from the first farm he owned. I was able to cash that in. I run the sawmill, and my business had done right well. I guess at one time back there, we had the largest-volume lumberyard in the county. Remnants of it is still standing. [I had] what we called a lumber sorter. It was the first one, I think, in the state. I believe that you had to have good equipment; even though technology was headed our way, it hadn't fully arrived at that time.

During this time was when I got acquainted with Clyde Turner. I used to call him Hooten Dasher. That was his nickname over in White County. Clyde was a big buddy of mine. He had Mount Yonah Lumber Company, and we used to trade lumber. When you try to fill a bill order to build a house, there might be a part of that order I didn't have in stock, so I'd go to Clyde Turner. And if he was short of something, he'd come t' us. We ended up partners. I had half interest in it. I used to tell folks that I had half interest in the product, and I was always the one who was successful in borrowing capital to expand the business. I sold out my interest to Donald Thurmond.

PLATE 28 "Even though I didn't have a basic formal education, I had become quite educated through on-the-job training." Tommy Irvin as a young man

I changed from cotton to the lumber business due to the boll weevil. The mechanized machines that you used to spray for the boll weevil didn't function very well in small crops like ours. I tell folks . . . I was real, I guess, self-gratified to know that when I got in the lumber business and got to be kind of a leader in the lumber business . . . I was in a meeting at one of our national meetings, and some of the technology people out of Washington, U.S. Department of Agriculture, said that they thought they knew how to get rid of the boll weevil. It thrilled me that I was one of the leaders in getting the boll weevil program implemented here in the South. That was quite an accomplishment, considering that the boll weevil had been so destructive to people who were producing that commodity.

Well, I tell people that the unusual thing is how one thing leads you into something else. We used to have our own milk cows. My barn's down there below the house—still there. One morning, I heard somebody coming down towards the barn. I recognized the voice. It was a person wanting to ask me to run for the state legislature. I told the individual that nobody would vote for me 'cause I didn't know anybody, and I didn't know anything about politics. He came back another day or two later with a couple of other people with him, still wanting me to run for the state legislature. On his third visit, he got me to tell him that I'd look into it.

I got out, and even though our incumbent member of the state legislature had already qualified, I went from door to door and knocked on everybody's door. When election time come, I won by a big margin. That's how my political career began, and that was in 1956. [Years later when] Nixon offered Campbell a position as deputy secretary of agriculture, USDA, somebody mentioned to Governor Lester Maddox that if Campbell went to Washington, under our constitution the governor has to fill the vacancy till the next general election. Everybody said that if Campbell goes to Washington, Irvin's gonna be agriculture chief. Maddox did that without ever—it never was mentioned to me—just one of those quirks that he had.

Well, here come the media—wanted to know what I'd do about it. I says, "Well, he never mentioned it to me." They said, "Well, whatcha gonna do?" I said, "Well, seems to me like I don't have a real big choice. If Governor Maddox wants to fire me as his chief of staff and name me to a constitutional-elected position, I can either [be commissioner of agriculture] or I can pack my bag and go home." People tried to get him not to appoint me. I think the unusual thing about this is that this thing got so hot. When I took that job, we just had got a telephone—rural Georgia, you know—and he called me at home, and I always said when I spoke to him, "Remember, this is not a private line." "Well, I don't mind if it isn't," he said. "You've done a great job for me. If Campbell goes to Washington, Georgia needs a new commissioner of agriculture."

Well, becoming commissioner of agriculture was a big challenge to me, but I was young. I was very active. Even though I didn't have a basic formal education, I had become quite educated through on-the-job training. If you're an active member of the legislature, you know a lot about how government works. If you don't after a small period of time, you oughta leave. The challenge was a great one. Even though I was appointed January of '69—the balance of that term was by appointment—[I had to run] for a full four-year term in 1970. I served two years; I ran in 1970. I had formal opposition from Mr. Bill Lanier, who was highly qualified. He had been Farm Bureau president for several years and had most all of the political insiders already committed to be for him. You didn't have a two-party system back then—everybody gettin' elected as a Democrat. I tell folks the way I won that race was that I just outworked him. He had the infrastructure they had. I think before the votes were finally counted, I made some inroads on that.

I've been a big advocate for world trade. I had worked in the political arena to get funding for a division of the U.S. Department of Agriculture called Foreign Agriculture Service. Well, if you feel the calling, opening these wider doors is important to fulfilling your mission. I've been one of the first trying to get Cuba opened up. Castro, he invited me to come see him. I was the first ag chief to go to Cuba. Well, I was very much a front-runner

PLATE 29 "Castro, he invited me to come see him."
Tommy meeting with Fidel Castro in the early 1990s

and a very active advocate of business. I knew enough about the Communist system to know that if we didn't have him on board, these deals would go nowhere. When he invited me to meet with him, he stole the role from me, telling me how bad he needed us to do business with him. I had already been very active in promoting trade with Russia and briefly active, probably as active as most any other leader, in trying to get China opened up. I think it'd be a great place to get these countries like that to buying our product.

You know, our own government don't want us to sell, to do business with Cuba, and the only reason is they think it might enhance the Communist system. Whether you're Communist or whether you're not, trade will bring us closer together, and I think freedom has been a great hallmark for me. I don't know of a thing I've done that's given me more satisfaction, been more important, than establishing trade with the Russians, Cubans, Chinese, and all of the other ports around the world.

I told someone in south Georgia when I first became Commissioner—they'd ask me, "What do you grow in north Georgia?" And I'd tell 'em, "Well, we're diversified," but I used to use the phrase "Our number one commodity is chicken." We also grew cotton, corn, and peanuts in south Georgia, tobacco in middle and south Georgia, and sweet potatoes. These different commodity groups have been kind of my base. We have what we call commodity commissions now. We have one on all these different commodities—allows us to generate funds, and we'll invest a major part of those funds in research. For every dollar we spend on research, with a little time, we'll give you back a dividend of ten to one. We were able to do a lot of that through innovation.

The farmer's biggest problem today is market—if you got a strong market, you'll see prices very strong. If the market is weak, the market will go down. I've always said, talkin' about the economy, it's kind of sick right now, but to go back up, agriculture will help lead it, and I think it will. Tobacco used to be a big commodity in Georgia. At one time, it was about a hundred-fifty-million-dollar-a-year commodity. It's practically down to just a small percentage of that now.

You see a lot in the media now about the green industry. Organic fruits and vegetables make up a large part of the green industry. We get a lot of those commodities that we do extremely well in. We have to police them. We've caught these people, what we call misbranding, trying to sell organic 'cause it pays a premium, when in some cases it's not genuine. We can seize that and have it relabeled, if it can be done, or destroyed. You're beginning to see aisles in the store now where it says "organic." Our folks will check it to make sure it's genuine. You, as the consumer, will be paying a premium if you take it home. I wanna get in one that you'll recognize: the Vidalia onion. That's come along under my leadership. It's highly recognized. I spent years and years to keep people from south Georgia, and unscrupulous people out in Texas, from getting a transfer load of their white onion, bring 'em here, put 'em in bags, and sell 'em as Vidalias. We got a law now that makes it a felony to mislabel them; I think we've done extremely well in accomplishing that.

When Jimmy Carter was governor, he come forth with a whole bunch of what we call consolidation, and he had in his consolidation plan to put gasoline with us because we have a weights/measures laboratory. We have a weights/measures law, and what it goes back to is being a good move that I agreed with him on and supported his efforts because automobiles now are very sophisticated. We refine gasoline different in the summertime than we do in the wintertime, so that you get performance. . . . You don't want to allow gas to be sold and put in your car, and you drive down the street, and it vapor locks, goes dead, and you can't get it to crank. That could happen if you allow an unbranded product to be sold.

I think it's important to have the power that we have. If we see some unscrupulous person trying to sell something not safe, I can stop it in its tracks. I can tie it up and force 'em to either correct it, if it can be corrected, or destroy it. I know I've been called on for years to strengthen the federal safety net; safety is better than it has been, but it'll never be as good as we like to see it. The feds oughta concentrate on lettin' us know what they know about the products that are comin' in here. We had some places in California that were shipping these products, and they did not meet our standards. I told 'em they had to fumigate it, or they couldn't sell it here. They took me to the U.S. Supreme Court. The feds came in and said, "We've approved it. You can't do what you're trying to do." I said, "I might not can in your sight, but I've already done it." Caution should always be a major factor in how a product is handled.

A major concern for the 1996 Olympics in Atlanta was piroplasmosis, a protozoal infection of horses that some of the horses to be competing from Europe had. Many horse owners here in Georgia did not want these horses to enter the state over fear of infecting horses here. We went to Europe with the equine leadership here in this state: My tale was that we needed to make sure we could host an international event. We could not do anything that was gonna cause piroplasmosis to be inflicted on our equine industry. Those racehorses are mighty valuable, you know. We had a special facility for those horses coming in from foreign countries—had a holding pen out at the airport where they were piloted in, and every one of 'em was fully inspected to make sure they weren't bringing in something that would carry a tick. Ticks are the vectors that carry piroplasmosis. All the areas where the horses were boarded or performed were treated for ticks—if the vector is not there, the disease cannot be spread.

We had a fellow named Bo Helander. He was one of the international leaders in the equine industry, and he came up to me on Sunday afternoon out here at Conyers the last day of the Olympics. He said, "I want to congratulate you, Commissioner. I didn't think you could do it." He says, "You proved me wrong." We put in place a system that we felt reasonably sure would be successful; our plan worked. Our plan became the international plan; I went with Dr. Lee Myers, my state veterinarian, over there to Sydney, Australia, to show them how we did it here.

Well, we skipped over several stories, but one I want to tell is, I was selected as a delegate to the [Democratic] National Convention in 1960. I was lucky to be there. I was kind of a nobody back then, but I was a member of the state legislature. I remember when John F. Kennedy came in the room where we were at, and I was fortunate enough to have a seat on the aisle as you go up to the podium. He came by, and I was able to say a few words to him and shake his hand. I came back from that convention all farred [fired] up, and I campaigned for the president.

I didn't support Jimmy Carter when he ran the first time, but I go to some functions occasionally now over at the Carter Center. President Carter shook my hand as we were going in, and I was the only person that he recognized in his speech. So you know, I made a good impression on him, even though, politically, he had a lot of critics to him.

I was always anxious to get messages to the "head man." If a president was coming to Georgia, we'd get invited to greet him as he got off Air

Force One. Sometimes you'd get in the car with him and go to wherever his destination was; sometimes not, but I come up with a smart idea. I says, if I have somethin' I wanna tell 'im, you don't know if you'll have an opportunity to tell 'im or enough time to tell 'im, so I would write me out a little note and two or three one-sentence bits of information, and when he come through the line, I'd say, "Mr. President, put this in your pocket. When you have time, please read it." I know that he did [laughs]. [**Editor's note**: Mr. Irvin shows an article printed by *The Atlanta Journal-Constitution* that shows President Bill Clinton reading Commissioner Irvin's notes while standing on the tarmac.]

President Clinton told me, I'm gonna be here in Georgia. I was in a meeting in that car with him with that [African American] lady who used to be in Congress out here in DeKalb County—Cynthia McKinney. He also called me and asked me to introduce him at that college out in Macon— Mercer University. They picked me up here at the Atlanta airport. I got on a jet, and he was already on the jet. It was his campaign jet, I guess. He was very sensible, and I suspect that President Clinton would have offered me some physical appointment, but I let them know that I didn't want it. Mrs. Clinton said, "Commissioner Irvin, you can't introduce yourself to me." Says, "I know you."

I have to say I've been absolutely lucky. I've been out front in so many of these areas. If something's gone wrong as far as the politics in this office, in this elected office, they'd show me out the door. It'd be like *The Atlanta Journal-Constitution* said: I kept the seat warm until the people of Georgia selected a new ag leader.

You know, a lot of people have wanted me to resign from this office so this current governor could pick a successor. I don't believe in that. Well, you know, with my health, I probably should, but I think the people of Georgia would find some fault in me if I'd had the position they had and said, "I don't believe in that," and then I'd contribute to that. . . . People ask me, now, would I have any advice for my successor? I say to most people who raise that issue that as quickly as we find out who our new commissioner is gonna be, I'm gonna invite him to come to the capitol. I want to spend some with him and tell him what he's really taking charge of. I happen to think we have one of the best departments of agriculture in the U.S., but it's not good because of me. It's because we had a good team—a lot of good people.

You know, I was able to accomplish everything that I even dreamed I thought I could. I know that Lester Maddox used to pay me compliments— said that I made him the proudest of my service to him of anyone else in his administration. That's quite a compliment coming from the governor.

The headlines in the *Atlanta Journal* and *The Atlanta Constitution*—

we had two separate papers back then, but they call themselves combined now—I think the *Constitution* editorial was "Irvin Keeps Seat Warm till the People of Georgia Can Choose a New Ag Leader." I kid folks today; I say that after forty-two years, I still keep it warm. A lot of things has changed in those forty-two years. We've got, probably, four hundred fewer employees than we had when I went there. Over the years, the legislature has given me more authority, more to do, and it becomes very important that you learn how to do more with less. We're right now facing a budgetary problem here of a magnitude we've never heard of before. It's gonna hit us hard. I wanna leave this department in just as a good a shape as I can for these next six months that I'll be here. I hope that whoever comes here will build him a team and move this department forward.

How I met my wife is a great story. We used to have a Southeastern Fair—leased that fairground there so they could start making movies here. We'd carry a busload down to the fair there in Atlanta. We got all the way in Gwinnett County, and the bus stopped for refreshments. Some young man was sitting back in the bus by this pretty young lady. He got up to go get a soft drink. I tell folks I got his seat, and he never got it back [laughs]. That's where I met her was on that school bus. We were both teenagers when we got married. I certainly was attracted to her. She was born in Delaware. Her parents moved back here to Habersham County, and she graduated from North Habersham High School. We went on our honeymoon instead of her going on what we call a senior trip. My wife, Bernice, has been a real partner in all of the things that I've been involved in. She would praise me when, I guess, I really needed it, and she also criticized me when I needed it.

I guess since I really had a very limited formal education, I wanted the best for my children. We have five. My oldest son is James. He's a lawyer and state court judge in Stephens County. My second son is Johnny; he runs Rabun County Bank. My son David was a CPA. He and Johnny opened up a chain of Burger Kings. My oldest daughter, Londa, is a paralegal. She works for the Whelchel firm in Gainesville, which is the most prominent law practice in northeast Georgia. My youngest daughter, Lisa, works in the home. My kids turned out real well. My wife and I, we were really blessed. Well, I tell folks the great thing about my children: I never had to get up in the middle of the night and go and get 'em out of jail. A lot of young folks mess up, you know. My grandson was here with me earlier today—the one who is running for state representative. He lives up in Stephens County, in Toccoa. I kid folks; I say, "He's starting exactly where I started."

As for other accomplishments, I used to go speak to the government class at the high school. I think one of the real rewarding things I did is, I would take the county registrar with me—these were seniors—and register 'em to vote and make that part of the teaching process. I was very pleased with the feedback you get.

I'm past Grand Master Mason of Georgia. Governor Maddox, he had been aware that I was gonna get appointed to this, his comment was to me, he said, "Being Grand Master Mason, that's more important than being in line to be governor."

Well, there are gonna be a lot of opportunities when I retire. I might work a day a month without pay, or I may not do anything. I find a lot of people in the university system want me to help get a good agriculture person on the Board of Regents. The Board of Regents [the University of Georgia College of Agriculture and Environmental Sciences] has most of the ag programs now. I would be honored if they wanted to talk to

PLATE 30 **Tommy Irvin as a Grand Master Mason, seated in a chair that George Washington sat in, at Solomon's Lodge in Savannah, Georgia**

me. See, you never know; I may be asked next year to do something, and if I really feel that I can make a contribution, I'll give it a lot of consideration. If I don't feel that I can do those goals, I will say no.

I am often asked why I didn't run for governor. If I had wanted to run, I would've run and won and served and then been forgotten about now [laughs]! I tell folks that power is very important, but with power you have to be correct. If it's misused, it can be very destructive. I try to weigh all that. I had reasonable amounts of success keeping the politics out of what's best for the people of Georgia and the department. You've heard me say this: "I don't know of a time that I hadn't felt we had more successes than we did failures." If our new commissioner will devote his time to what we have and build on it and not try to disassemble it and redo it, we'll both be winners. If you get too ambitious, you can do more harm than you can good. Being able to respond is a very critical thing to get along, especially if you're in an elected office. Nobody is gonna be a hundred percent successful and do everything exactly like it oughta be done, but if you get the bits and pieces and put those into the master plan, you'll establish yourself a genuine leader. I think it's very rewarding. I don't know anything I'd do any different if I could do it again.

Knoxville Girl*

I met a little girl in Knoxville, a town we all know well,
And every Sunday evening, out in her home I'd dwell,
We went to take an evening walk about a mile from town,
I picked a stick up off the ground and knocked that fair girl down.

She fell down on her bended knees, for mercy she did cry,
Oh Willy dear don't kill me here, I'm unprepared to die,
She never spoke another word, I only beat her more,
Until the ground around me within her blood did flow.

I took her by her golden curls, and I drug her 'round and 'round,
Throwing her in the river that flows through Knoxville town,
Go down, go down, you Knoxville girl with the dark and rolling eyes,
Go down, go down, you Knoxville girl, you can never be my bride.

I started back to Knoxville, got there about midnight,
My mother she was worried and woke up in a fright,
Dear son, what have you done to bloody your clothes so?
I told my anxious mother, I was bleeding at my nose.

I called for me a candle to light myself to bed,
I called for me a handkerchief to bind my aching head,
Rolled and tumbled the whole night through, as troubles was for me,
Like flames of hell around my bed and in my eyes could see.

They carried me down to Knoxville and put me in a cell,
My friends all tried to get me out, but none could go my bail,
I'm here to waste my life away down in this dirty old jail,
Because I murdered that Knoxville girl, the girl I loved so well.

Crime Close to Home

Killings and Other Crimes

---

*Precisely when and by whom this was written is unknown; the song has always
been credited merely as "traditional" whenever it has been recorded.

Knoxville Girl

Crime Close to Home

Life was simple back in "the good ol' days." Crimes were rare and murders were virtually unheard of. Doors were not locked, and windows were left open night and day to take advantage of the air-conditioning provided by nature. The few crimes that did occur were met with disbelief and disgust by the residents in and around the surrounding communities. With no electricity in most homes for news coverage, the stories of horrid crimes were spread by word of mouth from family to family throughout the area. These stories were passed down through the years from generation to generation. Several of these events were documented in the bluegrass ballads that wailed from an old wind-up phonograph, spinning the twelve-inch, 78-rpm recordings. These ballads, recounting stories of death and dying, were usually sad and often true. I remember as a child hearing The Louvin Brothers sing "Knoxville Girl," the Blue Sky Boys harmonizing on "Katie Dear," and Jimmie Osborne crooning out the words to "The Death of Kathy Fiscus." These songs saddened the hearts of listeners while bringing them close to the strangers whose life and death had been documented in the lyrics of a song. My mother and daddy often shared stories of crime with us as we were growing up. I will always remember the story my mother told of Grace Brock's murder. Approximately four thousand people had traveled to the little town of Cornelia, Georgia, to view the body in an effort to identify the victim. My mother and grandfather had participated in this viewing. Although my mother was a little girl, she often recalled the event and told of the body lying on an old sheet-covered iron bed. She distinctly remembered a sand-filled shoe and the necklace lying beside the victim.

Most of the stories that follow are based on actual murders, robberies, and other crimes that were committed years ago in the mountains of Appalachia. Some of the facts may have been slightly altered as the stories were recounted from one family to the next.

—*Joyce Green*

"A ripple of dramatic emotion swept over the courtroom."

~ The 1939 murder of Grace Bingham Brock ~

Saturday, September 24, 1939, would be a day that would shake up the residents of a little town in Habersham County, Georgia, for on this day the gruesome murder of a young woman, Grace Bingham Brock, would be uncovered. The discovery of Mrs. Brock's body in the cold waters of the Soque River would spur an investigation spanning from Habersham County to Greenville, South Carolina. The evidence that was soon to be uncovered would convince a jury to convict the husband of a beautiful young woman of one of the most brutal murders that has ever been committed in the state of Georgia.

PLATE 31 "Thousands of people filed past the body
of the young woman at Sosebe-McGahee
Funeral Parlor." Grace Bingham Brock

It was a Saturday when Sam McDuffie and Hoyt Standbridge, both employees of the C. M. Miller Company, accidentally discovered the body. They were hauling apples between the orchard in Cleveland, Georgia, and the packinghouse in the nearby town of Cornelia. They had made numerous trips throughout the day, traveling across a one-lane metal bridge that spanned the Soque. On one of these trips, Mr. McDuffie glanced down on the crystal waters of the river and caught a glimpse of something that would forever be etched in his mind: the feet and legs of a woman, protruding from the surface of the water, which was lower than normal due to the mill having been closed and the dam emptied. The two men went immediately for help.

The body had been thrown about three hundred feet below Cannon Bridge, with a heavy piece of iron tied around her neck with wire and her skull fractured in three places. A coroner's jury came to the conclusion that the victim had met her death by blows over the head with a sharp-edged bludgeon. The inquest revealed evidence of a huge struggle at the crime scene. Two pools of blood about two feet apart had been hastily covered with sand, but the blood had seeped through to the top of the mounds. Only one set of footprints was officially documented as leaving the scene, but a witness testified he found two sets of footprints, one a man's and the other a woman's, showing the woman was running, apparently trying to escape her assailant. She had circled a large tree several times, and when she was finally overtaken, there was evidence of a struggle. The bruises on the body indicated that the victim had been badly beaten before her death.

During an examination by a local physician, three severe wounds were found on the deceased's head, two of which were thought to have caused her death. One extended some four or five inches over the top of her head, and the other—a shorter but deep wound—was slightly above and behind the left ear. There were also many bruises on her face, neck, breasts, and legs, all of which, other than the three large cuts or wounds, could have, in the opinion of the physician, been inflicted by a man's fist. After this examination was completed, the public was invited to view the body in an effort to make a positive identification.

Finally, on the Monday following the finding of the body on Saturday, the victim was pronounced upon good authority to be Mrs. Grace Bingham Brock, who was raised in Turnerville, Georgia, in Habersham County and was the wife of Rufus Brock. A friend of Mrs. Brock, Mrs. Lelia Burns, was an important key to the identification. While she was unable to identify the swollen body, she recognized the dress and the shell-bead necklace that Mrs. Brock had been wearing. Mrs. Burns stated that she had made the dress for her daughter and it would not fit, so she had given it to Grace Brock. She also told authorities that she had been with Grace Brock when she purchased the necklace in Greenville, South Carolina, and that Grace was trying to dress up for her husband in an attempt to win back his affections. Grace Brock's father then made the final identification.

Well over a thousand people, the largest number of local citizens ever assembled during any court session, crowded the courtroom and halls for possibly the most sensational superior court case in the history of the county. The coroner and sheriff had worked ceaselessly since the body had been discovered. Their detailed account of the investigation resulted in the arrest in Greenville of Rufus Brock, the estranged husband of the slain woman.

During the trial, a ripple of dramatic emotion swept over the crowded courtroom when a slender, auburn-haired young woman, dressed in a blue-and-white silk dress and gray tweed jacket, took the witness stand. She declared that she was Clara Franklin Massey, a twenty-four-year-old silk mill employee, of Greenville, whom Rufus Brock had married September 3, 1939. In her testimony she stated that she had thought Brock was divorced and that he had abused her on several occasions when she questioned him about

PLATE 32 "We recommend that Rufus Brock
be held for murder." Rufus Brock

his marriage. Mr. Frankum, the prosecuting attorney, entered their marriage certificate as an exhibit in the evidence.

Several articles of Mr. Brock's clothing were also entered as exhibits, as was a forty-seven-pound gasket pin, which was traced to the Cornelia railroad yard. An automobile jack taken from Brock's car was said to have traces of blood mixed with the rust of the metal. Another gruesome exhibit was a torn, bloodstained shirt said to have been worn by Brock on the night of Monday, September 28, when he took his two little boys, ages six and four, to the home of his parents, who lived within a mile of the Cannon Bridge on the river near where the body was found. According to other sources, several strands of hair were attached to the dried blood, which had soaked the shirt.

Witnesses stated that Brock claimed that as he and his wife and children were returning to Habersham County, they were stopped near the Tugalo River Bridge on the Georgia–South Carolina line. He was attacked by two unidentified men, and Mrs. Brock had then gotten into the car with them and had not been seen since. While Rufus Brock and Grace Bingham were students at Rabun Gap–Nacoochee School, in Rabun Gap, Georgia, they had run away together and been married. Grace was sixteen at the time, and Rufus was eighteen. Four years and two children later, they moved to Greenville. Rufus claimed that Grace had grown tired of city life and returned to Georgia. According to him, she returned to South Carolina several times in an attempt to convince him to move back to Georgia.

Many holes were found in Rufus's explanation of Grace's death, and the fact that he had been seeing—and later married—a woman from South Carolina did not help his case. In 1939, South Carolina refused to legally separate a husband and wife, so divorces were rare. It was surmised that Rufus therefore needed a way out of his predicament, and this was the likely motive for Mrs. Brock's murder.

Nineteen of the thirty witnesses subpoenaed in the case were called to the stand during the trial. Evidence was presented, including the victim's clothes, beads, and shoes and Rufus Brock's bloody shirt, as well as a car jack on which blood appeared. Once the presentation of this strong circumstantial evidence against Mr. Brock concluded, the jury retired.

After deliberating for less than two hours, the jury filed into the courtroom to render its verdict of guilty of murder with recommendation for mercy, which virtually meant life imprisonment. They concluded from the evidence presented that Rufus Brock had brutally murdered his wife, Grace, while their two children slept in the backseat of the car. According to witnesses, as the verdict was read, the defendant maintained the same calm, composed manner that he had manifested throughout the trial, and he seemed to be much less agitated than his father and mother and other members of his family, who had remained at his side.

Since Grace Bingham Brock's death, many people have reported seeing her ghost, wearing a floral dress, walking on the cool waters of the Soque River in the early hours of the night.

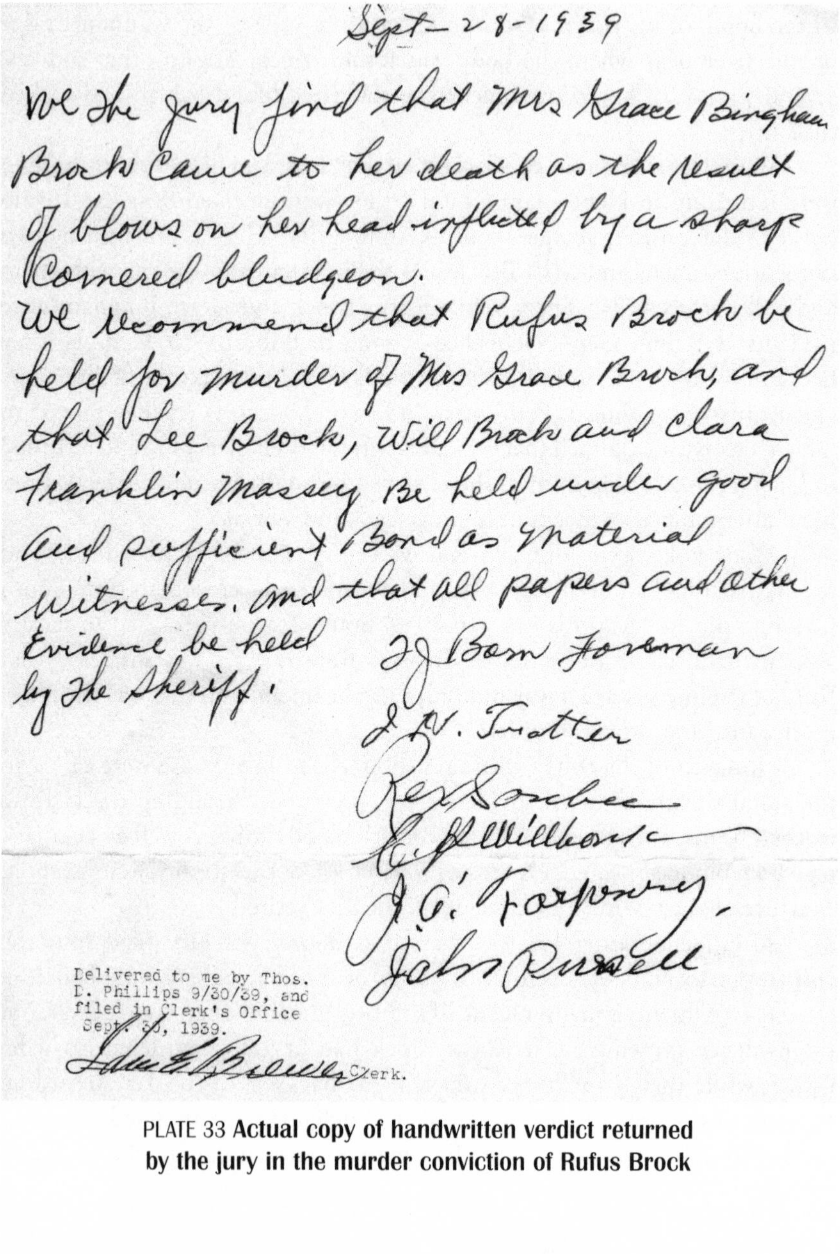

Sept-28-1939

We the jury find that Mrs Grace Bingham Brock Came to her death as the result Of blows on her head inflicted by a sharp Cornered bludgeon.

We recommend that Rufus Brock be held for murder of Mrs Grace Brock, and that Lee Brock, Will Brock and Clara Franklin Massey Be held under good And sufficient Bond as material Witnesses. And that all papers and other Evidence be held by The Sheriff.

T J Bam Foreman

J. N. Trotter

Rex Loudee

C. J. Willbanks

J. O. Forpony

John Russell

Delivered to me by Thos. D. Phillips 9/30/39, and filed in Clerk's Office Sept. 30, 1939.

[illegible] Clerk.

PLATE 33 **Actual copy of handwritten verdict returned by the jury in the murder conviction of Rufus Brock**

Hell-Bent and Whiskey Bound
A Scaly Mountain Murder
~As told by Lillie Billingsley~

Murder and crime in the mountains of Georgia and North Carolina were rare when our grandparents were growing up; however, some of the crimes that did occur were quite gruesome. The following story, told to us by Mrs. Lillie Billingsley of Scaly Mountain, North Carolina, was one we have never forgotten. Her attention to details and somewhat humorous nature as she shared her memories made a lasting impact.

—Joyce Green

I'll tell y'all a story about a man that liked to work in the whiskey business because he made whiskey, he drank whiskey, and he sold it. He was a bad old man. He looked like the boogerman [boogeyman] to me. He used to come by, and he'd say to my daddy, "How about you trade me them two girls and let 'em come stay with me for a while?" My daddy would tell him, "No, they better stay here. We don't let 'em leave the house too much. They got too many chores to do." He looked like the boogerman, and I believed that he *was* the boogerman.

So he came in one morning about four o'clock, and his wife was making breakfast. He was drunk—pretty well drunk. He had a good old lady—I mean a good'n. Her name was Sis. Sis is what they called her. I don't know her real name. He come in mad about breakfast, I guess, and he jumped on the poor thang. She was rollin' her biscuits now, and he just walked up to her and knocked her brains out, I guess. He hit her in the head, and she fell. Well, he seed that he'd killed her, and he didn't know what he was going to do with the body. He built a fire and drug her in the front room, out of the kitchen, and he put her in the fireplace and burned her. He crammed her head in, and then her shoulders, and then her whole body into the fire. She was a big old fat lady, and the grease run out of her, all down on the floor. It was just real bad, you know. And that grease is still on that floor, they tell me, but I don't know. I stopped by that house one time and Jim's sister said, "Lillie, that's where he killed her."

It was bad he killed her—threw her in the fire, and he killed her. He tried to live with that, but he just couldn't. He knew he'd done such a bad thing to kill his wife. Well, anyway, he decided to confess what he'd done. He tried to live on through the years, but I reckon his conscience got so tore up that he only come out of that house to get the mail. He had to go over this little branch by his house, and him and his horse would get to that branch, and that horse would not go across that branch. He would finally have to get off the horse, and he would have to pull the horse across that little branch. So he just went crazy. When he got old, he went to live with his daughter. Well, he went crazy; he didn't know what he was doing. They finally had to strap him down in the bed. They said he would just holler and scream. They said he said that he could feel the flames of torment—that they was going to burn him up. Well, he died tied down, and he did confess that he killed her right before he died. They buried him out there behind that old schoolhouse. Now there are five or six graves out there behind that old schoolhouse. I even went to school in that little building. It wudn't as big as from this table to the wall [motions with her hands]. Mary James was the teacher; she taught five or six of us out there. We walked to school back in them days; we didn't have no cars or nothing.

They didn't have no law in those days. Back then they'd just take 'em [criminals] to some barn—some old house—somewhere and take a rope and put it around their neck and make 'em stand on a chair. Then they would jerk the chair out from under them and then the rope would break their neck, but that's how they told me it was done, I guess; I wasn't born in them days. But anyway, that was awful bad, I thought, and it was awful. So then after the man passed on—well, they took him out there. He was buried out there at that school.

"Well, now, this is a true story."

~A story of birth and death from Melissa Rogers~

Occasionally, people share with us tales of strange and unexplainable happenings. Mrs. Melissa Rogers told us a story about a young woman who was apparently a witch, and explains why some members of her family believed this.
—Margie Bennett

Well, now, this is a true story I'm gonna tell. It's very true 'cause my mother and my older sister told me about it. This woman [they knew about] had had some girls, and they'd got messed up and had a couple of babies, but nobody never did know what went with the babies. After the others had done married, the younger one got like that.

One day the thrashers come to help thrash the rye fields. The daddy and the thrashers went out and worked till twelve o'clock, and the mama fixed dinner that day and they come in to eat. The younger daughter's name was Ada, and her daddy asked where she was at. Her mama said, "Ah, she's out around here somewhere." So she went out on the porch and she hollered and hollered, "Oh, Ada! Ada! Come on to dinner!" And she never did come or nothin'.

And her daddy got ready to go back to the field and he said, "Well, I'm worried about her." Said, "We better see where she's at and try to find her." Said, "This is not like her to not come when she's called." So he went on back to the field and worked a little while, and he got worried, and he come back to the house and he got to looking. He called in the neighbors, and finally, at last, they went in an old building, what they used to call a smokehouse, which was made out of just old puncheon-like boards where they stored a lot of stuff. And her mama had took some old plank and stuck it up in the cracks and had Ada a-layin' up on it, and she'd had that baby and she'd died. They all came in there, and they was a-gettin' her out and was gonna take her in the house. That's what they used to do, you know. They'd take 'em in the house and lay 'em out on a table or the bed or something like that for visitation and burial preparation. They didn't take 'em to the funeral home 'cause they wadn't anything like that.

One woman in there said she heared something a-makin' an awful queer noise, and there was big boxes of all kinda stuff packed up in there, and that woman got to listening and she said, "Well, I hear something." And the girl's mother said, "Aw, it's just probably a rat or something." Said, "They're all the time around in here." And she kept hearin' it, and she kept hearin' it, and after a while she got worried and she started a-huntin'.

And so she got to huntin' in all them boxes, and that mama had a big box of quilts packed up, and way down about middle ways under them quilts, this neighbor woman found this little baby. And it had the corner of the quilt stuck in its mouth, and she was gonna smother it to death like she'd already done two more. She had 'em out in the garden, and she'd buried 'em under an apple tree in a corner of the garden. And that's what she was gonna do with that one as quick as it was dead.

And this neighbor woman, she took the baby home with her, and she kept it and raised it, and I seen her myself when she was grown and married—that one that she had in that box. My sister showed her to me when we was havin' a big dinner on the ground at church one day. And she said to me, she says, "There is the little girl that was found in the box." And she is still alive. So that girl lived and stayed on with this woman until she married. She's a good bit older than I am, but so far as I know, she's still livin'. And she lives at Hiawassee where my sister does.

[That woman that killed the babies], they said she was just almost like a witch because she could almost do anything she set her mind to. And the ones that was there when she died—she died at home—they said that they had to hold her in the bed, and that when she died, the clock stopped—the big winding clock on the wall. They said it stopped, dead stopped.

Last words, in a choked voice: "Good-bye, men."

The hanging of Will Brown

"I was an eyewitness to the killing of the Negro known as Sweet," stated Charlie Williams. Thus began the trial of Will Brown, accused of murdering the man called Sweet at Lakemont, Georgia, on April 30, 1915. Numerous testimonies and cross-examinations took place in the courtroom that day, but no one testified on Mr. Brown's behalf. There were no witnesses, other than a mysterious lady named Elizabeth, to the prior scuffle or threat outside the dance where the murder took place. No one who was interviewed for this story was able to tell us why Elizabeth did not testify in defense of Mr. Brown, for till his dying day, he professed that the killing was in self-defense.

—Ann Moore

The following testimonies were taken from Rabun County Court transcripts.

The State v. Will Brown (Col.) (charged with the offense of murder in Rabun County Superior Court. August term 1915—Verdict of Guilty)

Charlie Williams (Col.) sworn for the State testified:

I was an eyewitness to the killing of the Negro known as Sweet. He was killed with a pistol. It was in April, I think, of this year on a Saturday night. We was having a dance. This fella that done the shooting, he just stepped inside the door. He had a bottle and both of his hands in his jumper pockets. After he had been in there a second, he just pulled out his pistol and shot Sweet, and when he did, Sweet got up and groaned a time or two and throwed his hands around this fella. Sweet run out the door and fell at the corner of the house. When I say the fella that did the shooting, I mean the defendant. The defendant run. There had been no words between them at all.

Cross-examination of Mr. Williams:

This occurred in April, as well as I remember, on Saturday night of this year. I was at the dance. I was working there at Mathis, cooking for the Northern Contracting Company. There was a dance there. The defendant was not in the house when I went in there. If he was, I didn't see him. He was there somewhere. The first time I saw him was when he came in the house. Sweet was soundly sitting by a lady and Dave Barrett. I was standing by Dave Barrett. This fella walked in and done the shooting is what I saw. I was with Richard Rose, Dave Barrett, and Slim Roberson. I was just standing there at the time. I had been dancing. I was resting then. We were standing there laughing and talking loudly. The first thing I knew, the defendant was in the house. I seen him when he come into the room with his hand in his jumper pockets. The man that was killed was sitting. The lady was sitting there by Sweet, the fella that got killed. When the defendant walked into the room, he seemed to be like he was hunting somebody. It looked to me like he shot the man he was after. He shot him and then turned around and walked out. He stood there about one step from the door, seems like he had one foot in the door and one foot about one step from the room. He just drawed his pistol out and done the shooting. I can't remember whether it was his left or right shoulder, but I think it was his right shoulder. I saw the place the bullet went in. It went in and come just under his left armpit. The bullet did not go upward; it went upward and lodged into his body, far as I know. I wasn't a physician; I didn't examine that far. There was a good many Negroes down there that night; there wasn't so many in the house, but there was some in the kitchen and in the other room. There wasn't any drinking there that I know of. We was having a dance there and having a very nice time in that room where we was, up until the shooting. Everybody was having a good time. Everything was going on quite well. The defendant just walked in there and shot this fella, Sweet. It wasn't a woman with me—it was a man. I don't know exactly what we was talking about at the time. It has been so long since this happened. I was talking to him. I wasn't looking him directly in the face. The woman's name that was sitting by Sweet was named Josie. They all jumped up and ran out.

Statement of the defendant Will Brown

I was down there one night standing there talking to this boy that had a girl named Elizabeth, and she come up there to get a pair of shoes, and when she walked up, we walked up to the house together. She tried on the shoes, and they seemed to be too small for her. She asked me to go back with her to get them changed. I said, "All right," and we went on back in and she changed the shoes. When she came out to where I stood, she went on up the hill and I stopped. After a while, this here other fella, George, came out there, and we stood up there and talked. This woman called me in the house wanting me to go and sell some chicken sandwiches to the boys at the camp. Then I come back, and this girl was talking to me and had both hands on my shoulder. About that time this fella, Sweet, he come from behind the house and says, "What you doing here, got my woman barred up like this?" and grabbed me and slammed me up against the house two or three times. I says to him, "Don't do that. You are liable to break the stitches in my side." I had been cut in the side, and it was all sewed up. He slammed me down in the ground and says to me, "If you cross my path anymore tonight, I'm gonna kill you." I wound up where the game was going on. A boy named Boss Nix or something like that says to me, "Let me have fifty cents on this gun, and I'll give you seventy-five cents Saturday." I said, "All right" and put the gun in my pocket. About that time, some of them said, "Let's go to the dance." I said that I didn't care, and when we got there, this fella, Sweet, jumped up with a knife in his hand like that and come at me and says, "What did I tell you?" Just as he come at me, I shot him and backed out the door. Sweet throwed his hands up in the air and went out the door. I backed out the door and come out. I went on and told this woman that I had shot Sweet, and she said, "You'd better leave here because you are a stranger and them boys will mob you." So, I got on the railroad and kept walking.

Although the other testimonies are very interesting, they are too numerous to include here, and we felt that the following interview by David Vinson was more insightful. The interviewee, Edward Vinson, was an eyewitness to the hanging:

It was a sad day for a ten-year-old. The hanging caused me to distrust lawmen, and I never did consider them to be a friend. It made an imprint on my mind that has never left me. Children should never have been allowed to watch hangings. The courtyard was completely covered with people from children to adults. People arrived there by train, buggies, and on horseback.

Luther Rickman was deputy sheriff and jail keeper. Luther was a kind and compassionate man, so Brown asked Luther to do the hanging. Luther told him he would do anything he could for him, but he would not hang him. Instead, the sheriff, John Beck Dockins, did the hanging.

Will Brown was standing on the gallows with his head down before they put on the black cap, when Chet Howard, the photographer, called to him and asked to raise his head. The crowd of people cursed Howard for asking him to do so.

They delayed the hanging until after the one o'clock train ran—for what reason, I don't know, unless it was a message from the governor. I watched Brown until they jerked the trapdoor out from under him; then after so many minutes, they opened the door, so I had gone down to where I could see him hanging. One shoulder was lower than the other. I don't know what they did with the body after the hanging. As I remember, there was not much said about the hanging afterward.

"A Hanging in Rabun County"
From *The Clayton Tribune*
Friday, February 11, 1916, page 1
By Col. T. T. Twisters

There have never been but two hangings in Rabun County since the establishment of the county, a-way back in 1819. The County Courthouse at Clayton stands on the crest of the hill, which, from the southwest corner of the building, slopes rapidly downward. On this sharp slope, the gallows, built for this occasion, was erected.

The crowd was very orderly, and not at any time or anyway during the trying scene did it give the officers of the law any trouble in the performance of their peculiarly painful duties. He had not killed a resident of Rabun, but a stranger to the county, a man of his own race.

The sheriff, upon whom rested practically the entire responsibility of conducting the execution, was exceedingly restless, moving here and there about the platform and consulting his watch almost every minute. I had heard that the hanging would occur at one o'clock. When the hour of one pealed forth from the courthouse tower, everybody present became, as if by a pre-arranged signal, keyed up to the highest pitch of expectancy. At about one-ten, a white minister of the Gospel talked with the condemned man (who claimed until the end that he did the killing in self-defense), but, I understand, only stated (from the gallows) that he was ready to go to his "home in Heaven."

The manacles were removed from the hands of the condemned Negro. His hands were tied behind his back with a white rope, apparently a piece of a brand new plow line. He was led upon the trap door. His feet were tied together. With quickly nervous fingers the sheriff drew the black cap of a very soft clinging material over the Negro's head, then quickly followed the noose of the rope, with its huge knot set under his left ear; then the drawing of the rope securely around the neck, and finally, the sheriff stepped back off the trap-door, motioned his deputies out of the way, and, with white face and a quick movement of arm and hand, sprung the trap. The Negro's body shot downward—out of sight!

Within an hour or so, I saw a wagon being driven up Main Street on its way to the cemetery on the edge of town, bearing a neat looking coffin, all that was mortal of a criminal who had expiated his crime in the manner in which the law decreed. Rev. George W. Seay offered a prayer.

Editor's note: *Local legend says that Will Brown was buried in Clayton across the street from the courthouse. It says that he is buried on the corner beside Shadyside Drive. Supposedly, there are ten or fifteen people buried there.*

"Yeah, that stuff's a-growin' wild up there."

~ Life and times of former sheriff Marley Cannon ~

Marley Cannon was sheriff of our county during the 1960s. The job was quite different then—there were only two or three paid deputies on his staff, and though there was a much smaller population, Rabun County covered a large area with mountains and lakes to patrol, in addition to the towns of Clayton, Mountain City, Rabun Gap, Dillard, and others.

—Margie Bennett

I had in my mind for a few years there that I wanted to be sheriff. I never knew that it would materialize as it did. I got to planning and talking about it. It was not that I had anything against the sheriff who was in office; he was a good friend of mine. I've studied a many of a night before I went to sleep wondering whether I would run or not. I made up my mind that I would run. I understood that I could get beat easier than I could win. I made up my mind that I was going to try it. If I won, then I won. However, if I got beat, I could go hide in the woods and cry, and nobody would know! Seriously, though, I wondered how I would make out being the sheriff if I got elected. Finally, I felt like the time was right for me to run—so I did and won!

Times were different in those days. To show you the difference in the times now, as to how they were then, there were hardly any firemen on duty. Usually, unless it was Friday or Saturday night, we only had one policeman on duty. There was a button in the fire department that would set the siren off. The police department had one, too. Almost always there was one or the other of us out all the time. If someone would call the fire department and find no one there, they would call the police department, and I would set the siren off. I would run uptown and tell them where to go, once they got back from wherever they were at.

I stayed sheriff for eight years. I started out with one deputy. We did not have any base radios. We only had a radio in the car. If my wife, Lorene, needed me, she would call on the phone to the courthouse, and they would call me on the car radio. The old jailhouse was two stories. The jail was upstairs. We had old metal steps that wound around that connected the first floor with the jail. We had a bullpen up there. A bullpen is a large room that holds a bunch of prisoners. Most of the time, these prisoners were only in jail cells, but occasionally the bullpen would be used if all the other cells were full. I put an old carpet out there in the living room. The old sheriff told me when he left, "I tell you right now, you won't keep that thing here very long. They'll flood it out!" We kept a lot of prisoners there, and we worked long hours. We had prisoners of all kinds in jail. We had murderers, fighters, thieves, and every kind of prisoner there was. You name it, and we probably had it at one time.

The old jail was in pretty bad shape. The old courthouse was in bad shape as well. There were big cracks in the floor at the old courthouse. Everyone was wanting a new courthouse. The government was expected to pay the other half of the cost of the new jail. The vote carried. However, the government was so long in getting their part done that we had to run another vote. Everybody that was interested in the new building really had to work hard in seeing the project through. There were so many people against it because it raised their taxes. A lot of people were having a hard time making a living anyway. However, the vote passed.

I believe my wife and I moved into the new jail on December 18, 1968. At the time, we had only one deputy. We moved in really before they were quite finished with the jail. The next spring, they got the upstairs done. Then they moved the people out of the old courthouse.

I never did have any trouble much when I was sheriff. The only trouble that I really had was keeping people from taking things up to prisoners. Sometimes someone would slip a hacksaw up to them. My bedroom was directly under the old jail. One night at the jail, I woke up, and I heard sawing going on. It was up over my head. I put on my socks and slipped on my pants. I eased on up the stairs. I went up real easy. As I looked coming around the bullpen, I saw this guy with a can opener about five inches long. He was making a key! He did not see me. He never got it working. Of course, it was a little funny in a way.

In those days, we could trust some of the prisoners. I had one prisoner that I let stay out all day and help me around the jail. He would go uptown and run errands for people. Well, this one other boy had a hacksaw. We worked long hours, and sometimes you work so long, and you lay down to go to sleep, you sleep real hard and cannot hear anything. Anyway, the man used the hacksaw and got out. Four of them escaped. What was funny about that to me is the fact that one of the four men who escaped was the boy who I let out during the day to run errands for me! He escaped with the other three. It seemed like he would have left whenever he wanted to. I got them all back in jail anyway. Two of them I got back the next day. One of them went over into South Carolina, and I had to get a bench warrant for him.

We had one boy in jail who had a child about a year old. He would take pins and pinch his little baby in order to make his wife do what he wanted her to do. I went and got a warrant for him. He was that type that could not stay in tight places—claustrophobic. I think this was planned, but somebody came to the jail and wanted to talk to this man. Well, when my wife opened the door, he ran out over her. She slapped him good, though! I never did want anyone caught as bad as I did this man. I guess I tried the hardest to get him than anyone else in my life. We kept after him, and I located him, but he got away from us again. Some way or the other, we found out where he was in South Carolina. We got out after him again. He got away from us then, and we found out that he went to Florida. After a while, I found out where he was and I went after him. I was going to pick him up down there. He got away from me once again. Of course, by this time, we were all pretty hot after him because he had slipped out between our fingers so many times. So he went to Pennsylvania. He never did come back. I will go ahead and say that he married again up north, and his wife killed him up there.

One time we had a report on a marijuana field in the Persimmon community. We observed this marijuana field from the woods. We went back to Clayton to get a warrant. There turned out to be an acre of marijuana at this field. There was some corn, too! It was fertilized pretty heavily. The corn was in roasting ears—ready to eat! In the meantime, we got three or four big plastic bags. I saw the man [who had the marijuana field] coming down from his house when we were raiding his field. The man was hauling the marijuana on a jeep. He come running off down there to meet us. I told him we had a search warrant for marijuana. I'll never forget what he said: "Yeah, that stuff's a-growin' wild up there. I'm trying to cut it down now and haul it off to get rid of it." So we arrested him and brought him on to the jail.

PLATE 34 **"I got the National Guard, after we bush hogged it, to bring diesel fuel to burn it." Marley Cannon and GBI Agent Henry Dillard in the marijuana field**

That was the first time marijuana was seized in the state of Georgia. I felt sorry for the family of this man. They all lived on a dead-end road going up to the house, so I put guards up there to keep anybody from going up in there that night. I did not know how to get rid of it legally because it was in a cornfield. So the Georgia Bureau of Investigation [GBI] and I went to the judge and solicitor and we talked to them about it. I thought we could get a court order to destroy it. He said he could not give a court order without having a hearing on it. I could not wait on that. The solicitor and I called the attorney general's office and asked for an opinion. We have not heard from them until this day. The judge and the solicitor told me to get rid of it the best I could, and they'd back me and support whatever I did. First, I got a man with a tractor and a Bush Gog. I had the field [mowed down]. I had the deputies to pull all the corn down around the edges. I piled it up as best as I could so it would not be a waste.

In the meantime, I got to studying about the fact that this was a private road, and I did not have any legal right to stop anyone from going up in there. I went and pulled my guards off the road. People from all over the country got on the television and radio and came in there. I got the National Guard, after we bush hogged it, to bring diesel fuel to burn it. Well, the search warrant got missing. Naturally, his lawyer tried to get the case thrown out. We tried to establish a court order by a hearing from the judge. I carried that to a higher court on them—the court of appeals.

Searching through the house, I found a hundred and some gallons of liquor and some bags of marijuana. I got the liquor and marijuana out of the house. We just dropped the other case of growing marijuana against him. We figured that it would save us time if we just dropped the other case. He was found guilty of possessing the liquor and marijuana in his house.

I brought a stalk of marijuana with me to jail. I kept it in a bucket. It got out in the news that I had the marijuana. I did not do anything there for five straight days but show people that marijuana. Nobody had ever seen any of it from this part of the country. I knew where the seed had come from, and I knew who bought it, and I knew where they delivered them to. I had all the information on this stalk of marijuana.

In the early part of 1972, which was the last part of my term, we had a prisoner that we caught in South Carolina. He stole some gas in Franklin, North Carolina. We got a call on him, and we caught him coming down Highway 441. We brought him on to jail, and he was tried for stealing gas. In the meantime, we checked his records out. It turned out that he was an escapee from a federal penitentiary in Florida. So they had the jurisdiction on him, but we tried him in Georgia for possessing stolen property. I believe they gave him three years, to the best of my knowledge.

I was holding a young boy from New York in jail the same time I was holding this man from the penitentiary in Florida. We were holding this young boy for Towns County. I forget what they were holding him for, but the main thing Towns County Police Department wanted to do is have him witness in a case to convict a real bad criminal. Well, this one day I came in late from work, and the deputy told me that this little boy from New York had sent a note out, and the note said he wanted to talk to us. We made out like he had a phone call or something, and I went back there and got him. This young boy was telling us about the guy we had from the penitentiary in Florida that planned to escape. Anyway, he said that he talked one of those boys into bringing a pistol in that night when they came back from church. I moved this feller from Florida out by himself in the back of the jail where we had two cells. The county had fixed a place in the back for storage space—mattresses, blankets, and things like that. In the meantime, we took everything away from him, except his matches and cigarettes and the normal things for anybody to have. So I went on to bed. We were all very tired.

That feller had planned an escape to happen during the night. He had rolled a lot of toilet tissue together, and he put a match in the middle of it. He throwed it through the jail cell into that storage part. He waited until real early in the morning to where there would not be any fire officers out on the road. He knew that a fire at this time of the morning would result in us having to open up the jail. He would have an opportunity to escape. Well, this plan did not work out for him. A quarter until seven, my wife woke up and found the jail full of smoke. I got three prisoners out, but there were two men in the back who suffocated to death. I went in the bullpen first and got all the young people out first. I stumbled over one who had passed out on the floor. I got him out, and he lived.

Fred Lee, the man who opened up the courthouse that morning, came in through the back of the jail. He came in through the back of the jail. He came in at six thirty. He did not smell any smoke when he came up by that door. He got upstairs, going about his duty, and he heard people hollering and going on. He thought it was a normal situation, due to the fact that we had every kind of criminal in that jail. It was real bad. That was an awful bad tragedy. My wife was overcome by exhaustion. She was in the hospital for almost a week.

I had got my third deputy a week before this happened, and I had one deputy that was still in school due to mandatory training. I left the new deputy on duty to do what had to be done. Well, it turned out that we had arrested two men from Clayton. My new deputy put them in the front cells, whereas if I'd been there, I would have put them in the back. This was fortunate for the two men because it made them easy to get out without dying from the fire.

This county grew too fast [when I was in office.] It grew fast, day and night. This county has always grown very fast. These mountains here are wonderful, and naturally everyone likes to live here. We've got all these woods and all these lakes and houses. A lot of people would not dream about the scenery that we have here.

Back then, we did not have any Mountain Patrol, no policemen at Tallulah Falls, none at Mountain City or Dillard. It was just work day and night for us back then. The police department did not have adequate help. I did not have a secretary, bookkeeper, radio operator, or anything. My wife, my deputies, and my prisoners helped me run the sheriff's department. I could not have made it if it was not for my wife. She was the backbone of the sheriff's department. She worked hard. I do not see how she made it. Come to think about it, we would not have made it if it was not for the prisoners helping around. You know, some of them you could depend on real good. They were a lot of help to me.

When I first went through office, you could basically do what you needed to do. However, I did not mistreat anybody. If I knew that someone stole something, and I knew it in my own heart and mind that I was right, I could get a warrant and would not worry about it. I could then go and pick them up and bring them into jail. I could question them then. At first, you know, they would not want to talk to you about it. If you kept on and on, you could break them down. I broke down a good nine out of every ten people that I questioned.

Things started to change. You could see people throwing things and breaking out glasses in store windows on the television. Illegal seizure and illegal search charges began to be filed. If you were to see a vehicle come out of a drive, loaded down with televisions, and if you did not have something like a taillight busted out, or a license check, or something like that, you could not stop them. If you did, it would be an illegal search and seizure, and the case would be thrown out. It just got harder and harder and harder to do anything. That trend is turning a little bit, but the crime rate is not.

I came to the realization that it had got to the point that it was not worth it. I made plans to quit two years ahead of the end of my term. So I had a job ready for the end of my term, making more money. My new job was only eight hours a day! I have to say that with no regrets. The people in this county were really good to me.

"Machine Gun Bandits Hold Up Bank Of Clayton"

~1934 bank robbery as recalled by Huell Bramlett~

My grandfather Huell Bramlett was born on May 21, 1914, in Clayton, Georgia. That is also where he grew up. He has lived in many different places and has done many interesting things, and he can tell you stories to prove it. He worked in Albany, Georgia, where he ran a record store and fixed broken jukeboxes. Granddaddy Huell was also in World War II in Okinawa when the war ended. From there, the American government sent him to help rebuild Korea. However, one of his most interesting stories was when, as a high schooler, he witnessed the robbery of the Bank of Clayton.

Kelly Cook and I told Mike Cook, our Foxfire teacher, about this story, and he was ready to send us to interview Granddaddy Huell on the spot. Mike got really excited because there had never been an interview about this bank robbery since students interviewed Luther Rickman, the sheriff of Rabun County at the time of the bank robbery in 1967, for the first issue of Foxfire. *There has never been an account of this robbery printed in* Foxfire *from a bystander's point of view.*

—*Erin Smith*

The Rickman interview was Foxfire's very first. It was printed in The Foxfire Magazine, *volume 1, number 1, and reprinted in the Spring 1988 20th Anniversary issue. Here are a few facts that Huell left out: The amount of money that was taken was about $1,830. The robber's name was Zade Sprinkle. There were some others, but Zade was the leader of the pack. The exact date was August 21, 1934.*

—*Kelly Cook*

This robbery took place in 1934, to the best of my knowledge and abilities to tell it. I was going to school in the tenth grade in Clayton at Rabun County High School. My principal and teacher, Mr. Reynolds, he had a' asthma attack, and he wanted me to drive him up to the drugstore. The drugstore was by the bank at that time. I drove his car up there with him, and he got out and went in the drugstore. While he was in there, I heard shooting in the bank. I didn't know what was going on. I found out later that it was Dr. Dover that was in there when it was happening. He was a prominent doctor there at that time and an official of the bank, but, anyway, the gunshots were shooting at the floor, and we still did not know what was going on.

The officers of Rabun County were not around at that time. So Mr.

PLATE 35 **Clayton in the late 1930s or early 1940s. The bank is located where Western Union is. Photo courtesy of Edwards Studio**

Reynolds came out with his medicine that he got in the drugstore, and he got in the car. I started to back out. This other man that was with the robber was sitting in the car next to ours, and he pointed his pistol over at us and said, "Pull back up in there and don't move." I still did not know what was going on and I was scared, too, I guess. At that time the robber came out with the money in the bag. I do not know whether it was a paper bag, a sack, or what. He got in the car, and the robber began driving.

They took off down 441 South to the Bogg's Mountain Road, but when they [the robbers] took off, I was sitting in Mr. Reynolds's car. I could see some kind of machine gun in the back of the car. I did not know exactly what it was, but the evidence [later presented in court] said it was a machine gun. Anyway, they strewed roofing tacks in the road so the people that were chasing them could pick up the tacks and puncture their tires, and that would delay their capture.

Naturally, the Rabun County law, Sheriff Rickman and Harley McCall, had time to get there, and they were chasing the robbers. Anyway, they went across Bogg's Mountain Road, and the county crew workmen that worked on the road were there scraping the road, and something happened, and they could not get their equipment out right then. Those two robbers told the workmen to move immediately. So they did; they moved it, and they went on and proceeded into South Carolina.

In North Carolina the police officers were alerted. At that time, there weren't any radios, I don't think, or any kind of equipment that they could get ahold of any of the other officers and let them know what was going on. So they were apprehended in Asheville, North Carolina. So this one robber—I don't know what happened to the other one that was with him—they put him in jail at Asheville.

Then they appointed me to go and verify him after they had found out that I had seen the robber who came out of the bank with the money, to see if it was him. So this man didn't have any hair, and he was a fat, chunky fella. And I had to verify him. When I verified him, Sheriff Rickman and Harley McCall got him to come on out, and Sheriff Rickman called this man's name and said, "Get in the backseat with me. I'm not gonna put no handcuffs on you. If you do anything or try to run, I'll shoot you." So he came on to Clayton Jail, and finally he had a trial. When he had the trial, he told Sheriff Rickman, he said, "Sheriff Rickman, I'm glad you wasn't in there 'cause I was in there after that money and me or you, one would have died." That's all.

PLATE 36 **The original newspaper clipping from August 23, 1934, two days after the robbery**

"I ain't made no liquor in a long time."

~Bass Dockery, "the Wild Russian"~

When we set out for Tennessee to interview Mr. Bass Dockery, we did not know what to expect. Mr. Hoyt Bryson of Mount Morris, New York, had written Foxfire telling us a little about Bass, suggesting that he would be a good contact. Mr. Bryson told us he grew up in the Tellico Plains area of Tennessee and had known about Bass for many years. "Mr. Dockery is a remarkable man," he said, "and has always been very much a part of the mountains. He lost his right arm in a shoot-out with a law officer many years ago. He had many years of making whiskey . . . and homesteaded the place where he lives yet."

When we finally found Bass Dockery's house, two hundred miles and a four-hour drive from Rabun County, Georgia, there was no one at home. Disappointed, we decided to go back down the mountain and eat our lunch, hoping that he would return home before we had to head back to Georgia. A few hours later, we retraced our way up the narrow, bumpy, one-lane road and forded the creek where the bridge was out. We knocked on his door once more, feeling hopeful because a Jeep was parked in the driveway and it hadn't been there before.

When we first arrived at Bass's house, I didn't see anything unusual about its construction. It was about sixty feet long and fourteen to sixteen feet wide, built of concrete block, and one story. Although I took the side of the house we drove up to as the front, there were no windows except for those in the shop at the end of the house. The front door, where we knocked, was the only visible entrance. Later, when I was on the inside and could see what the other long outside wall looked like, I knew why he needed no windows on one side; the outside wall was made of windows and led to a deck or porch about six feet wide, overlooking the valley we had just driven up from. There was something even more unusual: plate-glass windows between each room. By standing in the living room, you could look through the bedrooms and on into the kitchen, three or four rooms away. I think there were doors between the rooms, but I don't remember. Perhaps they were just standing open. Bass said he didn't want anybody sneaking up on him, and this way he'd be sure to see them first.

He answered our knock after what seemed like a very long time. We were contemplating leaving because we were hesitant about walking around to see if he was in the backyard, for fear he would think we were prowling. We didn't want to leave, though, when we were so close to what we felt would be a great interview. Finally, he opened the door, and we began explaining our reason for being there. His grandson J. D. (short for John Dillinger) Dockery was also there and helped explain to his grandfather about us. We told Bass who we were and showed him some Foxfire magazines and books to assure him we meant no harm.

He did talk to us some but did not want us to tape-record him or take pictures. He seemed somewhat apprehensive about being interviewed, though he showed us several newspaper articles that had been done on him over the past few years. We assured him that we would not publish anything until he had approved it. He said that we should wait a few weeks and then write him for a date, and he would have J.D. write and tell us when it would be convenient to return. We left a bit disappointed but excited about getting to come back later. I did write Bass a letter about two weeks later and waited anxiously. J.D. answered and gave us a date, and off we went again. On this trip, we were able to tape and photograph him.

Bass Dockery was born near Unaka, North Carolina, in 1894 and was one of four boys. His father was a farmer and a logger. When Bass was eighteen years old, he left home to work in logging camps. He worked for different logging companies and sporadically made moonshine until he was twenty-six. At that time, he married and started making moonshine for a living. He and his wife had nine girls and three boys, all we were told, named after outlaws he admired. The children have long since grown up and moved away, visiting occasionally, but usually Bass goes to see them now. Bass's wife died in 1971, and until very recently, he rarely left the mountains. Now he owns a beautiful late-model car and spends the winters traveling out west and anywhere else he takes a notion to go. He showed us souvenir longhorn steer horns from Mexico and other mementos from his travels.

Bass claims that he was, and still is, the meanest man around. He has many experiences to substantiate that statement, but to me he seemed very pleasant and interesting. His personality is warm and friendly, his sense of humor sharp and witty. He had me captivated from the moment we entered his house. Tale after tale, true stories of his life came from this thinning, white-haired man. He told of shooting at the feet of neighboring young men when they were all courting and being thrown in jail for disturbing public worship. I just found it all hard to believe, but many people around Tellico will reassure anyone who asks that Bass did do those things, AND that he has honesty and integrity in spite of those shenanigans.

—Bridget McCurry

I was born over the mountains here. We lived up back in Unaka, North Carolina. We had a nice home, good as anybody else's. We raised hogs and cattle, stuff like that. My father was a farmer that could do almost anything. No, he didn't make liquor, and he'd get after me for makin' it. I had three brothers. One brother lives in Franklin, North Carolina, now, and the other two are dead. Goldie, the brother next to me, made moonshine, but Raleigh never did make no liquor. He was kind of a meetinghouse [church] man.

My grandmother on my daddy's side died at my house. Now, she was a thoroughbred Cherokee Indian. Old Kiwooti was her daddy and lived on Hanging Dog back up in the mountains. They just had split-wood puncheons and moss for a bed. The dog and the cats crawled through every crack in that house. There wasn't a crack stopped up! She was staying with me and my family when she died.

I never went to school but a few days in my life. When I was growin' up, there wasn't no compulsory going to school. I didn't have to go. And we lived up back in Unaka, three or four miles back up in the mountains. I didn't want to go—boy-like, you know—and that's what happened. I got no education for nothing but meanness. I stayed at home till I was eighteen years and then went to work in logging camps. My father logged before me. At one time, logging was a big industry here. I've worked at Sunburst, Black Mountain, and Mount Mitchell in North Carolina, went over the mountain with the Brown Brothers down there and worked for Bancroft's down here. I worked at Helen, Georgia, and in Conasauga, Tennessee.

I've been in lots of logging camps, spent seven or eight years just in logging camps. It was a hard life. Made two dollars a day. It would be from seventy-five to one hundred seventy-five men to the camp. I'd change off jobs every once in a while. That's the way they do it now. They'll hear of a better job and a better place, and they'll travel backwards and forwards, changing jobs. That's the way it worked. I've stayed as high as six months in one camp—eat every meal and sleep there every night. I quit logging when I was twenty-six. That's when I got married and went to makin' liquor full-time. My wife was twenty years old when we got married. She died in 1971, had cancer for six years. I've lived alone ever since she died.

If people had to live now like I was raised up, they'd shoot theirselves. They couldn't put up with it. They've been living this high life, and if they had to go back to livin' the way it used to be, they'd shoot theirselves. My wife and I lived way down here on what they called Beaver Dam Bald till the kids got old enough to go to school. Then we moved up here, and I went back to mixing that liquor.

Bass moved onto some land just over the Tennessee line in North Carolina after he was caught making liquor in Tennessee. There was only a little log cabin there, and he moved his family into it. A logging company owned the land, but he just "homesteaded" it, not paying rent but living on it just as if he owned it. At some point, he paid back taxes that were due on it. He lived there for seven years, and it was considered his by some old law that was on the North Carolina books. We were not able to get all the facts quite clear on his homesteading the property, but when this story was written, he did own 126 acres.

I stayed here on this land for several years before I owned it. People kept on telling me, "That land's your'n. You can take it." The logging company that owned the land kept notifying me to move, or they was going to come out here and throw me out. They didn't come, though. There was this fellow who was the lawyer for that company that owned the land. He was an awful good lawyer. I'd run up on him in Murphy, North Carolina, and he'd notify me to leave. And, I'd say, "You'd better be quiet, old man, about that." Over the years there were different lawyers that had charge of this piece of land. They don't allow homesteading no more. They said I was the last man ever to pull a deal like that. All you have to do is stay seven years—you have to stay twenty-one years on government land—seven years homesteading, and you can take hold. They done away with it right then.

I had to pay one hundred and twenty-five dollars in back taxes when I homesteaded this piece of land. That's all it ever cost me. I've got a hundred and twenty-six acres left out of two hundred fifty-seven. I've sold that much off in lots for summer homes. There was a little old log house here. It wasn't much bigger than this room here. It was just a little old shack of a thing. We moved in there. We had about five or six kids when we come in here. That house is tore down now. Then I built a bigger place and finally built this concrete-block-and-glass house about twenty years ago.

I farmed and made moonshine, too. We didn't do much farmin' no way. It's hard to make corn here. It's too cold. Budworms in the spring will git your corn. You can't do no good. This land's more for weeds and gopher grass and things like that. My wife, Callie, and the younguns worked like dogs. Now, my wife was a worker! She didn't set around and twiddle her fingers and big toes. The children are all grown and moved away now. I've got a girl in Franklin, North Carolina, and one in Florida, and the rest of 'em scattered all over the United States. I've got a boy out in Oregon. There was a lot of money there when he went out there. Folks got a hundred dollars a day for work. He's cut timber ever since he's been there. I can't tell you how many, but I've got about twenty-three grandchildren, and I believe about forty or more great-grandchildren. That ain't many, maybe, but if I seen them all a-comin', I'd sure move out. I ain't having no reunion!

I never made any liquor before I was eighteen. Never got hooked up with it. It was something I just wanted to cultivate, I guess. I just got interested in it and got started on it and just didn't stop. Sometimes I had four sixty-gallon barrels, sometimes up to twelve and fifteen, like that. It's a job, too. At times I had people workin' with me. At times I didn't. I made liquor for thirty years, just the same as you'd be working on the job. And I broke the record of makin' the best liquor that was put out. I took mine off from one-hundred-ten to one-hundred-twenty proof. It took a man to drink it; a boy

PLATE 37 **"I made one-hundred-ten proof and along like that. It was high-powered. I've got fellows drunk, took clippers and clipped their hair off and greased their head with axle grease."** (*Monroe Life*, September 14, 1977)

couldn't. I was making it down there in Tennessee, in the general area where Bill White later had his huntin' lodge. Used to be liquor wasn't so high. I sold lots of liquor from four dollars a gallon on up to twenty dollars.

Most moonshiners make what's called singlings. This means going through the distilling process once. I put mine through once, clean up the still, and run the liquor through a second time. We call that doublin'. That's when you make your good liquor. I made a run one time using two bushels of rye, one bushel of corn, and one of Irish potatoes. If you've got beer that won't work, you just cook you a little poke [cloth sack or bag] of taters and put a rock in it and sink it in your beer, and it'll put it to work. I let a neighbor have a drink. I could hear him a-hollerin' for ten hours nearly after he left my house. I stayed in the moonshine business for thirty years, and in all that time, they never once caught me. I came nigh to gettin' caught a few times, though.

The way I kept from getting caught was, I stood in with the law. I was acquainted with the law and got along with them. I guess they just took a liking to me, and I got along. This talking about 'em and going on and all such as that won't work. I never give 'em a dime. I never give 'em no liquor as a bribe. Never bought them off or nothing. The federal men didn't watch moonshiners so close back then. However, they'd come in there sometimes. They didn't work at it then like they do now. I had a brother, Goldie, over here that helped build Fontana Dam, and he was acquainted with a fellow by the name of John Morton who was a federal man. Old John got word on me, and he came over where I had my still. He hung around in the territory playin' cards and drinkin' a spell. Me and Goldie had been up the river there on the ridge to see about the beer on our still, and we heared somebody drivin' up. We backed our car down, went back down the road, and come up like we were waiting. We wanted to throw them off from comin' down that way. The man asked if there was any liquor in this country that a man could buy, and I said, "Yeah."

I didn't know him, but Goldie knew who he was. The man asked, "How much would a half gallon cost?" I said, "It'll cost ten dollars." God! He fell over and went to kickin' like he was dyin'. He said, "Ten dollars?" I said, "Yeah." He decided he wanted it anyway. He said, "When you gonna bring that liquor?" I said, "I ain't going to bring it. You have to go get it." Well, we brought him up to right over there [near Bass's house]. Him and Goldie stood over there and talked. I come over here near the house and got this fruit jar washed out, and it was ready to go. I had that liquor hid right out there in the thicket, and I was about to go out there and get it. Goldie come over here. He said, "Don't you know that's John Morton?" I said, "No." He said, "That's that federal man." I just run over there and give his money back. I said, "Here's your money." He said, "What do you mean?" And I said, "There ain't no liquor for you. I don't know what went with it." I just turned around and walked off. He said, "Wait a minute." I come back over here to the house, and I had a thirty/thirty lever-action high-power gun. I walked over there to that big white oak. I said, "Come on over, Uncle John." And he never come. I didn't aim for him to come, for I knowed if he did, he might find this liquor. That's the closest I ever come to gettin' caught. He stayed in this section, though, and he went on over to Hanging Dog, and a cousin of mine was making liquor then. Morton said, "Can I get a quart of liquor?" My cousin said, "Yeah, I guess." And he turned around to his boy and said, "Go get this man a quart of liquor." He come back and handed the liquor to his daddy, and his daddy handed it to Morton. And Morton said, "You's all under arrest." He took 'em both and put them in jail right there.

I moved my still occasionally. I stayed in some places back up off in Rough Ridge that I cleared out—pretty good new ground. I made it all over these woods here. I didn't stay in one place all the time. You can't go to sleep there. You're lookin' for something you don't want to see, and that's the law. There's something or another all the time. You're busy. You've got something to do, not just sittin' there sleeping. The beer will scorch and ruin. I've made a run or two of apple brandy and peach brandy, too. Now, that's something that you can drink—that's good! You run them apples in this summer when they come in. You fix them where they won't freeze, and they sit there till next summer. Then you run them off. They're all rotten, just fermented. There ain't nothing much left in there, just juice. You get one quart of brandy out of a bushel of apples. That's all you get. That's a slow-runnin' business. You mix sugar with the juice, and you can make good drinkin' liquor and good brandy, too.

If you get a good run out of cornmeal, you get two gallons of liquor to the bushel of meal, and that's about all you'll get. If I make a run with syrup liquor using sorghum instead of granulated sugar, I might get a good mash *and* good liquor. Then next time the liquor might be just as foggy— nasty-looking stuff. It's not consistent. It don't run out the next time like it ought to.

Most of the people come and got it. I never took much liquor away. They come and got it. There's been fellows come out of Atlanta here looking for my liquor. I didn't carry my liquor out in a truck. I'd carry it out on my back. Years ago, my brother and I hauled crossties to Murphy, North Carolina, on a wagon. We'd put bundles of corn tops for the mules to eat on the top of

PLATE 38 "Whoa, mule, whoa." Bass, before his arm was
shot off, hauling fodder on a sled pulled by a mule

PLATE 39 **"I've been in jail a many a time—
just for packin' a pistol." Bass after
his arm was amputated**

the load. And in each bundle of tops, we hid a gallon of liquor. In Murphy, we'd find a friend who let us know the whereabouts of the high sheriff and the revenuers. If they were anywhere around, we'd get that liquor sold and get out of there.

About 1931, I was over at Unaka Valley one evening. There had been a meeting over there. A bunch of us fellows was sittin' on a' old, crooked pasture rail fence. One of the fellows' brothers was drinkin', so he and another boy took the one who was drunk up to his sister's house. I waited on 'em down there at the fork of the road. The others had gone on, and I was by myself. This fellow Johnson come up and said, "What's argon' on here?" And I said, "It ain't anything to ya." That's all I said, and he just hauled out his gun and went to shooting. The first time he split my hat brim right along there, and the next time, he hit me right in the neck there. I had my pistol stickin' out of my belt, and as I come off'n the fence, I came out with a gun. He throwed his flashlight down. Now, the sky was clear, but there was white clouds a-blowin' over along like that—the moon was shining—and he throwed his flashlight down. I grabbed my pistol and shot him right through the thigh. He shot six shots and hit me twice. He was a bad shot, but he'd killed seven men. I made the sixth man that man had shot that didn't die. He's dead now, but I don't know what he died from.

They put me in jail that night. I've been in jail a many a time—just for packin' a pistol and getting drunk and disturbin' the public worship and such as that. We'd get in a fight right in the middle of the meetinghouse. We didn't care. We didn't care for nothin'. I stayed in jail maybe a month. Three men signed my bond for me, but the doctor wouldn't let me out of jail before that. He said, "It's that big artery. If you were to sneeze or cough, and it was to break, you'd bleed to death. You've got to stay here till that heals over." I don't know. I may have stayed there two months. It was two years after I lost my arm before I was tried for that shootin'. They waited till my arm got well before they tried me.

The judge who tried me was a mean old devil. He handed down my sentence. Then he got to vilifying me, talking mean to me. He kept saying things to me like: "Shooting up the law. We've got to have lawmen. We've got to have the best citizens," and all such as that. I said, "Judge, you're just a d—— liar. There sits the outlaw. He's killed seven and shot me, and you call *him* a good citizen?" He said, "Get him, Sheriff. Get him out of here." The sheriff had me by the belt a-pullin' me toward the jail door, and I was a-cussing him. The judge said, "I wish I hadn't already passed sentence on you. I'd give you a hundred years." I served nine months in the chain gang, built nine months on the road for shootin' Johnson. I was a water boy on the road and that was all I had to do. They was good to me, and I was quiet. I didn't raise no disturbance, for I knowed if I did, I would just have to make more time.

Some people I knew had signed a petition for me to get out. One man told me, "Mr. Dockery, I'll not sign that. I'm going to write a letter in a day or two, and that will do more good." And it did. He wrote the governor a letter. Then he said, "Dockery," he said, "it looks like the chips are for us. It looks like you are going to get to go home in a few days." He said, "Everybody's for you." Well, that cheered me up. Then I heard from him sayin' that this big crook that drove a transfer truck and came down to a nearby logging camp every Saturday night, was telling the governor, "Keep Dockery there in jail the longest day you can." He says, "That's the meanest man that's ever been in this country. We're afraid to go to bed. We're afraid he'll burn the house on us. Keep him in there the longest day you can." And he wrote that. He wrote that to the governor, and the governor mailed it to me. I wish I'd kept that letter, but I don't know—I guess I just burned it then. That man was related to my family. Him and my daddy was first cousins. I made it hot for him when I come back from jail, though.

I was talkin' to one man who'd been elected sheriff four times in one town in North Carolina near where I lived. He was strict and straight. He was a tough one. He would convict you whether you was guilty or not. I was talking to him up there after he got out of the business, and he asked me if I was makin' liquor. I told him, "Yeah." He said, "Just keep on makin' it." It wasn't his job to worry about it anymore. I ain't made no liquor now in a long time. It got so dangerous around here. There is too many people in these woods. I ain't made no liquor in a long time.

Hooper's Bald is a prominent mountain in the vicinity where Bass was raised. We had heard of Hooper's Bald because it was once a famous game preserve. In our general conversation, we asked Bass if he knew anything about the preserve on Hooper's Bald.

Some people who developed a game preserve on Hooper's Bald brought buffalo and Russian hogs in here years ago. I seed the first ones they ever brought here. A fellow by the name of Brian Radford had one of them buffalo in a cage-of-a-thing. Them horns were about six inches long, and they was black from one end to the other. We boys would slip along, and we had a walkin' stick, and we'd jab him, and he'd stab them horns through that thing. Radford said, "Ah-ah-ah, you boys, don't do that. Don't do that. He'll break out of there." We'd jab him with that sharp, pointed stick, and he'd just let go and stab them horns through that cage. They was just little old pine boards. If he could've, he would have tore out of that cage and left. They brought them Russian hogs in here years ago, and these woods was full of 'em. They just ain't here no more. When they first brought them here, they was *mean*! If anybody got around where those hogs had little ones, they'd run the person up a tree. No, I never did have one to chase me up a tree, but I've witnessed it.

I do more trappin' than anything. Of the eighteen bears I've killed, I trapped most of them. I snared mine with a hollow log and spring pole and cable. I'd put bait in that log, and he couldn't pass it up. He'd go in there to get it. That spring would trip and catch him by the hand, and he couldn't do no good but run around. It's been about sixteen year since I've killed a bear. Last fall, down the road there, I seed signs of a bear, but I never did locate it. Something 'r 'nother happened to it.

"Let me tell you about Bass."

~Bill White says, "We hit it off good."~

Bill White grew up in the mountainous area around Tellico Plains, Tennessee. When he was a boy, he met Bass Dockery and tells us about that in this interview. We had not heard of Bill White before we went on our first trip to meet Bass. We stopped at his store and trailer park to ask for directions to Bass's house. In the course of that conversation, he told us some interesting things about Bass and how he had come to know him. We asked if we could come back and interview him later in the afternoon about his friendship with Bass. He said, "Sure," and the information Bill gave us helps to make this a more complete story about Bass Dockery. Without Bill's help, Bass's story would have been quite sketchy.

Several years after he returned from World War II, Bill bought property along the Bald River Gorge near Tellico Plains and bordering National Forest land in the midst of excellent hunting and fishing country. When this story was written, he and his wife lived in a house they built after their hunting lodge burned down. They ran a small convenience store and trailer park. People would leave their vacation trailers there year-round and stay in them throughout the late spring, summer, and early fall. Bill White is a very interesting person himself, and when we returned during the winter to have him approve the article as we had typed it, we took pictures and copied old pictures of his, and talked to him more about his life.

—Bridget McCurry

I have been right here sixteen years. I used to own a forty-room hunting lodge right up there [points to a location about one hundred yards from the store]. It's burned down now, and I now run this hunting and recreation camp.

I know a little about mountain ways. You take care of your own and let the other fellow take care of his own. It's not just Bass. It's everybody in these Appalachian Mountains. They are all like that. They've got their own code. They'd rather settle their own arguments, their own feuds, than have outsiders, The Law, come in and try to tell them so-and-so. Usually the Appalachian people back in the mountains think it's a one-sided deal because if a man killed my brother, say, then why should The Law or somebody else come in here and kill that person, take him out and put him in jail, or do *anything* with him? That's *my* grief. *I'm* supposed to go out there and punish the killer. That's strictly up to me to do. That's *my* revenge, not theirs, not The Law's. That's the code these people like to live by. If a man does something to you, then that man's the one to be punished by *you*, not the judge down

PLATE 40 "Let me tell you about Bass." Over the mantel, behind him,
are paintings Mr. White commissioned of famous Indians he admires.
A few of the many Indian artifacts he has collected are shown
hanging on the wall. He is very proud of his own Indian ancestry.

there sittin' on that stand. He ain't done nothing to that judge. He done it to
you. He stole your horse. He's done something to *you*. Well, go over there and
steal one of his horses. That's the way it's supposed to go down. If somebody
steals one of your horses, well, you go over there and steal one of his if he's
got any, and if he ain't, you steal his brother's horse. Then, if they don't like
it, they can take care of the brother that stole your horse. It cuts down on a
lot of things.

You know, they made all of these laws and a lot of people don't believe
you ought to take the law into your own hands that way, but that's the way
most of these old mountain people believe, just like Bass does—take care of
your own business. You'd be surprised how well it works. It worked a whole
lot better back when less law was practiced in these hills and folks governed
themselves. It worked for the Cherokee Indians, and they never had so much
murdering, stealing, and goings-on because they had their own rules and
enforcement. Their own families and people took care of their problems. You

take before World War II, all these people that lived in here were self-made people. They tended their ground, and they hunted and fished for a living. That's all there was to do. We didn't have nothing else. We were poor people, but we didn't know it! Nobody had ever told us we were poor, so all of us was that way.

When the big Depression hit the cities and areas away from the mountains, it didn't surprise us much. It hurt us less because we'd been having a depression for a long time. We didn't have much to begin with. We lived about the same as our families had for the last one hundred and fifty years—just off the land. We were happy. We didn't know we were poor until somebody out of the city came out here and told us we were poor people. We didn't know that the rest of the world was any different until we all got out of here and into the armed services. When World War II broke out, most of us young men were dying to get in that service, so all the young fellows around here in these mountains got in there. I went in the Marines. Several of them went into the Army, the Navy, or some other branch of the service. We were all patriotic anyway. Just a great big old rough bunch of boys, you know, and we thought fightin' those Germans and those Japanese was going to be a cinch. We was going over there and clean 'em up in a week or two, wasn't going to be no trouble with that.

Boy! Away we went—went in there, and they put us through this thing. Man! They gave us two pairs of dress shoes, three pairs of field shoes. Why, I'd never had but one pair of shoes in a whole year in my life, and I was in high cotton. They gave us five or six, seven pairs of pants, five or six shirts. None of us had ever wore any underwear. We didn't know what that was. And socks! They gave us twelve pairs of socks and seven or eight pairs of underwear. They gave us a good shooting gun to go with it. We thought we were on top of the world—went in there and they had this long table. They had all this food stacked up on there, beans and meat and everything else. We weren't eating thin gravy with a fork anymore! Man! We were reachin' over there and getting something we could put our teeth in. And then we got fat and sassy. No wonder we whipped them people over there. They hadn't been as hungry as we had. We went over there and looked around at New Zealand, Australia, and all of Europe. Those people lived in big fine homes. They had good stuff to eat, and we thought the U.S. was a wealthy country! We didn't have nothing to what those people had.

We came back over here after the war, and we was a little smarter than we was when we left. We found out that ninety percent of us hadn't been getting anything and only ten percent of this country had been raking off all the harvest, all the wealth. We wasn't gettin' nothing. So things began to change a little bit. We started moving along, and right now, I don't reckon anybody's hungry in this part of the country. They can sit down to three meals a day, and they don't go hungry as fast. You'd be surprised. You never got enough to eat back then, and that's the truth, but people ain't gonna tell you that because their pride won't let them. That's the honest truth, and Bass knows it, and I know it. We all know it. It's just been in the last few years that the Appalachian Mountain people, and the American people in general, has really got to set down and have three good meals a day, and have a car that's no more than ten years old to ride around in, and maybe go to a show and spend a little money. They didn't have it before World War II. They liked to have starved. They didn't starve, but they was hungry. They didn't need to go on any diets like now. They was on a diet all the time because they didn't have enough to eat. They was all skinny. I never saw anybody fat in this whole country. I remember those days. I was just a kid, and I grew up under that. I had to pick blackberries and grow apples and grapes to put up before we got through the winter. It was a long hard winter, and there were a lot of lean years and a lot of lean winters, too.

I met Bass Dockery with my grandfather. My grandfather used to buy a little whiskey from him. That's when the Dockerys lived back in the holler, and I used to come up here with Granddad. Bass made some of the best whiskey, I guess, in this country. Everybody from all around wanted to buy Bass Dockery's whiskey, just like my grandfather plum over across the mountain would come over here and buy it because Bass made his whiskey out of a copper outfit, a copper still, and he made double-twisted whiskey. It was pure corn whiskey. Just like I said—when you drink his whiskey, you can smell the man's socks that plowed the corn 'cause it's good whiskey. And they all came in here and bought it. He had a little garden right out here and had a little corn patch right on top of that mountain right up there. [Bill points out the door of his store.] He plowed his corn and made liquor off of it. Bass made a good living.

I never did make liquor myself, but I've been to Bass's still. I've helped him fire it up, throw wood on it. We was pretty good friends. He liked me, and I liked him. We hit it off good. I don't know of many people that get along with him really, except maybe his own kids, and sometimes he gets mad at them and tells them he's going to leave them out of his will. Bass had a spring right off the house. He had a tube run back in the bank with the spring water coming out. When I'd be up there, he'd give me a drink of liquor out of the jug, and I'd reach over there and get me some spring water to chase it with. If I was going to spend all night with him when I was a boy, I would pitch a pallet down there before his fireplace. Usually, we'd be getting ready to go a-huntin', and it'd be cold up there. In the morning, I'd get to smelling that coffee making and that bacon frying, and I knew it was time to get up. I'd get up from that pallet and go in there and have good eating, and then we would go hunting.

Bass had a house full of kids up there. They were small, like myself, then. He had nine girls and three boys. I've heard this tale about Bass. A fellow asked him, he said, "Well, Bass, how many kids did you have?" And Bass said, "Well, me and Callie had twelve, and there wasn't none of 'em worth a d——, so we stopped." And I've heard him tell a fellow that myself when I took him up to Bass's one day. Had all those girls and boys, and they had a great big long table, and he'd put jelly glasses, a row of 'em, down that table. He'd get a jug of liquor, and he'd go down through there pouring them about half full of liquor. Then he'd take a spoon of sugar and put in every one of them glasses. When the children got ready to go to bed, they'd go by there and drink it. Then they'd climb up that Jacob's ladder to the crow's nest [loft of the cabin] and just jump down on those straw tick beds that were thrown down up there. They all slept up there together. They kept warm. Bass and his wife slept in a room right off the kitchen. There was just one bed in there, I believe.

Bass wasn't an easy father to live with. Those kids had to work. And they had nowhere to go. And, like I said, they didn't wear enough clothes to wash up. They were all out, cuttin' wood, makin' corn, hoeing and plowin' that corn. Taking off bee honey, gatherin' apples and pickin' berries, and canning all that stuff. It took them all summer to can enough stuff to do them the winter, so they was working all the time. They had apple trees, pear trees, and peach trees, and those kids had to get out there and gather all that food in at harvesttime. They made apple butter and jelly and stuff like that to winter them with. And Bass'd go out here and trap turkey, bear, and hog, and cut them up for winter meat and winter lard. He used a big ol' trap he'd made. It looked like a big rabbit box.

Bear grease is used for cooking oil. That's the best cooking oil you ever ate. Anything you fry or cook in it is extremely good, and it won't make you sick. I've seen Bass take a jar of bear grease, about three inches, and just drink it down, just pure bear grease. I've drunk it, too, and it's good for you! Lots of people say, "That old yellow bear grease is nasty." I'd druther have it three to one than I would hog grease. They'd cook those roasts and that bear meat up and it's good. You can sit down there and eat a peck of it, and it won't hurt you one bit.

Bass had English and Cherokee Indian ancestry. Bass tells a story about his granddaddy, I think it was. He swapped a mule and his skinny wife for a great big healthy, strong woman. He was lookin' off down through there, and he saw this big fine stout-looking woman, and he said he wanted her pretty bad. He went off down there to this fellow's house and he said, "Listen, what would you take for that woman?" He said, "Now, I couldn't swap her off. She's a big stout woman, and she does a lot of work." Bass's grandfather had a pretty good mule, a young, big gray mule. He bridled his mule and got his old lady by the arm and went off down there and said, "Listen, I'll swap you the mule and her for your woman." He said that man went out there, looked over the mule real well, looked over the woman pretty good, and said, "I believe you've got a trade on your hands. I'll just take this mule and this woman off your hands." He went in the house and got her and gave her to Bass's grandpaw. His grandpaw took his new wife home and told Bass's daddy, "Every time I look at that man, I get plum sick. Boy, I really beat him. I've got the biggest, finest, stoutest woman you ever saw for that little old skinny woman and that mule down there."

Bass's children went over there in Hanging Dog to school, but it's thirty miles away. He had some kin people over there and the children boarded with them. He'd send them over there and let them stay and go to school. I think they sent them over there in sections. When those girls and those boys got up big enough to get out on their own, they took off. All they'd had to do up there was work—no recreation—and when they were seventeen, eighteen years old, they were gone, and they're not coming back to live. Some of them he hasn't seen for several years. He had one girl who disappeared, and he didn't hear from her for twelve years, never saw her for twelve years. She was about eighteen years old when she left. He finally heard from her about three years ago. She had been in Canada and had married some fellow up there. Bass's wife got to worrying about her so much that he got the FBI to looking for her. The FBI never located her. She just finally showed up one day—just walked up on him. He didn't know she was there until he looked up and there she was.

He has about twenty grandchildren and forty-three great-grandchildren. He's said he'd close the door if he saw them all comin' at one time for a family reunion. He couldn't have them all up there. He'd have the biggest bunch you ever seen. They'd be stringin' in there for the next forty days. They come in and see him for a while and then leave. They ain't goin' to live off up in those mountains because those boys and girls had a hard time up there. They had a hard time to live.

Bass had an old Indian motorcycle that he rode. That was before he got his arm shot off. He would make that liquor and ride that motorcycle on those trails up here, and couldn't nobody catch him. He could outrun anybody on that motorcycle. Did Bass tell you about the way he got his arm shot off? I'll tell you what happened. Now Bass was makin' liquor for this old man down in North Carolina. Him and Bass was makin' liquor together, but he was more or less haulin' it for the man. That's who started Bass in his

PLATE 41 **Playing cards was a favorite pastime at the hunting lodge that Mr. and Mrs. White owned and operated.**

young days to making liquor. Bass was real young then. He was just a big old boy.

Well, he was over here on top of Beaver Dam Bald makin' this liquor, and Bass broke some of the whiskey accidentally. Him and that old man (I'll call him Johnson, but that wasn't his real name) got into it over him breakin' that liquor. Bass had an old mule and a sled, and he used that sled to get the whiskey out from the still, and he'd sell it to some of these timber cutters right up here at the fishin' hatchery. They had a railroad roundtable up there and had a railroad track comin' through here. They cut that timber out of these mountains, drug it off down there, and put it on these cars. That's where Bass and Johnson were sellin' their whiskey at. Old Man Johnson had killed nine men. [In Bass's story he says seven men.] He was fast with his gun, and he was extremely dangerous—extremely dangerous. Well, him and Bass got into it, so Bass quit haulin' his whiskey down there to the loggers. Johnson didn't have a mule, so he had to pull his whiskey down there himself. That made Johnson mad, so he got to talkin' about Bass. Then him and Bass got into it again over *that*.

Bass decided that he'd have it out with Johnson, so he went over to Hanging Dog to the church house. Bass wasn't a religious man, just went over there, I guess. Bass was setting on a rail fence outside the church, and Old Man Johnson came walkin' down the street. Bass called out and said, "I'm the meanest Russian in the mountains," and he had already pulled his pistol out. Old Man Johnson, who was a deadly person—like a coiled rattlesnake—why, his pistol came out so fast, and he shot Bass so fast, shot Bass in the neck here, and shot his hat off, and shot him three or four times in his arm there. As Bass was goin' down off the back of that rail fence, he got one shot in and grazed Old Man Johnson in the leg. The law came over there and arrested Bass, took him to Murphy, and put him in jail. Of course, they had to take his arm off. Gangrene set in, and they didn't take him to the hospital until ten or eleven days after he got shot. And, of course, Bass never did like Johnson from then on. Finally, Johnson died and Bass told me a tale. He said, "Well, that old man finally died. It took seven to hold him in bed, he'd lied and killed so much." I don't know whether that's true or not, but that's what Bass told.

Bass had a still back there in that holler. The revenue officers slip-walked in here and went right up there in that holler behind this place I own now, and Bass had the liquor still back up there. He'd made some liquor and had it down at the spring. He was bottlin' it up in fruit jars, bottlin' it up to sell some. His wife gave him the signal that the revenue officers were comin' up the trail, so he took and broke all his whiskey against some rocks. Well, they came up the holler there and seen what he did. Some of the bottles still had a little whiskey in them, four or five drops maybe, and they poured it all together tryin' to make a case out of it. They arrested him and took him to a nearby town and put him in jail. He made bond, then went back for his trial. Those revenue officers came in there with a whole half gallon of whiskey, which wasn't whiskey he'd made. It was some that they'd planted on him, you see. In other words, they told the court it was his whiskey, and they stuck Bass—framed him—but Bass got away. He dodged the law back in these mountains for about a year, moved his family back up where he's at now just over the Tennessee line in North Carolina. He's been there ever since, right out of the state of Tennessee into North Carolina, on account of them framin' him over here. The revenue officers absolutely framed Bass Dockery.

They never did find his liquor still, so he moved it from here in Tennessee to over there on the North Carolina side. That's when he put these silver dollars down on the trail. And if he came by and he looked down and that silver dollar was gone, he knew somebody was up there at his liquor still, and he'd tie a little thread across the trail, too, and he'd come by, and if the thread was broken, he'd know not to go in to his still. The house Bass lives in now has just been built lately. The old log house was torn down. It didn't have no windows atall—just logs and a shutter or two on it. That's about all. He wanted his new house to have lots of glass walls and windows because he was gettin' old, and that way, he could see everybody that moved. He didn't want anybody sneakin' up on him, so he put glass all over the doggone place. Bass Dockery's always carried several thousand dollars on his person, all the time, and he didn't want an outlaw to slip around up there and whack him on the head or shoot 'im before he saw them, so he sees everybody that moves up there. He's got a .357 Magnum he keeps right there by him all the time—plays it around, you know, and tells everybody he's got it.

He's just started travelin' in the last few years. Listen, I couldn't get him out of here to go forty miles to anywhere a few years ago. He's just started doin' that. I'll tell you something else he wouldn't do. I'd take him out down to Athens, Tennessee, or somewhere. He wouldn't drink the water out of those spigots, city water. He wouldn't drink the water or any kind of soft drink. He wouldn't even eat anything. He said that water would kill you down there, and it wasn't fit to drink, and that stuff they fed you in those restaurants wasn't fit to eat and it was liable to kill you. He said, "They've got everything in the world in it tryin' to preserve it. I'll wait till I get home to get me some water. That stuff you're drinkin' out of—them old cola bottles and things like that—is poison. You put a piece of fat meat in that bottle, and it'll eat it up, so what do you think it'll do to your stomach?" So he'd come all the way back home and cut him up a strip of meat and fry it, and eat that and get him a drink of water.

He's not wrong, and I mean, he said that several years ago before they proved all that stuff. He's a smart man. The more I've thought back about what he told me and what they've found out about what we eat and drink, and about how some of it will kill you, the more I know that he was smarter than they were, 'cause he knew that years before they did.

Bass likes to say he was the meanest man around. And Bass was mean. You asked why he's called "the Wild Russian." A wild Russian hog is the meanest thing, I guess, you could ever come in contact with. He'll slip up on you, gore you, and bite you. He'll do *anything* to you, and it's hard to kill him. You can put a pack of dogs on a wild hog, and if they're not real good, extra good dogs, he'll kill all of them and then get away. A Russian can run for miles before you can kill him. He can tear you up, and he'll eat anything, even spring lizards, so that's why they named Bass "the Wild Russian." He lived off the land, and he was tough, and he done real well. And he could be just as mean as any old Russian hog, too—just as ornery and mean! He's mellowed a whole lot now. I'll tell you what he would do to people he didn't like [when he was young]. He'd see them goin' to church, and if they went with a girlfriend, he'd start shootin' at them with his pistol, and shootin' the ground all up around them and runnin' them off, runnin' them back. He'd do things like that, Bass would. Now, that was before he lost that arm, but he learned to use that stump pretty well, and he got a little mean again, but Bass Dockery is a very unusual person, and he's a self-made man, and he's smart. He's got more honor than most people you know. Bass Dockery is truthful, and he's honest. He wouldn't steal a dime off nobody. He wouldn't take a dime unless he had done something for it. He never bribed anybody. He wouldn't give anybody a quarter to leave him alone. That's just his way, you see. He's not a mean man, not a vicious man. Bass Dockery is a tough man, but he's not a mean, tough man. He just means what he says. He doesn't mean for you to run over him, and he doesn't intend to run over you. He's one of a kind, a self-made man. He's an unusual person because he has survived the way he has for the past eighty years.

"Oh, Lord, if you won't help me, don't help them."

~ The legend of the Moccasin gang ~

I have lived in the Satolah community in Rabun County almost all of my life. As a little girl I had heard stories about the untamed Billingsley brothers and the trouble they caused in the Moccasin gang war. When Brandie Rushing and I started this article, authentic accounts were hard to find. Relying on old newspapers and history books, we located enough documented information to piece the jigsaw together.

—Mandy Owens

The Moccasin gang war took place near the town of Highlands, North Carolina, in 1885, and alcohol caused it. Liquor and "spirituous fruit juice" were considered by society to be among the greatest and most appalling evils of the time. One 1885 newspaper, *The Keowee Courier*, of Oconee County, wrote in regard to liquor and the like, "I tell you, all strong drink is crooked, crooked cognac, crooked schnapps, crooked beer, crooked wine, crooked whiskey because it makes a man's path crooked, and his life crooked, and his death crooked, and his eternity crooked."

Liquor was believed to possess the power to destroy a man's country, as well as his life. Obviously, the problem of drunkenness was taken very seriously by society, and when the problem came to Highlands, Highlanders took matters into their own hands. Thus began the Moccasin gang war.

Highlands was a quiet, pretty town located in the western mountains of North Carolina. The beauty and tranquillity of the area were jeopardized

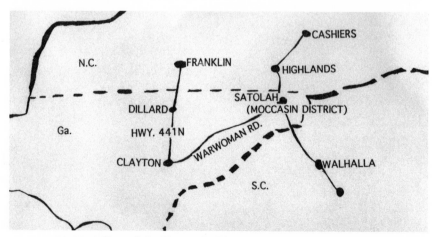

PLATE 42 **Map of the Moccasin District and surrounding areas**

when men and women from surrounding states came into neighboring communities, such as the Moccasin District, near present-day Satolah, to bring their "evil ways" to the law-abiding people of the town.

These newcomers established distilleries in the woods around Highlands, much to the disapproval of the townspeople. During their free time, these Moccasin dwellers rode through the town with their rifles in hand like cowboys, looking for trouble and creating chaos everywhere they went. When these "evildoers" from Moccasin began to bring liquor and moonshine into Highlands, a town strongly opposed to such things, the townspeople decided that it was the last straw. The beliefs and ethics of the town were being jeopardized, so they tried to shut down the distilleries and made it clear that anyone selling or bringing such evils into town would be arrested.

The threat was not really taken seriously until the spring of 1885, when revenue officers captured a moonshiner from Moccasin who was a friend to the Billingsley brothers. They brought the man back to Highlands and planned to stay at the Smith Hotel until they could transfer him to the state prison. While the moonshiner was there, one of the Billingsley brothers tried to free him but was arrested in the attempt. He, too, was held in the Smith Hotel.

A rescue party of eighteen was formed by friends and family of the Billingsley man. The infamous Billingsley brothers, nicknamed the Moccasin gang for the trouble they had caused in town, were included in the party. They declared war on the once-quiet town of Highlands.

This war lasted three long days. During those days, every animal or human that stirred was in danger, for any sign of movement was followed by a shower of gunshots from both sides. The nights were filled with dread of

PLATE 43 **The Smith Hotel, currently the Highlands Inn**

the day that would follow, as trigger-happy gunmen kept their weapons on hand and waited impatiently for daylight. Although the shooting continued, no one was shot or killed until the third day.

On that day, Highlander Tom Ford took a ladder and climbed to the roof of the Smith Hotel. He pointed his gun at the Georgia men and hoped he could hit one before they had a chance to kill him. His finger closed tightly over the trigger, and the bullet flew from the gun, killing a man from the rescue party. Before the rescue party had time to react, Ford began to fire again, wounding two of the other men.

The Georgia men didn't retaliate then. Instead, they retreated from Highlands to bury their dead, but Highlands had no cause to celebrate: The Moccasin gang knew that food and supplies had to be brought into town along the main Georgia road that ran through the Moccasin community. The gang intended to use this road to prevent such goods from reaching Highlands.

The Billingsley brothers sent a letter to the mayor explaining that they were planning to blockade the road from Walhalla, South Carolina, into Highlands and that any man attempting to pass into or out of town would be killed. The mayor took the threat very seriously. No one from town dared challenge the Billingsley brothers, so Highlands commissioned a Confederate War blockade runner, Joe Lovin, to infiltrate the blockade. He was "as brave a man that ever walked the Earth." He mounted his horse and started on the road to Moccasin. After riding awhile, he came upon an odd sight: The Billingsley brothers were walking single file toward him.

His heart leaped into his throat as he looked into their eyes, but he held fast. He grasped the reins of his horse in one hand and searched his mind for the appropriate prayer, but only one came to mind: "Oh, Lord, let us be grateful for what we are about to receive." Then, with his free hand, he reached for his gun and said, "Oh, Lord, if you won't help me, don't help them, and I'll shoot the d—— Yankees like I used to durin' the war!" The old man didn't know if it was the prayer or the threat that saved him that day. Joe Lovin passed by the Billingsleys' watchful eyes, waiting for an attack that never came. They let him pass by unharmed. That gesture ended the blockade, as well as what is known locally as the Moccasin gang war.

Sources

The Keowee Courier, 1885.

McIntosh, Gert. *Highlands, North Carolina . . . a Walk into the Past.* Birmingham, Alabama: Southern University Press at the Presses of Birmingham, 1990.

Rabun County Heritage Book Committee. *Rabun County and Its People.* Clayton, Georgia. Walsworth Publishing, 1992.

A Legacy Lives On
~Sam McMahan on the loss of the Woodards~

I knew Diane and Duane Woodard before they were married. Diane and I attended school together at Rabun County High. She was a sweet girl with a wonderful personality and very active in school. My father, Rev. Jesse Edmonds, was the pastor of Taylor's Chapel Baptist Church in Mountain City, Georgia. I remember him having Duane, a young minister, come to preach for us at our little church. Daddy also took us to a tent revival where Duane was holding services in Mountain City. Through the years I have often thought of Diane and Duane and was saddened by the memories of lives ending way too soon.

The Woodards' son Kevin shared these memories with me: He remembered hearing his grandparents talk about Diane wanting to marry Duane when she was fourteen years old. Her daddy refused to sign for permission for them to get married, and she cried for days until he finally gave in. Kevin told us that after this tragic event, his grandfather had mentioned on different occasions that he was glad he had gone ahead and signed for the marriage because it gave them more years together and allowed them to have their family. Kevin also told me that the murder of his parents is what influenced him to pursue a career in law enforcement. Although these tragic events took the mother and father of three wonderful children, and the son and daughter of two loving families, the legacy of Victory Baptist Church and Christian School lives on. The church attendance is unbelievable for such a small community, and parents send their children all the way from here in Rabun County, Georgia, to Dillsboro, North Carolina, approximately fifty miles, to attend and graduate from Victory Christian School.

—Joyce Green

Duane Woodard, a young minister, founded Victory Baptist Church and Victory Christian School in Dillsboro, North Carolina, in 1967. He was their first pastor and school principal. I started attending the little Christian school when I was in the second grade.

Duane's wife's name was Diane Carnes Woodard, and she was originally from Tiger, Georgia. Diane's parents were Boyce and Dorothy Carnes. Boyce worked for years for the city of Clayton. He played the guitar and did a lot of bluegrass stuff. For many years he played and performed with the Black Rock Quartet.

Duane and Diane were murdered during my senior year at Victory Christian School. Duane and Diane had three boys, Arnold, Kevin, and Shane. Kevin and Shane both graduated from Rabun County High School.

PLATE 44 **Victory Baptist Church, founded by Duane Woodard.
Victory Christian School is located just to the left of the church.**

Arnold returned to Victory Christian School during his junior year and graduated from the school his father had founded. Arnold is the oldest and Shane is the youngest. On January 9, 1981, Diane and Duane had taken two of the boys up to Duane's daddy's to spend the night. They had Shane with them, and they went down to the church. There was a man, Herman Franks, that was mentally challenged, who had got saved there. The best way to explain it is, I think that he was wanting to be pastor there and he thought, I guess, if he could get rid of Duane, he could be the next pastor. He told Duane he was called to preach. He tried to go to Bible college, and he wudn't able to do the work, so he came back and he started there at the church. He got it in his mind that if he killed Duane, that he would be the next pastor.

When Duane and Diane were leaving, Mr. Franks rammed into their car and knocked it up against the bank. Then he jumped out and stabbed Duane and Diane but never hurt Shane. Once he had killed them, I think realization set in, and he got in his car, shot and killed himself. It had been snowing, and there was about two inches of snow on the ground. The Woodards' car was still running, and Shane crawled up under the car. He layed under the car all night, and it run out of gas. When they found him he was still under the car, and the side of his face was real bad frostbit, but he recovered.

Our house was located right above the church, so we could see all the commotion that was going on after the murders. It was a sad time. That killing almost closed the church down when it happened. It got down to about twenty people attending. Now there's almost four hundred attending every Sunday. We are in the process of building a new church because we have outgrown the little church.

Diane was born February 23, 1954, and Duane was born October 27, 1946. Diane was about one month shy of her twenty-seventh birthday and Duane was thirty-five when they lost their lives. Diane's mama and daddy took the boys and raised them. Arnold has a beautiful voice and is a talented singer. He is going into the mission field. Kevin became a law enforcement officer. Shane, who was about two years old at the time, is in the construction business.

PLATE 45 **Family portrait of the Woodards:**
Duane (back), Arnold, Diane, Kevin, and baby Shane

Barbara Allen

In Scarlet town where I was born, there was a fair maid dwelling,
And many a lad cried well a day, for the love of Barbara Allen.

Twas in the merry month of May, when spring buds were a-swelling,
Sweet William on his deathbed lay, for the love of Barbara Allen.

He sent his servant unto her, and down where she was a-dwelling,
Saying you must come to my master dear, if your name be Barbara Allen.

Slowly, slowly she got up, and slowly she came nigh him,
And the only words to him she said, young man I think you're dying.
Well he turned his face unto the wall, and death was with him a-dealin',
He said farewell my comrades all, be kind to Barbara Allen.

Oh mother, mother, make my bed, make it long and narrow,
Sweet William died for me today, I'll die for him tomorrow.

Sweet William was buried in the old churchyard, Barbara Allen in the choir,
And from his breast there grew a rose, and out of hers, a briar.

They grew and grew, to the old church top, till they could grow no higher,
And there they twined in a true lover's knot,* for all true lovers to admire.

Tales and Legends
Place Names, Ghosts, and More

*See page 434 for instructions for tying a true lover's knot.

Barbara Allen
Tales and Legends

The fireplace, built from rocks gathered from a nearby stream and held together with just the red clay mud from the hills, served as the place for families in the mountains to bond and share the events of the day. Bibles were read by light from kerosene lamps, prayers were prayed, and many legends and stories, both true and imagined, were shared as families huddled around the glowing red embers that at times could be deceitfully hidden by the gray ash surrounding the bed of coals. Sometimes smoke would fill the room from winds that drifted down the open chimney. The smell of kerosene from the burning lamp permeated the air of the humble dwelling. It was often difficult to fall asleep after hearing the many tales of "haints," ghosts, and witches.

Just as the ghost of Grace Brock has evolved through the years, so have other legends and tales. Many of the legends have been recorded as songs. There are at least ninety-two versions of the tragic love ballad "Barbara Allen." The version I remember, the one opening this section, was recorded by the original Carter Family.

As you read these stories—some legend, some true—shared by some of our contacts, light an old oil lamp, gather around the fireplace, and get ready to hear strange noises during a sleepless night.

—Joyce Green

"This happened on a cold, windy winter night."

~Family ghost stories from Melissa Rogers~

This happened on a cold, windy winter night, where a brother of mine was walking down a road at Hiawassee, Georgia. He had been to visit a girlfriend that night. He had a great big old German shepherd dog with him ever'where he went, and that dog would fight for him and do anything he told him to. He didn't have to speak to him but one time.

He stayed with his girlfriend till about midnight that night, and then he had about two miles to go down the road and up through and around the cemetery. About a half mile before he got to the cemetery, he heard something coming behind him—the ground was froze, and it was real cold and the wind a-blowing—and he could hear its hooves a-cracking, and he said he was afraid to look back. After a while it got closer and closer to him, and he turned around to look back, and he saw this sheep a-coming as plain, and he told his dog to go get it, and his dog only got closer and closer to him till he rubbed up ag'in his leg. He said that sheep come right on down to the side of him and went on down the road out of sight, but he could still hear its feet a-ploppin' on the cold ground—just a regular-looking sheep, only it just didn't have no head!

My mother and daddy, at one time, lived in a house that was said to be haunted. People said that they had been some people that lived back several years before then that had killed a man there. They was two men and a woman killed this man there, and they cut his head off. And after they cut his head off, why, the woman kicked it over across the floor. They was some big ol' shoals off below the end of the farm, and they took 'im and put 'im over there in the big shoals where the water flowed off.

And they was a woman that her husband killed her in this house, and they said that he killed her because she couldn't have any children for 'im. They said that he abused her, and she died within a little while. He married this other woman, and they had about five boys and two girls, and they both lived to be real old. Well, anyway, this happened to my brother one night when he and my mother and my daddy lived in that old house. All the other children was married off, and he was the only son still living at home. The house didn't have no inside bathroom, so he had to go outdoors to the bathroom, and it was real cold that night. There was a big, long porch come all the way across the house, and when my brother got up and went to the door, he seen this woman sittin' on the banister of the porch, and he thought it was Mommy. So he went back into the house in a few minutes and stood at the door for a while, and directly Mommy called him from the bed and said, "H.P., what are you doin' up?"

He said, "Mommy, are you in the bed?" And she said, "Yeah." Said, "What's the matter?" He said, "Well, I thought that was you a-sittin' out there on the banister." Said, "There's this woman sittin' out there where you've got that quilt spread across the banisters." And she said, "No, I've not been out." And she got up and they both went out on the porch, and it wadn't there anymore. He said it looked just like Momma sittin' there with her apron on. The moon was kindly shining, and he couldn't tell how she was dressed, but . . .

And another time, when they didn't anybody live in the house, there was some men a-comin' up the road from way down on a place they called Persimmon. They was a-ridin' around this little crooked road, and it was gettin' just nearly dusky dark, and they seen a woman a-sittin' out there on the fence. They said when they got up close to her, why she got up and went towards the house. She had on a black dress trimmed in pink, and she sit down on the porch, and they rode on by and she was still sittin' on the porch, but they wadn't nobody lived there and hadn't been in a pretty good long time.

"Our cemetery is haunted. Did you know it?"

~Louise Tabor relates a tale for Halloween~

This story was told at Halloween. It could have been fiction, or it could have been true. A lot of tales had been told of a big man, with a hook on one side instead of an arm, who scared young people parked on a mountain called Lover's Leap. One or two had been killed. One night a couple was parked up there. All at once the girl screamed and said, "Get me away from here!" The boy didn't stop to ask questions but started the motor and zoomed away. When they reached the girl's home, she got out of the car and looked at the door. There was a hook grasping the latch that opened the door, and the door was scratched.

A woman told me this. She was part Indian and lived on the reservation when she was first married. She lived near an old Indian burial ground, and people told her that it was dangerous to live there. They assured her that spirits lived there. She was young and unafraid, and one night she sat up until late and her husband was already asleep. She was nervous for some reason and put off going to bed. She watched the moon come up. Finally, she decided to go to bed, and when she undressed and got into bed, she was careful not to awaken her husband. She laid down on the edge of the bed on her back, and when her eyes became accustomed to the darkness, she looked around the room and the moonlight made it bright. Out of the corner of her eye she glimpsed movement and turned her head and saw a man standing beside her with an arm upraised, and in his hand was a large knife that glittered in the moonlight. The scream she loosed raised her husband from the bed. As he was levitated, he grabbed her by the arm and dragged her out of the house. There was no sign of the man in the house, but they would not go back in there. They went and stayed with some of the family, and the next day when the sun was shining, the man went back and loaded the household goods on a borrowed wagon and moved them away from there.

My aunt Ellie lived in a house that was supposed to be haunted. By what, they knew not, because they had heard nothing. One night all the family went to church, except Aunt Ellie. She didn't feel like going. She was sitting in the living room, sewing, and she heard a noise on the stairs. "Now, that's probably the ghost," she thought. She wasn't afraid, but when the noise continued she became interested. It was a drag, and then a bump that sounded like someone on crutches. As it drew nearer the bottom of the stairs, Aunt Ellie grew more unsure of her courage. She couldn't just sit there. The thing would be in there with her in a minute or two. She jumped up, and, carrying a lamp, she hurried to the bottom of the stairs. There she saw a great rat dragging an ear of popcorn down the stairs. It wasn't told whether she was afraid of rats or not!

My grandpa told us one time about a cemetery just up the hill above their house where all of our relatives are buried. There was a path through the cemetery that was used as a shortcut to the house below. Grandpa said, "Our cemetery is haunted. Did you know it?" He continued, "You know when cousin Jed died? Well, the grave had been dug and left open that evening. Just about dark, a storm cloud came up, and I carried a load of board over there to cover it and keep the rain out. When I had the shelter set up, it began to rain, hard. I stepped down in the grave to keep dry. I heard somebody coming down the path lickety-split. I knew it was Wash Gibbey, on his way home. I stuck my head up out of the grave and said, 'Come in out of the rain, Wash.' I've never heard a man run as fast in my life! When Wash reached home he knocked the door down and was unable to talk for the longest time. Now he has been telling everyone that dead people up there called to him to *come in!*"

Mrs. Tabor wrote a book titled What Tales Are These? *that contains many of the ghost stories she heard growing up. These stories have been told as true and are all said to have happened in the Appalachian region. Here is an example*:

Did you ever see a ghost? Oh, yeah! I saw one. I was hurrying along a trail I had traveled a thousand times. The moon was almost down, and there before me was this big white thing. It looked like a woman in a wedding dress.

I said, "Howdy do," and it just stood there. I said it again a time or two, and it said nothing. Finally, I said, "If you don't speak, I'm gonna run right through you." It stood there! I took a long run and go and landed in a big Spanish needle bush. It had grown to that size since I was last on that trail. It had been covered with needles, and it took me a week to get them all out of my clothes.

PLATE 46 **"Did you ever see a ghost? Oh, yeah! I saw one." Louise Tabor**

"If you believe in spirits at all, like I do . . ."
~Bob Justus talks about the "little people"~

I got to looking, and you know, this theme of the "little people" is worldwide. Now, almost every culture and every age, they believed in little people. Isn't that strange? They call them fairies or elves or banshees. The Cherokees believed in them, and I've got a bunch of stuff down here on Indian culture; some of my relatives, like me, are part Cherokee. I've got a lot of information from them, and so, everywhere, all these tribes had a belief in little people. I don't know about you, but I've lived a lot in the woods. I love the woods and streams. I've met this little lady talking about little people, and here's what I wrote:

In the Days When Mighty Falls
In the days when mighty falls
Roared downward into Tallulah Gorge
Little people in granite halls
Wrought works of art with blazing forge.

In rock castles under the mount
They lived and loved thru the ages,
With tunnels and caves beyond count
In the gorge where the flow rages.

Rare would men of the outer world
Ever get to see the little folks
Who lurked by pools where water swirled,
Wearing nigh invisible cloaks.

The Indians knew and felt great fear
When the sounds of hammers rang out
From the deep caverns far and near,
And oft was heard a distant shout.

A dam was built across the flow
And the roaring falls grew mute,
Then the little folks had to go
Taking their hammer and flute.

They say when the river flows
Freely thru the roaring gorge
Once more will sound the hammer blows
And bright will glow the hot forge.

Will the flow roar in the new park
And the little folk live again
Like dancing shadows in the dark
And voices singing in the wind?

When the settlers first came into this part of the country, they heard these tales about little people from the Indians. The little people lived in the gorge, and they were afraid of them. They were suspicious, and so there were no Indian villages right on the gorge. There was one slightly north of there in Rabun County, Georgia.

Talking about the Indians and their belief in little people in the gorge, they believed in these little people, not just in the gorge, but that there were different types of little people. One type lived up in the hills of the Blue Ridge Mountains; then there were these that lived in the gorge, and they had caves hewed out under the falls. You know, it's a lot like the stories I've read about the trolls from Europe that dug caverns, mines under the mountains. So when settlers came to America, they heard the same stories about little people. I wonder sometimes if people, no matter what race or background they come from, handed down stories, whether there were little people at one time. It's often been discussed. Maybe the great flood that the Bible talks about killed them off, but they claim they have not found bones that prove there were such little people; anyway, I imagined what it was like when the first settlers got to the falls, and this is what I wrote:

We can only speculate of untold years when Indians stood on high
ledges and viewed with awe the raging river below and whispered
stories to their children of the little people who lived in great caves
under the falls.

Now, this is a legend I have heard about the gorge. When the first settlers, in the early 1800s, came to the falls, the Cherokees told them one of their oldest legends. There was a race of little people who lived all about in that region, but especially had their homes in the nooks and crannies of the great gorge overlooking the falls. Many, many moons ago a party of Cherokee hunters happened into that region and were never heard from again. A group of medicine men went to look for them and found a great fissure in the earth inhabited by a race of little people, who dwelt in the crevices of the rocks under the waterfalls. In trying to hold a conference with these little people, the medicine men found them shrieking and making menacing motions. Sensing that these little people were enemies, the Cherokees thereafter kept away from the falls as much as possible. According to another version of the legend of the little people, which was heard as early as 1819, there was a cave in the side of the precipice to which a marauding tribe of little people retreated and disappeared when they stole Cherokee women and children.

Cherokees feared the place. A few years later this Indian tradition was heard by white men and recorded, so this is actually passed on from the mouth of the Indians, dealing with the same rock house or cave. Its entrance was the door to the "happy hunting ground," for Indians who entered there never returned. Therefore, the Indians never hunted again in that vicinity, and they noted that the eagles raised their young in that cave.

The Indians are not the only ones that have built up legends about Tallulah Falls, Georgia, 'cause the white man came along and let his imagination play upon it, too. So when the white settlers first came into the Tallulah River country, a man and his children, working in the fields, were murdered by a party of Indians from the west, who were fighting the Cherokees. The widow, who escaped, bided her time for revenge. Years later these same hostile Indians came looking for the Cherokees. Under the pretense of showing them the way, she led them unsuspecting over a cliff into the raging waters of Tallulah Falls, and as the last one disappeared, she threw up her hands and with a shriek of fiendish laughter exclaimed, "It's finished; I have my revenge," sprang over the fearful ledge, and followed her victims.

Years ago, when Billy Long and I camped and explored the gorge, we explored the whole thing, from the bridge all the way down to the lake. Now, listen, at night you better be prepared 'cause we heard sounds like rolling bowling balls echoing. It reminded me of the story "Rip Van Winkle."

During the night rocks would fall, I mean really fall, and strange sounds came out of that river, like a knocking noise or almost like bells. I was out in this river, and I said to these two guys, the Reed brothers, "Do you hear voices down here?" One brother said, "No, are you nuts or something?" I said, "Well you just listen. You'll hear whispers and echoes and bells and all kinds of things." After a while he came back and said, "I wish you hadn't told me that; I began to hear those voices!" It was funny!

At times in the night, Billy Long and I would hear rumbling sounds like stones rolling in potholes in the riverbed. Sometimes stones, loosened on the heights above, fell into the gorge. See, they heat in the day, then when night comes, they cool off and it loosens those stones. That's why there's rocks as big as cars down there, that came off the cliffs. Even these little stones will hurt you or even kill you. So if you ever stay down there, stay away from the edge of the cliff. Anyway, we went on down . . . I can imagine the Indians hearing things like we experienced, like those rocks being thrown at us, or that rumbling that's kind of strange. Where did that echo or rumble come from? What caused it? It did sound like something in caves. No wonder the Indians felt this way.

The Cherokees were greatly impressed, if not frightened, by the falls, and they readily developed their myths about this gigantic display of nature, leading them rarely to hunt or fish there. One of their myths clothed the falls in a sort of mystic, supernatural atmosphere with a Rip Van Winkle tinge. It seems that once upon a time, two beautiful Indian maidens mysteriously appeared at a Cherokee dance in a town near the head of the Chattahoochee River. Dancing until the morning sun, they had greatly infatuated one of the young warriors. They promised to come back seven days later, and when they returned to their home, he accompanied them. On the journey, he passed through several supernatural adventures in which water and grass was confused as one being the other. They finally arrived at a cave in the high gorge towering over the Tallulah Falls. There certain mysterious formalities and rituals took place in which turtles, snakes, and a brother to the two Indian maidens played a part. The warrior showed great fear, whereupon the maidens' brother, staring at him, warned him never to talk about this experience and called him a coward. Then it was as if lightning flashed from his eyes and struck the young man, and a terrible clash of thunder stretched him senseless. When at last he came to himself again, he was standing with his feet in the water and both hands grasping a laurel bush that grew out from the bank. There was no trace of the cave or the "thunder people," but he was alone in the forest. He made his way out and finally reached his own settlement but found that he had been gone so long that people thought him dead, although to him it seemed only the day after the dance. His friends questioned him closely and forgetting the warning, he told the story; so in seven days he dies, for none can come back from the underworld and tell it and live.

I'll tell you someone who told me about the little folks was Ronald Vandiver. I used to sit with him; I would go to his home, and he would tell about it. They lived in granite halls; these little people lived in granite halls, and they had forges. They were miners. They had apparently magic powers; for instance, very few people could see them. Now, I don't know about you, but I've been in certain special places, and I feel almost a chill come over me in places, and I'll see movement out of the corner of my eye, and I'll look and there's nothing there. And these voices, it's amazing! I've heard voices and I look around; I'm not kidding you about this, but, at night, I don't know about you, but I've had someone say, "Bob . . . " and I'd wake up and look around and of course no one is there.

I'm a student of the Bible. I love the Bible. Some stories about the little people come from the angels, and angels I firmly believe work all around us; I really do. The Bible says that they'll appear in the form of a person, and I've had some strange encounters with certain people at certain times. Like when I was nearly killed in Vietnam and I was saved, if it wasn't an angel that was working through them, I don't know what it was. But here's the thing, going back to the little people. Rarely would men of the outer world, that's us, our world, ever get to see the little folks. One reason for that it is told, you see, they really live basically in a world within our world; it's co-joining with our world. I've never heard of the little people having anything to do with the big people. They did everything they could to avoid them. They had the ability, I think, to jump from this world to another.

PLATE 47 **"I believe in reality, but I also believe in the spirit world."**
Bob Justus sharing some of the stories he has written

I was up in Cherokee, North Carolina, and I was talking to the head of the Cherokee museum, and we got to talking about the Cherokees. To them, spirits were everywhere. We talked about how they lived in certain places like where two streams met, and why they did certain things like they did, and why even though they killed game, like I have, they would always give thanks to the Great Spirit. Always had the spirits in their mind and, to me, I think—and this is just my takeoff on this—but sometimes where people get the idea of little people, I think they can be sincere 'cause I've felt strange things. Anyway, I believe that these spirits are real, too; one thing is the angels, and there are also evil spirits.

If you believe in spirits at all, like I do, the Bible talks about that, although I don't think that spirits can really bother you. I believe you've got safeguards, not letting evil spirits bother you, 'cause the Bible gives you safeguards. I was going to tell you about what I saw: I was coming back from this hunt all by myself one day down along the creek. There was swamps and I'd stayed all day down there. Late in the evening, the sun is about to sink down, and I'm walking into the site of this old house there. There's a porch and I'm on the old road that went around the front of the house. Coming out of the woods there, I noticed there was a bluish haze and the sun was focusing in there slanting down, and I thought, "That looks like blue smoke." I looked; I got my first view of the house as I turned the corner. I shouldn't tell this [laughs], but just for an instance there, there was two rocking chairs sitting on that porch. There was an old man sitting in one, and an old woman sitting in the other, side by side. There was a young fellow like a teenager, and a girl standing beside them. I had that vision, or whatever, of that young man leaning over the old man's shoulder and pointing right at me and like that [snaps his fingers], all that I saw was a pile of stove wood! That's not the only time I thought I saw a vision.

I was in Truett-McConnell College; I must have done something bad or something. I don't remember what, but I was laying in my bed, and I was dozing off. Anyway, I remember opening my eyes and there over my head was a hand, stretched out right over my head! Just a hand. I'm glad it wasn't a fist! I don't know whether it's a blessing or a curse, but the hand was right over my head and, snap, it went out!

Now here's one: When Dad died, you know, he was the outdoor type, farmer, hunter, and all that. Well, you know, Mother had already died, and that was probably the worst experience of my life up until that time because me and her were [crosses his fingers together] not just mother and son, we were friends. But, anyhow, I was asleep here, upstairs and in my sleep, I don't know which came first, but I could smell the barnyard. If you ever worked around the barn, it smelled like manure or milk or whatever. And when Dad would come back from milking the cows, that's the way he'd smell. I could just hear voices like it was regular voices, "Don't worry; I'm all right." Funny thing, not long after that my daughter Amy said, "I had a dream about your dad, my grandfather, and it was a good dream!" So, you know, there's just things that hang with you.

I'm not really superstitious. I really am not! I believe in reality, but I also believe in the spirit world. Nanny Dickerson believed in what people would call magic. She had a remarkable affinity with the Cherokee beliefs. She had a lot of their medicines. She said she had no one to pass it on to. I said, "Can't someone learn it from her?" She said, "No. It had to be someone with the right spirit."

Nanny talked about the little people. She believed, too, that strange fires would be seen, especially along streams or swamps. She never really put a name to it. She told us kids stories that made chills run down you! Some of it was devil fire, probably. The devil was up to no good, especially in the swamps.

I shouldn't tell this story, but a few years ago, maybe ten years ago, we had a longtime hunting club near Thompson, Georgia. Daddy had got the family started in it to keep us together. He was dead by then. Anyway, I had been hunting in along the creek, and I was all by myself. We had this old house—two-story house—out in the woods. It had been an old farmhouse, and they say a man was murdered in it. I do know it was full of rats and snakes back when we cleaned it out; we killed a couple of copperheads inside the house. One night, I was sleeping in a room and the steps came down from upstairs and came out in that room I was in. I was in a room by myself. Well, that night I hear a knock, knock, knock, and it was coming down those steps. I thought, I'll just lay here, and when it got to the bottom steps, it quit. So I tried to go back to sleep; maybe I dozed off. Here it come again! This time I got my flashlight; when it got near the bottom steps, I shined my light and there wasn't anything there! Here's the clincher to this thing: The next morning I mentioned it and my brother, Dickie, he was sleeping in the room opposite of those stairs. He said, "You know, I heard that, too!" I never found out what it was. I heard it, but I didn't see it. To this day I don't know what caused that!

The Legend of the Deer and the Witch
~ Lillie Billingsley's "tale that my daddy told me" ~

There is this other tale I can tell you about Scaly. This is a tale that my daddy told me. He told me that there was an old lady who lived not too long a-ways from us. Daddy said she was a witch, and my daddy said that she would turn herself into a deer. As the men went by to work, she'd see them coming, and she'd turn herself into a deer. And she'd be that deer coming around that field pickin' along like a deer would, you know. So they got the guns, and they was going to shoot that deer. They went to work that morning, and she turned herself into a deer because she was a witch. I don't know anything about witches. They shot about three shots, and when they got back home, Dad said that they talked about it. One of them said, "Now, I'll tell you how we can do this. If it's a deer, we'll get it this way. We'll put some good stuff in the gun, and we'll get that old deer tomorrow." And the next morning they did, and they went on to work. That next evening as they come back from work, they went by that old lady's house. They went in and knocked on the door, and nobody come. They went on in, and she was lying in the fire. She fell in her fire and burned up. So when they shot the deer, they had killed her, too.

"You may not believe this, but they say . . ."

~Numerous Rabun legends from several people~

Legends are recurring stories told to be true. They begin, probably, as personal-experience narratives or anecdotes about people known to the teller. As they spread from the source, they take on the character of a legend. Sometimes the truth is stretched, but the stretch is not emphasized. For a legend to survive, it must be interesting, memorable, and believable. Printing legends can be touchy business. Some people are offended that we refer to their true story as a legend; others are skeptical of anything less than documented fact. Believe them or not, legends are important. They educate us, they entertain us, they validate our culture, and they contribute to our sense of community.

These legends are perhaps the most intriguing of all the narratives we have collected. There are many people who believe them even though they defy the laws of physical science, but the laws of science never bind legends. They instead are bound only by human imagination and human need. It is satisfying to believe that the unexplainable might be possible.

—*Julie Roane and George Reynolds*

Light in the Cemetery

Lynn Phillips told us, "My grandmother Allah Ramey told this legend to me about when she was a girl. Grandma Rhodes is my great-great-grandmother, Allah's grandmother. To get from Grandma Rhodes's house to Tom Roane's place you had to go past the cemetery where the floating lights was. Garnet Williams was a friend of Grandma and Grandpa Rhodes."

I's just spending the night at Grandma Rhodes's. Whenever Garnet Williams come up to see us one night and whenever he got ready to leave, I don't know, I guess he's afraid that he would see that light. So we stood on the porch, and Grandpa went to bed. Garnet went out towards the cemetery. Grandpa said, "Now, if y'all want to see that light in the cemetery, it's out there." And we went out on the porch just to look. He came to that branch that turns up to Maude Fisher's and right there it [the light] went up. It was just as bright as any car light you've ever seen. You could see the shadow of the leaves all up and down the porch. Garnet, he's scared to death, but he knowed he had to go home. So Grandma Rhodes said, "Garnet, why if you see anything, why, holler when you get out there." Garnet said that he would. He got down nearly to the cemetery and said, "I don't see nothing, Mrs. Rhodes," and we just went back in the house. And boy, when that happened, the light come down the bank on Garnet, and boy, he just run till he got home, and he run again' the door.

Mrs. Williams said, "What'n the world's the matter?" She said he just run out o' breath.

But it won't cross through water, though; it won't cross the branch. It just went as far as Tom Roane's. Mama lived there for years and she never did see it, but Gertrude did. It was a big light and there was a little one behind it. One night Virge Burton had blood poison, and they sent the Fisher boys down that road. That light got after them, and they come back to Grandma Rhodes's to call the doctor. They saw it as they went on, but they never saw it no more. Oh, they say a bunch of people seen that light. Papa said it was a mineral light. But it looked scary.

One night, Ernest was a-comin' to Grandma Rhodes's to get his hair cut. He's gonna ride down there and put his horse in a stable and stay till the next morning and go on back home. When he come over the top of the hill at Tom Rich's, why he seen that light coming out of the cemetery. He thought it was the Greens fox huntin'. So he got up there even with the cemetery, and that mare started jumpin' up and down and wouldn't go no further. Ernest turned and went back down to Tom Rich's to get Fred Henry to come back with him. Ernest had nothing to drink or nothin', but they never seen it as they come back. Papa said it was some kind of mineral in the ground and when it got damp, why, it looked like a light.

PLATE 48 **Abandoned homesites are fertile ground for the growth of spooky tales.**

The Witch's Grave

A student in our school told the folklore class about the witch's grave.

Where Lake Burton is now, there used to be the town of Burton, and to build the lake they had to move the whole town. There was churches and graveyards and things, so they had to dig up the graveyards and move all of the bodies to another graveyard. Redo 'em, you know, re-dig 'em. And a lot of people who knew people there, that were buried there, had kinfolks there, really protested. And they left some of the graves—it was a family graveyard plot, you know, family plot up above it. And they'd said that there's a witch there, and that every time you go, you'll find new flowers on the grave 'cause somebody keeps puttin' new flowers on the grave, but nobody knows who it is. And they say that you can go up there anytime, and they'll be flowers on the grave, and that weird things grew on it. Somebody went up there and tried to make it stop growing, whatever it was, and it wouldn't; it kept coming back. I don't know what it was, but they say that the woman that's buried is a witch.

The Big Shadow

One night, as a result of boredom, Julie Roane took a hike with her family. I think she might think twice before doing this again!

Last summer my dad, my uncle, and a bunch of us kids got together and were going on a nighttime hike. We didn't leave until about twelve o'clock that night. We walked the lines of our property, and when we were coming back down, we came by the pond over behind the Negro graveyard. We heard a big gushing sound. There was a big shadow of a big bird on the ground, but when we looked up nothing was there.

The Car That Rolls on Level Ground

Frank Miller wonders if you have ever parked your car on level ground and had something strange like this happen.

There's a place somewheres, I don't know where at, where you can park your car at night, and when you cut your lights off, something comes around and pecks at your windshield. You can put your emergency brake on or anything, and your car will roll from a level place. It scares you, too, they say, but it's never happened to me.

The Tale of the Haunted House

Billy Joe Stiles tell us about the ghost in Clayton. Or was it really a ghost?

Just outside of Clayton there's this old house that's been abandoned for several years, covered up with kudzu. This house is supposed to have ghosts in it or haunted or something like that. You can hear chains rattling at certain times of night.

One morning a man got up, found out that he didn't have any flour for breakfast, so his dear wife sent him out to town to get a fifty-pound sack of flour. So it was kinda drizzling and one of those mornings he didn't much want to be out. So he put on his big slicker coat, walked to town, and got fifty pounds and put an old piece of cloth or something on it, a rag of some kind to keep it dry. And as he started back home, he had to walk by this haunted house. It was one of those mornings. His old lantern had gone out, so he was stumbling up the road to get home. His wife was patiently waiting at home to make biscuits. He looked across the road, and he saw a fellow coming by; it was his neighbor, John. Well, being a good neighbor, he hollered out, "Hey, John." Well, John was very scary and very superstitious. He had heard that this house was haunted. Here John peeped across the fog and saw a big black thing with no head, and John broke to a run; as he run, his neighbor kept hollering, "Hey, come back here, John; help me, John." The more the ghost (supposed to be the ghost) hollered, the faster John ran.

As time went by, this fellow didn't say a word. One morning he was out in town talking to John about the tale of the haunted house, about seven o'clock in the morning when he started for work. Now this is the way, a lot of ways, tales got started. All that ghost was, was John's neighbor trying to be kind to him. He never did convince John that that house was not haunted and wasn't full of black ghosts.

The Faucet That Drips Blood
Helen Craig tells us about a house on Hellcat Creek that she once lived in. She said it dripped blood from the faucets.

There was this couple and they got in a fight, and his wife killed him and, now, like late at midnight, you can go in there and turn the faucet on and it drips blood. It was in Mountain City on Hellcat Road, but they tore it down. I'm not sure that it would really happen because I never got up and tried it.

The Ghost at Wall's Mill
Ricky Justus tells us about the old ghost house at Wall's Mill. He said his grandparents lived in this house.

Well, my grandpa and grandma, back in the thirties, lived in the old ghost house down at Wall's Mill. They gave it the name "ghost house" on account of there was a man killed hisself in the bedroom of the house. My grandma said after they moved into there, she went in to find an old patched quilt or something to cover up with, for it was in the wintertime, and it was cold as blue blazes. She said she went in there, and blood was just all over the walls and floors, and what was left of that old bed was rotten and falling all to pieces.

That night, my uncle and aunt, Ump and Grace, and one or two of their younguns had to spend the night. I forgot the reason. They spent the night and slept beside the bed where my grandpa and grandma slept. They made them a pallet on the floor beside the bed and slept there. Along over in the morning about two or three o'clock, gettin' up toward daylight, they heard a racket that sounded just like a man walking around in bare feet—sock feet, you know, on those rough pine floors and them boards a-crackin'.

Grandma said along about crack of daylight, they heard a man saying, "I want my house." She believes it and it woke Uncle Ump up, too—that man walking around pecking on the walls saying, "I want my house," and so Uncle Ump said, "Ah, if you wait till morning, I'll give the d—— thing to you."

Bloodstains That Won't Go Away
We collected this legend about a father who killed his son because of the way he treated his mother.

I've heard this story a many of times. Well, you know over there where Tom Brown and Tee-bone lives? That man shot his boy because he had been drinking and been jumping on his mama. His daddy finally got tired of it and just shot him. The boy was eighteen years old. He shot him on the porch of that old store building, and right there, every time it rains, there will be a thing come up like oil. You know how oil comes up in rain and beads? Blood comes up where that boy lay and died, but that one up there at Franklin, they never did find out who killed that woman. They could paint and sandpaper the walls and everything, but they said that blood just comes up in spots— just like it come plumb through the boards.

The Mysterious Man
Bessie Stancil tells us about a mysterious man who was walking out of the graveyard.

This old man was going by the graveyard one night, and he was going alone. This here man came on down to the road. He looked, and then he went walking up to the side of his wagon. He had a basket on this arm and a head in the basket.

The Headless Woman
Lisa Lovell, a folklore student, heard this legend from Terry Benfield, who heard it from someone else.

I heard there was a headless woman in Roane Cemetery. At certain times of the year, she would come around and ask people for a pail of water from their well.

Glassy Mountain Ghost
How would you like to be looking up on a mountain some night and see a light come gliding off? Ricky Hopkins actually saw this.

There used to be a boy that would fly off the mountain on a glider. He was killed out in Utah. On a full moon you can see a light up on the cliffs. About twelve o'clock or twelve thirty you can see a light fly off the mountain, and a 360 kite will land in the field down below there. Sometimes if he doesn't land there, it just keeps going till it's out of sight. I have seen the kite flying and the light, but it didn't scare me because I didn't know what it was. The last time I saw it was about the middle of last fall. He makes a screaming and squawking sound, but I don't know what it hollers like. When we saw it, we were supposed to have been coon hunting; me and these two friends of mine was up there. We were about polluted, ya know, but we don't think our eyes was playin' tricks on us.

Monster Catfish
One of our teachers told us about the catfish that are down in Fontana Lake. Word is that they are as big as a motorboat.

What I heard was that, see, there was a crack in the dam, and they had skin divers to go down and check it. And when they went down, they came back immediately. They said there was catfish down there the size of boats, motorboats, and that they wouldn't go back down again. You know, that's what I've heard and that's what several people have told me. I don't know. It may not be the truth.

One time I hung something at Fontana Lake; I don't know what it was, could have been a turtle, mud turtle, or something because we were in the boat. We were anchored out in the lake, and I was fishing. All of a sudden, then, the whole boat started moving with the anchor on it! I ain't kidding you; you can ask the guy I was with; he was there. He couldn't believe it. And the whole boat just started moving; then, all of a sudden—*pong*—he broke my line. I thought I was hung all that time until it started moving. That's about twenty-eight miles from the dam. You know, at the dam, I don't know the exact figures, I think from the top of the dam to the bottom it's eight hundred feet, but usually it's about halfway up—the water—so you know it's like four hundred feet or something like that. Myself, I can believe it because you know if there's that much water, that depth, there could be fish that big. If there's one that big at the end where we were fishing, there could just as well be one at the dam that large, or larger than that (that's what I'm saying). I know one thing, they keep the dam closed. You know, it's a road that goes across, and every time I've been over there it's been closed. And I don't know if it's because of the catfish that they can't get the crack fixed.

Place-Name Legends

The names these legends refer to were not imposed by any official source. They grew, instead, out of the communities themselves and are supported by narrative accounts. The legends may vary in content, but they answer the basic question of how things came about.

Wolffork

Billy Joe Stiles tells us how Wolffork got its name.

When I was younger, I was told this story, and I don't know how reliable it is, but this is the way it was related to me. There were some wolves coming down the mountain, killing sheep and so forth, around the place at the mouth of Wolffork Valley. Several men got together, and they killed this great big wolf. Everybody wanted to see it, so they strung him up in a tree, between the forks of a tree, and people came by and looked at him and admired the big wolf and went on. As time went along and they passed this tree, they simply referred to it as the wolf fork, and then from then on the valley got its name—it was called Wolffork Valley. How reliable this is I don't know. I've never seen a wolf in Wolffork Valley, but years ago there might have been.

Tallulah Falls

This is a story about the gorge told by the Indians and written down by Marie Mellinger.

Every year, the Four Winds held council on Wayah Bald. At one such meeting, the North Wind and the South Wind had a quarrel. She left in a huff, heading south, and the North Wind followed her, so she took her finger and drew a crooked line across the ground. There, a great, deep, crooked chasm opened up.

"Ha," said the North Wind, "I'll huff and I'll puff and make myself a way across. Foolish woman; I'll get you yet!" North Wind huffed and puffed and breathed on the chasm, and it filled up with ice, but before he could cross on his ice bridge, South Wind said, "Ha, foolish man, I will huff and I'll puff and breathe my warm breath upon the ice, and it will soon disappear."

South Wind breathed her warm breath upon the ice, and it began to melt. Water began to form, and run down the gorge, first in a trickle, then in a mighty torrent. Looking upon this with disgust, North Wind huffed and puffed his way back to the North Land.

As the waters rose, they formed rapids and waterfalls. The South Wind Spirit planted bushes and trees and pretty wildflowers and ferns along the sides of the rushing torrent. "This shall be called Tallulah," she said, "a place of winds." She set little frogs in the water to sing "tu-la-lu-yi."

This was long before the white man came and harnessed the waters, creating a dam and a lake, but if you come in springtime of the year, you can still see wildflowers and ferns planted by the South Wind. And if you sit on the edge of the gorge on a warm April evening, you can still hear the little frogs sing "tu-la-lu-yi."

Lover's Leap

We collected this Tallulah Falls legend from Mrs. Ollie Dyer, who used to work at the Tallulah Falls park.

I asked the man who owns this place if the Lover's Leap story that was on the card was true, and he says, "If it's not true, it must have some truth in it," because the story was told to his grandfather when he bought the land here just a few years after the Indians were driven out of here. So it's possible. There's a drop of about nine hundred feet from that ledge of the rock that's known as Lover's Leap to the riverbed, and it would've been quite the place to get rid of somebody because the river, then, went on through here, until Georgia Power Company bought and dammed it up. They say that Indians threw the white man off—he was one of the first men that came into, or settled, this area. He and the Indian girl [Tallulah] fell in love, and the Indians didn't want him in the tribe, and they didn't want her to leave, so they took him out on Lover's Leap Point and tossed him off into the river, and she jumped after him. That's the story.

Clarence Bramblett tells us the version that he heard about Lover's Leap:

Well, one time there was this little boy and his sister, and his mama and daddy got killed in a car wreck. They wouldn't put the kids in the same orphanage home and so they separated them, and when they were about eighteen years old, they met each other. They fell in love and about a year after they were together, they got married, and then they found out that they were brother and sister. They went to the Tallulah Falls Gorge, and they jumped off and killed themselves.

Tiger

Janie Taylor shares her version with us of how Tiger got its name.

In the 1800s British soldiers went over to fight the battle in India. While they were stationed there in service and fighting this over in the foreign country of India, they heard many sounds, including the Bengal tiger. Now, this tiger has a terrible wail, and these soldiers went back to England, then they migrated to the New World. So they came through South Carolina and found our mountains here in North Georgia. No sooner had they got here, they heard this piercing, screaming cry that sounded just like the Bengal

PLATE 49 **Janie Taylor sharing tales with students in a Foxfire class**

tiger back in India, and they all said that it sounded just like the tigers in old India, and so let's just call it Tiger. Now, you and I know that it wasn't a tiger at all because they don't have this habitat, but instead it was a black panther, the panther that we know and fear so much. And so all the time it wasn't a tiger at all, but it was the cry and scream of the black panther that terrified these early settlers.

Ann Carnes told us how Tiger got its name. When she was little she heard this legend from her grandfather.

When I was little my grandpa told me how Tiger got its name. There was a Cherokee chief named Tiger, who one day in the year of 1836 went up on the mountain with his tribe to get some furs, and he was killed by a tiger, so they decided to call it Tiger.

Screamer Mountain

George Kell shares his version of how Screamer Mountain got its name.

When the white people ran the Indians away from here, a woman ran across a mountain with a baby on her back, screaming. That's how I heard Screamer Mountain got its name.

Historical Legends

Historical legends are important, not so much as factual historical accounts but as accounts that satisfy the human need for drama and intrigue. The following legends represent an important link between people and places in our community.

The Hermit That Lives in Tallulah Gorge

Mrs. Ollie Dyer tells us this legend about an old man who used to live in Tallulah Gorge.

There was an old hermit that lived in a cave down there, but he has been gone for years. There was a man, I believe his name was Ledford, that used to live in down below what is the lodge, what was the lodge, down there below the power company village. He had been married and his wife had died, and it upset him so much he just didn't want to be around with people. That's why they say he went off in there, and he stayed down in there and slept in a cave that's down in the gorge for a time. And he just didn't want to be where people were. I've seen him. He used to bring old little bunches of kindling he'd cut, and bring it out and sell it and get whatever he needed, like salt and maybe a little bacon, at the store that was out there. And then World War II came, and he came out. He said that he had stayed long enough, that he'd come out and help win the war.

Doug Young tells us a legend he heard from his father about an old man who lives in Tallulah Gorge.

This feller back in World War I, when they had the draft, didn't want to go 'cause he was scared to go, I reckon. So he moved in the gorge in a cave where he had a bunch of old goats. They've still got goats down there, but

PLATE 50 **The Witch's Head rock formation in Tallulah Gorge, from a postcard predating construction of the hydroelectric dam**

you don't ever see the old man because he stays up in the cave all of the time. He hardly ever comes out, but people said they've seen him once in a while, and he wears old raggedy clothes and stuff.

And Bob Justus adds:

Around Tallulah Falls, strange things do happen. Ronald Vandiver told me that when his great-grandfather came here, when it was still Indian territory, a hermit lived in a little shack in the gorge. He said there was a little shack right on the edge of the gorge. And this hermit, old man, lived in it, but I can't remember details about what happened to him. I think, if I understand right, that the tourists thought he was like some kind of a troll. I guess he might have had a white beard or ragged clothes or whatever. Evidently, he was a real character!

Man Buried in Foundation
This legend was collected from Kirk Patterson, who heard it from his grandfather many times.

My grandfather told me that he used to work on the Fontana Dam. He said that when he was working overtime there, it was a long time ago; I don't know exactly what time of year it was. He said that they were working on pouring parts of the dam and that there was this man working over there with them, and he fell off some way into the dam, and they just buried him alive.

Helen Craig tells the folklore class about something that happened when her father was helping pour the foundation for Rabun County Hospital.

When I was little, my dad was telling me about when he was working at Rabun County Hospital, when it was first started. He helped lay the foundation. There was an old man there, and he had a heart attack or something, and they couldn't get to the ambulances, and he was already dead, so they just buried him in the foundation.

Billy Joe Stiles gives us some factual information about people falling into concrete dams.

There's a lot of controversy about people falling into dams, and so forth, and being buried alive. My dad did this kind of work most of his life, or a good portion of it, so I asked him about it. I had heard the same story when I was young. There's no report to it; he said he'd never heard of such a thing, but it still makes a good story.

The Bottomless Hole: Bull Sluice

Lynn Phillips told a story about a "bottomless" hole. Carroll Lee told her this story about his grandfather Leander Ramey.

They say that down there on the Chattooga River at Bull Sluice, there's a big rock, and at the bottom of that rock, where the falls are, it has no bottom. One time this man went down there and picked up about a seventy-five-pound rock and jumped in and went down a long way and never hit the bottom, so he finally had to let go of the rock and come back up.

Green (or Frog) Pond

Billy Joe Stiles tells us a legend about Green Pond. He says he's heard there is a bulldozer in there.

Up my way there's a rather interesting little place called Green Pond, and in the bottom of Green Pond, there's supposed to be a bulldozer and several things like that. Green Pond was made right after the turn of the century, in early 1905 or something like that. At that time they didn't even have a bulldozer. What happened was, they were blasting for rock. They'd get it out to put on the highway. Water seeped in and got on some old tools. The only bulldozer in those days was mules. To my knowledge, there's no mules left in the bottom of Green Pond.

George Bowen tells us the legend that he has heard from a lot of people about the Frog Pond in Rabun Gap. This is the same pond that Mr. Stiles refers to as Green Pond.

Well, I just heard that there's a pond up there at Rabun Gap where there used to be a rock crusher. When they were paving a new road through there, and it's just real deep there and rain had filled it all up, they say there's two or three cranes in the bottom of it; but, really, nobody knows just how deep it is and it's on the side of the road going up on Highway 441. That's about all I know about it.

"These old mountains have lots of magic."

~ Fairy tales and folklore from Clyde Hollifield ~

Sometimes people ask Foxfire students how we came up with the name for our magazines and books. Mr. Clyde Hollifield talked to us about the origin of the name because he was intrigued with the vegetation—foxfire or fairy fire or will-o'-the-wisp—and shared his research with us. He told us what he'd heard about the little people and how it ties in with the foxfire.

—Kyle Conway

I've been pretty curious about foxfire the last four or five years. In Scotland and Ireland, foxfire was called fairy fire for obvious reasons. I don't know where the term "foxfire" comes from, but I have a feeling that it's an anglicized word. In Irish fairy tales and folklore, it's usually called fairy fire or will-o'-the-wisp. Maybe they're talking about swamp gas, foxfire, or who knows what, but they call both by the same common name, will-o'-the-wisp or Jack of the little fire. Like a lot of Irish folklore, most of the stories I've seen didn't deal with foxfire directly, but it was just part of the story. Irish fairy tales are kind of gruesome, a little bit bizarre, and the fairies aren't to be trusted. The general story goes that somebody is going across the moors at night and sees foxfire and thinks it's a cabin. They go toward it and end up falling in the lake and drowning or getting led off into the moors by this foxfire, fairy fire, will-o'-the-wisp, or whatever. So they didn't think of it as a particularly good thing.

The stories I've heard locally around here are mostly about somebody that had seen foxfire on a hunting trip. "We got up there in the woods, and it was

PLATE 51 **Time exposure of foxfire glowing on decayed wood**

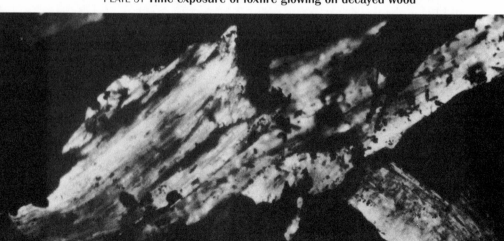

PLATE 52 **Clyde digging at the roots of a rotten stump to find foxfire**

just a-glowing all the way to the top of the mountain," that kind of thing. I'll give you my own personal ideas about the little people that lived on top of the Smokies. I don't know anyone else particularly that has the same feelings I have, but I know some Indian people that talk about the little people. This one Indian fellow I know talks about four different kinds of little people. All of them are white. Some little people lived on top of the mountains; some little people lived in broom sage, some in laurel thickets, and some just lived in deep woods. Fairy fire or foxfire may be their fire. It's sort of underground, the opposite of our fire. Their fire is cold and blue; ours is hot and red. Their fire is wet, yet at the same time it's burning, oxidizing wood, and giving off light. Their fire is at the other end of the spectrum, sort of opposite of our world. I think the literal translation of the Cherokee term was something like "cold fire" or "fire that's cold."

All the phosphorescent lights, the Brown Mountain lights, and all the others have some Indian legends about their association with spirits and stuff. I think that's one of the real magical qualities of these mountains. It's just the fact that on summer nights, they are glowing out there all over the mountainside—lightning bugs, glowworms, mushrooms, foxfire, and a few Brown Mountain lights drifting through. So who's to say what's an elf or a fairy if you see a light in the woods at night? To me, it has that elfin quality— that cool blue-green lunar sort of elfin color. Most people, especially kids, seem really fascinated by it. When they see a chunk of foxfire, they take to it instantly and want to handle it or break it up.

Foxfire is a real curious thing, which to me hints to the elfin world, but if foxfire is an elfin thing and if you mess with it, you're very apt to come to the attention of the little people. You'll be noticed if you play with something that's in their element. Foxfire is just barely in our physical world. It's more in their element. Not only is foxfire one of the real mysteries and magic of these mountains, but also things like the Brown Mountain lights, things that nobody quite understands. I just wonder sometimes if these natural lights aren't somehow connected to a part of a larger phenomenon. These old mountains have lots of magic, and the glowing things are just some of it.

"I wasn't hallucinating."

Greg Stancil's true encounter with the devil

Have you ever ridiculed tales of superstitions that surround some places? So did Greg Stancil as a young man out drinking and partying with his buddies. This is the story of his conversion.

Before I was saved, we were over off Highway 20 on Sawnee Mountain. Actually, I was told later that there was an old Indian reservation–type deal on the grounds up there, and there were a lot of evil spirits up there. But before my encounter, I thought, "Yeah, right, whatever." Anyway, we were all partying again, and we all were loaded up and went up there on the top of the mountain, and we were sitting there, and we were all scattered out somewhat. It was summertime, and it was hot, still weather, not even a breeze.

The next thing I know, the wind started picking up, and we looked at each other and we thought, "This is weird, ain't it?" Then we started hearing, like, a little jingle sound. So we just sit there with our beer and everything and just went on listening to AC/DC, and all that. The next thing we know, we started hearing from the very back this roar, like all these voices of all kinds: men, women, and whatever voices you could put with it, all kinds and they were roaring, screaming, growling, and snarling. It was like something bad, and these chains started rattling and shaking. The wind picked up, and the sound started from the back and was coming toward us. At first I thought I was the only one hearing this, but the other guys that was with me actually heard it, too. One boy actually busted the beer bottle in his hand; that's how bad it was. We took off running and jumped in the truck and took off down the hill. When that happened, it let me know that the devil was real. It was something letting me know that that was Satan. I think that was God's way of giving me an awakening.

As we went to town, to the shopping center, that place could never have been no fuller than it was that night. It was packed. We pulled up there, and I got out of the truck, and I fell to my hands and knees right there, and said, "God, if you'll help me, I'll quit alcohol and drugs." I didn't know how to pray 'cause I was lost, but I was asking God for help. I knew what I had heard was real; I wasn't hallucinating; I wasn't tripping on no drugs, just alcohol; this was real. Everybody looked at me, and there was so many that laughed at me and, of course, there was some that was concerned, but I told them, "If you experienced what I just experienced, you would be right here, too. If not, you would be crazy." That night I realized I could be in hell that quick.

Echoes

Delbert McCall

I've been singing for my Savior,
I've been singing for my friends,
Soon I'll sing with all the angels,
When my earthly life shall end.

I hear echoes over Jordan,
I hear praises round the throne,
I hear singing over yonder,
Praise the Lord, praise the Lord,
We've made it home.

Let me sing through all my valleys,
Until the mountaintop I see,
Let the music bring me laughter,
Let my burdens from me flee.

Sing praises to God, sing praises: sing praises
unto our King, sing praises.
—Psalms 47:6

Mountain Music Fills the Air

Traditional Bluegrass & Gospel

Echoes

Mountain Music Fills the Air

Bill Monroe once defined bluegrass music in the following terms: "It's Methodist and Holiness and Baptist. It's blues and jazz, and it has a high-lonesome sound. It's plain music that tells a good story. It's played from my heart to your heart, and it will touch you. Bluegrass is music that matters."

Before electricity, there were no electrified instruments or deafening drums rattling the walls and shaking the whatnots from the mantels. The music of our elders was as pure as the maple wood from which the instrument had been precisely shaped and molded. You could hear the banjo ringing loud and clear as mountain music filled the air. When the bar was slid across the strings, the Dobro would almost speak to you as the music resonated from under the steel cone embedded into the wooden top. From the "convicting" power of the traditional gospel hymns to the sad and happy stories the music told, bluegrass serves its purpose well.

The song "Echoes" was written by Rev. Delbert McCall, who has preached the Gospel and entertained thousands throughout the years with just his voice and a single guitar. Whether it be in a church, nursing home, hospital, or the home of a shut-in, or just singing the final song for a friend who has departed, Reverend McCall provides music and laughter to untold thousands. To the preacher and the groups featured in this section, music is a passion. It's not performed for money but echoes to lift the spirits of those who travel from far and near to listen, clap their hands, pat their feet, and often join in. The stories of the groups featured in this section will allow you to briefly pull back the curtain and peep into the lives of individual members of several, mostly bluegrass, groups with some southern gospel interspersed. A CD with musical selections from all the musicians featured in this section may be ordered from Foxfire at www.foxfire .org or by calling 706-746-5828. Listening to the CD will define for you what the high-lonesome sound really is.

—*Joyce Green*

"We went to the Grand Ole Opry in 1960."

~ Curtis Blackwell ~

I decided to write my third Foxfire article on a type of music that is very popular in the mountains but that I had not often been around: bluegrass. I learned about Curtis Blackwell from his son Shane. Mr. Blackwell was born just over the state line in South Carolina and is now living in North Carolina. He has six children; three sons are following his footsteps and playing music.

Shane and I made the trip to his house in neighboring Otto, North Carolina, and the interview began. Mr. Blackwell's humor was apparent as he went and changed for pictures and came out in a "Curtis Blackwell and the Dixie Bluegrass Boys" shirt.

Mr. Blackwell immediately made me feel right at home as he began to tell me stories of his past in bluegrass music. He began playing at family reunions and then started his own high school band. Later he played on the Grand Ole Opry and was a member of Bill Monroe's band. As I began working on my article, another student, Erik Lunsford, who was also doing his article on a bluegrass musician, asked me if we could combine articles. I said yes, and the following is the finished product.

—Amy York

My name is Curtis Leland Blackwell. I was named after my daddy. My birthday is September 13, 1942; it's the same as Bill Monroe's, but different years, of course. When I was real young, probably six or seven years old, we used to go to my uncle Ben Burton's house for family reunions, and my brother and a couple or three of my first cousins all played. One of them played the guitar, one played the fiddle, and one played the mandolin. They used to play a lot when we were done eating dinner. I just got to listening to that and liked it. I guess that is really what got me interested in bluegrass music.

In the later years, me and some of the boys in school got to playin' together, and I got real interested. I played in a high school group. It was just a little band. We had electric guitar, mandolin, and a guitar. That was Fred Burton, Junior Lee, my older brother Haskell, and myself.

After I got on up and got to playing music myself, we used to go to a place above Walhalla, South Carolina, called Cuzzins. We used to go up there and play a lot on Saturday nights—before I got into where I had to travel most every Saturday night. We used to do that a lot, and I think that is where I learned a whole lot, really. After that band busted up is whenever me and Haskell and Junior Crowe got together. We called ourselves The

PLATE 53 **"My birthday's the same as Bill Monroe's."**
Curtis as a young boy

Sunshine Melody Boys. We did our first recording, which was done in about 1959, or something about that. Then we won a contest and went to the Grand Ole Opry in 1960.

After we come back from the Opry, we played a lot of shows over in Toccoa, Georgia, and in that area for a good long while because it was sponsored by WLET Radio in Toccoa. Gene Bowlenger was the man that took us to the Opry, and we played a lot of shows at high schools for a couple of years; then we eventually broke up. Then I formed Curtis Blackwell and The Dixie Bluegrass Boys. I've had that band ever since, and that was probably in 1965, or somewhere in that neighborhood. Then I got my brother-in-law, Sam Cobb, who plays bass, and me and Al Olsteen, who picked banjo, and Larry Jefferson, who played the mandolin. To begin with, it was just a four-piece band: mandolin, banjer [banjo], guitar, and bass; then Randall Collins joined us later on.

One of the most memorable people that I have played with, of course, is Bill Monroe. He was one of the biggest stars I've ever played with. We have played with quite a few other people, too. I played in Bill Monroe's band, so I would have to remember him better than anybody. We have backed up people like Chubby Wise and Mac Wiseman; some of those fellows was a real pleasure to play with because they was real entertainers. I played with Bill Monroe for just a little while. We had the Dixie Bluegrass Boys band, of course, and we played around where he was at a lot. A fellow by the name of Lewis Olsteen, which is Al Olsteen's (who used to be my banjo player)

PLATE 54 **Junior Crowe, Haskell Blackwell, Curtis Blackwell,
and the Opry announcer. Junior Crowe is the father of the
Crowe brothers, who are featured in the next story.**

brother, mentioned to me about why didn't I take the job when somebody quit. I said, "Well, you know I would like to try," so he called Bill and set me up a thing backstage at the Opry. I went and tried out with him. I didn't even get to come home. I had to take my clothes and go on.

Bill was real easy for me to work with. A lot of people kinda had a different opinion of him. He was real good to me. He treated me like a son. Of course, I never will forget that powerful voice he had and the great mandolin playin' he did.

Some of the most memorable places we have played has been the World's Fair in 1982, and, of course, I have played at the Grand Ole Opry. That was a big thing. Those are probably the two most memorable places that I have played.

I play the guitar in the band. I do play the banjo, the fiddle a little bit, the mandolin, the bass, and I play about all the bluegrass instruments. I'm not real good on all of them, but I can play them enough to consider myself being able to play them. I like the fiddle better than any of the other instruments. We have produced three albums. We have two CDs, and we've got six tapes. I'm on three forty-fives, from back in the older days. We recorded the first one in New York in 1969 at Columbia University. Then we did a square dance album down in Aiken, South Carolina. I was on one album with Oliver Rice.

The latest two things we have done have been on CDs. We've got six albums in all, and four of them are on CDs. *Walking on a Highway* is the latest gospel album we got, and it is named after a song I wrote. We did *Our Traditions to You*, *She's a Rose in the Master's Bouquet*, *On My Way Back to the Old Home*, *Where Did the Good Times Go?*, and *On and On*.

I do have three sons that also make music. Terry, my oldest son, played with the band for about thirteen years, then he quit to go into the ministry. He plays a mandolin and sings high tenor. My second son, Victor, has never really been a member of the band, but he has done a lot of fill-ins for me through the years when somebody couldn't go. He plays mandolin or guitar, whatever is needed, and he sings high tenor and lead. Shane, my youngest son, played with me for a couple of years, and he plays flattop guitar and sings lead and tenor. Then Terry, Victor, Shane, and Randy Crowe formed their own band called The Blackwell Tradition. All of my boys are really good musicians, and Shane performed on the Grand Ole Opry in 2004.

I do write some of our songs. Some of the other boys write some. It is hard to say what my inspirations for songs are. When they come to ya, ya just have to write them. I don't write music. I put the tune to it and everything like that. The reason I chose bluegrass is because I liked the acoustical sound that bluegrass has. Another thing that interested me in it is Daddy used to listen to Earl Scruggs and Lester Flatt every morning at, I believe, five forty-five. I liked the sound of the banjo; that kinda got me interested in the bluegrass part of it. I just always liked that sound. I was probably influenced a lot by Bill Monroe and Lester Flatt and Earl Scruggs back in the fifties.

The main difference in bluegrass and country music is bluegrass is all acoustical instruments. Country, of course, is electric music with drums. Of course, bluegrass has always been associated with a high-lonesome sound, which country is not.

I think probably the most influential person in bluegrass would have to be Bill Monroe—of course, Flatt and Scruggs and Wiseman, also. They all influenced it, but I think Bill would have to be the biggest influence of them all. Bill influenced the music in the early years. In the later years, though, you have got people like Alison Krauss and Ricky Skaggs and those people that have been on the Opry, and they will play a little bluegrass along with the country that they are famous for. It's probably boosted it a whole lot. Alison and Ricky and those people are making them play it a little more on the market than it has normally been played. Ralph Stanley, Reno and Smiley, and all the older groups that have been around a long time have also had an influence on bluegrass music.

When I was real young and gettin' started, I had some first cousins that had a group called the Burton Trio. There was a gentleman that came through Westminster, South Carolina, that had been transferred in to manage one of the department stores over there, and his name was J. W. Hardwick. He was

PLATE 55 **Curtis and The Dixie Bluegrass Boys: Sam Cobb (bass), Chuck Nation (fiddle), Curtis (guitar), Charles Wood (banjo), Vic Blackwell (mandolin)**

a real good singer and a real good musician, and he taught me to play bass. I played bass with him and the Burton Trio. That kindly influenced me, a little bit—their type of music, too.

Bluegrass music seems to be growing all the time. The festivals get bigger and more of them. They're everywhere now. I can remember when they was only three or four festivals in the United States: Bean Blossom; Berryville; one in Fincastle, Virginia; and the one over at Shoal Creek in Lavonia, Georgia, used to be all they was. Now they's at least two or three in every state. I think that the future of bluegrass music is pretty good. It keeps gaining every year. The crowds get bigger at the festivals and whatnot, so we hope it will continue on.

The Dixie Bluegrass Boys are a very talented group of musicians. Band member Sam Cobb has been a member of The Dixie Bluegrass Boys since our inception in 1965, but we were musical partners even before then. His musical roots are deep, and he and I have played every major bluegrass music venue throughout the eastern U.S. Sam brings his own unique blend of warmth and humor to the band. You just have to hear him sing "The Rooster Song" and tell his latest favorite joke. He blends his great baritone harmony, singing with a precision seasoned over many years, and provides rock-solid bass picking that draws from a lifetime of music experience.

Vic Blackwell grew up in our musical family as the second born of my three sons, and he has been a member of The Dixie Bluegrass Boys since 2003. He is a talented songwriter and musician and exemplifies that famous high-lonesome bluegrass sound with his crystal-clear lead and tenor vocals. Vic is personality-plus onstage and communicates to the audience with a warmth and sincerity that delights and entertains fans of all ages.

Charles Wood has won banjo contests from Maine to Colorado and all points between. He is a two-time Winfield National Banjo Champion (1999 and 2006), Colorado Rockygrass Banjo Champion, Renofest South Carolina State Banjo Champion, Merlefest Banjo Champion, Georgia State Banjo Champion, and more. In 2005 he performed with Steve Martin, Earl Scruggs, Pete Wernick, and Tony Ellis in concert in New York City and on the David Letterman show—"Men With Banjos Who Know How to Use Them." He has performed on Garrison Keillor's *Prairie Home Companion* show and has toured extensively in Europe. Charles is a consummate musician whose playing style encompasses musical genres from traditional bluegrass to classical.

Chuck Nation is a past Louisiana State Fiddle Champion. He can play mandolin, guitar, banjo, and bass equally well and has won numerous awards and contests throughout the South with all instruments. He was a member of Louisville, Kentucky's, legendary Bluegrass Alliance from 1972 to 1974, whose alumni include Vince Gill and Tony Rice. Chuck has played across the U.S., Alaska, Canada, Japan, throughout eastern and western Europe, and has been on the stage of the Grand Ole Opry, New Orleans World's Fair, TV, and radio. Chuck has worked as a studio musician, traveled extensively with various professional groups, and opened shows for a diverse list of folks from Ernest Tubb to Mother Maybelle Carter to Mac Davis to John Hartford. He has shared the stage and played with the likes of bluegrass luminaries Bill Monroe, Mac Wiseman, Sam Bush, Vassar Clements, the Whites, Dan Crary, Byron Berline, Allen Shelton, and many others.

Editor's note: *Curtis is a member of the Atlanta Country Music Hall of Fame. Having received numerous awards over the years, he was officially recognized again in July 2010 as a legend of bluegrass at the International Bluegrass Music Museum in Owensboro, Kentucky, while attending the Pioneers of Bluegrass Reunion being held at the museum. While there, he also performed on stage with other former members of Bill Monroe's band during filming for the museum's video archives.*

**Curtis Blackwell and The Dixie Bluegrass Boys' music
is available at www.curtisblackwell.webs.com.**

PLATE 56 **Curtis in August 2010 with two of his many awards, including his
1960 First Place Award from the Third Annual Grand Ole Opry Talent Contest**

"I like the ol' brother-style duet stuff."

~ Wallace "Josh" Crowe ~

Grand Ole Opry performers several times over, worldwide bluegrass travelers, and frequent holders of the number one spot on bluegrass radio stations, the Crowe Brothers are extraordinary musicians. When people hear about them, they assume the talented brothers, Josh and Wayne, come from a large town and had many music lessons from famous teachers. No one would ever think they come from Warwoman Road in Clayton, Georgia, and were taught by their father, also a wonderful musician. Today they continue to astound the music industry. Joyce Green and I spent the evening with Josh, learning about the band and hearing his stories, and I was pleasantly surprised that Josh has remained a grateful, well-mannered small-town boy who has not let fame go to his head. The Crowe Brothers are a prime example of rising above obstacles, making a good life for yourself, and following your dreams.

While at the concert the evening of the interview, we had the opportunity to meet Harold and Ann Williams from Wingate, North Carolina, longtime fans of the Crowe Brothers. They had driven over three hours to Maggie Valley, North Carolina, that weekend just to be at the Stompin' Ground for the Friday night concert. Harold said, "They are the best in bluegrass; it just doesn't get any better than this. If I had a million dollars, I would buy them and have them play for me all the time!"

—Casi Best

My name is Wallace "Josh" Crowe. I was born in Clayton, Georgia. My dad was in the music business and got me and my brother, Wayne, started in it. We didn't know anything else because we grew up in music and thought that's what you were supposed to do. As time went on, we played with the more local and regional groups like Oliver Rice and those guys. We started out at home like everybody else, playing and singing in somebody's living room and going around in the community playing in churches. When we got our first job, it was with our buddy Raymond Fairchild, here in Maggie Valley, in 1975. I had just turned seventeen years old when that happened. That's where the Crowe Brothers' career started. We'd sung in other groups before, but we never had called ourselves the Crowe Brothers. Now we've been going for the past thirty-five years, traveling and singing and working in the music business.

My daddy and Curtis Blackwell and Haskell, Curtis's brother, got started in this business when they done a contest with all of the radio stations all over the United States. The PET milk company out of Nashville, Tennessee, did a talent search and hosted the show. It's kinda like *American Idol* is today to your new music. Back then, it was for your country, bluegrass, and that type of music. Bluegrass music wasn't perceived like it is today. Now it's all a music on its own, whereas back then it was combined with country. Daddy, Curtis, and Haskel won first place nationally in that PET milk contest in 1960, then they got their first shot to go to Nashville and play at the Grand Ole Opry. When they played at the Opry in 1960, it was as big as being on a national television show today. Radio used to be like television is today, and the Grand Ole Opry was the biggest thing on the radio. I remember I was three and living down on Warwoman when Daddy performed on the Opry. I can still remember how much it changed our lives, just them making that one appearance on the Opry. When they played the Opry, that really set them on fire in the music business. Curtis at that time wasn't but eighteen years old, so he was young. Their band didn't stay together, so Daddy went on to play with other groups.

I'd say the other most successful group in that era would have been the Chestine Brothers. They were actually nephew and uncle, but that was their name. I think Daddy told me that the first time he ever met those guys he was doing some kinda little show out there at the old high school gym, which

PLATE 57 "We've traveled coast to coast."
Wayne and Josh, the Crowe Brothers

is now the civic center in Clayton, and those two boys come that night, and that's how they struck up a friendship and started in the music business together. They done a lot of stuff together for several years and even up till Daddy got disabled and quit playing and being on the road, so they all played together up till about eight or ten years ago.

Today I could go play the Grand Ole Opry ten times this summer, and y'all would never know it unless it was on our website or they televised it, but the Grand Ole Opry, to our music, is still the stage you want to make it to. In country and bluegrass music, that stage is your ultimate goal. It's not that you make that much money playing the Opry like they used to. People used to make a living by playing the Opry, if they were a member. In today's time a country music star's used to making half a million to a million dollars a night in these big coliseums and things, so even if they're a member of the Opry, they can't afford to give up a million-dollar show to go do something that's going to pay 'em maybe four hundred dollars for the night.

The Opry served its purpose. It still does for people like us, the bluegrass people that are still able to play there. It gives you clout that you otherwise wouldn't have in the music business. That's the way I see the Opry today for us. We started playing there in March of '78. The Grand Ole Opry changed our whole music career all through the eighties. Having that kinda clout does things for ya that you otherwise wouldn't get done. Just being able to say, "Well, I've done the Opry so many years or was a guest on the Opry," helps your career. I can remember hearing all the country music stars when I was growing up back in the sixties and seventies, and a lot of them's dead and gone now, but you sit around and think about how you want to meet these people, and you just crave getting to meet 'em. In our career we not only get to meet 'em, but become great friends with 'em. I go to their house and sit down and talk to 'em just like we're talking now because we've become that kinda friends.

Roy Acuff, when he died out, it changed the whole scope of Nashville, the Grand Ole Opry, and just everything about Nashville. It definitely changed our career in the sense that the whole Opry itself changed, the personnel, everything. So it's not like it used to be. It's still a great thing to be there, and I wouldn't want to see it gone, by no means, because it still means too much to our business. I think bluegrass has roots in the Opry. People like us or others in bluegrass go there, and the Opry means something to us.

I've played on shows and with people who were my idols when I was a kid. I never thought I'd grow up and work with these people. Money can't buy that stuff. You can be a millionaire, but it can't buy you the experiences you've had. If I had an idol in the music business, that would have been Ira Louvin with The Louvin Brothers. I like the ol' brother-style duet stuff, and

that was even before Wayne and I started singing. I was twelve years old
before I ever heard the first Louvin Brothers album because we didn't have
access to music like kids do today. I was at somebody else's house spending
the weekend when I got to hear that album. They just happened to have those
ol' records laying around, and he told me that he had something he thought
I'd like. That changed my whole way of looking at duet music.

I remember the first thing that we ever did that I got paid money for
[laughs] was there in Clayton where there used to be a Belk's [Belk department
store] up on Main Street. They had a grand opening or something there
when I probably wasn't but about eight, maybe, just really learning to chord
and strum on the guitar. Wayne was already playing guitar. Our daddy had
taught us how to play, and he took us that night to Main Street. I remember
they paid me about eleven bucks.

The guitar's my main instrument. I've done a lot of mandolin playing
and bass playing. We started here in the Stompin' Ground in '82. In the
fall of that year, a television production group come here and filmed a pilot
show for the *Fire on the Mountain* program. They took it to Nashville, and
The Nashville Network bought 'em out and started doing the filming. David
Holt was the host of that show.

I have two boys, Quentin and Shelton. They are both musicians. Quentin
took Wayne's place with us there for a good little bit, and also Wayne's son,
Shane, did the same thing for a little while. For a long time, I called my
group the Josh Crowe Band. In '93 I teamed up with David McLaughlin
out of Winchester, Virginia, and we worked together for about five years as
Crowe and McLaughlin. Both of us still had things going on individually,
too. That was a good five years with him and one of the best recordings that
I ever did in the music business.

Wayne wanted to take a break and quit for a while because of all the
traveling and not being at home. We'd come in a lot on Sunday night or
Monday morning, wash our clothes, get ready, leave out again on Wednesday
or Thursday, and be gone again. I remember that both of my boys were born
in Clayton at the old hospital. Quentin, my youngest son, was born at four
twenty in the morning. I was there but had to leave at eight that morning,
and we was gone for two weeks. We were in Ohio doing two weekends back
to back, so we couldn't come home. That was the most miserable two weeks
I've ever spent in my life. I said, "No more," after that. I wouldn't do what
we did that week again.

We've traveled coast to coast, and David and I did some overseas things,
over in Ireland and Mexico and a few other places. When we went to Ireland,
we flew into Dublin, and we were about sixty miles out of Dublin in a little
ol' town where they were having this festival. Rabun County, our home,

looks a lot like Ireland; the mountains are just a little higher here. It reminds me more of when you go up into Kentucky, you're kinda in the hills, the real lush green pastures and rolling hills; that's what it reminded me of.

I write quite a bit of our stuff. The rest of it comes from people that send us songs and different songwriters that pitch us some of their songs. The record companies want their bands to do some new material, but also do some recognizable songs, too. Some fans will let the companies know that they want to hear the same traditional songs, but they want the Crowe Brothers' version. It's just like Christmas songs. Every group does all the same Christmas songs because their fans want those songs, but by their favorite artists. That's the way that record companies look at that kinda stuff, but new material is a must-have, too. Even if it's somebody that is unknown sending you songs, you are always interested because the best song that you've ever recorded might be one of them that some nobody is sending you.

It's kinda hard to say what the turning point for bluegrass was because there's a lot of different turning points for it. Business-wise, to bring bluegrass to being just a type of music where you go out and play festivals, I think the International Bluegrass Music Association in Nashville and the record companies has got a sense of what they had to do in order to commercialize this music to a certain extent, and they've helped it in that sense more than anything I've seen. You can count almost on five fingers how many times that bluegrass really got a peak, and then it'd come back down. Movie-wise, it would be *Deliverance*. Although it was bad on one hand, it was good for bluegrass music because now if someone hears the banjo, that's what they are reminded of. So that was good publicity. Even though a lot of people perceive the locals there in Rabun County to be that way [that was depicted in the movie], and we know that's very well not true, but that still put bluegrass on the national map, just like Earl Scruggs did on that movie *Bonnie and Clyde*, when he played the "Foggy Mountain Breakdown," and the more recent *O Brother, Where Art Thou?* has done to bring it back to the front lately. Steve Martin has done a lot to promote bluegrass. We've all seen a lot out of him this past year, but he's no better of a banjo player than some of these other guys out here; some of them are probably better than he is, but he's got that movie-star status to go along with being a good banjo player. He is good at what he does and has been for years, so with him coming in, he took bluegrass to another level that some other groups wouldn't have been able to. His playing put him on the Jay Leno show, the Letterman show, and the list goes on, but without having that movie-star status, any other group's not going to get on those shows that he did.

Bluegrass has definitely had its ups and downs, but a true bluegrass fan will always be a bluegrass fan. As we travel all over the country, we find the crowds are different everywhere we go. You get down in Alabama and Mississippi, and down in there, you get more in the Bible Belt area. There's a show out in Mississippi that we played at called the Legends [of Bluegrass] Festival, and there's two or three thousand people sittin' there, but it's the oldest crowd that I think I've played for [laughs]. There was fifty percent of them either on a walking cane or wheelchair, but they enjoyed the music to death. Then, the more you go north up into New York, Pennsylvania, Ohio, and around in there, then your crowd will start mixing up, and you'll get more of the young people coming out. It's really always been older folks in this part of the country, though. It'd be eighty percent is older, and then you may have a few young people if their parents or grandparents brought 'em. It's one of those things of if they like it, they like it, and if they don't, they'll never be back [laughs].

The best thing that's happened to our music here in the last few years is SiriusXM Radio. I don't say that because they've really been good to us, as opposed to the bluegrass charts and some of these other things, but because it's a good thing. There's two things that's happened in the past couple of years that I've never seen happen as long as I've been in this business. First, I've got paid more royalties than I've ever got paid. I'm not talking about a few hundred dollars; I'm talking about in the thousands of dollars. The other thing is that when I'm out settin' up for these shows or festivals somewhere, a lot of people come up to you and say, "I want to buy your new album that's got your hit song on it." That's never happened in bluegrass before, not with me anyway. That's started happening because people's hearing the music every day. I'll always have people come and tell us that they've seen us on different television shows and heard us on different radio stations.

We've had a lot of funny things that have happened to us over the years. There's some things that I could tell ya and some things that I probably can't [laughs]. We was going one day to Cleveland, Ohio, and it was back in the early eighties. We'd actually borrowed a van that my daddy had to travel up there in. I didn't have nothing that we needed to drive that far, and Raymond's rig was tore up, so we borrowed this van from Daddy. All up through Kentucky we had nothing but problems out of it. We had a water pump go out and everything else

PLATE 58 **"A true bluegrass fan will always be a bluegrass fan."** The Crowe Brothers following a concert, spending time with young admirers

possible. All night long we worked on that van. We was stopping in garages here and there the whole way. Finally, right above Lexington, Kentucky, it was just coming daylight, and we had a bed in it. Wayne was back there asleep, I was driving, and Raymond was sittin' in the passenger seat. It was one of those ol' vans that when you raise the doghouse thing in the middle you was looking right down on the motor. Well, when Raymond raised that, there was a flame that shot right up to the ceiling [laughs]! We pulled into a rest area there, and it was absolutely pouring the rain. Wayne woke up and come outside in his socks in that deep water. We's unloadin' everything we had out of that van. He didn't know what was going on. Finally, we got the fire out. We sat there for eight hours, and a guy we knew in Columbus, Ohio, was actually the engineer on a recording session we done with Raymond back in about '76 for Rural Rhythm Records. Well, he and his wife came all the way from Columbus to Georgetown, Kentucky, picked us up, and took us back to Columbus. We rented a car and went on to do our show in Cleveland and somewhere else we had to be. Then another buddy of ours that was in the music business up there that was also a mechanic brought us and everything we thought we was going to have to have all the way back to Georgetown. He fixed all the wires and everything on that ol' van, and we drove it back home. They's lots of them old stories like that, some of them I've tried to forget over the years [laughs]. They're funny now, but they sure weren't then.

Right now, we are on the road about thirty dates a year. Playing thirty dates a year means that you're probably on the road for sixty to ninety days. That don't sound like a bunch, but it is if you're out there doing it. When you look at the way things have been, Wayne and I are lucky to even be back in this business with all the talent that's in it, and much less to have done what we've done in the last year and a half. It's kinda mind-boggling to me that we could even throw our hat back in the ring and hit anywhere close. There's just some great young kids, young bands, and a lot of things going on out there. It's a hard time, but it's a good time.

The Crowe Brothers' music is available
at www.crowebrothers.com.

A Story and a Song

~David Holt~

I have known David Holt for many, many years—not personally, but through his music and his many connections to Foxfire. When The Foxfire Boys, students in George Reynolds's Foxfire music class, were just starting out as a band, they were graciously invited by David to perform on his program, Fire on the Mountain. What a treat it was to have our young students performing on such a terrific program. It gave them a wealth of experience in live performance and one they'll never forget. Many years have passed since then, but when we decided on a music section for this anniversary edition, I just knew that David needed to be included. When our museum curator, Barry Stiles, told me that David would be performing with Doc Watson in nearby Franklin, North Carolina, I seized the opportunity to have our editors interview him, and I personally contacted him to see if he (and Doc) were willing. David immediately agreed, for which we were so thankful, and he spent a good deal of his personal time in helping us write his story—valuable and limited time, as he was traveling and performing. Unfortunately, after all the years of giving interviews for TV and radio and national magazines, Doc preferred not to give yet one more interview! We were proud to honor that wish, but Sheri Thurmond and her dad, William, sure enjoyed the performance of both of these great musicians that evening in Franklin after David's interview. Just as Foxfire students continue to preserve a part of our Appalachian culture through oral history interviews, David has spent years of his life preserving our wonderful mountain music, as related in this short biography.

Every young man dreams of a life of adventure. In 1968, David Holt found his life's journey in the heart of the Appalachian Mountains. With a passion to become an old-time banjo player, David traveled to remote mountain communities like Kingdom Come, Kentucky, and Sodom Laurel, North Carolina, searching for the best traditional musicians. Holt found hundreds of old-time mountaineers with a wealth of folk music, stories, and wisdom. There were banjoist Wade Mainer, ballad singer Dellie Norton, singing coal miner Nimrod Workman, and 122-year-old washboard player Susie Brunson. Holt learned to play not only banjos but also many unusual instruments like the mouth bow, the bottleneck slide guitar, and even the paper bag.

For over three decades, David's passion for traditional music and culture has fueled a successful performing and recording career. He has earned four Grammy Awards and performed and recorded with many of his mentors, including Doc Watson, Grandpa Jones, Bill Monroe, Earl Scruggs,

Roy Acuff, and Chet Atkins. Today he tours the country performing solo, with Doc Watson, and with his band, the Lightning Bolts. David Holt is a musician, storyteller, historian, television host, and entertainer, dedicated to performing and preserving traditional American music and stories. Holt plays ten acoustic instruments and has released numerous recordings of traditional mountain music and southern folktales.

We appreciate David's efforts toward the documentation and preservation of our traditional music and are honored to include him here with Curtis Blackwell and the many others who have continued throughout the years to carry on the tradition—a tradition that we are grateful for having younger folks like The Foxfire Boys and Mountain Faith to continue for many years to come.
—Ann Moore

I grew up in central Texas, where I saw some traditional music and lots of traditional storytelling. The only traditional instrument in the Holt family was a pair of wooden rhythm bones made by my great-great-grandfather in the 1850s. My grandfather and father played the bones and taught me when I was a child. It opened my ears to unusual kinds of music and made me realize early on that there are other kinds of music besides pop music.

My father was an inventor, and, when I was ten, he decided he was going to move our family from Texas to California. In college in California, I met Ralph Stanley after a concert at UCSB. I really loved the clawhammer-style banjo he learned from his mother. After the concert Ralph told me that if I wanted to learn the old-time style, then I needed to go back to North Carolina, Virginia, or someplace in the Southern Mountains. So, in the summer of 1969, I traveled throughout the Appalachians from north Georgia all the way to West Virginia with my banjo-picking buddy Steve Keith, looking for traditional musicians. We were amazed to find hundreds of old musicians born in the late 1800s. It was clear they were a different breed and the last of that pioneer generation. This generation would be gone in a short amount of time. So I just finished college and moved back to Asheville, North Carolina . . . and that's how my interest in mountain music began.

In the late 1960s and early '70s, there was not much differentiation between bluegrass, old-time, and even country music. It was all kinda one thing. There were banjo and fiddle players, of course, but there were also ballad singers, old-time piano players, harmonica players, and mouth bow players. There were even old-time people that played panpipes. There was tremendous variety. It was generally referred to as mountain music. Styles were not so segmented like they are now. These days people are shut off in their little niches.

When I moved to Asheville, I started really working hard on learning the banjo. That was my only goal in those early days . . . to be a really good clawhammer banjo player. As time went on I began to learn other instruments. In the last ten or twelve years, I've been working really hard on the slide guitar and Doc Watson's style of fingerpicking guitar. Doc and I started working together in 1998, and I realized I had a rare chance to watch him and learn from the master. I've actually gotten pretty good at it and learned a lot, which is amazing considering I started learning in my fifties.

Performing with Doc has had a huge influence on me, and winning a Grammy with him for *Legacy* was a career highlight. Doc learned a lot of his repertoire from old seventy-eight rpm records. He has a very wide-ranging view about what kind of songs he will

PLATE 59 **David Holt with the slide guitar and banjo—two of the many instruments he plays**

sing. As Doc says, "If a song has something to say, I might sing it." One song I learned from him is "Ready for the Times to Get Better" that Crystal Gayle actually recorded first. It's a fingerpicking song, very beautiful. It has the feel of an older song, but words that a modern audience can relate to. Doc is a real master of taking an old song and making it sound new, or a new song and making it sound old. He has been able to attract a huge audience because of this. I have tried to follow his example: I try to play great songs really well and engage the audience as I go along with stories.

I do a lot of songwriting. I enjoy writing when I am inspired. On every CD, I usually record one or two of the songs that I have written. I think I've written some really good songs, but songwriting is not my emphasis. My real love is with the traditional material. I like learning the old stuff, and I love playing it for other people. Traditional music is where my passion is. One of my main goals has always been to keep the old-time mountain music alive. I just love it. Being a guy born outside the Southern Mountains, I could look over the whole scene and see what needed to be done. To give you an example: I lived up in a little community in North Carolina that was way up in the mountains. There was a kid up the road from me that had known me his whole life. He could've come to me at any time and taken banjo lessons from me; I would've been happy to show him. His grandfather and I were good friends and played music together. This young fellow didn't get interested until he saw me on satellite television on the *Fire on the Mountain* show (on The Nashville Network in the 1980s). It was seeing the music he had all around him on television that got him interested in learning it. I started thinking, "There's a lot of power in making sure that the music keeps on going by trying to get it on television and in front of young people." That was one of the things I tried to do back in the eighties and nineties.

The *Fire on the Mountain* show was started after the producers that worked for The Nashville Network saw a show I host for North Carolina Public Broadcasting System called *Folkways*. They asked me to host the new show. We did ninety-five half-hour shows, featuring everybody from Bill Monroe to Etta Baker. The show ran from 1984 to 1989 and is without a doubt the best collection of traditional music of the 1980s that exists. Unfortunately, when CBS bought The Nashville Network, they just put the tapes of *Fire on the Mountain* in storage. Maybe someday they will release them to the public.

On the other hand, the PBS *Folkways* series can be downloaded for free on iTunes! Or you can look at it on the website unctv.org [University of North Carolina Television]. All of these shows are downloadable, so you can look at them any time you want. They include everything from old cooking ways to traditional crafts and, of course, mountain music.

I got into storytelling when I was collecting songs and heard the old-timers telling me tales about things that happened in the mountains. I remember banjo builder and player Stanley Hicks; he was a good friend of mine. He told me about an elephant that was hanged in Erwin, Tennessee, in 1916. I said, "Hanged? That seems impossible!" So I researched the story from old newspapers, and, in about 1973, I told the true story in a concert for the first time. I realized people would sit moderately still for a three-minute song, but they'd be glued to their seats for fifteen minutes for a good story [laughs].

In 1976, I was invited to tell stories at the National Storytelling Festival in Jonesborough, Tennessee. There were about a hundred fifty people there. Today the festival has grown to about twelve thousand people. I was lucky to be part of the storytelling revival from the very beginning. In those early days, I told a lot of folktales and true-life stories I had heard from mountain people. Today I'm using storytelling more to set up songs. I use my storytelling ability to make a song interesting to a modern audience who doesn't know anything about the music. For example, there is a song I do called "The Cannonball." Well, there was an old ballad-singing lady, Inez Chandler, that I used to go see up in Sodom, North Carolina. She had an unusual chorus for "The Cannonball." To get the audience interested in the tune, I introduce it with a little story. I tell them that Inez had a wonderful way with language, and she always had an unusual ballad or song that had been passed down through her family. I would stop by her house, and she'd always say, "David, you want some coffee?" I'd say, "Sure, I'd be happy to have some coffee." She'd say, "I've only got the ol' 'decapitated' kind [laughs]." "Well, that's all right; I don't like coffee with a 'head' on it anyway." She said, "Excuse the smell. I cleaned the place from top to bottom with 'pneumonia.' It's so clean though that you could hear a pin drop [laughs]." She'd just say things like "You've buttered your bread and now you can sleep in it." That's the way I'm using storytelling now, to set up a song, make it more interesting to the audience. Most everything I do I've learned from mountain people throughout the years. I rarely get material from books or CDs.

I don't really come from a musical family except for five generations of rhythm bones players. There were lots of natural storytellers, though. My family, being from Texas, had lots of stories about battling terrible weather, Indians, and everything else. I had a great-uncle who had emphysema, and he still smoked nonfiltered Camels. He had a tracheotomy hole that he could blow smoke rings through. He used to tell me stories about Jesse James and how I was related to him. Just so happened that about a year ago I had the genome testing, and it turns out that at the top of the list of famous people I was related to were Frank and Jesse James. I thought he was "talking through his hat" when I was a kid, but Uncle B. was telling the truth [laughs]. Storytelling in my family, like in most families, just happens, and it's not formal or done in performance style. They just launch into something that happened in the old days. I guess that's why I ended up really liking true-life stories. I love folktales, too, but I really like the storytelling where you don't even realize you're being told a story. You're just being told what happened, and you're captivated by it.

I talk to people everywhere to try and find stories—to find a good story, you really have to dig around. For example, Micaville, North Carolina, was one of the largest mining capitals of America. People would go out and dig in their backyard for mica. A big chunk of mica sold for seventy dollars a pound back in the late 1800s. That was a lot of money back then. They could split the mica real thin, and then they would sell those sheets that were used in potbelly stoves for the window so that you could see through it. The mica wouldn't burn or get hot. Now, that is not a story, but it is an interesting premise. So now I'm looking for a true story about something that happened to one of the mica miners—how he struck it rich or something. To have a good story, you have to have an interesting setting and something compelling has to happen to the characters in the tale. A story has to lead to a climax. I am in the process of talking to people, following leads, and hoping to come across some bit of history that will make a great story about mining in Micaville, North Carolina.

Many people have been an influence on me and my music. If you look on my website, I have put up photos I've taken of some of my mentors. Doc Watson, as I mentioned, has been a huge inspiration to me. An old fiddler named Bayard Ray was a great help to me. When I first came to Asheville, he'd come over every day and teach me a new tune. He was from that same little community as Inez Chandler. Dellie Norton was a singer who sang old ballads handed down from her family for four hundred years. She also knew all about how to heal with herbs and old-timey ways of making a go of it in the mountains. I give credit to Grandpa Jones and Roy Acuff, who were good friends of mine. They knew how to entertain an audience with old-time music, and I learned a lot by watching them. I tell you another person I admire, Wade Mainer. He is still alive now, and he's one hundred and three years old. He was from Waynesville, North Carolina. He has been a friend for almost forty years. Wade was a professional old-time musician. Etta Baker, the wonderful blues guitarist from Morganton, North Carolina, was a great friend to me. Walt Davis from Black Mountain, North Carolina, taught me a lot about old-time music because he was a professional old-time musician back in the 1920s and '30s.

I try to learn as much as I can from these folks who made a living in the music business way back when because, even back in the thirties and forties, it was still old-time mountain music. My inspiration for storytelling came from Ray Hicks and Stanley Hicks, who were superimportant to me, as well as to a lot of young folks. Even though I don't tell their stories, just to be around people who are traditional tellers is so powerful. You can see how storytelling naturally fits into their lives. I hope I've absorbed some of the soul of music and storytelling from these people because I think that's the key thing—having the power of some of the music come through you is just amazing. That makes the music engaging and soulful. All the old-timers added their own personality to a song. The music always has to come through you.

The best thing about this job is being with old-timers and other musicians. I still love to visit folks way back in the mountains and spend time with them. That is a great joy for me still. Certainly, one of the highlights of my career is getting to work with Doc over the last thirteen years. We tour two or three weekends a month, and I treasure every concert.

I hope that years from now, I will be seen as a guy that helped to open the door to traditional music in the Southern Mountains. I want people to see what an incredible treasure mountain music is. It doesn't exist everywhere. Only the southern Appalachian region has these kinds of songs, this wonderful music, and traditions imbedded in the culture. This is really powerful music. I want people to see me as a good player and a person who presented the music well; someone who was easy to get along with and helped open the doors so other people could experience what I have experienced. It is very important to me to see the music carried on. It is a wonderful living tradition, and each generation has to pick it up and bring it into the future. I'll do whatever I can to help make that happen.

David Holt's music is available at www.davidholt.com.

PLATE 60 **David with his mentor, Doc Watson**

"It's been real, and it's been fun, but it ain't been real fun!"

~LV and Mary Mathis~

"Mary, Mary, quite contrary . . ." These could be the words LV Mathis would use to describe his soul mate of fifty-four years, Mary Walker Mathis. Of course, "Lyin' Varmint" might be the quick response from Mary. The truth is, this couple has weathered the storm, held on to God, and survived the test of time. They are a loving, talented couple who live in a beautiful home on the lake in the mountains of Tuckasegee, North Carolina, a home crafted, designed, and built by LV himself. The soft hand of a mostly self-taught pianist joined the hand of a soon-to-be carpenter, and a true love story began on the swings at a carnival in 1954. The Mathises have written the recipe for relationship survival. They have worked together, played together, laughed together, and cried together. Friends who visit feel the warm welcome extended by this couple, and no one ever leaves with an empty stomach. I would guess they have never met a stranger. Mary and LV Mathis are a blessing to know and love. I am thankful for the opportunity God has provided for me to become their friend.

—Joyce Green

Mary: My name is Mary Alice Walker Mathis. I was born in Townsend, Tennessee, March 21, 1939. I am the oldest. I have four brothers and one sister. They all live in Tennessee except my oldest brother; he lives in Candler, North Carolina. They are all still living.

The times were hard when I was growing up, you know, 'cause we were dirt poor; most of the folks were. We had a lot of fun, though, and I don't know how much we considered ourselves to be poor. My daddy was an alcoholic, but my mama saw to it that we always had something to eat. She just worked in the home there and just raised all six of us. I remember she made banana pudding in a dishpan. That was a big banana pudding! I still remember her doing that. There was not much left of it by the time she would get some. LV remembers my mama for her biscuits and her gravy.

I don't know how old I was when we got electricity. I was probably eight or ten years old. I was a lot younger than LV was when he got electricity. He can tell you when he got electricity, but we had it when we came here to Cullowhee, North Carolina, because we had an electric stove.

LV: We hadn't got modern inside when you got here.

Mary: Before we had electricity, we kept things cold in the creek. They had a little house that was built over a creek or stream, and we kept milk

PLATE 61 **Mary Mathis's grandpa Walker's homeplace in Wears Valley, Tennessee**

and cream and stuff in it. We had cows at one time, but I guess we got more modern. I don't know how long we had a cow. Daddy worked construction, and we moved a lot. That was why we moved here to Cullowhee. Daddy helped build the lake here. We never had a really big house, and we were constantly moving place to place.

My daddy was a good worker when he worked. He was raised to that. He never knew anything different. When he was growing up, his dad (my grandfather) had stills, and my dad carried the sugar to the stills when he was five and six years old. My grandfather went to California when I was about five or six years old, and I didn't know at the time why he left. He left a beautiful farm in Wears Valley, Tennessee, and it's still there today. I found out later that my grandfather had left because the revenuers were after him. He lost everything he had in Wears Valley when he went to California. He never came back, so I really don't remember a lot about him. That's all my dad knew growing up, and there was a lot more than one running still in the county. None of us ever drank; I hated it.

I went to so many different schools when I was growing up. I think one year I didn't go to school at all. I think I should have been in the first grade that year I didn't go. Back then they didn't come to get you, so I just didn't go to school. They probably didn't even know we existed. I grew up going to so many different schools that I never really got established anywhere. When I went, we had quite a few kids in a class, and sometimes we doubled up in classes [more than one grade] and only had one teacher. Mama took us to school when she could.

PLATE 62 "I don't know how much we considered ourselves to be poor." Mary Mathis as a child, seven or eight years old

We had a television when I was probably about fifteen 'cause we didn't have one when I was a kid living in Cullowhee, but we had one after we moved back to Tennessee. You know, I don't remember much about television, and I don't remember watching it because there wasn't that much on it, but maybe one channel. I can tell you the first television that I ever saw was in Maryville, Tennessee, at this drugstore combination grocery store, and they had a television up on the wall and *Howdy Doody* was on, and that's the first time I ever saw a television.

I sung as a little girl in school. I loved country music and I had my little songbook, and I'd listen to the songs on the radio. I listened to Loretta Lynn, "Coal Miner's Daughter." I liked all that stuff. I was never able to afford her records, but I loved her music, and I loved her singing. I would go to the classroom sometimes, and I would sing. We also listened to Hank Williams, Johnny Cash, Kitty Wells, and all them older ones.

Daddy had a car. Should I tell her what kind [to LV, laughing]? Daddy fixed up pieces of junk and whatever he could get for a car. We had an ol' ambulance one time that we rode in. I must have been six or seven years old, and we just got in the back of that thing and rode like we was in a limousine. We had a hearse one time, too. It still had the rollers in the back of it [laughs]! It had a big, wide side door on it, too; you could go in that way or go through the back where they shoved the caskets in. We had a good time, though. It didn't bother us [laughs]. We were glad to have anything that had wheels that we could go in. My dad, many times, wouldn't go anywhere with us. He'd just want to stay home. I loved to go and travel, so since we've been married, we've traveled a lot, since I didn't get to when I was growing up.

I moved to Cullowhee in January, when I was eleven years old. I thought it was the most lonely, forlorn place I think I have ever been to. It was blowing snow, and it was just a very bleak place, I thought. Then later we moved around to the Vernon Painter place and lived there. Vernon was a teacher in Cullowhee. I basically grew up there. We lived there till I was about fifteen, I guess, and then we moved back to Tennessee. During that time I knew LV and his family 'cause he lived just around the road here. In fact, he was born right over here in a log cabin, which I have a picture of.

I didn't go out on dates because my dad and mama wouldn't allow me to do that. I never really went on a date. The first time I ever saw LV was at a church in Cashiers, North Carolina. He was with Pete Jones, his cousin. After that I knew him, but I never actually dated him, never

PLATE 63 "We went to the carnival, and there was my mama, daddy, and brothers following us around." LV and Mary Mathis at the Maryville, Tennessee, county fair in 1956. Mary was seventeen, and LV was twenty.

talked to him, for probably a year I guess, but he would go to Cedar Baptist Church, which is right around the road here, on Cedar Valley Road. I would go there some, and I talked to him a little bit during those times.

His mother told him, "There's a girl you can date." She said, he said, "I wouldn't date her if she was the last girl on earth." Of course he was plottin' then [laughs], even though we didn't talk to each other at that time. I finally began to talk to him, and then I dated him about two years. One year of that was after I had moved back to Tennessee. I was fifteen and he would drive across the Smokies to see me. LV was really the only boy I ever dated. I talked a little to a boy they called Corny. He was LV's cousin, but I never really dated him. His name was Cornelius, but they called him Corny. LV came to the house and picked me up, and that was the first time Daddy had let me go on a date by myself, but I really wasn't by myself because my daddy and my whole family followed us. They really did. Anyway, we went to the carnival, and there was my mama, daddy, and brothers following us around. We rode the swings for a while, and LV got behind me on the swings, and he held my hand on the swings. I still have a bowl that was gotten at that carnival. Cornelius and LV are about the only dates I had. Cornelius is dead now.

LV's name is just LV. He has no name, just the letters. I asked LV's mother what the initials stood for. I said, "It's got to be somebody." Well, no, she didn't name him after anybody. So we got to calling him Lyin' Varmint 'cause we couldn't figure it out.

I was seventeen and LV was twenty when we got married—just mere kids—but we've been married fifty-four years in October [2010]. He says, "It's been real, and it's been fun, but it ain't been real fun!" He always tells everybody that. LV didn't sing back then. I've taught him everything he knows [laughs]. After we were married, I took piano lessons for six months. I finally got this lady to agree to give me piano lessons, and I know that God had everything to do with that, too. I went to see her, and she was teaching

PLATE 64 **"I've taught him everything he knows [about singing]." Mary and LV Mathis on their wedding day**

a room full of little children. I went to the screen door and asked her if there was any way she could teach me, and she said that she just didn't think she could take anyone else, but she just stood there. Then she said, "Yes, I will." So I took about six months with her, but I couldn't keep it all up, work eight hours a day, come home, and raise a family, keep house, and all that stuff, and I had to quit because I was working, too. But I told myself, "I *will* play the piano one day." So that's what I did. The woman teaching me didn't believe in a lot of rhythm, so I never really learned rhythm, but I knew I was going to play one day, even if I had to teach myself. I played guitar when I met LV, and I was doing pretty good at it, and we got married and that's when I stopped playing and didn't play guitar anymore. Anyway, I've always loved music. It was just in me, and I loved it. I loved to sing and play, and whatever else I could do.

When I was growing up, my mother took me to church when she could because she didn't drive, and if Dad took us once a month, then he thought that was enough. So we didn't go very often. When I was about six or seven years old, I went outside and I told my mama to come outside because I wanted to show her something. She came out and I said, "See up there; there is where God lives, and I'm going up there someday." I remember really clear about a church we went to with my aunt. It was a Church of God. She would come get us sometimes and take us with her. I remember as a child seeing the power of God. I've never forgot it, and I knew it was real. There were things that happened, that I remember, that made me know that God was real, but I was never saved until I was going to Oak Ridge Baptist Church. That was a long time ago. When I was twenty-seven, I had gone to the altar a couple of times, but I never really was saved, nor did I ever say I was. Sometimes when you'd go to some of the churches, they'd drag you to the altar, and they'd tell you when to get up—that you was all right. I even got that said to me when I was saved. The preacher told me to get up and I said, "There's more to it than that." I just knew there was, and I stayed on my knees until I was sure. And there *is* more to it than just getting up.

The way we started singing was, I was saved about five years before LV, and I guess that after I took the piano lessons, and I got to where I could play around pretty good on it, then we started singing together. Our two sons sung with us. I guess we sung together about ten years, if that long. When Allan, one of our sons, got married, that ended. Vernon, my other son, continued to sing with us until he decided he was grown up and knew everything there was to know.

LV: My name is LV Mathis. I was born May 24, 1936, and I'm almost too old [laughs]. I was born right down in the holler here in Tuckasegee, North Carolina, in an ol' log cabin that used to be down in there. They's seven of us, two brothers and four sisters. I'm second to oldest of us all. I had one older brother, and he passed away when he was nine years old.

Life was rough when I was growing up! We was poor. Everybody was poor, but we didn't know it. It didn't make no difference because everybody was just about the same, and if I had to go back, I wouldn't change a thing because I learned a lot.

Mary: We grew up in the town and not back here in the mountains like he did, so we did know people who had a lot more than we did and that were a lot better off than we were.

LV: We had the farm. It was just an ol' mountain hillside farm. We had to raise what we ate and all that. I remember when we didn't have power. I remember my grandmother would grow a big patch of punkins [pumpkins], and when they first bloomed, she'd pick the blooms off, roll 'em in cornmeal, and fry 'em. They was just as good as squash, if you didn't have squash. We'd keep everything that we needed to keep cold in a spring box. That's a box about eight foot long—the one that we had was 'bout eighteen inches wide or somewhere along in there—and water would run in one end of it and then stay in there because there was a lid on it. We'd put our milk, buttermilk, butter, cucumbers, watermelons, and different things in there.

We always had two cows. We'd always churn our own buttermilk. They wudn't no Wal-Mart around! My grandmother had a porch on her house, and she had these great big ol' barrels made out of a log, and she'd keep her

PLATE 65 **LV's birthplace. LV's mother, Lettie Mae Hopper Mathis, at right with LV in her arms, brother Frank sitting in doorway**

PLATE 66 "Life was rough when I was growing up." LV Mathis school picture from Rocky Hollow School, Tuckasegee, North Carolina, age ten or eleven

PLATE 67 Rocky Hollow Baptist Church and School, where LV attended first through fourth grades

kraut, corn, and pickled cabbage in 'em and get out whatever she wanted, whenever she'd need it. It'd be fine out there because anything pickled would stay good. We made leather britches, dried apples, peaches, and all that, all the time. In order to live, that's what we had to do if we wanted to eat. By the time I was big enough to hold a turning plow, I was out there turning the land with our two horses.

Mary: See, he can tell you about all that old stuff, whereas I can't!

LV: On a typical day we got up at four o'clock in the morning, whether you needed to or not. We worked all day until it was about dark. We'd take about half an hour to a' hour off for dinner, if you could hold off that long, because most of the time they's a-needing you to get back out there to work. We'd put in ten or twelve hours a day in the summertime. Then, in the wintertime, we'd put in time getting the wood. It never ceased; we's always working. We never knew when Saturday come because we'd work right on through it. They wasn't none of this "Let's go to town" business, but we always knew when Sunday come because we didn't work on Sunday.

For fun, we mostly just climbed sapplin's, had grapevine swings, fishin', huntin', swimmin', and just anything because we had to make our fun. In the summertime we'd fish the river here all the time because they wudn't no lake there then. It was a great big ol' river running through there. We fished that river and all the creeks around that had any speckled trout in 'em. Then, in the wintertime, we hunted. I never bear hunted or deer hunted, but did lots of coon and squirrel huntin'. We'd catch 'em possums and feed 'em buttermilk and bread, and then we'd cook 'em. They's just good white meat, and it was as good as chicken if you didn't have chicken. We had chickens, too, and got our own eggs and stuff from 'em. Barnyard chicken makes the best chicken and dumplin's. There was none of this going down to Wal-Mart and picking the chicken out. Mama'd grab up that chicken, and its neck would be wrung before you'd know it.

I went to church until I was about twelve or fourteen years old, then I stopped going. When I was a kid, I would sing in church and Sunday school. Mary got to going to church. It was about five years after she got saved when I started going to church with her and got saved. I was going, and I'd hear her and the boys singing, so I just joined right in with 'em.

Mary: He did sing at the Church of God that I went to when I was a little girl.

LV: We've been going to Oak Ridge Baptist Church about forty-five years now, but I've only been saved about thirty-five years.

Talking about how me and Mary got married, well, I just tried to outrun her, but I couldn't [laughs]. We met there at the carnival. I had seen her before that, though. My cousin she was with wouldn't ride the Ferris wheel with her, so I rode the Ferris wheel with her. It was sometime after that I asked her out. I walked her home from church a few times, and then we started datin'. In about a year Mary's family moved back to Tennessee. She thought she had saw the last of me. That didn't break my heart, but I did hate to see her go [laughs].

Mary: He rode to the top of the Smokies with me in an ol' International pickup truck that looked like it was about to fall apart.

LV: It was 'bout three months before I went there and saw her. We dated about a year. We couldn't call each other, so we'd write to each other.

PLATE 68 **Mary and LV in the Smoky Mountains on Easter Sunday 1956. They married that October.**

Mary: I still have most of the letters, too. We wrote a lot because that's the only way we had to communicate with each other back then.

LV: We were married awhile before we had a telephone. We barely had power up here. We lived in an ol' store building with a bedroom, kitchen, and a living room. We lived in that for a couple of years.

Mary: You know what we had as a roof over that store building? It was a Pepsi-Cola sign. That's what was out hanging over the door.

LV: That house was right up here on this same road around the curve.

Mary: We put up wallpaper, and we thought it was purty. When we built a fire in the heater, that wallpaper paste got hot, and I can still hear the wallpaper going *pop, slit, crack, splat* because it was getting so hot! But that was our home until we could get by. Then we bought a little single-wide trailer. That's when we bought Allan a little carpenter toolbox because I reckon that's what he was destined to be. So we bought him a little toolbox, and we had a new red Naugahyde couch, and it was beautiful. First thing Allan did was, he got out the little saw, and he just sawed away at the arm of that couch. He was about three or four, and when he got to that brand-new couch, he knew what

PLATE 69 **Mary, age twenty, at her and LV's first home. It had been an old store. Note the Pepsi sign for roof over the door.**

a saw was for. So today he still knows what a saw is for because he's still a carpenter. Vernon, our youngest son, is a good carpenter, too. They took over the business when we retired.

LV: When we first married, I was in construction work, and I did that for probably ten years. Then I quit and went to work in the pulpwood business. Pulpwood work is when you cut the tree down and cut the wood into pulp so it can be made into paper. So basically, I was working for a paper mill. We had a truck and a skidder to help us cut the tree and drag it out. I did that for about seven years, and then they went out of business. I didn't want to fool with going to Canton, North Carolina, to work—that was where the plant was then—so I quit. I come home to rest for a day or two, and a boy up the hill here come down to see me one night. He said, "You want go to work?" I said, "Well, not really, but I guess it's a pretty good opportunity to go." He said, "Well, I need a carpenter." I said I would. I worked with him for about five years. In the meantime, while working for him, Arnold Rigdon was my boss man. He was the best carpenter I ever met. After working with him about a year, I told him I was going to hang with him and learn everything he knew, and I did. I stayed with him five years, and then he quit and went to driving a truck. So I just kept on. I went to Maggie Valley, North Carolina, and worked for a guy, and I worked with him for nine and a half years. I drove to Maggie Valley every day. It was a long ways—little over an hour or more. I done that for nine and a half years, and then there wasn't much building going on in Maggie Valley, so the boss sent me to Asheville, North Carolina, to work on building some condominiums. I went over there and built one. They had another one that was about ready to be built, and the feller said, "Why don't you build this one yourself?" I thought about it, and prayed about it, and I told Mary, I said, "I believe I will." So I give him a bid on it, and he took it. He said, "You're the one that's doing the work, so there's no point in working for the other feller, since you're doing it anyway." So I built two there before I come back to Cashiers to work, and I stayed up there till I retared [retired]. I worked there about thirty years. I enjoyed it. I've gotta few tools left, but my boy has got most of 'em. I give 'em to him when I retared.

I built this house we live in. I always had ten or twelve men working for me at that time, and they helped me build this house. I had the gradin' done, and Mary and I had prayed about this house, so I had the church people come over one Sunday after morning service. They all come down, and we got down here where the basement's at now and had prayer. Then we built the house. We had almost enough money to build it. I had to bary [borrow] twenty thousand. The bank didn't want us to bary twenty thousand; they wanted to let us have thirty thousand. I told 'em that I didn't want that much, and they told me to just take it 'cause I'd need furniture and other things, too. I give in and took the thirty, but we finished the house, and I took 'em ten thousand dollars back.

Mary: When we took it back, they said, "Don't y'all need some furniture?" I said, "Yes, we do, but I'm not going to finance furniture, so y'all can have this ten thousand dollars back."

LV: We started building in '88 and finished in January 1990. We had an old couch in the living room, and we just slept on the floor on a mattress and springs.

Mary: We'd bought two bar stools for the kitchen, too.

LV: Later I got to thinking about a gazebo we had built up there in Cashiers and decided I needed me one out there, off the deck. I set in and got it all laid out. I got Sam Crawford, he was working for me at that time, to come one Saturday and help me. I'd already dug the footers, and the Saturday he come, we set the posts and got it all framed. Then the next Saturday we put the floor on. I got the men who worked for me to come help me put the roof on it. Allan did the work on the inside of it. Then I started loaferin' [traveling], gettin' ol' antiques to hang in it. When I got it filled up, I just kept buying. So now I've got the basement full.

Mary: Well, at first he'd come in, and he'd just set it up on the mantel. At that time this mantel wasn't there, and the one that was, was an ol' rough piece of wood. It wudn't smoothed, planed, or nothing. It still had the splinters all in it. You couldn't even dust it, it was so bad. He'd come in and set them things he'd bought up there, and I'd say, "We don't have any more room for this stuff!" We just had no place to put it all, so I told him to hang it in the gazebo, and he started hanging it in the gazebo. What's out there now wasn't all of it. He sold a lot of it.

LV: I've collected stuff from California, Maine, Washington, Florida,

PLATE 70 **LV and Mary on a Caribbean cruise in 2005**

from everywhere. We've done a lot of traveling. We had a motor home. The man I was working for one week in Maggie Valley couldn't pay me, and he had a motor home. He told me, said, "We're going to try to sell that motor home, so I can pay y'uns for this week." I said, "Well, how much do you want for it?" He told me, and I said, "Well, I believe I'll just buy it." So I bought it. It was a Class C, and I just couldn't hardly stand to ride in it [laughs]. Nevertheless, I bought it anyway. We kept it for about ten years, I guess. We didn't use it a lot because we just didn't have the time. If I was working and she was working, then we just didn't have the time to travel. Sometimes, in my business, I had to stay pretty close by, so we couldn't travel much. So we sold it. We bought a pop-up [camper] and traveled in that a little while, but that wudn't no good. It was more work than it was anything. If you was just going somewhere for a one-night stay, then you had to get it all ready, hook it up, and so on, and it just wudn't worth all that. So I sold it and I bought another motor home. I bought it over in Asheville, North Carolina. It was a nice motor home. We did travel in it a lot, but I didn't like it because of the bed in it. The only way to get in the thing was to crawl up in it. You couldn't just walk around and get in. We had it for a long time, and Mary's brother finally bought it off me. When he bought it, then I found the one that I've got now. We took this one to Alaska. We've been to Hawaii a couple of times. We went one time and stayed three weeks. I went over there and built a man a room on his house.

Mary: We'd took a cruise there the first time, and this man had a shack on the island and invited us back, so that time we had to fly.

LV: I dried him in a living room on it [the shack]. I dried it in, put the windows, door, and sidin' on it.

Mary: We were invited back this year [2010], but not to do any building, just to come and have the house to ourselves, but we ain't going. I don't like the plane ride, and that's just a long way. Anytime you get on a plane, you never know what you're gonna get into, whether it be storms or anything else.

LV: The world has changed a lot since I was a boy. Today things are all outta whack. I think our government needs to seek the Lord and His guidance 'cause you can't run nothing without the Lord. It's got outta hand, and the people in our nation don't wanta think about God, and they've got it in their head that they can run this place without Him. I can warn 'em right now that you can't run nothing without Him in it. You can't even have a good business; you can't even have a good home or nothing else without Him. Unless He's the head of it, you ain't got nothing. That's the way I feel about it.

Mary: The government is trying to take God outta everything instead of invitin' Him in. They're working hard every day to make sure there's no prayers, no name, and no mention of Him. They shouldn't want to keep Him out. They should invite Him in.

**Mathis music is available from LV Mathis,
PO Box 125, Tuckasegee, NC 28783.**

A Family Tradition

~ Mountain Faith ~

There is no sweeter blending of voices than that of sibling harmony. The band Mountain Faith is certainly a good example of some of the finest family harmony in the field of bluegrass music. Sam McMahan; his daughter, Summer; son, Brayden; and nephew, John Morgan, not only take the soulful sounds of traditional music to a higher level, but are also one of the most talented groups of musicians and able to compete with the best of 'em. Their interest in music, commitment to family, and love of God are shared with audiences across the country. They are a blessing to know and a joy to hear perform, whether it is from a stage during a concert up north or echoing down the "holler" from the outdoor pavilion at Old Mater Farm.

—Joyce Green

Summer McMahan

I'm Summer McMahan, and I'm sixteen years old. My cousin, John Morgan, is fourteen, and my brother, Brayden, is fifteen. We live close to Dillsboro, North Carolina, and John lives in Sylva, North Carolina. When we started playing music together, John was seven, Brayden was eight, and I was nine. We've been playing about eight years, I guess. I started first. I started out on piano before the fiddle, and I knew how to read music then, but I don't remember it. I usually just play by ear. We all play by ear. My interest in the fiddle began when I saw the Fiddlin' Dill Sisters, a local band. I saw them at a singing at Mountain Heritage Day, a festival sponsored by Western

PLATE 71 "Mom, I want to play one of those."
Summer McMahan playing the fiddle

Carolina University, which features a display of Appalachian heritage and is attended by thousands. I was really little and said, "Mom, I want to play one of those," so she called a man, and he started giving me fiddle lessons.

I started taking fiddle lessons and, after about a year, Brayden and John started taking fiddle lessons, too. They didn't like it, so John decided he wanted to play the guitar, and Bray decided he wanted to play the banjo. I just mainly play the fiddle. The way we started playing and singing was, Dad had played the bass in church all his life, and so we got asked to sing at our church. We played "I'll Fly Away," and then my grandmother's church booked us. After that the churches just started calling.

The band mainly consists of Brayden, John, and me, but my dad also plays with us. Sometimes we have a mandolin player. A lot of the time it's a different mandolin player every time. I sing lead and alto. Brayden has a good lead voice. John has a good singing voice, too. His voice is deep. We pretty much all sing all of the parts [lead, tenor, alto, bass]. We just kinda switch around.

We travel to sing about every weekend. We usually play and sing three times every weekend, starting about May till about October. Our traveling doesn't really cut into our social life, though, because usually we'll miss like a Friday or something at school, and then we're back. A lot of our friends go with us on trips we take. We travel and sing all over the United States. The farthest north we've been is Delaware. We go to Chincoteague, Virginia, every year, and we sing at the blueberry festival that they have. We've sung in Colorado, Florida, Texas, South Dakota, Wyoming, Alabama, and all the states around here. Those are just some of the farthest places we have been.

We go to Victory Christian School. Our school is run by our church. The school is right beside the church, as you start up Cowee Mountain in

PLATE 72 **"We travel to sing about every weekend."**
Mountain Faith at one of their performances

North Carolina. There's a lot of people in our school that sing, so we're not really different. Our school is very small [laughs]. In kindergarten through twelfth grade, there's like fifty-something students. We have a lot of one-on-one time. I like going to a Christian school. I like how it's a lot smaller. I've never been to public school; I've always been in the Christian school, so I don't really know what public school is like. I think I like Christian school because I like to get busy and get stuff done.

I don't know what Brayden and John plan to do, but when I finish school, I'm thinking about going to Tennessee State and majoring in bluegrass. Then on the weekends, I can keep doing what we're doing [performing]. If you get a degree in music, then you can do studio work, keep singing, and really work in any aspect of the industry. A lot of professors at Tennessee State are members of groups, and they teach and keep traveling and singing, too.

Sam McMahan

My name is Sam McMahan. I was born February 5, 1963. We were raised at Punkintown [Pumpkintown], right up here through these mountains. I've been in and around music all my life; I remember, growing up, my papaw singing at all the churches around here. He'd make us grandkids get up and sing, too, so I've always been around music, but Summer, Brayden, and John really got me into it. When they started playing, they wouldn't get onstage without me. That's how we started playing and singing as a group in our church. They got up to sing and play and said I had to get up there with 'em, so I got the bass and went. I had learned to play the bass as a teenager. I actually learned on the electric, but I switched to the stand-up [doghouse bass] and now that's all I play.

PLATE 73 **The cover of Mountain Faith's latest CD, *Billy Red***

My brother has played piano for a southern gospel quartet for years. He's played with The Inspirations, The Florida Boys, and several others.

Where we live here and have the music shows was a tomato farm for seventy-five years. The main part of the house here is over one hundred years old. The ol' man, Claude Buchanan, that owned it laid his last crop at age ninety-four. He was always called the Mater Man and that's how I always knew him. He had an old Ford truck, and I don't think he ever got it out of second gear, so if you met him on the four-lane road, he was going twenty-five or thirty miles an hour, tops. He would haul tomatoes out by the truckloads, and he washed every tomato by hand. One time some people did a video of him. They was going out west and wanted to take it and show the people out there. Claude was washing tomatoes with a big ol' chew of tobacco in, spitting and all, and the lady told him to say something to the people out west. He'd look at the camera for a minute, and then go back to washing. She said, "Now, Claude, you've got to find something to say to the people." He looked up at the lady and said, "It didn't flash [laughs]." He thought she was taking a picture, and she had been videoing him that whole time. His daughter put the farm up for sale right after he died. She had several golf clubs wanting to buy the property and offers from other developers, but she wanted to keep the land as a farm, so we were able to buy it from her. This whole area [motions to the area surrounding his home] was all a big tomato patch. We tried growing tomatoes, before turning the farm into a bluegrass farm, but didn't have much luck. That's how our Bluegrass on the Farm got started. This is our fourth year [2010] having it, and we start shows in June and run through October. We change the lineup of groups every year. We just have a wonderful time. Claude's daughter lives in Canton, North Carolina, and still comes to a lot of our singings here.

It usually works out where we have music scheduled for every other Saturday night. Now, this year, we will have Dailey and Vincent here on a Friday night because that's the only day that they had open in their schedule. Then we will have shows on the second Saturday of July, August, September, and on the second Saturday of October, we'll finish up. We usually have a good turnout in the fall because the leaves are all changing and there's a beautiful view from out there at the pavilion. For our festivals we have about seven hundred come through here, give or take a few. Some of the night singings and things, we'll have about three hundred or so. We have people come from Virginia, South Carolina, Tennessee, all over, so it's a good time. We just got the septic system put in this year for campsites and hopefully, by next year, we'll have about ten sites.

We donate the money made at the Mater Farm singings to different organizations. We donated to the Make-A-Wish Foundation the first three years, and this year we're contributing to Life Challenge. It's a shelter for abused women and children, and it's run by the Baptist Association. We usually are able to donate about two thousand dollars.

We have recorded three albums. We recorded a "chipmunk" album when the kids were seven, eight, and nine; Brayden was as wide as he was tall, and John's guitar was bigger than he was, so we called that the chipmunk album [laughs]. We've made two more CDs that we sell now. One was all gospel, and we just got the proofs back from the newest one. It is our first bluegrass CD, and it contains five bluegrass and five gospel songs.

Playing and singing is our hobby and our ministry combined. That's a hard thing to balance out. We all like to perform at bluegrass events and at church. We like to go to Long Creek, South Carolina, on Friday nights and play bluegrass and gospel and have a good time. Then we also want our music to be a ministry when we go into church on Sunday. I think all three of these guys are well balanced. They understand what we're trying to do. When we go into a church or anywhere to play, it's easier to play and have a good time when the audience responds well. Some churches where we go are more contemporary and don't have an appreciation for bluegrass music, and you can't even tell if they like the music. If you know the people are enjoying it, then you are enjoying doing it.

Along with all the traveling and singing, I also own a business. I change a lot of tires [laughs]. I have a tire store here in town. I put these kids to working, too. John and Brayden help, and Summer runs the deli. She gets up at five o'clock and works until time to go to school.

I was the administrator at Victory Christian School for several years. I prefer a Christian school to public school because of the content of the subjects. In a Christian school even the math word problems are teaching morals instead of just the core stuff. They also have Bible classes, too. It's a place where kids can go and be a good Christian without all of the peer pressure. There's still some there, just not as bad, I don't think. Hopefully, when they get older and get out in the world, their Christian education will help them make better decisions. I do, however, believe there are Christian teachers that are called to teach in the public school system, my wife being one of them. I believe the Lord can call you into the teaching profession because my wife has a great ministry there in her classroom and school.

Several of the private schools around here join together and provide the opportunity for the students to participate in sports just like public school. Summer, Brayden, and John all love sports. Summer played on the summer volleyball team for private schools this year; they won the volleyball state championship. The guys play basketball and golf.

Editor's note: *Brayden and John are long on talent but short on words. Brayden did tell us that he'd rather pick than sing. He said he was content and happy with music and traveling and that he enjoys it as long as the sound system is good and it's not too cold.*

**Mountain Faith music is available from Sam McMahan,
138 Old Mater Farm Road, Sylva, NC 28779;
www.mountainfaith.bandzoogle.com.**

Fishers of Men
~The Primitive Quartet~

There are some singers who sing "a little bit of country and a little bit of rock 'n' roll," and maybe a gospel song somewhere in their performance. Then there are singers who have dedicated their lives and careers to working strictly for the Lord. The latter would include The Primitive Quartet. The Primitives have traveled the country spreading the Gospel for many, many years. They are steadfast and have not wavered from their faith or their commitment to God. They walk the walk and talk the talk. If you spend just a few minutes with any one member of this group, you will realize what true, sincere Christians they really are. They have blessed untold millions with their CDs, videos, and live performances. I'm sure the angels perk up and listen as the voices of Reagan, Norman, Larry, Jeff, Mike, and Randy blend in sweet traditional harmony that flows with the ripple of the river and echoes through the mountains of Candler, North Carolina, where their annual gospel singing is held each July. The members of this group have never lost sight of where they came from. They are down-to-earth, generous, true friends to family and fans alike.

—Joyce Green

Larry Riddle

I'm Larry, and I was born on April 15, 1952, to Glenn and Lois Riddle in Marshall, North Carolina. I lived in the era when we didn't have inside plumbing and when we had cows, chickens, hogs, and raised most everything we ate. I had a wonderful childhood, roaming the mountains, playing and fishing in the creek, swinging on grapevines, and climbing jack pines. My uncle Hilliard taught me how to make roosters fight, and I dearly paid for that. Every time I went to gather the eggs, a rooster would flog me. Finally, the Lord called it home, with a little help from me. The world is a different place today; it really is a different place to live.

My mom and dad sang in church when we were small and traveled to many singings in the area. I grew up singing a little bit with them and got gloriously saved when I was eighteen years old. The group was born in '73. We started on a fishing trip, and we're still fishing, singing, and huntin', and enjoy it. We started out singing as two sets of brothers—me and my older brother, Reagan, and Norman and his older brother, Furman. Furman kinda took me under his wing when I was first saved, and we spent a lot of time huntin' and singin' and goin' to church.

I've been singing with The Primitive Quartet for thirty-seven years. We've been singing this mountain music a long time. I was twenty-one when

PLATE 74 **The Primitive Quartet: Larry Riddle, Norman Wilson,
Randy Fox, Reagan Riddle, Mike Riddle, and Jeff Tolbert**

I started singing with them. During the first five years of singing, they'd take up an offering for us, and we were so embarrassed, we'd try to give it back to them. We never, ever intended to do this for a living; it's just something that happened. We sang five years locally, close around home. Then Archie Watkins with The Inspirations was having some problems with his vocal cords, and they asked us to travel with them for a while. We actually traveled with them for eighteen months. That was a tremendous gift and a blessing to be able to travel the country, meet all the promoters, and be introduced to all their people. If it hadn't have been for that, we probably would never have sung professionally, but God just kinda laid it in our laps. We all were self-employed at that time, so we could both work and sing until the one [the singing] took over the other one [working] and made it possible. God has been good to us. He has really been good to us. I'm very thankful.

We have always gone with acoustic music—just our ol' mountain and bluegrass music with mandolins, guitars, basses, fiddles, and banjos. We sing shape-note music. It used to be in all the songbooks, but now it's round notes. That's the way we learned to sing, by shape music, and it's kinda progressed along as time went on. Reagan writes a lot of the songs that we sing. We get songs from other writers, and we still try to put a couple of shape-note songs on every CD. Our music has gotten away from all shape notes, though. We cut our teeth on the shape-note music that you heard on albums for years, but now we put the music to original songs ourselves.

We are very proud of our homecoming singing, Singing in Hominy

Valley, that started in 1981. Hominy Valley is just west of Asheville, North Carolina, on Highway 151. We advertise all year long to our friends, inviting them to come to visit the beautiful mountains, and it doesn't take much to get people into these western North Carolina mountains, especially if they like gospel music, too. We have groups from all over the country come to sing with us, usually about a week around the Fourth of July. We also have two weekends of singing in the fall at Hominy Valley in Candler, North Carolina. Candler is our home, and it's easy to get people to come see our beautiful fall colors during the second and third weekends in October.

We average traveling twelve days a month. We have done that for thirty years now on a regular basis. I don't even know how many states we have performed in, really, just all over. We are thankful that people everywhere enjoy our kind of music. I feel like it is a ministry for Christ, or I wouldn't be doing it. He is very, very precious to me. I can't imagine life without Him. If it wasn't for Him, then I wouldn't have been able to stay on the road for thirty-seven years.

It's a little bit embarrassing for me to talk about things like the awards we have won. Last year at the Bluegrass Awards at the National Quartet Convention in Louisville, Kentucky, Mike got Musician of the Year, and we got Group of the Year. Jeff got Top Vocalist, and Reagan got Songwriter, and we have been nominated several times for Band of the Year. They inducted us into the Blue Ridge Music Hall of Fame a couple of years ago. In September of 2010, we were blessed to be awarded the Norcross-Templeton Award at the NQC. I guess what I am as proud of as anything is that we have been consistent. The Lord has blessed us to have songs in the top-forty charts for the past twenty-five years, and that's in the southern gospel music field.

We sing at more southern gospel venues probably than anything else. We sing with all the southern gospel groups, and we do a few bluegrass festivals a year—nothing like as many bluegrass as we do southern gospel, though. We probably sing at one church and two other venues per weekend, so about one in three times in a church. Still, that's my favorite way to sing, like we are here tonight, in a church. We go, and they feed us a wonderful meal, treat us unbelievably well, take good care of us; we sing, and then when we are done, around nine o'clock, we can go home. God has blessed us with precious friends all over the country that makes this possible.

I would like for young people today to know that if there wasn't even a hereafter, which I absolutely believe there is, God has proven Himself to me many times that He is real. He has been such a very present help in so many times of need for me. He's just a precious friend that nothing's ever gotten too big for. He changed my world; you'd just had to know me before. Christ is the best thing that's ever happened to me. He has blessed me in so many ways. One example of this was how I prayed God would send me the girl He had for me to marry. He showed me my wife was the one. I spent a day in the mountains praying. When we first started singing, I started praying that God would send me a good, godly woman that I could live with. I knew He loved me; I knew I loved Him; I knew He knew the future; and I knew that I didn't. So why not consider Him, if He knows the future, in something as important as picking a mate? I went to the mountains and said, "God, I need your help; show me if she's the one." I've never had a more heavenly day in my life. I believe He was pleased that I wanted to consider Him in this big decision. He said, "Consider Me in all your ways." I poured my heart out to God, asking if she was the one, and He just blessed it. Consider Him in all your decisions; He knows the future. That would be the advice that I'd give a young person, but most importantly, give your heart to the Lord while you're young. When you're old it will get hard and change will be harder for you then, but when you're young and tender, that's the time to trust the Lord, and He'll bless your whole life. I started right, tried to live right, and I'm more determined to finish right the older I get. We've made so many precious friends around the country singing, and I would so hate to let them down, too.

If I had my life to live over, I would pick the same path again, without a shadow of any doubt! I don't see how people make it without the Lord, especially in hard times. A year ago I found out that my eldest daughter had breast cancer; my mother had breast cancer at forty-nine; my wife was diagnosed with breast cancer at forty-nine, and my daughter at twenty-nine. It's just a privilege to have Him to turn to all the time, in good times and bad.

A lot of people ask my advice on how to succeed in the world of gospel music. I tell them three things: One, be a little bit different; two, have original music; and three, have the touch of God on your singing. Especially, have the touch of God! Praise Him for being so good to me!

Reagan Riddle

My name is Reagan Glenn Riddle. I was twenty-seven when The Primitive Quartet started singing, thirty-seven years ago; you do the math [laughs]. I'll be sixty-four on June 30 [2010], but I don't feel it most of the time. For the first six years of my life, we lived on Foster Creek in the Big Laurel section of Madison County, North Carolina. My first school was the Foster Creek School, a two-room school with no indoor plumbing. At age six, we moved to Candler to be closer to my dad's work. At age fourteen, Dad bought me a brand-new Gibson factory left-handed guitar. I'll never forget how thrilled I was with it! As I look back and reflect on the monthly singings that my parents took me to, I realize God was preparing me for what He had in store.

I have been blessed with health all my life. I was raised in church, and that's where my love for music comes from. I used to sing with Mom and Dad a little. We attended Missionary Baptist Church, and that is where I still go today. I have two daughters and six grandchildren. My youngest daughter is married to Randy Fox, a member of our group, and they have two children. My older daughter is married to the pastor of one of the best churches in our county, North Asheville Baptist. They have three biological children and one adopted from Kazakhstan. The song "I'm No Longer an Orphan" that The Primitive Quartet sings is the little girl that story is about. She was eleven years old when they brought her to America, and she is now nineteen. She loves her Poppy, and I love her, too. Both my girls are involved in music. Tracey, my older daughter, sings in church all the time, and Tammy, Randy's wife, is a good singer and can play the piano and upright bass.

We started singing in 1973. It was just an accident. We went on a fishing trip and picked a little bit and sung two or three songs. Today, we are accepted in southern gospel music and at the National Quartet Convention, but our style of music is the mountain style. We sing the shape-note style of music and play the bluegrass instruments—guitars, mandolins, and fiddles. Shape-note music is a very elementary form of music. You remember learning the do, re, mi, fa, sol, la, ti, do in school? They just put a shape to those notes. In about three months anybody can learn the shape-note-style music. A lot of churches years ago had the shape-note-music schools, and in two weeks, they could about have everybody singing their part. I mean, it just works beautifully.

I play the guitar by ear, and I am left-handed. Believe it or not, I play cello right-handed. That was kind of a challenge. I've always played the left-handed guitar. I just turned the strings around when I was younger and before Dad bought my new Gibson in 1960. That was the first left-handed guitar I ever had. I was like the lightnin' bug that backed into a fan; I was delighted [laughs].

I've written a lot of songs over the years. I usually write about two or three, sometimes four or five for each new project. We get a lot of songs in the mail, so it just depends on whether we are able to use them. We got some songs recently from Texas. I'd written four or five for the recording we just made, but I liked the songs we got in more than the ones I'd written, so we recorded them.

We just had our new bus special-built for our group of six people. It has nine bunks. We have had four buses since we've been singing. We started with a van and a trailer just like everybody else. I love it. The joy of singing is still in it for me, and I hope that shines through when we sing. I love the Lord, and I just appreciate the privilege of doing it, and it *is* a privilege. People hear you on the radio and perhaps see you on television and come to see you just out of curiosity one time, but if nothing touches their heart, you'll never see them again. If something touches the inner man, they'll want that again. That is the Lord's part. This tells me that we can do nothing within ourselves.

I don't regret a mile that I've traveled for the Lord; however, my daughters were on the homecoming court just about every year in high school. I guess if I had it to do over, I wouldn't have missed those homecoming games like I did. We were always gone. Those were special events for my daughters and if I had it to do over again, I might make a change or two like that, but that is all. For some reason my family really wants to support us and travel with us when we go on that cruise every year [laughs].

If I had any advice for young people today, it would be about serving others; what you give away is the only thing you're going to take away, just serving and being a help to others. I believe that's the most important thing that we can do in this life, just being an encouragement to others. That's what this music is all about—just spreading sunshine.

Mike Riddle

My name is Michael Dean Riddle. I was born on May 1, 1957, and live in Candler, North Carolina, which is in the city limits of Asheville. I have three brothers and one sister. We were born about five years apart. All the brothers play music or sing except our youngest brother, Darren. Reagan is the oldest, then my sister, Geneva, then Larry, me, and Darren.

The first instrument I learned to play was the bass guitar. I played the bass with a group in Haywood County called the Happy Travelers when I was thirteen years old. They actually picked me up to go practice and sing 'cause I was too young to drive. I played with them about a year and a half. They just played locally around here in four or five counties: Macon, Haywood, Buncombe, and Jackson. Then I played with the Seeker's Quartet from Asheville. When I was sixteen I played bass guitar for one summer at Fontana Village Resort. They had a bluegrass group called the Fontana Ramblers. We played five nights a week from April through October. Doyle Barker played lead guitar, and Vance Trull played fiddle. These guys were very kind to me and taught me a lot about music.

Dad had an old Silvertone guitar and later bought a Gibson B-25 guitar. I would come in from school and play the guitar for two or three hours every day after school. I never did play sports in school; I played the guitar all the time. I had three albums that I practiced with to help me learn to play. They were by The Inspirations, Conway Twitty, and the Peace Maker's Quartet from Asheville. I thought I would never learn to play lead guitar. I actually laid it down for about six months and kinda gave up on it. Then it was like God revealed to me the pattern of how the scale of music works, even though I play by ear. So I picked it back up, and it all fell into place. Before that, I could play rhythm and a few runs, but I never could really learn where to place licks in behind singing, where it fit at the right spots and didn't take away from the singing. I'm thankful to God for that 'cause I was just about to give up. I was probably about fourteen or fifteen when I really started catching on and played lead guitar. I'm fifty-three now, and I'm still learning. Of course, I forget more than I learn [laughs].

I've never moved from the farm where I've always lived. I met and married my wife, Diane Hicks Riddle, who was raised in the Biltmore area of Asheville. We don't have any kids of our own, but we've always enjoyed our nieces and nephews. My dad gave us all lots on the farm to build on, and my family has always been there close by.

Besides lead guitar, I play bass guitar and the mandolin some. I had a steel guitar one time, but I never did get it mastered. I've fooled with the Dobro and banjo but never really got good on them. I also play the organ and piano a little. There was a dear man, Lane Worley, who was with the Happy Travelers, that got me started on the piano. He showed me how to play the bass notes with your left hand, like you were playing a bass guitar, and then chord with your right hand. We didn't have a piano at home, so when we would get to church early, I would practice. That's how my playing got started. Lane passed away about four or five years ago. He was a great encouragement to me.

I started singing with The Primitives when Furman Wilson left the group to start pastoring a church. Furman sung with them for the first five years, from 1973 to 1978. They were singing locally at that time, maybe five or six counties, and would occasionally sing in East Tennessee. I had been playing off and on some with them. When Furman started pastoring full-time, I joined the group and started playing lead guitar and singing baritone. I have now been with the group for thirty-two years. Some of the dates we fill each year we have been doing annually for twenty-five years, like the Georgia Mountain Fair and our anniversary singing in Gainesville, Georgia, with our dear friend Hayne Tatum.

We have been truly blessed working for the Lord. We have been nominated for several awards. Working for the Lord is the biggest reward of all, but it is an honor to be recognized for your work. In years past the quartet has been nominated for Group of the Year and Band of the Year at the National Quartet Convention. We were fortunate to win Song of the

PLATE 75 The original Primitive Quartet in the 1970s:
Reagan Riddle, Norman Wilson, Furman Wilson, and Larry Riddle

Year with a couple of songs, "That Soldier Was Me" and "Walking in the Highway." I've won Favorite Instrumentalist a couple of years in a row, 2008 and 2009, at the Front Porch Fellowship Bluegrass Gospel Awards. I was honored to be nominated, much less win it.

I think it was God's will that everything has happened like it has. I know I have failed the Lord in many ways. If I could do things over, I would probably try to lend a helping hand more to people that are hurting and try to be an encouragement to them. I was saved at Maple Ridge Baptist Church when I was thirteen. The pastor was Claude Surrett. I started attending Maple Ridge when I was six months old, when my parents moved to Candler from Madison County. All the members of The Primitive Quartet attend Maple Ridge.

My advice for anyone is to accept Jesus as their Savior and live for the Lord. They will never regret it. It's tougher now than when I was growing up. When I was a kid, there were so many folks, like my parents, who were just good, godly people. They set an example before young people. That upbringing doesn't ever leave you. I never will forget it. A lot of those people who were role models for me are dead now. I think we need to be more Christlike, set better examples, and do our part to show the world that Jesus is real. It is my prayer and the prayers of The Primitive Quartet that God will use our music to draw people to Him and to touch and comfort people who are hurting and going through valleys.

Randy Fox

My name is Randy Dale Fox. I was born on June 26, 1962. I grew up in a little town in Indiana called Williamsburg. They were still taking baby pictures in black and white then. As a child I can remember we didn't have air-conditioning, but I don't remember missing it too bad. We could get about three channels on the television, and we changed those channels with a pair of pliers. Life seemed to be at a slower pace back then. I went to church, went to school, played baseball, and went hunting and fishing with my dad. Mom was, and still is, a great cook, so we had plenty of good food to eat. I cherish my youth most because my parents took me to church and taught me about Jesus.

My dad was part of a quartet for twenty-six years, so gospel music has always been a big part of my life. After I was saved at the age of twelve years old, I developed a love for the music. My dad was in the process of trading guitars and noticed I was starting to learn how to play. He told me if I would learn how to play and use that talent for the Lord, he would give me his old guitar, which was a 1962 D-18 Martin. Long story short, I got the guitar, and just recently I told my thirteen-year-old son the same thing my dad told

PLATE 76 **Randy Fox with his wife, Tammy, and children, Cessali and Carson, taken on the Singing at Sea cruise**

me, and I passed it on to him. About that time, Dad's group had slowed down, so we started a group called the Gospel Fishermen. We traveled and sang together for about five years. At that time I had moved on to playing the mandolin. I can play a little bit on the banjo, but I currently play upright bass with The Primitive Quartet. I don't formally read music, but I can follow shape notes a little. I have written a few songs down through the years.

I still enjoy the traveling our group does. God has kept the joy in that and also the fact that our schedule does not keep us gone all the time. We average three days a week on the road, and we are home most Sundays, which allows us to be active in our home church. Our fellowship on the bus is great, and I think that shows when we perform onstage.

My favorite place to sing in general would be smaller churches. That's not to say you can't have great services in other venues because I've also felt His presence while singing on a street downtown. Our homecoming singing is always special, and it's at Hominy Valley in Candler. I like it because it's at home and that ground has been dedicated to God for the purpose of praising God in song.

The recognition we have received has been great, but it's something I never really think about much. We received the Song of the Year on a song I sang lead on, "Walking in the Highway," a few years ago from the radio show *Front Porch Fellowship* and have won other awards from them also, including male vocalist, Jeff Tolbert; musician, Jeff and Mike Riddle; as well as Group of the Year. We were also honored to be inducted into the Blue Ridge [Music] Hall of Fame last year.

PLATE 77 **Randy playing with Doc Watson when they were being inducted into the Blue Ridge Music Hall of Fame in June 2009**

I've been married twenty-two years to my wife, Tammy. Tammy is the daughter of Reagan Riddle, one of the founding members of The Primitive Quartet. We have two children, Cessali, fourteen, and Carson, thirteen. Our family has adjusted to the lifestyle my profession brings. They go with me once in a while when we are close to home, but most often they stay at home. My kids are really involved in activities in school. I miss some things that happen on the weekends, but I think I get to spend more time with them overall than the average father does.

My life thus far has been wonderful. I've made mistakes and bad decisions like everyone else, but through it all God has been faithful, and I hope to think I've learned some things down through the years. I'm still learning because I have two teenagers now—pray for me! The Lord has changed my life forever. I was headed for a place that was not prepared for me, and He changed my direction and now guides my path. One day I'll get to see Him and thank Him for what He has done for me. My advice for young people today would be to seek God in everything they do, stay faithful to church and the things He has given them to do. We all have a work to do, and He will direct our paths if we will listen to him.

Jeff Tolbert

My name is Jeff Tolbert. I'm from Mount Airy, North Carolina. I've been raised around music all my life. My mom and dad, Troy and Phyllis, had a lot of musical background on both sides of their family; music was a way of entertainment for us. I just started learning to play, I guess, from being around it all the time. Dad taught me a lot. He would put my fingers on the strings and show me the chords, and that was where my music began. Dad and I started singing together when I was very young. We would play at a lot of the churches and community gatherings all around my hometown.

When I was fifteen years old, I started traveling full-time and what you would say professionally, with The Easter Brothers. They taught me a lot and are still some of my heroes today. I went on to travel with Jeff and Sherri Easter, The Lewis Family, and also The Isaacs for about five years, and when I went off the road with The Isaacs in the fall of 1996, I had the opportunity to work with Ricky Skaggs. I enjoy recording, playing, and producing with many different artists in the recording studio.

Reagan Riddle called me right before the Hominy Valley singing in July and said, "Jeff, I wish you would come down here this week and sit in with us and pick and play some." So I thought about it and decided to go to Hominy Valley and enjoy the weekend with them. It's amazing how God puts things together. I had played with them some off and on when other groups I was with performed with them, but after this particular singing, God opened up a new door in my life, and I've been traveling with The Primitives going on fifteen years now.

It's an honor to be with the quartet. It's just amazing how God has blessed us and used the songs that we sing. Reagan is such a great songwriter, and what a privilege it is to sing a lot of his songs. It's been a great experience traveling and singing with these guys.

During that whole process I was just telling you about, I got married. It's ironic that we're here at Hominy Valley because I met my wife here. Her name is Shaytonya, and she was standing in the coffee line at the concessions, and when I saw her I was in love. I thought, "Well, a good way to meet her is, I'll go get her a cup of coffee and meet her in line." You can say a cup of coffee introduced me to my wife. Somebody told me the other day, "If I would have known that you could get her with just a cup of coffee, I would've given her a doughnut." I took her back to the same spot, and while looking at the mountains, I asked her to marry me. We got married in May 2004 at Maple Ridge Baptist Church. My wife and I live in Candler [North Carolina]. We built a new home about three years ago, and we are so thankful for what God has given us and blessed us with. We have a five-year-old son; his name is Briley. He is such a joy to our life; he is now picking and singing some also.

PLATE 78 **"A lot of people say he's a mini-me."**
Jeff with his son, Briley, plucking on the ol' banjo

Singing keeps us on the road quite a bit. Sometimes it is a sacrifice for us, but it is more of a sacrifice for our wives in a lot of ways. I definitely thank God for the wives of the quartet for standing by us and for their support and encouragement. We couldn't do without them! They've sure been a blessing to us.

I'm very privileged to do what I do; I love to sing and play. This style of music is my heritage, and I hope to pass it down to my children, and to have God to bless it would just be amazing. We've been nominated for several awards in Louisville, Kentucky. Mike's won instrumentalist, and I've won it a few times, also. We have won group and song of the year many times, and I've won male vocalist. It's kinda like a little boost, or a pat on the back, when you do get those little kind of things [awards] from time to time. It's a humbling experience knowing that God is using us in what we do.

I presently have a solo project called *Mercy and Grace*, and I'm working on another one with my dad. We (the Primitives) are hoping to do an instrumental project soon.

It's rewarding when we have people come up to us and say, "I bought your DVD or CD not too long ago, and it has been an encouragement to me," or have them tell us that someone was saved while listening to the words of our songs. A gentleman came up to me yesterday and said, "Jeff, I want you to know that my brother-in-law was dying" (he was very ill and on the verge of death), and I got to talking to him and asked him if he knew the Lord; "No," was his reply. Reagan wrote a song that I did on my new solo project, *Mercy and Grace*, and the name of the song is "Don't Die Without Jesus." The man said, "I just left the CD with him, and I told him that this was a young man who sings gospel music, and I'd love for him to listen to it." He went back the next day, and his brother-in-law was playing "Don't Die Without Jesus" over and over and over. He asked the Lord to come into his life, and he got saved. Just a few weeks after that, he passed on. It's just rewarding for someone to come up to you and tell you things like that. It helps you to keep going.

I've heard Norman say many times, "Without the Lord's touch on what we do, it would be nothing." What we're singing about comes from the heart. You can sing songs and sing a lot of words, but when you can actually sing songs and know what you're singing about, and know there is hope, that's what makes it real.

It is an honor to sing and play gospel music. Each and every one of us has a different talent that God has given us. Let's use those to lift Him up. Psalm 150:6.

Norman Wilson

My name is Norman Wilson. I was born July 2, 1944, in Macon County, North Carolina, on what they call the John Dean place down on the Little Tennessee River, but that's only history, and it is only as accurate as those who record it [laughs]! We moved and left over there where I was born in Franklin and went to Buncombe County, North Carolina, in the middle fifties and made a life there. Things changed some with the different locations. When you leave one place and go to another, there are different ideas and different standards, but overall, life's been good to this Wilson family.

In my family there are three boys, and we have two sisters each, so five. Us boys are quite a bit older than our sisters, and we were kinda grown when they came along, so we helped raise them, too. My brother's names are Furman and Truman. My sisters are Judy and Peggy Jean. Now, she don't like the Peggy; she likes the Jean part.

Life was not as stressful when I was growing up, as it is on kids today. We didn't expect a lot, and when you don't expect a lot, you're not disappointed. We were self-sufficient. We had what we needed; we grew what we needed and made the rest of it. Life was simpler, but our values were absolutely great. Our raising has been a good road map for the rest of my life, and Heaven will be my retirement due to my raising. Life was tough, but like I say, it was simple; didn't have a lot of stress. We just had what we had and gave thanks for it.

Daddy was a' old-time mountain preacher who preached fifty-seven years before graduation [going to Heaven]. Dad was an odd little man. He just wanted things right; he wouldn't accept nothing but right. There was no gray area for him. If you ever get to a point in life where you don't see the color gray, you won't be liked too much. Our society has got to where they want to gray everything. My daddy might have been strict, but he was the best example. We were simple people, but we were proud people. Growing up, we farmed, logged, cut timber, et cetera. Dad always had a truck, and he would do hauling for other people, and that is where the money came from to support our household. We were fortunate. A lot of folks during the late forties and early fifties didn't have any kind of transportation, so if they had any hauling to do, Dad done it.

In 1954 is when we got electricity. I remember the first time we had electricity. A fellow came and put us in two little lightbulbs, one in the living room and one in the kitchen, hanging down on a wire. They had a string hanging down from it to turn on the light. It had a forty-watt lightbulb, and we sit up about all night long looking at those lights. We thought the sun was shining in. We just had one window in the living room, and it was a small window, and we hadn't seen the corners of the house. It was a single-box house. A single box means it didn't have no two-by-fours, it was just a single box. The cracks were stripped. They took paper or cardboard, or newspaper, and put it on the inside. They would take flour paste and put paper up on the wall. It was purty. Some of it had designs on it, and that was cool. We had linoleum on the floor, and you just had one floor, the subflooring, and the cracks of the boards would start coming through the rug, but it sure was purty when it was new.

I know about the running water, too; we run and got it, not out of the well but out of the spring. We kept our milk cold by setting it in the spring box in the branch. As time goes on we can look back and laugh and remember and give thanks. God's blessed our nation. Our nation has come from struggling to the land of plenty. That's the reason our immigrants has come. I've been south of the border, and I don't wonder why they want to come to our country. God has blessed America—not that He hadn't blessed all—but, I'll be honest with you, God will honor his own. When America stops honoring God Almighty, then we're gonna be in trouble.

My interest in music started when I was young. Dad played guitar and the French harp—harmonica, but it's French harp for us mountaineers. He had a little ol' guitar I'd look at. Kids weren't allowed to play with the instruments, but I was intrigued with it. Dad showed me a couple of chords. My fingers weren't long enough to make anything but the G chord. I could barely make a D, and I couldn't make a C. My granddaddy was also a great old-time backhand banjo player. When I was about four or five years old, he lived with us. My grandpa would get up at four o'clock every morning. He didn't sleep much at all, and he'd come to where I slept, and he'd say, "Norman, how about getting up and let's pick a little bit." That's where my music started. I know kids don't play well when they first start, but he would say, "Boy, you're doing good. You're really doing good." That would encourage me. Music has made me a good life, and that's where it started. My granddad really instilled in me the drive, and the want-to, to play. Most kids want to play ball, but I wanted to learn how to play music, and that's why I do what I do today.

We started singing as a family in the fifties. My daddy and my older brother and my grandmother started singing together. My grandmother was a singer's singer. Dad sang bass, my brother sang the lead part, my grandmother sang the alto part, and I sang the high tenor. We sung together until my grandmother died in 1957. Then me, my dad, and my brother and a Crane boy started singing as a quartet. We called ourselves The Wilson Family. That was a seventeen-year tenure. We never made any recordings. Dad wasn't gung ho on recordings. He didn't think that was the right thing to make money off your recordings. I'd give anything now if we'd made some recordings back in the sixties.

Over in the Fontana, North Carolina, area is where I got acquainted with my wife, Kaye. Her name is Wanda Kaye. She was a Whitehead. I met her daddy about two years before I ever met her. I loved that man. He was the best preacher I'd ever heard; we just bonded. He invited us to come down to his home church in Tennessee. He pastored Meadow Branch Church. He said, "Come early, and my wife will have supper for you." Well, we went down there, and we went early, and there was the purtiest little girl standing by the driveway that I had ever seen in my life, and I said to myself, "That right there is gonna be my wife." She was probably about seventeen or eighteen. I talked to her, and she had a boyfriend. I seen her again after that and asked her out, and she said, "No, I got a boyfriend." I don't like noes. Noes don't cut it. We got married on Valentine's Day in 1970. I'll tell you right now, these long-distance romances, they're not pleasant.

I started with The Primitives the first of April in 1973. My wife loves for me to be on the road singing; it gives her a rest, and she loves it. Actually, she has been very supportive. Without our support at home, our quartet would not be what it is today. Every man is only as good as the support he has at home. If you don't have support at home, you won't last long. Our wives have a lot to do with the things we do, and we certainly don't take that for granted.

The Primitive Quartet always done their own thing. That was what we had going for us back in the seventies. We were doing old primitive original-type music, and we never stopped, and I hope we never do. When we first started, we called ourselves the Riddle-Wilson Quartet. We got to thinking, "We need another name." I thought, "'Primitive' means original," so that's where I came up with the name Primitive. So we started calling ourselves The Primitive Quartet. In the beginning, we traveled in cars or trucks or whatever we had. In 1973 we cut a record. It wasn't tapes, and it wasn't CDs; it was a record. We also made a few eight-tracks. Then in 1974, we bought us a little van, and we traveled in that for a while. As progress went along and the funds started coming in, we bought us a new van in '77 and bought us a little trailer and painted it up, and we were big-time, full-timers. In about '77, The Inspirations came over, and we sang on the program with them, and the rest is history.

We got our first bus the last of 1979 or the first of '80. None of us had had a bus, and we didn't know what to do. We are now on our fifth bus. We bought a new Prevost in 1999, and we bought a new, custom-built MCI last year. It's made traveling a lot more comfortable. We don't do but about a hundred sixty dates a year. We try to be at home at least four nights a week. That's helped our longevity. We're home every week and try to be home every Sunday for church. Some Sundays we sing away from home, but not every Sunday.

What makes singing good is that little sweet touch of God in it. It's kinda like cornbread or biscuits. Now, you can have biscuits, and you can have flour; you can have milk, and you can have eggs; but without grease, it ain't much, and it don't rise too much. That touch of God puts the grease in the bread. Some of the best singing you'll ever hear is back in these mountains. It's a different sound, pure harmony. We try to do everything [music and voice] when we record, and then we can duplicate that when we sing live. We do most of our recording at Horizon Studios in Arden, North Carolina. A lot of your well-known groups are recording there where we record.

My advice to young people today is to find some vocation in life that they enjoy doing. Life's a short trip. If you really enjoy your work, it will never become a job to you. Then do it with all your heart, with all your might. I believe that's the road to success: Find something that you enjoy doing, and do it to the best of your ability. Always do your own thing; don't do what everybody else is doing. I encourage young people to learn how to play an instrument, learn how to make music. It's good mind therapy. You can be having a bad day, and you can pick up an instrument and play some kind of little tune, and it's better than the alternative—taking some kind of medication. I have built sixteen mandolins. It is just a hobby. I take a piece of wood, and everything that don't look like a mandolin, I cut it away! If you don't do something in life, you won't be remembered too long. If you build a good instrument, it will last a long time. I always put my dad's name on the mandolins I build, just to honor and remember him.

The best part about my life is I made a lot of friends and got to meet a lot of precious, precious people. I think the people we meet enhance our life because we learn from each other. That's about the story of it, and I'm about twenty-one or twenty-two now, but I hope to keep learning till the day I leave here. Life is what it is. Yesterdays are what's made us what we are today. Happy trails.

Rev. Radford Wilson

Had it not been for Rev. Radford Wilson, there might not have been a Primitive Quartet. He was the father of two of the original members, Norman and Furman, and he also taught Larry and Reagan Riddle to sing shape-note music.

—Joyce Green

Rev. Radford Wilson was born to Bart and Lela Bell Mize Wilson on November 21, 1912, and grew up in the Scaly Mountain, North Carolina, community. He lived in Macon County until he moved to Buncombe County in 1955. Radford was a man of integrity and honor. He announced his calling to preach the Gospel at the age of twenty-five. He was ordained at the Flats, in Scaly Mountain, and was Baptist minister for fifty-seven years. Reverend

PLATE 79 **Rev. Radford Wilson and his soul mate, Virta Berlene Anders Wilson**

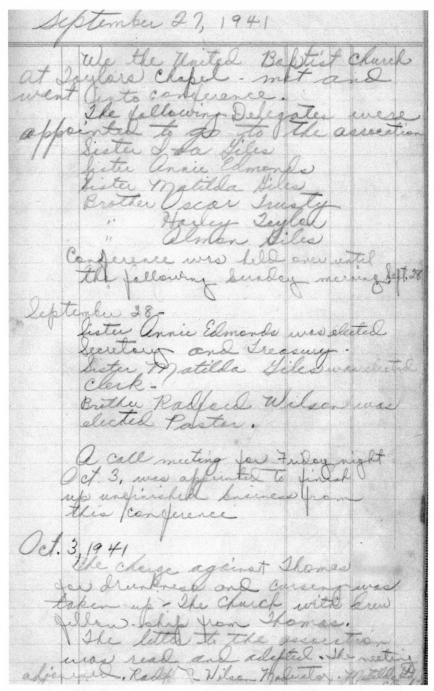

PLATE 80 A copy of the church records from 1941, when Reverend Wilson was elected pastor of Taylor's Chapel Baptist Church in Mountain City, Georgia. Note where a member of the church was taken out of fellowship for drunkenness and cursing in these minutes of one of the church conferences.

Wilson served as pastor of churches in several North Carolina counties. He also pastored in Rabun County, Georgia, and was instrumental in winning many souls to Christ. Radford not only preached, but he also knew his music quite well and taught his children how to sing the shape notes, which is the traditional mountain-style music that The Primitive Quartet still sings today.

On May 8, 1941, at the home of Oscar Nix, Radford married his sweetheart and soul mate at the age of twenty-eight. Her name was Virta Berlene Anders. She was not only his soul mate but also his prayer warrior. She was very quiet and soft-spoken, but her ability to shine always shone through. She loved everyone, welcomed everyone into her home, and always had a bountiful spread. She was truly the backbone of Radford's ministry with her quiet and humble demeanor. Radford and Virta had five children: Furman, Norman, Truman, Judy, and Jean.

Radford loved to sing. He was elected choir director of his home church at age eleven and competed in many singing events. For many years he had his own singing group, which included two of his sons, Furman and Norman, along with Ronald Crane. Radford taught Reagan and Larry Riddle how to sing shape notes, which was instrumental in forming The Primitive Quartet.

Reverend Wilson was a very good mentor and counselor. People came from far and wide to seek his advice. He would tell them, "It's not what I think, but let's see what God says in His Word." He truly was a man of God. Norman states that he will never forget what his daddy told him on his dying bed. He said, "Honey, live right and you can die right." Without a doubt, Radford and Virta were both people that you knew lived for God. They are gone, but they are still missed and will never be forgotten.

**The Primitive Quartet's music can be ordered
at www.primitivequartet.com.**

A Band Is Born

~George Reynolds and The Foxfire Boys~

As I quickly ran into class the day of my first Foxfire interview, I was extremely nervous because I was going to meet Mr. George Reynolds. I didn't know what he looked like, but I had heard many stories about him already, so I was excited to get to meet the legendary teacher. I enjoyed listening to his recounting of how Foxfire came to be, how the Foxfire Boys started, and of his life after Foxfire. Also, I learned of his experiences as a Foxfire folklore and music teacher. Not only did he play his guitar and sing, but he played the jaw harp, as well, and Joyce Green even joined in and helped. Other classes also got to enjoy George's interview because after he stopped talking he started singing, and he sang all the way through two more classes. It is easy to see how he motivated his students with his enthusiasm and talent.

George left Rabun County High School when he married, and he moved to Knoxville, Tennessee, where his wife was teaching. He stayed at home with his son for a while before beginning to teach school. He even told our teachers that people would come up to him in the grocery store when he had his son and say, "Well, I guess Granddad is out with the grandkid again."

He currently teaches music at an elementary school in inner-city Knoxville, where he still uses the Foxfire teaching approach every day. His elementary students make their own instruments out of flip-flops and cardboard tubes, and they love it! He is still listening and learning from his students today, and he feels blessed to be doing what he loves to do. Even though we miss his presence here at Rabun County High School, we are so happy that he is carrying on the Foxfire tradition.

—Ana Merino

I didn't take education courses in college and did not plan to be a teacher professionally. My parents were teachers, and everybody said, "Well, I guess you'll grow up to be a teacher like your mom and dad." So I ended up being a teacher, and I got an opportunity to work for Foxfire. I guess you could say the timing was just right. Foxfire did not have a real true folklorist on the staff, and they were publishing materials about folklife—southern mountain folklife. They hired me to be a folklorist, and along with that they also expected me to teach. All the Foxfire staff were teachers, advisers, editors, and everybody did everything. We were still at Rabun Gap–Nacoochee School then. It was the tenth year that Foxfire had been around. I taught one year there at Rabun Gap. I didn't have to be certified as a teacher because they could cut the red tape and count me as the Foxfire teacher's aide. I learned to teach in the classroom from spending time with the Foxfire staff.

Everybody was so excited and dedicated to being the right kind of teacher. We were involved in this process where we were actively engaging the kids in helping us learn how to do our job. I guess you might call it a profession. It was never based on what we learned at college, but much of it was in what we had learned from just paying attention to what the kids told us. The most important thing about being a Foxfire teacher was paying attention to the students you were teaching and becoming a learner in the process so that everybody shares a learning experience and nobody is the boss. No one is the center of attention, although someone has to be the adult in the room and be responsible. The whole process is a shared learning experience, and that is how I learned to teach—I listened to my students. Well, it turns out that that was a really good way to learn.

We started the Foxfire music program with the idea that we would collect music tapes and turn them into recordings and sell them in order to support the music program. It was the same way that the spoken word was published in the magazines. The magazines, by that time, had become quite a big producer of material but not necessarily income. The books themselves were incredibly successful. As you may know, *The Foxfire Book* was the biggest-selling book at that time in Doubleday's publishing history; its corporation was one of the big five publishing companies in the world. So that was a real plus, because not only was Foxfire a great place to work, but everybody knew about Foxfire—it was real famous.

The magazines were published from '67, you know; the class started in '66. It wasn't like the other magazines; it was like a school literary magazine. They invited poetry and prose from other communities. There was artwork, and there was all kinds of things that were pretty much along the lines of the typical high school arts journal. The turn of events that changed the magazine forever was when they first interviewed Mr. Luther Rickman, the sheriff, about the first great bank robbery back in the thirties. People were just fascinated by seeing printed word about somebody in their community and about an event that happened up there that was dramatic. They all wanted copies of it, so the kids decided to sell more and more and do more interviews and include more community people in the magazine. The popularity increased dramatically with the introduction of the personal interview and material that was collected. I don't know how many issues the magazine sold, but it was 1972 when the first book was published, and so all the collected materials, up to what would have been 1971, were organized in the first book.

Most of the people were Betty's Creek folks because the community kids who went to Rabun Gap–Nacoochee School were mostly from Betty's Creek. The county would pay Rabun Gap–Nacoochee a certain amount to provide teachers to handle that number. It was an unusual combination of private-school kids that boarded there, who had no transportation away from the school, and kids who lived in the community. The combination was pretty cool. The kids who lived in the community knew all the folks up on Betty's Creek. They were kin to them, as well as friends with them. They could introduce them to the boarding-school kids, and the kids at the boarding school were just dying to get out of there. It was a pretty contrastive atmosphere. They would just jump at the chance to leave campus and do something out in the community.

One interesting thing I learned while we were doing the *Foxfire: 25 Years* book was that it was sort of a self-study. We interviewed other people who had been in Foxfire. Some students were interviewed and also people who had been Foxfire students. The kids who were A students didn't want to take Foxfire because they had figured out and insisted that they knew how to get A's. They knew exactly what was going to be on the test, and they knew how to make the system work. The kids who were not doing really well in school were a perfect match for Foxfire because it gave them opportunities to use their gifts and the things that they knew. They were kids who knew culture. They didn't like school very much and didn't care about an English book. They were really good about going and interviewing the locals, and they learned the language skills by organizing the words so that they could make the spoken word interesting and easy to read. I think that the whole phenomenon of how Foxfire started was a really fortunate combination of a lot of different factors that nobody might ever even have planned.

Having a connection to the real world out there, doing things hands on, creating things, and working with each other in small groups—all those aspects about Foxfire came from young people telling the teacher what works. Being able to cut it down to something that simple where you just say, "Okay, we're just gonna ask the kids." That's so simple; it's genius. Nationwide, there was this yearning for something that wasn't made out of plastic. There was this movement that occurred that was bigger than Foxfire, which they call the back-to-the-land movement, where everybody was kind of struggling to find things that were naturally grounded and simple with healthy and earth-friendly dimensions. When Foxfire came out, people just soaked it up like water to a thirsty person, and it sold all over. It was a best seller for weeks, but they couldn't print enough copies of it; people just loved it! The royalties generated enough money to hire other folks to work for Foxfire and help meet the needs of other kids. Maybe they didn't want to do a magazine, but they would rather do a television program or make a record of different types of music. They hired me because I was a musician and a card-carrying hillbilly and folklorist all combined.

Guy Carawan, who was on Foxfire's National Advisory Board, was a musician for social change who was employed at the Highlander Center. He took me under his wing and took me around to do concerts and stuff with him. He recommended me to Foxfire. He brought me down here for a concert to meet the kids. They all talked first, and then he and the kids said, "Well, we want to sing." They found out what I was all about, and they were going to talk about hiring me. They brought me down here to do a concert at Rabun Gap–Nacoochee School, and resulting from that and other things, they eventually hired me. There happened to be this really famous television documentary producer who is still around, Geraldo Rivera. He was really famous for some documentaries that he did. The kids wanted to see what a real documentary producer looked like, and the benefit was in the information video program, so they invited Geraldo Rivera to come down here and be there for the weekend when Guy and I came to sing. We're at the concert, and there are all these television cameras and lights and stuff hitting us in the face and this big ole ABC lens right in front of my face while I'm singing my song. Boy, I was really impressed—ABC is here filming me. I'm

PLATE 81 **"I was a teacher for Foxfire for nineteen years."**
George Reynolds recalling his Foxfire experiences

gonna be on television, yeah! Well, Guy wasn't impressed, and he realized that these guys were in between him and the kids, and he said, "Turn that camera off and get out of my face! You didn't ask me if you could do this, and I bet that you didn't ask these kids if you could do this. You're messing up this concert, and I want you to just be quiet for a minute because I've got a song I want to sing, and I don't want you bothering us." The kids gave a standing ovation. They didn't care if this guy was famous; they didn't care if this was ABC. They wanted to hear the song. So Geraldo gathered up his film crew, flipped that little scarf around his neck, got into his car, and got back to Atlanta. We never saw anything on ABC. Basically, they ran them off, but the kids didn't care. I thought, boy, I was so impressed by ABC, but I'm in the presence of people who are not impressed. That, in turn, impressed me.

I was a teacher for Foxfire for nineteen years. After one year at Rabun Gap–Nacoochee School, Foxfire moved lock, stock, and barrel down here to this high school [Rabun County], which was a brand-new building. Everything was exciting.

I [didn't work on] the magazine at first; it wasn't in my job description. I'll never forget this: [the *Foxfire* teacher] and I were sitting up there on the hill, up there on the mountain [The Foxfire Museum and Heritage Center], looking at this house that was partially completed, and we were talking about how it would be the house where I would live. We were talking about my salary at the time, which was twelve thousand dollars. He said, "Now, I want you to start a music program." Four words ["start a music program"]— that was my job description; there was an underlying idea that I would do that when I first came here in 1976. I was asked to start a music program, and it was just that simple. That simple idea came from the fact that the publications supported the magazine program. If we documented musical traditions and sold records, we could support a music program. There were already the beginnings of a video productions program, and the idea behind it was that we would produce videos. It would be self-supporting, too. Foxfire Records was immediately part of the idea, and I was asked if I wanted to teach some courses, and I said, "Well, I will teach the folklore course, and I'll teach the folk music course, so I will do a record production course, too." When I first started teaching folklore and folk music, I was sort of teaching about music. The kids would go out and study other people playing music, but they didn't play music at that time. In the conversations that the staff had with each other, we were constantly thinking about how we could do our job better by including the kids in the way it was designed. Everything we did has evolved; it evolved pretty much from scratch because we decided we weren't going to teach like teachers but more like advisers, counselors, or coaches. Instead of deciding what to do, we were gonna work with the kids to figure out what the next step would be. When I got here, I was teaching about folk music, and Filmer Kilby had been in my class at Rabun Gap, and Filmer said, "You know, George, when we get all our work done, can we bring our guitars in and play a little bit?"

I said, "Once we get all our work done," so he brought his guitar, and it was great. We had a great time, and that became a regular thing. Next thing you know, it was the next semester and the next school year, and I'm saying, "Well, I'm just going to offer a course in music to teach students how to play." We could teach anything we wanted to teach at school at that time. We let the kids sign up, and we had a terrific amount of kids to create new things from scratch, and it was incredible. We had the money to do something very interesting, very new, and on the cutting edge of education because we had the brains to do it and the schoolrooms to do it and the kids to do it with; it was a very serious responsibility. At the same time, it was just joyous to be able to decide, "Well, I'll teach a course," so I taught a musical performance class. I requested that my kids bring their guitars to school. We started a performance class, and I had maybe twelve or fifteen kids, and we had most kids bringing guitars. I brought a bass fiddle in and a banjo, and some wanted to do pop music, I remember. One student was singing Beatles songs, and Steve McCall was doing some Hank Williams songs. We had a couple of people doing some gospel music. They all had different things in mind they wanted to do, and I didn't decide they were gonna do this kind of music or that kind of music. I just said, "Okay, now you've got your instruments here, what do you want to do?" The first year (I think the first semester), they performed for us and for each other. We had a little boy named Dan Barnes who said, "You know, my sister is in the second grade over at Tiger at South Rabun Elementary. Could we take our class over there and do a concert for her second-grade class?" Well, I thought, that's gonna be a lot of trouble to gather this group up and get a bus or van or something and get them over there. Dan and I thought about it and decided that it was worth giving it a try, so we loaded up and went over to Tiger and performed for the second-grade class. It was a big hit at Tiger, but on our way back home, I realized that it was a big hit with high school kids, too. They thought, "Man, I'm really gonna practice 'cause I want to do this again," and so when they got back to class, there was absolutely no doubt about it; they were seriously motivated, and they didn't even have time for any kind of foolishness. Everybody worked really hard, and we went back and did another concert as a result.

Another dimension of the music program came out of that, too. It was expected that when you walked in the classroom, you were gonna be working up something to perform for someone else outside the classroom. It became clear that people were gonna have opportunities to work in small groups. People were gonna have opportunities to choose what they did, and I felt I would be the facilitator person who helped them learn what they wanted to do, but I became the person who decided what to teach when they decided what they wanted to learn. I didn't make any of that stuff up, not that anyone can make that up. It's just a combination of all of us putting twenty heads together.

The performance program became a real performance program where there was no question about it: If you walked in that room, you were gonna be expected to do something for somebody else, and it also became clear that as the teacher in the room, I wasn't gonna be able to work and teach everybody what they wanted to know. The kids had to teach each other, so the rule was as soon as you learn something, your first responsibility is to show someone else how to do it. Teaching is no longer in my corner; it's everybody's responsibility for helping each other to get better at what we do.

When I asked George Reynolds what he is doing now, he replied: I do the same thing, except I do it with little-bitty people in the inner city who have never seen a cow. I teach elementary school in Knoxville in an inner-city school next to a seven-hundred-fifty-unit housing project. I tell people I've changed planets from here to there. First of all, going from high school to elementary school is a big change, but going from good ol' Rabun County to good ol' inner-city Knoxville is more than just going to another place; it's going to another kind of life. My son goes to that school. He's a real smart boy. It's a magnet school, and they draw people in from all over the country to participate in the things that the school offers, but it also shares all those goodies with the community kids who don't have the same kind of opportunities that kids out in the suburbs might have. It's good for my boy, too. He's got buddies that live out in the community, and his best buddies are the community kids. You've got these kids that come in and are academically accelerated, and then you've got your community children, some of whom the parents don't read to, or maybe the parents have other problems like not being able to read, being in jail, or being drug addicted. There are a lot of folks that are struggling people who have jobs and are working to get out of the projects. Then there are people who live very modest lives and live around the edges of the projects, but they have real low-income jobs. It is a very interesting community. I left here [Rabun County] because I married a woman who lived in the inner city, and she had her career, and I had this career. One of us had to quit our job and go to the other place. She also had our child on the way, so I decided to go there and be a full-time daddy for a couple of years and see if I could find another career over there. It was kinda like jumping out of a plane, and I didn't know where I was gonna land. I never imagined that I would find a career that I enjoyed as much as Foxfire, but they gave me the same opportunity that I got here. I was looking at all kinds of different options. I was thinking about maybe applying for a job as a band director or something. The paradigms of what music teachers do out in the world were getting pretty narrow. I knew, or at least I thought, I was never going to find anything as wide open as everything I was allowed to do here at Foxfire, but they hired me through several events that just sort of fell into place. There was a position open at this elementary school, and the people who ran the magnet program decided that this would be a good match for me, and I thought, "Man, I'm a high school teacher; I'm not sure this is exactly what is the best, but I'll take your word for it." So they put me in this instrumental music position in a school that already had a regular choral music teacher, but it was specialized to be instrumental music on the school level from kindergarten up, which was the only position like that in the whole system and maybe in the whole state.

I teach kindergarten through fifth grade—every kid in school, pretty much. They understand that I was coming from outside of the box here and that I was interested in doing things that were creative and different from typical elementary school classrooms, so the principal said, "Okay, do all that stuff and have a good time, and I know you will figure it out," so they left me alone. They just left me all alone and let me create what I did because there was no curriculum in place to tell me what I should do. There's state guidelines and national guidelines as to what should be in music curriculums, but they are very broad, and they don't tell exactly how to meet those guidelines. This course has to do with teaching basic principles of music, teaching music to kids that can be used in the real world, and showing what connections it makes to occupations. Here I was all over again in a classroom making up what I do from scratch, and this time employing the wisdom of the kids was a little bit different because teenagers can articulate what they mean or what they want more skillfully than five-year-olds or even ten-year-olds. I figured out how to ascertain by observing their behavior and observing what gave them joy and what picked up their curiosity. It's been a brand-new challenge intellectually as a teacher, but the lessons I learned here in Foxfire about how to teach are all still there, and it all still works. It's just as important to pay attention to the kids and learn from them now, too.

I teach instrument building; we build instruments out of tin cans and used guitar strings, bamboo, and stuff that we recycle that other people were gonna throw away. That's a whole lot of fun. Right now we're working on an instrument built out of cardboard tubes. Last year somebody asked me if I wanted some eight-foot-long and three-foot-in-diameter cardboard tubes. I said, "Sure, bring them in here; I'll figure out something to do with them."

So we made these vertical-tube percussion instruments out of them. You can try this at home if you want to. I bought these pairs of flip-flops—they have terry cloth on one side of them. They're kind of like house flip-flops. You take that cardboard tube and hit it with the flip-flop, and it makes a pitch. I was experimenting and practicing some measurements, and I started whacking on that thing, listening to what kind of sound it would make. I got this *doot, doot, doot* sound. And I said, "Wait, what's going on here?" All of a sudden, one night, it just sort of came to me; there's this song that I learned when I was a kid called "Pipeline" where one of the guitars is going *doo, doo, doo, doo,* and the other guitar was going *doo, doo, doo, doo* in a different pitch. The whole thing shifted to another chord *doo, doo, doo, doo,* so we decided we were gonna play "Pipeline" on cardboard tubes. We found some leftover electrical conduit in the hallway. I took them back to the room, and we cut it into two lengths. I don't know if you've ever tapped on a piece of steel conduit pipe, but it rings like a bell. So we made this metal tone out of electrical conduit. We did *doo, doo, doo* on the cardboard tubes, and we had ourselves a song!

"Kickin' Around with The Foxfire Boys"

Entering my senior year as an editor for The Foxfire Magazine, *I wanted my last article to be special. I wanted to go out with a bang, not a whimper. I met with a fellow senior editor, Austin Bauman, and we came up with an idea of doing an article together. We looked over previously attempted interviews and decided to interview all six of The Foxfire Boys and compile their stories in a larger article. [Only partial articles are included here. The complete interviews can be found in the Spring/Summer 2008 issue of* The Foxfire Magazine.*] The members of the band had some wonderful stories about their beginnings and their rise to stardom. All of them credited George Reynolds, high school Foxfire music teacher, as having inspired them. Just ask Dean, Mike, Filmer, Tom, Steve, or Wayne, and I'll bet they'll tell you how much they love playing the music of Appalachia.*

—*Jared Weber*

Getting to know The Foxfire Boys was quite an experience. I was inspired by their musical talent, as well as their outlook on life. They were some of the most enjoyable people that I have ever met. I was amazed by their stories of playing at the Olympics, at the Grand Ole Opry, and with John Denver, and my face was sore from laughing at their stories of practical jokes and pranks. For me it was an adventure, and for them, like everything else, it was a lot of fun.

—*Austin Bauman*

Filmer Kilby

The Foxfire program was at Rabun Gap–Nacoochee School when I was in school, and that's the first time that I became acquainted with George Reynolds. He had started a folklore class. It wasn't really a music class, but it had a lot of musical background with it. He was a real good musician on all different types of instruments. He was playing a mouth harp [harmonica], too, and that was right down my alley. I started building a bigger repertoire of different styles and types of music. I was learning more new songs and a lot of different types of hot licks on the guitar. It was just an all-out learning experience for me—a lot of fun. George was just a real open-minded fella. He helped just about anybody with whatever type of music they wanted to pursue or any kind of instrument they wanted to try to learn on. If he knew somethin', he'd show you. He'd help you along and get you started. When I met George, he was just influencing to the third power. He kept me interested in it.

In the Foxfire class, we would usually just get in a little circle and play our music. We'd accompany each other, and if somebody had a song they wanted to work or somethin', we'd help 'em with it. It was kind of like a group effort. We probably started our first band in about '78. It was me and George, Scott Stewart played the banjo, and Clinton Kilby played kinda like a rhythm guitar. I played the mouth harp mostly. I guess that was the first Foxfire band. We started it off, and then Tom and Wayne and Dean and The Foxfire Boys came along a couple years after that.

I know all the guys in the band today. We was always just a big circle of friends. We were always playing music together and stuff. Lots of times, we'd be gathered at the same place playing music. Course, everybody usually practiced at George's. We were constantly running into each other up there. We became friends, and we played music together for years. I usually filled in when somebody was out, and I knew George real well. Then he gave me an opportunity to step in when he had to move on, but there'll always be a spot for George anytime he wants to come play with us. That's the way it all came down. We were just all pickin' buddies.

When we formed that first band, our first performance might have been for the faculty and the school. I was real nervous—like a long-tailed cat. My knees were shaking. I was playing that harp, and it's a wonder I didn't swaller [swallow] it. Getting in front of a crowd is part of the learning process. I play the bass now, and I'm kind of in behind 'em. I can hide out right there. That's not too bad. You get over that nervousness the more you play. It gets to where you can handle it. We've done some pretty big gigs; we played down at Warner Robins in a big festival. There was quite a few people in on that deal. Another big place is at Stone Mountain. We get invited down there

PLATE 82 **Steve, Dean, Tom, Filmer, and Mike performing at a 2004 event held at The Foxfire Museum and Heritage Center**

ever' so often to play at some of their festivals. There's usually a pretty huge crowd at those festivals. I didn't get to play with John Denver. I was kind of substituting in between when all that was goin' on. I didn't go with 'em to the Grand Ole Opry either, but I listened to 'em play on the radio.

You have the same professional composure when you play outside of Rabun County as when you play at local places. The sound has a lot to do with how smooth everything goes, when you get everything sounding good and you get into the groove. That's where the last song made you feel real good, and the next song makes you feel even better. You get your adrenaline pumping, and it really don't matter where you're at then. That's a good feeling.

I'm a better musician now than I was when I started. I know about twice as much as I knew then, and I didn't know nothin' to begin with. Now I can play all different instruments: banjo, Dobro, and a little bit on the mandolin. When I was in high school, I couldn't play much on any of those instruments. George has helped me tremendously, I'd say. He's a highly intelligent guy. He kept me interested, and he's responsible for me being where I am with these guys. I hated to see 'im go. I had a lot of good times with 'im. We went to a lot of interesting places in the musical arena. We met a lot of folks, from West Virginia coal miners to guys like Doc Watson. Some of the folks are pretty old to still be playing music. It's fantastic!

I've wrote a few songs, too. When I'm writin' a song, I pick the tune out first. Sometimes I'll think of some verse or idea in my head, or maybe I'm humming along and I sing a few words with it, and it sounds good. Then I'll come home and put that with some music. The majority of the time, though, I guess I pick the melody out first and then put the words with it later.

Bein' a big star like Garth Brooks or John Denver never really appealed to me. That's not my bag. I'd rather be a songwriter. If it were somethin' like "Achy Breaky Heart" and it was a success overnight, I'd be pretty happy with that, too. One song's all it takes if you get it into the right hands, but if I can just get the message across or the sound that I'm trying to achieve, that's good. I just do it for entertainment mostly—I entertain myself mostly. I like music. If I didn't, I probably wouldn't even fool with any of it.

I love to play with these guys. It's great to just watch 'em perform on the stage. Watching Mike's face is pretty good entertainment itself 'cause he really gets into it. He gets in the groove, and then I get in the groove. Watchin' the expressions on these guys' faces is somethin' else. You can tell they like it. If you ever watch 'em, you can tell how much feeling they put into their music. The whole thing's been a good experience. It's been a lot of fun. If it wasn't for the fun part, I probably wouldn't have fooled with it. Speaking for me, I love music, and I know they all do, too, so we're just doin' somethin' that we enjoy. We're all buddies. We usually go on fishing trips and huntin' trips. We've got a lot of stuff in common, and we've always got along real well.

Mike Hamilton

My first performance with The Foxfire Boys was in a talent show, and I played guitar. Dean played banjo, and Steven was the only one that would open his mouth and sing. I think Richard Hembree [an original member of the band] played bass, and we entered the talent show. We did two songs, "Blackberry Blossom" and "Cripple Creek," so we did two or three songs in the talent show. I said, "Well, let's put together something." So me and Dean and Steve were kind of founding members, you know, a little bit older than the rest of those guys. Wayne's the same age, but Wayne and Tom kinda came into the picture later. George kind of coached us along and helped us with our approach and how to get from the beginning to the ending of a song and actually play a song all the way through. He was encouraging right there from the very beginning.

They got the band name from the Foxfire music class. It wasn't a real big creative thing. It started out The Foxfire String Band, then the "Boys" thing kind of got thrown into there when Roy Acuff introduced us at the Opry as "The Foxfire Boys."

George was just really, really some extra-special teacher. He helped and encouraged us to get started. He made me get up in front of the school in the ninth grade and play. I was playing banjo at the time. I played guitar, but I was picking up the banjo, too. I learned about three or four songs on the banjo. Dean, our banjo player, was out in the audience. He heard me playing the banjo, and he said, "Well shoot, I ought to be able to do that." He went that summer and took banjo lessons from Freddie Webb. He came back in the fall of the following year, and he knew about four or five more songs than I did. He was really just primarily staying on banjo, and I said, "Well, shoot, you know these songs. I'll just play guitar. You play banjo, and we'll get a band together. Steve will sing. We'll get Richard Hembree to thump on the bass, and we'll go from there." So we kind of got it together, and George would coax us in the right direction. He wouldn't jump in and direct everything. He would help us if we'd ask for help, but he was good about lettin' us do our own thing.

When we played at the Grand Ole Opry, we were nervous, but we pulled it off good. Roy Acuff got us back in his dressing room and took up time with us. Everybody was like, "Mr. Acuff, we need to do this and do that," and he was like, "Y'all go on. I'm talking to my boys back here." He was saying, "Son, when I was your age, I was so scared I was playing more behind the bridge of the fiddle than in front of it. Don't worry, y'all. Y'all will do fine. Get out there and be comfortable and have a good time." He really made us feel at home, just like we were sittin' in his living room. He took up a lot of time with us and bragged on us. We were nervous 'cause it was live radio. My brother, Dave Hamilton, was on a boat out in the middle of the Gulf, off the coast of Mobile, Alabama, and he heard it on the radio. They called 'im out there and said, "Your little brother's fixing to be on the Grand Ole Opry." They had like a live Saturday night radio show, and just knowing that you're gonna be nationwide on the radio, you're thinking, oh Lord, don't let me mess up. We squeezed it off. It was really somethin' because I'd been there with my dad, William Hamilton, two times before that, seein' other people on stage. I made the comment to my parents at the time, "You know, next time I come up here, I'm gonna be on that side of the stage," kind of halfway joking, you know. Then he looked up, and I could see 'em back there, and I was up there on stage. That was pretty awesome 'cause a lot of people that are really good musicians never get that kind of opportunity. I think we got a lot of opportunities that we normally wouldn't have by being associated with Foxfire and having a nationally known name. Gosh, that's a long time ago, '84. We got several calls like that from the governor's office to the National Endowment for the Arts, several pretty high-profile gigs.

When we did that, I guess I was out of school a couple of years. Tom and them were, I think, still in school. I was in college. One of our most memorable performances was the first paid gig we had over in Canton, North Carolina, over at this place. We did a little Saturday night show, and I remember it got us a hundred bucks. That 'as the first one. That was memorable and so was the Grand Ole Opry, and the music we performed in Norway when we got to go to Lillehammer in '94 for the Winter Games.

We got to play with John Denver at the high school. We didn't know that we were gonna play with him, but he did a few songs, and then there was a rock band. They played their act, and we played our gig. Then we went back out again and sat in the audience. Then I see George going across the football field with a big giant bass on his shoulder, walking over there, and I saw this limo pulling up on the visitor's side and John Denver getting out. They paged us over the microphones. So we go over there, and he wanted us to do backup with 'im. He had seen us at Ed West's, who was having a reception for all the movie people that were in town—Hallmark Hall of Fame was filming *Foxfire*. We did like a little private party for 'im, and he was watching and said, "Dang, where are y'all playing?" Tom said, "We're playing for this kid that needs an organ transplant, and you really ought to try and come." He really kind of puts the guy on the spot. He says, "Well, heck, I'll try to be there." And you know, word gets out that he might be there, and the next thing you know, there's four thousand people at the high school. That was pretty memorable. We did a jam session with 'im; we grew up playing "Grandma's Feather Bed" and then "Country Roads" and all that. We'd go through it, and everybody'd come in on the harmonies. Then he'd go, "Gee, we got that one, let's go to the next one" and "Okay, the bridge goes up to B," and everybody would come in and they already pretty much knew the songs. I remember Dean English onstage leaning over to me going, "Do you believe this? John Denver at our high school, four thousand people here; we're playing onstage with John Denver. Do you believe this?" I said, "Heck, no, I ain't believing this."

I guess it was politically correct for him to come. It was a benefit. He was a really nice guy. I never really was that big of a fan until I got to meet 'im and he got up there and did "Rocky Mountain High" and the "Annie" song, just with one guitar. He just brought the house down. He was a killer musician, a really good singer. He worked hard at making us feel comfortable with him onstage 'cause we were nervous. He'd put his arm around us and say, "Ahh, let's have a good time," and just made us really feel comfortable with 'im. He really worked hard at remembering all our names and stuff. We got a little part in the movie after that, a little two-minute scene in there. We were the band during the dream scene. So he came up in the middle of the night when we were still shootin' up there. "Mike, Dean, Tom, what are y'all doing?" He talked to us and got the fiddle and started playing "Country Boy." He really was an extraordinary musician and singer. Until you see 'im in person, you don't realize what a good musician he was.

I play the lead guitar in the band, but I end up doubling as the soundman. I end up settin' up everything, and I enjoy that part of it, too, 'cause I've played in rock bands and country bands over the years, which have been more electric oriented. I'm kind of more into the equipment part and gettin' everybody's sound right 'cause that really makes it.

An audience's response when you really pull somethin' off good is great—when you're gelling and you pull off a great solo part and everybody's, as we call it, in the zone. When everybody's in the zone, and everything's clicking, and the sound's good, and the monitors are right, and you just have that magical connection with the audience, it's just an unexplainable feeling. It's in my heart when I really am totally one hundred percent happy. It is very spiritual. Oh, I love it, whether it be rock 'n' roll or bluegrass or whatever.

All of us are best friends. You won't find more honest, good-hearted, Christian guys anywhere—good musicians. Plus, they got a good sense of humor and have a lot of fun. We cut up, and we joke. We've got to do stuff that we normally would never have gotten to do and got to go many places and open up for some big-name Macs [stars] that we normally wouldn't have got to do. We have been good friends through it all and have done some good. I guess that would probably sum it up. They're just the best guys in the world. I would like 'em and think the world of 'em if we didn't play music, but fortunately, we get to get that music released, too. They're all really good musicians, and I've seen 'em just grow up and get more and more professional about it. We all go huntin' and fishing together and stuff. We go out on a fly-fishing trip every chance we get out west and spend a lot of time together. We set around the campfires playing in front of somebody; we're setting around the campfire rehearsing or setting in Wayne's basement playing. We got to do a lot of stuff that I wouldn't have never got to do. I'd 'a' been sittin' at home playing with a rock 'n' roll band somewhere, but it's helped me in all my other bands. It's helped me as far as getting out in front of people, just out in the general public, and seeing people and meeting new people. I feel more confident about looking people in the eye and shaking their hand and getting out in front of the crowd. I feel more comfortable 'cause we have done it so long, and over the years I don't get flushed and red anymore. I just feel a lot more confident in any aspect of life, whether it be a job interview or anything like that. If I'm talking to a group of people or startin' young folks out and playing music and encouraging 'em—I guess a lot of the stuff George Reynolds laid on me subliminally. I find myself doin' the same thing, and I'm seeing young kids that are just learning to play guitar and all. I know how the fire was, how excited I was about it, and how excited George would get about us and encouraging us. I find myself doin' the same thing, and I want them to experience some of the same things I have and the joy that I've got out of it, 'cause it's been one of the most rewarding things in my life.

Steve McCall

I got into George's class when I was a senior. Just before we started the band, that's when I started learning more, I guess, and playing. He played guitar really well, and he offered guitar lessons, so I took lessons with him. I was really impressed with his ability. That's probably the biggest influence on getting me started in playing. We were able to travel when the band did start. George took us all over to different high schools and a few colleges and this and that just to play, and the Tennessee Reunion at John Rice Irwin's Museum of Appalachia, and it was really good for us. We got to play at the '82 World's Fair in Knoxville, and it wasn't long before we got to play on the Grand Ole Opry.

Probably Doyle Lawson influenced us a lot. Ricky Skaggs influenced us a lot 'cause he was just coming out. You know, he played a lot of bluegrass before he went to country. He was in his heyday about the time we were working on stuff and learning stuff, so we learned a lot from his tapes. As a matter of fact, we got to open up for him one time in Atlanta later on. Doyle Lawson influenced us, especially with the a cappella numbers that we do. I don't know, there's Doc Watson, you know—we'd listen to a lot of his stuff—and Tony Rice. We used to listen to him a lot.

We just did it for fun. We sat down a couple of times and talked about whether we should try to play at festivals and do it for a living, but it always come out as a no 'cause we just wanted to have a good time and not get tired of it. We've had a lot of good opportunities through the years. I really couldn't say what my favorite part about performing is 'cause I like it all. The worst part is puttin' the sound system up and taking it down, especially late at night when you play till twelve or one in the morning and you gotta take the sound system down. We play for a lot of different things, like wedding receptions or background music for parties. I don't enjoy doing that as much as I do concerts. We played down at Truett-McConnell College [Cleveland, Georgia] in the chapel there one time, and that's probably one of the best things that we've played at in a long time—as far as people sittin' and watching and paying attention to what you're doing. I enjoy that type of thing a lot more than just playing for background at a wedding reception.

Well, it takes a lot of practice to be good enough to be asked to play for people. You just gotta stick with it, and you gotta constantly learn new material until you get your reputation built up. It's a lot of fun. I've really enjoyed it, and I wouldn't take nothing in the world for it. If you've got a group that can get along as good as we have, you're very fortunate. Try to look for somebody that you can get along with to start a band with. That's one of the main things, being able to get along. As far as everything else, I guess you just gotta take it as it comes and play at every opportunity you get. You want to help your community any way you can.

I thank the Lord for keeping us together. We are all really good friends. A lot of times when we practice, we'll talk for two or three hours before we get to playing the music because we don't see each other that much. We want to know what's goin' on with all our lives and get caught up. Sometimes we don't get a whole lot done 'cause we'll sit up and talk until it's time to go to bed. We're all like brothers; I'm an only child, so they're the closest thing I got to brothers, I guess.

Dean English

The Foxfire music program when I was in high school went through a couple of phases. The main thing I remember about George Reynolds's class was that every week, what you had to do was you had to learn somethin' from somebody else. That was what you were required to do. And once every week or every two weeks, he would have an in-class show, or whatever you would call it. So everybody could show and tell what they'd learned. It worked out good for the people that really wanted to learn. He'd give 'em a good chance to learn any kind of music or whatever they wanted to do. George was always there to help you keep things in tune or work out any kind of problems with the vocals or whatever.

When we started the band, I think we did a talent show. There was a little talent show that came up, and we decided to get a couple of songs together for the talent show. I think there was four of us at that time; I think we got second place. After that, we started doing other little things and stayed together. Someone offered us a paying job, and I don't remember what that was, but it probably wasn't but fifty bucks or something. We just kept goin' from there.

George was a real good fella; he had a way of firing people up, and he'd get all excited about music, whatever it might be. It didn't matter to him what kind of music it was, but he knew a lot. I guess you'd call it music theory, and stuff like that. It didn't matter if it was rock 'n' roll or old-time or gospel, he could help you do it, and he could do it himself. He was a big influence. I hate that he had to move off and leave everybody else here. He was well liked by the students and people in the community. He was also known to be really good with kids.

We're a lot older than when we started; I guess we know more types of music and stuff. When we first started out, we only had about eight to ten songs. People told me that it's unusual for a band to stay together this long. We've never really been on the road and just played music as a profession. We've always enjoyed what we do, just like out here at the Foxfire Festival, we just have a good time. We might play music together; sometimes we would go on fishing trips together or huntin' trips. We've always been that way. We aggravate each other sometimes, but we get along. I've heard a lot of bands don't stay together like that. If they do, it's just a huge struggle, and I think part of the way we do this is we don't take it extremely serious. It helps us kinda keep the fun, I guess you'd say.

It definitely makes it better if you got a good audience. No doubt about that. There'll be some places we play where there'll be two thousand people there and somethin's goin' on and nobody's really paying attention that much. Then there are places where there ain't but ten people, but they're paying attention, and we just play better. Otherwise, it's just like we just jam! If we're somewhere playing, and we realize that somethin' else is goin' on, some huge event or whatever, and we're just playing, we'll just play whatever we want. We're okay just to please ourselves. You want to enjoy it, and generally we do, but you definitely enjoy it more and it makes it the best when you got a really good audience.

There's just tons of memorable moments in our musical career. We've had so many funny things happen. We've got to go play at a lot of places and meet a lot of people that we would never have been able to meet otherwise. We've had a real good time. I'm so glad that I was here and able to be a part of it—and I still am—and I'm real glad that it was with these guys.

Tom Nixon

I started playing music when I was in, I guess, the first grade. I was always interested in music and beatin' around on the piano and beatin' around on an old guitar that we had. My grandfather was very musically talented. He could play anything, and the whole family on my dad's side was, too—some on my mother's side, but mostly my dad's side. I guess that's what sparked my interest. My cousin, Filmer Kilby, gave me my first guitar when I was in the second or third grade. I can't remember which one. He showed me a few chords on the guitar, so did my dad, and that's where the interest started. From there, I again used to beat and bang on the guitar. I showed a little more interest in that than I did something else. As time went on, by fourth grade I kinda backed off a little bit. I'd be more interested in sports and that sort of thing. That went on until about the eighth grade, where I met some of The Foxfire Boys. I was still playing a little music at home and at church. I was singing some and learned how to play the bass at church and the guitar some. When I saw The Foxfire String Band, at that time, they had a music class, and some of that class was playing in the gym. I remember being in the eighth grade and goin' down to an assembly. We went down, and I seen some of them play. I had my buddy with me, and I remember saying, "Ah, they ain't no good," but they were, actually. I really wanted to be down there with 'em. One of the members playing the banjo was Dean English, who lived on Persimmon at that time and rode my bus. We didn't have a whole lot to say to each other because he had just come to the community. He just moved here to go to school. His family is from here, and we got to know one another on the bus. He'd heard a tape of me playing with my cousin, Filmer. We got to talking 'bout it, and he invited me to come down to the music class. This was in the eighth grade during Georgia history class. I would tell the teacher I had to go to the bathroom; I started taking regular bathroom breaks. Mrs. Brown began getting a little concerned, wanted to know if I was sick as a couple of weeks went by. Then, of course, I told her what was goin' on. Then she let me, once I got my work done, go ahead and go down to George's class. The music performance class is what it was. She let me go down, and I would go down and just pick with 'em and have a good time participating in whatever was left of the class. That's the story of how I got affiliated with the band to begin with.

Then as I moved on to the ninth grade, I was able to take Foxfire classes. I took music performance with George as an elective. That's how I got to know the guys in the band a little better. They were staying after school for practice on Thursday evenings. I played the guitar—everybody played the guitar. They didn't need a guitar player. They had a bass player, banjo player, and a guitar player. They really needed a mandolin—nobody played the mandolin. My grandfather had an old mandolin. I wish I had got to play with him some, but I never did. He passed away in '76. I sang some with 'im, but I never really got to play a lot of music with 'im. He had an old electric mandolin, and I got that and took it to school. I would mess around with it, but I didn't know the first thing about it. I guess that's where I became more involved 'cause George knew some about the mandolin, showed me how to tune it, and showed me some chords. He gave me some tablature, and I learned some songs. There was a benefit at the Clayton Elementary School; that was my first public performance with the band.

Obviously, I was the last to graduate 'cause they were all older than me. I guess the highlight of high school was the tenth grade because Dean and Wayne were there. They were in the twelfth grade, and I was in the tenth grade. Mike had just graduated, and Steve had graduated a couple of years before that. Those were considered our successful years. We got to play a lot of places and travel a lot with Foxfire and play at high schools and some colleges and met a lot of girls. We thought that was really cool and neat. We were pickin' up jobs and making money for our music, but after the other boys graduated, the cycle continued on. I can't speak for them, but I began to play in what we called The Foxfire String Band, which, by the way, used to be our original name. And then we changed it to The Foxfire Boys after our appearance on the Grand Ole Opry. We were introduced as The Foxfire Boys.

That name was an accident. I know it was. I don't know, maybe Roy Acuff just could remember Foxfire, and we were a bunch of boys, which makes sense. It kinda has a bluegrass ring to it. Foxfire String Band has more of maybe a "folksy, old-time" ring to it. We primarily played bluegrass at that time. We still do, but we do a lot of other types, too. I was in the ninth or tenth grade when we went to the Opry. That was an experience—very exciting, real nervous, but it was a really big deal, especially at that young age.

Meeting John Denver was another fun time, and we've warmed up for several big-named bands: Mark Collie, Terri Gibbs, Billy Joe Royal, and several others. We've been real fortunate to get to open shows for some of those folks. The Atlanta Olympics was not so much a big deal to us because Atlanta's just right down the road. It was just like goin' to Atlanta to play, but it was a fun experience. We had a good time. It was very crowded. Playing somewhere far away for a few thousand people, you feel like you're performing, and you're just trying to perform. If the crowd's caught up in it, it can be just wonderful. You get that charge of energy from the crowd, and you just play hotter, and you play better. On the other hand, [I like] playing for a benefit in Rabun County, and one of our favorite places to play is the Satolah Fire Department. It's more enjoyable to do that. We know everybody. There's that sense of community and family, and we're just having a good time. We're playing for us, too, and we can let our hair down instead of being puppets—doing a puppet performance. We can just jam. I guess that's the major difference. They're both fun.

We've always aggravated each other, not in a bad way but pulling jokes and that sort of thing. There've been some comical things that have happened. Mike Hamilton most of the time gets the butt of the jokes. From the very beginning he has always gotten that, I think, because he's such a great guy. He's easy to get along with, besides the fact, I guess, Wayne and myself are the two meanest in the group. We've played some pretty bad jokes on 'em.

We all go camping together, huntin' together, fishing together, and hanging out together. Besides the music, we're a family. We're just family rather than just band members. Every time we get together, somethin' funny always happens.

PLATE 83 **Dean and Tom are the owners and operators of Blue Ridge Music, where they use the Foxfire teaching approach with their students. See the Spring/Summer 2010 issue of *The Foxfire Magazine* for more details.**

It's really extraordinary that we have been together this long, most of us. 'Course George has gone on [moved to Tennessee]. We all like the same things. When we come together to practice, we hardly ever get any practice in because we're interested in what's goin' on with each other and talking about huntin' and fishing or guns. We all have similar interests—talking about family. That's probably one of the main reasons that we've stayed together and that we don't have a clear boss. We have Wayne, who schedules most of our gigs and holds some things together for us, but we don't have a band leader. We all become leaders at particular times when the situation calls for it. I think that helps, and I think that team play works best. Those two reasons, I would say, are the reasons that we've stayed together so long, and it's a blessing, too. I just can't believe we have been together this long. It must be the grace of God, literally!

I think I've been lucky and been blessed to be able to hang out with these characters, to be able to play at some of the places, meet some of the people. It has just really worked out well. I feel fortunate to have been a part of it. The music is great, and we all have such a strong friendship. We've been through a lot together, but we've remained friends throughout it all. I hope it continues on, and I believe it will.

Wayne Gipson

I can't even remember the first time that I performed with the Boys, but it was pretty scary for me gettin' up in front of all those people. It's just like anything else; the more you do it, the more comfortable you get with different cultures. It was a wonderful experience. It's actually easier to perform for somebody you don't know than it is people you do know. I know that sounds kind of strange. I think you want to do everything just perfect for people you know. I've gotten to the point now where it really don't bother me. Just like any other kind of performing, I guess there's always butterflies. I really don't have stage fright or anything like that.

Your favorite song is probably the one that you've just learned. You've got so many songs and you do 'em over and over and over. They don't get boring, but they're just not as fun to do as new songs. I guess the one right now that's my favorite is "Last Day at Gettysburg."

Nowadays, we actually play less together, practice-wise. We hardly ever get to practice, but we play probably as much or more than we used to back when we were in school. We usually play during the summer and on up into fall.

I think you can learn to read music. Anybody can learn to read music, but that's not really what we were. I think George might have had a class or two that taught how to read music, but mainly we done it by ear. You know, just everybody can't do it by ear, and I just think you gotta have the ability. I think some folks got it; some folks don't. You really gotta be interested in it. My advice would be that just whichever instrument you want to play, it's gonna take a long time. It's not something you do overnight. Just get off to yourself and just practice.

I think George influenced all of us. I think we all kinda looked up to him. I don't know that any of us really considered George a teacher, although he really was. He was more of a friend, you know. He just knew so much about music and different instruments. It was a big influence on me.

I guess one of the reasons that we've stayed together so long is that we are all such good friends, all the guys in the band. To really know what I was talking about, you'd really have to be in the band and know just the camaraderie between the guys and just the friendship mainly. I mean, we make a little bit of money here and there, but we really don't do it for the money. I think it takes a special kind of people, and we were all friends before we began playing music together; well, I was with most of 'em, but I think it takes a special kind of people, you know, for that longevity. To be able to stay together that long, you gotta be able to not be too serious about anything. I really don't think we've ever had any kind of dispute between any of us. You know, there's some times when somebody's late or somethin' that we may get a little bent out of shape, but it's forgotten in about five minutes. We've been lucky.

The Foxfire Boys' music may be ordered directly from Foxfire at www.foxfire.org or by phone at 706-746-5828.

"Because He Loved Me"

~ Morris Stancil and his son, Greg Stancil ~

Open any church hymnal, look on the back of award-winning southern gospel groups' CD cases, choose the gospel playlists on airlines, even travel to other countries, and you will most likely see the Stancil name or hear the encouraging words written by Morris. However, Morris's exceptional songwriting ability came with great loss. Through the tragic murder of his only sister, Morris begged and pleaded with the Lord for a way to cope with his grief. "It was Lord led," says Morris, because a few days after pouring his heart out to God, words and a melody just came to him from out of nowhere. For over forty years since then, God has given Morris a song every few days. Through unbearable pain and loss, Morris and the millions of people touched by his music have been blessed. "God was in on it even back then," he says, and exactly right he is. Who else could have turned the hardest time in Morris's life into such a glorious and blessed ministry?

—Casi Best

Morris: I'm Morris Stancil. I was born February 26, 1943, in Alpharetta, Georgia. My daddy and most everybody were farmers back then. That's all we knew to do, so everybody was poor. There wasn't too many public jobs, and most people didn't have much of an education and so forth. I had one brother and one sister. My sister was tragically killed at Christmastime in 1967, so it's just me and my brother now. She was only nineteen when she was killed. She was the youngest of the three and, of course, that was really bad. Now Christmastime's always a sad time for us. Mama and Daddy always took us to church, but they just didn't sing. I always grew up in a Christian home and am thankful for that.

Growin' up, I'd get up on Sunday morning and watch *The Gospel Singing Jubilee*, which had all the older groups that I grew up listening to on it, like the Spear Family and the Lafevers. They were all my inspiration and I loved 'em. My parents never sang, so me getting into music was odd. The Lord gave me, my sister, and brother all three good voices to sing. There never had been no music in the family, on either side, so it had to be God. So I think me getting involved in music was just the Lord calling me into it. I was twelve years old when I got saved. When I got home, the same day I was saved, I had this feeling that I wanted to play the piano. I'd never had that feeling before. It was like my fingers were just wanting to touch the piano keys. I kept talking to Daddy about gettin' me a piano and, like I said, money was not easy to come by back then. I begged and begged, and he finally bought me this old upright piano for fifty dollars. Well, that was a huge deal for me.

Mama'd tell me that even before Daddy bought me the piano that I'd sit in the window[sill] and act like I was playing the piano. So to do that I knew it had to be a calling. When I got the piano, I started taking lessons from this old gentleman not far from us. I didn't take them very long, about six or eight months, maybe a year. Then one day he told Daddy, "I can't do anything else for this boy. He's got the natural talent. Just let him go." So that's the way it was. I just took enough to know how to read music, which is the four-part, shape-note, harmony-style music. That helped because now I can read music enough to play any song, usually, that's put before me out of the church book. To learn the rest of it, I just took out on my own and the Lord showed me that I should just play it like I feel it.

My songwriting is another thing that I think God intervened and was in on. I told you about my sister, and I had never written a gospel song before her death. The Lord gave me, my sister, and my brother all a talent to sing. We started out just as small children, and after I was saved and got my piano, then we had a little trio. I was about fourteen years old and my sister and brother were younger. We sung at churches around the area—in revivals, singings, and so forth. After she was killed, I had a hard time dealing with that death. We were all very close. I told the Lord one day that I just needed some comfort with it all because I just couldn't handle it. We were never told the truth, never told why or how it happened, or anything else about her case. Then, one day, the words from out of nowhere started coming to my mind, "By an eye of faith, I can vision Heaven portals, it helps me when my load is hard to bear, when the river is hard to cross, and the hill is oh so high, keep me humble, Lord each day, increase my faith." So I wrote the full song as it came to me, and it was called "Let Me Look over the Hill"—first song I ever wrote. It just started from there, and every few days I would start hearing another song. I could hear it in my mind, just something feeding the words and the tune, and I'd go to scribbling it down on some paper. That's how it all started. That was just another calling that the Lord gave me. Why He used it through the death of my sister, I'll never know, but my sister was saved two or three years before she was killed. I could see it all over her face and heard her testimony, and I know where she went. There's no doubt that she went to be in God's paradise.

When I was born, my right arm was completely paralyzed and laid up against my left shoulder, but I had a good, old-fashioned, praying Mama. She said that she started praying that the Lord would let me use that arm in His service someday. She didn't ask that it be healed, just that I could use it for Him. Well, as time went on, when I started to school, it had moved down some, but not down to my waist yet; however, Mama kept praying. When I started to high school, it had moved on down some more and continued to move slowly down. Even today, it still is not straight and does not have much strength at all in it. Of course, I am left-handed, and do everything with my left hand. There is hardly enough strength in it to lift anything at all, but it [my arm] will play the piano for hours at a time and never get tired. Now, you tell if that is not an answer to a good ol' mama's prayers and a miracle from God. That's important to me because when it comes to getting the Lord's work done, even later down the road, He'll do it. The Lord knew that I would play the piano, so He provided the way. Hallelujah, praise His name! It all started as a humble beginning, and now I have been in the gospel music ministry for over fifty years.

I don't know exactly how many songs that I've written, but it would be well up in the hundreds. I alone have recorded over two hundred of my songs, and there are a lot at home that I've never done anything with. I'm thankful that my songs have gone out to other gospel groups and been a blessing. Here again, it must have been what this was all about, that He could use me to bless somebody else.

The Primitive Quartet has sung several of my songs, I'd say about ten or twelve. The most popular one that they've recorded is "Because He Loved Me"; that's the first one they did of my songs. "Flight Without an Airplane," "The Fire's Never Gone Out," "I'll Never Walk in the Valley Again," those are a few that come to mind right off.

Gold City has done a few of my songs. One of them was "Angels Move Over 'Cause I'm Coming Home." The Inspirations did a few, and one of them was "I Found a Treasure." The Kingsmen have done several of my songs. The most popular song and one of their most requested still today is "Beautiful Home." That song has been recorded by many groups, and you will find it in many church choir books, along with "Because He Loved Me." They are also played on several commercial airlines' playlists. I wrote "Holy Angels" and "I'll Get to Lay It Down"; those are real popular songs, too. The Perrys picked up "Holy Angels" and recorded it.

I've never written anything but gospel songs. The Lord just can't let me. I've had people ask me to write them a country song, but the Lord has never given me a country song. He's only given me gospel. I feel honored when I hear my songs on the radio by the different groups but then, at the same time, feel humbled that God would use someone like me.

I had my own quartet before Greg, my son, and I started singing. Over the years I've had two or three different group arrangements. My brother and his wife sang with me for years. He sang bass and was a real good bass singer. His wife sang alto, and we had this outside friend who sang with us, too. As times change, people change, and they leave for this reason or that. So finally it wound up just being me and Greg, which everybody seems to like, so that's the way I'm going to keep it. Greg and I've been singing for about ten years, just the two of us. He's been playing bass for me even back when I had different people with me, so for about twenty years total. We mainly stay in the Southeast to sing, but we've done a few trips up north before.

Churches have changed a lot throughout my life; of course, the music is a world of difference. Way back when we only had a piano, then a little later we had a bass guitar, and then gradually other things came along. It's usually always been the four-part harmony, but the style has changed a lot. We always just had the old-fashioned, foot-stompin' southern gospel, and now it's more on the contemporary side with the praise-worship music. The whole thing has just really changed from what it used to be. It used to be those good, old-fashioned women would get so excited they'd go to shoutin' and running across the church. We just don't see that anymore, in most churches anyway. I think that people are longing for those spirit-filled services today and longing for those old-timey ways.

I would tell young people today to follow their calling. If they know for sure that God's wanting them to do something, then they need to do it. Financially, they may not get rich, but they'll be paid many times over by blessings and the blessing of seeing others get saved from their ministry.

PLATE 84 **"It wound up just being me and Greg." Morris and his son, Greg**

"I Saw the Light"—Greg Stancil

Greg Stancil is an integral part of a well-loved vocal duet. He plays bass guitar, sings backup for his father, Morris, does some of the lead vocals, and brings humor to the stage, but he has not always walked the straight and narrow. He once was on a downward spiral of alcohol, drugs, and rock 'n' roll. I've always heard people say, "When the Lord gets ahold on you, you'll never be the same." I knew this statement was true; however, I did not realize how true prior to meeting Greg Stancil. Greg's life has taken a complete one-eighty since the day he received God's gift of salvation and traded rock music for the sacred hymns penned by a talented father. Greg attempted to outrun the Lord for many years, but quickly learned after an encounter with the devil and his demons [read about this experience on page 194] that Jesus was the much better choice. Today Greg is living for the Lord and following through in the music ministry God has given to him. Greg has been an inspiration to many by sharing the comparison of his life before knowing the Lord. Greg says the best thing in his life was when he "saw that white light."

—Casi Best

Greg: My name is Greg Stancil. I was born in 1967. Life growing up with my daddy, oh boy, I guess I would say that I'm just thankful that I grew up in my daddy's home, because actually Mama and Daddy had got divorced when I was about six years old, and I was sorta like in between. Anyway, it all boiled down to one thing: My daddy's mama, my granny, practically raised me, pretty much. I grew up in the home with them [his grandmother and father], and thank God it was a religious home. You know, it's like the Bible says: If you bring one up in that way, they'll never forget that, but I was also the one who also wanted to experiment in the world. I wanted to have the Christian atmosphere, but at the same time, I thought I wanted to live life like everybody else was living it. I realized, through time, that wasn't the life to live.

A lot of it has got to do with your environment, who you hang with. Where we grew up—now, don't get me wrong, there was a lot of good people, but also there was these kids that was in the wrong. A lot of 'em were drinking alcohol and doing drugs and all sorts of things. I sorta fell in that category with them. The next thing that I knew, one thing led to another, and I won't lie: It started off as a good time and I had fun, but looking back on the results of it all, it didn't turn out as good as I thought that it would turn out; it had a flip side to it. A lot of things can start off good, but if you leave God out of anything, you won't have anything, and you won't be anything. I believe that the only thing that saved me were the prayers that were going out for me. I remember there was a lot of times when I was about eighteen, nineteen, or twenty years old, I would come into the house maybe two thirty or three o'clock in the morning, and I would hear just this loud voice, and I would think, "God, what in the world?" I thought somebody was dying. I thought, "What's going on?" I'd go through the house, trying to sneak in, of course, but after hearing this loud voice I'd think, "That sounds like Granny," and I would think something was wrong. So I'd go hauling off through the house and open her bedroom door, and she'd have that little night-light on in there and you could see; it wasn't bright, just that dim look in there but, man, there she was on all fours, on her hands and knees, and, I mean, she was hollerin' out to the top of her voice to God. I would keep hearing her bring up the name Greg. She kept bringing up my name and asking God to watch over me and all. At the time I just thought, "Well, whatever; that's good, I guess," but that would linger with me 'cause so many times I would come in late like that, or maybe a day or two later, and hear her doing that same thing. At the time I couldn't see the whole picture 'cause I was lost, and to me all that was nonsense, but I thought, "So be it."

My turning point or last straw came when I realized the truth about my surroundings and about those I thought were my friends in that environment of drugs and alcohol. It just seemed like everything started closing in and something started bothering me, tugging at my heart. I had always been raised in church, and I'd hear preachers preach on rock 'n' roll, drugs, Heaven, hell, and so on. There'd be a lot of times I would think to myself, "God, am I really saved?" At an earlier age I did go up to the altar and ask God to save my soul, and I thought I was saved, but I really just never got a connection to make me sure of that, and I started questioning myself. When all that started taking place, I was hearing those preachers' words going over and over in my head, "If you died today, do you know where you're going?" or "Are you saved, and if you are, are you really saved? Do you really have that assurance? Do you know that?" I got to thinking more and more about that 'cause I'd heard them say that if you're saved, you don't really live the life I was living. Of course, we all make excuses for everything, trying to avoid doing that better thing. We don't want to give up what we are doing, and we don't realize it at the time that what we are doing is killing us. It is what's gonna take us out of this world. All that had started bothering me.

Finally, I was invited to go to a church one night. Me and a friend of mine were up at Cumming, Georgia, at the mall, and of course we were alcohol and drug loaded. At that time in my life, it did not matter who was around me; I spoke what I thought. I was who I was; I would say, "You live your life, and let me live mine," and that's the way it was. Nothing really bothered me. Anyway, we were up there minding our own business, doing our own thing, and we noticed these two girls coming up through there, and

I recognized the driver 'cause we hung out with her brother a lot. I knew she was real religious, real Christian-fied. For some reason, there was something that started bothering me and making me feel like I needed to hide the alcohol, the beer we were drinking. For some reason I said, "Jimmy, hide that beer."

When she pulled up, she said, "Well, hey, Greg; hey, Jimmy. What are y'all doing?" I said, "Ah, nothing much," and she said, "I can already see that." For some reason I just felt lowered; I mean lowered. I thought, "What's wrong with me?" I thought somebody had spiked my drink; I never had felt that way and I didn't know what was going on. I guess I was under conviction. She said, "Greg, I wanted to pull over here to invite you—now, Jimmy can go, too, if he wants to—but the Lord wanted me to come over here to invite you to come to our revival. It starts tomorrow night." It was Church of God—Pentecostal; 'course I was always raised Baptist, which I was always taught that denomination is just a symbol but salvation is the real thing, and I said, "Yeah, I'll go." She said, "Are you sure you're not saying that just because of the shape you're in?" I looked over at her and said, "I promise you, I will go." I said that probably about five times, and each time I said that, I'd become sober. The more I said, "I promise you," the more I became sober.

I looked at her and I said, "I promise you, I'll go." I was really warped in the head 'cause I couldn't figure it out. Here I am, all distorted in my mind from alcohol and drugs, and the more I'm saying, "I promise you," the more I became sober. Now, Jimmy is the type that had never been to church. He could care less about church, don't care about going to church, but he said that he would go. That sorta threw me for a loop, too. She said, "Okay, we'll meet back up here tomorrow evening, and y'all can follow us up there." About two thirty or three o'clock that morning, I took Jimmy home and, being in our situation with what we were doing, I thought, "This is it; I'll never hear any more from Jimmy." You see, the way we actually started our day was, we would smoke it, and we would pop the top. That would be our breakfast and how we started our day and everything, the first thing every morning.

I went home and got some sleep and woke up, and I was feeling pretty good, actually, for the first time. I went up to town to get something to eat. As I was coming back and getting to the red light there between Highway 9 and 20, the thought came to my mind, "Didn't you have fun last night?" I sat there and thought about that and I thought, "Yeah, I did." "Wouldn't you like to have another good time like that tonight?" I set there and started thinking 'bout that, and I know the windows in my car were sealed tight, but there was this still breeze that came blowing through my vehicle and went right across in front of me and this still voice said, "You made a promise." I've never questioned that. I slid up behind the wheel of my car, and I said, "I'm going to church; I'm going to church." Nothing would change my mind, not drugs, alcohol, or money, nothing; I knew I was going to church.

Jimmy called me two hours ahead of time and said, "Are you gonna come get me?" I said, "Are you going?" He said, "Yeah." I said, "Have you been drinking?" I knew him and I knew that was the first thing we did every morning. He said, "I ain't touched a drop." Well, I couldn't believe that, and I said, "Are you sure?" Well, he started gettin' mad at me then and he said, "Greg, I swear to you, I have not had one drink; I have not smoked anything; I ain't took nothing; I have not done anything." Then I was startled, and I just could not believe that, but I just took his word for it, and I picked him up, and we met those girls up in town there and we followed them. The church was over in Buford; I never will forget. I remember that I was about twenty-three years old. We pulled up in the parking lot, and I thought, "Where's the church?" Here's this big parking lot and I thought, "Is that the church? This is a big place here. Is this the church?" You gotta remember that my hair was real thick then, way down on my back and real long. I had earrings, and I thought I was somebody, something, you know. I played the eighties rock 'n' roll music and all that stuff, and I thought about the Bible saying, "Come as you are," and I thought, "This is the way I am, and I ain't gonna change for nobody. They accept me or they don't accept me."

We got out of the vehicle and met them up there at the front, and we start to go in there, and, man, we get in the door, and I look around at the balcony, and I thought, "This is a big place." The girl that invited us said, "Greg, we're going up closer to the front. Y'all are more than welcome to come sit with us if you like." Me and Jimmy both said, "Right here's good," and it was the very back seat in the whole place. We start to go in, and I tell Jimmy to go ahead and he said, "Oh no, you go ahead." We were arguing over who was going to sit on the very end of the seat. I gave in and let him have the end seat. So here we sit.

Brother Jentezen Franklin, he hadn't actually made it big at the time, was helping with the revival. I didn't know him. I didn't know anybody. The only people I knew were Jimmy and that girl and her friend. I didn't really even know her friend. We were just sitting there, and I had heard preachers preach drugs, Heaven, and rock 'n' roll, hell and all, and it sunk in somewhat, but it didn't really. That night, when Jentezen got up there, the spirit of God come through him. When he started preaching, it became 3-D. You gotta remember that pulpit was a long way off, and it was like somebody zoomed him in. When he started preaching, that preaching was for me, and I knew that, even with all those hundreds of people there, that message was for me. When he starting preaching God's word, the Spirit was coming through him, and here I sat and I thought, "Okay, well, this is all right, but we can just ease off a little bit; there ain't no need to jump on me."

About that time he started getting a little more involved in the message about the drugs, alcohol, Heaven, hell, and how all this worked. I thought I'd slide over to the left side, hiding behind this bigger lady, but for some reason it was just like his face was visualizing, coming direct at me, and it was the Word. The Word coming from his mouth was coming straight at me, and I thought, "Well, I'll slide over," and I slid over and leaned toward Jimmy behind that bigger, heavier man, and I thought, "This is good." Well, let me tell you, the Word was still coming through, and right there was Jentezen's face; it was just coming in 3-D, and he was just zoomed in to me. There was no avoiding that. My heart was pounding; I started sweatin'. Something was letting me know I needed to get up, and there were a lot of people there, and they are not giving an altar call at the time. I was scared to death. Then this still, silent voice said, "Come on; get Jimmy to go with you." So I looked at him, and I said, "Come on, Jimmy, let's get up and go." He said, "Go where?" And I said, "To the altar." He dropped his head and put his finger over his mouth and went "Shhhhhh." When he went "Shhhhhh," it sounded like it delayed and reverberated and filled that whole place. It was like we was in an empty hall and it just carried. I thought, "Wow." He sat there and he said, "Unh-uh, no way." So I sat there, and I knew it was me.

This lady beside me said, "You want to get up, don't you?" There was something telling me no, but there was more yes, and I said, "Yeah," so she said, "I'll pray for you." I sat there trying to build my courage, and they hadn't give an altar call yet. A few minutes later he asked if anybody wanted to come down, and I started to get up, and on the left side of me, it was like a hand slapped me on the shoulder and set me down. I shook my head, and I thought, "Surely that lady did not just set me down after she just said she was gonna pray for me." As I started to stand back up, it hit me again on the left shoulder, and I looked to my side; there was nothing there, but the weight was, and I started to push up, and it pushed me down. It sat me down, and after about four times of that, on the fifth try, I said, "Jesus, I can't see you, but I believe in you," and I said, "If you'll help me get up from here, I'll meet you down there at that altar." When I started to stand up again, that same thing hit me again on the left side and started pushing. Well, my encouragement was to push that much harder, and I said in my mind that I was not going to quit and I pushed, give it all that I had, and it was like trying to pick up a van; it was almost impossible, but I kept pushing, and once I got halfway, that hindrance snapped. I heard a noise in my left ear, and it went straight down to the floor, *zzzzup*. Next thing I know that whole place turned white, and I was like floating, and the next thing I know, I was at the third pew at the front. I looked to my right, and there were three ladies with a glow to their face and the prettiest smile that you've ever seen, and I was a stranger there, but I knew they were there for me, without a doubt; for some reason they were there for me. I knew that.

I got down on my hands and knees, but I did not know how to pray. I thought, "What's God want me to say?" Only thing I knew to say was "God, what he preached on is in my life, drugs, alcohol, rock 'n' roll; it's all in my life, and I can't quit. I tried to quit; I can't quit. I feel that I'm gonna die this way, but the preacher just told me if I believed in you and asked in your name if you would you save my soul, you'll do that. So that's what I'm gonna do 'cause I don't know what you want me to say." I said, "In your name, Jesus Christ, would you please save my soul?" I just kept asking Him, "Lord, save my soul." I didn't feel anything different. I said, "Lord, I just don't really feel the change. I've always been told there'd be a change; you'll feel a change." All of a sudden a little vision of people appeared around me, and that still voice spoke out and said, "People of the world are holding you back," and there was a little vision of a white robe, and hands and feet, that's all I saw, just a little vision, maybe about two inches tall, just a little vision. I said, "Jesus, that's you, ain't it?" I said, "Would you please save my soul, please?" Next thing I know, when I come up from that altar, I came back so far, and 'bout that time something started pulling me backwards, and I felt like I was gonna fall, so I thought I'd take my left leg and put it back there and brace myself so I wouldn't fall. My feet was anchored; they were not movin'. They were there to stay. And something just kept pulling me back. I felt like I was gonna fall. That still, silent voice came in my right ear and said, "Let go; I gotcha." I said, "Jesus, with all my mind and all my heart, I believe that you've got me," and I let go. When I did, I came a way back and my head dropped down. I saw a white, bright light come from my heart, through my flesh, through my shirt, all the way across to the other side, and there was a still, silent voice came dead center in my right ear. I almost had to quit breathing to hear it and just listen. When I caught hold of it, it was crystal clear, and he spoke to me and said, "You made the right choice, and you will be rewarded for it in Heaven."

I looked up where those ladies were at, and it was like white floatin', like a spirit, like angels floatin', and I don't even remember being in my body. Everything was totally different. Talking about the peace, love, the joy, and the happiness that I had, that's the first time that I've ever experienced anything like that. The best way to describe it is, you can't see the wind, but you can feel it, and that's how it felt.

As soon as I turned and laid eyes on Jimmy in the back, every bone in my body started crushing and hurtin', and I dropped to my hands and knees achin', in so much agony and pain. I said, "God, what is wrong?" That still, silent voice came to my right ear and said, "Jimmy is a part of you; Jimmy shoulda gotten up; he will now probably regret it." That's just been one more true experience for me that makes me know that my name's been written in the Lamb's Book of Life. Over in the years I have strayed away, and it's been a constant battle in life, but I have made a commitment to serve the Lord.

Well, let me tell you about my Copenhagen deal. Now, there again, just like with anything else in your life, you can have whatever you want and think there is nothing wrong with it. Of course, we all do that. We make excuses for what we do. There's nothing wrong, if we look at it the way we look at it, but in God's eyes, it's a totally different situation. We say that we want to do what God wants us to do, but at the same time, we avoid the right thing. I started smoking, dipping, and the whole nine yards, at six years old. I knew I was gonna die from my cigarettes because I watched my grandpa suffer for six years, laying in his home on a hospital bed from smoking. I'd hear him begging God to take him. He was on oxygen like you wouldn't believe, turned wide open, and he still couldn't breathe. I was watching this, and I crushed my cigarettes, and I said, "I'm gonna quit." So I gave up my cigarettes in 1990, and I stayed quit for three years, but I craved a cigarette the whole time. I'd walk around smelling and breathing in other people's smoke. Somebody said, "If you're gonna do that, you might as well light up one 'cause you've not quit." I had never in my life, even as a kid, been sick on cigarettes—tobacco, yes, but smoking, no. About that time, I just gave up on quitting, and when I went back to try smoking again, I got real bad sick. It took me two weeks, but of course I kept forcing myself, and before I quit the next time, I got up to about four packs a day. I kept doing that for about two more years before I gave it up.

My dipping, of course, I kept doing that. I kept praying and asking God to help me quit dipping and all the time packing the can, and packing it in my mouth and saying, "God, will you help me quit dipping?" I was wanting God's help, but at the same time, I wasn't putting forth an effort to help myself or be a part of this. When people's prayers are going on, God hears those prayers and He knows, and I guess He started helping me out a little bit 'cause each time I would put a dip in, I was not feeling good about what I was doing, so I'd try to hide it. I'd cover my mouth, and I'd never done that before. Same as with the alcohol deal. Why did I do that? I couldn't figure it out. There was something there bothering me. Then I started getting sick. Each time I would put a dip in, I would start getting sick. I would think, "God, why am I getting sick?" Here I don't realize I'm praying, asking God for help. Finally God let me realize one day, when it got so bad and I was so sick, that I just couldn't really deal, that I needed to get serious. I fell down and asked God for help. I said, "Lord, I've always been the one to give in and give up." I said, "I can do that easy, but trying to accomplish something, that's been the hardest thing for me to do." I'd just give up. The least little thing that rattled my nerves, I'd think, "Well, gotta get a dip; gotta calm my nerves." Anyway, I said, "God with your help, I've got to do this." And I've always prayed, "God, before your coming, I just hope and pray that it's your will, and you'll have me cleaned up 'cause you said that only the pure and holy enters in the Kingdom of Heaven." It kept bothering me, realizing that this dip is making my temple unclean. That made me try that much more. When I turned it over to Him and started confessing to Him, and I would have these trials and temptations come to me, and I could have given up, but I was honest. I fell down and said, "God, here I am with this same problem. I got this craving coming in, and you know I'm about to give in. I'm not gonna lie to you. I could go to the store right now and buy about two cans of this stuff and start dipping," but I said, "I don't want that. Will you deliver me from this? I want to be strong." When I started doing that, things started changing. He heard me and knew how serious I was. I finally was able to quit. I told Daddy, "It seems like now I understand more how God wants things and wants us to do. I said, "If you'll abide with Him, He'll abide with you, and now if you'll stay connected with Him, locally, not long distance, but locally, He'll answer your prayers. He's proven that to me." That's true with anything in our lives.

When it comes to drugs and alcohol, my advice to young people is, first, don't do it. That's the first thing. You've always got that first invitation to smoke your first joint, drink your first alcohol drink, take your first downer, coke, whatever it is; there's always that first time. I know we can tell people not to do it, but most people are gonna wind up trying it. That's the wrong thing; they need to take advice from somebody that's been there and done that. Find the right surroundings, and find somebody in the church that's really close to God. Pick the right environment, and don't socialize with the wrong crowd. You can be tempted, and the devil will say, "Hey, you can do this and do that," but remember, it's not the greatest thing. That's just the devil, leading you off on his little trail, to pull you away from God. So pick the right environment because you become who you hang with, and that's the bottom line. So choose to hang with the right people, you are more likely to do good. You need somebody to guide you there.

**The Stancils' music is available from Morris Stancil,
1825 Lakeside Trail, Cumming, GA 30041.**

The Banjo Can Also Touch the Heart

~Dale Tilley~

It's obvious from the first moment you speak with Dale Tilley that he feels very passionate about life—from being an evangelist, his life's calling, to being a loving husband, father, and musician. He speaks from the heart and is energetic in expressing his thoughts and feelings, for as he said to me, "As you notice, Teresa, I have the gift of gab." A naturally talented musician, Dale, with his wife, Jan, welcomed us warmly into their home in northwest Georgia on a June afternoon. Surrounded by family photos on the walls and Dale's guitar and banjo on music stands, Dale openly shared his brief music career, his acceptance of Jesus as his Savior and Lord, and how he was able to bring his musical skills of playing, writing, and singing into his call to the ministry. A passionate man with a story to tell, he has traveled to many parts of the world sharing his music and God's love.

As our interview neared its close, Dale gave us a miniconcert, featuring some well-known favorites and a few songs that he has written himself, including "David's Delight" and "Ephraim's Blues." And just before we said good-bye, he showed us his library, where he prepares for his sermons and studies—a room filled with bookshelves on each wall where he knows every book and can tell the story behind each. I hope you will enjoy getting to know this man as much as we have.

—Teresa Thurmond Gentry

I was playing the guitar from the time I was ten—taught myself—and I always wanted to play the banjo. I remember in early elementary school one day they had hobby day. They asked, "What do you do?" I told a lie. I said I was a banjo player 'cause I wanted to be so bad, but I couldn't play. If they had said, "Okay, here's one, play," I couldn't have, but I wanted to because I used to hear Lester Flatt and Earl Scruggs on the radio on *The Martha White Show* early in the morning before we went to school—six fifteen in the morning—and all the family up, and there's Flatt and Scruggs playing. It was great.

I had to quit school because I had to leave home at fifteen—had nowhere to live, nowhere to go. For twenty-two days, I had nowhere to go. They write you off in school if you don't show up. You would think they woulda sent somebody for me, but anyway, after twenty-two days, my buddy Larry found me and said, "Mama said you come stay with us." At first I said naw. I was very ashamed and embarrassed, you know. It's bad enough to not have anywhere to live, but you do what you have to do to survive. That was a

PLATE 85 **"I left North Carolina at age eighteen
and went to traveling to see the world."**

Christian family that I moved in with, a poor family. I thought we were poor until I moved in with them. They were poor, but they were rich in love. Oh, my! They were very huggy people, tell-you-they-loved-you people. That was a different world for me. They were churchgoing people, and so I got a little bit involved in church. I had already been around them. That's how I knew Larry. I met him when I was eleven or twelve years old. Got around old-fashioned preaching—an independent Baptist church—with guitars, fiddles, and stuff like that. At that time I was playing music a lot.

I never dreamed I'd really play until I was seventeen. A buddy of mine had an old folk banjo that didn't even have a resonator on it. He played the style of Grandpa Jones and those people—Stringbean and David Holt and some of them—what they call drop thumb, ol' mountain-style drop thumb. You didn't use picks, but I couldn't play like that. I started playing with picks like I play with the guitar, so by the time I was seventeen and a half, I was playing banjo. My dad had played music. He had a guitar. He could only play like G, C, and D. That's it. Then my brother Steve bought a guitar and he wanted to play. You know, here I was playing already. You see, it came natural to me. I always said music is a gift from God. A lot of people take lessons. Back when I started learning, you didn't have DVDs, and you didn't have lessons, lesson books, hardly at all. You had to put the record on and try to learn flat full speed, nothing to slow it down, but I played with one of these cassette recorders. I listened back to it and heard what I was doing wrong and tried to get it just right—listen to the record, play, and then listen to the record and play.

At the age of eighteen, I met Kenny Baker [Bill Monroe's fiddle player] at a bluegrass festival. All of these guys back then, they drank alcohol. Aww, they drank. Whew! My first time ever around moonshine was in the back of an old car. We were going to pick, and I had some popcorn. I told one of 'em, "Pull over there, and let me get me a Coke." And he said, "Ahh, here." And I said, "What is it?" It looked like water, but he said, "Why don't you just . . . it's all right . . . take you a swallow." Whew! It liked to burnt my toenails off. It was moonshine. They laughed; these old men laughed at me. I was a kid and that was my only taste ever in my life of moonshine. It was enough. That stuff'll pickle you. You know, forget formaldehyde and all that.

Anyway, Kenny told Betty Fisher in Marietta, Georgia, about me. She's the band I played with—Betty Fisher and the Dixie Bluegrass Band—my first professional job. So I started at seventeen and a half, and by the time I was nineteen, I was playing the Grand Ole Opry with Betty's band. I played every day for five and a half hours a day, practicing the same thing—the same songs—till I got 'em right. I was also a studio musician. A lot of country singers wanted to record a song, but they didn't have a band, so they would call me.

PLATE 86 **"By the time I was nineteen, I was playing the Grand Ole Opry."**

This was in the early seventies. They would pay me a hundred dollars to come in for thirty minutes.

We made the cover of *Bluegrass Unlimited*. Anybody in bluegrass, this is the magazine that they subscribe to. We dressed up, every one of us; we all matched. A lot of bands came on in blue jeans. Ricky Skaggs had a group called Boone Creek, and they'd come on in blue jeans and casual shirts and stuff. It was a very good, clean show, and I thought the music was good. Of course, Betty was one of the few women in bluegrass at that time, and she had a good group. I stayed with her from the age of nineteen till I was twenty-three, when I got saved. I got saved in 1976 in August. I left bluegrass. I told the band, "Don't book any more for me, but whatever you've booked, I'll honor."

They said, "Well, what are you gonna do?" I said, "I don't know, but the Lord has saved me—got something for me to do. I gotta find out what it is." I didn't see anybody for at least a year and a half. I didn't see none of the people in bluegrass, although they called at first after I was gone. They quit calling after I said, "I sold my banjo, and I'm preaching." I would witness to them. I'd say, "Listen, let me talk to you about the Lord." They'd say, "Well, I ain't got time." I'd say, "Okay." So that ended most of the conversations. In about one year, I had to get rid of my banjo because people kept calling and wanting to hire me, and it was tempting—people throwing money at you. I said no. I was twenty-three years old, and I sold my banjo. I found something serious. I thought, if I'm gonna devote my life to this, I can't be torn between it. After a year, the Lord had given me victory to be able to say, "Hey, guys, look. I'm gonna play my banjo in church—play for the Lord," and at this time, Jan and I were dating. We married in October, and I started preaching not long after that and have been ever since. I still play bluegrass. I still play "Shuckin' the Corn" and "Groundspeed" and all that stuff. I just don't play bluegrass at festivals; I play in church. I have people in church all the time say, "Play 'The Beverly Hillbillies,'" and I say okay. I mean, pastors ask me to play "Foggy Mountain Breakdown." I'll say, "Okay, you're the pastor."

We have fun with the music, but the Lord has just used my music to assimilate it into my ministry. It's become part of the ministry—not the dominant part. The preaching part has been the dominant part, but this has been a great door opener. I've gotten to win a lot of pickers to the Lord because I pick. Music ministers to the heart in a tremendous way. It prepares the heart. A banjo is a joyful instrument. You can't help it; if you play it any speed at all, it affects your foot.

So what I do in my ministry is that I play the banjo before I preach, and I play slow stuff on the banjo, not just fast. That's the difference in playing by yourself and taking the banjo where normally you wouldn't—jail, prison, hospitals, nursing homes, churches. They don't normally have a banjo player, so it's been an honor to be able, all these years, to go play for people who otherwise would not hear a live banjo player—to see one live—unless they see one on TV or something.

Then I started writing songs. Even before I got saved, I wrote songs, but after I got saved I started writing more songs. I've written a pile of songs, and they are totally different than my bluegrass. I'm trying to get my songs done while I'm still able to be here to sing because once I die all those songs, unless I have 'em recorded, are gonna be gone. All my instrumental banjo songs that I've written I'm trying to put on tape—on a CD—because, number one, a lot of 'em are hard to play; it's going to take somebody real special to want to learn to play these. Any banjo player can play "I'll Fly Away," but to play some of the other stuff that I play, it's very difficult.

A buddy of mine up in Indiana helped me put all this stuff together. He told me years ago, "You need to start puttin' your songs on CD. You could sell 'em when you go preach." I didn't have the money, so he helped me put my first CD together and then the second and so on. So everywhere we go, especially now, I sell my CDs. I sell 'em for ten dollars apiece, or I give 'em away. I tell people, "If you don't have ten dollars, take a CD. You can have a CD, but one per family," because I was in a church preaching, and a man and his wife had a pile of kids. When I said, "You can have a CD," they all got a CD. I'm not kidding.

I've written a bunch of songs. When you hear my music, it's totally different. To get my music out, it's a blessing that people have recorded my songs. We just had a group up in Indiana, a gospel group, record three of my songs. They had already recorded two of my songs, so they've recorded five altogether. This ministers to the foot [pointing to his banjo], and my music that I've written ministers to the heart. Some bluegrass will minister to the heart when you play it right; some of that old stuff—the old slow gospel bluegrass, even "Cabin on the Hill," a Flatt and Scruggs tune. Every time I hear that song, boy, it makes me think about going home. A lot of those bluegrass songs had that touch to them, like old country. Old country music is different from new country today. Well, old bluegrass is different than new. We have newgrass now—Béla Fleck and the Flecktones. I met him [Béla Fleck] and witnessed to him, and got to talking to him, and he said he was a Jew. I said, "So was my Savior." "But are you saved?" is what I asked him. He's a great banjo player in his style.

All that I've accomplished in life is what the Lord has helped me do—my traveling—all the countries that I've been to, places I've been. At eighteen, I walked the Grand Canyon; I walked to the bottom—three and

PLATE 87 "We have fun with the music, but the Lord has just used my music. . . . It's become part of the ministry."

a half miles—and walked back up. I've got pictures of me in the Grand Canyon. I stood on the San Francisco Golden Gate Bridge, on top of the Empire State Building, and the Twin Towers. They were building 'em when I was standing on the Empire State Building. I saw the Twin Towers coming up. They hadn't finished them yet. To go out of this country, to get to go to Alaska, to fly within hundreds of miles of Russia and preach to a village of four thousand people—it's an honor to have written these songs and written poems. And then to go preach and see so many saved; somebody might think that I've done a lot, when really I haven't. It's just that the Lord has let me utilize what I have.

You're born with the gift of music. I've had people say, "Brother Dale, will I ever learn to play a banjo like that?" I can say, "Practice hard," but people are born with the gift of music. In the Old Testament, God gave Asaph and those people the gift of music. He put it in them. He put the ability to engrave in people that didn't have it. That's in the Old Testament. He gave them the gift of engraving, embroidery. They couldn't do it, but he put it in 'em.

So as a child I had the gift of music. I didn't know I had the gift of music. I had to grow up, and I was on up in age in preaching before I realized, "Hey, this is a gift."

Dale Tilley's music is available from Dale Tilley,
PO Box 252, Ringgold, GA 30736-0252.

"I'm a musician."

~ Gary Waldrep ~

I had the opportunity to meet and listen to Gary Waldrep and his band at a bluegrass festival in Long Creek, South Carolina, a few years ago. I was not in the stage area when the group began to perform, but the group's rich harmony, echoing through the hills surrounding the park, drew me up front and close to the stage. Talking with Gary later, I realized he was a huge Foxfire fan, and that day he made plans to stop by my classroom at Rabun County High School, at some point in the future, to pick up a set of the Foxfire books. True to his word, a couple of months later, he and his mom came through Tiger, Georgia, and purchased the entire collection of Foxfire books. I found Gary to be not only a very talented musician and performer but also a loyal friend to his fans, both on and off the stage. He always has time to talk or play a tune with a stranger, who quickly becomes his friend. God has truly blessed Gary with talent in so many ways. I feel privileged to call him my friend.

—Joyce Green

I started playing music when I was five years old because my family played. It was just something that we picked up. I never had a music lesson; I didn't even know what a music lesson was. We were just blessed with a God-given talent—the gift of playing by ear. When I was little, maybe four or five years old, I started playing my first instrument. It was a shoe box and two pencils. I would sit there while the folks played, and I would beat the pencils on the shoe box for a drum, and that was the rhythm. That's how I learned to beat rhythm and keep time.

The first true instrument that I ever had in my hands was a mandolin, which I still have out there in the office. It belonged to my aunt, and she let me borrow it and play it one day. She showed me three chords—G, C, and D—and I started playing and getting my rhythm down with just three chords on the mandolin. Today I'm really a banjo player, and I make a living playing the banjo, but it all started with the mandolin.

My first prize was a silver dollar when I was five years old. My family was playing at a local rescue squad fund-raiser, and this old man walked up to me and gave me a silver dollar. That was the first money that I ever made. During my preteen and teenage years, my aunt was playing bass in the family band. They played gospel and old-time country music. At this time there was not a lot of bluegrass, so they were playing southern gospel and old country gospel—stuff like the Carter Family, Roy Acuff, and Hank Williams. They loved country music, and my aunt started showing me some

PLATE 88 "It's come apart. It's terrible, but on that mandolin is where I learned to play my three chords—G, C, and D." The mandolin that Gary started playing when he was five years old

runs on the electric bass guitar. I learned a few runs and moved from playing the mandolin to bass guitar.

I played bass guitar for five or six years until my aunt fell in love with this guy, Kenneth [Kenny] Townsell. He loved bluegrass and while they were dating, he brought an old banjo over there to my grandparents' house and started playing it. Well, I picked it up naturally, after he showed me a few licks. You know how musicians are; we want to go around learning to play different instruments, and so I started playing it, and I kinda liked the sound of it. You know, I thought the banjo was pretty cool 'cause I'd always played country and gospel and didn't really know what bluegrass was. Kenny kind of brought the bluegrass influence and old-time music into the family. So I got my driver's license so I could drive and started going to some fiddlers' conventions and square dances—anything that I could find that had old-timey bluegrass music—and I would play the banjo. Thirty-two years later, and I'm still playing banjo and making a living with it. That's where I got started into bluegrass.

My family played music, but they didn't tour extensively like we do today. They mostly stayed in the community. They would go to different people's houses on Saturday night and pick, or to church singings and nursing homes and play for the folks there. My mother was a wonderful singer. She didn't play an instrument hardly—just the guitar a little bit—but she taught me and my sister how to hear the different parts in singing. I owe all my singing ability, which is not a whole lot, to my mother 'cause me and my sister grew up listening to her sing. She'd be singing a song like "Will the Circle Be Unbroken," and she'd tell us, "Now, don't sing my part 'cause I'm singing my part. Sing high above me or below me." She said, "You get a part, and you get a part." Well, that's how she taught us to sing the harmony. I lost my mother three years ago with colon cancer. She was sixty-five. My dad is still living. He's seventy years old and on the road with us. He helps drive the bus and sells my CDs.

I didn't know what I wanted to do when I got out of high school. I thought, "Well . . . I don't want to be a dentist, and I don't want to be a lawyer." You know, I'm thinking, "I'm a musician." I was in the band in high school, and I loved the band. I was drum major. If it hadn't been for band, I probably would've flunked school [laughs] because I didn't like school that much. Thank God for band!

When I finished school I was already playing bluegrass music. I would go to fiddlers' conventions on Saturday night, and they would hold contests for banjo playing, fiddle playing, and buck dancing. Well, I'd enter in every category because I thought I could play a song on something, and I would end up winning prize money. When I'd get home, I'd have two or three hundred dollars in my pocket. And I thought, "This is something. I might could do this for a living. Why not?" My parents didn't push me to play, but my mother always encouraged me in my music 'cause she loved music; however, my dad wasn't very keen on the idea. He wanted me to be the big football player type, but I was not into sports much. I'm an Alabama fan; that's about as far as it goes. I thought, "Well, I don't want to do that, so what am I gonna do?" Basically, I started playing for money. I'd enter contests and get in these little bands, and we'd enter contests and win five hundred, a thousand dollars, or whatever.

I started in my first, I guess you'd say, professional band when I graduated from Boaz High School in 1981. I graduated in May and that summer, in June or July, the Warrior River Boys offered me a job playing banjo, and I started touring with them. They were a traditional bluegrass band that played Bill Monroe–type music. We had to wear the hats and the suits and all that, which I did for a while. During that time I learned a lot of banjo tunes and practiced singing harmony a lot. I sung baritone mostly. I stayed with that group from 1981 through 1985. Then I joined Wendy Bagwell and the Sunliters, a gospel group from Hiram, Georgia. I'd always loved their music, and Wendy was a great entertainer and a friend of our family. I got to watching him a lot onstage, and I saw how he could get the people just right there, so he helped me learn how to entertain. Playing with them gave me a lot of southern gospel background because they were southern gospel stars. They were big time back in their day. I toured with them a year before I got back into bluegrass 'cause my heart was wanting to get back into the old-time music. When I left Wendy's group, I went back to playing with the Warrior River Boys for a couple of years. After that, I gave them my notice because I was basically wanting to do something different. I wasn't what you'd call a band jumper because I would always give my notice and say, "Well, you know, I wanna do something else." And they'd say, "Okay, bye. See ya." And they'd keep playing. They are still playing today, and we play on some of the same shows sometimes.

After that, me and my uncle Kenny formed a group called the Sand Mountain Boys, which was a national touring group. We were four guys—me and my uncle and two guys from Florida, but me and Kenny were the Sand Mountain people. We kind of did our own thing. We quit wearing the hats and went a little more radical with the music. We basically got out of most of the traditional and did some stuff that we wanted to do. We even wrote some of our own songs. I don't write much, but my uncle's a good writer, so we were doing some of his stuff.

That went on till about '96, and I got tired of that. I wanted to do something else; something else was calling me. With all the groups that I'd played with, I was the one that got out there and kind of emceed, and I was kind of the leader of the band, but not really. People would see me and they'd think, "Well, he's our favorite 'cause he's a banjo player, and he talks and he dances." People started telling me, "You need to form your own group; put your name out there. Put Gary Waldrep out there instead of the 'blah, blah, blah boys.' Put your name and your face out there." So that's what I did. In 1996 I just quit all of the groups I was in. I thought, "I don't want to be a sideman no more. I'm either gonna do this thing and be my own leader, or I'm just gonna play for the fun of it and go get a job," so I put my name out with The Gary Waldrep Band. I let everybody in the band shine. I don't hog the show. Mindy sings half the songs in our group. Donna don't sing, but if she wants to do a special, she does. Kenny plays his specials on his fiddle. It's not just Gary Waldrep; I let everybody do their own thing, so that's why we call it The Gary Waldrep Band. It's not The Gary Waldrep Show; it's the band. Letting people know who you are was one of the smartest things I ever did.

During the time from '81 to '96, I only played in three different groups, so in '96 me and my sister, Susan Waldrep, helped me get a band started. She's a great singer. We formed the group and it was kinda like a brother-and-sister act, and we got some good breaks. We had some people listen to us in Nashville, and we got some people filming documentaries out here.

PLATE 89 **"I let everybody in the band shine. I don't hog the show." The Gary Waldrep Band**

Things happened, and all of a sudden our family was kind of thrown into the music spotlight, per se. We started recording CDs and putting out our music. That helped because it got our music out to radio stations. We started winning some awards in Nashville at the SPBGMA, which is the Society for the Preservation of Bluegrass Music in America. In 1993 and '94, I won Best Banjo Player of the Year, Clawhammer-Style, and Old-Time Banjo Player of the Year. It helps when you get a few national awards. Newspapers were coming out and doing stories on us.

My sister had to retire a few years ago because of some medical problems, and she basically turned everything over to me, so it's my band now, and it's The Gary Waldrep Band. My family is in the band. My aunt and uncle that I was telling you about—Kenny and Donna—they're in my band. Kenny plays the fiddle and drives the bus. Aunt Donna plays bass guitar, and Mindy Rakestraw is the lady that I have from Dallas, Georgia, and she plays guitar; then I have Stan Wilemon from Snead Crossroads. He plays mandolin for me. We've got a five-piece band, and we just go play bluegrass and gospel music. I do all the booking for the group. We play festivals and churches. We try to give our audiences what they want to hear. If they like and want bluegrass and old-time music, that's what we give them.

For thirteen years we produced our own bluegrass festival here on the farm. It was called Festival on the Farm. We had thousands of people out here on the farm every year, anywhere from seventeen hundred to eighteen hundred people for the weekend. Our stage was the back porch here at the house. One of the reasons I started the Festival on the Farm was to give back to the community. I wanted them to be able to come out here on the farm and see us because a lot of these folks don't get out of town. They would never see us because we tour out of town a lot. We stopped it three years ago when my mother passed away because she was such a big part of it, and we just couldn't go on with it. We've got one of the largest fan clubs in bluegrass today. We've got over fifteen hundred members, and that's pretty big for bluegrass. They're real good to us, too. They hold fund-raisers to raise money; if we need something for the band, like a tire for the bus or whatever, they pretty well take care of it for us. They're great. The building where my bus is parked was donated to us by the fan club. It didn't cost me a dime. They were tired of sitting in the sun, I guess. The fan club all raised money and had a guy from Georgia come out here and bring the materials and build it so they would have a place to sit during the festivals. It was a big honor to know people care about you that much.

I play nine different instruments. I would play an instrument for a year or two, and then I'd see someone else play another one, and I would want to try that. I guess I didn't get bored with an instrument but just decided I wanted to try to play all of 'em. Then, if I needed to get a job playing something, I could. I've had jobs playing fiddle, banjo, and mandolin, so it's been good to learn all the instruments. The clawhammer banjo style is basically what I'm known for in the country. In the clawhammer-style banjo picking, you don't use picks. I do a lot of clawhammer today. Clawhammer is a style of banjo that's old as the mountains. It started in the Appalachian Mountains and is one of the first styles of banjo playing in the history of the banjo in America. The banjo did not originate in the United States; it actually came from Africa and is an African instrument. The slaves brought the banjo to the southern plantations years ago. Other people that come in—the Irish people and others—picked up the instrument. Everybody wanted to play the banjo, so the clawhammer style basically started with African Americans. Three-finger banjo-style picking is like Earl Scruggs plays. He didn't actually invent the three-finger style, but he made it popular. He was their spokesman because he was the first guy that got out and started touring with a band where people could hear the three-finger style. With the three-finger style, you use a thumb pick and two finger picks. With clawhammer, you just use your fingernails. You don't use picks. It's more like a dance rhythm, I guess you'd say. There's lots of other banjo styles. In New Orleans there's the strumming banjo—the Dixieland. We kind of feel like we've got our own brand of mountain music up here on the mountain 'cause years ago Sand Mountain was so isolated. You couldn't get up here except for only two or three roads going up on this mountain, so we just kind of got our own little brand of old-time music, I think, and you can hear it in the recordings of the artists around here, too. I like this ol'-timey stuff. Even though I play professionally on the road, we still get together here on the mountain and pick and have jam sessions and food with the neighbors. The food's a big part. Certain communities have musicians that live there, and the music's even more popular than in other places. Holly Pond is forty-five minutes from here. They have two or three families that play. We used to go over there and play, and then they'd come over and play music with us. It's kind of like a network. You get to know where all the musicians are and where and when they're picking.

I was a DJ for years. You know, musicians have to have little side jobs, and one of mine was the host of a radio show. Of course, I talked a lot, and sometimes Mindy tells me I talk too much onstage. She tells me to shut up and sing—no dead time. I did the DJ thing for a gospel station. I loved that 'cause I could play what I wanted. I also sold jewelry one time when I was between bands, and I loved that because I wear a lot of jewelry onstage. I have also worked at a car wash, and that helped me decide to get back into music. That was work! Oh my gosh, I bet you I lost probably thirty pounds that summer working at that car wash. It's a good way to lose weight because those cars keep coming in. We were hand-washing them. I told my boss, "I'm getting back into music. This is for the birds." So I did.

I have also been teaching music for years. That helps supplement my income pretty good. I get a grant from the state of Alabama that pays me to teach kids and adults. It's an apprenticeship grant where the students complete an apprenticeship with me. I'm considered a master artist by the state. There's grant money there, and they're gonna give it to somebody, so I always fill out the application. Sometimes I get it, and sometimes I don't. The people who give these grants know I've been doing this for years. I've played for them down there in Montgomery at the capitol, and they know who I am, and they know I'm legit. I've used the money to buy books for students and helped buy their gas if they can't afford to come for lessons. That's what the money is for. It's not a whole lot, but it helps buy an instrument for a kid sometimes. I teach thirty-minute lessons on the banjo, fiddle, mandolin, bass guitar, and guitar. I can do dulcimer and autoharp if somebody wants to learn them. I try to pass on what I've learned to them. I've been teaching for twenty years.

The music business has been really good to me. People have been great. We've got a great following. It's just been a great ride. I'm forty-six, fixing to be forty-seven in a few weeks, and I never would have thought that I would have been playing music all this time and making a living with it. I'm not getting rich, but I'm paying the bills. If I can just do that and keep my bills paid, then I'm doing okay. Our music now is all over the world through the

Internet and radio. Everybody says, "Why don't you move to Nashville? Why are you still in Kilpatrick, Alabama?" Well, this is my family's farm. I grew up here, and when I was little, this is where I was running around. There used to be a cotton patch or corn or whatever Papaw grew, where my house is now. I built my house here in '94, and why would I want to leave here when I am only two or three hours from Nashville? I can drive up there and back if I need to take care of business. I want to be here where I grew up. This is home. My friends and family are here. We just take the bus and go where we want to go and come back. My memories of the music are right here. That's why I love this place so much; it all started for me right here on this farm.

I have been honored numerous times for my music. Governor Bob Riley issued a proclamation declaring every September eighth as Gary Waldrep Day. Two years ago, I was inducted into the Alabama Bluegrass Music Hall of Fame. I was one of the first inductees in there. Me and Charlie Louvin, Jerry and Mae Hinton, Claire Lynch, and Three on a String were the inductees. I've got two commendations by the governor. The county named a road after me; 479 is the Gary Waldrep Highway. I also received the Gary Waldrep Road Resolution from the DeKalb County Commission.

We're active in our own church. I go to Fairview United Methodist, which is over here in Albertville, Alabama. We like to be at home on Sunday mornings to go to our own church. That's why we don't play a lot of churches, because we all have our own church that we like to get back to. If we do a church service, it's usually on Saturday night or sometimes a Sunday night.

PLATE 90 **Gary started playing music when he was five years old at his grandparents' farm, on which he built a house and now lives.**

We love bluegrass gospel. We sing a lot of bluegrass gospel. Part of my heritage is singing the old spirituals. As a matter of fact, if we're at a festival two days and we're gonna do four shows, you can bet one of those shows will be all gospel. When we do an all-gospel set, people love it.

Canada, Colorado, New York—the further up north you go, the more they love old-time southern Appalachian music. I found that out just traveling. We travel twenty-eight to thirty states a year and play music from Sand Mountain here. I've been able to take my music to most of the United States and Canada. We've played on the biggest cruise ship in the world, the *Oasis of the Seas*. I'd never been on a cruise, and I thought I'd probably get sick, but I didn't. We went to the Bahamas and played music on the ship. We played down in Saint Thomas. It's always nice to have a great time and do something you like. I just got back from Ontario, Canada, a few weeks ago. It's like getting a paid vacation every weekend I go somewhere. Of course, we don't get to sightsee a lot, but we get to see a lot of the country just driving back and forth.

I've met a lot of the big stars—Ricky Skaggs, Steve Warner, Earl Scruggs, and Grandpa Jones. I loved Grandpa Jones. He was one of my idols 'cause he played the banjo in the style that I love—the clawhammer. Most of the stars that I have had contact with are bluegrass stars. I've picked with Bill Monroe and Ralph Stanley. We record on Tom T. Hall's label now. I've been to his house, and he and his wife, Dixie, are just like us. Mindy is involved with a group called the Daughters of Bluegrass [all women bluegrass stars], and they record special CDs. She was on the label with Tom T. and kind of helped me get my foot in the door with him. They heard a sample of our music, and they liked it and wanted to hear more from us. I sent 'em a CD, and all of a sudden they wrote a song for us. We recorded it. It's called "Trust and Pray." We have pitched it out now to radio stations, and it should be getting some airplay.

A record label can help you get your songs played on the radio. For instance, if you were a DJ and I sent you a copy of The Gary Waldrep Band, and you don't know Gary Waldrep, you might just throw the recording in the trash can. But if you see Tom T. Hall and Dixie—Blue Circle Records—you might take time to listen to the recording. That's what this label is doing for us now. When we record a song for them, they're gonna get radio royalties. So it's good for each of us. There's no big money in radio royalties, but it does help you get bookings. If I was to get a chart song, promoters look at that, and they think, "Well, Gary here's got a number three. Let's call him up and book him."

About forty percent of the songs we do are public domain. I don't write. I've wrote maybe two songs in thirty years. I entertain the crowd and pick.

We have writers that write for us. My uncle Kenny writes, and I've used two or three of his songs. We've recorded two of our mandolin player's songs. He's wrote some songs for a lot of the big groups. Me and Mindy—we don't write. We just stand up there, sing, and look pretty [laughs]. Writing is just something that I guess I haven't been inspired to do. I would love to write, and I need to write, but it just don't come to me that easy. I guess it's just like people say, "Well, you play by ear. I wish I could do that." Well, I wish I could write a song. We also have people who write for us in Nashville, and they send me tons of songs—independent songwriters that know I play music. I've been doing this thirty-something years, so they pretty well know my name and address. One of the songs we recorded, "Mountain Pines," was written by a Cherokee Indian lady.

I love being a musician, and I love to pick instruments, but I had rather sing two to one as to play. I love just to sit down with two or three people and a guitar and just sing. We love to do that as a band, and our band is known for its harmony ability. We work hard at it. People have told us that we have the best harmony than any band they've ever heard. We're real proud of our harmony.

I don't want people to think that I'm just in it for the money, 'cause I'm not. I do a lot of charity work like Relay for Life, United Way, and the American Cancer Society, but in order to play music for a living and not have another job, I have to charge a certain amount to run the bus. I am so fortunate and blessed that I can make a living with my music. It's like somebody fishing or hunting for a living. It's something you really enjoy doing and can do it and sustain yourself with it. Of course, I live by myself. If I had a wife and kids, I might not be doing this. That hasn't happened yet. I'm married to my banjo, and it don't eat a lot. Anyway, it's just fun. It's a fun ride, and I'm still ridin'. I don't know how long I'll be on it, but for now that's what I do; I just play music. I thank God I can make a living at it.

**Gary Waldrep's music is available from Gary Waldrep,
1958 County Road 479, Albertville, AL 35951;
www.garywaldrep.com.**

"Emergency services pronounced me dead at the scene."

~Young Harmony~

Blessings—we receive them every day, but the majority of times we are too busy to realize it. However, when you receive a blessing like Johnathan Bond did twenty years ago, and even hearing or reading his story, you learn to never take things for granted and cherish every moment God has given you. Just like Johnathan, when we are teenagers we believe we are invincible and nothing will ever happen to us. Johnathan learned very quickly when he was struck head-on by an eighteen-wheeler, flew across the median, and was hit by two cars at great force that he was anything but invincible. He learned how quickly your life can be taken from you, and most of all he learned who the Master Physician truly is. When the Lord raised Johnathan from eighteen and a half minutes dead, even the medical staff agreed it was nothing short of a miracle.

Prior to the interview, I had heard bits and pieces of Johnathan's personal testimony but mainly knew the multi-Dove-winning southern gospel group he leads, Young Harmony. Had it not been for God's healing hand upon Johnathan, the music industry and millions of people would never have experienced this blessed group. Young Harmony has recorded a total of fourteen projects to date. They have been featured in several national magazines, including the Singing News, New Church Connection, US Gospel News, Reader's Digest, *and many others. The group has received numerous Dove Award nominations, and in 2004 it was named Group of the Year. In 2007, "God Is Still God," written by Jonathan, was nominated as southern gospel and gospel music's Song of the Year. In 2008, the group was inducted into the North American Country Music Hall of Fame.*

During the interview I sat listening to Johnathan, Noel Walters, and Darlene Chapman recall stories from their group's ministry and their personal experiences. As I sat there I kept thinking, "Wow, what an inspiration!" At eighteen years old, I was diagnosed with cancer. At the time of this interview, it was a few weeks before my one-year checkup, which is the make-it-or-break-it visit. The Bible says that in everything there is a purpose, and I know without a doubt that the purpose of me having had the opportunity to meet Johnathan was to remind me that God is still with me, and God is bigger than any problem I have.

—Casi Best

Johnathan: I'm Johnathan Bond with Young Harmony. I was born in the Phoenix, Arizona, area on October 11, 1967. I was eight years old when we moved to Dalton, Georgia. I only moved because my parents did. There wasn't really much choice in it for me [laughs]. I lived in that area until '90. Then I moved to Chattanooga, Tennessee.

My whole family is in music and has been for years, but I got started in music because in '91 I had a major car wreck, and I will share what God brought me through. My cousins traveled with a gospel group, and they started asking me if I would go with them. Before you knew it, I was sharing my testimony and singing a song. It just sort of evolved into a trio from there. It wasn't a plan as far as on my part. I actually had no idea; it took me a while to even realize, "Hey, we have a group [laughs]." The group was me and two of my cousins, Murray and Tuwana McClure. The McClure family traveled, and as my great-uncle and his wife got older, they didn't travel as much. People would call and say, "Well, what about the 'McClure Trio'?" and that was the name that we went by for a couple of years. As the McClure Trio, Murray and Tuwana worked full-time jobs and couldn't travel places. I was still under doctor's care and wasn't able to work, so when people would call and say, "Hey, would y'all come and sing," they couldn't go. So I'd go do some solo work. Eventually, I just got other people to help me and formed Young Harmony. The McClure family still sings some in Chattanooga, but they're not traveling anymore.

I've always been raised in church, and I've always believed in God. I didn't even know there was an option to not believe in God. I've always believed that He was the creator of the universe. Growing up in church, I never realized that I needed Him as a personal Savior. I believed other people did but I was fine. I lived my whole life that way. I'd been to the altar; I'd done everything that everybody expected, but in my heart I had never accepted Him as a Savior. My mom, dad, brother, and sister traveled, singing for many years, and on September 23, 1991, a Monday evening, my mother called me. She said, "Your brother is not going to be able to go with us this coming weekend. I need you to fill in for him."

I said, "Mom, I can't do that; I've got a lot going on." She said, "We're practicing at the church in the morning at ten o'clock, and I *will* see you there, right?" I went to church with them that Tuesday morning to go over their songs, and I could sing, but I didn't. All the songs were great songs, but they weren't personal to me. Then we began to sing a song that my mom and dad used to sing a lot called "Miracle in the Making." As we began to sing that song something began to happen within me, and I knew what that was, but I wasn't ready for that. I was scared of that, and I remember when we got done with that song, I brushed a tear from my face, and I didn't let them see me. I told my mom, "I need to leave."

She knew what was going on, so she said, "Well, let's just go over that song one more time." I said, "Mom, I've gotta go to work." I left for work, and it was raining really hard. An eighteen-wheeler pulled over in my lane and hit my car. When he hit me, he knocked me across the median, and two other cars hit me at a force so great that my seat belt snapped in half. At one forty-five in the afternoon, the emergency services pronounced me dead at the scene.

My mom was on her way from church, headed home. She heard on the radio that there was a fatal car accident on Battlefield Parkway [Highway 2], which was not the direction I was supposed to have been going to work. As soon as the radio announcer said they were rerouting traffic because of a fatal collision on Highway 2, she turned to my brother and said, "That is Johnathan." Keep in mind now that the DJ said nothing at all about sex, race, car model, car color, or anything.

My brother said, "Mom, that's not the way that he goes to work." She said, "There's not a doubt in my mind that it is Johnathan." She turned around and went toward the hospital. She knew with the traffic being so backed up that she could get to the hospital about the same time. When she went in the hospital, through the emergency room, she went up to the counter and said, "I'm Johnathan Bond's mother. He had the wreck over here on Battlefield Parkway just now." She didn't ask because she already knew it was me. One of the doctors heard her say my name and came out. He put his arm around my mother and said, "Mrs. Bond, I'm really sorry to tell you that we did all we could."

She said, "Would you pray with me?" While they were praying, the nurse that was cleaning me up for identification ran out screaming, "Help! This man is *not* dead!" I had begun to strangle while she was working. The doctor got up from his knees praying and went to help. My mother stayed on her knees. A nurse told me this later, she said, "Your mom stayed on her knees even after they said you were alive."

I asked my mother later, I said, "After you knew that I was alive, why did you stay on your knees?" She said, "We've always taught you if you ever ask someone for help, then you always take the time to say thanks." They put me in the trauma unit, and I was in a coma. They told my parents what all was wrong with me: My back was broken in nine places, I was paralyzed from just above my waist down, my right eye had dislocated, my skull was cracked, my head was swollen and was hemorrhaging, I had two broken ribs, my arm was broken, my shoulder was broken, I had lost all of my blood except for half a pint, and the most critical part was the eighteen and a half minutes of unaccountable [loss of] oxygen to the brain.

The doctor said to my mother that day, "At best case, Johnathan will live as a vegetable"; however, my mother wasn't accepting that. Two days later my heart stopped. The medical team ran in with the paddles and got my family out of the room. When they were done, they came back out, and Dr. Tom Odum, the doctor from the emergency room, said, "Mrs. Bond, we did everything we could, but we have lost him this time." She said, "Do you remember the day he came in here? Would y'all pray with us again?" While they were praying, I came out of the coma. My heart had started beating again, and I was aware, awake, and talking. The wreck was on a Tuesday, and on Saturday I walked out of the hospital, completely healed!

The first thing that my nurse said when I started talking was "I want to serve the Lord." That was her first phrase to me. She has since been to many of our concerts and shared her own testimony. The paramedics have been to many of our concerts and shared how they never expected anything at all to come from the wreck but how God brought me totally, one hundred percent, from it.

I was under doctor's care for two years following the wreck. They have never done surgery. They thought they were going to have to do some plastic surgery because of the cut on my face and the scar that was there, the aneurysm, and my head swelling the way it did, but they never did any kind of surgery. God healed me all the way through.

It's been since '91, and I never have back problems. I travel and lift all the time, which are the worst things that you can do with back issues. It's not anything that anyone should get any of the credit for, except God. Through that, that's how I started sharing my story, and they'd ask if I would sing a song and, of course, I would. If you know me now and knew me then, you'd see the difference. I'm very outgoing and thankful for what God's brought me through. He has given me the joy of the Lord and my salvation. I have joy wherever I am, and before I was real timid and shy. Anyone that knows me now is like "no way" [laughs].

That's my testimony. When I look back at it, I'm thankful for not just what He did physically, but also spiritually. I went into the hospital a broken man and came out standing on the rock. We have a song that says, "He took my past and made it whole," and that's what He did for me. I'm thankful for that.

I've got a little over one hundred songs that I've written. They're all very personal to me. I can tell you exactly what was happening in my life that encouraged every song.

Darlene: Some famous people have picked up his songs.

Johnathan: Mariah Carey, "Inside Your Heart"; Alison Krauss, "I Need Your Grace"; and I've got two songs on hold for Christmas [2010] right now, one with Vince Gill and Amy Grant, and the other with Wynonna Judd. The one with Wynonna Judd is "Do You Know Jesus?" and it's a really cool song. We were at a church, and I just wrote it in the midst of a major battle. I was at a church that I mostly didn't want to be at because I was in the middle of this struggle. A lady asked the kids, she said, "Is there anything you'd like to hear Mr. Johnathan sing?"

This kid said, "Rudolph the Red-Nosed Reindeer." I was going, "Oh, great." [Laughs.] Of course, I did it and as I started singing it, I got this other song. I wanted to say, "Hey, can I just take a quick break?" It's the whole Christmas story, all right there in the song. I got that from being in a place I didn't really want to be because I had so much going on. That's something else I've learned, too, is a lot of times the reason that we don't succeed or get through our situations is because if Satan can get us to focus on our problems, then he's taken our focus off of God. If we can take the time to get our focus back on God and off of us, then we can overcome whatever the situation.

The scripture that says, "Those that wait upon the Lord shall renew their strength," I was always taught that it meant when you've done all you can do, just sit and wait on God. I've learned to believe that it means those that wait upon the Lord like a server would do at a restaurant can renew their strength. When I'm having a bad day or feeling rough in a situation, then that's the very thing I do, is say, "God, what can I do for you, because I'm needing to wait on you today?" That's where my strength has been.

I was talking to one of the little boys at that same church, and he was probably nine years old and seemed like he was by himself. He was in a corner and wasn't really part of the whole group. I went over to him and I said, "So, what are you getting for Christmas?" He said, "The same thing that I get every year, probably." He was an orphan. I said, "What if God were to bring you a family for Christmas?" That's what I started praying for, but when I said that, this song just came to me, "The Gift Made the Difference." In the song, he was placed into a family, and the second verse says, "I wasn't there when Jesus was born, but I know what He's done for me, and the gift made the difference for me." All the songs have a story and are all personal to me.

These are the two people that I get to travel with, Noel Walters and Darlene Chapman, and I'm so thankful for them. It is just the three of us that travel. We are the band. I play the piano, but I didn't take piano lessons. Just being around music all my life, I picked it up. I play by ear and read music, too. We were always taught the do, re, mi, fa, sol, la, ti, do, so I learned all of that. Growing up, our church had a choir and a band, so I learned by being around that as well.

Noel: I play the bass guitar.

Darlene: I play the piano. I've been singing since I was three. My daddy was a pastor, so I grew up in church, so I've been playing and singing since I was born [laughs]. That's just what our family did.

Johnathan: And you'll see why she's been doing it a long time tonight. It's just the three of us now, but I love it! They have been with Young Harmony six months. I met Darlene sixteen or seventeen years ago; she was traveling with a group, and we were friends, and we traveled in the same circuit kind of thing. I met Noel about six years ago, and he traveled with Mel Tillis for about sixteen years. God just put us together at a tremendous time, and we sang here at Country Tonite Theatre in Pigeon Forge, Tennessee, our very first time together. I said, "Why can't this be one of those churches with only like twenty people for our first time?"

When I think about the name of our group, I think, "Oh mercy, we are a little past the name [laughs]."

Darlene: Watch it [laughs]!

Johnathan: The name came about when we were at a church, when we first started singing, and the McClure Trio couldn't go that night. I had gotten a couple of people to go, and we didn't have a name or anything. This older lady stood up after the concert and said, "How beautiful it is to see young people in harmony with their calling that God has given them." When she said that, the Young Harmony part just sorta came out at me. I didn't think about years to come.

We sing in any venue, from small churches to big churches to restaurants, just anywhere we are led. We got to sing on the History Channel on National Prayer Day in Washington, D.C. Year before last, I had to read all of the "begets" [fathered a child] from the Bible on television. I was going, "Oh, have mercy," at all these names I couldn't even really pronounce. One year we were asked to sing at a bar on National Prayer Day. The woman said, "We want you to come, but we want you to know we are still going to serve the alcohol."

I said, "You be you, because we're still going to serve what we serve, too." And it was just beautiful. It was difficult for us mentally. We went in and wouldn't even drink a bottle of water because we didn't want to leave the wrong impression. We got there in time to go around and talk to each person that was there. We just chitchatted, got up, and sang, and then we left. It was probably about five or six months later, and I was at Goody's, a former clothing store, because they had this really big sale [laughs], and a lady came up to me and said, "You won't recognize me, I'm sure, but I was at the bar in Lookout Valley, Tennessee, when you sang on National Prayer Day. I just want you to know that you made a difference in my life."

I was just amazed at how God works. Scripture says, "Go unto the highways and the hedges," and those places are the hedges. I know that you do have to be careful, but we shouldn't let anything keep us from sharing the good news. We have a job to do.

We were called and asked to sing at a revival, and it was just about a' hour, hour and half from our house. We truly wanted a spirit-filled service, so we fasted. I can tell you that we don't miss a meal for anybody, except for God. We'd fasted that whole day, and the plan was that as soon as that service was over, we were headed straight to Burger King. We were going to get a Whopper with cheese [laughs]. As the service was nearing the end, the pastor stood up and said, "We're going to take up a love offering for the evangelist that has come from Florida. Before we take this love offering, I want you to ask God what He would have you give." I had in my pocket eighteen dollars. I had a ten, a five, and three ones. I was going to just put three ones in the offering, and then we could eat on the other fifteen. God spoke to me, and He told me to give the eighteen dollars, and I was starving! So what I was going to do was just give eight dollars and let my wife eat later; just kidding [laughs]. Actually, I gave the entire eighteen dollars because that's what God had instructed me to do. When we left the church and we were on the way home, I told her that I didn't have any cash and that we were about a hour and half home and surely we can make it. My stomach was just growling. I got on the interstate, and we were headed home, but in about three exits I turned my blinker on, and she said, "Where are you going?"

I said, "We're going to Burger King." She said, "But we don't have any money." I said, "I know, but the Lord told me to go to Burger King." We got to Burger King and, as we pulled in the drive-through line, there were three cars ahead of us. I got to the speaker, and I said, "We want two Whopper with cheese combo meals, one supersized, one with Diet Coke, and one with sweet tea."

We headed to the window, and she said, "Johnathan, what are you going to tell them when they ask for the money?" I said, "All I can say, really, is hold on. The Lord sent me here, so He'll send the money." I didn't know how God was going to do it, but I knew He would. I didn't know if we were going to have to mop or what, but I knew He would take care of us. We got up to the window, and the lady opened the window, handed out our drinks, she had the bag of food in her hand, and she said, "The lady in front of you just paid for your meal. Have a good evening and come again." She was just as amazed as we were, too.

Man, oh man, we feasted that night [laughs]! It was just so cool and just to think that God cares about every aspect of your life. There are a lot of entertainers, a lot of people who sing, a lot of people who minister, but I don't believe that God has called any of us to be exactly like each other. Our prayer has always been for God to use us, especially since He has brought me from the shyness. Even now, we sing all the time when we go to restaurants, and it's been amazing to see how God uses that in people's lives. That's been our desire, to not just be typical singers, but that we want to be used. That's what He's been doing and I love that.

One Saturday after an all-day singing that we had in Kentucky, a couple of the groups decided to go to Shoney's and have dinner. When we entered the restaurant, the hostess asked the ordinary question, "How many do you have tonight?" I said, "Wait, hold on just a minute before we're seated. We want to sing a song." All of us gathered around there and the hostess just said, "Well, okay, I guess; whatever."

We sang "This Little Light of Mine," and the hostess took us to the very back corner of the restaurant. On our way back several people stopped us and said, "We couldn't hardly hear you. Will you sing another song?" To make a long story short, before that evening was over, we had spent four hours there at Shoney's restaurant, and we had sang at least eight songs in the course of our dinner. The last song that we sang was "Amazing Grace." We sang the first verse and the last verse. Then a lady tapped me on the shoulder and asked if we would sing the verse that says, "Through many dangers, toils, and snares."

As we began to sing that verse, a little girl, probably thirteen years old or so, bowed her head on the table and began to cry. Right there, in the middle of Shoney's, she gave her life to Jesus. I was just so excited! I looked around

PLATE 91 **"How beautiful it is to see young people in harmony with their calling." Young Harmony members Johnathan Bond, Noel Walters, and Darlene Chapman**

and there were several people in the restaurant that were singing, and I said, "Let's finish the song." We finished the song with just the verse "Praise God, praise God." As we left that night, I could feel a pat on the back from God above, knowing that He was pleased with His servants. I want to remind you of Psalms 27:23: "The steps of a good man are ordered by the Lord, and He delighteth in His ways." Today, wherever you go, just remember that your steps have been ordered.

While we were at Shoney's, there in Kentucky, a man came to me and said that his wife had just passed away and that they had come to Shoney's just to get away from the crowd and be alone. It was a good ways from their home. He told us that he and his family were preparing for the funeral, and they didn't have anyone there to sing. He said, "Would you be willing to come back up and sing at the funeral?" I told him, "That would be great. We would be honored to do that."

The funeral was the following Tuesday, and we went back to the church that he had given us directions for. As we got there a lady came to me and she said, "I don't know who you are, but the Lord spoke to me and told me to tell you to be obedient to Him." I just said, "Thank you," and asked her to keep me in her prayers throughout the service. I got up to the piano and began to prepare for a song, and they had told me to pick out the songs. When I sat down there on the stool, the Lord began to speak to me and He dealt with me about singing "Consolation on Your Knees." The words to that song actually say, "Whatever brings you to your knees is good for you." I started thinking of the circumstances, and I thought that is really not a song that you would sing at a funeral. Then He reminded me that He sent a servant to come and tell me to be obedient to Him, and that He knew I would be weak at this time. I started playing the song "Consolation on Your Knees"; as I began to sing the song, the altar began to fill up. There was seventy-two people that came and gave their life to Jesus there at the funeral. I was just truly amazed by this. All it goes to show you is that obedience is better than sacrifice. No matter how off the wall or unusual it may seem, God has a plan and a reason for everything.

Traveling and singing, you never seem to find time to get in bed early, but one Tuesday night we all got in bed early. Right when I got to sleep, the Lord woke me up and He told me to go to Nashville. I didn't know why He had told me to go; I only knew it was late. I got up and got my clothes on, and I left for Nashville. I didn't have a clue where I was going, but I just drove and prayed all the way there. I said, "God, I've got to have your guidance because I've never done this before." He told me exactly where to exit and when to turn, and then He told me to stop. I stopped there and looked around, and right across the street from where I was, there was a nude bar. Not a brand-new bar, I want to make sure you understand, but a nude, as in no clothes, bar [laughs]. I just said, "God, I wasn't raised like this. What's going on?" He began to speak to me in a way that I had never heard Him before. He told me to go and ask for a girl named Angie. I walked across the street and knocked on the door. Two people came to the door, and one was a big ol' guy, and then one was a girl. The guy said, "Can I help you?" I said, "I need to see a girl named Angie."

The girl looked at him, and then she looked back at me, then back at him and then back at me, and she said, "I'm Angie." She was really amazed because it was her real name and not her stage name. She walked out on the sidewalk there with me, and I told her, I said, "The Lord told me to tell you that He was there for you when you were seven, when you were fourteen, and when you were twenty, and now the time has come for you to be there for Him. He has a great work for you to do, and He told her what that was. The last thing that the Lord told me to tell you is this is your last warning."

When I said that, I turned and walked halfway across the road to get to my car. She grabbed me on the shoulder and said, "Wait a minute. Who are you?" I gave her a card that said, "Young Harmony." I said, "I'm a preacher from Chattanooga. I know this is weird to you, but God sent me all the way up here just for you, and now I'm on my way back home."

She started crying and said, "No, this is not weird to me. My dad is a preacher, and he told me the exact same thing you told me two nights ago, except he told me that God was going to send me one more warning. Would you give me a ride home?" I was in complete amazement. She got in the car and we left. We went about thirty miles from where we were and drove down this long driveway. It was about two thirty in the morning at this time, but every light in the house was on. There was a man standing out on the front porch. She opened the door of the car, and she ran and said, "Daddy! Daddy!"

He said, "Your mother's inside on her knees. The Lord just woke us up and said, 'Your little girl's on her way home.'" Again, I was in complete amazement. I sat there in their driveway and began to realize how strong of a God that we serve and how caring of a God that we serve. I realized that night that the God I serve is bigger than the gay bars, the nude bars, the biggest bottle of alcohol you can find, and the largest dose of drugs. All we have to do is just like that mother and dad did. They asked, they believed, and they stood on faith. If you've got family out there that you've been praying for, I would encourage you to ask and believe, and they'll be home.

Noel: It's kinda like Johnathan when he talked about six months ago, him going through a trial, and that's what I've felt like. I grew up in the ministry, too. My dad had a gospel group and still pastors today. The flood in Nashville a few weeks ago [in 2010] flooded us out. We lost our home and everything. I'd been moving stuff that was left out all day, and I guess I was tired and hurrying, trying to get it all done. I went to step off the back of the truck and fell out. I was going to fall on my head, so I broke my fall with my arm, which crushed my wrist. The doctors are trying to fuse my hand and my arm back together. I'll probably never have any wrist range, but at least I'll be able to move my hand.

Johnathan: You may have, because they said I'd never walk.

Noel: Just the other day I thought that I've testified all my life and sung about God's goodness, and I've felt like when all this happened that I'm not gonna travel and sing anymore. I didn't get shushed, like Johnathan did, but the Lord spoke to my heart and said, "I know exactly where you are, and I know everything that's going on." I thought how bad would it be for me to quit and all of sudden turn my back on all the things that I know are true and all the things that I've sung about and testified about. That would be like the biggest lie that there ever was. All of the songs mean more to me now than they ever have in my whole life. I have come to the fact that it is just stuff and it can be replaced. I know that God's bigger than all of that, so it's been a huge blessing to me, too. We've all got testimonies, and we can testify to God being much bigger than anything that ever happens in your life.

Johnathan: My personal belief is, not that it's right or wrong, but the scripture says, "All things work together for our good, for those that love God"; the best thing that ever happened to me was my car wreck. Now I know that God has His focus on me all the time, and I'm thankful for that. If you are able to say, "Here's what God's done for me," and help somebody else, then it's worth everything that you've went through.

My advice for young people today would be to realize why you are here. Realize that it's not just something people say but that God really does love you. I would have loved to have realized, years before I did, that He really loved *me*, not a group of people, not a congregation of people, but me individually. If I had realized that, I would have had a happier life and also been a part of helping other people to be happier. Just realize that God really does love you.

**Young Harmony's music is available
at www.youngharmony.com.**

~Experiencing Traditional Music~

*Near the end of this book, beginning on page 493, we have included
an extensive listing of music festivals held around the southeast—Alabama,
Florida, Georgia, Kentucky, the Carolinas, Tennessee, and the Virginias—
with the hope that you will find an opportunity to experience firsthand
the various styles of traditional music that are so deeply ingrained
in the lives of the contacts featured in the "Echoes" section.*

Daddy Was a Farmer

Joyce Green

My daddy was a farmer,
He was just a simple man,
He never owned a tractor,
But he toiled to work the land.
He followed that old mule
To the end of every row,
And the fruits of his labor
Came from the seeds he'd sow.

God always blessed my daddy
With more than we could eat,
He shared with all the neighbors
And the strangers he would meet.
His hands were stiff and calloused
From the hard work he had done,
But his heart was kind and gentle
Till the day his race was run.

Now, the life of an old farmer
Is a gamble every day,
He prays for rain and sunshine
From the very first of May.
He hopes his crops will prosper
As he toils from week to week,
And many times he worries,
There are nights without much sleep.

School Farm Families

At Rabun Gap–Nacoochee

Daddy Was a Farmer

School Farm Families

Mountain folk know how to live off the land. They have survival skills that have been lost in many other areas of our country. Most of the older generation knew that in order to eat during the winter, food had to be grown and preserved during the spring and summer, so they farmed. There were no fancy tractors, Rototillers, or cotton pickers. The farmer, dressed in overalls and an old straw hat, with his calloused hands to the plow, walked behind a stubborn old steer, or maybe a team of just as stubborn old mules, day after day, tilling the land. Fields were planted by hand, harvested by hand, and the women of the home preserved the crops. Green beans were picked, broken, washed, and packed into quart fruit jars before being carefully submerged under water in an old iron pot sitting over an open fire. The jars were boiled for four hours to make sure they were sufficiently preserved. Every member of the family shared in the responsibilities of running the family farm.

Many families were sharecroppers who gave half of their harvest to the owner of the farm in exchange for housing. Some private schools ran school farms, and families lived on school property and shared their crops with the schools. This section will highlight the memories of some of those school farm families who once lived on the Rabun Gap–Nacoochee School Farm. Rabun Gap–Nacoochee School still sits on a hill against the backdrop of the Blue Ridge Mountains, but the school farms are long gone. The memories, however, will live forever.

—*Joyce Green*

Rabun Gap–Nacoochee School Farm Family Program

I grew up in Rabun County, attended and graduated from RGNS (Rabun Gap–Nacoochee School), and thought I knew just about everything there was to know about the school. Boy, was I wrong! I had no idea what a huge impact the Rabun Gap–Nacoochee Farm Family Program and junior college had on so many families in our community until we begin interviewing families associated with the Farm Family Program. I was amazed at how grateful these families were for the opportunity not only to work hard every day, but also to take great pride in the hard work they did. As these people spoke of their experiences at Rabun Gap–Nacoochee School, it was evident from their expressions and their enthusiasm that the Farm Family Program meant a lot to each and every one of them.

The Farm Family Program was a dream of Andrew Jackson Ritchie and Addie Corn Ritchie, founders of Rabun Gap–Nacoochee School. When the school began, tenant farmers were allowed to live on the school farm, but only as a supplement to the labor of the boarding students. When World War I started, many of the older boys at the school joined the military. Therefore, more families were brought in to continue the farming operations. The Ritchies' guiding principles for the Farm Families included taking large families in order to have the largest impact, limiting their time on the school farm to five or six years in order to help as many families as possible, and choosing families with the greatest potential to succeed.

Rabun Gap–Nacoochee School would accept applications from families to live and work on a farm owned by RGNS and then choose families they believed would gain the most benefit from being a part of the Farm Family Program. The application for admission, provided courtesy of Rabun Gap–Nacoochee School Archives, included questions such as:

Do you want a better chance to educate your children than you now have?

Do you want a chance to become a better farmer and to make a better living?

Do you and your wife want an opportunity to improve

the position of your family as a member of a good
community?

Do you understand that if admitted to this school you
and your wife enter as pupils?

Adults had classes in agriculture and home economics. The
men studied care of the farm boundary, farm crops, livestock, soils
and fertilizers, gardening, fruit growing, farm mechanics, and farm
management. The women studied health, foods, cooking, sanitation,
home nursing, sewing, and laundering. All adult members of
the family were expected to attend meetings; be enterprising,
industrious, and thrifty; possess qualities of workmanship; be good
citizens; be dependable; and keep their children in good standing
in school.

According to the general rules and regulations provided to
us by the Rabun Gap–Nacoochee School Archives, families were
admitted for one year at a time and were told each year if they
were invited to stay another year. Each family had to operate a
model farm with all the land yielding its share of income, and each
was given a house, a barn, a one-acre garden, pasture for two milk
cows, and firewood for fuel at no cost. In return the families were
expected to maintain their home and farm and do all minor repairs
to their buildings and land. Large repairs or improvements were
the school's responsibility. Each family had to keep a farm account
book showing what they made, spent, and saved each year. Adults
were required to attend educational meetings organized by the
school, and all school-age children had to attend school.

Most of the families came with very little in the way of
material possessions. They did possess a strong work ethic, faith,
and determination. With the help of the Farm Family Program,
when they left Rabun Gap–Nacoochee they had money saved and
were better educated, which meant a brighter future for them and
their children.

Every person we spoke with had nothing but good things to
say about the school, the Farm Family Program, and what a benefit
it was to their families. The Ritchies' dream became reality, thanks
to many Farm Families' hard work and sacrifice.

—*Kaye Carver Collins*

My family history is intertwined with Rabun Gap–
Nacoochee School. I was introduced to the school when I was just
a few months old. My parents, William and Jo Thurmond, moved
to a house owned by the school, and my dad worked at the school's
dairy, but my roots had already been planted at Rabun Gap long
before I came into being. The Thurmond family moved here from
White County, Georgia. According to my great-uncle Pledger,
"We moved all our belongings here in a wagon and a Ford Model
T. The house we moved into was not finished. Dad was a carpenter
and he finished the house." Not only did my papaw's family move
here, but his wife's (Annie Lee Dowdle Thurmond's) family also
moved to the school to be part of the Farm Family Program.

I spent lots of time in my childhood listening to my papaw
spin tales about his childhood, his mischievous games, and his
courtship of my grandma. I can still hear his voice as he talked
about catching the Tallulah Falls train (TF) as it chugged north
on a Sunday morning and the details of the day spent with my
grandma attending church, eating dinner with the family, and
sitting on the front porch. After a day in Otto, North Carolina, he
would catch the TF as it traveled southward back down to Rabun
Gap and jump off to head home to his awaiting chores.

Once, when we lived in what is now the Rabun Gap–
Nacoochee Middle School building, he told us about a young lad
who liked to pick on other students. My papaw and his friends
were tired of the bully and decided that one day they would pay
him back. As it so happened, there was an outhouse located on
the hill just above our house, and on the other side of the hill was

the Methodist graveyard. The twinkle in Papaw's eyes as he shared how he and a bunch of boys waited until that young lad went into the outhouse, and then how they turned that outhouse over on its side and sent it flying down the hill, told me of his satisfaction.

It was a time when families still ate supper together without the interruption of telephones and televisions, when hard work, sweat, and honesty were as much a part of living as eating, and when a man who wanted better for his children earned them an education and a way through a school rooted in those values. Andrew Ritchie knew there were capable families in and around this area who just needed a little assistance, and then they and their children would be able to fly off on their own. Logan E. Bleckley—chief justice of the Georgia Supreme Court and a good friend to Andrew Ritchie—said it best in a letter to obtain funding for the start-up of Rabun Gap–Nacoochee School when he wrote, "I know their needs and their resources. With a few rare exceptions, they are an excellent population—none better anywhere within the range of my acquaintance—but they are poor. There is no school above elementary grades within the limits of the county. Children in that region abound; the valleys and hillsides literally swarm with them, and many of them have as bright a mind as can be found on earth."

I am proud to be a grandchild of those wonderful, hardworking Farm Family Thurmonds, and I greatly appreciate the head start in farming and the education that Andrew Ritchie and the Farm Family Program provided to my family.

—Sheri Thurmond

Rabun Gap–Nacoochee School Farm Family Housing Occupants

House 1*
Elcaney Jenkins
Benny Eller
Duel Garrett
Herbie Bradley

House 2
Joseph Sosebee
Gaither Gibby
Claude Penland

House 3*
Old Sutton Property
Raz (Erastus) Mason
Lee "Farmer" Jones
George Dowdle

House 4*
Millard Buchanan
Grady Ashbrenner
Homer Woods
Deverest Pointers
Clayton Ramey

House 5*
Luther Adams
Doc Phillips
Alex Hopper
Ralph Peterman

House 6*
W. C. Neal
Julius York
Dan McDowell
Jay Bird Dills
Betty Webb family

House 7*
Wilbur Tatum
Frank Foster
John Will Thurmond
Milford Kell
Woods family

House 8*
Lake Stiles

House 9*
Andrew Ritchie

House 10
Faculty House
H. L. Fry
Jim Burden

House 11
House on the Rock
Paul Williamson
Garnet Nix
Luther Sanders

House 12*
Norman Coleman *(1st house)*
Lawton Brooks

House 13*
Alex Hopper
Hubert Woods
Jerry Kilby

House 14
Gordon Canup
Onie Carver
Frank Forrester

House 15
Faculty House

House 16
Dan McDowell
Luther Adams
Andy Cope

House 17
Grover Webb *(1st house)*
Lee "Farmer" Jones
Lester Cody

House 18
Luther Adams *(2nd house)*
Ralph Robinson *(2nd house)*
Fred and Doris Carpenter
Lawton Brooks
Boyd Parker

House 19
Norman Coleman *(2nd house)*
Zeb Bryson
Lee Williamson
Grover Webb *(2nd house)*

House 20*
Ranson Brown
Joe Arrowood
Roy Roach

Houses 21 and 22*
Clarence Thurmond
Earl Holt
Ernest Holt
Ralph Robinson *(3rd house)*

House 23
Jeff Chastain
Clint Whitmire
Elem Stockton
Ralph Robinson *(1st house)*

***House has been torn down or moved.**

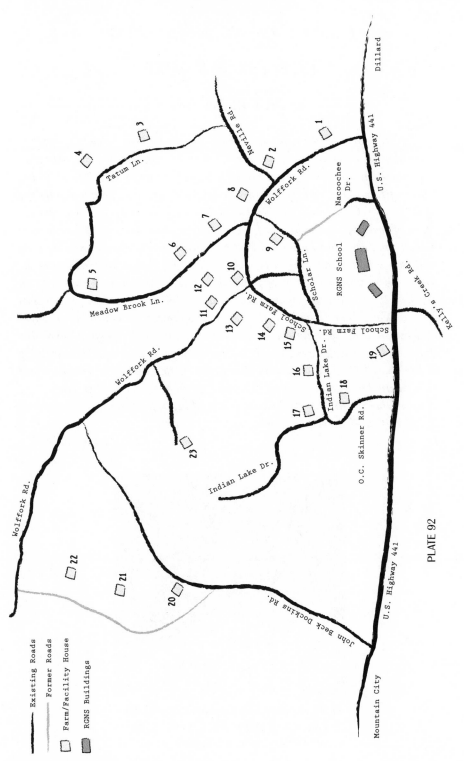

PLATE 92

Rabun Gap–Nacoochee School Farm Family Program

~Dr. Karl Anderson~

Karl Anderson first came to Rabun Gap–Nacoochee School in 1950 as a member of a Southern Association of Colleges and Schools Accreditation Committee. At the time, he and his wife, Lib, were faculty members at Toccoa Falls Institute (TFI) and had learned to love the work and family atmosphere there. Mr. O. C. Skinner, president of Rabun Gap–Nacoochee School and the board of trustees, had approached Dr. Anderson about leaving TFI to become business manager and business education teacher at RGNS; in addition, Dr. Anderson would be training to possibly replace Mr. Skinner as president of the school. There were a number of problems facing the school at the time. From 1932 to 1945 it was a junior college, but in 1945 the program was stopped because World War II had cut the school's enrollment. In addition, an angry student had shot a dormitory houseparent in the stomach. Although Dr. and Mrs. Anderson were not eager to leave TFI, they saw a greater need for their training at RGNS. They were also assured that Rabun Gap–Nacoochee School wanted both spiritual and academic growth, so the Andersons packed up their belongings, using a School Farm truck as moving van, and began their many years of service at Rabun Gap–Nacoochee School.

—Kaye Carver Collins

PLATE 93 **"Here was a school that provided education for families living on its farms, as well as serving as a boarding school."**

When I became a member of the staff at Rabun Gap–Nacoochee School in the fall of 1952, the Farm Family Program had been under way since 1917. Rabun Gap–Nacoochee was unusual among high schools in Georgia because it had both day students from the local community and boarding students from other communities and other states.

One of the special programs at Rabun Gap was the Farm Family Program. This intrigued me when I first visited the school on the accreditation team. I discovered that here was a school that provided education for families living on its farms, as well as serving as a boarding school for young people from many different states and as the high school for the Rabun Gap and Dillard communities.

As with other programs at Rabun Gap, this unique program developed from facing a difficult challenge that was turned into an opportunity by the Ritchies and their colleagues. The challenge? Under the leadership of Andrew "Andy" J. Ritchie, a native of Rabun County, Georgia, a school had been planted in the beautiful Tennessee Valley of northeastern Georgia by 1905.

Andy and his red-haired wife, Addie Corn Ritchie, were a talented and trained pair of educators raised in the mountains of northeastern Georgia but educated at the Georgia State College for Women for Mrs. Ritchie and Baylor, Harvard, and the University of Georgia for Dr. Ritchie. Their story is an important core of the Farm Family story.

Local high schools were rare in the mountains during Andy and Addie's youth. To get a high school education, it was necessary to go to a boarding high school after elementary school. Unless the family lived in a community large enough to support a high school through their own taxes, education

PLATE 94 **"I discovered that here was a school that provided education for families living on its farms, as well as serving as a boarding school for young people." Fathers and sons plowing with a team of mules. Rabun Gap-Nacoochee School is in the background. Photo courtesy of Rabun Gap-Nacoochee School Archives**

normally ended at the elementary school level. Addie Corn and Andrew Ritchie first met at a boarding high school near Hiawassee, Georgia.

Following this, Addie went to the Georgia State College for Women in Milledgeville, Georgia. Andy went for a year at Emory at Oxford, Georgia, and then to Baylor College in Baylor, Texas, for a year. Running out of money, he read that at Harvard University a poor student might obtain a job and earn tuition. Andy obtained a railroad ticket and a small amount of money and left Rabun County for Boston for the possibility of an education at Harvard. After a year at Harvard, illness forced him to return to Georgia. He then enrolled at the University of Georgia and did the work required for an AB and a one-year course of the law school. After recovery he decided to go back to Harvard to prepare to teach English composition and literature at the college level.

Upon completion of his master's degree, he obtained a position at Baylor University and married his high school sweetheart, Addie Corn, whose home had been Hiawassee, Georgia. On summer vacations in Georgia, they were reminded again and again of the inadequacies in education for mountain children, their own relatives, and others. From Baylor University, where Andy was teaching, they first traveled to Atlanta and then to Tallulah Falls

PLATE 95 "Few would have funds enough to go outside of these mountains to get the needed high school education and maybe even go beyond." Griggs Farm Family, photo courtesy of Rabun Gap–Nacoochee School Archives

Gorge by train. That was the end of the railroad, so they returned to their mountain home in Rabun County by horse and buggy.

There in the beautiful mountains they were confronted with a kind of ugliness—educational poverty—that they had experienced themselves as youngsters. Now, as trained educators, they began to wonder why they were teaching in Texas, when the needs were so great for their relatives and friends in the mountains.

In 1903, they decided to work with people in their home community to raise funds to build a central school that would replace the smaller, poorer-staffed schools scattered throughout the area. This, I think, is the marvel of Rabun Gap–Nacoochee. Andy Ritchie was born on a farm located on what is now called John Beck Dockins Road. It is now the site of the thread plant called Parkdale. His father was a prosperous, hardworking farmer. Now, Andy and his wife, Addie, saw the lack of hope for most of the young people growing up where they had lived. Few would have funds enough to go outside of these mountains to get the needed high school education and maybe even go beyond.

Andy resigned his position at Baylor at the end of the academic year and set out with a dream to begin a school for the mountain children who were too remote to get a decent education beyond the first few grades. To people who had money, wherever he could present his case, he said, "I've been a part of that community, and there are people who could advance if we could give them an education."

He gathered the people of the community together and presented them with his dream. They raised what money they could from the local community, and Andy Ritchie developed friends in Athens and Atlanta and renewed contact with some of his Harvard classmates. After two difficult years of raising money, buying materials, and building the classroom facility, including dormitory space for the girls, a living facility for men was also erected at another site on the campus. The new school was opened in 1905.

[With the means they had], people were as self-sufficient as they could be. In those years students who came to the school from places beyond Rabun County were often fully grown adolescents from way back in the mountains who had little or no educational training beyond the elementary level.

Following the example of a few other schools, which tried to produce some of their own income, the Ritchies acquired land around the classroom building where they might raise crops and livestock to feed the students and to sell to make money to operate the school. The boys could work on the farm two days a week and go to classes for four days. Using the rotating schedule, they could help supply most of the labor for the farm. Girls had a similar schedule but centered more on food preparation and other activities needed

PLATE 96 "Some of the girls even worked at tasks on the farm, like hoeing."
Photo courtesy of Rabun Gap–Nacoochee School Archives

to keep a school going. Some of the girls even worked at tasks on the farm, like hoeing; we have pictures of them working in the field.

In 1917–18, America declared war on Germany. World War I armed forces now took many of the male students at Rabun Gap, who were often older than children in today's high schools. They were at an age to become involved as volunteers and draftees. Now, with land for more extensive farming activities, the loss of boys to the armed forces presented the school with a serious problem of trying to produce crops on the acquired land without sufficient available labor.

The Ritchies saw a possibility in this challenge. Some of the land they acquired to be farmed by students still had the houses of the families who had sold the land. The Ritchies brought families from this area with children to these houses to farm the land that students had once farmed. Andy and Addie were not interested in simply having tenant farmers to till the land and raise the crops. They saw another opportunity from this challenge. They would limit the time a family could spend at the school to five or six years; then the family would go to a farm they had purchased or another farm somewhere to use their newly obtained skills.

At the school they would be replaced by a new family, which would come to farm the school land. This was the birth of a unique adult education program called the Farm Family Program. The children of the Farm Family Program would be expected to stay in school. In the early years of the twentieth century, many children would drop out by eighth grade to work on their own farm or to find some kind of local employment.

Mr. Lee Fry was in charge of the farm families, serving as farm manager. Under the direction of Mr. Fry, the men could be trained in more modern, more scientific methods of farming; then, after five or six years, they would

Rabun Gap Industrial School

Plan of Operation and Terms of Admission
For the Mountain Family

The object of this mountain school, in its family plan, is to reach the humblest family and the poorest child in the mountain cabin, and to educate men and women, as well as children, to remain in the mountain country and make it a better country to live in.

The plan is to take groups of families in rotation, settle them around the school on a fertile valley farm for a few years of training in farming and home-making, and then send them out into the surrounding country to make better farms, better homes, and better citizens.

The school undertakes to do three things:

1. To give these families a better chance to educate and train their children. It provides for the children of each family a good school for nine months of the year in which each school day is divided equally between the work of the schoolroom and the industries of farm and home.

2. To give these families a better chance to make a living and improve their financial condition.

3. To make these families better farmers, and to make it possible for them, when they leave the school, to establish themselves on farms of their own prepared for a profitable and happy life in the mountain community.

The whole place is an educational institution. Every foot of land in the 1,500 acres, every garden, every kitchen, every barn, and every cornfield is a part of the school curriculum. Each home on the farm is a school dormitory, and each family is a part of the school organization.

Therefore, when a family comes to the farm for a term of training, the father and the mother, as well as the chldren, come to school. The heads of the family come under a system of rules and regulations which they must obey just as students obey the rules of any well-governed institution.

No family should apply for admission who is seeking a place simply to rent land. Such is not the purpose of either the school or the property. The whole establishment is for purposes of education, and especially education in farming and domestic industries.

Rules and Regulations

1. Families are admitted for a term of three to six years, depending on the age of their children and their financial circumstances. Young families with children coming into school age and with a future to make are preferred to older ones.

2. A written contract is entered into between the school and each family as a tenant for one year at a time, or from the time of planting a crop to the end of the calendar year.

3. Each family is placed in a boundary of land and required to do good farming. All crops suitable to the mountain country are planted, and crops are rotated so as to improve the land and increase the yield. Clean and intensive cultivation is strictly required.

4. Each family is expected to make a model crop and to make its boundary a model farm. Suitable rewards and increasing income are offered in proportion to the attention and care which a family gives to the boundary of land and premises for which it is responsible.

5. Each family must share with the school in the normal up-keep of the property which it uses by furnishing its labor to make repairs to the house and barn, and to the fences, gates, and roads about its premises. It must also keep all fence rows and hedges and the banks of all streams and ditches in proper condition without expense to the school.

PLATE 97 **"This was the birth of a unique adult-education program called the Farm Family Program." Photo courtesy of Rabun Gap–Nacoochee School Archives**

move from this setting to other communities, sometimes a farm of their own. While the men were directed by the farm manager, the wives got together for meetings and trainings, at regular intervals, with the school's home economics teacher. When the family would leave to go to a farm of their own, they brought this training to other communities, benefiting themselves and the community to which they moved. Another family would then take their place, and the cycle would begin again.

One of the early families was the Thurmond family. Mr. and Mrs. Thurmond and family moved to the Farm Family Program in the late 1920s. Mr. Thurmond then died, but Mrs. Thurmond and the family stayed on in the Farm Family unit that was provided to them. There were eight or nine children in that family. And from that they went their separate ways. One family was [that of] Clarence Thurmond. He became a longtime farmer up on Wolffork in the Rabun Gap community. He had a dairy farm. These were people of quality; they had something to work with. I say it that way because these were individuals that inherited certain capacities, and their families pushed them.

To become a Farm Family, you completed an application, and Mr. Fry and Mrs. Pleasants, or Dr. Ritchie in his time, studied the family, saw the potential within them. They were the people chosen, and not all of them succeeded! Some came in, and they weren't willing to do what was required to be successful. You had to have a family, obviously. In other words, a man and woman by themselves without any children would not be eligible, nor would an older couple. The program was for the purpose of building a family in a good setting.

PLATE 98 "The men could be trained in more modern, more scientific methods of farming." Photo courtesy of Rabun Gap–Nacoochee School Archives

You got to live on a tract of land, including a home, barn, et cetera, and you got half of the end product. The other half went to the owner of the land, the school. "Sharecropping" in some places is a bad word because people have taken advantage of it, but this was sharing the crops. So the farmer got half of the corn; if you grew cattle, you got half. Several other families got started in what were once dairy units because they developed a herd and, when the time came, they bought a place, and they took their portion of the herd with them. Others did not follow through, but they had five years to bring their children up in a good place, a good setting, better homes.

Andy Ritchie sought and got financial backing for the Farm Family Program from foundations like Rockefeller and Carnegie. Other kinds of financial backing came only when Andy had raised money from other friends to match the funds coming from the foundations. Each Christmas, since I came to the school, and extending back, I don't know how many years, each Farm Family was given citrus fruit and candies as a gift from the school.

With movement of small manufacturing plants into the South because industry found an abundance of labor willing to work, it was no longer necessary to earn a living from working on a farm from "can to can't"— daylight to dusk. When I came in '52, we still had what we call a house and a path. Do you know what was at the end of the path? A privy, yeah [laughs]! We got to the point where water was brought into the home spot, so we eventually had it so that every house had a house and a bath instead of a house and a path! You can't visualize what it was like when there were no industrial-type factories here. There was nothing else to speak of. All you had was what you had on the farms.

With the entrance of small industry, a forty-hour workweek became a reality. Since the first large plant in Rabun County primarily employed women for sewing tasks, the men were called go-getters. Do you know what that means? It wasn't because the men were lazy; the men didn't have employment outside of their work on their farms at the time. So they would take the women to work in the morning, go home and do the farming or do whatever they were going to do, and then they'd go get her at the end of the day. Soon other plants like James Lee, the carpet-manufacturing company, came in to provide jobs for both men and women. The small farms, which had been the backbone of agriculture in Georgia, gave way to jobs in plants. By the mid-1960s, the day of the small farmer was over, and the need for the Farm Family Program had vanished.

The school used some of the land for a dairy unit of its own, using students to carry out many of the tasks under the work program. At one period of time, the school had four Farm Family dairy units. When families left the school Farm Family Program for local textile plants, the school consolidated these smaller milking units into a larger unit, which then milked about eighty cows each day. Some of the labor to operate the dairy unit was provided by school students through the school work plan.

According to a list gathered by the Farm Family Organization and staff at Rabun Gap–Nacoochee School, there were 162 families and 824 children identified. The Farm Family Organization includes members and descendants of those families who participated in the Farm Family Program.

It would be difficult to measure the impact this large number of children from this many families had on the communities into which they moved and lived after their time at Rabun Gap. In all the contacts I have had with former Farm Family members, there has been appreciation expressed for what the years at Rabun Gap meant to them and to their family, for being given a leg up in life.

The Ritchies, and others who worked with them, had the ability to face problems, consider them as opportunities, and thereby develop new programs that enriched the lives of those attending the school, whether they were younger children in the classroom or adults living and working on the school farm as part of the Farm Family Program.

PLATE 99 "It would be difficult to measure the impact this large number of children from this many families had on the communities into which they moved and lived after their time at Rabun Gap." Farm Family children circa 1950. Photo courtesy of Rabun Gap–Nacoochee School Archives

"I think it was the people that made it so special."

~Frances Fry Deal~

Frances Fry Deal attended Rabun Gap–Nacoochee in the late thirties and early forties. Her father was responsible for many aspects of the day-to-day operations at Rabun Gap–Nacoochee. He was the farm family manager. He taught adults farming skills at night and students agriculture during the day. In addition, he was a coach and bookkeeper, a jack-of-all-trades. Frances also met her future husband, Jimmy, while attending RGNS.

—Kaye Carver Collins

The Farm Families were there early. My dad came from Athens to Rabun Gap in the thirties, primarily to work with the farm program. He did some teaching also. That was his main job, I think. He came first to organize the Farm Family Program and, besides doing that, he headed up the kids on the baseball team for a while, so wherever he was needed, that is what he did.

Dr. Ritchie would come down to our house, sometimes at six o'clock in the morning, because he thought of something he had to tell Daddy. He would come in and have a cup of coffee and talk to Daddy before he ever went to work, so I think my dad worked from six in the morning to seven or eight at night sometimes—really long hours! Daddy also did bookkeeping one time when they were short of a bookkeeper. There wasn't much he couldn't do. Dr. Ritchie would walk just like everybody else. He would walk from where they lived; they lived in a little house. It was not an awful big house at all. They were a fantastic couple! He would come walking down at six o'clock in the morning, just as hard as he could come.

Dr. Ritchie always had presents for all the Farm Families and a big tree at Christmas. It was held in the dining hall, usually, because that was a big place. They always had presents for all the little ones especially. I don't really remember too much about it, but I am sure the presents weren't anything expensive. The women met, I don't know how often they met, but they had sort of a club, or a get-together, because I know Mother, Martha Eleanor Fry, always went to those. She enjoyed going. She enjoyed being a part of the Farm Family unit.

I remember the Farm Families who had children my age. I remember the Thurmonds and the Swansons were ones we were most fond of. They were special people. The Webbs lived not too far from the old house where I lived. I used to visit back and forth with Betty Webb. I remember our house was very cold [laughs]. You did not have furnace heat then. You had coal stoves and woodstoves. Our bedrooms were very, very cold. When we would

PLATE 100 "He taught the adults things like dairying and beef cattle programs, and just farming in general." Frances's father, Henry Lee Fry, at left. Photo courtesy of Rabun Gap–Nacoochee School Archives

get up of the morning, we would run to the room that was the warmest. It was cold in that old house, but it was a wonderful time! There were always a lot of children around us; one time my mother had a lot of the children playing out in the yard, and somebody came by and asked her if that was an orphanage. There were five of us, plus five or six more of the neighbors, so they thought for sure that it was an orphanage!

We used to go camping over on Scruggs Rock. We would get together, a group of us, and go over there and cook breakfast, spend the night out there on the hard ground. I don't know how we enjoyed it so much! We were probably ten or twelve years old. We liked to tease each other about that the graveyard on Scruggs Rock. We also went frog gigging. Have you ever heard of that? [**Editor's note**: Frog gigging occurs at night. The participants use a lantern or flashlight to locate frogs along the banks of a river or pond. The light reflects in the frogs' eyes and also stuns the frogs for a moment, making them easier to catch using a four- or five-tined stick. Once the frogs were captured, their hind legs were removed and cooked for eating.] We did that at Green Pond. Scruggs Rock was a big playground for us. It was within walking distance without getting run over; of course, we didn't have a lot of traffic then anyway. In fact, we would ride bicycles. My grandparents lived in Clarkesville, Georgia, and we would ride bicycles all the way from here to Clarkesville [about thirty miles]. When we got tired, we would stop, and the conductor would let us put our bicycles on the train. So we rode part of the way on bicycles and part of the way on the train, the Total Failure [Tallulah Falls Railroad]; you know, that is what it was called! We had a lot of fun growing up because we all had a lot of children around us who were the same age, so we had a really good time growing up.

Going back to the Farm Families, they had certain criteria; there were certain things they had to have before they could come. I am sure they had to have a good, big family and real need. I am not sure exactly how they decided. I remember my mother—she was not a nurse, but Dr. Neville, who was the doctor for our community, if somebody was expecting a baby, especially if it was a Farm Family, he would come get Mother to go with him to help take care of the babies. I remember one time (this was not a Farm Family baby) the mother died. They didn't have help and the rest of the family was small children, so Mother brought that baby home with her, and we kept it two or three months and cried when it left because we felt like it was family.

I remember mostly my years at Rabun Gap. We had wonderful teachers;

PLATE 101 **"Of course, every reunion that we come back to, they are getting fewer and fewer at our age, but for years we had such a large crowd of ours that came back."**

Miss Lennon and Miss Clayton and all of them were really marvelous teachers. Miss Jones was the librarian. They knew how to teach you! I also attended the junior college there. We had a lot of good home economics teachers and had a really good home economics department at that time. They had a nice kitchen set up, and we learned how to cook. We had a lot of machines—we had sewing instruction. We got to make a dress. Every year we could choose something that we wanted to do, a project. I ended up making several dresses that way.

The students used to pick blackberries and make blackberry pies and blackberry jam. They canned and had gardens. I didn't do that up there at Rabun Gap–Nacoochee, but I did it in my own home. Everybody had more than one job!

Jimmy and I dated in high school. We had basketball games and plays, and we had a lot of stuff happening. We had a lot of different activities on campus. We stayed busy all the time. Most of the things were on campus. We did have a theater in Clayton we could go to, but if you were dating someone in the dormitory, they didn't have a car. If you were dating somebody who had a car, you might get to Clayton to the theater. Of course, I went off to college after I got through school here; I went to finish my degree, then I got married.

My fondest memories are of meeting such a variety of people, and it seems like every one of them is special to you. Of course, every reunion that we come back to, they are getting fewer and fewer at our age, but for years we had such a large crowd of ours that came back. It is always such fun to get back together. I think it was the people that made it so special.

"Jack Acree . . . washed my mouth out with soap!"

~Jimmy Deal~

Jimmy Deal was a boarding student at RGNS in the late thirtiess and early forties. His father had passed away before he was two and his oldest brother died forty-five days later, leaving his mother to raise seven children alone. The boarding students were required to work just as hard as the Farm Families did in order to pay for their tuition. There were two dormitories when Jimmy first went to Rabun Gap, but later a third one was added to accommodate more male students. According to Jimmy, Mr. Shotts, the admissions director, had a bet with Dr. Ritchie that he could enroll one hundred boarding students that fall, and he did, winning a new hat from Dr. Ritchie.

—Kaye Carver Collins

They didn't have room enough, so they built a new boys' dorm down below where the gymnasium is now. We must have had twenty rooms there, I think. I guess we had four men to a room. It was called the annex. Each room had a woodstove. That was one of the good things we had going because in the wintertime when it snowed, Dr. Ritchie would close down the school, partly because the day students had trouble getting there, but the rest of us would go rabbit hunting. We would track rabbits in the snow. We tracked them, found them under a bush, and grabbed them! So what we would do if we caught a rabbit is dress it out and take it back to the room. We could cook on top of those little stoves. It was pretty good eating! I think we were very humane. We would take a stick and whop him right back of the head just as hard as we could. He didn't know what hit him! We got along pretty well under the circumstances.

We were a pretty responsible bunch of youngsters. There was a joint chimney between two rooms, so there were two stovepipes running up the same chimney. We didn't have to go get wood, per se, but we did have to bring it there. We went up into the mountains and cut firewood because the dormitories and main building, Hodgsen Hall, were wood-fired in those days. We would cut pulpwood and stuff and haul it to the dormitories. Now, we didn't use wood in my dormitory. We burned coal, so we got along very well. We had a small apartment that was occupied by two male teachers and, in some cases, a third one. They were like houseparents, but they also taught. Jack Acree was one of them. He later became Executive Secretary [Director] of the Georgia School Boards Association.

Miss Hackney taught history. Miss Lennon taught math. They taught Bible, too. Yes, that was a required course, both in the junior college and the high school. I have never been sorry about that either! It was very helpful. I remember one time Jack Acree, a former student who came back to teach in the junior college, washed my mouth out with soap! I was saying a few words I shouldn't have! He just grabbed me because I was right outside his door, since my door and his were opposite each other. I don't remember what I was saying, but it was something I shouldn't have. He reached out and just grabbed me! You know, he was a pretty tough little guy. He had me well under control and before I knew it I had a mouth full of soap! It didn't stop me from swearing, but it taught me not to under certain circumstances!

My principal work at Rabun Gap was in the dairy department. My first year at Rabun Gap–Nacoochee School was the summer of '38, and I started out working in the garden department. I was a long way from home, so I never was able to go home and visit during the holidays. I grew up in eastern North Carolina, about one hundred miles from the coast. So I was there at Rabun Gap to work during the holidays. My first Christmas holiday, I started working in the dairy, and I milked cows for the next three years! The result was that I majored in dairy science at the University of Georgia, taught there, and spent fifty years in the dairy industry.

We didn't have all this mowing equipment; the cows did that. We would take the dairy herd out and let them mow grass. We had to be at the barn at four o'clock in the morning. We had alarm clocks, but actually what we did, because most of the time all the guys who milked at the dairy were in the

PLATE 102 "I remember one time Jack Acree . . . washed my mouth out with soap!"

same dormitory, there was one person in the dormitory that was responsible for getting the others up. While we were working the dairy, another crew took care of the hogs and another crew took care of the beef cattle. All of those were at different times of the day. We also butchered the beef and hogs. We had lots of things going on.

Whoever got there first had to get the cows in; each of us had our own assignment. One person would be assigned to go get them and bring them in, in three different groups. They had to be put in certain locations, and then when they went into the milking barn, we had it set up. It is amazing how fast cows learn their stall! If people were as smart as cows sometimes, it would be a lot simpler. We had twenty-four cows that four of us were milking. It was all hand done in those days. There were eight cows in a row, and each of us had two cows. The most memorable occasion I had was one time a fellow named Foster Goolsby, who was a junior college student, was sitting just the cow beyond me. (He later became a school superintendent.) He had on a brand-new pair of overalls, and his hind pocket was just sticking way out, and I was sitting right behind him. I just filled his hind pocket full of milk until it started getting good and wet and he started feeling it. (The devil made me do it!) When he jumped up, I jumped up; he chased me around the feed room! I just knew he was going to kill me! I had a bucket half full with milk, so when I went around the last corner, I knew he was right on top of me, and I just turned around and threw that whole bucket of milk right in his face! I have told his wife many times since then that the reason he is such a good-looking fellow is because I gave him a milk bath when he was a youngster!

We would milk in an hour and a half. From the time we would start to the time we got through, it was usually close to a couple of hours, but that involved getting the cows in, milking them, and then they got put in the location where they were supposed to be, or we turned them out to pasture. We didn't usually turn them out except in the summertime. Of course, we had to be responsible for getting the hay in. We didn't have hay bales in those days—that was forked! We did everything from plow and plant corn to harvest it as silage, filling two upright silos. We hauled the feed off to have it ground. We didn't have a grinder. When we got it back, we mixed the cow feed by hand. You don't think that is fun; you work in there, and you work it in a little at a time, throw your feed in there, and have to turn it over five or six or seven times. It was dusty, but we managed to get along very well. My job, usually, after we got done milking, was to clean up the milking equipment. That took a little time, too. Thank goodness we had a good water supply. During World War II all the men were in service and the girls ran the dairy.

Our water supply was from a real good spring up on the mountainside, and it came down into a monstrous big cistern that held all the water. Gravity from there down, enough pressure so that even though that cistern was, of course, at a higher elevation than the main building, we had adequate pressure. We would get the water just by natural gravity. It was already electrified when we got there. The electrical system was over at Estatoah Falls.

The chicken houses were started while we were there. We had small chicken houses, but they put in a big chicken house. One of my former roommates worked at the chicken house. Do you girls want to leave while I tell her this?! Anyhow, he was chewing gum, and he dropped his gum, and he said he tried three or four pieces before he found the right one [laughs]. That is a true story. I wasn't involved in it; it is just hearsay.

Dr. Ritchie never learned to drive. He either had a student driver, or Mrs. Ritchie drove him everywhere he went. His home has been torn down. It was right across the street from where the industrial arts building is now. There was a one-story cottage there that the Ritchies used to live in.

Dr. Ritchie did not want us to have tractors because he wanted the kids to have the jobs. The only people who had tractors were some of the Farm Families. Occasionally, they would do some work for the school when they got caught up on their own work. We had four pairs of mules, plus a spare, so we did everything with mules. I still remember the names of all of them! It was fun. We weren't supposed to work them but six days a week, but on Sundays sometimes we would slip out some of them and go riding around the country. We went over on the road by the quarry and I was riding a big, tall, raw-boned mare mule named Kit. She was about sixteen and one half hands—big and tall. Peter Williams was riding another mule, and he came along behind me. He had a piece of hose about five feet long in his hand. When he came by me, he hit my mule in the rump and she made a surge, like that! I bounced all the way from her rear end to her shoulders and ended up hanging underneath her! My arms were locked around her neck before I ever got her stopped. We all rode bareback. That is the closest I ever came, I guess, to getting absolutely killed! If I had fallen under that mule, there would have been no way to keep me from getting stomped. We also had a couple of bulls, and we were responsible for making sure the cows got bred naturally; we weren't doing artificial breeding in those days. We had two big bulls, and, I mean, they were big! We learned to be very cautious.

We didn't have any sports besides baseball and basketball. They did play baseball—in the cow pasture! I remember one time a fellow slid into what he thought was third base! They had a gym, but it has been completely remodeled now. There is a great story they told on the athletic director; his main activity would have been as athletic coach, basketball partly. Somebody

PLATE 103 **"We had small chicken houses, but they put in a big chicken house."**

asked him how he had managed to get such a good center for the basketball team. "It was very simple," he said. "I sent him out across the pasture where the big bull was, the big bull got after him, and there was one tree in the field. He made a beeline for that tree, and there was one limb twelve feet off the ground, and he jumped!" They said, "Did he get it?" He said, "Not going up, but he got it coming down!" So that is how he became the center for the basketball team.

We had a canning house where all the girls did all the cooking. The old dining hall was where the industrial arts building is now. It was a two-story building, and the girls who worked in the kitchen lived upstairs. One of the good features about working in the dairy was that on Sundays we had to carry the milk down to the dining hall after we got it cooled. We had a surface cooler that the milk flowed over, so we would take it down to the dining hall. On Sundays when we got down there, there were always some Sunday desserts left over. The girls who worked in the dining hall were very kind to us. They made a point to be sure that we got plenty of special food when we got down there with milk on Sunday afternoons. Let's see, I can't think of the dietitian's name right now. Anyway, they were pretty good to us! The crew that had to work on Sunday fared pretty well!

Frances and I were high school sweethearts! She lived on campus, so I had to go down to her place. We didn't marry until after she got her degree. I was planning on her putting me through college, and she did help [laughs]. Her final degree was a PHT—Pushing Hubby Through!

We graduated from high school in 1940, and Frances graduated from the junior college in 1942. I attended junior college at Rabun Gap for my freshman year, but the year after I finished high school, I couldn't go to school anymore because I didn't have any money. So I joined the CCCs [Civilian Conservation Corps] for a year and then went back for my freshman year. For my three years there, nobody in my family put a nickel into my education. We didn't have any money. The only way I could go there was just simply the fact that we were able to work on campus and earn ten cents an hour.

Gosh, the kids who went through that Farm Family Program ended up fantastic people. Ursery Dillard ended up as a major professor at North Carolina State. Irwin Dyer became dean at the graduate school at Washington State. We had some really top-notch people there in those days, myself excluded!

All the students who were part of the Farm Families went to school there. An awful lot of the kids who went to the junior college went on to Berea College in Kentucky to get the rest of their degree. Several of those became department heads in major colleges and other places. I became head of the Department of Agriculture at Berry College. That was after the war because I had only completed my freshman year at Rabun Gap before the war came along. In fact, I was there when the war came along. That summer I went ahead and joined the Navy, where I served for almost four years.

I think the fact that all of us who were at Rabun Gap–Nacoochee School needed some help to get an education and that helped make it a great experience. In fact, if you could afford to pay for your education, you couldn't go. Everybody that went there had to work and pay for part of their education. A few people had a little backing from home, but I certainly didn't! A number of them were in the same shape as I was in. If I had not gone through Rabun Gap–Nacoochee, I would have never gone to college, much less become a college professor and head of the Department of Agriculture and Forest Resources at Berry College. I owe Rabun Gap–Nacoochee School a great deal.

"What I've got now, I picked up from Rabun Gap School."

~James Adams~

When James Adams's family came to Rabun Gap, it was a great adventure. James had never really been out of Habersham County, Georgia. He, his dad, and his brothers were on top of a truck loaded with all their earthly possessions as the truck swayed and twisted around Tallulah Gorge. James said he thought, "Where in the world is Daddy takin' us?" When they arrived, they moved into a little house, way up in a holler. His dad started working the land, and the children went to school and helped on the farm.

—*Kaye Carver Collins*

Well, we lived in Habersham County and about starved to death [laugh]! No, we wasn't starvin'. Daddy always made us somethin' to eat. Anyway, Daddy and Mama had some friends that lived up there at Rabun Gap. Daddy went and talked to 'em, and then he put in an application. Dr. Ritchie come down and interviewed us. My mother kinda knew the Ritchie family. We lived in a big pasture, and we looked out and saw a car comin' out down that little dirt road. We wondered, "Who in the world is that?" Dr. Ritchie got out and opened the gate. Mrs. Ritchie drove in, and he closed the gate back and got back in the car. We still wondered who it was. He come on up, and Mama got to where she could see him. She said, "Well, that's Andrew Ritchie!" They come on up and we sat out on the front porch, all of us family was there, and he interviewed us. Dr. Ritchie asked was we church members or attended church, did we stay in school, and how many they was in school. They was three of us in school at that time. He asked how many they was in the family; of course, we was all sittin' there. He asked about our lifestyle kindly, 'bout workin' and farmin'. He said, "As far as I'm concerned you can get ready, but we don't have no house for you yet." So we just set still, and finally we got a letter that said we was accepted to move in December of '37.

I was nine years old when we moved. I was born in '28, and that was '37. Mama and Daddy raised us right, Christian livin' and all. The first Sunday that we got up there, Mr. Sam Bleckley come by. He already told Daddy, said, "I'll be goin' by, so y'uns can ride to church with me." We rode to church with Sam Bleckley as long as we lived up there; of course, he went up on the hill, and we went down on the highway. We was Methodist. He'd stop there at the road that goes up to the Baptist church, and we'd get out and walk on up there to the Methodist church. We attended church regular; my mother, she never did. She claimed she had to sit home and have dinner ready for all of us! She'd have dinner sittin' on the table, of course, when we got home from church. She never did go to church except for when they had a conference. She'd fix the dinner and we'd take it over there, and she'd go that day. We was raised in church, though I got out for a while after I got to where I thought I knew more than they did [laughs].

We started in goin' to school and workin'. The elementary school was over there at Dillard. That's where we went through [ninth] grade, then came to Rabun Gap in [tenth]. They did have the eighth and ninth over there at Dillard; then one year they moved it [eighth and ninth] over there to Rabun Gap.

Families always had somethin' to do, places to go. I remember fondly we always had ball games to go to. Here, in Habersham County, we never did have nothin' like that then. The junior college had a baseball team. We

PLATE 104 "As far as I'm concerned you can get ready, but we don't have no house for you yet." The Adams Farm Family in 1945: John, James, Reba, Ruth, Gordon, Luther (father), Lamar, Lassie (mother), and baby Branson

was connected with everyone, more or less, just like one big family; all of the school farm folks was just like one big family. When we had a ball game or somethin' or another, we'd all gather right there in the forks of the road. There was a road that turned and went up Wolffork and turned and went where I lived. There was a place where we could set right there in the fork of the road and talk and go on. One night we set there for a right smart little bit and talked. We was talkin' about goin' home, and I said, "I think I'll go. Y'all come home with me." One of 'em said, "Let's do that!" I started home, and every one of 'em got up and went with me! We got down there where we turned down to my house, and I thought, "Well, now they'll go on that way." They didn't do it! Right into the yard and into the house they went with me—Fred Williamson, Hayward Bryson, Sam—Sam Foster was the one that said, "Let's do that." So they come on in and sat in there for a while, and then they got up and left. The next mornin' Daddy said, "What was goin' on in here?" I told him. He said, "Well, next time you keep your mouth shut [laughs]."

At that time they allotted each family so much land for row crops and all. Anytime a man didn't have work to do on his own place, they tried to find somethin' down there around the school to do to make a little money. Daddy done anythin' they asked him to do—if it was dig ditches or whatever it was, he done it.

[A typical day was] get up, go milk the cow. When I learned to milk,

PLATE 105 "The elementary school was over there at Dillard. That's where we went through [ninth] grade, then came to Rabun Gap in [tenth]."
Photo courtesy Rabun Gap-Nacoochee School Archives

PLATE 106 **"It had runnin' water but didn't have no bathroom."**
Photo courtesy of Rabun Gap-Nacoochee School Archives

Daddy turned the milkin' over to me until we got two cows and then John got old enough to start milkin'. We had a cow apiece. We usually took care of the milkin' and all. Daddy would go feed the horse stock and the hogs. We took care of the milk and the chickens. We'd shell the corn for the chickens and feed 'em of a mornin' and leave. We'd get in wood and cut wood; stove wood for the stove and wood for the heater. We done stuff like that of a-mornin', and of an evenin', we always had somethin' to do—milkin' and feedin' and stuff like that.

Every day that Daddy didn't work on his property, they usually gave him somethin' down there on the school to work. He learnt carpenter work, and he learnt paint work. At that time the women had to go in about once a month to women's meetin's. Mama didn't like it; she said she already knowed it, but she didn't know everythin' [laughs].

Each year they sent out a letter askin' if we wanted to stay or either tellin' folks to move, whichever the school wanted. If they wanted you to stay, they'd ask you, and if you hadn't been satisfactory to 'em, they'd tell you to prepare to move by December. So we stayed on. Mr. Fry just sent another letter saying, "If you don't send it back, we'll consider you want to stay; if you don't want to stay, send it back in." Daddy just stayed on as long as he had a good thing. He wasn't gonna lose it. Daddy, I think, bein' the man he was, was why we stayed there ten years.

We stayed up there in that little house next to the Bleckley place for two years, and then they built this house down there at the point of the school road and the road that takes you out toward the lake. It was new, and we moved into it and stayed in it eight years. When we moved out, there wasn't a pencil mark, or crayon mark, or no screens broke out, or no windows broke out of the house. It had runnin' water but didn't have no bathroom. Well, I saw 'em puttin' out posts toward the house to put up electricity! They got electricity in pretty soon after we got there. That was the first house we lived in with electricity, and the first house we lived in with water in the house. We lived there eight years; I graduated in '47.

One of the fellers fell off a bale of hay and hurt hisself. Daddy and other people went out and got his hay, finished gettin' his hay up for him. If you got behind on anythin' like that, the other farmers would go help him an' all. It was a helpin' place.

That's all Daddy ever done was farm. Even though it was hard times, we always had a big garden and had chickens and had cows to milk, and hogs to kill, and most of our livin'. Then we traded eggs for flour and sugar and stuff we couldn't raise ourselves—saved our eggs instead of eatin' 'em. We'd eat biscuits and gravy and stuff like that instead of eggs. Once in a while we would get ahead to where we could eat an egg.

Well, altogether I'd say Daddy farmed about twenty-five acres. We always had corn and hay. Of course, we had one free acre that we could plant in anythin' we wanted to. Daddy would always plant it in whatever could be

PLATE 107 "Even though it was hard times, we always had a big garden and had chickens and had cows to milk." The Lillie Billingsley family. Photo courtesy of Rabun Gap–Nacoochee School Archives

sold at the market for that extra money comin' in. One year he set out bell peppers—just different things that were a cash crop.

He bought his seed, and they paid for half of the fertilizer. Most of the time he saved seeds, beans and stuff like that, corn seeds—he always picked out. He had a big barrel that he threw 'em in as he was shuckin' corn, savin' the seeds for the next year. He'd save his tobacco seeds and raise his plants, save tomato seed and sow 'em, plants like that; he'd save his own seeds for anythin' and raise his plants, set out stuff as he had to set out.

Daddy was paid when he went down there to the school and worked. We got to get some money to use. He was out doin' carpenter work and paintin'. When he couldn't farm, or if we didn't have anythin' to do at the barn, he done that. They'd come get him when some of the rest of 'em didn't have no work to do. I guess it was on the count of he done anythin' you wanted him to do.

Soon as me and John got old enough to do things down there, we'd go with Daddy, and they'd give us somethin' or other to do; I worked for Fred Kelly, Mr. Fry, Mr. Pitts, and Mr. Miller—done a little work with all of 'em, but we just worked and worked. The first work that I done was when they built that barn over there—that big beef cattle barn on Wolffork. When they built that, me and a Foster boy and a Hollifield boy took our daddys' teams of horses and hauled rock out of Betty's Creek over there between the school and the Dillard House. We hauled rock over there out of that creek to build that barn with. That was the first time that I was kinda put on salary. I got seventy-five cents a day, seven and a half cents an hour, ten hours a day. Daddy got seventy-five cents for his team [of horses]. That was the first work that I really done. Then I got to where I would do anythin' [laughs]! I done anythin' that there was to do. A man took us over there to what used to be the dairy barn the other day. I told 'em, "The last work I done over in this barn was me and two of my buddies cleaned it out." I always tried to do whatever they asked me to.

They'd always have a Christmas gatherin' down there and give gifts. Another thing that they done, the boys would take mules and wagons and deliver boxes of gifts and clothes and all that to the Farm Families. The school paid for it, I reckon. The family never had to pay for it. It was through the school, and they was shippin' in stuff from all over the country, gifts and things like that. I remember that's the first toy I ever had—a little truck, metal truck; that was before plastic. The Farm Families all got a box for Christmas. They done that for two or three years. It had clothes, all different sizes; they knew what children and what size they'd need. It had a small bag of apples and a small bag of oranges. We'd get firecrackers and oranges and apples for Christmas.

PLATE 108 **"He run back in the house, and if he hadn't have had to go back in the house to get his gun, we'd 'a' been shot."**

Of course, there were all the time things goin' on; me and one of my friends . . . when a new family moved in, we'd serenade 'em. Well, we serenaded the family one night, and me and one of my friends hid up in the cemetery—we was gonna scare his brother. We waited and waited and waited, thought he'd come on; well, directly the lights went off in the house. Oh, he'll be on in a few minutes; we waited and waited and he never did come. The next mornin' we figured out he stayed all night with 'em [laughs]. You know what serenadin' is? Well, when they had a new family, we'd just all gather around and somebody usually had a gun—shoot it to start off with and we had bells or pans, somethin' to beat on, somethin' like that, and get all the way around the house. When that gun went off, we started beatin' on the bell or on the pan, makin' a bunch of racket around the house. Of course, we'd do that a little bit, and then they'd come out and invite us in. That night the friend didn't come home; he stayed all night. Another thing that happened, this friend, me and him was good buddies all the time I reckon. When they first moved in, they built that little house down there that they was gonna teach the girls how to cook and all down there. Well, the first night me and him got up in the woods, got a handful of rocks to start with, and got up in the woods—we was gonna wait till the lights all went out, and we was gonna throw rocks down on the top of the house to see if we could scare 'em. Well, about the time their lights went out, here come a dog down the trail; uh-oh, we knew that that dog was follered [followed] by Robert Philp [laughs]. So we took out through the woods, and they had chicken coops all over the hill up there. I'd run into a fence and jump back, and he'd then go over it. He'd run into a fence and fall back; we'd help one another. Mr. Taylor, he lived in a little house right there next to the road; he would come out, and he heard his chickens start. He run back in the house, and if he hadn't have had to go back in the house to get his gun, we'd 'a' been shot [laughs]. We kept goin', and we got down there to where Melvin Dickerson lived on Wolffork Road at the four-way stop. I said, "See you tomorrow, Fred."

Another thing that happened to me and Fred and his brother Ned—they went home with us from church one Sunday. We went to the barn, got us a tow sack [burlap bag], and then ripped it out and got down in the creek and started "sangin'" for fish. We had a pretty good bunch of little ol' fish. Goin' back toward the house, I said, "Fred, you can carry these fish home with you; we don't eat fish at our house." When we started to school Monday mornin', we got up there nearly to the road and there lay those fish on the side of the road. I went on up to school and said, "Fred, what did you throw 'em fish out down there for?" He said, "The same reason you didn't take 'em home with you. You knew we'd get tore up for fishin' on Sunday [laughs]!" I had a lot of good friends up there—Hayward Bryson and Fred. We just had a good time.

If I hadn't gone to Rabun Gap, I probably wouldn't have graduated high school; I doubt it, for I hated school with a passion. The first day I went to school, the teacher made me mad somehow or another. I told Daddy I was through with school! He said, "Well, get your hoe and go to the field [laughs]!" I started in the third grade when we moved here and failed the first year. Then I went and made it on through high school, finished high school in '47. I doubt if I woulda went through high school if we hadn't come to Rabun Gap. We had thirty-five in the whole school down in Habersham, and there was thirty in my class up there at Rabun Gap. They was one thing different: They took more time with you at Rabun Gap and worked with you; you could understand things better. I doubt if I had went through high school if I hadn't went to Rabun Gap.

My sister, Ruth, was in the last junior college class. There was a junior college there when we went there. She went to Berea in Kentucky for a year up there. Mr. Floyd up there at Clayton got her a job in Banks County, Georgia, for a year, and she taught down there. The last year she taught up there in Mountain City, Georgia, and she decided she didn't like school teachin'!

That's about all I can remember about the way it was; it's just altogether a different situation than what we have here. I enjoyed it all the time we was up there. Had some good friends up there, and the Philp family took me in.

He was a fine teacher. If you didn't learn anythin' from him, there wasn't a teacher nowhere that could teach you.

We just prospered every year we stayed up there, as far as I'm concerned. We was the first regular family that stayed ten years. Mr. Bellingrath said, "Mr. Adams, I hate to tell you, but I guess you can just go ahead and move this time." When we first moved up there, we weren't promised but two years, and if you didn't satisfy 'em the first year, one was all you had. We stayed two, three, four, five, and we was the first family that stayed there ten years.

Hard to describe what all I got out of Rabun Gap School: how to live a life that's worth livin', how to carry on your life, what to kindly expect out of life; what you put in it is what you got out. It's just about the way I can describe it, really.

I think that Rabun Gap School brought us out. What I've got now, I picked up from Rabun Gap School—the way I try to live, and do, and work, and all. I worked thirty years for the state, retired from the Agriculture Department of the state—worked all my life, from the time I remember goin' to the field workin' to the time I retired, and still try to help here some. Anyway, Rabun Gap School was a blessin' to us is the main thing that I can say. It was a good life. Always up there we made good, done good, and that's just about all farmers and workers can ask for.

Farmer's Daughter

~Jo-Anne Stiles Hubbs~

Jo-Anne Stiles Hubbs's family moved to Rabun Gap in 1938. Her father and mother, George and Agnes Angel Stiles, moved the family into house number 2 on the school farm. During World War II they moved to Knoxville, Tennessee, but eventually made their way back to Rabun Gap–Nacoochee School.
                                                                    —Kaye Carver Collins

The first time we lived here, we did those fields over next to Betty's Creek, down in the bottom, and over the hill to the road. We done all of that. We had a garden right next to the house, and, of course, we had the barn and the chickens. Daddy raised little chicken broilers. When I was twelve, we started making sorghum syrup. Daddy had a pretty good patch of cane, and other people on the school farm raised cane, too. We made it for everybody—six hundred gallons was made that year.

The sorghum mill was down below where the old post office was in that field. Fred Williamson would run the stalks through the grinder. My daddy was real particular. He didn't want any fodder left on it. He wanted it all picked off, which was pretty hard on the little hands, but we had to pick all of that fodder off. He topped it, and the cane tops were used for feed for cows and chickens. I skimmed the sorghum, and my daddy kept the fire goin' and run it off. Those days that I worked there, I wore a brown wool skirt. When we got through, my skirt had so much sugar in it, it stood alone. We made sorghum from daylight to dark, along in October. It got dark a little earlier than it did in the summertime.

We lived there in house number two till 1943. It was during World War II because my daddy went to work at Oak Ridge, and we went back to Franklin, North Carolina, a little while and then moved to Knoxville, Tennessee. When he finished his job in Oak Ridge, we came back to the school farm. It was in 1945 just before Christmas. We lived in house number eight when we moved back. It was a big two-story house across from the rock. Paul Williamson lived on the rock at that time. Julius York, the Webbs, and the Holdens were living on the school farm, too.

This time, we tended the bottoms next to the Little Tennessee River down below Hodgsen Hall, the whole bottoms between the highway and the river. I hoed corn all the way across those bottoms, and it was hot. One year, Daddy had cane and something else planted there; I don't remember what it was, but I do remember hoeing corn in long rows in those bottoms. I know that we got a share, but I don't remember what the shares were. I think it was one-third, but I'm not sure. I do know that we had a free patch or acre that we didn't share with the school.

Since I was in the eighth grade when we moved back, I attended school at the old Dillard Community School. In the ninth grade, I came to Hodgsen Hall at Rabun Gap–Nacoochee. We always walked to school. On Sunday Mr. Bleckley would pick everybody up on that road and haul us to church. He had an old black truck, and we all sat in the back. We would sing all the way there and all the way back, just as loud as we could! You couldn't do that anymore. They would probably lock you up now and not let you out with that many kids in the back of a pickup truck, but he picked us up every Sunday morning to go to church and every Sunday night to go to training union at church.

It really was a great time to grow up. It was a great time! The more things I see away from here, the more I'm convinced that this was one of the greatest blessings in my life. I might not have thought it then, but I do now!

"You just enjoyed living."

~J. T. Coleman ~

J. T. Coleman was four when his parents, Norman and Ruby Coleman, and his sisters Betty, Texas, and Carol moved to the school farm in 1933. They moved everything they had in a school bus. The people in the Wolffork community had built the school bus body on a truck chassis, and Norman Coleman bought it and started the first school buses in that part of the county. Dr. Ritchie had told the people on Wolffork that if they could work out transportation, the children of the community could come to Rabun Gap–Nacoochee School for free. In addition, the Colemans could live on the school farm for ten years.

—*Kaye Carver Collins*

The people on Wolffork had been meeting for quite some time to try and get their kids to Rabun Gap School. They were meeting in the Baptist church up on Wolffork. So, anyhow, the deal was that my dad would buy a truck chassis, and the people up on Wolffork built the first bus body. That was the first bus route in 1934. Then, a couple of years later, the people on Kelly's Creek wanted the same thing, so he bought another bus and hired a fellow by the name of Arthur Norton. He lived with us and helped Dad on the farm and drove a school bus. He got drafted in World War II, and that is when my mother started driving the bus. Over a period of time, he had three buses. He picked up the route on Bald Mountain, Kelly's Creek, Wolffork, and Betty's Creek. Those were the bus routes. He operated those until he retired after thirty-five years, when he reached age sixty-five.

Dad's primary job when we lived on the school farm was that he would drive the bus. That was the agreement. At that time people would come and work on the school farm for five years. Dr. Ritchie said, "If you will buy a bus and start the routes, you can live on the school farm." Our first house is no longer there. It was a big two-story house across from the "house on the rock" on the Wolffork route. It had no electricity and no indoor plumbing. It did have an outhouse. I remember when electricity came in. We didn't have a telephone until years after that. We did have pianos and a square radio, but that was long before television. One house had a spigot in the kitchen. We lived in that house five years, and then they built a new house on the hill there across from Rabun Gap Post Office and we moved into that brand-new house as the first family.

Dad also did some farming at the school; in the fall when you gathered your crops, you would take two loads to your barn and one load to the school barn. We did that for eight or ten years. We had a team of mules that we used

PLATE 109 "My grandfather was born there and my father was born there, and all of his brothers were born there." J. T. Coleman's family home in the Persimmon community

to cultivate the corn. When I was about ten, I could do that. I could hoe corn when I was nine or ten. We never used any of the school's equipment.

It was a lot of fun because you had families with children of your age. We had an open pasture between our house and the Frys' house, and that is where we played football games, baseball games, whatever games we wanted to play. We had hoops and would roll the hoops. That was a big thing when we were growing up.

We didn't get into much mischief, at least none that I want to tell about [laughs]! Playing in the barns and throwing hay down when we wasn't supposed to—when you are feeding the animals, that is all right, but when you are just throwing hay bales at each other, it isn't! Stuff like that, if it gets out of place, you are in trouble! The Williamsons were the closest family to us. They lived right across from us in the house we call the house on the rock. Fred and Ned Williamson were close to my age. We had good times together playing. We didn't get in a whole lot of trouble, come to think about it.

The one thing my daddy believed in was me working—anything that needed to be done from the time I was old enough to plow a mule, eight or ten years of age—me. Arthur Norton, who lived with us, helped Dad, too. My dad bought one of the first tractors in this area about 1938 or '39, and we—dad, Arthur, and myself—did what everybody else called public plowing, a dollar and a quarter an hour for the tractor and the driver. People would come to Dad and say, "Norman, can you plow this field?" It happened that the fields were on the same routes as the school bus went on, so I would get on whichever bus route where the tractor was needed and work till it got dark because Arthur and Dad were driving the buses. Then on Saturdays—all day Saturday until midnight Saturday night—we didn't plow after midnight on Saturdays. You don't plow on Sunday! At that time I was about twelve. I would ride the bus route to wherever the tractor was and work. It was good times. You just enjoyed living.

At Christmas, the Farm Families met in what was at that time the dining hall, and there would be before Christmas, as I recall, an exchange of names among the families, and you brought your presents for whichever family's names that you drew to the party and put them under the Christmas tree. We had singing and laughing and we'd tell jokes. It was a lot of fun. The Ritchies gave items like candy, suckers, stick candy, and stuff like that. There was nothing elaborate, just small gifts.

I was fourteen when I started driving the bus. My birthday is September eighteenth. At that time you could get a driver's license at fifteen. The highway patrolmen came to the Rabun County Courthouse once a month to give driving tests. We went out there in August; I was one month short of being fifteen. My dad talked to the patrolman, and he said, "No, sorry, we can't do that, give a license ahead of time, especially to drive a bus!" My dad

PLATE 110 **"Those were the best years of my life, of my growing up, you know."**

kept talking and talking and finally he said, "Why don't you take him and give him a test and, if he can't pass it, then I will understand why you won't give it to him." So finally they said, "All right!" The highway patrolman got in the bus with me, and we left the courthouse there and went out toward Germany Mountain and got there, and the patrolman said, "Take this road." So we went up it almost all the way to the top, and he put me through ever' turn and twist you can think of, turn here, back up here, this and that. We got back to the courthouse, and he stepped down and looked back at me and said, "Boy, you can drive the h—— out of this thing, can't you!" So I got my license. It was just kind of a technicality. I think school started on the fourth or fifth of September, and I was going to be fifteen in just a few weeks. No big deal!

I think going to RGNS made a difference in who I am. It was a combination of living on the school farm, associating with the people who lived on the school farm, and having teachers who stressed that you work hard in your schoolwork, specifically Miss McKinney, Mrs. Hackney, and Mr. Fry, who taught agriculture. Mr. Fry, whose job was connected to the school, taught agriculture to the students in school. I don't remember him teaching the farm men, but that could have been something my dad was doing that I wasn't aware of.

Those were the best years of my life, of my growing up, you know. I have had a good wife for fifty-five years—family and children is better—but it was my best years of growing up. Overall, it was good times and a good upbringing. It was just the basic things that I feel like I was a-taught. All my teachers stressed being a good student and working hard to get the best grade you could and working extra hard to do that. They stressed going on and getting a higher education and, of course, my dad was always stressing that, too. He said all his children would have a college education. That was one thing that he regretted. He left Rabun Gap School and didn't go on to a higher level. A better education was just a day-by-day thing in my family. You didn't give a lot of thought to it. You knew what was expected. After I graduated from Rabun Gap, I went to North Georgia College; at that time it was a compulsory military college. You had to get your commission after four years and serve two years in the military after graduation. It just so happened that I graduated from college in '51, and the Korean War had started in '50.

"Mama ordered one hundred little biddy chickens."

~ William Thurmond ~

William Thurmond, my dad, was a third-generation Farm Family member whose family moved here from White County, Georgia, where my great-grandfather Thurmond worked some for Nacoochee School before it burned down. My grandmother was also part of the Farm Family Program, having moved with her family to the school farm from nearby Otto, North Carolina. She graduated from RGNS in 1932 as class valedictorian. Granddad Thurmond was two units short of graduating when he went into the service. Upon his return from World War II, his family moved to Rabun Gap–Nacoochee School and became part of the Farm Family Program, learning the dairy industry and creating a family business from the skills he obtained. It is there on the school farm where my grandparents also met. Being a former Foxfire student, as were my sisters, Teresa and Sandra, it is with great pleasure that I share a part of my family history with you here in this 45th anniversary edition.

—Sheri Thurmond

In February 1946, we moved to Rabun Gap–Nacoochee School on the Rickman Creek boundary, and became part of the School Farm Program. I was five or six years old when we moved. Carl Vinson moved us from Dillard over there one day in a truck; the house we moved into was just a boxed-up house. It had two bedrooms plus the upstairs. It was not painted inside or out, no electricity, and no running water. We had the well out back of the house, and we had a stone trough there next to the well where Mama put her milk and butter and kept it cold. The kitchen end of it had been added onto the house. That room was sealed on the inside but didn't have no insulation in it. It had a fireplace on the north end of it and a fireplace on the east side of it.

After we moved, Mama ordered one hundred little biddy chickens from Sears and Roebuck. We raised them up. She sold some of the roosters and some of 'em she killed and canned the meat. She sold part of the pullets, but the rest she would raise out and would get 'em started laying first, so that she would have extra eggs. Dad would take them to the store and sell 'em or swap 'em for goods that she needed. She made a lot of our shirts by buying cloth with the money she made from selling eggs. Mama would make some of 'em, and Grandma Thurmond would make some. Grandma was a real good seamstress herself. We usually got one pair of shoes a year. We got them about the first of November, or it might have been a little bit later. When

PLATE 111 **The Clarence Thurmond family when they first arrived at Rabun Gap–Nacoochee School**

they wore out that next spring, we went barefooted from then up until shoe time that next fall. I remember one time Harold, my brother, and I were playing around the front of the fireplace. Dad had built up a big fire, and I mean, it was a good fire. That fireplace was the only heat we had besides the cookstove, and that's where our beds were. Well, Harold had pulled his shoes off, and me and him was a-playin'. I had done something or another, and he didn't like it. Well, he picked up one of his shoes and throwed it at me. Well, I dodged that shoe, and it went right straight in the fireplace. By the time Dad raked it out, it was done charred—I mean good and charred [laughs]. He did get two new pairs of shoes that year.

When we moved to the school, Dad didn't have any work stock to work the farm with, so he went down to Franklin, North Carolina, there at the Stamey boys and bought a pair of mules. I don't remember what he gave for them, but he worked them up until he bought his first tractor in the fall of '52 or '53. Now, at that time, the dairy farm was not there. We farmed to pay rent. We planted corn in the upper and lower bottoms. The rent down on the bottomland was half of what you made. If you had an acre of corn, half of that acre went to the school as rent. Now, on the upper land, the rent was three-quarters to one-fourth. So if you had four wagonloads, one would go to the school, and the other three was kept by the farmer to do with as he pleased. We mainly raised hay and corn in our fields. The school had a stationary baler that you used to bale their share of the hay. When the school farm crews slowed down, they would come to the fields and bale the hay. A gasoline motor ran the baler, but you did not move it like these here balers are nowadays. You pulled it up to the stack of hay, fed the hay in it by hand or pitchfork, and this arm pushed it down in the baler. Then a plunger pushed it back in there. Dad's part of the hay was left loose in the field. We hauled it into the barn on a wagon and fed it to the livestock loose. His part was not baled.

Our first garden was up there behind the old house. In that garden we had onions, carrots, radishes, cabbage, beans, squash, pumpkins, and cucumbers. What we raised, Mom canned. Dad also had a big syrup cane patch. He hired Mr. and Mrs. Lon Dover to make the syrup. She was good at making syrup. Dad had raised up about an acre to an acre and a half of the syrup cane. He stripped that fodder off of the cane and hauled it with his wagon over there to the syrup mill, which was right across the branch from where the house was on the rock. The syrup mill was right along beside Wolffork Road. He hauled the cane over there, and he got Fred Williams to feed the cane mill. By that, I mean the cane mill mashed the cane stalks flat, and that mashed the juice out of it. It run from the cane mill down to the shed where they had the furnace set up, and that was where the syrup was cooked. Mrs. Dover didn't use a thermometer either. As the juice was cooked, it had an ole green skimming on it, and they skimmed that off. They would put that in a container, then you could take you a biscuit or a piece of corn bread, rake down through it, and eat that [laughs]. I think, if I remember right, that the acre to two acres of cane made three hundred gallons of syrup. The school charged so much for Dad using their syrup mill, but I don't know how much that was. It was a certain percent of the syrup. Then Mr. and Mrs. Dover charged so much or got so many gallons of the syrup for the making of it. In the end, Dad had something like one hundred fifty gallons of syrup left that he sold or swapped. A lot of it he took to the store at Dillard and swapped it for stuff that we needed, like coffee, flour, salt, and spices.

We hadn't been on Rickman Creek too long before Dad ended up with three cows. Then he started buying calves and letting 'em nurse on that third cow. When the calf got up to weighing about two hundred to two hundred fifty pounds, he would take 'em to the sale. Since he was selling them as veal calves, he got more money than he would have if he had raised them up.

In 1948, the school built us a new house that was sealed. It had electricity, a bathroom, and running water in it. In 1949, the school built us the new barn. I don't know exactly what the process was, but Dad went in and talked to them about running a dairy, and it was just something that they worked out. The school farm had four other dairies on it, plus ours. So in October of 1952, Dad went into the dairy business. At that time, he had seven cows and twelve calves. When Dad went into the dairy, he started paying cash money on the land instead of paying a share of what he raised.

Up until they built the new barn, we had been milking the cows by hand. The first time we milked—Dad, Harold, and me—it took us two and a half hours to milk seven cows. We didn't know what we was a-doing. In that new barn, we had electricity, so we had International Milkers that were run by a vacuum. That was all three of us. Well, we put the cows in there, and they had a feed trough in front of them where we put the feed for 'em while we was a-milkin'. Well, one of the milkers had a big ole pulserator that caused the vacuum to hit this way and then that way [William moves his hands in a crisscross motion]. Well, that pulserator was supposed to switch the vacuum from the front two teat cups to the back ones and, at the same time, squeeze the cows' teats. One of those pulserators, in shipment from the factory, had gotten bent. It wouldn't hit nary a lick, and that was our biggest problem. That day it took us two and a half hours to milk just seven heads.

When Dad started the dairy, whoever owned the cows had the right to

PLATE 112 **Clarence Thurmond (left) and William Thurmond (right) on the Rickman Creek boundary land when they were in the Farm Family Program**

sell the milk. So Dad was paying rent on the land, and now he also paid rent on the house, but he had the right to sell the milk to whomever he wanted. Dad sold to Sealtest Dairies in Asheville, North Carolina. We started off milking the milk in five-gallon pails. We had one extra pail. We would just swap the lid off this pail onto another one, and then we took the milk to the cooler room and poured it into a strainer that set on top of a ten-gallon can. When the can filled up, we set the strainer off on an empty can, put the lid on the full one, and put the one with the ten gallons of milk in it over into the cooler. The milkman come by every other day and took the full cans of milk and left the empty ones.

I started helping Dad when I was old enough to carry a lantern. I would get up of a morning before daylight. We would light the lantern, and I would carry the lantern for Dad to see how to get to the barn. Once at the barn, we would feed the mules, slop the hogs, milk the cows, and take them to pasture, and take the mules to the creek and water 'em. That was the start of my day. We done those chores seven days a week. On Sunday, we mainly did the chores at the barn, but we didn't do any fieldwork on Sundays. On Sundays, you got up, went to the barn, and got the chores done up. Then when you had done that and eat breakfast, you went to church and mainly you walked to get there.

When Dad went into the dairy business, he was going to pay me and Harold four dollars a month for working in the dairy barn, and he was going to pay Annette, my sister, four dollars a month to go to the barn and wash the milk cans up. Well, Harold—he took his four dollars a month in cash. I had been wanting a heifer calf, and so Dad sold me one for four dollars a month. It took me ten months to pay the heifer off. That was in 1952. When she calved, I started selling milk, paying for the feed. Mr. H. L. Fry had a registered Guernsey cow and a heifer calf. He wanted to sell 'em, and he wanted two hundred fifty dollars for 'em. This was in 1953. I had saved up enough money in a year and a half to buy 'em.

One thing that Dad always done for a lot of Farm Families was castrate the pigs or the yearlings. Whenever it came time, they would ask Dad about helping 'em. Dad would always ask, "Is the signs [of the Zodiac] right?" They would say, "Yeah." I remember one time Mr. Keener lived over on the hill there where Jeff Chastain built his house. He came over there and said, "Clarence, I've got a little job over there I need you to do." Dad said, "Mr. Keener, when are the signs right?" He said, "Tomorrow." Dad said, "I'll be over there about eight thirty or nine." We went over there, and he had three pigs he wanted Dad to castrate. Dad, he worked on them.

Mr. Keener said, "I've got another little job up there, but I hate to ask you to do it." Dad said, "Mr. Keener, what is it?" He wanted an ole billy goat worked on. Dad said, "I've never worked on those billy goats. It might die." Mr. Keener said, "I don't care if he does die. I'm tired of smelling him." So Dad went ahead and worked on him and the ole bill lived.

I mentioned before about Mr. H. L. Fry; well, he was the farm manager there at the school. He would go around to each farmer and meet with him. The farmers' wives had meetings, too. They were supposed to attend one day a week or once a month. Mrs. Knox was in charge of that. They was taught and showed how to can and clean house. Mr. Fry would say to the farmers, "You need to do this, or that and the other." One thing he believed in was a-cuttin' off the creek banks every year. If any of the farmers were on a boundary of land that had wet land, they ditched it with a shovel to dry the land out. They would go in there and ditch it out by hand, usually in the wintertime, and go to a wooded area and cut poles, six or eight inches in diameter, and they would roll two of 'em in that ditch length-wise. Then they would go to the woods and saw 'em down a pine and saw it up according to how wide their ditch was. They would block the pine out with a crosscut saw, and then they split that block up in slabs. They would haul or sled those slabs to the field and laid them down on top of those poles. That held the dirt up off of those poles; therefore, the poles would let the water run out of the fields into the branch or creek. It would let the field or the dirt dry out to where you would not mar up [get stuck] in wetland. Now I've got a scar on my leg where I was pulling a crosscut saw and that saw hit my leg. It just laid it open. It was no stitches then; you just had kerosene-oil bottles—poured [the wound] full of kerosene and went right ahead and worked. It just kept it from getting infected.

Always right before Thanksgiving, we would have a Farm Family supper there in the old gymnasium where the administration building is now. Well, back then the school had that old '40 model Ford bus, and they would bring it around and pick up all the Farm Families and haul 'em in there. The Farm Families would fix up a box supper, take it in there, and everybody shared. Then they would have games. One game I remember of them having there was, they got four or five of the Farm Family men and set 'em down in a chair. They said that they knowed they was all good milkers because they had milk cows at home. But what they done, they had these here baby bottles filled up full of milk, and they wanted to see how fast those men could empty out those bottles of milk a-sucking on it. Well, Dad was one of 'em. He got that nipple of his bottle between his teeth and bit a hole in it [laughs] and won that game.

'Long in November, when the temperature of a morning would get down below freezing, you killed hogs. It would give you enough of that cold temperature at that time of year to where the meat would cure out and not spoil on y'uns. Well, say Dad killed hogs—Mama would fix up a mess of meat for all the neighbors. Then when they killed hogs, they fixed up a mess of meat and sent a mess back to you. Back then the school had a slaughtering house over there. The farmers could either have a barrel, heat water at home, pour it in the barrel, and scald the hogs in that barrel, or take them to the school slaughterhouse and kill 'em that way. Dad killed hogs there at home a year or so, then he took 'em to the school's slaughterhouse, which was much easier and faster. Grandma Thurmond always cut up the fatback meat to be rendered out for the lard, but she took the skin off of the fatback and had the skinless cracklings. Nowadays, the skin is left on the cracklings and that makes 'em tough.

Well, we all got into our share of mischief while living there. For amusement we would fix us up a sliding board in the fall of the year. We would take the widest board we could find, and we'd take that board and take it out to the chopping block, slope that one end off. Then if there was any beeswax around and we could get our hands on it, we would turn that board up and put that beeswax on it and wax it down good. Then we went to the woods, found us a hill, and trimmed us out a trail. We'd do this from one year to the next. Then the leaves would fall on that trail that we had trimmed out last year. We would get right back up there and lay that sliding board down, sit down on it, and slide down the hill. We would also fish. We used a pole off of the creek bank and used the red worms as bait. We used a string off of a fertilizer sack as a line to fish with. And one of the things that us boys always had was a slingshot. They stayed in our back pockets. Generally, we had rocks in both of our front pockets, and anything that got up in front of us that we wanted to shoot at, we shot; and generally, we'd hit it, too!

I went to school at the Community School over there in Dillard. Then in the eighth grade, I went to Rabun Gap–Nacoochee School, and, at that time, the eighth graders did not rotate from class to class. Miss Perdix was my eighth-grade teacher, and she taught us every subject just like we were in elementary school. Then in the ninth grade, we went from teacher to teacher. Mr. Billy Joe Stiles taught me in biology. I think he's about eight or nine years older than what I am. He was going to Berry College before his seventeenth birthday and, before his twenty-first, he was teaching at Clayton High School [Rabun County High School]. Then he came back to Rabun Gap–Nacoochee. His family was in the Farm Family Program, too. Mr. Morris Brown and Billy Joe were two fine teachers! Let's see, Mr. Philp was the principal then and, in the late forties, Mr. Bellingrath was the president.

The farm program wanted you to be thrifty with your money. Most of the Farm Families that lived there went on and bought land of their own when they left the Farm Family Program. Most of the families, a lot of them, borrowed money through the Federal Land Bank or through the Farmers Home Administration to buy their land. Mr. Fry would help 'em with that. I would say that the Farm Family Program gave Dad the ability and the knowledge, and I'll say the financial backing to where he could buy his own property and have his own farm. I learned the knowledge of how to work or do chores on the farm. Later on I was in the Future Farmers of America program, and I am the only member from Rabun County who has ever received the American Farmer Degree. I was involved good enough in farming to where I made out the applications on it for two years and got it. You had to be established in farming to get it. Well, at the time, I had twelve head of registered Guernseys, plus I had paid for that Oliver Super 66 diesel tractor while I was in high school. I received the American Farmer Degree after I finished up high school. An FFA member can stay active in FFA for three years after he has finished up high school. I applied for two years, and on the second one, I received the degree, and I am still the only FFA member from Rabun County that has been awarded the degree.

"Life was hard, but there were fun times also."

~Harold Thurmond~

Harold Thurmond is William's brother. He was four when Clarence and Ann Thurmond moved their family to the school farm. He remembers the first house they lived in as being "old and rough." It had no underpinning, the wall studs were showing inside, and there was no electricity. In addition, their bathroom was a one-holer with a catalog for paper. Baths were taken in a galvanized tub with water drawn from the well and heated on a wood-burning cookstove. He also remembers his dad and mom saving up to fulfill their dream of owning their own farm.

—Kaye Carver Collins

Life was hard [on the school farm], but there were fun times also. One day Dad came in with an old bicycle in the mule wagon. It had no fenders, a loose chain, and bad brakes. My brother William claimed it and, being unable to ride, promptly plowed into a sticky-hedge bush. He wouldn't give up or let me try it. Two hours and many scrapes, scratches, and bruises later, he made a circuit of the house, and I finally got my chance. I didn't achieve success as quickly as he did. Rickman Creek ran through our farm. It served as a playground, a swimming hole, and a summer bathtub. Once when Dad was planting corn, I saw a large trout in the creek. I told Dad about it. He cut an alder pole, made a hook from a fertilizer tag staple, and tied the hook to the pole with a length of string from a fertilizer bag. I baited the hook with a grasshopper and caught that trout. Mama fried it for my supper. Some things that happened were downright funny—two had to do with our mules.

My favorite: Ol' Alec was a slacker, smart, and stubborn, but then Ol' Alec was a mule. His mate, Bob, caught all the heavy loads. Whether they were hitched to wagon or hay rake, Alec would gradually ease up on his chains so that Bob was doing the pulling with Alec merely strolling alongside. It was a constant battle slapping Alec with the reins or prodding him with a stick just to keep him tight against the traces and doing his share. I saw him get in a hurry just a couple of times. Dad was plowing corn with Alec and a spring-tooth plow, scratching in the laying-by fertilizer. A thunderstorm came up over Smokehouse Knob and swept down into the valley. By the time they got to the end of the row, it was raining hard with lightning and thunder at full pitch. Dad unhitched the plow, tucked the reins under Alec's harness, slapped him on the rump, and watched Alec race alongside the creek to the bridge. A scared mule making a run for the barn in a thunderstorm didn't have time to contemplate the dangers of a wet wooden

PLATE 113 **"That night we milked the cows in our own barn, slept in our own house . . . living the dream that Dad had envisioned." Left to right: siblings William Thurmond, Annette Pressby, and Harold Thurmond**

bridge. Ol' Alec simply disappeared in a clap of thunder when his hooves slid out from under him, and he sailed into the creek. By the time Dad got to the bridge, Alec was standing up, shivering a bit, soaking wet, unhurt. Dad laid down on the bridge, got ahold on Alec's bridle, and led him out of the creek, through the bushes, and up the bank. He turned him loose, but Alec didn't break for the barn, just plodded along beside Dad. He seemed to be a bit embarrassed by his fall into Rickman Creek. The sun was shining by the time they made the barn, but Dad didn't take Alec back to the field; he figured that Alec deserved a break from his trials and tribulations.

The second one is funny only in retrospect: On that hot, dusty afternoon, I was wading in the creek and running through the hayfield, barefoot and shirtless. Being only seven years old, I was too little to help with the haying, but I liked to watch Uncle Pledger and my brother, William, stack the hay around the pine pole that Dad and Pledger had planted in the ground. It was also fun to run alongside the mules as Dad raked the cut hay to the stack. The two-wheeled metal hay rake rattled and clanked, bouncing over the clumps of grass. Dad sat in a cloud of dust as he drove to and from the haystack, all the while trying to keep Alec from slacking off. Pledger was on the haystack to cap it off—must have been five or six feet up. William was forking the hay up for Pledger to place and tramp down. I was running with the mules when the bumblebees attacked. They ambushed us from underground. In seconds the mules and I were swarmed by black-and-white demons that had burning stingers for tail guns. I ran screaming toward Pledger and the haystack, slapping at the buzzing insects around my head. The mules broke and galloped willy-nilly across the field with Dad holding on for dear life, pulling on the reins and yelling "Whoa!" Pledger threw down his pitchfork, vaulted off the stack, grabbed me up, and ran into the shelter of a nearby cornfield. He finally got all the bees swatted off me and my yowling reduced to pitiful moaning and sobbing. Dad got the mules reined in after a not-so-joyous ride around the hayfield. I had ten or twelve stings and a swollen face and shoulders for a couple of days. I remember Dad saying that Ol' Alec had no problem pulling his weight with those bumblebees urging him on.

That same field was also the scene of a childhood tragedy. A stray black feist took up with our family. I thought he was the best dog ever and claimed him for mine. We were always together except for in the house. Blackie had to stay outside. He was a ratter, loved to catch mice and rats and sometimes snakes. Someone from the school was plowing our field with a tractor. I was watching the plowing; Blackie was watching for field mice. The tractor finished a furrow, lifted the plows, and made a turn to the next furrow and ran over Blackie. Mercifully, he died instantly and was buried there in that black loam.

Speaking of rats reminds me of Esco Pitts and a rat killing. Esco was a handyman for the school—could drive a tractor, run a pipeline, wire a house. Whatever needed doing, Esco could do it. Esco was helping with the razing of our old house and barn after the new ones were in use. The barn had been cleared except for a pile of corn in the corncrib. Knowing that the pile contained rats, we prepared with sticks and dogs, hoping to kill as many of the pests as possible. Esco derided our preparations, and he said the way to do it was to "just ketch 'em with your bare hands, then squeeze 'em to death right quick-like." Well, of course, he had to put up or shut up. The corn pile was pushed over, and rats ran in about twelve different directions—up the walls, across the floor, between legs, rats everywhere. The dogs were pouncing and shaking rats, William and I were flailing with our sticks, Esco was grabbing at rats, and Dad was about to fall over laughing. Surprisingly, Esco caught one and squeezed it to death in his hand but suffered several bites before he subdued it. Esco had a way with honeybees. I saw him catch a swarm of bees that were hanging off the back of a trailer. He simply closed a tow [burlap] sack around the teardrop-shaped swarm, shook the sack a bit, and the bees dropped into the sack. There were several bees still on the trailer. Esco raked them into the sack with his bare hand. He wasn't stung even once.

Esco had a neighbor, Uncle Virgil, who could conjure warts. Uncle Virgil smoked a pipe—not just any pipe, a genuine briar that was as old as Virgil himself and looked it. The stem bent over his lower lip, swooped down to his chin, and flared out into a bowl that was worn smooth in places by Virg's calloused fingers. The inside was charred and thin from fire and scrapings, the rim burnt by matches, scarred from being rapped on posts and rocks. He looked like a gnome with his battered felt hat cocked on the back of his thinning gray hair, chewed pipe clamped in yellowed teeth, faded blue overalls over a plaid work shirt, short legs barely reaching the ground, and beat-up high-top work shoes that had seen better days. He wasn't really my uncle; everyone called him uncle. Virgil smiled as he took my small hand. His wrinkled face seemed to become smoother as he examined the wart on the back of my hand. He took his glasses from his overalls, bent down, and peered more closely. He smelled of Prince Albert tobacco and Aunt Sally's strong black coffee. "How long has it been there?" he asked. "Three weeks, a month . . . I don't know." "Is it sore?" he said. "No, just itchy," I replied. He took a puff on his pipe, lifted my hand, and blew smoke over the wart. He bent his face over my hand and mumbled unfamiliar words while gently rubbing the wart with a rough thumb. Another puff of pipe smoke completed his conjure; a tousle of my hair sent me off to play with Aunt Sally's cats. "That should do it," he told Dad. "Come back in a week if it's still there." But we didn't go back; the wart dried up and dropped off in five days. Each time I smell pipe smoke now, I think of Uncle Virgil, look at the back of my hand and wonder, "Did it really happen?" and then knowing that it did, "How the heck did he do it?"

Through all the hard times and the fun times, Dad held to his dream of his own farm. The dairy operation enabled Dad to realize that dream. It brought in money—cash money that was saved for a down payment. It bought a new Chevrolet pickup and a used tractor and equipment. Sadly, the mules were sold. In 1955 Dad bought a beautiful farm in Wolffork Valley and built a dairy barn there. When it was ready, we drove the cows three miles to their new home. That night we milked the cows in our own barn, slept in our own house, and awakened the next morning, living the dream that Dad had envisioned. That dream was fulfilled because of the opportunity in the Farm Family Program. Dad continued to live his dream till the end. Several years before he passed, I spent a couple of hours walking the farm with him. I later wrote these words:

Autumn Walk
Autumn leaves spiral down,
Shades of red and gold
Swirling in hued depths.
White-cold clouds harbinger winter's advent,
Wood-smoke curls low on the land
Bearing odorous memories of
Childhood past.

He leans on his stick to
Survey the hilly pastures and
Dark bottom lands.
A breeze ruffles his white-cold hair, the
Lowering sun shimmers in the grass and
Flames yellow-hot on the
Mountaintops.

Thirty-four autumns have passed with
Him and his land, autumns of
Hard work and satisfaction.
The land remains unchanged,
The body and the buildings
Slump and lean where pushed by time's
Relentless passage.

A broken arrowhead is unearthed and
Pocketed to join a pot of
Similar treasures.
What primeval hands shaped those edges?
Could it be that this land was
Loved and revered by
Other ancients?

The valley sinks into shadow as
Eastern mountains stand pale
Purple in the gossamer twilight.
Moments become ages as
Quiet stillness pervades.
He calls to his dog and they move
Toward home.

For Dad, August 1998
© J. Harold Thurmond

"Being on the school farm was a wonderful thing!"

~Doug Nix~

Twenty years ago, I was a Foxfire student at Rabun County High School and senior editor of Foxfire's 25th anniversary edition, which, not by chance, is proudly on display in my office, begging coworkers to ask, "What's that book about?" I jump at any chance to brag on my experiences with Foxfire and tell them about my heritage in the foothills. Foxfire: 25 Years is a shameless plot device I use to evoke such conversations.

This story marks my second interview with Dad, the first being an article published in the Summer 1991 issue of The Foxfire Magazine *(volume 25, number 2) about the closing of Rabun Mills, the impact the textile mill had on the local economy, and the implications of the recession of the early 1990s. Like several hundred families in the area, my family felt the impact deeply. The closing of the plant meant an end to Dad's thirty-year career built on hard work and sacrifice. The story you are about to read is the prequel to this magazine article.*

Dad's story, here, tells about his family and their start in life in the early 1940s. At the time, the country was recovering from the Great Depression. Unemployment was still rampant, averaging over 15 percent nationwide. The Great Depression, either directly or indirectly, is a very common theme or frequently referenced period of time for Foxfire. The fortitude, resolve, and strength of Appalachians who grew up during this time period are evident in the body of work at Foxfire. The stories of our elders during this time are remarkable, to say the least.

Part of the Foxfire experience as a student is the knowledge that is gained and the learning that occurs about Appalachian heritage. For many students, Foxfire provides a mechanism for learning new things or additional details about their family that would go untold otherwise. Grandparents and great-grandparents make great first-time interviews for new Foxfire students! My grandparents Robert and Edith Cannon were Foxfire regulars throughout my illustrious high school career, and my mother, Judith Nix, was a Foxfire Community Board member. I recall learning many things about my grandparents that I believe would have passed unmentioned had I not had a reason to ask.

Prior to this article, I knew that Dad grew up on the school farm and even recalled some of the stories. However, I didn't have a clear understanding of the circumstances that brought him and his family there. Like many Foxfire students, I gained a deeper understanding about the school farm and Dad's upbringing through the production of this article. I'm astonished that his family went from having nothing to being able to purchase property and build a house in a ten-year period, which was no small feat at the time. It's very clear that Dad and his family worked very hard on the farm, but that was a family trait, and they thrived because of that. I am very thankful to the school farm. I'm sure that my existence and my station in life [a licensed civil and environmental engineer who graduated with a master's degree from Georgia Tech in 1998] today are due to the opportunity the school farm provided Dad.

—Chris Nix

We moved to the school farm in 1948 when I was six years old. Living on the school farm was an opportunity that my family had heard about, and we wanted to give it a try. Jobs at the time were very scarce, and my daddy didn't have a trade skill, so we got in with the school farm. My parents were grateful for the opportunity to work and make something out of themselves and provide for the family. The school farm gave me, my brothers, and my sister a chance to make something out of ourselves, too. The main thing about living on the school farm was that we had to work! Living there helped us in several different ways. It helped us to be able to put food on the table. It helped us to be able to buy clothes, and it helped us learn how to do stuff. I learned a lot about farming while doing it over there on the school farm.

Daddy was working for the school, and my younger brother Ernest and myself took care of the family livestock and garden. We farmed the land down there; me and Daddy took the plow, and we would take it time about, resting, while the other one went to one end of the field or to the other plowing.

To me, being on the school farm was a wonderful thing! It got us off on the right track. I don't know anybody that didn't appreciate the school farm. When I went to school, I didn't have but two pairs of clothes. One pair of clothes were on my back, and the other pair were in the laundry. All the kids on the school farm were like that.

We always had something to do. The people who ran the school farm liked to see you working. They liked to see you keeping your grass cut good, and keeping your creek banks mowed down. Mr. Fry would come around and look and see how everything was going and to see if you were taking care of the house. Sometimes you would have a problem with the house that you lived in. When we first moved there, we didn't have bathrooms in the house. It wasn't too long after we moved to the school farm until we got bathrooms. It was a while though because they came and moved the outhouse twice! I'd say we lived there two or three years before we got a bathroom.

When I was in the first grade, I had to walk to school from the house. The school had a bus at the time, but if you lived on the school farm, you didn't get picked up by the school bus. I walked the railroad track, up the road, and into the school. There was a group of us who walked together.

Some kids would pick a fight—there was one group that would just about pick a fight every day. We had to be good friends with those boys!

We were in clubs in school. We started out with the 4-H Club. I was in the sixth grade when I got my first steer for 4-H. From the sixth grade on, I had a steer every year, and, at one time, I had fifty little pigs. People would come to our house, and they'd say, "I want that pig right there," and they'd just reach in the lot and get it. Well, that was ten dollars; that's what I got per pig—ten dollars. I started saving my money.

The school would let us have all we could make on the farm except for one rule regarding our corn. If we grew corn, we had to give the school a third of it. I was in the FFA [Future Farmers of America], and they wanted us to grow a hundred bushels of corn on one acre of land. Well, the school encouraged us to do it, and FFA challenged the students to do it. The school was set up to enable the families and their children to learn to farm and live off it.

Most of the time, my acre of corn checked out a little better than one hundred bushels because we replanted it. My brother Ernest and I replowed it, took care of it, gathered it, and put the hundred bushels of corn up. Dad was working for the school farm for seventy-five cents an hour. He started out at sixty-five cents an hour; back then small change was big money! I thought, "Now I'll sell that hundred bushel of corn to Furman Vinson over in Dillard." It was yellow corn, some of the prettiest corn you ever laid your eyes on. He said he'd buy ever' bit of it if I would haul it over there to him. Well, my brother Ernest and I did; I hauled the corn over there, and he give me eighty cents a bushel for it. At that time, that was a lot of money! Living on the school farm taught me to raise livestock and farm the land; it also taught me how to make and save money!

I had steers, and my brother helped me with the pigs. I have to say that I did give my brother Ernest some money for helping me with the pigs. Before we went to bed, we'd have to shuck two bushel of corn so that it'd be ready to throw in the hog lot to feed all the hogs in the morning. Also, we had to feed the horses, and we had two cows. My brother would milk one cow, and I'd milk the other one. We took care of the outside.

My daddy got into the chicken business through the school. He had to get permission from the school to do it, and the school allowed him to raise chickens. Daddy would take care of the chickens, and me and my brother would take care of the barn work. My sister and mother would take care of the housework. When it was time to plant the garden, Daddy would plant it, and we'd have to work it. We had to do what it took to keep everything growing. We'd raise chickens and sell them for five cents a head, which was not a lot of money for the amount of work. We got to the point with chickens that we transferred from the grower business to the egg business. There was a company that would buy them, and the eggs would go to a place and be hatched, and they would turn around and either hatch or sell the chickens.

We grew our own potatoes; we had our own eggs; we had our own meat. Chickens! We had chickens by the boochoos [bunches]! Every Sunday they'd be two chickens in the pot for Sunday dinner. We killed hogs. We had plenty to eat! It was because we worked for it! We produced everything you would want to buy at the store really.

We had plenty to eat; I mean, I never did go to bed hungry, and I never did get hungry living on the school farm. We had some of the greatest apple trees over there on the school farm that you could imagine—and we had cherry trees. I believe there were about eight cherry trees that we could pick cherries off of.

Daddy would decide that we needed to kill hogs and make an appointment at the school slaughterhouse. There was one time Daddy had his pickup backed up there loading meat on his truck bed; he'd have shoulders, hams stacked up about three or four feet tall, and two lines of big shoulders and hams stacked in there. Mama really enjoyed the tenderloin. That was the choice of the pig meat. We'd take it and put it in the smokehouse, hang it up, and Daddy would salt it and smoke it. We had to keep a smoker in there to keep flies away. You smoked to keep the greenflies down. If the summer was really hot and you had a lot of meat in there, you'd have to keep it going a couple of weeks.

We seldom killed livestock in the summertime; most of the time it was fall of the year. That was because of having to deal with the flies. It was just ever' once in a while we'd slaughter in the summertime. We had to put the smoker out there to keep the meat from ruining and turning green. You had to put salt on it to keep it purified. That was the biggest reasons. You have to keep a close watch on it.

When we killed three or four hogs at a time, we'd have hot biscuits, tenderloin, and gravy for days and days. You know, believe it or not, we didn't eat eggs even though we raised them. We just didn't care for eggs. We got to where we didn't care for chickens. We just got to where we got tired of it and ham, too! We eat mostly soup beans [pinto beans] and potatoes.

A man named Edward Pitts had a dairy. His family was similar to ours. He moved on the school farm just like us—just like my family, the Pitts came to the farm with nothing. That is a harsh way to look at it, but that's how it was with both our families! The Pitts were our best friends and the Woods family, too. Our families would work together and help with the gardening. Once all the beans came in, the women would get together, and they'd come to your house and get about four or five bushels of beans picked. Then they would break beans, and I mean a lot of beans. Mama would rinse them clean and put them in jars. Then we would take them over to the cannery on the school farm. The cannery was ran by Mr. Jim Burden. We'd can a hundred and fifty cans at one time at the cannery. As you can imagine, we didn't go hungry while we were on the school farm.

My mother would do most of the planting in our garden. The tools Mama had was her apron—with her bean seed in her apron, she'd drop them, just by hand. Daddy would cover up the seed by using a plow called a gee-whiz. Then after the beans grew up tall, we'd plow the corn with a plow called a five-foot. It had five feet on it that would just go through there and leave the corn standing. That was the hardest thing I done on the school farm, was to learn to plow with a five-foot. It was hard to learn!

The school farm encouraged us to grow livestock! The agricultural teacher, John Anderson, was the 4-H Club teacher, and we had Mr. Patrick and Mr. Burden in FFA. If you were in the FFA, you had to have a project. Some of the guys had pigs. A pig is a stupid animal! They would try to lead that pig through town, and I'm not making fun of them because they had pigs, but they'd have a walking stick, and they'd tap that pig there on its side to try and get it going in a certain direction. It just didn't work good sometimes! Some of the boys learned to raise high-quality pigs. As I said, we were encouraged to have a project in FFA and also in 4-H.

PLATE 114 **Doug standing on the location of the old slaughterhouse. The old red barn behind him used to house the Clothes Closet (page 389) talked about by Lucy Webb in her Farm Family interview.**

PLATE 115 "It was just the corn they wanted a third of, and we grew a lot of it." Doug pointing to the field where he grew his one hundred bushels of corn.

Every year from when I first joined 4-H to the twelfth grade in high school, I showed steer. Only one time did I have a case where I couldn't take a steer to Atlanta to the show. This particular steer went crazy, and we couldn't do anything with it. I had several steers to choose from. I led them through Clayton; we had livestock judging down there under the gym, and we'd have to take our steers up there and bring them down Main Street in Clayton when we showed them off. Then we'd take them to Atlanta, and our teacher, which was the agricultural teacher, said, "Now, don't let your calf have any water, not until we get down there." I couldn't understand why he didn't want us to give them any water, so I asked him. The teacher said, "Because if you do, your steer will drink a tub full of water, and it'll weigh a hundred fifty [or] more pounds." I never did get a ribbon for any of my steer until my senior year. However, I did get ten dollars every time I went to Atlanta. The last time I went during my senior year, I had a pretty steer, and this steer would mind you like nobody's business! Mr. Burden told me, he said, "You're going be lucky if you get choice out of that steer." I took him out and started leading him around; the judges were all up there, and that steer stopped with his front feet just right and his back feet were just right. For some reason, the steer slowly turned his neck, and you could just see the tenderloin flexing on the back; it was a perfect sight! I got twenty dollars that year and, finally, a ribbon. That was my last steer.

Our parents didn't mind our projects as long as we did our work and chores; we all had chores to do. Me and my brother Ernest's deal was to milk two cows and shuck two bushel of corn every night. We would have to milk the two cows the next morning and then just throw the corn over into the pen. Now, this was all before you went to school. After Daddy got into the chicken business, it changed my school projects. I didn't have a whole lot of time to fool with my steer. I took my own corn, my yellow corn, and I'd take it to the crusher mill. I fed my steer a special grade of corn that they taught us there in FFA how to do. It was a mixture of cottonseed meal, yellow corn, syrup, and stuff. I'd take it over to the crusher and have it mixed. Then, at the last, I started feeding them shelled corn. Daddy bought me a sheller, or somebody give him one. I'd shell corn with it. Our projects didn't interfere with any of our work over on the school farm. As a family, my projects didn't interfere with my chores or the school farm.

One crazy thing I done over there on the school farm was a bike stunt. Often I would go to a creek and ride my bike with the other kids. I decided that I was going to show everybody how I could jump that creek on my bicycle. I got up on that hill and down through there I went—fast! I jerked the handlebars up to jump the creek, and that front wheel went right into the bank and just rolled me over!

My aunt moved across the creek from us. They had two girls, my cousins, JoAnn and Mary Ann. My sister, Marie, played with them. One time all of us were up in the pasture playing, and we all got into a fight. We decided that we had had enough of that! We told them to stay across the branch [creek] over there, in their territory, and we'd stay on our side of the branch in our territory. A couple of days went by, and we decided that we would meet down at the branch. We went down there, and nobody said anything. I believe I was the one that suggested that we get a spool and put it on a post and run a string from one side of the creek to the other. I had a Prince Albert tobacco can; we took it and shut the lid on the string, and it would go around the spool and keep right on going. I said, "If you have anything to say to us, you write it down on that paper and send it down to the branch." We did that for about a week, and then things kind of smoothed over. First thing you knew, all was forgiven, and we were playing again.

There was a swimming hole out in the pasture, and there were three or four good-sized girls who were our neighbors that swam there. They'd have their bathing suits on, and we'd be in there with our blue jeans on. They'd come down and tell us to go on out, and that they wanted to play down there. We'd have to leave the swimming hole until we saw them leave, and then we'd make another dive!

A funny story: I actually went thirteen years to school. You probably don't want to know about my second grades. The teacher would say, "We are going to have a test tomorrow." Mrs. Barnard Dillard, she was a great teacher and person, she would hand the papers out for the test. When she finished handing them out, she'd say, "Now start the test." We just had that one classroom, so the same teacher taught you everything. In the second grade, I didn't see that what she was teaching had anything to do with growing pigs and plowing a field, so I'd just sit back and rest while everybody else was moaning, groaning, and writing to get through with their tests! I'd just write my name up at the top of the paper, date it, and hand it in. I did that for a year. She never did say anything to Mama. I never did take my report card home! That next year when school started, the teachers would come around and talk to her pupils that she was going have in her class for the next year. So she came over to our house, and she told Mama, said, "Mrs. Nix, I like Doug so well that I am going to have to keep him another year." Boy, Daddy told me, said, "You'd better get your lessons up every night." I used to listen to the Lone Ranger on the radio instead of doing my lessons!

Daddy learned to be a plumber and helped a man by the name of Mr. Lake Stiles. They went around from house to house seeing if there was anything that needed to be done, something that needed to be fixed, plumbing to work on, or a door or something, you know. He worked for the school. He did maintenance on the school building, and he also painted. Daddy did whatever they needed done.

Me and Donald Woods got our first Social Security card working for the school farm. They let us help do jobs over there, like digging ditches. We worked with a guy named Tommy Lee Norton. He'd go out with me and Donald and show us stuff to do, and we'd do it. We'd plow or do whatever needed to be done.

Each family had ten years to live on the school farm. When my family's ten years was up, we were asked to leave the school farm when I was still in the eleventh grade. Mr. Fry said if we wanted to, we could pay rent and stay one more year, so that is what we did. In the meantime, while we were paying rent, my grandpa Harkins told us about some land for sale on Kelly's Creek. So Daddy went over there and bought four acres. We built a house over there, and then we moved.

I was graduating, and my brother Ernest and sister, Marie, were in the tenth grade. Ed, my youngest brother, was in the seventh grade. Daddy got a job over there at the plant in Rabun Gap [James Lee and Sons—Rabun Mills carpet plant] painting the steel. He was going to be a steel painter. He got into the company that did the construction of that place.

I saved money working on the school farm while I was in school. I had saved enough money to buy my first car. It was one hundred twenty-nine dollars for my first car, a '49 Chevrolet. When we left the school farm as a family, we had a home to go to on Kelly's Creek and a few dollars in our pocket and clothes on our back. We were ninety-nine percent better off than we were eleven years prior when we moved onto the school farm. We didn't have anything when we went to the school farm. Afterward, we had a truck; we had a television, which was unusual for people. We had a living room suite. We had three bedroom suites. We had a stove, refrigerator, and a kitchen table, which was very unusual. People couldn't afford that stuff. The school farm was something that was really, really helpful to our family. Daddy was able to work and provide us clothes and everything for us to go to school. It was an opportunity that you couldn't turn down! You got a chance! You had to be people that would work the farm, and you would work! That's what we did. We worked!

To me, what the school farm did was one of the greatest things that could happen to a family that didn't have anything to start with. To be where we are today, really, it is because of the opportunity provided to my family by the school farm! It gave us a good start. It gave me an education, not only me, but my brothers and sister. It gave us an education and gave me an idea of how to farm.

"I knowed there wasn't nobody else for me."

~Lucy Webb and her daughter Mary Webb Kitchens~

Lucy and Grover Webb fell in love and married young. When they moved to the school farm, they had a young family of five boys and two girls. Grover worked with maintenance and supervised dormitory students working on the farm. He, Lucy, and the children also farmed a plot of land. Lucy stayed home, cooking, cleaning, canning, and providing support for her husband and children. Her niece, Ann Henslee Moore [Foxfire's president and executive director], would often visit and has warmhearted memories of having chocolate gravy and biscuits for breakfast at the Webbs' home and playing with her cousins on the hillside above the current-day Indian Lake.

—Kaye Carver Collins

Lucy: I was born October 19, 1925, to Will and Dealia Henslee, and was raised in Rabun Gap, Georgia, near the York House and over there on Kelly's Creek Road where the slaughter pen [Blalock Meats] is now. Daddy moved us over here to Dillard, Georgia, and that's where we lived.

Grover and me started goin' together when I was about thirteen. I knowed there wasn't nobody else for me. I went with him, and we got married when I was nearly sixteen. Right after we got married, Welborn Garrison came down from Horse Cove in Highlands, North Carolina, to get Grover. They needed him to work, and he was gone for two weeks [laughs]. He never came back until he got enough money to buy a cookstove, then he come by and picked me up. We stayed in Highlands until Junior [Grover Webb Jr.], my oldest son, was about a year old, and then we left and came back down to Dillard.

Mary: We moved to the school farm when I was six; that was around 1960. Mr. Fry and Farmer Jones offered Daddy a job and he got it. I think it was Fred Kelly that helped him get on with the RGNS School Farm Program.

Lucy: It was. He worked with them men putting in bathtubs and all of that. Tommy Lee Norton and them would be settin' out there a-talkin', and you could see Fred Kelly comin' down the road. They'd go in that house then and get to work. I loved Tommy Lee and L. D. Hopper. They was good people, but, yeah, Fred Kelly helped Grover get the job with the school.

Mary: Daddy worked the schoolboys that were dorm students. He did the farming there and was over the dormitory students doing the farming; they planted the cornfields, done the plowing, and raised strawberries, all for the school farm. He was paid by a straight check from the school. He got so

PLATE 116 **"Grover and I started going together when I was about thirteen."** Grover and Lucy at home on Betty's Creek, many years ago

much money from the school, and the house we lived in was part of it. They furnished our home and the place around it for us. He probably didn't get but thirty or forty dollars a month for the work he did.

We lived in two different houses on the farm. We lived there in that house right by the three-way stop where the turn to Indian Lake is now and then around there by Esco Pitts on Wolffork Road. Our second house had three bedrooms, and they were on the back side of the house. They were big, old, huge bedrooms. The bedroom that Mama and Daddy slept in had a fireplace in it. Me and Clara, my sister, always roomed with Mama and Daddy. Then four of them [the boys—Jimmy, Calvin, Freddie, and Ronnie] would sleep in the middle room, where Mama had two beds, and two would sleep in each bed. Then Junior had the end room 'cause he was the oldest. Then when Junior was gone [grown up and moved out], Calvin and Jimmy got it, and then one time Clara and I finally got our own room. In the front was the living room, the dining room, and the kitchen. The living room had a fireplace in it, too. The bathroom was kind of on the side between the back bedroom and the kitchen. You could go in it from the house. I loved that school farm house. I wish I had a house there now.

PLATE 117 **"Mama and Daddy raised everything we had."**
Photo courtesy of Rabun Gap–Nacoochee School Archives

Lucy: I tended the kids, kept house, canned, and cooked.

Mary: Mama worked the garden right down below the house, too.

Lucy: I guess there was an acre there between the house and the barn.

Mary: We had one garden below the house, and then we had one out there between us and where Reverend Jack Beaver lived. Jimmy raised hogs out there, too. Mama and Daddy raised everything we had. Daddy planted corn and sugar cane because they made cane syrup. The cane syrup mill was located on Wolffork just past the house on the rock. The school grew and collected their own cane and then made syrup out of it. Farm Families could use the mill if they wanted to, but Mama and Daddy raised everything we ate.

Lucy: We had to live. I couldn't work on a job because I had to feed seven of 'em [her children].

Mary: We raised raspberries on the school farm and carried them to the farmers' market in Dillard to sell. We also raised rhubarb. Daddy would crate it and carry it to Atlanta to sell at the state farmers' market. Then we would help Jimmy. He was in FFA [Future Farmers of America], and he raised tomatoes and bell peppers, and we helped plant 'em. He raised prizewinning hogs, too. Daddy would buy the bell peppers and tomato plants. They would be wrapped in a little brown paper bag. There would be hundreds of those tomato plants and bell peppers.

Lucy: We sold taters to Miss Louise McKinney, too.

Mary: Yeah, that was for the Dillard Community School to use. Mama was a home person. She stayed at home. She raised us, washed our clothes, fed us, and bathed us. She wudn't one for going out into the community to work. She was a home person. She worked the garden and canned.

Lucy: I did help Mrs. Vivian Tatum up there in the Clothes Closet [an old chicken house on the school farm that was used to sort and house used clothing donated by community folks for local schoolchildren] and bought my kids' clothes from there. The girls had beautiful clothes from there. People would give Mrs. Tatum the clothes.

Ann Henslee Moore: Though my family wasn't a School Farm Family, we could buy 'em for like a dollar apiece. It was full of clothes, and that old chicken house is still standing.

Mary: They was cheap, too.

Lucy: I worked for her, and she would give me clothes for the girls. People would come in there, and then you would see them out dressed so fine, and you'd think they wore thousand-dollar dresses. They'd bought 'em at the Clothes Closet for fifty cents a dress! The money made from sales was for the school.

Mary: It was to help the campus. Dormitory kids shopped there, too. I loved it there, the school and all. They had some good teachers. They were strict, but caring, too. I loved Mr. Billy Joe Stiles. I did.

Lucy: And Mr. Brown.

Mary: Yes, and Mr. Morris Brown, the principal, too, and there was no difference shown in the kids [community or dormitory]. Mr. Stiles would get on to Donnie Anderson [community student] just like he would anybody else. They treated you right. Mr. Brown, you couldn't ask for a better principal. We were all friends, dormitory and community students, and some of 'em our best friends; they still are. If the boarding students done something that they weren't supposed to do, they had to go. They didn't keep 'em. They would send them back to their homes around the country. I can still remember when they brought the first African American student to Rabun Gap–Nacoochee. He played basketball, and we got along with no problems, not a bit.

Lucy: When I was growing up, me and Cecil [her brother and Ann's dad], I remember the school would come and pick blackberries back up there in the mountains on Kelly's Creek and carry 'em out in big washtubs. The schoolkids, or the boarders, as they called 'em, would pick the berries. They had to work to go to school there back then like pickin' those berries and makin' a garden.

Ann: That's how the boarding students paid tuition. They had to work just like we did at home. It was a whole community. It was like a big huge family.

Lucy: All of us!

Mary: We really were a big family because we were all friends. We walked to their houses and played with each other. The dorm students were our people, too.

PLATE 118 **Lucy on her birthday in 2009, in Alto, Georgia, where she lives with her daughters, Mary and Clara**

Ann: Andrew Ritchie started the school and the Farm Family Program for the local families because he wanted to help folks like Aunt Lucy and all of the folks in Rabun County. He started it to help the mountain children get an education.

Lucy: And my grandpa went to school in a little ole house 'cross from the present post office up there at Rabun Gap with Andy Ritchie.

Mary: That was my great-grandpa, Dock Henslee.

Lucy: Yeah, it was a good time. It was a lot of hard work, but it was good having them kids all home. I wouldn't mind going back either if I was able. It would be nice.

"Raise 'em, feed 'em, and kill 'em."

~Doris Carpenter and her son Jim Carpenter~

Fred and Doris Carpenter, along with their two girls and two boys, moved to the school farm in 1961. By that time, factories had started production in our county, and many people, including Fred and Doris, worked outside the home at paying jobs. The school allowed them to live on its land and divide any crops grown with the school, providing them with better housing and a better living with which to raise their children.

—Kaye Carver Collins

Doris: We moved there to Rabun Gap–Nacoochee School in 1961. Dorothy is my oldest child, Marie is next, then Jim, then Thurman, and he is the baby. We stayed there seven and one-half years. We was supposed to have been there just five years, so they let us stay overtime because they didn't have nobody to move in. When they had somebody else to move into the house, they asked us to leave, and we left. While we were livin' there, I was workin' at the shirt factory.

Jim: Dad was workin' at the A.I.D. Corporation for Mr. Leslie. I'll start with where we lived then. We lived in the house over across the field from the Green Frog Pond. Dad farmed sixteen acres, grew corn, sharecroppin'. That's the way he paid for livin' there—he'd get half and the school would get half. He'd make cornmeal out of part of it, used some feedin' the hogs and cows, and he sold part of it to other people for feed or whatever [laughs]. Some of 'em he sold to, it was probably "whatever" [moonshining]!

Doris: The house I moved into at Rabun Gap was better. It was bigger and in better shape. The one we owned out there in Clayton wasn't very good. We had runnin' water at the school farm house. I enjoyed it myself. It was out of town, and I just enjoyed bein' there.

Jim: The one we lived in down on Highway 76 didn't have runnin' water; we toted water from the branch out beside it to fill up the washin' machine and do the laundry. Gallon glass jars, candy jars, 'em candy jugs— we used to get them from Gordon Lane's store. After he'd sell out of candy, he'd give Dad the jugs and we used 'em to carry water. We wadn't [wasn't] big enough to carry the five-gallon buckets. Thurman, he fell one time and broke one of 'em and laid [cut] his hand open. Mama grabbed a washcloth and held pressure on it. We had a '47 Chevrolet, I think, at that time. She put pressure on it, drove that car, and it was a straight shift, to town to the doctor's office. She drove and held that pressure on there with the other hand.

Doris: I made it to town in five minutes, too!

Jim: They sewed it up, fixed it. That same place, I got cut one day; Mama and Daddy was at work and Grandma, Mother's mother, was there with us. I was out in the yard and stepped on a piece of glass and sliced my foot open. I went a hobblin' in the house and told 'em what I'd done. Grandma said, "Yap, you've sliced it a little bit," said, "hold it up behind ya and let me wash the blood off of it." She come in there with the washrag in one hand and the other hand kind of behind her. I didn't think nothin' about it, and I was a-holdin' that foot up. She come out with a bottle of alcohol and turned that thing upside down and just poured it! You talk about doin' some hoppin', one-legged hoppin'! It fixed it! They had a way of curin' stuff!

It was bad for skunks there where we lived on the school farm. We called it Skunk Holler. One time Dad killed a skunk; he run and chased it on down through the field and shot it with him a-runnin' full tilt! Didn't think he killed it. He went back that afternoon, after he got off work, and found out that he had shot it and killed it. Him and Little Brother backed one in the corner of the barn stall and told me to get him somethin' to kill it with. All I could find was a little ball-peen hammer with a long handle on it. He backed that thing in the corner and beat it in the head while it was a-sprayin' him and him just a-laughin'—me a way back out of the way so I didn't get sprayed!

Doris: I filled the washin' machine up with water; it was an ol' wringer type of washin' machine that was on the back porch, and I put the Clorox to it. I would not let 'em in the house with them clothes on. I brought their clothes out there, and they changed on the back porch. I just throwed 'em in that Clorox water and washed 'em and that scent come out. They told me you had to bury your clothes if you ever got sprayed, but that Clorox brought it out.

Jim: Me and Little Brother, Thurman, would set a rabbit trap, and all we ever caught was skunks or possums. If we caught a possum, we'd take it out to Uncle Clyde Cannon; he'd put it in a fifty-five-gallon barrel and feed it and fatten it up and then have possum to eat. He liked it. I couldn't stand the thoughts of it myself! I wouldn't try it. They was always somethin' goin' on!

Dad got livestock after we got there. We didn't have 'em before that. Jerry Ayers was who Dad got his cows from. Jerry always had good milk cows. Dad would get 'em from him. He'd just get the hogs wherever he could find some and raise 'em, feed 'em, and kill 'em.

Doris: Thurman also had a calf that he took to the show with the FFA [Future Farmers of America]. I forget now how he did; seems like he won. He got a ribbon of some kind. I believe he got second place or third place.

Jim: The school just had one tractor that they let the Farm Families use, and it was used from one to the other. You put the gas in it, even had headlights, believe it or not, so Dad could work at night! Dad, he farmed till midnight lots of nights. Get up the next mornin' and be at work at seven!

Doris: I stayed up. I was a-cannin' most of the time, except in the wintertime.

Jim: Uncle Ott [Arthur] Dills had an ol' mule we'd borrow. When the school's tractor wouldn't be available, we'd go borrow it. He lived over past the rock crusher [the rock quarry], and we'd go over there and get it. Me or Little Brother one would ride it back. Dad would follow us in the car. We'd come to the branch [Darnell Creek] there before you'd get to the plant [Rabun Mills factory] and it'd stop. You could jerk on the reins, kick it; it wouldn't do nothin', just stand there. Dad would have to get out, put somethin' over its eyes, lead it across the bridge and get on the other side, take it off, and he's ready to go then. He'd go right on down there and walk across the bridge at the Little Tennessee River, never even stopped! Right on down there we'd go and we'd take it down there and plow with it.

I was a-tryin' to garden one day, and it decided it was dinnertime, I reckon. When I got to the end of the row and tried to turn it around, it kept

PLATE 119 "It was bad for skunks there where we lived on the school farm. We called it Skunk Holler."—Jim Carpenter
"They told me you had to bury your clothes if you ever got sprayed, but that Clorox brought it out."—Doris Carpenter

goin'. I stood up on the plow and jabbed it in the ground as deep as I could and was a-leanin' back on the reins. It just pulled that head down and just keep a-goin'. Didn't pay it no attention. Before he tore up the road around through there, I finally just laid the plow over and let him go on. He went up to the barn walkin', walked in his stall. I got a' ear of corn and put in there. It eat the ear of corn, and then it was ready to go again. He come out and headed back towards the garden. We got back and finished plowin' it then.

I'd go out in the field or in the pasture behind the barn to try and catch the mule. It'd be right there behind the barn, and I'd walk out there with the bridle, and it'd take off to the other end of the field just as hard as it could go. It'd get out there; I'd go out there after it; it'd run right at me and look like he was gonna run right over me and, just before he got to me, he'd rear to the side when I raised that bridle up, like I was gonna slap him with it. He'd rear to the side and go around and then go back out towards the barn. I run back and forth two or three times and got tard [tired] of it. I went in the house and told Dad that I couldn't catch that mule. He kept runnin' away. Dad said, "That mule ain't no problem to catch." He went out there and put an ear of corn in the bucket, walked out the back, and shook it. That mule come a-flyin' up there, put his head in the bucket, and started eatin' the corn. Dad slipped the bridle over his ears. As soon as he got through eatin', he put the bit in his mouth. We went on and plowed then; had to use gee-haw. Gee is right and haw is left. That ol' mule—I was a-plantin' corn with it on a Saturday before I went in the service on a Tuesday, back in 1966—with a one-row corn planter, put fertilizer in one hopper on it and the corn in the other hopper on it. It went out through the row there, and the fertilizer would drop in and cover it, and then corn would drop in and mix it. That was a handy rig. We usually had somebody with a corn picker to come and pick it. It takes a long time to pick corn; they wadn't enough of us to pick it fast enough by hand!

We'd go back and pick up a lot of corn that the corn picker missed. We'd go back and get that. Plowin' them fields and usin' that fertilizer, I was a little boy, but I couldn't do it now! I'd throw a one-hundred-pound bag of fertilizer on my shoulder, get another one under my arm and go out through the plowed field, and there I went! I was a little more slim and trim back then. I was a hundred and sixty pounds.

I grew a' acre of peppers for the Campbell Soup Company; we grew bell peppers for them. I planted an acre of it, and we had these fifty-five-gallon drums that we put out in the field that we mixed the plant starter in to water the plants and help them get started. It come up a storm one day, started boilin' up a storm. Dad said, "Boys, you had better get them barrels out of the field before it washes out from under them and breaks a bunch of pepper plants down." So we went out there to get 'em. Dad just picked his barrel up and walked out of the field with it. I picked mine up, and bein' not too bright at the time, I throwed it up over my head and it a-thunderin' and a-lightnin'. The static off of that lightnin' hit that barrel and made the hair stand up on both of my arms, plumb up to my shoulders. I throwed down the barrel and broke down more plants than if I had washed out them barrels probably. I didn't throw it back up over my head when I went to retrieve it and get it out of the garden!

Doris: I had a pea patch out beside the house there, and we made so many peas there that year that I give I don't know how many away 'cause I couldn't can 'em all! One time the school asked me to go to Atlanta with 'em to sell some canned foods. I loaded up my canned food and went with 'em. We sold it ever' bit, and they wanted us to come back and bring some more, but we never did go back.

Jim: We shelled peas, broke beans. I couldn't eat 'em all! I hate 'em once they're cooked! Just go out there in the garden and shell 'em out and eat 'em.

Grover Webb lived right around from us. Jay Bird Dills; his real name was Lester, same as my middle name. They called him Jay Bird all the time. He run one of the dairy farms. Uncle Ralph Robinson and Aunt Marjorie, Morris, Gary, and Judy, they run one of the dairy farms. We would go over there sometimes and help with the milkin' or help put up hay, helped put silage in the silo. We done that quite regular.

We was back and forth all the time. Uncle Ralph and cousin Jay Bird, they had a tractor duel one day. Jay Bird had a John Deere he thought could just outplow anythin' in the world. Uncle Ralph had a big ol' orange tractor. He had big ol' disc plows for it. Jay Bird had the regular plows. They got out there a-plowin' a field, and Uncle Ralph would make two rounds to Jay Bird's one—just had Jay Bird all tore up! So he just kept raisin' his plows up a little higher, plowin' a little less deep, tryin' to catch up with him. Uncle Ralph had his down just as far as they'd go and was just a-plowin' circles around Jay Bird—just beat Jay Bird to death! It was fun! They was all the time fun with somethin' like that a-goin' on. We loaded two flatbed wagons; we stacked them things just as high as we could with hay. That ol' orange tractor of Uncle Ralph's, it didn't even slow it down. It was a hoss [powerful] tractor; it could pull.

At the dairy, they always had that one cow that liked to kick. It was a black Holstein. She liked to kick, try to get you, surprise you and get you, so you had to watch her. She never got me, but I seen her get one or two—catch 'em on the arm; they'd have a big ol' scratch mark all the way down their arm. Jay Bird and them had one that liked to do that, too. She liked to kick.

Freddy, their boy, when he was little, that ol' cow kicked at him one time, and he got a short-handled shovel and walked up around and got in the feed trough. They had their head locked in there. He got in that feed trough with that short-handled shovel and started a-beatin' that cow between the eyes! He was just a little ol' bitty thing, but he got up in that feed trough in front of that cow, and he got that short-handled shovel, and he went to workin' on that head!

Raz Mason lived on the school farm, too. He did some work for them at the school, just general work. They lived around off the Betty's Creek Road, the back side of Betty's Creek there. That's where Raz lived. I'm tryin' to remember who it was that lived on out there past Jay Bird, the Phillips[es], I think. He was two or three years ahead of me; he was about Morris's age, I think.

Doris: Now, the Woods lived there when we was there. They had two boys, I know.

Jim: The boys was twins, I think, best I can remember. I think they lived in the house up past Grover Webb; they lived on the same road we lived on [back of the old post office].

Doris: Grover lived in the house back behind us.

Jim: I think at that time the land was actually owned by the United Daughters of the Confederacy, or they donated to the school to help build those houses. We lived in the first one there and you went on around, and Grover Webb lived there.

I caught chickens at night and went to school durin' the day for several months, me and Jimmy Webb, for Furman Vinson. He'd come around in an ol' Chevrolet van, a panel van, no backseat in it, just a driver's seat and one other seat. Turner Enloe helped catch; he was one of the ones that helped catch. I'm a-tryin' to think of that little feller's name. There was a little dried-up ol' man that helped catch. Julius was his first name; I can't think of his last name. It was fun. You was wore out when you went to school. It made it kind of hard to learn; it was an experience! Me and Jimmy usually worked on the truck. We handled ever' chicken that come out of the chicken house. We usually caught ten thousand a night. They was seven of us, five that would catch 'em and bring them to us. Me or Jimmy one would be stackin' crates, and the other one puttin' chickens in 'em. Put fourteen chickens to a crate.

I guess I was about seventeen. They'd come around in the ol' panel van and pick us up, and we would go to wherever we was gonna catch that night. We worked from Tallulah Falls to the other side of Franklin, North Carolina. We went to the other side of Franklin to get roosters and layin' hens, some of them with them big spurs on their feet. We'd catch three of 'em at a time and bring out there. They'd just kick and just about jerk your arm out of socket! We'd put them in. We started out from there. The road down was down a bank, I guess you'd say, just about washed. Billy Long was a-drivin' the truck, and he turned around that curve and the truck started rarin' up, and five of us grabbed ahold of the chains that was holdin' the crates on and held on to 'em and rode on the upper side of the truck to hold it down enough for him to get around that road. That'd be a little against OSHA [Occupational Safety and Health Administration] regulations now! Back then, you done what you had to, to get the job done. We had some fun times a-doin' that.

Doris: I wouldn't call that fun.

Jim: We had kinfolks that come by and everythin', and we'd pop dishpans full of popcorn and eat popcorn. You worked all day and half the night, but it always seemed like there was time for family back then.

Doris: We didn't have a television, but we got one before we left Rabun Gap–Nacoochee School.

Jim: You went to school and church; I didn't even get to go to a ball game until I was in the twelfth grade. Tuesday night was church night at our church and that was ball game night, so I was in twelfth grade and FFA had the concession stand. They let me off one night there from church to go work the concession stand! Due to old age and poor memory, there is no warranty—expressed, implied, or otherwise—on this information!

Editor's note: *Doris and Jim lost their wonderful daughter and sister Marie shortly after this interview was conducted in summer 2010. Marie was a loved and loyal member of the Foxfire family as well, having been comanager of Foxfire's gift shop, along with her sister-in-law, Jim's wife, Paulette, for the past six years. She was such a blessing to us every day through her strong faith, and she will truly be missed.*

"I can remember in the fall of the year . . ."
~Bobbie Dills Carter~

The Dills family moved to the school farm in 1962. Jay Bird and his sons ran a dairy farm, while wife, Bobbie, worked at a nearby factory. Bobbie reminisces about a wonderful home, good neighbors, and cherished family memories.
—Kaye Carver Collins

We moved to the school farm in 1962, I think. Fred Kelly come and asked us if we would be interested in goin' to work on the school farm. My husband, Jay Bird [Lester Dills], and I decided we would do it. I had a really gentle, good milk cow, and my father-in-law traded me a car for the cow when we moved. I was workin' at Rabun Mills while Jay Bird and the boys run the dairy farm. So havin' a car was a necessity. I loved it when we moved to the school farm. We got a house with water and a bathroom in it! It was somethin'! We stayed four and one-half years! We had six kids altogether— Jerry, Lee, Allen, Elizabeth, Fred, and Gail.

A funny thing happened when we moved over there. Jay Bird was helpin' Ralph Robinson with his hogs, and he was goin' over a fence, tripped, and fell in a big mud hole where the hogs had been. He was covered in mud from his head to his toes! The feller he was helpin' said that it was so funny that he had to laugh; even if Jay Bird had killed him, he had to laugh.

We had a dog named Bossy, and he was really good at helpin' get in the cows. All you had to say was "Bossy, go get the cows." And he would go gather them in! One day Jay Bird said he didn't believe that dog would bite anybody. He said, "I'll prove it to you." So he snuck off to the barn and put on a big old coat and covered hisself up and come sneakin' up to the house. When he got close, Bossy started growlin' at him. Jay Bird come on up there and reached out like he was gonna grab the dog. That dog took off after him! Jay Bird run and went up a tree! He kept sayin', "It's me, Bossy! It's me!" We like to have never got that dog away from the tree so Jay Bird could come on down!

I can remember in the fall of the year, they would have a big get-together and make sorghum syrup. Every family got some to take home with them. We had lots of good neighbors there. We was all the time helpin' each other and havin' fun together. One time Raz [Erastus] Mason was over at the house, and Fred and Gail always run around barefooted. Well, Raz took out his pocketknife and told my younguns that if they didn't put on their shoes, he'd cut off their toes with his knife! Ever time they saw Raz a-comin', they'd run to find their shoes and put them on!

Sod [Cliff] Conner would come by and leave supplies for the cows ever'

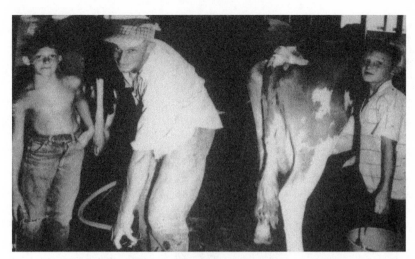

PLATE 120 "When they got them up and movin' toward the dairy barn, he and Lee would lay down where the cow had been layin' to get warm." Jerry, Jay Bird, and Lee Dills

once in a while. One day they was puttin' up the stuff, and Gail and Fred was runnin' all around them, and Sod was afraid the kids might get hurt, so he got out this big sack and told them, "If you don't quit runnin' around out here, I'm a-gonna put you in this here sack and take you home with me!" They took off runnin' to the house and dived under a bed to hide. After he left, we got to huntin' them kids and couldn't find them anywhere! We hunted in the barn, in the house, everywhere! I finally found them up under my bed, sound asleep!

Jay Bird and the boys worked the dairy barn. Jerry helped with the milkin', and Lee cleaned out all the milk containers. Jerry told me years later that sometimes they couldn't get Bossy to gather all the cows in, and he and Lee would go out in the pasture barefooted to bring in the cows. He said it would be cold and some of the cows would be layin' down. When they got them up and movin' toward the dairy barn, he and Lee would lay down where the cow had been layin' to get warm.

Jay Bird had a tank with gasoline in it outside that he used for some of the farm equipment. He got to noticin' that his gas was missin', so one night he decided to go out and wait and see who was stealin' his gas. We went on to bed and after a while I heard a gunshot! The man took off runnin' and left his gas cans! Jay Bird had hit him and was able to track him back on an old road up behind the house. He must have left his car parked there while he come down and tried to steal the gas. We found out later that Jay Bird had shot him in the hind end. He had to go to the doctor to get shot out of his backside!

PLATE 121 **"I cried and cried when we left."**
Bobbie Dills Carter

At Christmas, most of the Farm Families would go up to Buddy Gibbs's store on Wolffork to buy stuff for their kids. You could get good stuff and get it cheap! So we'd gone up there and bought BB guns for all the boys and big ol' dolls for our girls. We hid it at the house and while we was gone one day, the kids found it. We found out years later that they would get the guns out and shoot birds while we was gone. The girls would get the dolls out and play with them. One day, Elizabeth had her doll out playin' with it, and it was really cold. So she took the doll in the livin' room, set down by the stove, and put her and her doll's feet out toward the stove to warm them. Well, the doll had on plastic shoes and the shoes melted!

I remember one year, I growed a big garden of okra! Ever time I would go pick okra, I'd come back with a bushel hamper full! I don't remember what I done with all that okra—sold it, give it away, I can't remember!

One day, a couple was a-visitin' us. Every few minutes Jay Bird or the other man would leave the room. They just keep a-doin' it! After a while, I told his wife that I was gonna see what they was doin'. So the next time they got up and went out of the livin' room, I snuck over to the dining room door and watched. Jay Bird had a quart of liquor hid in the closet, and they was goin' in there to get them some. Jerry had a little chicken, and after a while they put some of that liquor in a saucer and give it to that chicken! It would take a sip, pull its head up to swallow, walk around a little, and go back and take another sip. It was sort of staggerin' around and after a while, it just fell over! Jerry thought his chicken was dead, but it come to after a while, got up, and went on its way!

I really hated to leave the school farm! I cried and cried when we left. We had really good neighbors, and the school was really good to us, but Jay Bird decided it was time to go back to our little log cabin on the hill!

"They provided the house, and we provided the labor."

~Marjorie Robinson and her son Morris Robinson~

Marjorie Robinson and her husband, Ralph, raised two sons and a daughter. They lived in Gastonia, North Carolina, for several years. Their son Morris hated living in Gastonia and especially hated going to school there. By the time he was a seventh grader, he was waiting for the day he turned sixteen so he could quit and never go to school again. Fortunately for him, times were hard and Ralph lost his job at Firestone Tire and Rubber Company. The family moved back to Rabun County, eventually settling on the school farm, where Morris discovered a renewed passion for learning.

—Kaye Carver Collins

Marjorie: I lived in Rabun County all my life until I was married. I graduated from Rabun Gap–Nacoochee School in 1937; then I was lucky enough to attend junior college there. I got two years of junior college, and then I taught school two years here in Rabun County. I'd been dating my husband for four years, and he got tired of waiting, so we got married. He was living in Gastonia, North Carolina, at that time.

While we lived in Gastonia, things got slow just like they are here now. Ralph was working for Firestone Tire and Rubber Company, and I was working at a sewing plant as an inspector. The children were all in school. The only place they had to play was a small yard.

Morris: It was a very small yard, plus we went from a grammar school of one hundred twenty-five students to a grammar school that had about twenty-five hundred in it. Now, talking about a culture shock, that was a culture shock. There you had kids, I would say, that came from broken families, and they were just allowed to do anything that they wanted to. When we say that you literally had to fight every day just to exist, that's the way it was. I wanted to move back. I had told Mama that I longed for the day that I turned sixteen years old because when I did, I was quitting—that was going to be my last day of school.

Marjorie: He was coming to live with my mother and daddy.

Morris: I was in the fourth grade when we moved to Gastonia, and I was in the seventh grade whenever I made that revelation. I had been through three years of it and hated every day of it and wanted to come back to Rabun County.

Marjorie: I worked at a cotton mill.

Morris: Daddy had been with Firestone for fifteen years when they laid him off. I remember we was sitting there at the table one night, and Daddy said something about "Well, Margie, this is it. We're going back to Rabun County because I do know that, in Rabun County, I can raise enough food to feed my family." So sure enough we moved back. We moved to Clayton, Georgia.

Marjorie: We lived right there at the shirt factory [Clayburne Manufacturing], so I went and put in my application. My husband went everywhere and put in applications, and he hadn't got a job. I got on the evening shift, and he was at home with the kids till I got off.

Morris: Ernest and Bernice Holt lived on the school farm. Bernice was Mama's niece. They told Mama and Daddy that the school might have a couple of openings coming up on the school farm. They told Daddy that he and Mama should go up to Mr. H. L. Fry, who was in charge, and put in an application if they were interested. Daddy did. In December of 1958, Mr. Fry came and saw them and told 'em they had been accepted for the Farm Family Program.

Marjorie: We had to apply to the program.

Morris: They asked Mama and Daddy questions like were they thinking about continuing their education? Had they had any experience farming? Were they raised on a farm?

Marjorie: Of course, your daddy did have experience farming when he was growing up.

Morris: Yes, he did. The first house that we lived in on the school farm was where the beef cattle barn was. You know, it's burned down now, but when it was there, we lived in that house right there next to it. I remember that house well. We moved in on Christmas Eve, December 24, 1958. It was exciting getting a new home and setting up the furniture so that we could live there, but most importantly was going to the woods and finding a Christmas tree. It was a long day, but we were ready for the visitor from the North Pole by ten o'clock p.m. We stayed there about a year, and then they moved us over here, off Highway 441, where Green Pond is. That first house you see there is where we moved. We tended all of that land from the house to the road and then all the way back to where you turn and go back to Indian Lake. We had that in corn. At that time, Bernice and Ernest decided that they were going to leave the school, and they had a dairy farm. The dairy farm was over there where the Gap Manufacturing plant is today. I think Daddy went to the school administration and talked to them to see if we could do the dairy when Bernice and her family left. They told us yes. We took and gathered all of our corn up that we had in the barn and took it all over to the dairy farm.

Marjorie: Rent was included in all of that. We didn't pay rent. They paid my husband to farm.

Morris: It was fifty percent. They provided the house, and we provided the labor, and it worked out good. You bought your own seed and equipment. The first tractor we bought was a little Farmall A Cub. It was fine just for corn, but when we got to the dairy farm, we needed something bigger because not only were we doing the hay for the cattle, but we were also raising corn and cutting it for silage. So you had to have power takeoff, which that little A Cub didn't. Then he got an Allis Chalmers tractor.

Marjorie: Then you got a percentage for the milk.

Morris: We got a percentage of the sale of the milk. We averaged right at about fifty to fifty-five cows that we kept milked. By then, we had electric milkers. It was the type where you just changed the top off. You washed 'em, changed the top off, and then went to the next cow and put them on it.

Monday through Saturday we were at the barn milking at five o'clock in the morning. The first run went in at five. The reason I say Monday through Saturday is because you had to know my dad. My dad was a teaser, and he'd always say on Saturday night, "Boys, I'm gonna let y'all sleep in the morning. Get you some rest. We're not going to start milking until five thirty in the morning [laughs]!"

Marjorie: They got thirty minutes' extra sleep.

Morris: We'd get thirty more minutes [chuckles]. So we started at five and we finished at about seven or seven fifteen. We had time to quit milking, come to the house, eat breakfast, get our baths, and go to school.

Marjorie: Now, no profit was shared out of your own garden, and we had a huge garden.

Morris: We had an acre and a half to two acres. It was huge. We had everything. It started out with the little onion sets, so you had the little spring onions and English peas. We had green beans, carrots, radishes, turnips, turnip greens, mustard greens, cabbage, lettuce, and, of course, your tomatoes.

Now, on the school's part, we planted mostly corn, but they didn't tell us, as I remember, what to plant. A lot of people would raise the corn because they got half of the corn crop, which could be used to feed their own animals. Whenever they divided the crop, what you did with your half was yours. You could sell it, if you wanted to, or you could keep it to feed with.

We would usually average between ninety to a hundred five bushels per acre of corn. We did. I'd have to say one thing: We were very fortunate, but I think that was due to my dad being raised on the farm. I can remember one time that we had a really rainy spring, and corn got so high that we couldn't side-dress it and lay it by because it was so wet here in Rabun County. We had to do it by hand, and we walked through every row of corn. We started at nine o'clock every morning. We come home at noon to eat, and then we'd go back and do it again that afternoon. Some years as we added the ammonia nitrate to side-dress the corn and laid it by for the year, we would throw out soybeans. When you harvested the corn, you would plow in the soybeans. This was done to enrich the soil for a better crop next year.

Marjorie: I worked during the day. In the summertime, Ralph and the boys would gather in tomatoes. We grew a lot of tomatoes. They took 'em to the cannery and canned them—took their jars, and they put 'em through the sieve and canned them in big half-gallon cans. As far as green beans and things like that, they would have a run of them ready when I got home. Ralph would put 'em on, you know, to blanch 'em. When I got home, I would put 'em in jars that had been scalded good and ready to put 'em in. Ralph sealed them, and I put 'em in the pressure cooker. I would take the last run off, some nights, about twelve thirty. Ralph and I would stay up, and we'd can two or three runs because, in the pressure cooker, you didn't have to cook 'em but about thirty-five minutes under pressure. Then you had to let 'em cool down till you could open the canner.

Morris: One year Daddy sent me over here to Dillard, me and my brother, Gary, to the farmers' market to see if they had any tomato plants. I said okay. I went and I heard Furman Vinson tell this guy that he didn't have any tomato plants, so me and Gary, we started to turn and walk off.

PLATE 122 "Their daddy always insisted that they get a good education where they wouldn't have to work like that for the rest of their lives."—Marjorie Robinson "Somewhere in the conversation with Daddy, it would always come up. He'd say, 'You know you need to get you a good education, then get you a job.'"—Morris Robinson

He said, "Hey, Morris, hold on a minute." He walked on over to where we was at. He said, "Can I help you? What are you looking for?" I said, "Well, we were looking for some tomato plants, but I heard you tell him that you didn't have any."

He said, "Let me finish up here. Don't you go anywhere; stay right here and talk to me." So he finished up with them and they left. He came over and he said, "Morris, let me show you what I've got." He went over there, and he had about a half of case a tomato plants. Now they were drooped, and he said, "I'll tell ya, these are good. They're just drooped. They need to be watered, and I think they'll be fine. If you want 'em, take 'em and set them out because I'm gonna throw them away. I'll give 'em to you." So I took them and went back to the house. We had the land already fixed ready to plant. I said, "Daddy, here's what Furman gave me."

Daddy said, "Huh, it's fixin' to rain. Let's get a little rain on them and by tomorrow morning these will be pretty." So we set in to set them out. We set out a little over three hundred. I can't remember the exact number, but we set out three hundred plants, and that's why Mama will tell you we had plenty of tomatoes. I gave them away; I sold some, too. I had a guy from Florida drove up in the yard one day and asked if he could buy some tomatoes. I guess he got a half of bushel or a little more of tomatoes.

He said, "What do you want for them?"

I said, "Whatever you want to give me for them." He handed me some money. I can't remember how much, but Mama comes out there and she said, "Did I hear you say you sold them to that guy?"

I said, "Yes, Mama, I did." She said, "Well, Morris, you know we are giving these away."

I said, "Mama, he didn't ask me if I would give him some. If he had, I'd have said yes. He asked me if I would sell him some." She said, "Yeah," and I just reached and handed her the money.

I said, "That goes on the fertilizer [laughs]." Just like that and, like I said, if he had asked me to give 'em to him, I'd have give 'em to him, but he didn't ask that. One thing about it was, it ended up that a friend of his ran a truck route of produce out of South Carolina, so he started coming over and buying from us. So we did pretty good off tomatoes that year.

Marjorie: That's true. It was real good, but it was hard. It was a blessing, too, because all of the farmhouses had running water.

Morris: We had a bathroom with a bathtub there. The house where we were living in Clayton only had an outhouse, so the house on the school's property was a step up for us.

Marjorie: We had three bedrooms, an indoor bathroom, kitchen, living room, and an upstairs, and, like I said, we had running water to the house.

Morris: Plus, everybody worked together. If Doc Phillips over there needed hay cut next week, different ones would go from their farm to Doc's farm. They would cut all the hay, get it ready, bale it, and then we'd all show up after school or after milking, and we'd get in a few loads before dark. The men would work together during the daytime, too. Then when we got ready to cut our hay, they'd all come over to our farm and help us out.

Marjorie: They worked as a team.

Morris: And I think that I really and truly had more fun, if you can have fun, doing hard work during that time because all of them were big teases. They'd cut up, and the things that we did to each other were so funny. Like when we were cutting silage, Raz Mason and Jay Bird Dills drove the truck. Tommy Lee Norton drove the tractor with the cutter that was cutting the corn for silage. We had to ride the trucks, me and my brother did, and keep the corn pulled back so we could get a good load on there. Every time you'd come to the end of the field, Raz or Jay Bird would put us under the blower. They did it just to be doing it, so I got to the point where I would take my big fork that I was raking back with, and I'd get me up a shovel full, and as I went under the thing, I put a big shovel through the truck window. So when we got the truck loaded, they may be sitting in about three feet of silage, but, of course, now I was the one, too, that was covered. You can imagine when we got home at night, and we'd take our clothes off with all that corn juice on them, they would stand up by themselves! Like I said, we enjoyed it. It was hard work, but I think really and truly it taught us a lot. We could accomplish anything that we set out to do, but it wasn't just the situation; it was all of your neighbors, too.

Marjorie: Their daddy always insisted that they get a good education where they wouldn't have to work like that for the rest of their lives.

Morris: I don't think I can remember a time that at least four times a week, somewhere in the conversation with Daddy, it would always come up. He'd say, "You know you need to get you a good education, then get you a job." Education came first and then a job. Daddy would say, "Now, you can't go anywhere unless you got that education." I don't think children today are taught or told that enough. I think kids today need to hear more of that, and it needs to come from the homes, not just from the school system.

Marjorie: That's right. The parents ought to say your education comes first because you're gonna use that for your living when you're grown and have a family.

Morris: It was emphasized at home to get an education, but then also at school with people like Morris Brown, Billy Joe Stiles, and Dr. Karl Anderson. They talked about getting your education, finding your profession that you wanted to go into, and that would prepare you for the future, but you did it through education! We not only heard it, but we also saw examples of it because that's what they did. Billy Joe Stiles, of course, he was Farm Family. He was raised there, and he had gone on to Berry College and then came back and taught at Rabun Gap. He didn't mind to tell you that he was raised right there on the school farm. So you saw an example through him. They worked here. He worked here. He knew what it was to work, but yet he went on and got his education, and look what he's doing now! It was inspiring. Then, of course, Mama was raised with Morris Brown. We knew what kind of upbringing he had. It was the same as the kids in this area at the time had, but he had gone on and got a college education, and he was back teaching and then became principal.

Marjorie: He and I started the first grade together and graduated together. And then he went off to college, but I couldn't afford to go off. I got to stay at home, which meant sometimes I had to walk two and a half miles to and from school. In the wintertime, we had chemistry, and it was extremely cold. I wouldn't get out until late because we had lab after the three o'clock class was over. One time I thought I was going to freeze to death. It was cold and a north wind blowing, and I had to walk about three miles. Back then, girls couldn't wear pants; we had to wear dresses. I got to Dillard and Mr. Miller Grist had a store, and we bought all of our groceries there. So I stopped in there to get warm 'cause I thought I was going to freeze to death, and he gave me two pairs of lady's long cotton stockings. He made me sit down and put them on. I got them on and started on home. I got about halfway from the store, and my first cousin, his wife, and his mother lived together, and I stopped in at their place and got real good and warm again. I made it home, but I thought I wasn't going to.

But anyway, I went two years there at the junior college, and then I was able to teach. If you were a community student, you could just tell them that you wanted to attend the college. We were on semesters, and we only had to pay thirty-nine dollars per each semester. With other fees, it came out to about ninety-nine dollars for the two semesters, and that was a lot of money back then. I worked during the summer and saved the money. One summer I worked for our neighbor. His wife was sick, and they wanted me to work down there and help her. I worked all that summer, seven days a week. I had to cook, wash dishes, clean, sweep, and work some in the garden, and can food, but I didn't have to do the wash. They had somebody else to do it, but I had to iron all the clothes and everything else. On Sunday morning, they went to the Methodist church at Dillard, and I got to go home. But I had to get up, cook breakfast, and clean up the kitchen before I left. They ate out for Sunday lunch, so I got to stay at home Sunday night, but I had to get up early enough to go to their house, which was about a mile, and cook breakfast for them on Monday morning. On Sunday when I left, they paid me two dollars and fifty cents for seven days of work. I saved it for college. I helped buy my books and, back then, we couldn't go to the store and buy ready-made clothes. I bought material, and my mother was a good seamstress. She could take a catalog, look at a dress, sit down, and cut the dress out and sew it. She and I together made all of my dresses. I bought the material, and we made them on an ole treadle sewing machine.

My oldest sister was a schoolteacher, and she helped me, too. She told me, "Now, I'm going to help you all I can so that you can get your two years of college, then you will help our brother, who was younger than me, go to school." When I finished junior college, I taught school and helped my youngest brother.

Kaye Carver Collins: *So in the seventh grade, Morris, you had already made up your mind that you were going to quit when you turned sixteen, and then you decided, when you got to Rabun County, that you were going to be in the medical field. What happened?*

Morris: I think I knew I wasn't going to quit because now I came to a school that I could go in, in the morning, and start school. It was a whole different situation. There were no fights. Nobody hounded anybody. We just come in and went to school, had fun, and hey, I didn't want to leave that. I think that was the biggest thing. It was just the whole atmosphere. In Gastonia, you had to be in a certain clique. Your mama and daddy had to be bringing in some big bucks. If you chose to participate in something, whether you got to participate was based on what your mama and daddy made. I never saw that at Rabun Gap. It was not how much your mama and daddy could pay to get you into this or that. It wasn't like that.

There was no difference between community students and dorm students at Rabun Gap–Nacoochee. I guess my class, I graduated in 1962, was one of the closest classes because it didn't make any difference whether you were community or a dorm student. Let's say some of the dorm students had more money than we did in our family—that didn't mean they [the students] had more. They wore blue jeans just like we did.

Marjorie: And the dorm students had to work on the farm along with the other boys.

Morris: They had specific work crews for them to work on. The dorm students were assigned to a work crew. Then somebody like Farmer Jones, he had the dairy over there at the school, was in charge of those boys. Then they had the field crew. They would go out and maybe hoe strawberries and then pick them when they were in season. Then you had the trash team. They went around to all the dorms and all the buildings, picked up the trash, and then carried it out to the dump. There was a certain area out there on the farm that was designated for that. Then they'd meet on a Saturday, go out there, and burn all the trash, so there was no difference in us because we all had to work.

I remember one time, Doc Phillips got his arm hung in a corn picker, and it crushed his arm. He had a son, Clyde, who was in my class, and Betty and an older boy, John, who was in the service. He had a lot of problems with that arm, but there was six weeks there that Doc couldn't milk. There was our dairy farm, Jay Bird Dills had one, the school had one, and Doc's. Each milking time, morning or night, one person went from each farm to help milk. We'd go over and help Clyde milk, and we did this until his dad could come back to work and that was about two months. He was so grateful. Doc was so grateful that we came to help him, and all he could say was "Fellas, you just don't know how much I appreciate this. If there's anything that I can do, you call me." It was one of those situations where he could not wait to get back to work. I look at today and there are people out there, if they got hurt like that, they'd never work again, but he didn't do that. He just could not wait to get back to where he was able to work. He appreciated people going and helping him. He would say, "I might not be able to go and do anything, but I can talk to you." To me that was just great. It was great to be able to do something to help somebody and know that he appreciated it. He didn't want to be in that situation and, as soon as he could get out of it, he wanted to go back to work full-time. Everybody worked together and helped each other out. This was the Christian thing to do. You looked out for your neighbor and friends, and they looked out for you. If you had extra produce from the garden, you shared with the other Farm Families.

Marjorie: We always got a big box of stuff—just different kinds of things given to us at Christmas.

Morris: I remember that. I guess the one big thing that I remember was our times at Christmas. You didn't expect a whole lot at Christmas. Kids today would laugh at what we expected. What did I expect? I knew what we'd have. We'd have coconut cake, a chocolate cake, and a couple of different kinds of pies, especially pumpkin and apple. Mama makes those old-fashioned, stacked pumpkin pies, and she still does it today.

I know that there's one thing that I probably never even told Mama that I really appreciated. There's one thing that I knew I would always get—a long-sleeved shirt. They wasn't the ones that you went to town and bought. She could get scraps of cloth from Clayburne Manufacturing, and sometimes there would be pieces in there that would make two or three shirts. Well, if it did, Gary got one, I got one, and Daddy got one. They were the flannel shirts, long sleeves for the wintertime. Mama would sew those while we were in school so we never saw them until Christmas; then we got our shirts. I have to say I looked forward to seeing them. I think today that that's neater than anything. The fact that she could make 'em and keep 'em hid, and we never found them; never saw them. But I do remember the Christmases with the Farm Families all gathered together.

Marjorie: And, at that time, there was about fifteen Farm Families living there, I think.

Morris: Yeah, they had the dairy farms, the corn crops, and the hog farms where they raised and sold hogs and, of course, that provided meat for the school. Some of the families there were the Grover Webb family and Lester Cody's family. He was in my class in school.

Let me tell you this: On the first day of school, I went in and they introduced me and my brother to Dennis Spruell and Lester Cody. Well, me and Dennis have kept in touch all of these years. Dennis was married twice and, during his second marriage, they had two children, Denise and Andy. Denise got married in March, and we went to her wedding. Me and Darlene [my wife] are Denise and Andy's godparents. They come to our house on a regular basis. I talked to him this week. I mean, it is just something. For the first five years, we had sort of lost touch because he went into school and then into service. Of course I went to school. We came back for our five-year reunion, and he was there. I met up with him, and we got started talking, and we've just kept in touch ever since. He calls me and I call him. His kids call and say, "Hey, Uncle Mo. How are you doing?" I say, "I'm doing fine."

They say, "We just thought we'd call and check on ya and make sure you were doing okay." Friendships like that are not unheard of for Rabun Gap. It would be in most schools, but not here. If you are back to any of the reunions, you see these from Mama's class on down.

Work, worship, and study—lessons we learned at Rabun Gap got us through the hard times in our lives. We knew we were blessed with what we received. I can say that with the hard work of my family, I never went to bed hungry at night—not even one night. Education prepared us to choose and succeed with a career. That prepared us for the future. I hope that I can pass these lessons in life on to my children, grandchildren, and great-grandchildren:

- Be thankful for the many blessings God grants you, serve the Lord, and strive to advance his Kingdom.
- Be alert to the needs of your fellow man and strive to help him achieve his accomplishments.
- Live every day that others will see Jesus Christ through you and your actions and reactions to life.

"It was really a blessing for us."

～Tommy and Emma Chastain～

Tommy Chastain's family lived on the school farm about a year and a half, raising corn "on the halves" with the school. Emma and her family moved to Rabun Gap from Waynesville, North Carolina. Her father traveled for work, and according to Emma, they lived "all over everywhere, in Arizona, California, and different places." Emma's dad finally settled in Rabun County, and they, too, became part of the RGNS Farm Family Program. Emma and Tommy met and fell in love while attending Rabun Gap–Nacoochee School.

—Kaye Carver Collins

Emma: The Chastains actually lived over next to the rock quarry when Tommy was little. They lived so close to the quarry that rocks would actually come through the roof of their house. Boulders would come through the house where they lived. Claude Kelly was so scared for them to stay in the house any longer that he found them a school farm house. Tommy's daddy worked at the rock quarry. When they moved to the school farm, he worked at Dillard Builders' Supply and sharecropped. Tommy's mama stayed home a short period of time when her children were small. She worked at the shirt factory for years and years and years. She worked there before Highway 441 was built.

Tommy: We bought a tractor in 1953. We were living where the rock crusher was then, about where the shop is now. We moved from the quarry in late '55 or early '56. We farmed and sharecropped with the school. I can't remember if it was a year and a half or two years that we stayed there. We put in one crop there, I know. Then we bought the Keener place. I am sure that being a part of the school farm helped my family some. We was used to working! We had chickens when we lived on Kelly's Creek. We had about four or five thousand. When we moved to the Keener place, we built a house in '58 that would hold

PLATE 123 **Tommy with his father's tractor, still stored in his barn just off the RGNS campus**

ten thousand chickens. Daddy growed chickens for T. F. Vinson. On the school farm, we didn't have chickens; we just grew corn.

Well, I don't know if I was old enough to work, but I got involved in it! I was five or six years old. Age didn't matter back then. There was no corn pickers [machinery that picks corn]. The only corn pickers you had was your two hands. There was no front-end loaders, so we had to shovel to clean the chicken houses out. I was just big enough to get into something when we lived on Kelly's Creek. When we got over here on the school farm, I was big enough to work.

Emma: We moved here in '59 and lived on the school farm from '59 to '70. We moved from North Carolina. Daddy found out about the school farm. We were very, very poor. Like everybody else back then, we didn't have nothing. He found out that you could come live on the school farm and work and be able to raise your kids and educate us there, too. Joe, Jack, and myself are the only three that went to school at Rabun Gap. I was the youngest, and I was in the sixth grade. I was about eleven.

Daddy logged with horses and mules. He had his mules or horses so well trained that he would actually take the boys to the woods. They would hook the mule to the log, and it would take it down. They would unhook the log, and the mule would go right back up to where Daddy was working. We used those horses to plow with, too—all fifteen acres. We lived up right across the mountain here, up where they have their water facility. The house is gone now. A hog farm was down below us. Raz and Myrtle Mason lived on the hog farm, and we were in the house above them. I don't know who lived in that house before we did. Since then, that house caught on fire and burnt after we moved from there. When we lived over there, law, we did peppers, cabbage, onions, beans, a lot of different things. At that time, we were toward the end of the School Farm Program; we paid rent and we did not have to divide our stuff. The school farm was phasing out, and they would rent out some of the houses. Some of the school farm people were still there, but anybody new that came in, like us, paid rent. Of course, before we came to the school, some of the houses we lived in, they didn't have running water and didn't have bathrooms. The water was just a-runnin' from a spigot there all the time. The school farm house had just one bathroom, and it was a small little thing. I don't think they was even a tub in there, just a shower.

Leroy Carpenter used to come to the house. He was from Scaly Mountain. He used to come 'cause he was a friend of Joe's. Leroy made this little thing that looked like your finger and your thumb [stuck out like your index finger and your thumb]. He would put his thumb on that thing and push it down in the ground and plant pepper like you would not believe, or plant onions. It made an indention and was just long enough to put the root down in the ground. Leroy probably still has it. They'd get on their hands and knees and crawl through that field. They had them rows of pepper plants or whatever planted in just no time flat! We planted everything you could possibly plow over in there. We did onions one year—that was a sight! We had to wash the onions and wrap five or six onions in a rubber band. We had to take the dirt off of them with running water. Lord! We did that for days and days. We just did edible corn; we didn't have farm animals. Daddy would take it to the farmers' market and sell it.

One year Daddy decided that he would rent all the ground behind where the Rabun Gap Post Office is now. It was a five-acre tract. Now, this is before they bottomed out the creek and got out all that silt and stuff out. It flooded ever' single year. He decided that we would take that field and plant it full of tomatoes. We planted tomatoes and strung them up. We had a tomato crop like you would not believe. They were about ready to take to market—five acres of tomatoes. It started raining and that creek went up, and it went up, and it went up. We had big old thirty-gallon barrels that we used to spray them by hand. The next morning when we got up, we rode by it in the old logging truck; Daddy logged on the side in the wintertime. He got all of us in the truck to drive down here and see the tomato patch. It was completely underwater! Them big barrels were floating! We lost the whole entire crop of tomatoes after we had worked and worked and worked. He didn't lease that piece of property from the school anymore! That one season got him!

We paid thirty-five dollars a month rent. That was a lot of money back then! Other places to rent was about the same. After they had to move, they lived in the sawmill houses [a row of workers' houses near the old sawmill north of Mountain City, Georgia], and they were thirty-five dollars a month also, but at Rabun Gap we also got all the land up around the house to farm. We probably farmed at least fifteen acres. It was a very interesting experience. Earl got married first; he was the oldest. He married Shelby Jean Browning, who was Benny Browning's daughter. They had the Browning Sisters; they sang and were a very popular group. Shelby Jean played the piano for the Browning Sisters. Earl met her through Carolyn. Carolyn and her were in the same class. When they got married, there was a little tiny red house out beside our big house; it was just one room. Mother and Daddy fixed that up for them. They didn't have a stove to cook or a bathroom or anything, but they were just as happy as they could be. They had just a little living area and bed, all in just one room. That way they didn't have to actually live in the house with us. After that, Carolyn married Phillip Roberson. We all got married just right in a line, and then Joe got married. He married Laura Chastain the first time. He is married to Wanda Ledford now. Jack married

Lou Ledford, and then I married Tommy. Every one of us got married in a five-year span. We are ten years apart. Mother had all of us in that ten years. Jack is the only one who has passed away.

After I graduated from high school in 1970, the school wouldn't even let you rent from them. That's when my folks moved to the sawmill house. There was still a few people on the school farm. We were there, the Lanichs were there, the Carpenters, the Arrowoods, and the Jenkinses were still there. Lake Stiles was still there. The Burdens lived in the house where they now have the Alumni House. Seems like Pope Bass lived on the "rock." We had a little tiny post office over there. At that time most of them was paying rent.

There is one thing I have kept through the years, and this is very important to me. Every year we would plant greasy-back cornfield bean seed. That bean seed was Daddy's bean seed that we brought from Waynesville, North Carolina, over to here. We have given bean seeds to everybody—I don't know how many people in Rabun County. I have kept the bean seed all these years. There were no greasy-back beans in the county until Daddy came. One time I lost the seed, and this is what I had to do to get my seed back: We gave a man seed who was one of our neighbors. We lost our seed because what you have to do is let it dry. If you don't let it dry good, it will mold, and it won't come back up. Apparently that year, we didn't let it dry enough. We had give this man some seed. We never charged for the seed. We always just give it away. I went back to this man and said, "I have lost my seed." He said, "Well, that is tough!" He said, "I've got 'em, and I'm not givin' you none!" I said, "Okay, one way or another, I will get me some seed!" This particular man brought some of his beans to Darnell's Grocery Store in Dillard, Georgia. Hubert and Butch would buy local produce. I am sure the good Lord just sent me over there to the store that morning. Here come in two bushels of the greasy-back cornfield beans. I said, "Hubert, can I pour those beans out and get the yellow ones out of it?" I said, "I'll pay you for them. I have got to have them yellow beans." He said, "Emma, what are you gonna do with the yellow beans?" I said, "I've lost my bean seed, and I can get my seed back if you will let me get them yellow beans out of there." He said, "You just go right back there and pour them out on the floor and do whatever you want to with them beans." So I got back there and got me some paper bags. I poured them two bushels of beans out on the floor and picked out every yellow bean I could find. I brought them up to the counter, and I paid for them yellow bean seeds. I brought them home, and we dried them bean seeds, and we kept our beans! If I had not been in the store that particular morning, I would have lost them seeds forever. Those beans came from that man that would not let me have the seed. He brought two bushel in there that morning and sold them to Hubert. I got 'em back! I was determined to get my beans back! The Lord has blessed us, and we have never lost our seed again. That is one thing I have still got that belongs to the family.

Mother never worked outside the home until Daddy was diagnosed with black lung in '67. Mother started working over at the Rabun Gap Craft Shop as a weaver. That was the first job Mother ever had. That was the year that Jack graduated from high school. Daddy always provided for us the best he could. We didn't have nothing, but that was all right; nobody else had anything either! They wudn't but about three people in our class that had over three pair of breeches [pants]. We couldn't wear breeches except on the days when it got really, really cold [fifteen degrees or below]. Then we had to wear skirts over the top of them. We definitely had to go to school dressed up all the time.

Every single one of us graduated from high school, and that might not have happened if we hadn't been able to move here. Mother said, "All of you *will* graduate from high school no matter what!" Now, Daddy did not graduate from high school, but he was a very intelligent man, very smart. Daddy quit school at the age of fourteen and had to get out and work. Mother did graduate from high school. When she said, "My kids are going to graduate high school," we knew she meant business. When Mother

PLATE 124 **"Like everybody else back then, we didn't have nothing."**
Emma and Tommy Chastain with two of their four grandchildren

spoke, you listened! We respected her very, very much! We did not want to disappoint our mama! It was just like smoking; she told us girls, "Ladies do not smoke, and if I catch you with a cigarette in your mouth, I will slap it down your throat!" We never smoked! She wanted to raise ladies, and she did. Every one of us actually married while we were on the school farm, and we all married in five years' time.

Daddy was a very rough man, and he was very much a mountain-type person. In his own way, though, he was very loving and giving. He would give stuff away, just like those bean seeds. He would have never thought that the man he gave them to wouldn't give them back. When we were growing up, he never did go to church, but he made sure us kids did. He'd put us on the back of that logging truck, and we'd go to church. We went ever' time the doors were open! While we was at church, he would go to the store in Dillard and buy little cakes or a big old washtub full of drinks. He used to cut everybody's hair. I've still got his hand clippers. He'd cut their hair, and there would be big gaps in it. We couldn't afford haircuts. Poor old Jack, he had a big knot in the back of his hair, and every time Daddy cut his hair, Jack would have the biggest gap back there!

I have to tell you about poor little old Myrtle Mason. She was a cook at the high school. We walked home from school with her every afternoon. If there was any leftovers from lunch, they didn't want to leave the leftovers. She would always bring one of them gallon buckets with whatever she had left over from the school for Raz's supper, so she wouldn't have to cook. Us kids would eat ever' bit of it before she could get home. She would bring home fried chicken and say, "Now, don't you eat that fried chicken! Raz is gonna have fried chicken tonight. I don't want to have to cook for him." We would eat it all! We'd leave Rabun Gap School and walk through the field over next to where Lake Stiles lived. We didn't walk the road; we walked through the field. She would get on to us for eating that every single day. We never did leave nothing for Raz! Myrtle used to make chocolate gravy. It was the wildest-looking stuff you've ever seen in your life, but it was different. It was real good. Some of the mischief we used to get into—you'd really have to talk to my brothers about that [laughing]. I didn't get into as much as they did! They was the ones that was always into something. Now, Tommy got into some stuff; he used to go to the girls' dormitory and harass Dr. Karl Anderson!

Tommy: It's a wonder they let me graduate!

Emma: Poor old Morris Brown [principal at Rabun Gap–Nacoochee]. Why, Tommy had a seat in his office with his name on it. Poor little Mrs. Oscar Cook [the school secretary], she couldn't hear. She'd say, "What are you doing in here for?" Tommy would always tell her some yarn. She'd say,

"Just sit down over there; Mr. Brown will be in here in a few minutes." They would take Mr. Brown's car; he had a Volkswagen, and they'd take it and turn it around one way, and the next day it would be turned around the other way! They might hide it! They'd pick it up and just tote it around. He was probably standing in the office watching them. We had some good times over there at that school! It was fun! There wasn't the peer pressure there is today.

Tommy: We straightened the dorm students out in about the first two weeks of school [laughing]. Some of my best friends was dorm students. My class—there is seven or eight of us that get together every year, and it has been that way since we graduated.

Emma: We were just as close to some dorm students as we were to our own community students. We all were close. That is just the way it was. There was very few that were snobby, and they were the ones that came from the really rich families. There *was* some rich families back then, too, but very few. Mostly, we all had a lot of fun. We were starving before we moved here. The way it rains here and all, you don't log and make no money in the wintertime. We needed a place to come. It was really a blessing for us. We weren't completely starving, but we didn't have enough of what we needed. All of us learned work values; Tommy's family, too. His family had the chicken farm, and if it wasn't taken care of when Jeff Chastain got home in the afternoon, there was no tomorrow! We learned what it was all about to make a living and how important things are. I am real happy that we were able to do the things we did. Who knows, we might not have been able to get a high school education if we hadn't moved to Rabun Gap. We have been blessed so much to be able to raise our three children here in Rabun County. Wesley married Rhonda Watts, and they have two boys, Dalton and Cole. Crystal married Stan Baker, and they have two girls, Anna Beth and Bella Grace. Joseph is not married. The Lord is good!

Cotton Gins and Sawmills

~ The Jordan Family ~

The stories reflected in the lives of farm families are pretty much the same whether they are told in the mountains of northeast Georgia or in the hills of northwest Georgia and neighboring Alabama. The School Farm Families of Rabun County, Georgia, planted, labored, and reaped the bountiful harvests from the rich soils of the Rabun Gap–Nacoochee School Farm in order to provide food, housing, and an education for their children. Other devoted farm families, like the Jordan family, continue in the family farm tradition today. They have farmed for generations and have experienced the same joy, apprehension, and disappointments that only a farmer can know. Spending the day with the Jordans renewed my sense of appreciation for the modern-day farmer. The equipment has been updated and technology has changed the farming industry, but just like the farmers of past decades, they must depend on faith, nature, and fate to provide for their families in what may become a losing battle. I met the Jordans through their ties to the textile industry in Rabun County. Cotton produced on the Jordan farms was shipped to Rabun Gap and used by Fruit of the Loom, which at one time was one of Rabun County's largest employers. Jim Nixon, a good friend of Foxfire who was employed there, introduced us to this wonderful family. The mill has now closed, just like textile mills across the South, but the Jordans are true farmers, still loving and clinging to the family farm and the "sometimes good life" it provides.

—Joyce Green

Tom Jordan

My name is Tom Jordan, and I was born in 1919. My great-granddaddy George Washington Jordan and his wife, Emeline, came here and settled on one hundred sixty acres bought for them by her mother and father. They came from Greenville, South Carolina. He married a lady from South Carolina who was filthy rich. There is a creek right here—Cowan Creek—and the Indians were in here. The Jordans brought mules and wagons to South Carolina and had to settle where they were. They made a livin' with farms. My granddaddy was James Thomas, and his wife's name was Nobie. That's what they called her. This land was sorta her gallery when they got married. She had a garden out there, a flower garden. I bet it was a half an acre. She cooked three meals a day, and then she would get out there with a hoe and dig up dead grass outta that garden; she would even pray in the garden. You could hear her down there by the creek. She would sing about the pains and the heartaches of the world.

PLATE 125 **"Cotton farming was passed down through the family."**
Tom and George Jordan, courtesy of the Jordan family

This land we're on right now was homesteaded by George Washington Jordan and Emeline. We still have that one hundred and sixty acres of land today. I think they started years ago, using the land for growing cotton. I can remember, in 1928, when we had a steam engine over there in the cotton field. When they came here in 1846, they started using the cotton gin. Cotton farming was passed down through the family.

The gin workers that would do the ginnin' come from south Texas. They would get through there before we started here. They weren't like migrant workers or anything because they'd go back home and have their checks mailed back there. Not many people were required to live on the farm. One time here on the farm in Centre, Alabama, we probably had three thousand acres—not the hundred and sixty acres, but the other land. Most times on a farm we shared as sharecroppers. Sharecropping is a system of agriculture where a landowner allows a sharecropper to use the land in return for a share of the crop produced on the land. Another change in operations was how we accumulated more land. A lot of land we had was for our sawmill. When we got done farmin' in the fall, we started with the sawmill to make and sell lumber. The crop was so-called laid by. From about the first of July till cotton-pickin' time, we sawmilled, made lumber, and sold lumber. The people that farmed also worked for us at the sawmillin' operation. We hauled truckloads of lumber to Rome, Georgia, from Alabama. We made some money; they were paid a dollar a day. You got ten or fifteen dollars for a load of lumber. Today, it would cost you about four or five thousand. We did that for years and years. Many times we would buy the land, cut the timber off of it, keep the land, go buy more land, cut the timber off of it, and keep the land. Our way of life and a major part of our income was the farming and milling. Income didn't have anything to do with cotton bales or anything like that. We grow the cotton, we gin it, send it to warehouses, and then we send out a bid on who will give us the most for the quantity and quality of cotton we have. That's how we have the connection with Jim Nixon, because a lot of it was sold to Fruit of the Loom, which was one of the mills in Rabun Gap, Georgia. We've had a store here forever, a store and a filling station. We got Standard Oil in 1908. It wasn't for engines back then; it was for lamps to see by. That was the beauty of it. They called the kerosene lamp oil.

The price of cotton is a hundred and fifty years old. Cotton is sold in approximately five-hundred-pound bales. There are several thousand bales. Cotton had usually been handpicked until about 1960, the beginning of mechanical cotton pickin'. A few years before, there was probably one or two scattered around. It probably took about fifteen to twenty years to get away from all handpicked to all machine picked. This was just a typical farmland county out here in Cherokee County, Alabama. There were people that lived on the farm and worked a few acres of cotton and corn. The corn was mostly used for livestock feed, and mule power was used to till the soil with. There wasn't much corn, but they knew it was for the cattle and hogs. A lot of work went into growin' the corn; the corn was used to feed the horses and mules that pulled the plows to cultivate and till the soil to grow the cotton.

Jamie Jordan

I'm Jamie Jordan, and I'm from Coosa, Georgia—River Bend Farm. Actually, my family's from Centre, Alabama, which is about eight miles from where we live now, down the river. I was born in 1953 at the main headquarters of our farm, which is where my dad and uncle live now; it is also where our cotton gin is. I went to school in Centre, Alabama, and when I was a kid, they didn't have mechanical cotton pickers. Everybody used to pick cotton by hand back then; everybody from six to eight years old, all the way up, if they were able to pick, they picked. I remember that going on until probably junior high, which would have been about 1963 or so, and that's when the mechanical pickers came out—slowly it started phasing out the handpicking days.

Back then, when everybody did the handpickin' before the mechanical pickers, we used to start school a little early, say the middle of August, and we would go to school for three or four weeks, and then the schools in the county would let out for three weeks. It was called Cotton Pickin'. Really, back then I was so young that I didn't do a lot; I helped them around the gin a little bit. Probably when I was about twelve or fourteen, mechanical pickers came in, and then at that age I started helping at the cotton gin there on the farm, when I wasn't in school and when I wasn't playin' football or basketball or something. So the older I got, the more responsibility I had.

When I was in high school, that's when my dad and uncle started working the land and getting more equipment, and the people working on their farm were down to maybe six or eight. I guess my family was probably working six hundred acres or so. Cotton pickers and tractors were still slow. Thinking back, we thought it was fast, but compared to now, it was real slow and small. The work still took a fair amount of people, but now over the

PLATE 126 "We called it lay-by when we'd lay the crops by, when we got through plowing . . . about the Fourth of July." Hardy Naugher and Jamie Jordan

years—I can remember when I was a kid—we started farming with two-row planter, one-row picker. Then it got to be four-row planter, two-row pickers. Then a lot of people went to six, but when I started cotton I went with eight rows, and the first picker I had was a two-row. When I was a senior in high school, I was working a lot, and then, when I finished high school, my dad wanted me to stay and help out on the farm in the summer and in the cotton gin in the fall. So that's what I would do, and it took me seven years to get through college.

I finished college here at Berry College in Rome, Georgia. It took me seven years, and I was taking big loads because I wasn't going but half a year out of a year. So I'd work on the farm for my dad and uncle in the summer, and then we called it lay-by when we'd lay the crops by, when we got through plowing them. Usually, it would be about the Fourth of July.

Then there would be about three or four of us off the farm go into the gin, and we'd start greasin' all the grease fittings and adjusting the belts and repairing parts that needed repairin' from the season before. We'd do that in July, roughly the first of July until about mid-September, and then that's when the cotton would start coming in, and then we'd start ginnin'. Then we would usually gin, a lot of time depending on how good the crop was, on up until close to Thanksgiving or Christmas. Then I would go back to school after the first of the year. I did that until I finished college, roughly by age twenty-four.

Berry used to have a major for agriculture, and then people got away from agriculture, so then they didn't have a major for it. So, during that seven-year period, they came back with a major, and I had a dual major in animal science and science, and I minored in industrial technology. When people around the country ask me where I went to college, I tell 'em, and they say, "We never heard of it; is it a private school?" They say, "Where is it?" I say, "Rome. I'm surprised you haven't heard of it; it's the largest campus in the world." They say, "The largest campus in the world and we haven't heard of it?" They only had eleven hundred students when I was there, but the size of the campus was thirty-three thousand acres. I think it's down to twenty-eight thousand acres now. You know, college teaches you about your majors, but it also teaches you how to do research and be persistent and to work hard and not give up. I don't know, I never really thought about it a lot—about what might have happened if I didn't go on to college. I know in our area most farmers are in their fifties or up, but very few farmers went to college. Most of them grew up on the farm, and they just usually continued working for their dad. Then, as their dad retires, they just gradually take over and continue farming. Most of them have been successful. Anybody who has stayed in it this long has had to be pretty successful, or they wouldn't have stayed in it because the margin of profits have plummeted down. I don't care how hard a worker you are, how smart you are, how you learn, what year-to-year signs you look for, when to do this, and when to do that—you can have years like we had this year and, no matter what you do, you can't prevent a loss. One more year of full-time on the farm and the gin, and I had growing pains, and my dad and uncle didn't. So I sorta split off. I really asked them, I said, "Will y'all give me the responsibility of either the gin or the farm?" They talked it over, and they said that they really wanted me to stay and help them, but they had it about the size they wanted it. I respect 'em for that, and they didn't want to get any bigger, so that's when I broke off and started farming on my own. Even though I continued to work with them, we would swap out work and all. That was 1978, and then in the summer of '80 I hired my first farmhand, which happens to be sitting across the table from me. [The interview was in the dining room, and his wife, Kelly, was sitting on the opposite side of the table.] That would be the summer I fell in love with her. It was seven years later that we got married; I can't believe it took us seven. I wanted to make sure she wouldn't quit on me, I guess. On the farm she would go with me and help me keep the trucks pulled around. Now, as time goes on, she really works a lot more now than back then. Back then she was more or less a companion and a helper and helped me move equipment around; now she actually does a lot of tractor driving in the spring. She picks up chemicals, seed, and parts for us. Y'all don't get me wrong, she doesn't go out there every day and sweat and labor and get greasy, like an old farmhand. I know she's got a lot of responsibility with Jesse, our son, and with her mom and dad and my mom and dad. Kelly probably works three weeks in the spring and three weeks in the fall, driving the tractor for me, and the rest of the year as a housewife and mother.

I've been around farming all my life, being from a cotton family, both on my mom's side and my dad's side for four generations before me. On my mom's side, her grandfather bought cotton on the cotton block in downtown Rome, Georgia. On my dad's side, they were cotton growers and buyers in general. Both families were in the cotton business pretty heavy, so when I had the opportunity, I started growing a lot of cotton. The most I have ever grown in one year was nine hundred acres. Farming has gotten more and more risky, especially over the last five to ten years. The cost of production has gone up so much that we try to spread our risk, machinery, and labor out. That's why I have broken it down into three crops (cotton, corn, and soybeans), and I pretty much stick with that.

You see, farming has changed a lot since I was a kid. Of course, growing up on a farm in the fifties, sixties, and seventies, you didn't have the Wal-Mart in town or major highways. Like most people, we lived seven miles

PLATE 127 **The Jordans—Jamie, Kelly, and son, Jesse—standing in high cotton**

out of town, so we usually went to town about once a week—we went to church on Sunday—other than going to school. We caught the school bus and rode to school. Back then, your community had a community general store, a church, and some kind of school in the community. It was almost like one big happy family, with all the sharecroppers working on the farm. It was an experience I will never forget because back then everybody's work ethic, morals, and values were different than in this day in time. Back then, everybody had a lot in common because they all worked together, lived close, played together, and went to school together. That's when we'd get off work and we'd get together and go out and play football, basketball, or softball in someone's backyard. I have a lot of good memories with real good people.

Two of those real good people have influenced my life more than anybody, other than my mama and daddy. One was the head ginner and manager on the farm, Junior Dawson, and the other one was a black woman, Jo Wood, who helped raise us as a babysitter at times and helped clean the house as a maid. Neither one of them had more than a fourth-grade education, but they were two of the best people and really as smart as anybody, not by studies or by education but by good common sense and wisdom. Both have been dead for fifteen years, and I wish I had them around today to ask them questions.

I keep farming year after year, no matter how bad it is, because I love it. But there will come a point when I'll say I've had enough if it doesn't change. My theory is, when I got in it in '78, I thought less land because there's more houses, more roads, more buildings, more shopping centers, less land, more people. We'd get what we deserved one day. Well, my dad said about the same thing when he started, way back in 1946. I don't know, I always thought the people who toughed farming out would get out of it what they paid, what it was worth one day, but I don't know if it will ever happen. The reason I say it may not ever happen is America has let several industries go; that is really what America was built on. What I can remember is that America was built on small business and family farms—the main businesses being the automobile industry, steel industries, textile industry, and agriculture, those four. The textile industry is almost extinct in this country. The steel industry is about extinct, and the automobile industry has been lost to a lot of the foreign market; it's looking like the farming industry might. Even though you think logically, things don't always work logically. I'd hate to see America depend on foreigners for their food; it's bad enough that we depend on foreign trade for our energy, our fuel. I'd hate for us to depend on it for food. Even though most of y'all are young and all and don't think you could survive without fuel to ride around on, you can. But you can't live without food and water, and I hope that our government realizes that.

It used to be that the whole South was in the cotton industry; the southern part of the United States was planting cotton—you know, when they used to say cotton was king. We are number two in the world, and China's number one. It gets tougher to find markets for my cotton. When we were kids, within a thirty-mile radius with all our cotton left to gin, we would load it on a flatbed. One guy would haul all day with one truck, and maybe another guy would haul. Usually, most of it would go to Berrytown, Lindale, or Trion, all within about thirty miles. Before then, it was all brought into town by the farmers, and the buyers bought it on the cotton block. They put it out in a warehouse, and then the buyers sold it. That's what my great-grandfather (on the Horton side) was, a buyer. In our part of the country now, Trion in Leesburg, Alabama, still buys cotton or Fruit of the Loom in Rabun Gap, Georgia—most of my cotton goes to one of them. The reasons why the cotton mills are closing, I guess, is because they can't compete worldwide with labor. In a way we can still market pretty decent because we can do it over the Internet. So in that way it's better, but then you get into distant trucking. Just the difference in going to Rabun Gap and Leesburg amounted to about two dollars a bale, which was two hundred dollars a truckload. Leesburg is just down the river from Centre; it's really close.

I don't use the old almanac signs, but some of the older guys that used to help me used to talk about it. The size of corn grows about as tall as the ceiling. Sometimes the ear will be down low to the ground and then other times in the middle, and I would say, "Why? Why is that, Hardy?" Hardy Naugher planted in the signs of a shoulder or a chest or knee or whatever. But on our scale—eleven hundred acres of row crop—I don't have the manpower or the equipment to just blow through there and do it quick. On our scale, I go from when it starts warming up, and I do what I got to do. If I run out of time on corn, then I will start on soybeans and cotton. If I run out of time on cotton, I will go back to soybeans. I try to watch the weather, but the weatherman will run you crazy if you watch him too much. You really have to just go with the flow, and that's another thing you never know. You got gut feelings on it, so then do it if the weather's good. Normally, you don't plant cotton before the first of May, but if the weather's good in late April and the corn's finished, come the twenty-fifth of April and it's hot outside, sixty-degree nights and eighty-degree days, I would say, man, I got to change the planter out and plant cotton. Get it in early to make more, you know, and go to plant a hundred twenty-five acres in one day, and you say this is going to make two and a half, three bales an acre, everything's perfect. I've had the weather change in a week's time, and it didn't look like a hundred and twenty-five seeds came up on that hundred twenty-five acres, because if it's cool and damp, you have to replant it all. Or you can plant it and it come up looking bad and skimpy, and you end up having a good growing season. Then you think, "I really need to replant it over, but I don't have time." Then you end up having a good growing season and that crop be one of the best crops. I've seen some of the best-looking ones be some of the sorriest-looking ones. So you can't ever give up. You have to keep working all the way through.

As far as people helping me, I have one Guatemalan living on the farm helping me full-time. He's the first full-time helper I think I've ever had, other than Kelly. On a farm my size, to really be efficient, I need four people—three including myself. At times I could use more, and I do have a few part-time guys come through, but they may come through when you're busy, they may come through when you're not. You just never know 'cause they usually work other jobs. So I have Felipe. He and I do the majority of it, and then Kelly and Jesse do some. So you do what you got to do. That's one reason why we have gone to bigger equipment. Now I'm on ten-row equipment. I plant with a ten-row planter. I pick five rows at a time, six rows of corn. I've found out that a lot of people are going to bigger equipment. A normal day for me has changed a lot, too, over the years.

I used to not think about giving up on farming and doing something else. I think about it sometimes now because it keeps getting harder and harder to make ends meet. I think this is twenty-eight years I've been farming, twenty-nine maybe. To start with, I get up at six thirty, eat, get my chemicals and seed ready, and go to the farm. I drive fifty miles, work till dark—sometimes after dark—and then drive home. Dark may be at six o'clock this time of year, but in the summer, it's nine o'clock. Then, in '86, we bought a used cotton gin to keep up with the pace. So we bought a used cotton gin in Arkansas, went out there, and moved it back to Centre. The same year, we got in the aerial application business, which is also called crop dusting. I bought eight hundred acres when Kelly and I got married. I would get up early enough to be at the airstrip before daylight. I would do this because our first load would need to be out at daylight. While the heat's not up, the chemicals work better. I would start then, and we would either go to the farm or stay at the airstrip until dark. I'd get home nine or ten o'clock and eat. So it was a long day. Backing up a little bit, the older guy that used to go with me, he said, "Jamie, you're gonna make an old man out of yourself fast if you try to burn a candle at both ends." I used to laugh at him. When I was in my twenties, I'd say, "Cicero, you can't wear me out." If Cicero was here now, I'd say, "Yeah, you know what you're talking about, Cicero." He was about eighty years old. A year or two after I got married, I hurt my back bad. I'd never slowed down enough to realize how tired I was getting until I was laying in the bed and thinking about things I was doing right and doing wrong. I realized how I was wearing myself out. It was a way of God telling me, "You need to slow down." I still work a lot of long hours, but as time's gone on, I've gotten up later and come in earlier. Instead of working sixteen to eighteen hours a day, I'm down to working ten to twelve hours a day, depending on the year. A lot of times when I'm not in the fields, I'm on the phone or with a lawyer, farm officer, banker, or tax man or whatever. So it's still work, but used to, we used to work year around, and we even did winter projects. When Jesse was maybe five or six years old, I said no more am I doing winter projects; I'm gonna spend my winter resting and with my family. I pretty much have stuck with that. Now most days we'll work ten or twelve hours, but I still see some sixteen or eighteen. Like this time of year, when it starts getting later with cotton in the field, you can't pick any of the crops with dew on them. You have to wait till the dew dries off during morning, and then when the dew comes on early after dark, you have to quit. You can do the cleaning, service, and maintenance work, you know, at other times, but if it's cloudy or windy, you can pick all night; I mean, you can harvest all night. I guess the longest I've ever worked at one time, which is not good, but you do what you got to do—it was me and a Mexican, Santiago. We worked thirty-two hours straight one time, and it went back to the weatherman. He said it was one hundred percent chance of rain. It was getting close to Christmas. I've had crops in the field and lost a bunch of money because you can't get it out when winter rains set in. The weatherman was giving one hundred percent chance of heavy rain by daylight, and it was December twentieth, and so I said I was going to pick as long as I could. I kept saying, "Santiago, you can go in anytime." He'd say, "No, I'm gonna stay with you, boss." About every two hours I'd say, "You go in, you go in." Well, we made it to daylight, and they brought us something to eat. My other helper came in, and well, it didn't rain. It didn't rain until dark that day. Even though we were tired, yeah, I felt like I couldn't make it. The last day, the last ten hours, were tough because I thought, "Rain at daylight, I can go in. It's gonna rain." And it didn't, and you can't go in when there's cotton to pick and bills to pay. That's the longest day but we still get into some fifteen, sixteen-hour days. You know, your priorities change in life. I mean, I still got the bills to pay and I go to pay 'em, but I also realize that if you don't take care of yourself then nobody else is either. So a lot of times my fourteen, fifteen hours, I don't do that very often. I go to the house. I just say if that's not good enough, then it's just not good enough.

I know it's a little scary to think about my long working hours, 'cause I've had several friends that their wives leave them. It's no fun working long hours, because you don't always get to eat and see each other and wind down at night and all. Then, at the same time in the back of your head, you know that this isn't year-round. This isn't like a dairy. After we get over the rush of it, then we just spend a lot of time together. I guess we always got that to look forward to. Kelly has a nursing degree. She worked four years at the hospital; then, when we got married, she started working at a doctor's office in town and worked there four years. When we got Jesse [their son] in '90, she quit and didn't go back.

Kelly's really a main part in the operation. She keeps the clothes clean, keeps us fed, takes care of Jesse, takes care of me, picks up chemicals and seed and parts, pays the bills, sends the bills out, and drives a tractor six weeks of the year.

Well, Jesse really enjoys being around farming; it's a good experience, a good place to grow up. Even though he enjoys being around it, I don't think he's going to be a farmer. It's a good job, and he has a lot of respect for it. Something that keeps me going is, it's just a dream of mine. I mean, it's as good of a farm as there is in the country, I guess in the world. I have a lot of guys come in and say they would like to live here if I ever left, which I never would, of course.

Jesse, for about the last ten years, has had a sweet-corn patch. The main reason we got into growing corn is, I just didn't have the manpower and equipment to get a big cotton crop out timely. Our land is bottomland, which usually produces corn good, and so it spreads our risks out in three different crops. If corn prices are good and cotton's bad, you know, it spreads out into the growing seasons. You may have a good year growing corn [and a] bad year growing cotton. It spreads the risks out; plus, you can start planting a month earlier, and you can start harvesting a month earlier. So really it makes you two to three months more efficient. Plus, rotation is very good for the land. It's about the one and only thing that we can control that will pay a big dividend. The harvest time for corn is first, and then it depends on the variety of soybeans. Some soybeans are before cotton, some are with cotton, and some are after cotton. I spread the work out over a period of time so that it spreads your work, equipment, labor, and risk.

The five-row cotton picker I bought was a year old, and I rented it as a new one. To rent it a year is twenty to thirty thousand dollars, and you don't use it for about two months out of the year. So it was used when I bought it. I think it would have been about a hundred and sixty thousand dollars new. Now that same picker would be two twenty [$220,000]. I know they're coming out with a cotton picker that builds its own module. You cut out labor and equipment, and it builds half a module. I don't remember the list price, but I think they sell for four hundred fifty thousand dollars. I really don't think anyone could pay for any of this equipment, but you can't do it without it, so you just make your payment on it. I look at paying for it, but a lot of people look at buying it, using it for a few years, and trading it, and so it's like renting.

We worked hard when we were young, but we had a lot of work. Now, with the big equipment, if we're not working, there's nothing being produced. It's like that because we don't have people out there working. In other words, when you had two four-row planters, if one of them broke down, the other one was still going. Now if you break one down, it's a lot more stressful. It's sorta sad that I remember more bad experiences than good ones. I'm not a negative person, but I remember when I've been hurt, you know, when I hurt my back, when I hurt my leg. There has been a lot of good times, too. I'd say one of the best experiences that we have now is usually, once a year, we'll have our church, Sunday school class, and close friends out and have a cookout and a cotton ride. Instead of hayrides, we have cotton rides. Sometimes we do it for the youth, sometimes we do it for our class, and sometimes we'll do it for all age groups.

Editor's note: *We would like to extend our appreciation to Jim Nixon, who traveled to Alabama to introduce us to the Jordan family. We'd also like to express our sympathies to Jamie, Kelly, and Jesse, who lost the beloved patriarch of their family, Tom Jordan, in spring 2010. He will be missed by us all.*

With His Own Two Hands

Joyce Green

While strolling along in the mountains,
Beholding the sun's golden glow,
Adoring the wildflowers there blooming,
Around the old log cabin door.
My grandpa had built it for Grandma
With love and his own two hands,
A reminder of love once unshaken,
Empty and lonely it stands.

On the porch sits a cane-bottomed rocker,
It had once rocked my mother at night,
But the chair only rocks in the wind now,
'Neath the shadow of the sun's early light.
With his own two hands he once labored
In the fields at the breaking of dawn,
Providing a life for his family,
From the old home he seldom did roam.

At the end of the path an old barn stands,
With some old handmade tools and a sled,
Not needed or wanted for years now,
Since Grandpa and Grandma are dead.
In the hall of the barn hangs the bullwhip,
As a child he had helped me to braid,
With his own two hands he would teach me
With a love that I know will not fade.

We'll Tell You How
The Traditional Ways

With His Own Two Hands

We'll Tell You How

Our ancestors relied on knowledge, skills, and their own two hands to make, build, or repair homes, toys, tools, furniture, clothing, and other items needed for daily living. The following articles include detailed instructions for braiding a bullwhip and building a shaving horse. Directions and steps are also included for a drawknife and a five-in-one sled. These items were necessities for families who once inhabited many of the log cabins scattered through the mountains of Appalachia.

As depicted in the lyrics of "With His Own Two Hands," log cabins served as the dwellings for early settlers in Appalachia. Many have stood the test of time and are still standing today. There is just something about an old log cabin that can't be explained. Crossing the threshold takes you deep into another era before progress spoiled the tranquillity of life. It is a safe place with a homey feel. The walls seem to tremble with the kindred spirits of dwellers from the past. Many families were born, raised, and died within the confines of this one-room shelter, which they called home. The carefully hand-hewed and hand-notched logs, split-shingled roof, and wooden windows, held closed by wooden latches, protected its inhabitants from the wind, rain, and snow. The cabins were crafted to last for at least a hundred years, pending an occasional roof repair with newly split wooden shingles. Wildflowers and native azaleas surrounded the humble dwelling where fireflies glowed in the night and the lonesome sound of the whippoorwill could be heard from the distant "holler" (hollow). Children played with rag dolls and wooden wagons and skipped around the cabin with June bugs on a string. The dolls were hand sewn by mothers and grandmothers, and oftentimes Grandpa spent countless hours building the wooden wagons that raced down the hills and through the valleys of the old homeplace.

—*Joyce Green*

Tying a True Lover's Knot

~Research by Lee Carpenter~

For this common variant of the true lover's knot, also known as a fisherman's knot, two simpler knots lock together to create a strong join between two pieces of line. The face of the completed join will have a distinct appearance—the two individual lines are locked together perfectly side by side.

Begin by making a simple overhand knot. Hold the first piece of line (rope, string, yarn, etc.) in your right hand, with the free end hanging to the left. Grab the free end with your left hand and bring it down, around, and behind the line to make a loop. **(A)** Pull the end over the line and through the loop, pulling it far enough through so that the knot will not unravel, but do not pull the loop closed yet.

Still holding the first knot with your right hand, take the second piece of line with your left hand and **(B)** feed it through the first knot's loop, coming from

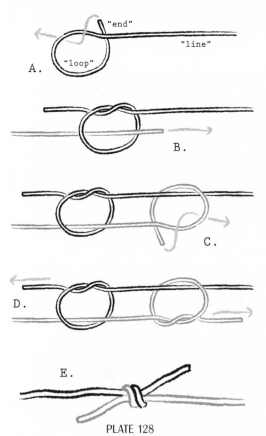

behind the loop. Hold the knot and second line together with your left hand. Grab the end of the second line with your right hand, bring it up and over the first line, down behind both lines, then **(C)** over the second line and through the new loop to form the second overhand knot.

Next, **(D)** gently snug down each overhand knot by pulling each end and its matching line. Now grab each line and pull to bring the two knots together. After a firm pull, the dangling ends will usually appear to move up or down from their initial positions as the knot sets when fully tightened, and then you will see **(E)** the two closely paired strands of line that give this knot its name.

PLATE 128

The Adaptable Five-in-One Sled

~Kyle Bolen~

At a festival held at John Rice Irwin's Museum of Appalachia in Clinton, Tennessee, we met Kyle Bolen, who was demonstrating how to construct wooden sleds. Even though we have done articles about traditional wooden sleds in the past, we became interested in Kyle's methods because the parts he uses can be interchanged and combined in different ways to make at least five distinct, functional sleds. The parts all fit together without the use of nails, so they can be quickly dismantled and reassembled. With the help of his grandson (shown with Kyle seated in the city sled on page 438), he can take a sled apart and put it together in different form in just a matter of minutes.

On the following pages, the five different sleds Kyle makes from interchangeable parts are shown. The parts he uses are listed with approximate measurements. Should you wish to make such sleds, you would probably want to use your own measurements to make the sleds fit your particular needs.

—Brant Sturgill and Rance Fleming

PLATE 129

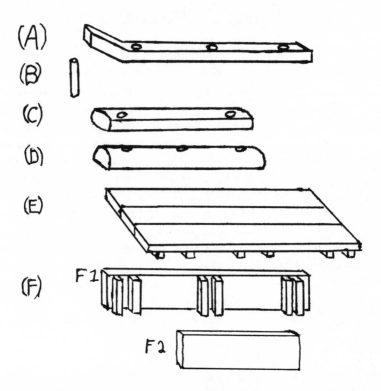

PLATE 130 **The parts needed to make the sleds on the following pages:**

A. Two sourwood sled runners, 6½' long by 8" by 5" wide

B. Six short wooden pegs, 8" long by 2" in diameter

C. Six main support beams (three to hold up the floor of the sled
and three that can be used as seats), 4' long by 4" thick by 5" wide

D. Two long support beams, 5' long by 4" thick by 5" wide

E. Enough 1"-thick boards nailed onto six cross braces
to form a floor 3½' wide by 5' long. The six wooden cross
braces are spaced under the floor so that they straddle each
of the three support beams (C) to keep the floor from sliding.

F1. Two sideboards, 5' long by 12" wide by 1" thick, with vertical wooden
strips nailed to the outside in pairs, spaced so that the long wooden pegs (G)
will come up between them from the runners to help stabilize the bed

F2. Two end sideboards, 3½' long by 12" wide by 1" thick,
that slide down into vertical wooden strips nailed in pairs
to the inside corners of the long sideboards

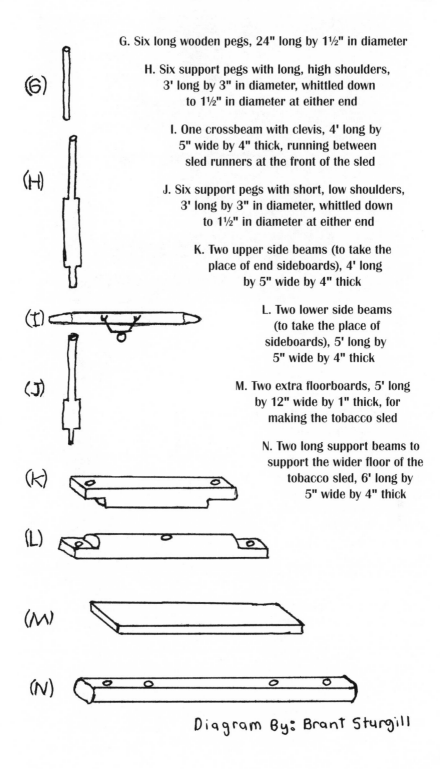

G. Six long wooden pegs, 24" long by 1½" in diameter

H. Six support pegs with long, high shoulders, 3' long by 3" in diameter, whittled down to 1½" in diameter at either end

I. One crossbeam with clevis, 4' long by 5" wide by 4" thick, running between sled runners at the front of the sled

J. Six support pegs with short, low shoulders, 3' long by 3" in diameter, whittled down to 1½" in diameter at either end

K. Two upper side beams (to take the place of end sideboards), 4' long by 5" wide by 4" thick

L. Two lower side beams (to take the place of sideboards), 5' long by 5" wide by 4" thick

M. Two extra floorboards, 5' long by 12" wide by 1" thick, for making the tobacco sled

N. Two long support beams to support the wider floor of the tobacco sled, 6' long by 5" wide by 4" thick

(6)
(H)
(I)
(J)
(K)
(L)
(M)
(N)

Diagram By: Brant Sturgill

PLATE 131

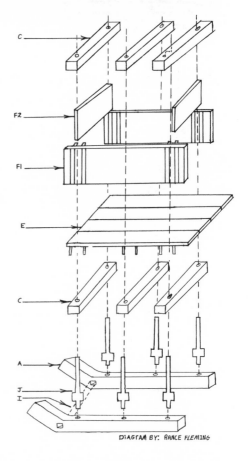

PLATE 132 This sled is named the city sled, and it is used for going back and forth to town. The one-piece standards (J) are designed to raise the bed up off the ground and to hold the sides firmly in place at the same time. These standards (visible on sled to left in photo above) are long enough to extend up above the sides so that extra beams (C) can be fitted down over them and used for seats. Nailed under the floor of the sled (E) are cross braces that fit over the floor beams (C) to keep the bed from sliding.

DIAGRAM BY: RANCE FLEMING

PLATE 133

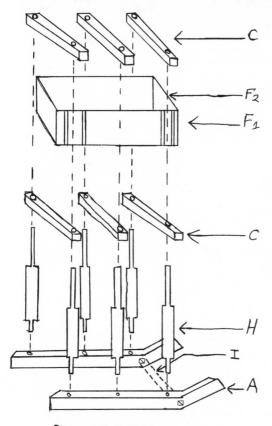

PLATE 134 The Ford Creek sled was used to haul people through obstacles, such as creeks or deep mud, that required the bed to be raised well above the ground. The standards are designed to keep the bed supported up off the ground. The top beams (C) slip down over the tops of the standards to serve as seats.

Diagram By: Jeff Giles

PLATE 135 The country sled was made very sturdy and low to the ground for use on cleared hillside fields and flat ground. It could haul anything from rocks to firewood to hay—anything not requiring sideboards.

PLATE 136

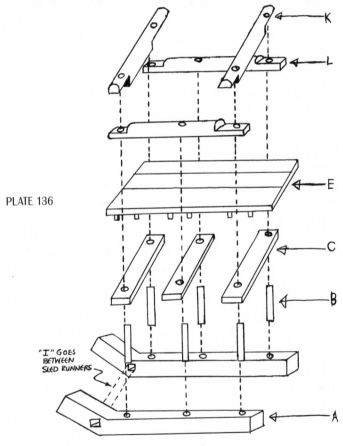

"I" GOES BETWEEN SLED RUNNERS

Diagram By: Brant Sturgill

PLATE 137 The tobacco sled was made to haul tobacco from the fields to the barn. It was designed wider so that it could hold more. It is built like the country sled, except that it has longer beams (N) to hold additional floorboards (M).

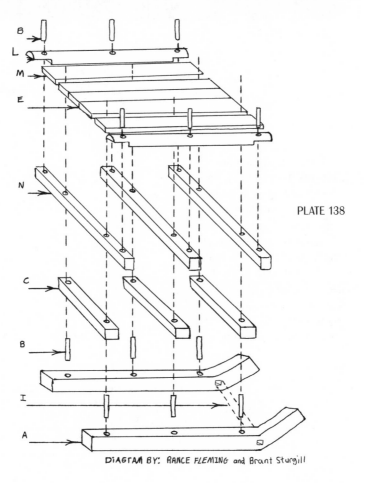

PLATE 138

DiAGrAM BY: RANCE FLEMING and Brant Sturgill

PLATE 139

PLATE 140 The rock country sled was designed to haul rocks and wood. It was constructed well so that it could stand rough use. The rock country sled has three long pegs (G) on each side (F1 and F2) to hold it together. Unlike the country sled, which has very short sides, this one has tall sides so that it can haul larger loads.

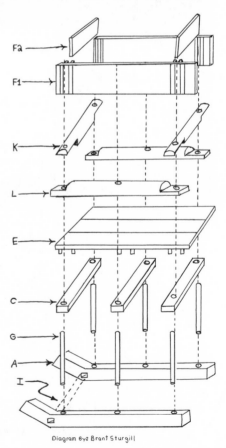

Diagram By: Brant Sturgill

Building an Oak Shaving Horse
~with Claud Connell~

Claud Connell, a longtime Foxfire friend, taught himself to work with wood from a series of books called The Woodwright's Shop *by Roy Underhill and* The Foxfire Book. *During the spring of 2009, Foxfire student Keifer Phillips spent time with Claud, learning how to build a shaving horse. Although it was tough work, the finished product is one that not many can claim to have spent time on, and Keifer doesn't regret the hard work that he put into making his very first shaving horse. Keifer took what he learned from Claud and later created his own shaving horse.*

Sadly, just as we were completing the first draft of this anniversary book, we received the news that our friend Claud Connell had passed away. We'll be forever grateful to Claud for demonstrating his great gift for woodworking at our events and for passing along some of those skills to the younger generation here at Foxfire. He did not want his craft to be a dying art, a concern he expressed to us over the many years we knew him, and just as he had hoped, some part of it will live on with Keifer.

The Foxfire Magazine class would like to give special thanks to Lyle Phillips, industrial arts teacher, and Barry Stiles, Foxfire museum curator, for their help throughout this project.

—Ben McClain

PLATE 141 **Keifer Phillips initially worked with Claud at The Foxfire Museum and Heritage Center during spring break in 2009.**

My parents encouraged me to get an education. They instilled in me confidence that I could accomplish anything I wanted if I was willing to do what it takes to get it done. I have found that to be true. When I wanted to learn how to make wooden buckets, I read all I could find about the subject and then set out to make one. I made lots of shavings and mistakes before I made the first one that even resembled a bucket. I never gave up. I can now do it pretty well, although there is still more to learn and improvements to be made.

The only thing I can say about my experiences that young people can benefit from is that they can accomplish anything they want to, provided they are willing to do what it takes to get it done. I have found that true. I have pretty much done anything I set out to do. It did not always come easy, but I just kept at it, made changes, and kept a positive attitude.

I don't remember just when I started, but about twenty to thirty years ago I was reading in *The Foxfire Book* and other books and became interested in traditional woodworking. I also read Roy Underhill's Woodwright books and whatever others I could find on the subject. Then I set out and, by trial and error, I learned how to build traditional furniture and chairs using mostly hand tools and traditional methods. I use hand-cut mortise-and-tenon and dovetail joints whenever possible. I have built pie safes [wooden cupboards] with hand-punched tin panels, gun cabinets, swinging baby cradles, a blanket chest, tables and chairs, and numerous other items.

Reading about butter churn making in *The Foxfire Book* interested me, so I obtained a blacksmith forge, anvil, and some blacksmith tools, and I made the rest of the tools I needed to make the buckets and churns. I became acquainted with Mr. Lee Tippett of *Foxfire 5* and learned a lot about blacksmithing from him.

I then learned to make buckets and churns by trial and error. It took a while for me to develop the required skills. I just kept making shavings and mistakes until I made more and more shavings and less and less mistakes. I can now do it pretty well. I enjoy going to craft shows and festivals, demonstrating bucket-making. I try to sell a few items to help pay expenses. I don't make any money doing this. I could never make a living at it, because it takes too long to make things.

Making a Shaving Horse

A shaving horse is a combination of a workbench and a simple wooden vise, actuated with a foot pedal underneath. The pedal is connected in such a way that it can hold one piece of wood firmly, leaving the hands free to use a drawknife. One of the main uses of the shaving horse is making chairs and tables. Before chairs were available through retailers and furniture stores, those building their own houses were under obligation to craft all of their furniture from logs. A chair is not the only thing that can be made by a shaving horse. Objects such as stools, butter churns, wooden buckets, and handles for other tools were also made with the shaving horse. Before you were able to build all these things, you had to be able to build your own shaving horse.

Things You Will Need:

The first thing that is needed is a log. The preferred wood to craft the shaving horse with is red oak, 6 feet in length and around 12 inches in diameter.

The following tools are needed:
- adze
- broadax
- drawknife
- hammer or mallet
- handsaw
- hatchet
- 2 timber wedges
- ½-inch and 2-inch drill bits and auger
- plane (optional)

Getting Started

The first step is to find a log or tree that is the right diameter and cut it to a length of approximately 72 inches (6 feet). It should be approximately 12 inches in diameter. Split the log in order to create sections. The log should

PLATE 142 **Claud steadies the red oak log with a cant hook as Keifer drives in timber wedges, working on the second split.**

be split into three pieces, one center piece that will have a rectangular shape approximately 3 inches thick, and two side pieces that will be approximately 4½ inches thick, with one rounded side and one straight, flat side.

To split the log, use timber wedges. A wedge is a thin pyramid-shaped object that is driven into a log or piece of wood to split it. The leapfrog method of wedging is an effective way to perform a controlled log split using two timber wedges. To perform a leapfrog split, drive the first wedge into the log approximately 4½ inches from the end. After the first wedge is driven in, a space will appear approximately 3 to 6 inches past the first wedge. Drive the second wedge into this space, thereby loosening the first wedge and allowing for its removal from the log. While the first wedge is removed, the second will remain in place. Insert the first wedge into the new space in front of the second wedge. Repeat this process down the entire length of the log until the first piece completely splits away from the log. Move to the opposite side of the log and repeat the process.

PLATE 143 **Shaping the bench with an adze**

Shaping the Bench

After the log is in three sections, use the middle section (approximately 3 inches thick and flat on two sides) to fashion the bench for the shaving horse. It may be necessary to use an adze to remove inconsistencies and unwanted slivers of wood. This can be accomplished by standing on top of the beam and swinging the adze in a downward motion toward the toe of your boot. The object is to skim the blade of the adze across the top of the log, removing a thin layer with each stroke. Be careful not to remove large chunks of wood or make the surface more uneven. [Warning: Improper use of an adze can cause bodily damage.] Once the bench has been roughly shaped using an adze, it can be further smoothed using a wood plane or a drawknife to level and smooth the eventual upper seat surface.

PLATE 144 **Smoothing the bench with a hand plane**

Creating the Legs

The next step is making the legs of the shaving horse. Use one of the two round-sided sections from step 1 to make the legs. Saw the section into two 19-inch sections. Using the broadax, split both lengths into roughly 3-inch-square pieces.

PLATE 145 **Rough shaping of the legs with a hatchet**

After the four sections have been split, use the hatchet or ax to trim down the edges of the legs until they are roughly round. They should be about 3 inches in diameter on one end (the bottom of the leg), and then taper them down to 2 inches on the other end (the top).

On the tapered end of each leg, use the handsaw to make a 2-inch-deep cut perpendicular to the grain of the wood. These cuts will have small wooden wedges driven into them in the next step.

PLATE 146 **Slitting the top of a leg with a handsaw**

Attaching the Legs

Using an auger with a 2-inch bit, drill two holes on each end of the bench, working from the top (smoother) side of the bench. The holes should be centered approximately 4 inches from the respective ends of the bench, 3 inches from the sides, and drilled at a slight angle to the outside. The holes should be drilled all of the way through the bench.

After the holes are drilled, insert the tapered ends of the legs into the holes. If the legs are tapered correctly, they should fit snugly. Use a mallet to make sure that each leg is snug in its hole. Insert a wooden wedge, perpendicular to the grain of the bench, into the cut in the top end of each leg. Use the mallet to drive the wedges securely into place. This will cause the tapered end of the leg to expand and tighten within the drilled hole. Use the handsaw to trim away any part of the wedge or leg that sticks above the surface of the bench.

PLATE 147 **The top of a leg in place through the bench, with a securing wedge inserted and trimmed flush**

Once the legs are securely in place, they should be checked to ensure they

PLATE 148 **The bench (on its side) with legs inserted**

are of equal length and that the bench itself sits level. If the bench rocks, place the bench upside down on a flat surface. Measure from the flat surface to the end of each leg to find the shortest leg. Measure and mark the other legs at the height of the shortest leg, and use the handsaw to trim each of the legs to the same length, cutting parallel to the flat surface.

Creating the Dumbhead

The dumbhead is the actual vise part of the shaving horse that holds the wood you are shaving in place. It applies a downward force against the piece of wood, locking it in place against the shelf. This allows the woodworker to use both hands to work the drawknife.

To create the dumbhead, cut the remaining log section into a piece that is roughly 32 inches long and 6 inches wide. (It's better to have too much than not enough.) The finished length of the dumbhead will be about 30 inches. Begin by making a cut about 6 inches from the end of your log section, square across the face [flat side], to a depth of 2 inches. This cut defines the gripping surface along the bottom of the dumbhead. Next, saw in along this cut from both sides of the log, leaving a 2-inch-thick trunk in the center of the log.

Using a wedge, split the extra wood from the sides and face of the log section, on the long side away from the face cut, leaving a solid 2-inch-square center section intact for the neck. Shape the dumbhead itself with the broadax or hatchet, rounding the top end, away from the face, and narrowing the head to about 6 inches across by splitting away the thin, rounded edges of the log section.

PLATE 149 **The dumbhead with all mounting holes drilled: foot-pedal hole at the bottom (right), mounting holes just below the head**

The final step in creating your dumbhead is drilling the mounting holes. Measure approximately 2 inches down the neck from the base of the head, and then use the auger and ½-inch bit to drill the first mounting hole in the neck, parallel to the face and at least ½ inch from the front edge of the neck. Move down the neck approximately 1 inch each time, drilling at least four holes. Move to the far end (bottom) of the neck, and drill one final hole, centered in the neck and approximately 2 inches from the end. This hole will be used to secure the foot pedal.

Creating the Bench Inset for the Dumbhead

To create the rectangular hole in the bench where the dumbhead swings, use the auger and 2-inch bit to drill a hole, centered across the bench, approximately 16 inches from the end of the bench. Follow this hole with three more, leaving ¼ inch of wood between holes, moving away from the end. After the holes are drilled, use the hatchet to cut out the remaining wood and square the corners of the hole, leaving a rectangular hole about 2 inches wide and 9 inches long. (A chisel can be used instead of the hatchet for a more accurate cut.)

Creating the Shelf

To create the shelf, use one of the leftover sections split from the original log. Cut and split the board to approximately 30 inches in length, 2-inch thickness, and 8-inch width. To create the angled surface where the shelf joins the bench, make a handsaw cut across the width of the board, starting about 6 inches from one end and cutting through the board at a shallow angle, aiming for the center of the board's narrow end. This surface may need further cutting or hatchet adjustments to create an even join with the bench.

The next step is the stabilizing block, which raises the vise end of the shelf above the bench. Cut and split a 5-inch-tall, 8-inch-wide plank, around 2 inches thick, and square both ends with the saw. One end (the bottom) remains square to join the bench. The other (top) end needs to be angled to join evenly with the shelf. Place the saw approximately 1 inch from the end of the block and cut, across the width, at an angle toward the opposite corner of the board. This surface may also require later fine-tuning to create an even, solid join to the shelf.

Mounting the stabilizing block is the next step. Measure about 28 inches from the end of the bench (the end with the dumbhead mounting hole), and drive two small finishing nails partly into the bench, about 4 inches in from each side. Hold the stabilizing block on top of these nails, square end down, making sure the block is perpendicular (square) with the bench, and tap it down firmly a few times with the mallet. Do not drive the block down very far onto the nails—all that is needed is to score matching marks onto the square bottom end of the block. Remove the block and pull the nails out of the bench. Now use the auger and ½-inch bit to drill 1-inch-deep holes into the bench, centered on the nail holes. Then drill matching 1-inch-deep holes into the bottom of the block, centered on the score marks left by the nails. Drive 2-inch pegs, approximately ½ inch in diameter, into each of the holes in the bench. Line the pegs up with the holes in the stabilizing block and use the hammer to firmly tap it into place. The stabilizing block should now be secured tightly to the bench.

Now test-fit the shelf by holding it in place with the square end extending past the stabilizing block by 2 inches or so, and the angled end, facedown, resting on the end of the bench. Use the hatchet or handsaw to trim the angled surfaces of the shelf and the stabilizing block, if necessary, until an even, flat join is achieved.

Once the fit is satisfactory, have an assistant hold the shelf in place, likely by putting his weight on it. Using the auger and ½-inch bit, drill two 4-inch-deep holes through the shelf, vertically, straight down into the stabilizing block. The holes should be centered in the thickness of the block and roughly 2 inches in from the sides of the shelf. Next, drill two 3-inch-deep holes through the bench end of the shelf, also straight down into the bench. These holes should be 3 inches from the end of the shelf (not the end of the bench) and 2 inches in from the sides of the shelf.

Remove the shelf, and drive two ½-inch-diameter, 4¼-inch-long pegs into the holes in the top of the stabilizing block. Drive two ½-inch-diameter, 3¼-inch pegs into the holes in the bench. Align the holes in the shelf with

PLATE 150 **A wooden mounting peg, driven through the shelf into the stabilizing block**

the pegs, and apply pressure to the shelf to begin seating it into place. From this point, the hammer or mallet may be used to finish completely driving the shelf down onto the pegs to securely attach it to the bench and the stabilizing block. Work evenly around the shelf, driving in small steps at each peg, being careful not to split the shelf or the stabilizing block. Once the shelf is solidly against the stabilizing block and bench, use the handsaw to cut the pegs off even with the shelf surface for a smooth, finished appearance.

Once the shelf is attached to the bench, make the dumbhead mounting hole in the shelf much the same as it was done for the bench. Drill the first 2-inch hole, centered across the shelf, about 8 inches down from the high end of the shelf. Follow it with two more holes, leaving ¼ inch of wood between them, working down the shelf. Use the hatchet to clean out and square the corners, leaving a 2-inch-by-6-inch rectangular hole.

Attaching the Dumbhead to the Shaving Horse

The first step in attaching the dumbhead to the shaving horse is drilling mounting holes into the shelf. Measure and mark a line across the shelf, about 2 inches down from the upper end of the mounting hole. Using the auger and ½-inch bit, move to the side of the shelf, center the bit in the thickness of the shelf, align the drill with the mark made across the shelf,

PLATE 151 **Mounting holes for the dumbhead, drilled through the shelf**

and drill horizontally through the narrow edge of the shelf, into the rectangular mounting hole. Move to the opposite side of the shelf and drill an identical hole.

Once the mounting holes are drilled, it is time to mount the dumbhead to the shelf. Mounting requires either a 6-inch-long dowel with a diameter of ½ inch (made from wood in the same manner as

PLATE 152 **Installing the dumbhead**

the legs) or a metal rod or anchor bolt with the same dimension. Slide the dumbhead down through the rectangular holes in the shelf and the bench. Slide the dowel through the hole in the side of the shelf, any mounting hole on the dumbhead, and finally through the other side of the shelf. The dumbhead should be securely mounted in place and swing freely.

If the height of the dumbhead needs to be adjusted, simply remove the dowel, select a mounting hole at a different height on the dumbhead, and reinsert the dowel. When working on a very thick piece of wood, use the holes lower on the neck; for thinner pieces, use the higher ones. This ensures that the dumbhead keeps a tight grip on the wood.

Creating the Foot Pedal

The next thing to make for your shaving horse is the foot pedal for the bottom of the dumbhead neck. To do this, find a piece of scrap log from the earlier splitting. Use the hatchet or broadax to split a piece at least 1 inch thick (can be more), 12 inches long, and 6 inches wide.

Using the ½-inch bit with the auger, drill four holes in a square pattern, approximately 1½ inches apart, centered across the width of the pedal, and about 2 inches from the center along the length. Use the hatchet or chisel to square the hole in the pedal, which should be about 2½ inches square. This is where the neck of the dumbhead will be inserted.

Once the pedal is in place, to keep it from falling off of the neck, place it above the hole in the bottom of the neck and insert a ½-inch-diameter wooden peg, 4 to 5 inches in length, through the hole so that it supports the pedal on both sides of the dumbhead neck. [A piece of metal may be substituted for added strength.]

PLATE 153 **The foot pedal is held on the dumbhead shaft by a peg.**

Finished Product

Once the final pieces are in place, the finished product should look very similar to the shaving horse pictured below. The shaving horse will be approximately 6 feet in length, 12 inches wide, and 18 inches high from the floor to the top of the bench [seat]. All that is left to do is find a piece of wood, sharpen your drawknife, and begin using the shaving horse. It is always a good idea to test the strength and mechanics of the shaving horse fully before using it. This will prevent injuries and will allow troubleshooting of any minor problems.

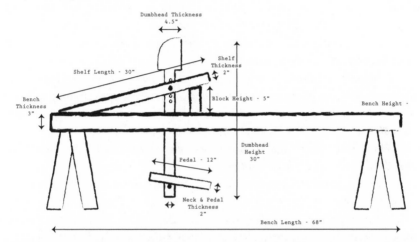

PLATE 154 This diagram provides rough dimensions for the major parts of the shaving horse, and can be used to create a materials list if not using a full log.

PLATE 155 This is the shaving horse that Keifer and Claud built in spring 2009. It lives on a porch at The Foxfire Museum and Heritage Center and is routinely used for woodworking demonstrations during guided tours and other museum events.

Chair Bottoming with Poplar Bark

~Harriet Echols, Elvin Cabe, and Nelson Cabe~

We have published articles in our Foxfire book series on chair making before and on bottoming chairs with corn shucks and oak splits, but we have never done one on using poplar bark (from the tulip poplar, or Liriodendron tulipifera*) to bottom chairs. Mrs. Harriet Echols told us that her parents used to bottom all their own chairs and she had been unsure about what time of the year the bark should be taken off the tree, so she checked with her neighbor, her son-in-law's mother, Mrs. Mary Cabe. Granny Cabe told her the bark should be stripped from small poplar trees in late April or early May, as this is the time when the bark separates best from the tree.*

On our first visit to her home, Mrs. Echols took us down to a field behind the house and showed us where some young poplar trees were growing that were suitable for making bark strips to use for chair bottoms. We tried splitting the bark off one of the poplars, then peeling the bark off the inner layer. It wasn't easy for us to split the strips, so Mrs. Echols suggested that we come back another day and she'd have some of her neighbors help us.

On our return visit in early May, Nelson Cabe and his brother, Elvin Cabe, cut down a tall, straight poplar, about 6 inches around, and showed us how to strip the bark from the tree, then how to peel off the outer bark, leaving the inner bark to bottom a chair with. They even came on up to Mrs. Echols's house and split the inner bark into 1-inch-wide strips, then helped us bottom a chair—an old one we had in our Foxfire classroom—as Mrs. Echols showed us how the pattern worked. It took us about an hour and a half to get the strips ready and to actually bottom the chair. We all felt so good about the job we did (with Nelson's and Elvin's help, of course) that we were ready to go home and bottom all the chairs at our own houses!

—*Melanie Burrell*

PLATE 156 **Johnny Ramey (left), Mrs. Echols, and Fred Sanders on the porch, discussing how the chair bottoming will be done**

PLATE 157 A tall, straight poplar tree with few branches is the best
kind for making poplar bark strips. The one Mr. Elvin Cabe
is cutting is about 3 to 4 inches in diameter.

PLATE 158 The thin part of the log at the top is cut off, and the branches
are trimmed off. Using a sharp pocketknife, Mr. Cabe slits the
bark lengthwise, from one end of the log to the other.

PLATE 159 He then runs his knife down the bark in a slit about 1 to 2 inches from the first cut and pulls off the first strip of bark. He and his brother, Nelson, continue to cut strips off the tree until it is completely stripped of bark all the way around. They got about four or five long strips from this tree, which was plenty for the chair we were bottoming.

PLATE 160 When they got to Mrs. Echols's house, they peeled off the outer bark, leaving the white, pliable inner bark, which was used to bottom the chair. Nelson, left, and Elvin, right, splitting a piece of inner bark (that they've already scraped the rough outer bark off) into two pieces, about ¾ to 1 inch wide

PLATE 161 **Mrs. Echols scraping off another piece of the bark, using a kitchen knife**

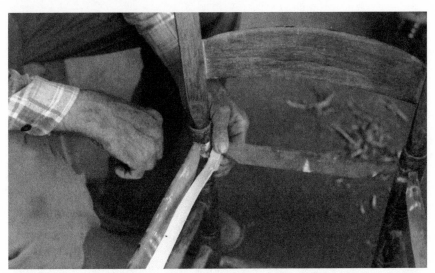

PLATE 162 **To begin bottoming the chair, a strip is folded over the chair round at the back of the chair. To hold the strip in place, tiny notches were made on either side of the strip, above and below the round, and then tied with a piece of string, looping it over and over about ten times.**

PLATES 163 and 164 **This strip was about 20 feet long. We began looping it around the front and back rounds as shown in these two pictures.**

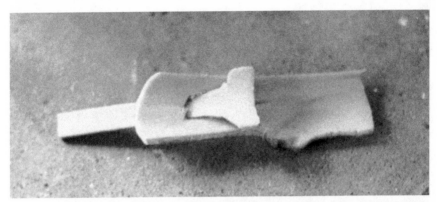

PLATE 165 As we came to the end of the first piece of bark strip, Nelson showed us how to connect it to a second piece with a notch like the one pictured. This works quite well while the bark is still green. If it has dried out, simply soak it for a few hours before bottoming the chair. Also, to secure the notch, we tied a small string around the strips.

PLATE 166 After completely wrapping the seat in one direction, Nelson started weaving the strips across the chair. The pattern he chose was a simple under-over pattern. Although the weave felt loose at first, it began to tighten as more rows were woven.

PLATE 167 **This shows the underside of the chair. It has to be woven just as the top side is. Note the notches where separate strips of poplar bark are connected.**

PLATE 168 To complete the chair bottom, the end of the last strip is woven back through the last two or three vertical rows, leaving no loose ends.

Raising Native Azaleas from Seed

~ Coyl Justice ~

**"About publishin' [my] secret, I don't mind because
at eighty-four, it don't make a lot of difference.
None of my family is gonna do it anyway."**

*In their nursery tucked into a hillside of the Betty's Creek community in
Dillard, Georgia, Coyl Justice and his wife, Mildred, demonstrated for me the
steps of gathering and then planting the seeds of the native azalea bushes that
provide beautiful color in the mountains each spring. As he described to me
each step of the process of growing these azaleas from seed, Mr. Justice told me
not only what he does in his nursery but also how a layperson could copy what
he does, using materials frequently found in the average home. As we walked
their property, I witnessed the thrift and ingenuity that have undoubtedly been
contributing factors in the success of their nursery. No container seemed to be
wasted; even old medicine bottles were recycled and put to good use. Long before
"green" was anything other than a color, Mr. and Mrs. Justice, and so many other
people of the southern Appalachian Mountains like them, were making do with
what they had, saving anything that could be reused, and wasting little, simply
because doing so just made good sense.*

*During my time with them, I found Mr. and Mrs. Justice to be patient
with the many questions of a novice gardener and generous with their hard-
earned knowledge. Their passion for their work was clear as they enthusiastically
showed me all their many plants and gave advice for some of my own gardening
dilemmas.*

*The Justices maintain several greenhouses in which they grow various types
of plants that they will later
sell in their nursery. Through
hard work, study, patience,
and determination, they have
created a business that they
enjoy. The fruits of their labors
have beautified homes in the
surrounding area for many
years, ensuring that long after
they've retired, their legacy
will continue.*

—Lacy Hunter Nix

PLATE 169 **Coyl Justice holding an immature
seedpod with evidence of bug infestation**

Gathering and Storing

After the native azaleas have bloomed out in late spring, a seedpod will form where the blossoms were. Allow the pod to remain on the plant until it begins to brown, usually in late September. Mr. Justice explained to us that if the pod remained on the plant for too long, it would burst when picked, spilling the seeds onto the ground.

Place the seedpods in a container—the Justices use an open cup for this step—sprinkle with insecticide, and then place the cup in a sunny windowsill, where the seedpods will dry for approximately two months. Mr. Justice describes his initial experiences with trying to sprout azalea seeds before he added the use of an insecticide to this step: "They wouldn't [sprout] because if you don't put some sort of insecticide on the seedpod, the weevils gets in it, and by the time you get 'em hulled out, they done got it eat up. They don't look like it 'cause you can't see where the weevils has eat 'em, but if you put Sevin on 'em—I use Sevin dust and just shake it up, you know, and let 'em dry. Then hull 'em out, and then they'll come out [germinate]."

In November, hull the seedpods by pinching the brown pod with a pair

PLATE 170 **Mr. Justice holding azalea seeds and chaff**

of pliers, then rolling the pod between your fingers over a container such as a plate or pie pan until the seeds fall out.

After shelling the seeds, rub them over a fine screen to separate the seeds from the chaff. The seeds will fall through the screen while the chaff remains on top. Then place the seeds in a container and store them in the freezer until you are ready to plant. "I gather the seed and freeze it. I have planted [them after I] had them five years in the freezer, and they still come up. If you gather the seed like this year, they'll come up this year, but one year is all they'll [usually] come up." Mr. Justice told us that he always plants during the December after he's gathered the seeds, though he believes that the seeds will germinate in the correct conditions up to a year later when stored in the freezer.

Germination

During the month of December, prepare the seed trays for planting. Mr. Justice told us that while he uses nursery seed boxes for his planting today, in the past, with great success, he has used plastic shoe boxes into which he had drilled drainage holes. To prepare for planting the seeds, screen peat through a wire screen. Place the peat remaining on top of the screen into the planting box first. Then mix part of the screened peat with warm water until it is wet. Squeeze the wet peat almost dry and place a 1- or 2-inch layer on top of the material already in the seed box. Then sprinkle the seeds on top. Finally, sprinkle a very small amount of the dry, screened peat—Mr. Justice said, "Pour barely enough to cover the seed; maybe not even one-sixteenth of an inch on top of the seeds and pat down gently." Mist the planted seeds with warm water—preferably the same warm water used to moisten the peat—and cover with plastic sheeting to keep the seedbed from drying out. Mr. Justice places his seedbed on a heating cable that maintains a temperature of approximately seventy degrees Fahrenheit at this point in the process to keep the azalea seeds warm enough to germinate. However, he said that before he had a heating cable, he would place the seedbed in a sunny windowsill in his home. Keep the seedbed slightly moist with occasional mistings but not overly damp—allowing the environment to be too damp will be counterproductive—as Mr. Justice says, "Too much dampness will kill them. Some of 'em will sprout a little bit later, but most of them will sprout in about four weeks."

After the seeds have sprouted, place them under a grow light or in a location that is warm and sunny. A window with eastern or western exposure should provide good light, though Mr. Justice says that one with eastern exposure is ideal. When the seedlings have sprouted, continue to maintain a slightly damp but not overly wet environment. When the seedlings have a pair of leaves, Mr. Justice makes a very weak solution of fertilizer with which he mists the seedlings approximately once per week. He says, "Keep the cover on 'em and mist about one time per week with a very weak solution. I only put about one-fourth teaspoon of Miracle-Gro per spray bottle."

Potting

When the seedlings are approximately 1½ to 2 inches tall, place into individual 2-inch seed cups. Patience is key, as Mr. Justice warned us that it takes a while for the seedlings to grow to this point. Mr. Justice uses 2-inch breakaway plastic seed cups, though he says that any cup that holds approximately the same amount of soil mixture and has drainage holes will do. A container that is too small will allow the soil to dry too quickly, jeopardizing the health of the plant. In years gone by, Mrs. Justice and three other ladies would perform the task of moving the seedlings from seed tray to cups by using a toothpick to lift the seedlings from the seed trays without harming their roots. The seed cups should be filled with a mixture of perlite and peat that has been soaked in warm water and then wrung almost dry.

PLATE 171 **Seedlings in seed cups**

PLATE 172 "I been takin' [azalea seedlings] out as they grow and puttin' them in individual cups. I leave them over winter, and then next year, I put 'em in gallons [to sell]. At three years, they'll bloom for seeds." At three years old, Coyl's plants are typically knee-high.

Once the seedlings are in the cups, keep them inside in a sunny windowsill or protected outside in a cold frame or a greenhouse. Mr. Justice told us that he had grown "hundreds of 'em in a windowsill" until he obtained a cold frame. Keep the soil "moist but not too wet."

Maturation

Allow the seedlings to grow in the seed cups through the rest of the year until early the next spring, almost a year in total, at which point they will be large enough to move to gallon pots. When Mr. Justice transplants his azalea seedlings to gallon pots, he plants them in "pure pine bark" that he mixes with slow-release fertilizer. If not using slow-release fertilizer, he recommends watering with Miracle-Gro regularly.

After moving the azaleas into the gallon pots in early spring, clip them back to encourage branching out; otherwise, they will grow straight up. Move the plants outside, but keep them protected. Mr. Justice told us that if they are planted outside while still too young, "the rabbits and deer will eat them." The plants will be ready to transplant into the ground when they are approximately 12 inches tall.

Forging a Traditional Drawknife

~Barry Stiles~

If you read the article on how to build a shaving horse, then you already know that a drawknife is an all-too-necessary tool. Therefore, if you plan on using your shaving horse, one of two things must be done. You can either go to your local hardware store and purchase a drawknife, or you can read this article and learn how to hand forge one of your very own. Although just hopping into your car and heading to the store might sound like the more rewarding option, I believe the final product of the second option, a hand-forged drawknife, is by far more pride-worthy and will be an altogether better tool. If you put forth the effort to create your own tool, you will have one that can be used to create products of extremely superior quality and can be passed down through generations, each family member knowing that his or her own ancestor forged that tool with the sweat of his or her own brow.

What is a drawknife? A drawknife is composed of three main features: wooden handles on the left and right side, a blade stretching between them, and the tangs. Inside the wooden handles are sections of metal that have been hammered down to thin, long points and hammered again to an angle. These sections of metal on the side are the tangs, and they are only visible while the knife

PLATE 173 **Inside the blacksmith's shop at The Foxfire Museum and Heritage Center**

is being made. The tangs, although simple, are where most of the work on your drawknife will be focused. Also, along with sharpening, honing, and tempering your blade, they require the most skill to forge. In this article we will make sure to describe everything down to the smallest detail to ensure that you, the reader, will have no trouble.

—Ben McClain

To make the drawknife, we used the blacksmith's shop at The Foxfire Museum and Heritage Center. The blacksmith and his shop were crucial to every community years ago. He made and repaired tools; some even made wagons for hauling. Although our drawknife project is not necessary for our community's survival, the tools and techniques used are identical to those of early blacksmiths who helped shape this country. Our blacksmith's shop is pretty typical of any blacksmith's shop from one hundred years ago. We have a forge, which is just a fire about 9 inches square and 5 inches or so deep. This is the place where we heat the metal. We burn soft coal as our fuel in the forge, and to get the fire really hot, we have an old hand-crank blower that blows air into the bottom of the fire. The fire in the forge can exceed three thousand degrees Fahrenheit, which is hot enough to melt steel. When we are heating metal in the forge, we are constantly looking at the color to know when it's hot enough. The color is our thermometer, and to really see the true color, you need to be in a shaded area. Another tool we rely on in the shop is the anvil, which is basically a large chunk of metal that you hammer heated metal against. I've heard the anvil described as the most perfect tool ever made by man; perhaps it is. It has evolved from over two thousand years of use, making it something pretty special. There was a time when blacksmiths were thought to have mystical powers. Hopefully, in the article ahead we will demystify some of the blacksmith's craft.

—Barry Stiles

Selecting a Metal

When selecting a metal to use, try to find a piece of steel with a high carbon content. For steel to be hardened and tempered, which makes for the most durable blade, there must be over 0.2 percent carbon present, and that steel would not harden very much. Ideally try to use steel with a high carbon content, such as spring steel or tool steel. For our drawknife we selected an old leaf spring from a vehicle. The size of the metal is also important. Depending on how large you want your drawknife to be, you may have to cut your material to match that size, leaving excess metal on the ends for forging your tangs. We decided to make a smaller drawknife; the measurements of our piece of steel are as follows: 3/16 inch thick, 15 inches long, and 1¼ inches wide.

Cutting Your Metal to Length

We used a hot-cut hardie to cut our metal to length. The hot-cut hardie is basically a blade that is inserted in a square hole in the anvil's face known as the hardie hole. Heated metal is cut by hammering it down against the hardie's blade. Assuming that the fire in the forge you are using is already going, you will need to use it to heat your metal. Measure the metal for length and mark it with a piece of soapstone. Soapstone markers are available at hardware stores and are commonly used by welders to mark metal because the mark will not burn off. Place the area of the metal

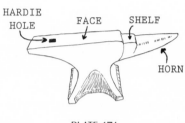

PLATE 174

around your length mark in the fire and cover it with coals. Keep turning the blower of the forge slowly to ensure the fire stays hot. Leave the metal in the fire long enough for the metal to turn orange, and then remove it from the fire. Place the heated section on top of the hot-cut-hardie blade and hammer directly above the blade against the heated section and your length mark to cut the metal. If the metal cools off before you have completed cutting it, simply place it in the fire again and repeat the process. After cutting your metal to length, it may need to be flattened back out. This can be done by simply heating the entire material in the fire and laying it on the anvil with

PLATE 175 **The end of the leaf spring being cut off on the hot-cut hardie**

any curve or bow in the metal facing downward like an upside-down U and hammering down the high spots. Most leaf springs will have an arch to them that should be flattened out in this manner.

Cutting Your Metal to Width [Note: This step requires two people.]

To cut the metal, you will need a hot chisel. A hot-cut chisel is not, in fact, a heated chisel but a chisel that is meant to be used with heated metal. Vice versa, a cold chisel can be used with nonheated metal. Placing the chisel against the heated section of metal, you will need to hit it very sharply on the back with a large hammer; this causes the metal to split. To cut your metal to width, you will have to heat it in sections in the forge. Three-inch sections should be wide enough. After the metal is heated, one person must hold the metal flat against the shelf of the anvil. This is the small stepped-down portion of the anvil between the horn and the face. You should never cut metal on the face of the anvil; doing so could damage the anvil. It is very important that the metal be completely flat against the shelf of the anvil; if it is raised, the hammer strikes on the other end can cause a painful jolt to the hands. As you near the middle of the metal, the holder may need to use

PLATE 176 **Ben holds the hot metal with tongs as Barry strikes the hot-cut chisel with the hammer**

PLATE 177 **The piece of leaf spring being cut lengthwise using the hot-cut chisel**

tongs because of the close proximity to the heated section of metal. One person will be holding the metal while the other person is using the hot-cut chisel to create the slit in the metal. The slit is begun on one end of the metal and slowly worked across the entire piece by moving the chisel and striking it until the other end is reached.

Creating the Tangs

To create the tangs you will need to heat the metal on one end to a bright orange. After doing so you will place the end of the metal against the face of the anvil. Only about 1½ to 2 inches are actually on the anvil; the rest of the piece is off the anvil. You will then proceed to hammer the top of the metal in order to elongate the tang and create the shoulder. Your hammer strikes should land with half of the face of the hammer landing over the face of the anvil and the other half of the face of the hammer landing off the anvil. This drives down the metal and begins to form the shoulder of the tang. Continue hammering the metal on the face of the anvil to create a long, slender section of metal. If you need to lengthen the metal rapidly, turn the hammer over and hammer the metal with the peen of the hammer. A straight-peen hammer works best for this. The peen on this type of hammer is wedge shaped, with the wedge parallel to the handle. When the metal is struck with the straight peen, it becomes longer without becoming wider. The straight peen creates little valleys in the heated metal, which are simply

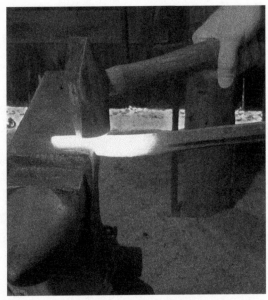

PLATE 178 **A shoulder and tang being formed by hammering down with the hammer face half over the anvil and half off it**

hammered flat with the flat face of the hammer. It is necessary to rotate the metal 90 degrees and hammer as well to create a tapered tang; otherwise, you would just flatten out the metal. The finished tang should be about 4 inches long by ⅜ inch wide by 3⁄16 inch thick at the shoulder. It should have square corners, not round, and taper gently to a point at the end, much like a hand-forged nail. Once you have one tang made, repeat the process on the other end of the metal to create the other tang.

Creating the Cutting Edge

To create the cutting edge, I find it easiest to use an angle grinder with a sanding disc installed, although a bench grinder or even a file could be used. It is also much easier to grind down the cutting edge before the tangs are bent, because after they are bent they can interfere with the grinder, making it hard to achieve a smooth, angled edge. Start by clamping one of the tangs of the drawknife in a vise. The drawknife will be held up in a vertical position. Hold the angle grinder on a 30-degree angle to the knife and start grinding down the length of the blade until the cutting edge and bevel are created. Make sure you grind the proper side of the knife or your drawknife will be reversed. You also may need to lightly grind the back of the blade to create a smooth, flat surface on the back side. It is almost always necessary to finish the drawknife with a whetstone, and the final sharpening should be left until after the blade has been tempered.

PLATE 179 **The cutting edge of the drawknife being ground with an angle grinder. The back of the blade is being lightly touched up after heavier grinding on the front.**

Bending the Tangs

To bend the tangs, heat one of the tangs in the forge until it is orange in color. The tang should be heated to at least the shoulder of the drawknife. After it has reached the proper color, bring it over to the horn of the anvil, place the shoulder of the knife tightly against the tip of the horn, and hammer down the tang until it has reached the proper angle. Shorter drawknives tend to have tangs bent at around 60 degrees to the blade, while longer drawknives tend to have the tangs bent at 90 degrees to the blade. Once you have done one end, repeat the procedure for the other end. If either tang goes out of alignment or is twisted with the blade, simply heat the tang and shoulder of the knife and hammer it flat on the face of the anvil.

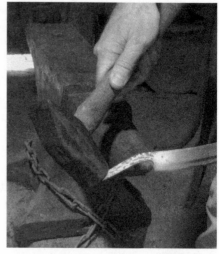

PLATE 180 **A tang is hammered down while being held against the point of the anvil horn.**

Tempering the Blade

A tempered blade is more durable than steel that has not been tempered. There are a lot of misconceptions about tempering steel. Most people think that tempering steel actually hardens it, when in fact tempering actually softens it from a hardened state. To temper our knife, first we must harden it. To do this we heat up the blade in the forge until it is just barely a visible red color in subdued light. Then it is quickly cooled off by plunging the whole knife into a tub of water; this is referred to as quenching the metal. It is important to move the blade around in the tub while it is cooling off; this helps the metal cool more evenly. The tool is now hardened, but when a tool is hardened it is also very brittle. It's actually too brittle at this point to be very useful, so we will take some of the hardness out of the blade by tempering it. The first step in tempering the knife is to polish the surface of the knife, removing the black on the metal that was formed in the forge and exposing the bare metal surface. Then we will reheat the knife in a low fire on the forge. The back of the knife should be sitting on the fire, and the knife should be sticking up vertically with the tangs standing straight up. As the metal heats up, oxidation colors will appear on the surface of the metal and move from the back of the blade to the front of the blade; this is sometimes referred to as running the colors. A little rainbow of colors forms and moves across the blade as it heats up. You must watch the metal very closely to see these colors form and move across the blade. A pale straw yellow will form, followed by bronze, followed by violet. When the violet color reaches the cutting edge, quickly quench the entire tool again. Now the tool has been hardened and tempered. Care must be taken not to overheat the tool once it has been tempered. Heating the tool beyond the tempering colors will undo the hardening, and it would have to be hardened and tempered again.

Attaching the Handles

Drawknives usually have wooden handles attached to the tangs. For our drawknife we "hot set" the wooden handles. Two handles were turned on a lathe, each handle being about 5 inches long and 1½ inches in diameter at its widest point. If you do not have access to a lathe to make your own handles, you can purchase wooden file handles at most hardware stores, which will work fine. Each handle has a metal ring on one end called a ferrule. The ferrule keeps the handle from splitting while it is being installed. We first drilled a pilot hole into the handle about 3 inches deep, then heated up one tang of the tool until the tip of the tang was just turning red. Remember not to heat the entire tool; just heat the tang from the bend to the tip, or you will undo your tempering. With one of the wooden handles clamped in a vise, the hot tang is forced into the pilot hole, burning a larger hole and creating a perfect fit. Push the handle down on the tang until the handle is about ¾ inch from the bend in the tang. The tang may have to be reheated a time or two to achieve this. Now remove the handle and cool off the tang by dipping it in water and pour a little water inside the handle to cool it off as well. Then place the handle back onto the tang and hammer the handle on the tang ¼ inch more. This will seat the handle securely so that it won't come off. Repeat the procedure for the other handle.

Final Sharpening

To get the final razor-sharp edge on the drawknife, a coarse whetstone should be used. Hold one handle of the drawknife in your left hand with

PLATE 181 **A wooden handle being pushed into a heated tang, creating smoke**

the cutting edge facing upward and press the other handle firmly against your chest. Take the stone in your right hand and rub it back and forth on the bevel, over the length of the blade, until the high spots are ground down. Then do a few passes on the back of the blade as well. When that is done, use a fine whetstone and repeat the process until the cutting edge has a mirror finish. A very small and thin ribbon of metal may form on the edge of the

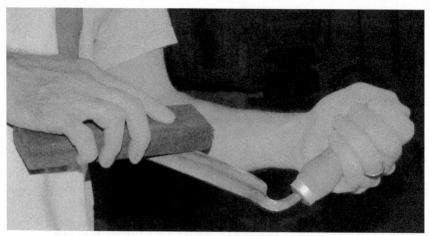

PLATE 182 **Sharpening the finished drawknife with the whetstone**

PLATE 183 **The sharpened edge of the drawknife**

blade, and this is easily removed by bending it back and forth until it breaks off. A leather strop works best for this. If you have ever seen a barber rubbing a straight razor back and forth on a piece of leather, this is what he is doing.

Using Your Drawknife

The proper way to use a drawknife is this: While sitting on top of your shaving horse, press your foot down on the pedal in order to ensure that the wood you are working with is properly secure and doesn't slip or wobble. Stretching your arms out to their full length, place the drawknife against the wood and pull with the blade facing your body. Make sure that when doing so you keep the blade almost completely parallel to the wood; that way you pull off only a small shaving, and the integrity of the wood is well maintained. If you do this correctly, the wood should be very smooth to the touch.

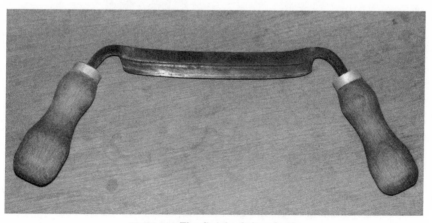

PLATE 184 **The finished drawknife**

Braiding a Leather Bullwhip

~Frank Vinson~

Frank Vinson is my grandpa. I've stayed with him and my grandmother Eva Vinson quite a bit since I was a small boy. I've wanted to do a Foxfire article on him for a long time, and when he said he'd show us how to make a bullwhip, I brought friends of mine, Cecil and Adam Wilburn, over to our house for the interview. We kept the tape recorder running as he showed us all the steps in making the whip, and he told us something about his boyhood and adult life.
—Cary Brown

Back when I was just a small boy, I lived with my pa and ma. We lived in old log shacks that my pa built out of old chestnut slabs. We didn't have goodies like kids have these days. We ate dried blackberries and apples; the only sweet thing we had was sugarcane. There was thirteen of us, including Ma and Pa; eleven kids, you know.

I remember when my daddy told me to go down across the field and

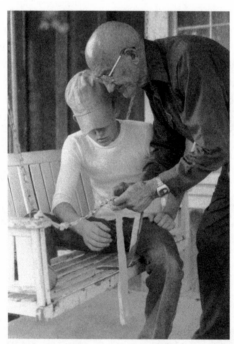

PLATE 185 I began to learn how to braid a bullwhip myself. I wasn't too good at it at first, but I got the hang of it. Grandpa showed me how, and it didn't take too long after that.

see about the cows. I'd cut my little toe about off with the ax, and I had to go barefoot, even though there was a big frost on the ground. My pa'd buy a cowhide in the fall and make us new shoes, and if we wore 'em out, we done without until winter.

He told me, "Frank, go get the cows." I got down there and one ol' cow was laying there with all four legs sticking straight up in the air. When I got back home, I was crying, and my daddy asked me what was wrong. I told him about the ol' cow and it made him mad, and he whipped the living stuff out of me for crying over that ol' cow.

I helped build the towns. There wasn't many families who lived up there—just a few here and there. Back when I built houses, I just used plain things like a handsaw, squares, and chisels. We didn't have such a thing as a skill saw or a drill. That ain't all I ever done—building houses. I ran the mail route, too. I had to use an ol' horse and, boy, I couldn't stand to ride a horse! But I did for a good spell—up to Highlands and to Franklin, North Carolina.

And now [1982] I'm ninety years old, and I've been married seventy years, too. And I've got six kids of my own. The oldest is sixty-five.

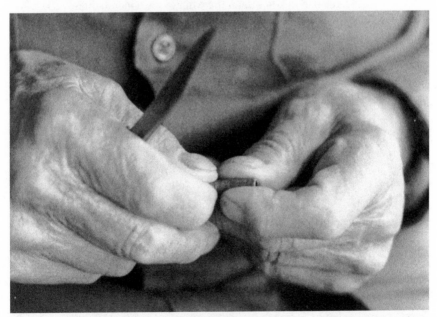

PLATE 186 Grandpa first cuts a hole, a ¼-inch circle, 1 inch from the end of each strip of leather that he will braid to make this whip. He uses four strips of leather, each 6 feet long and tapered from 1 inch wide (where the holes were made) down to less than ½ wide at the ends that attach to the cracking end of the whip.

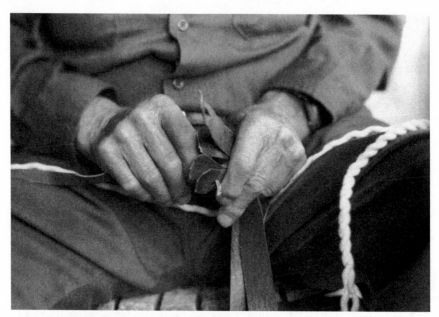

PLATE 187 He runs another strip of leather, about ½ inch wide and 12 inches long, through the holes in the four long pieces. He calls this a loop and will later use this to attach the whip to a wooden handle.

PLATE 188 He cuts a ¾-inch-long slot near each end of the 12-inch loop. See the diagram on facing page showing how this is drawn together and worked into the braiding of the whip.

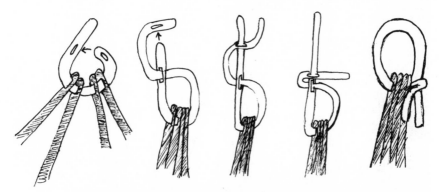

PLATE 189 The steps for stringing the strips onto the loop, fastening it together, and tightening it are shown here.

In a later step, the ends of the loop are slipped around and disappear into the whip as the four strips of leather are braided together. (Diagrams drawn by Cary Brown. They are not to scale but exaggerated to show detail.)

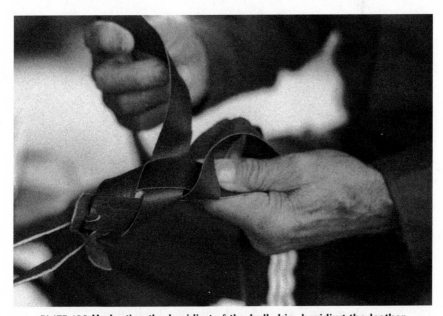

PLATE 190 He begins the braiding of the bullwhip, braiding the leather tightly around several strands of cotton rope. (He prefers a thick piece of rope to give more bulk to the upper section of the whip but used a piece of unraveled clothesline in this demonstration. The rope is doubled and pulled through the leather loop so that it will not pull out as the whip is braided. Note one of the loop's ends protruding from the top of the braiding to show how it has been worked into the whip.)

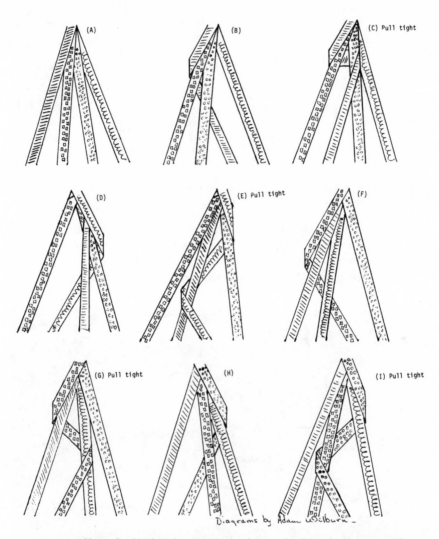

PLATE 191 Have the leather loop with the four unbraided leather strands attached, clamped, or tied to a nail. Spread the four strips of leather out, two in each hand. (To get the knack of braiding the strips into the proper pattern, you may want to practice with four 1-inch-wide strips of different-colored fabrics.)

This diagram shows the steps involved in braiding the whip. After each strip has been brought under and back over the other strips as indicated, pull the braid to a uniform tightness.

PLATE 192 Grandpa is getting to the end of the braiding, and the whip is getting smaller and smaller in diameter. (The leather strips are tapered.)

PLATE 193 Cecil Wilburn (center) and I are helping my grandfather measure out lengths of twine for the cracker. The cracker, made of many strands of tough string, is the object that makes the popping sound heard when someone cracks a whip.

PLATE 194 Cecil holds the whip so that Grandpa can begin braiding the cracker in with the last 6 to 8 inches of the leather section. He uses the same braiding pattern he used for the whip.

PLATE 195 Periodically, he cuts off three to four strands of string so that he is braiding with fewer and fewer strands. As the cracker gets longer, the diameter will be smaller at the tail end than the part around the braided leather. When he gets to the end of the cracker, he ties off the ends to keep the cracker from unraveling and cuts off the excess string.

PLATE 196 Grandpa chopped a handle out of a piece of hickory
wood. He smoothed the surface of the handle with a wood rasp.
He then carved a groove around the narrow end of the handle.
He attached the whip there by putting a slipknot in the loop,
sliding it around the groove, and pulling the loop tight.

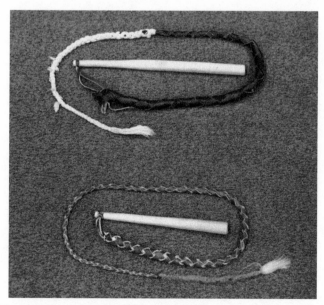

PLATE 197 At the top is the finished bullwhip my grandfather made to
show us how it's done. Below is another bullwhip made by my grandpa.

The Past Meets the Present

A Closing Letter from Foxfire President Ann Moore

Ann Moore joined Foxfire in 1976 as its bookkeeper and soon became an irreplaceable asset to the organization. Over the years Ann assumed many roles: circulation manager, editor, historian, administrator, and second mama to many students. The board of directors, in one of its wisest decisions, chose her in 2000 to become the president and executive director of Foxfire.

—Kaye Carver Collins

Ann Moore: A native Rabun Countian, I was born in May 1956 to two wonderful parents, Cecil S. and Ellie Ramey Henslee. While my father worked two jobs, day and night, struggling to pay the bills and put food on our table, my mom stayed home to raise my brother, Billy, and me, while also caring for Dad's parents, Will and Dealia Henslee, and his aunt, Belle Henslee, all three of whom lived with us most of my childhood.

As Dad was always seeking a better home for us at a less expensive rent, he moved us a lot from home to home in Rabun County, including into and out of several houses on the Rabun Gap–Nacoochee School (RGNS) Farm that you read about earlier in this book. Though we weren't a School Farm Family, we were able to rent from the school when the houses were unoccupied by Farm Families. One home I particularly remember living in on the campus was on the old hog farm. The house was so cold in the wintertime, with little money for which to heat it, that all seven of us

PLATE 198

would sleep in the kitchen and dining room area on makeshift beds near the stove. My fondest memories of the school farm and of my young life are of spending many nights throughout those years with my aunt Lucy Webb and uncle Grover and my seven cousins, who *were* one of the School Farm Families. My wonderful aunt Lucy would spoil Billy and me by making us "cakey bread" (a flat pan of biscuit bread) and hot chocolate gravy for breakfast! Uncle Grover would strum his banjo for us in the evenings, and we'd all sing; we played cowboys and Indians with the cousins at an old corral on the hill behind their house that now overlooks Indian Lake on the RGNS campus. Oh, what I'd give to have those days back, but then my wonderful nephews and nieces—Ramey, Jamey, Joy, Matthew, and Madison Henslee—wouldn't be in my life! What joy they have brought me . . .

I recall nights spent at the home of my maternal grandparents, Leo and Mae Ramey, when I would lie in bed in the back bedroom under a pile of quilts, snuggled in for warmth, way too comfortable to slip out from under the covers in an icy cold room to use the chamber pot, much less brave enough to dart outdoors in the dark of night to use the outhouse that sat on the banks of the Tallulah Falls Railroad in Dillard, Georgia. I am too young to remember the train, as the service was halted when I was very small, but I do remember my grandpa Ramey's stories of driving the "pitty-pat" (motor car that sometimes had to be hand pumped) down the tracks to the men whom he supervised. I especially remember the story of his near-death experience from one of the high banks caving in on him, for as a child, hearing that story made me realize that I might never have known him. His and Granny's treat to us that I remember so well was a five-cent ice-cream cone from Barnard Dillard's drugstore just a few hundred yards away from the house on what is now a four-lane, paved Highway 441. Granny Ramey tried to teach me to crochet, as she loved to do that; it was a necessity in her earlier life, along with knitting, but it became a pastime in her latter years. The one doily that I managed to make is still attached to that ball of yarn, wherever it might live today. Knitting was not my forte either!

Though our family was dirt poor and times were often so very hard, there was always gracious food on the table and love in our home. My daddy slaughtered hogs and grew vegetables in the garden to feed our family; Grandma taught me to churn butter in the old crock [churn]; and my mama made sauerkraut (which I avoided like the plague) in that same churn. Mama also tried to pass down her delicious culinary skills to me, too, but to this day I have to have a recipe from which to cook more than a basic meal. Her talent of adding a dash of this and a pinch of that turns into an inedible meal when created by me! I thank the Good Lord every day that I received other talents and skills from my dear mama, since the homemaking ones were not something at which I excelled!

Our family would listen to the radio together in the evenings after chores were done and, in later years, watch the old black-'n'-white TV. On Sunday afternoons, with no money for anything other than a bit of gas, Daddy would take us on drives in our old car to visit family members. My brother and I both, at age eight, began working outside the home in the surrounding community to help make ends meet. My summers, from age eleven to seventeen, were spent living and working at the old Boxwood Terrace Boarding House in Dillard. From seven in the morning till seven at night, I helped garden, milk cows, clean rooms, cook, wash dishes, and wait tables three meals a day. My after-school hours were spent working as a waitress at the Old Villager restaurant. Billy and I thought that if we could just provide for our own personal needs, life would be so much easier for our parents.

As you can see, I was a child who was reared in these Appalachian Mountains that I love so much—the customs and traditions and expressions preserved throughout the pages of *The Foxfire Magazine* and Foxfire book series were a part of my everyday life and influenced the person that I am today. My family has lived here for hundreds of years. I hear so much of my grandma Dealia in me at times, especially when someone tells me they've been ill or having trouble. "Bless your heart" will come right outta my mouth without hesitation, and I will immediately be reminded of my loving grandma and how I grew up hearing her use that expression and so many others that I still use today.

The lifelong lessons that my mama, now age seventy-five, taught me, like caring for family and others, sharing what little you have with those in worse need, respecting your elders, and always smiling through adversity, are instilled in me, as is my daddy's work ethic. Daddy's strong hands produced a lot of hard work in his short fifty-seven years of life, as he strove to provide for our family. The song "Daddy's Hands," written and recorded by country music star Holly Dunn, brings tears to my eyes, still today, 'cause when I hear it, it reminds me so much of my beloved daddy.

Of course, like my mother before me and both my grandmothers before her, I was a traditional Appalachian young woman of the time, marrying at a young age: Just a month after turning the ripe old age of seventeen, I married my husband of thirty-eight years, Larry Moore, whom I had met and square-danced with for many summers at the old Mountain City Playhouse, the main source of entertainment back in those days.

I am *proud* of my heritage passed down to me by my daddy and my mama, and therefore I have devoted my entire adult life to the work of Foxfire and the preservation and documentation by our Foxfire students of that Appalachian culture from which I come.

I was a mere ten years old when Foxfire was born; at that time, I was too young to know about the program. Just three years later, I learned of it when I started eighth grade at RGNS. Tenth grade through twelfth grade, I spent my free class period working on the RAGANA [Rabun Gap–Nacoochee] annual staff with one of my favorite teachers, Mr. Billy Joe Stiles. We shared an office in the administration building with the Foxfire teachers and students. On a few occasions (when there was no annual staff work to do, of course), I would go on interviews with my Foxfire friends, thoroughly enjoying the stories I heard of "haints" and ghosts and growing up here in the mountains—a life I knew so well from stories from my own grandparents. Little did I know at that time that just a year out of high school, I would receive a message from one of my other favorite teachers, Mrs. Melba Huggins, that Foxfire was seeking a bookkeeper. She was my role model when in high school, teaching me to type and do bookkeeping and operate office equipment, giving me all the skills I needed for the workplace. Foxfire staff members asked the teachers sharing lunch with them one day in the RGNS dining hall whom they might know that Foxfire could hire to replace their former bookkeeper. Mrs. Huggins recommended me and sent me a message to please go to Foxfire's office that very night at eight o'clock for an interview. The rest, as they say, is history.

As *The Foxfire Magazine* celebrates its forty-fifth anniversary in 2011, I celebrate my thirty-fifth year with Foxfire. It simply astounds me, even today, to think about the fact that a small magazine started by an English class at my alma mater, RGNS, in the northeast Georgia mountains, could still be in publication today and be the very cornerstone of this organization. Many, many changes have occurred at Foxfire since I began here as a young nineteen-year-old girl. I find it amazing, still, that I grew up with Foxfire as the organization expanded, taking on many new roles as the years passed by, and having now served as its president and executive director since 2000. When I joined Foxfire on May 1, 1976, had it not been for the mentoring of "Mama Margie" [Margie Bennett] as the students and I called her, I would have never survived this learning experience. At age nineteen, with all of the intelligent, educated adults on the staff, I felt quite out of place as the youngster among them. Margie and her husband, my dear friend Bob, took me right under their wings and taught me so much, guiding me through my new job. Years later, when I worked with Kaye Carver Collins and Robert Murray, two of the most wonderful people I was fortunate enough to have in my life, the mentoring continued. Though they encouraged me to move into the president's role in 2000 when the board offered me the position, either of them would have been the more appropriate person for the role—Kaye, a former Foxfire student, community board member, staff person, and great intellect, would have brought so much more than I to the position; Robert, such a natural-born leader and so admired by the masses, as well as an engaging teacher and brilliant man, would have been a great president and leader for this organization. Their confidence in me and their support of me in this wonderful but sometimes stressful job has meant more to me than mere words could ever express. I tried to share my appreciation with Robert over the twenty-two years he worked with me, and especially before his passing in 2008. I continue to try to relay that to Kaye and Margie every time I have the opportunity. Both have continued to support me here at Foxfire by returning to work with me whenever asked; their work on this anniversary book is just one example of that.

Foxfire is not the same as *the* Foxfire of yesteryear—staff members have come and gone and programs have changed—but during all of the organizational changes over its forty-five-year history, one thing has remained constant: our belief in young people and their ability to have an active hand in their own learning by immersing themselves in their community. Just as my grandparents and parents inspired and influenced me as I grew up here, so have Foxfire's contacts, whom you've read so much about in the magazine and books. Determination, perseverance, and life skills have become ingrained in me through the values I learned from *all* my elders; these are values that you have heard the Foxfire students talk about throughout their years with Foxfire, while they, at the same time, learned the skills they needed to be active, critical citizens in their communities and workplace. As Aunt Addie Norton so eloquently shared with them:

I tell you one thing: If you learn it by yourself, if you have to get down and dig for it, it never leaves you. It stays there as long as you live because you had to dig it out of the mud before you learned what it was.

Through this teacher-learner-community connection, the students not only learned those life lessons from their elders like Aunt Addie while learning about their culture and heritage, they also:

- preserved a part of that culture for future generations;
- learned interpersonal, communication, and publishing skills;
- came to value the importance of family and community;
- learned many traditional hands-on skills that they would use throughout their lives; and
- learned important lessons on persevering through hardships and difficulties in life.

Little did our students know that while documenting this vanishing way of life, they were also developing a teaching style, the Foxfire Approach to Teaching and Learning, that would be refined by thousands of teachers around the country as they used those core practices to teach their own students in a fulfilling and meaningful way.

The students also learned respect for their elders and that those elders have so much to share with younger generations that matters, if only given a chance to share their wealth of knowledge, for as our elders share stories of the past, they provide insight into history yet to be made. That teacher-learner-community connection and the history of the Appalachian area are what we hope to continue to share with generations to come here at The Foxfire Museum and Heritage Center.

We do continue to make a difference every day through our educational programs, as evidenced by many e-mails and letters we receive each day, including the following from former student Chris Crawford in New Jersey:

The year after high school was a tough one for me. . . . I fell back on the skills I developed with Foxfire: "construction." Yes, I became a heavy construction worker. . . . I got the job at the company I'm at now and I love it. I am a foreman/ heavy equipment operator, and we install natural gas and water pipelines. Between all of that, my kids grew up and one graduated high school last year. Both are attending a community college; [one] being in his second year is gearing up to be a teacher and [the other] wants to do the culinary arts . . . what a beautiful family I am blessed with. In closing, I owe so much to you [Ann] and all the teachers at Foxfire. You were the family I was blessed with through my youth [that] guided me through my troubled times. The guidance I will continue to use throughout my lifetime, and the memories will warm my heart forever. . . . I know if it weren't for Foxfire, things would be different for me. I understand the changes [in Foxfire], but I was given a chance to take classes in 7th grade and was hired for the summer maintenance program [several years]. . . . I laugh because I don't think there was a Foxfire class I didn't take in high school. I know I wasn't the ideal student, but if it wasn't for Foxfire's approach to teaching, I would have been lost in the so-called "Text Book" rules of teaching and been pushed through the system as an "under-the-rug" statistic with a lost education. So, when asked about high school, I always explain to friends how lucky I was to have Foxfire and what it was. If you could major in anything in high school, I would say I "Majored in Foxfire!" THANK YOU!

The work product of some of those students, The Foxfire Museum and Heritage Center in Mountain City, still thrives today. Built by the hands of Foxfire students like Chris, with adult supervision, the museum, a collection of twenty-two historic and replication log structures, provides rich educational programs steeped in the Appalachian culture. Living History Days are conducted each year on a Friday and Saturday in April, with hundreds of visitors learning about life in the early 1800s through Foxfire volunteers on-site at the museum, dressed in period clothing, demonstrating the skills of the era. Preachin' and traditional music can be heard throughout the hills from the chapel; ladies will be quiltin', churnin', makin' soap, weavin', and cookin' over the open hearth, while the men are hewin' logs and blacksmithing and doing intricate woodworkin'. At the same time, children will be learning lessons on the old slate boards in the one-room schoolhouse, the chapel that served as both school and a place of worship, or playing old-timey games on the grounds, or making a piece of rope on the old rope maker.

Children's Heritage Days are also conducted throughout the summer months; *Foxfire Magazine* students are on-site in leadership training courses or writing books such as this one; the magazine is in continuous publication at Rabun County High School, with the full support of principal Mark Earnest and two great classroom facilitators; an archive of historical significance for the region now exists and is available to the public as a result of that oral history collection by our students; guided and self-guided educational tours are provided to thousands of visitors each year, including school and home-school groups, individuals, clubs, and families; teacher-training courses in The Foxfire Approach to Teaching and Learning are held on-site each summer, conducted by our partners in education at Piedmont College; $25,000 in college scholarships is awarded annually to local Rabun County students in the Foxfire program, with over $850,000 having been awarded since 1976; a strategic plan is in place, governed by our board of directors; and my dream of having a year-round, active Living History Center is still alive.

Thanks to my great staff who help me to accomplish all of Foxfire's established goals and more, the leadership from our caring board of directors, the advice and assistance of our community board members, current and former students, and other volunteers who assist us each and every year, as well as our generous financial contributors, Foxfire continues to flourish and, like its namesake, foxfire, the luminous fungus that glows on decaying wood in these beautiful Appalachian Mountains, so does the glow of our Foxfire organization continue to shine!

With sincere love and gratitude, I dedicate this book to my mom and to those wonderful contacts who invited our young students into their homes and shared their stories, for had they not welcomed us with open arms into their lives, this wonderful educational organization called Foxfire would not exist today.

Experiencing Traditional Music in the Southeastern United States

To explore the world of gospel music, you need look no further than local churches to be presented with a wealth of opportunities. Ask around the community, and folks should be able to point you in the direction of notably musical worship services or churches that are known for hosting traveling gospel groups for special singings.

In the southeastern United States, good bluegrass music is fairly easy to locate. The list on the following pages is just a sampling of bluegrass festivals in the region, included here to help you find your way through the door of the bluegrass world. The festival listings here are based on information available while this book was in production in 2010–11. We hope that each and every one of these festivals are still being held when you read this, but please understand that websites, dates, and locations may have changed. Don't worry, though—once you've met a few people, searched the Internet a bit, and visited a festival or two, you should have no problem locating even more possibilities, both close to home and at family-vacation-worthy destinations.

∼ALABAMA∼

Great American Bluegrass Festival
April, Dothan
www.greatamericanbluegrassfestival.com

Tennessee Valley Old Time Fiddlers Convention
October, Athens
www.athens.edu/fiddlers

Foggy Hollow Bluegrass Gatherin'
June and September, Webster's Chapel
www.foggyhollow.com

Ol' Timey Crafts and Bluegrass Festival
September, Estillfork
www.prvlodge.com

Chimney Corner Celebration
October, St. Clair Springs
www.whitesmtnbluegrass.com

∼FLORIDA∼

Bluegrass and Clogging Festival
March, Auburndale
www.intlmarketworld.com

Dixieland Music Park
November, Waldo
www.dixielandmusicpark.net

Everglades Bluegrass Festival
February, Miami
www.southfloridabluegrass.org

~ FLORIDA *continued* ~

MagnoliaFest
October, Live Oak
www.magnoliafest.com

Palatka Bluegrass Festival
February, Palatka
www.aandabluegrass.com/FestivalListing.html

Riverhawk Music Festival
November, Brooksville
www.lindentertainment.com

Suwannee Springfest
March, Live Oak
suwanneespringfest.com

Yeehaw Junction Bluegrass Festival
January, Yeehaw Junction
www.yeehawbluegrass.com

~ GEORGIA ~

Bear on the Square Mountain Festival
April, Dahlonega
www.bearonthesquare.org

Blairsville Bluegrass Festival
September, Blairsville
www.unioncountyhistory.org

Dillard Bluegrass and Barbecue Festival
August, Dillard
www.dillardbbq.com

~GEORGIA *continued* ~

Foxfire Mountaineer Festival
October, Clayton
www.foxfiremountaineer.org

Georgia Official State Fiddlers' Convention
October, Hiawassee
www.georgiamountainfairgrounds.com

Hillside Spring Bluegrass Festival
May, Cochran
www.hillsidebluegrassrvpark.com

New Year's Bluegrass Festival
December, Jekyll Island
www.aandabluegrass.com/FestivalListing.html

Top of Georgia Bluegrass Jamboree
March, Dillard
www.gabluegrassjamboree.com

~KENTUCKY~

Bluegrass in the Park Folklife Festival
August, Henderson
www.bluegrassintheparkfestival.com

Carter County Shrine Club Bluegrass Festival
July, Olive Hill
www.cartercountyshrineclub.org

Festival of the Bluegrass
June, Lexington
www.festivalofthebluegrass.com

~KENTUCKY *continued* ~

Goin' Back to Harlan Bluegrass Festival
June, Harlan
www.harlanbgfestival.com

GrassStock
August, Harrodsburg
www.grassstock.com

Jerusalem Ridge Bluegrass Celebration
September, Beaver Dam
www.jerusalemridgefestival.org

Crowe Fest
September, Wilmore
www.jdcrowefestival.com

Newgrass Festival
August, Bowling Green
www.newgrassfestival.com

Poppy Mountain Bluegrass Festival
September, Morehead
www.poppymountainbluegrass.com

River of Music Party (ROMP)
June, Owensboro
www.bluegrassmuseum.org/general/romp.php

Rudy Fest Bluegrass Festival
June, Grayson
www.rudyfest.com

Sally Gap Bluegrass Festival
June, Williamsburg
www.sallygapbgfestival.com

∽KENTUCKY *continued* ∽

Salt Lick Bluegrass Festival
February, Shepherdsville
www.saltlickbluegrassfestival.com

Vine Grove Bluegrass Festival
September, Vine Grove
www.vinegrovebluegrass.com

∽NORTH CAROLINA∽

Big Lick Bluegrass Festival
June, Oakboro
www.biglickbluegrass.com

Black Banjo Gathering
March, Boone
www.blackbanjo.com

Bluegrass First Class
February, Asheville
www.bluegrassfirstclass.com

Charlie Poole Music Festival
June, Eden
www.charlie-poole.com

High Country Musicfest
August, Boone
www.highcountrybluegrassfestival.com

~NORTH CAROLINA *continued* ~

Hoppin' John Old-Time and Bluegrass Fiddler's Convention
September, Silk Hope
www.hoppinjohn.org

Kinston Winter Bluegrass Festival
February, Kinston
www.ibluegrass.com/kinstonbg

Lil John's Mountain Music Festival
May, Snow Camp
www.littlejohnsmountainmusic.com

MerleFest
April, Wilkesboro
www.merlefest.org

North Carolina State Bluegrass Festival
August, Marion
www.aandabluegrass.com/FestivalListing.html

Ola Belle Reed Music Festival
August, Lansing
www.olabellefest.com

Fiddler's Grove Ole Time Fiddler's and Bluegrass Festival
May, Union Grove
www.fiddlersgrove.com

Red, White and Bluegrass Festival
July, Morganton
www.redwhiteandbluegrassfestival.com

Shakori Hills GrassRoots Festival of Music and Dance
April and October, Pittsboro
www.shakorihills.org

~SOUTH CAROLINA~

Aiken Bluegrass Festival
May, Aiken
www.aikenbluegrassfestival.org

Congaree Bluegrass Festival
October, Cayce
www.congareebluegrassfestival.com

RenoFest Bluegrass Festival
March, Hartsville
www.renofest.com

South Carolina State Bluegrass Festival
November, Myrtle Beach
www.aandabluegrass.com/FestivalListing.html

~TENNESSEE~

Americana Music Festival
October, Nashville
www.americanamusic.com

Boxcar Pinion Memorial Bluegrass Festival
May, Chattanooga
www.boxcarforeverbluegrass.com

Dumplin Valley Bluegrass Festival
September, Kodak
www.dumplinvalleybluegrass.com

World of Bluegrass
October, Nashville
www.ibma.org

~TENNESSEE *continued* ~

Raccoon Valley Bluegrass Festival
October, Powell
www.raccoonvalleyfestival.com

Pigeon Forge Winterfest
December, Pigeon Forge
www.smokymountainwinterfest.com

3 Sisters Festival
October, Chattanooga
www.3sistersbluegrass.com

Uncle Dave Macon Days
July, Murfreesboro
www.uncledavemacondays.com

Union Bluegrass Festival
October, Farragut
www.unioncpchurch.com/bluegrass

White Oak Mountain Bluegrass Festival
July, Cleveland
www.whiteoakbluegrass.com

~VIRGINIA~

Bluegrass in the Blue Ridge
August, Luray
www.bluegrassinluray.com

Central Virginia Family Bluegrass Music Festival
May, Amelia
www.ameliafamilycampground.com

~VIRGINIA *continued* ~

Clinch Mountain Music Fest
June, Gate City
www.clinchfest.net

Graves Mountain Festival of Music
June, Syria
www.gravesmountain.com/bluegrass.htm

Menokin Bluegrass Festival
May, Warsaw
www.menokinbluegrass.com

Mineral Bluegrass Festival
July, Mineral
www.aandabluegrass.com/FestivalListing.html

Oak Grove Folk Music Festival
August, Staunton
www.oakgrovefestival.com

Roanoke FiddleFest
July, Roanoke
www.roanokefiddlefest.org

~WEST VIRGINIA~

Appalachian String Band Music Festival
August, Clifftop
www.wvculture.org/stringband

Pickin' in the Panhandle
September, Martinsburg
www.panhandlepickin.com

The Foxfire 45th Anniversary Book
Singin', Praisin', Raisin'

PLATE 199 **Editors: Casi Best (left) and Joyce Green (right)**

Joyce Green is a former *Foxfire Magazine* facilitator, having served in Foxfire's classroom for over thirteen years before retiring from Rabun County High School. She has been involved with Foxfire since the mid-'80s, serving on the community board as well as the scholarship committee. She was chosen as Rabun County's Teacher of the Year in 2003. She currently (2010) teaches part-time at Mountain Education Center High School, a nontraditional Georgia charter school.

Casi Best is a former *Foxfire Magazine* senior editor who worked on the magazine staff during most of her tenure at Rabun County High School. She is a remarkable young lady, cancer survivor, outstanding role model, and dedicated Christian. Casi is a Foxfire Julia Fleet Scholarship recipient who is currently in her second year of nursing school at Piedmont College in Demorest, Georgia.

Teresa Gentry is a former *Foxfire* magazine staff member and editor. As a Foxfire student, she helped to write and edit several of the books in the Foxfire Press series and worked with Foxfire during the summer months. Teresa was a Foxfire Scholarship recipient who graduated from Berry College. She is currently working for WebMD and, with her husband, John, is raising a son and a daughter.

Ben McClain, a 2010 graduate of Rabun County High School, is attending college to focus on photography—a field he became greatly interested in while a *Foxfire Magazine* student. While assisting on the anniversary book this summer, Ben also worked with Foxfire's curator, Barry Stiles, to replace several roofs on the cabins at The Foxfire Museum and Heritage Center.

Ann Moore, Foxfire's president and executive director, started with Foxfire in May 1976, just two years after graduating from Rabun Gap–Nacoochee School. While working with Foxfire full-time, she went on to obtain a diploma in accounting from North Georgia Technical College and attend night classes through Truett-McConnell College. She came to Foxfire to serve as bookkeeper and, over the years, moved into various roles within the organization, including administrator and acting president, before being named president in 2000.

Kaye Carver Collins has been one of the cornerstones of the Foxfire program for many years. A Foxfire student in the seventies, she later served on the staff as the community and teacher liaison. She is currently teaching math at Rabun County Middle School but continues to spend some of her summers with Foxfire, helping write and edit books. Kaye provides valuable input and resources and devotes her personal time to any project that arises, while also serving on Foxfire's board of directors and community board.

Lee Carpenter, Foxfire's computer and design "hired gun," provides contract work on an as-needed basis. He graduated from Rabun County High School in 1990, then went on to Young Harris College and Valdosta State University, earning a BFA in television production. His day job is working as a prepress operator at Gap Graphics & Printing in Clayton, Georgia, but he spends many nights and weekends working for Foxfire in several capacities, and also writes and edits Foxfire's newsletters and maintains the website. Lee is truly a jack-of-all-trades.

PLATE 200 **Book staff back row: Teresa Thurmond Gentry, Ben McClain, Ann Moore, Kaye Carver Collins; front row: Lee Carpenter, Margie Bennett, Lacy Hunter Nix; not pictured: Sheri Thurmond**

Margie Bennett taught the *Foxfire* magazine class during its later years at Rabun Gap–Nacoochee School and then at Rabun County High School. She has been a valuable asset to Foxfire in numerous capacities, living at The Foxfire Museum and Heritage Center for many years with her husband, Bob, to be full-time hosts to visiting teachers and students; guiding the summer work program; helping to write and edit books and magazines; and just being available wherever and whenever needed. You could never write a history of Foxfire that did not include Margie Bennett.

Lacy Hunter Nix is a former *Foxfire Magazine* student and scholarship recipient who has returned on several occasions to help write and edit several Foxfire books. Lacy has the ability to connect and form a bond with contacts that always develops into lasting friendships. She graduated from Brenau College in Gainesville, Georgia, with a degree in music, and now is a full-time, stay-at-home mom, raising with her husband, Chris, their two beautiful girls. Like her mother before her, Lacy is a wonderful pianist.

Sheri Thurmond (not pictured), a Foxfire Scholarship recipient, graduated several years ago with a degree in social work from Truett-McConnell College, then returned to school in 2009 to receive her teaching degree from Piedmont College. During her time at Rabun County High School, she was a *Foxfire* magazine student who worked with Foxfire during the summer months in the archives. Sheri has continued to work with Foxfire as a volunteer, though her time is limited due to her working two full-time jobs while searching for a teaching position.

Summer 2010 interview and transcription staff, left to right: Brittany Houck, Alyssa LaManna, Kelly Smith, and Katie Lunsford (not pictured: Kayla Mullen) are students at Rabun County High School. They will be leaders in the 2010–11 *Foxfire Magazine* class, as well as for the remainder of their high school years.

PLATE 201 **Student staff from** *The Foxfire Magazine* **class, from left: Brittany Houck, Alyssa LaManna, Kelly Smith, Katie Lunsford; not pictured: Kayla Mullen**

Contributors

Staff

Margie Bennett
Casi Best
Lee Carpenter
Kaye Carver Collins
Teresa Thurmond Gentry

Joyce Green
Brittany Houck
Alyssa LaManna
Kate Lunsford
Ben McClain

Ann Moore
Kayla Mullen
Lacy Hunter Nix
Kelly Smith
Sheri Thurmond

Students

Allison Adams
Austin Bauman
Russell Bauman
Terry Benfield
Casi Best
Clarence Bramblett
Cary Brown
Melanie Burrell
Ann Carnes
Gloria Carpenter
Kyle Conway
Kelly Cook
Greg Darnell
Hedy Davalos
Dennis Dodgins
Melissa Easter
Al Edwards
Aubrey Eubank
Rance Fleming
Candi Forester
Lacy Forester

Samantha Fountain
Jeff Giles
Curt Haban
Kasie Hicks
Ricky Hopkins
Ricky Justus
Hope Loudermilk
Lisa Lovell
Erik Lunsford
Bridget McCurry
Erin McDowell
Ana Merino
Frank Miller
Viola Nichols
Chris Nix
Max Norton
Mandy Owen
Alex Owens
Kirk Patterson
David Lee Payne
Anna Phillips
Keifer Phillips

Lynn Phillips
Carol Ramey
Johnny Ramey
Tombo Ramey
Dennis Ritchie
Julie Roane
Brandie Rushing
Fred Sanders
David Scroggs
Erin Smith
Anthony Stalcup
Cindy Stewart
Brant Sturgill
David Vinson
Tim Vinson
Jared Weber
Chet Welch
Adam Wilburn
Cecil Wilburn
Amy York
Doug Young

Contacts

James Adams
Karl Anderson
Lillie Billingsley
Vaughn Billingsley
Curtis Blackwell
Kyle Bolen
Johnathan Bond
George Bowen
Huell Bramlett
Lawton Brooks
Morris Brown
Elvin Cabe
Nelson Cabe
David Callenback
Marley Cannon
Doris Carpenter
Jim Carpenter
Eula Carroll
Bobbie Dills Carter
Darlene Chapman
Emma Chastain
Tommy Chastain
J. T. Coleman
Claud Connell
Helen Craig
Ada Crone
Wallace "Josh" Crowe
Wayne Crowe
Frances Fry Deal
Jimmy Deal
Bass Dockery

Ollie Dyer
Harriet Echols
Allen English
Dean English
Randy Fox
Wayne Gipson
Sammy Green
Mike Hamilton
Carlee Heaton
Clyde Hollifield
David Holt
Jo-Anne Stiles Hubbs
Tommy Irvin
Jamie Jordan
Jessie Jordan
Kelly Jordan
Tom Jordan
Coyl Justice
Bob Justus
George Kell
Filmer Kilby
Mary Webb Kitchens
Carroll Lee
LV Mathis
Mary Mathis
Delbert McCall
Steven McCall
Brayden McMahan
Sam McMahan
Summer McMahan
Marie Mellinger
Madge Merrell

John Morgan
Doug Nix
Jack P. Nix
Tom Nixon
George Reynolds
Larry Riddle
Mike Riddle
Reagan Riddle
Marjorie Robinson
Morris Robinson
Melissa Rogers
Jim Smith
Bessie Stancil
Greg Stancil
Morris Stancil
Barry Stiles
Billy Joe Stiles
Louise Tabor
Janie P. Taylor
Harold Thurmond
William Thurmond
Dale Tilley
Jeff Tolbert
Edward Vinson
Ernest Vinson
Frank Vinson
Gary Waldrep
Noel Walters
Lucy Webb
Bill White
Norman Wilson